SH

D0208202

DICTIONARY
OF
AMERICAN
MILITARY
BIOGRAPHY

DICTIONARY
OF
AMERICAN
MILITARY
BIOGRAPHY

Volume I
A–G

ROGER J. SPILLER
Editor
JOSEPH G. DAWSON III
Associate Editor
T. HARRY WILLIAMS
Consulting Editor

Greenwood Press
Westport, Connecticut • London, England

Library of Congress Cataloging in Publication Data

Main entry under title:

Dictionary of American military biography.

Includes index.
Contents: v. 1. Creighton W. Abrams—Leslie R.
Groves—v. 2. Henry W. Halleck—Israel Putnam—
v. 3. John A. Quitman—Elmo R. Zumwalt, Jr.
1. United States—Armed Forces—Biography. 2. United
States—Biography. I. Spiller, Roger J. II. Dawson,
Joseph G., 1945-   .
U52.D53   1984   355'.0092'2 [B]   83-12674
ISBN 0-313-21433-6 (lib. bdg. : set)
ISBN 0-313-24161-9 (lib. bdg. : v. 1)
ISBN 0-313-24162-7 (lib. bdg. : v. 2)
ISBN 0-313-24399-9 (lib. bdg. : v. 3)

Library of Congress Catalog Card Number: 83-12674
ISBN 0-313-21433-6 (lib. bdg. : set)

First published in 1984

Greenwood Press
A division of Congressional Information Service, Inc.
88 Post Road West, Westport, Connecticut 06881

Printed in the United States of America

10   9   8   7   6   5   4   3   2   1

Contents

Introduction

Armed, they came ashore, watchful of attack at any moment. Once the landing was made they searched for a defensible place. Fortifications and shelter were thrown together quickly. Then, they began patrolling. Before long, they clashed with hostiles and then began a period of raids and counter-raids, pitched battles, decision, and the desolation that so often accompanies the return of peace.

To students of American history this is a familiar scenario, one that could encompass the landing at Jamestown in 1607, Scott's Mexican War campaign of 1846, the Allied landings at North Africa in 1942, or the Marines' arrival at Da Nang in 1965. It reminds us, too, that military affairs have had a continuing and important effect upon the course of American history. Indeed, so much of this nation's energy has been spent in military pursuits of one sort or another that one wonders how we can lay a reasonable claim to a peaceful tradition. But because this unlovely fact is so, those who are interested in an informed view of the past are obliged to take notice.

Perhaps most readers, encountering a book of this kind, will search out their favorite military figure. They will want to find their hero's deed retold and discover once more his original appeal to their imagination. This is only natural. The story of a life, artfully told, has an eternal fascination. Why this is so, and what it may say about us, philosophers are best suited to discover. Today, the life that comes into view, the notable life, arrests the imagination no less than it did in ages past, when ancient listeners were entertained by ancient ballads.

Of all the lives held up for display, the military life often has seemed the most compelling. The life at arms possesses its own special drama, one replete with familiar themes—heroism and sacrifice, cowardice, emergency and recovery, victory and defeat, deadly genius and deadly chaos—all played out often in bas relief to the life of a nation itself. For centuries, it was in such terms that man knew and understood his history. Heroes and their acts were taken somehow to reveal the essence of an event or an age. So General George Pickett's charge was meant to characterize the Battle of Gettysburg and in turn, the Civil War in its entirety. Yet the Civil War had seen many such murderous assaults, many even more deadly than the one made by Pickett's men. At the battles of Malvern Hill, Antietam, and Cold Harbor soldiers were shot down in windrows because their commanders did not have enough imagination to see that the weapons of the day made their tactics obsolete. Yet the battle at Gettysburg is now seen as the high point of that war, and Pickett's charge as its centerpiece. By some means, perhaps only partly explainable, it was Pickett's charge that passed from fact to symbol for future imaginations.

A dictionary of military biography would seem a curious place to contest this way of seeing the past. A work whose object is the collection of biographical essays about individuals significant to the making of American military history would benefit, no doubt, from such a view. But there comes a point when symbols, however uplifting, however much they promise to inform, cease to tell us as much as we want to know. To say that Pickett's charge was the "high point of the war" is merely to indulge in historical fiction. At the time Pickett's men went forward, other men in uniform across the country were fighting battles—with the enemy, with themselves and their fear—that allowed no leisure for contemplation about events at Gettysburg. Nearly half the continent away, at Vicksburg, Mississippi, a siege that had been consuming lives and treasure for months was drawing to a close. For the men who participated in those battles, what was happening at Gettysburg was of little moment. The war everywhere lasted for nearly two years more, and what seems so clear to historians now was not at all clear to the combatants then. If the cause was lost after July 1863, how did the fighting go on for so long? But the fighting did, in fact, go on, and each action created more symbols and their human counterparts, the heroes.

On the whole, military history has dealt too often with heroes, and badly. We single out heroes by their differences from the rest of us. What ordinary people may do in a situation sets the standards which heroes exceed. Their actions are believed to have causative effect, a power to overturn predictable events, to disappoint sure plans, to dispute certain odds. Sergeant Alvin York, whose biography is included here, was chosen at least in part to demonstrate the susceptibility of the plain man for heroism. York came to his remarkable feat in the Belleau Wood on the Western Front with no special predisposition for the heroic act. An ordinary man, he was trapped in an extraordinary situation. No doubt other men would have succeeded as York did, but other men were not there. Later, York could say what he did that day, but not why. For military history, as with other kinds of history, description is always easier than explanation.

Heroism, like battle itself, does not easily submit to intellectual probing, for these are elemental rather than reasonable events. Writers may through their prose discuss what brought on a war, describe the raising and moving of an army to the battlefield, detail the plans and expectations of the various commanders, and assess the results of battle, but they have not been able to penetrate the mysteries of battle itself, and its human equivalent, why men fight at all. If battle is yet a mystery, then heroism is more mysterious to us still. Description will uncover some of the habits of heroism, however. Like any other event, the heroic act is not often repeated. A soldier may be, like Henry Flemming in Stephen Crane's *The Red Badge of Courage*, a coward one day and a hero the next. Flemming's story ends with his having passed through the fire of cowardice on the battleline to become a man and a hero, but there is no assurance that this soldier will not recant his maturity at the next opportunity. And although Flemming received the hero's acclaim, he was in the end not more accomplished as a soldier than when he began. Among professional soldiers who lead other men into battle, there seems to be a consensus that heroism is not, after all, very useful. However much heroism seems a particularly military affair, the lack of ability to sustain it diminishes its utility in a military operation that always depends upon regularity, discipline, and predictability. Military leaders spend a great deal of time to ensure that their operations unfold consciously, and that is why they would prefer, not battalions of heroes, but battalions of ordinary men.

Heroism is often thought of as one dramatic act only, but there are other kinds of heroism that are less often recognized. How would one describe Paul Baumer, the hero of Erich Remarque's *All Quiet on the Western Front*, who came to understand that he and his comrades lived under a death sentence that would be handed down before the peace came? There have been men like Baumer in all wars, the Everysoldier, but they very seldom appear in history books except in the collective—"the division moved at first light to take its place on the line." But in the end the Baumers are not so very different from all of us, and so we do not single them out.

There is a third sort of hero, a favorite of history. These are the grand figures who sweep across events, seemingly oblivious to the fates that control the rest of us, the Washingtons, the Grants and Lees, the Pershings, Eisenhowers, and Pattons. Far more than symbols, these men personalize history for us, and history cannot be properly explained without reference to their presence. That we often submit too much to the powers of such individuals for our knowledge of events is regrettable. When we say that Robert E. Lee, for instance, was the Confederate Army, we have reduced understanding to mere imagery. When we look closely, heroes and heroics seem too transient to sustain understanding, their effect too limited, too accidental. Lee was on the field at Gettysburg when Pickett's charge was launched. How much did his presence have to do with the men in the battlelines who attacked the Union positions? Images offer little protection against volley fire. These men, as all others who have found themselves in combat, were sustained by reasons at once more profound and simpler. In 1863 and long before, heroes such as Lee were believed to have great power over the course of history. Today, the importance that we are willing to assign any one person in the making of great events and obvious explanations will no longer suffice.

Has biography, the study of the history of individual lives, therefore lost its usefulness? The answer is no, if only because human life is the currency in which history most effectively deals. Far from being overtaken by new historical tastes, biography still is put to uses that go beyond the confines of an individual career. As the reader will see in the essays that follow, the authors have made judgments on their subjects. Some will say that the importance of a figure's life has been overrated, that the influence he had over affairs was less than expected, and that past images have misled us. Other essays will claim that a person is undeservedly obscure, explain the person's role in events, and suggest that the essay be only the beginning for further investigations. By this process of reordering historical judgment, a new picture of affairs is created. The process is one that historians carry on constantly; the difference in this dictionary is that so many historians have turned to the same task—the reevaluation of historical figures in the military past—in the same general way. If the *Dictionary of American Military Biography* accomplishes only this, the effort will have been worthwhile.

Interestingly, none of the writers who contributed to this dictionary claimed what the editors regarded as too much for their subjects, as if by studying their careers their images became less compelling. Once it might have been thought that by reading such a book as this, one would have achieved a complete picture of American military history. This premise has launched more than one such book, but no such claim is made now. Very like the contributors, the editors do not wish to claim too much. The historians involved in this project all understand that history is comprised of more than the lives of famous individuals. Therefore, we claim only that biographical knowledge is an essential part of history, but certainly not the only part. Like other categories of knowledge, biography will enliven and inform an understanding of American military history, but it cannot be said that biography stands alone to provide all that is required.

All this being said, it is important to emphasize that the *DAMB* is not a random collection of biographical essays. From its conception, the essays were meant to be a set, one essay in some way building upon and complementing others. Although the essays are arranged alphabetically, they are cross-referenced (with asterisks) to other essays on people who were associated with the subject under consideration. No major event in American military history is unrepresented in the pages that follow, and several are discussed by different scholars from different perspectives. By moving from one reference to another, the reader may collect these views and come to his own understanding of affairs. This applies not only to those individuals who are the subjects of essays, but also to many who are not. In the index one will find references to historical figures who, for one reason or another, were not given essays of their own. What this means is that many more figures appear in the pages that follow than the list of essays would imply.

The mechanics of effecting such a list were therefore important in the making of the *DAMB* set. There was first the matter of choosing from thousands of candidates those who should have an essay and those who should not. Furthermore, a reference work of manageable size was required, one that did not consume shelves of library space. At the beginning of the project, the editors fashioned a tentative list of essays and asked nearly fifty leading American military historians to consider how they would change it. The list of essays went through twenty-five editions before it reached its present state in an exercise that was in many ways as enlightening as the essays themselves. These historians were asked to view the list of candidates with the most critical eye. The real significance of even near-mythic subjects had to be reassessed for their own worth, as well as for their importance in competition with other candidates. Interestingly, one of the first standards established by this process was that no one would be included merely by virtue of the position he had held. To have included all the secretaries of war and navy, chiefs of staff and naval operations, generals above a certain rank and so on would have meant an abdication to the mere appearance of importance. Obviously, not everyone who holds an important office is important. The dignitary should impart more to the office than the office imparts to him. Certain candidates had inspired what could only be called "historical fan clubs," and their supporters prosecuted vigorously the case for their inclusion. In some of these cases, the sheer weight of truly significant individuals merely drove these candidates out of the running. In others, the editors were forced to end the argument. But the process was important, for from the outset the *DAMB* was intended to be at least in part an exercise in historical judgment. Many other judgments were made as well.

Some of these other questions were more difficult to resolve: how many entries should be devoted to a particular period or category, and should these numbers imply a certain scale of importance? What number of essays should be given over to subjects from the American Revolution, for instance? How many would seem disproportionate, and how many appropriate? In a long process of negotiation and discussion, the list took on a shape that was dictated less by quantity than quality, although numbers could never be entirely avoided. The early lists, it was decided, contained too many names from the Civil War. There were several reasons why this war made such a large claim for essays. The amount of historical work done on this period of American military history—by one count, from forty to sixty thousand volumes—was far and away the largest. Because of the massive historical projects to capture this war's official records (such as the 128-volume *War of the Rebellion*), historians knew more about the war's operations than any other war in American history. Obviously, the entire dictionary could have been consumed by Civil War entries alone. To a degree, this is also true of naval history. No doubt, a dictionary could have been made that covered only those who had some connection with land warfare, but such a definition seemed altogether too narrow. Military history has been construed in its widest possible sense, therefore, in order to include essays on naval subjects, and these make up roughly one-quarter of all the entries.

Further categories have been included as well. Subjects from the early Air Service, Army Air Corps, and U.S. Air Force have been taken into account, for while in terms of longevity the place of air power in American history has been relatively small, it has nonetheless exercised a significant alteration in warfare everywhere. Native Americans were included, not because they fought on the American side in one war or another (some did, some did not), but because they did exert an influence upon American events far greater than their numbers would predict. The long fighting retreat of the American Indians from the first landings at Jamestown to the last action at Wounded Knee affected all who were involved and imparted a legacy that scarcely can be separated from the life of the nation itself. And, finally, there are the civilians, which was perhaps the most severely circumscribed of all the categories. Even here, the standards for inclusion were hardly straightforward as they might seem. How might one deal with Theodore Roosevelt, a minor notable in strictly military terms, but one who, from his days as assistant secretary of the Navy to his presidency, dealt with military questions large and small? Should a civilian such as J. Robert Oppenheimer have been included on the basis of his work at Los Alamos in designing the atomic bomb?

Compounding all these difficulties was the consideration that scholarship is nowhere applied with an even hand. Historians and biographers tend to follow their own particular interests and to satisfy their own curiosity without much regard for the "state of scholarship" at any given time, and how a scholar may decide to investigate one subject or another is a process so varied as to defy correlation. Depending chiefly upon written records, historical scholarship tends to favor the more literate periods and people. No doubt the Civil War is studied because it is of obvious importance to American history, but the war also produced an enormous volume of personal recollections and official records that is also attractive to scholarship. On the other hand, the preliterate cultures of the Native Americans have been closed to historical work until very recently.

Fashions and habits of scholarship have also meant that figures once accorded a good deal of importance have gone out of vogue, victims of interests more modern. Until the very eve of the Civil War, few could contest General Winfield Scott's claim as the most important American soldier in the century. It had been a period that was not heavily peopled by military geniuses, after all. But then came the Civil War and a new class of general appeared with a newer style of warfare, one that in some ways seems closer to twentieth century combat. Apparently, Scott's position slipped below the threshold of historical notice. The standard Scott biography was written by Charles Eliot nearly fifty years ago, and no historian would say that the last word had been written on this important soldier, but the lack of attention paid to him recently would so imply.

Views of what exactly comprises "military history" came into play constantly during the making of the *DAMB*. Despite a good deal of writing recently that has challenged the old style of "drum and bugle" military history and has argued for a broader and more critical approach to the military past, there has been a persistent scholarly and public interest in wars and battles and in those who participated in them. Without much difficulty, the *DAMB* could have been made into a litany of battle captains and their deeds. It was in this case that heroes made their most insistent applications for inclusion. Did the trials of combat create some panhistorical fraternity, and if so, could it be said that only its members earned an entry in such a dictionary? Did their claims supersede those of William Duane, for example, who spent his career translating Continental military knowledge to the United States and winning little recognition for his efforts? American soldiers would depend in some way upon Duane's work for the better part of the century. Where should Sylvanus Thayer and Arthur Wagner, two of America's pioneer military educators, stand in the competition?

In the end, such questions as these were interesting exercises only. It is true enough that battles still dominate the study of military history and that all else is decidedly secondary in terms of the scholarship devoted to it. The Chronology of American Military Developments that makes up Appendix I is largely a chronicle of conflict, even though a considerable effort was made to include other important military affairs. It remains a fact, even so, that the frame of reference for all who are involved in military enterprises is either the last war or the next war. All energies seem bent to such matters, and given the sorry record of conflict that the chronology details, it seems a sound enough view for one to take. But it is also true that in the course of military history, the time given to actual battle is important but also relatively brief, and the time a man might spend during a battle in actual combat smaller still. What weight should be given, then, to those who sustained an important life as against those whose significance derived chiefly from one dramatic act? The answer can be seen in, among many others, Dr. Timothy Nenninger's essay on General Arthur MacArthur. Had MacArthur's only claim to note been his Medal of Honor winning assault up Lookout Mountain during the Battle of Chattanooga, it is doubtful that both MacArthur and his son Douglas would have essays here. In this case, both father and son have been included by virtue of their whole careers rather than any one particular accomplishment.

The MacArthurs of military history will, of course, always be attractive. But beyond these most visible lives stand others whose contributions sometimes worked influences far greater than anyone could reckon while they lived. Some never saw a battle (or wanted to) and devoted their lives, like William Duane, to pursuits that were by the lights of soldiers only vaguely military. Far from the deadly rituals of warfare, these men and women nonetheless figured importantly in the course of American military history. A place had to be found in the *DAMB* for such people. That is why one will find heroes here and great captains, but also inventors, writers, educators, physicians, explorers, and others.

The actual shape of each entry was easily decided. For reference, a detailed narrative of career was required, including exact facts of birth and death where possible. In these respects, the *DAMB* is very like any other biographical dictionary. About half of each essay is taken up with the narrative of the subject's career, but no rule was imposed on the authors to prevent their best judgment in any case. Similarly, the length of the essays was set at roughly 1,500 words, but the author was asked to stay only generally within that limit. For that reason, the length of any one essay is not to be taken as indicative of a judgment on relative importance. The latter half of each essay is devoted to the author's appraisal of his subject's importance to the course of American military history. Again, rules, conventions of interpretation, and given historical wisdom were not imposed. The editors refused to interfere with their contributors' views of their subjects, even though they might not themselves have agreed. Following each essay, the author presents a list of books that will give the reader an opportunity to pursue his interest in each subject. These works were chosen on the basis of scholarly accuracy and availability to the general public. Each essay is signed by its author. An asterisk (*) following a name indicates a cross-reference to another entry in the dictionary.

Every essay posed its own particular challenge to its author. Some of the more obscure subjects required substantial research before the essay could be completed. Probes into these lives sometimes uncovered new information or contested commonly accepted facts. Confusion in the records over Claire Chennault's date of birth set Professor William Leary off on a search that lasted for several months. Dr. Charles R. Shrader (also lieutenant colonel, U.S. Army) was one of those scholars who proved especially adept with such figures: his essays on Adolphus Greely and Frederick Funston are models of what can be achieved with even the most recalcitrant subjects. Dr. William Glenn Robertson's work on Homer Lea calls into question that figure's own account of his romantic infatuation with the armies of early revolutionary China.

Famous subjects were a different matter entirely. Consider the prospect before Professor Don Higginbotham, when he turned to write his essay on George Washington. Even the most casually informed would blanch in the face of such a project, but Higginbotham has devoted his career to studying the times in which Washington lived and so had to determine what should be included in an essay of less than ten pages. Perhaps even more to the point, how was Professor D. Clayton James to deal with his essay on Douglas MacArthur after studying that life for more than fifteen years of his own and in the process writing what is now considered the preeminent MacArthur biography?

These and other feats of scholarship came as no surprise to the editors of this work. Over two hundred scholars from the United States and abroad participated in the making of the *DAMB*. One contributor wrote his essay at the University of Aberdeen in Scotland, another at the University of Zambia. Professors both in and out of uniform at all the military services' academies and several of the staff colleges contributed. Another author completed his assignment while on a Fulbright in Thailand, while yet another wrote at very long range indeed, off the coast of Antarctica on an expedition to circle the earth from pole to pole.

Still other writers came from outside the professional trades. In the list of contributors that follows the biographical entries, the reader will see quite a few military and naval officers, most of whom are still on active service. All of them have done graduate study in military history and were asked to contribute because of their scholarly interests. Added to these is a group of younger scholars, some of whom are still in graduate school, working toward doctorates. A special effort was made to invite those who were just at the beginning of their careers, an effort that without exception was most worthwhile.

All these men and women cheerfully submitted to the standards of scholarship demanded for this dictionary. In this regard, at least, all were treated the same. More than a year was required to select the contributors to this work. Each was selected on the basis of his special interest in the subject he was assigned, whether through original research in the life of the subject or the period and class of enterprise that encompassed the subject. Some few contributors were so well and widely versed in military and naval history that they were asked to write essays on several different persons. Others had so well demonstrated their expertness on a given subject that there was no question as to who should write the essay.

The size, complexity, and time required to complete the *DAMB* make it a unique work of reference in the field of military history. No other work in the United States has called upon the energies and talents of so many military historians. For these reasons, the *DAMB* can reasonably be taken as a picture of the state of scholarship in military history in this country, a field that, for all the work that has been done, is still a relatively undeveloped one. The editors hope that the *DAMB* will contribute to the scholarly evolution of this field, and it is for this purpose that it has been written.

Shortly after the *Dictionary of American Military Biography* was conceived, Professor T. Harry Williams agreed to act as the consulting editor. He died before the dictionary could be completed. What this preeminent biographer, military historian, teacher, and friend has taught lives on, and his spirit animates the work that has produced this dictionary. The good that is here is his. This work is dedicated to him.

ROGER J. SPILLER
JOSEPH G. DAWSON III

DICTIONARY
OF
AMERICAN
MILITARY
BIOGRAPHY

Biographical Essays

A

ABRAMS, Creighton William, Jr. (b. Springfield, Mass., September 15, 1914; d. Washington, D.C., September 4, 1974), Army officer; commander, U.S. Military Assistance Command, Vietnam.

Creighton Abrams spent his boyhood in rural Massachusetts, graduating from Agawam High School, where he was captain of its undefeated football team and valedictorian of his senior class. Inspired by a lecture delivered at Agawam by a West Point graduate, Abrams successfully sought appointment to the U.S. Military Academy and matriculated there in 1932. At West Point he excelled in horsemanship and lettered in football. In 1936 he graduated 185th of 276 in his class and was commissioned a second lieutenant of cavalry.

The next four years Abrams spent as a troop officer in the 1st Cavalry Division at Fort Bliss, Texas, receiving regular promotions to first lieutenant (1939) and captain (1940). During 1940 he served with the old 1st Armored Division, but in 1941 he was transferred to the newly activated 4th Armored Division, located in California. Following his promotion to major in February 1942, he took command of a battalion of the 37th Armored Regiment. Only a few months later he was promoted to lieutenant colonel. He served as executive officer of the regiment until he assumed command of the 37th Tank Battalion at Camp Bowie, Texas.

Abrams and the 37th Tank Battalion went into action in Normandy in July 1944, and subsequently they participated in all campaigns of the 4th Armored Division. A serious student and practitioner of modern mobile combat, Abrams built a deserved reputation as one of the best tank commanders of the war, earning the respect and compliments of his comrades and superiors. General George Smith Patton, Jr.* commended Abrams, saying that "I'm supposed to be the best tank commander in the Army, but I have one peer—Abe Abrams."

After his distinguished battlefield service in World War II, Abrams received numerous and challenging postwar assignments in the United States and abroad, as well as completing courses of instruction at the Command and General Staff

College (1949) and the Army War College (1953). For two years (1946–1948) Abrams served as director of tactics at the Armor School, Fort Knox, Kentucky, where he revised the Army's manual on armor tactics. Some years later (1954–1956), he was chief of staff at the Armor Center. During the early 1950s he commanded the 63d Tank Battalion and the 2d Armored Cavalry Regiment in Europe. During the Korean War, Abrams gained valuable experience at the corps level, serving successively as chief of staff of I Corps, IX Corps, and X Corps. In these positions he planned defenses against the last major Communist offensives of the Korean conflict. Subsequently, Abrams was promoted to brigadier general (1956) and major general (1960). For three years (1956–1959) he held the position of deputy assistant chief of staff for Reserve Components, General Staff, Department of the Army.

In the early 1960s Abrams usually found himself at or near points of crisis. He was assistant division commander and commander of the 3d Armored Division in Europe during the Berlin crisis (1962). In September 1962 he was placed in charge of federal soldiers deployed at Oxford, Mississippi, to quell rioting that had occurred over the admission of a Negro, James M. Meredith, to the University of Mississippi. In May 1963 Abrams commanded troops that had been alerted in case it became necessary for them to intervene in Birmingham, Alabama, during racial unrest there.

In July 1963 he became commanding general of V Corps, one of the two corps-sized American ground combat forces in Europe. He was promoted to lieutenant general (1963) and general (1964), and then became vice chief of staff, U.S. Army, in Washington, D.C. These and other important assignments all were prelude to the greatest challenge of Abrams' career: his service in Vietnam.

In April 1967 President Lyndon B. Johnson assigned Abrams as the deputy commander of the U.S. Military Assistance Command, Vietnam. His principal responsibility was to improve the fighting capabilities of the South Vietnamese forces. During the Tet Offensive of 1968, Abrams supervised allied military operations in northern Vietnam, specifically ordering the recapture of Hue.

In July 1968 he assumed command in Vietnam following the North Vietnamese psychological victory in the Tet Offensive of 1968. For the next four years, Abrams' mission required the reduction of direct U.S. military involvement and the training of the South Vietnamese forces to assume increasing responsibilities for defense of their country. He departed Vietnam in June 1972 following the North Vietnamese Easter Offensive.

While serving in Vietnam, Abrams was nominated to be chief of staff, U.S. Army. The Senate confirmed his appointment on October 12, 1972, by a vote of eighty-four to two. For two years, until his death from lung cancer on September 4, 1974, Abrams worked diligently to rebuild the Army which had suffered the traumas of a rapid reduction in size, repositioning of forces occasioned by the end of military operations in Vietnam, and the political effects of the war itself in the United States.

He was interred at Arlington National Cemetery on September 6, 1974.

As a battalion commander in World War II, Abrams established a reputation that would follow him for the rest of his career. Throughout the Army he was known for aggressive, fearless leadership in combat. During the American Army's advance across France and into Germany, Abrams' battalion was the point battalion of General Patton's Third Army.

On December 26, 1944, Abrams' battalion was the first American unit to reach the 101st Airborne Division, which had been surrounded at Bastogne, Belgium, during the Germans' Ardennes Offensive (the "Battle of the Bulge"). On the way to Bastogne, when a concealed German antitank gun held up the advance of his armored task force, Abrams went forward in his command tank to destroy the gun and keep the advance moving to Bastogne. He was awarded his second Distinguished Service Cross for valor for that action.

Although Abrams held important and sensitive positions following his World War II service, he did not become well known outside the Army until he assumed command of the U.S. Army Military Assistance Command, Vietnam. Alert to the problems of the presidency during the difficult post-Tet period, Abrams also understood the internal and external political characteristics of the war and prompted quick changes in American military tactics. At Abrams' direction, the Army placed greater emphasis on defense of populated areas and deemphasized the massive sweep operations used under General William Childs Westmoreland.* Search and destroy tactics were replaced by tremendous numbers of small patrols and ambushes. Abrams' tactics were to get inside the enemy's system and, in his words, to "hound and harass and drive the enemy's influence from the land." Allied cross-border operations into Cambodia in 1970 and Laos in 1971 were conducted to push the enemy away from South Vietnam's borders, ensure the security of the American withdrawal, and give the South Vietnamese additional time to develop the Vietnamization program.

In his advisory role, Abrams' efforts rearmed and trained the Army of the Republic of Vietnam, including its militia—the provincial and district forces. A measure of his success came when the South Vietnamese Army withstood and eventually repulsed a massive North Vietnamese invasion in the spring of 1972 with only American advisors and air power in South Vietnam for assistance. Furthermore, Abrams instituted the nation-building pacification programs, which were designed to improve the educational, medical, transportation, and agricultural systems in South Vietnam. He was particularly sensitive to the war's impact on the hapless Vietnamese people and constantly stressed cooperation with local Vietnamese authorities.

Abrams' command of the U.S. Army Military Assistance Advisory Command from 1968 until 1972 was one of the most difficult tasks in American military history. The Nixon administration's policy of giving the South Vietnamese a chance for survival after America's military participation ended was achieved. While in Vietnam, Abrams' remarkable character and complete candor enabled him to achieve the respect of the virtually uncensored American news media, which was often hostile towards the Army.

As chief of staff of the U.S. Army, Abrams guided the rebuilding of the Army's professional and ethical standards in the bitter period following the American withdrawal from Vietnam in January 1973. He directed the introduction of a voluntary enlistment system, although he stated publicly that if the volunteer Army became racially and intellectually nonrepresentative of America, "then it's not an Army of the United States." He stressed modernization of the reserve forces and began implementing a reserve reorganization plan.

Abe Abrams is one of the unsung military figures of American history. He was inspirational, brave, bold, and wise. As division commander of the 3d Armored Division, Abrams was rated by his superiors as being "the outstanding armor commander of his generation." He was considered to be the "number one fighting general in the Army" according to General Bruce C. Clark. Aside from his combat prowess, Abrams excelled as an advisor to America's top civilian leaders, whether in the Department of Defense, Congress, or the White House. His success in this difficult role for a military officer was the crowning achievement of his illustrious career.

BIBLIOGRAPHY

Johnson, Lyndon B. *The Vantage Point*. New York: Holt, Rinehart, and Winston, 1971.
Millett, Allan R. *A Short History of the Vietnam War*. Bloomington: Indiana University Press, 1978.
Palmer, Dave R. *Summons of the Trumpet*. San Rafael, Calif.: Presidio Press, 1978.

VAN M. DAVIDSON, JR.

AINSWORTH, Fred Clayton (b. Woodstock, Vt., September 11, 1852; d. Washington, D.C., June 5, 1934), doctor, Army administrator and bureaucrat, archivist.

Fred C. Ainsworth was the elder son of a modestly prosperous Woodstock family. He entered Dartmouth College in 1869, but he left as a result of a breach of discipline and turned instead to a medical career. After three years of study in Woodstock, he enrolled at the University of the City of New York in 1873, proved an able student, and graduated in 1874. He held a junior medical post at Bellevue Hospital in New York City before applying, in September 1874, for an appointment as an assistant surgeon in the U.S. Army. His first assignment was to West Point in November 1874, but in July 1875 he was ordered to the Department of the Columbia where he served at Fort Vancouver and at Sitka, Alaska, before being reassigned to the Department of Arizona. His duties were routine, although he saw service but not action in the 1878 Bannock Indian War. In November 1879 he was promoted to the rank of captain and in April 1881 transferred to the Department of Texas where he served at Fort McIntosh. In July 1881 he married Mary (Bacon) Cranston, a widow with one child, but there were no children of the marriage. In 1885 he became recorder of the Army Medical Examining Board in New York City, and somehow catching the eye of those in authority, he was ordered to Washington in December 1886 to take over the Record and Pension Division in the Surgeon General's Office, thus entering upon an administrative and bureaucratic career that would last over twenty-five years.

The Record and Pension Division was responsible for supplying the medical records of pension claimants, and by this time Civil War pension legislation had reached such generous proportions as to threaten to swamp the division with requests for data. Ainsworth overcame cumbersome administrative processes, lengthy delays, and a considerable backlog of work by streamlining procedures, redistributing clerical staff, and dismissing those chronically inefficient. His most famous innovation was the replacement of the existing faded, fragile, and incomplete records with a system of index-record cards that were eventually to number many millions.

Ainsworth's achievements received immediate recognition from a Senate committee on government business methods and from the War Department Board on Business Methods. As a result, additional records were placed in the custody of the Surgeon General's Office, military and medical records were consolidated, and in July 1889 the Record and Pension Division was merged with certain divisions of the Office of the Adjutant General to form the Record and Pension Division of the War Department, part of the Office of the Secretary of War, with Ainsworth heading the new organization. With his usual energy Ainsworth reorganized work, introduced new business methods, and despite increased numbers of pension claims and the need to complete the index-card system, he cleared another large backlog of cases.

President Benjamin Harrison recognized Ainsworth's accomplishments with favorable mention in three consecutive annual messages between 1889 and 1891, but when Congress sought to reward him by making the Record and Pension Division into a separate and independent bureau Harrison vetoed the bill, because by specifically naming Ainsworth as its head and promoting him to the rank of colonel, Congress had infringed upon an executive prerogative. However, Ainsworth did attain the rank of major on February 27, 1891, the day after Harrison's veto, and in 1892 the president signed a bill creating a separate Record and Pension Office with a head to hold the rank of colonel. No officer was specified, but as expected Ainsworth received the appointment on May 27. By this time Ainsworth had under his direct control half the employees in the War Department, and the only shadow on his rising reputation was the abuse he unfairly suffered following the Ford Theater disaster in June 1893, when twenty-two clerks were killed and nearly a hundred injured when the building, used by the Record and Pension Office, partially collapsed during alterations.

During the 1890s records relating to Indian Wars, the Mexican War, the

American Revolution, and the War of 1812 were brought into Ainsworth's province, and later those relating to the Spanish-American War and the Philippine Insurrection were added. Ainsworth's ability to get things done led to the expansion of his responsibilities, which included in 1898 the task of completing the publication of the mammoth 128-volume *Official Records of the War of the Rebellion*, and within three years the final volumes were produced. His successes, and his claims to have effected economies in money and manpower, led to further personal reward when Congress granted him the rank of brigadier general on March 2, 1899.

Not everyone shared the congressional appreciation of Ainsworth, for his determination to protect the integrity and safety of records led to conflict with other bureaus and departments, with state authorities, and with individuals and even historians whose attempts to gain access he repeatedly thwarted. In 1912 many of the nation's most distinguished historians publicly protested his obstructions, and one even suggested that Ainsworth be made ambassador to Tibet for life. Not until after Ainsworth's retirement was access more readily available.

The shortcomings in military organization revealed by the Spanish-American War produced a considerable reform program which included the creation of a general staff, headed by a chief of staff, thus, it was hoped, replacing the constant bickering between the secretary of war, the commanding general, and the virtually autonomous and mutually jealous bureau chiefs. However, the Adjutant General's Department (reduced in size and function by the creation of the General Staff) and the Record and Pension Office continued to squabble over prerogatives until they were amalgamated in April 1904 as the Military Secretary's Department, with Ainsworth at its head with the rank of major general. Although the title of military secretary had been chosen deliberately to emphasize the break with the past, friction between the chief of staff and the military secretary persisted. In 1907 the name was quietly changed back, and Ainsworth became adjutant general of the Army.

His prestige was increased when he served as acting secretary of war in 1906 and again in 1907. He also worked to improve procedures for recruiting and for the apprehension of deserters, and he played a large role in obtaining the act raising Army pay in 1908. By 1910 he was at the apex of his career and expected, so many thought, to be chief of staff, but that year the post went to Leonard Wood,* ironically another doctor. After a brief honeymoon period, Wood and Ainsworth were soon at loggerheads over paperwork and Army reorganization as Ainsworth (and his close ally, the new Democratic chairman of the House Committee on Military Affairs, James Hay of Virginia) supported increasing the three-year enlistment to five years, thus creating a long-term professional army. In opposition, Wood proposed to cut the three-year term to two years and to prohibit most reenlistments in order to create a reserve of trained men.

The situation exploded in February 1912, when Ainsworth contemptuously and sarcastically rejected proposed administrative changes favored by the General Staff. Secretary of War Henry Lewis Stimson* suspended Ainsworth on February

15, but a highly embarrassing court-martial was avoided when Ainsworth was permitted to retire on February 16. The bitterness in Congress between the supporters of Wood and Ainsworth lasted some time, and only after one veto by President William Howard Taft and the threat of a second were specifically anti-Wood provisions defeated and the enlistment controversy compromised at four years with the colors and three in a reserve.

For a decade after his retirement, Ainsworth continued to exercise a very strong influence on military affairs through a circle of senior Army officers and powerful congressmen, and he is credited with a sizable role in the formulation of the 1916 National Defense Act. His wife died in May 1925, and Ainsworth himself succumbed to bronchial pneumonia on June 5, 1934, at the age of eighty-one. He was interred beside his wife in Arlington Cemetery.

Ainsworth's almost religious devotion to ordered procedures made him one of the Army's greatest business experts in an age that admired system and efficiency. He acquired a deserved reputation for administrative drive and an ability to complete any undertaking, and much of his lasting fame rests on his gift for creating order out of the previously prevailing chaos, confusion, and delay. In the long run, however, his insistence on habitual practice may actually have inhibited further administrative reform necessary to meet changing circumstances, and in the eyes of his opponents he was little better than a bureaucratic imperialist.

He always retained a tight hold on the dissemination of information, and he excelled at cultivating political contacts and influence through mutual favors. He developed the technique of taking personal credit for economies or positive decisions, while persuading others to sign unfavorable endorsements. Virtually every post he held was created for him by a grateful Congress, and he reputedly had more personal influence with Congress, usually exercised discreetly, than any other man in the government, not excluding the president himself. Ainsworth enjoyed close relations with the *Army and Navy Register*, one of the two contemporary service weeklies, but he received less favorable comment from the rival *Army and Navy Journal*. He could be charming and courteous, but his brusque manner, self-assurance, and ambition frequently made him appear arrogant. His injudicious, even contemptuous, and ultimately insubordinate remarks about those with whom he differed led to implacable enemies and numerous controversies. He was a general whose battles were fought in the offices and corridors of the War Department and in the halls and committee rooms of Congress. The enemy were rival bureaus and departments, the General Staff (which he referred to as the "General Stuff" and whose powers he repeatedly sought to restrict), and the chief of staff of the Army.

The tempestuous trial of strength between Wood and Ainsworth from which the adjutant general emerged with a damaged reputation, though he retained a considerable residue of influence, ought not to obscure Ainsworth's real abilities and his considerable contribution to the welfare of the Army and the rationalization of recordkeeping and military administration.

BIBLIOGRAPHY

Abbott, Lawrence F., ed. *The Letters of Archie Butt: Personal Aide to President Roosevelt*.
    Garden City, N.Y.: Doubleday, Page and Company, 1924.
————. *Taft and Roosevelt: The Intimate Letters of Archie Butt, Military Aide*. Garden
    City, N.Y.: Doubleday, Doran and Company, 1930.
Deutrich, Mabel E. *Struggle for Supremacy: The Career of General Fred C. Ainsworth*.
    Washington, D.C.: Public Affairs Press, 1962.
Hagedorn, Hermann. *Leonard Wood: A Biography*. Vol. 2. New York and London:
    Harper and Brothers, 1931.
Hagood, Johnson. *The Services of Supply: A Memoir of the Great War*. Boston: Houghton
    Mifflin Company, 1927.

EDWARD RANSON

ALGER, Russell Alexander (b. Western Reserve of Ohio, February 27, 1836;
d. Washington, D.C., January 24, 1907), Civil War officer, businessman, secretary of war.

Russell A. Alger was the eldest of three children of Russell and Caroline
Moulton Alger, Ohio pioneers. His parents, farmers of limited means, died when
young Russell was only eleven, leaving him to support himself and the smaller
children.

Alger's early life followed the pattern of the boy's success stories written by
his probable distant relative, Horatio Alger: orphaned poverty overcome by a
mixture of "luck and pluck." Subsisting as a farmhand and later as a part-time
school teacher, Alger managed to obtain a secondary education. He "read law"
with a local attorney and was admitted to the Ohio bar in 1857. Two years later,
he moved to Grand Rapids, Michigan, in search of the wider opportunities offered
by the expanding lumber industry. In Grand Rapids, Alger enjoyed modest
business success and married Annette Henry, the daughter of a prominent citizen.

The Civil War interrupted Alger's business career. An early adherent of the
Republican party and friend of his local congressman, Alger recruited a volunteer
cavalry company and in October 1861 received a captaincy in the 2d Michigan
Volunteer Cavalry. In April 1862 he was promoted to major in the same regiment.
At the minor Battle of Booneville, Mississippi, on June 1, 1862, under then
Colonel Philip Henry Sheridan,* Alger won distinction by leading a mounted
charge into the rear of a much larger Confederate force.

In October 1862 Alger transferred to the Army of the Potomac as lieutenant
colonel of the 6th Michigan Volunteer Cavalry. The following year, on June
11, now a colonel of volunteers, he took command of his own regiment, the 5th
Michigan Cavalry. This regiment, with the 1st, 6th, and 7th Michigan Cavalry,
made up the 2d Brigade, 3d Cavalry Division, Army of the Potomac, nicknamed
the "Michigan Brigade" and commanded by the flamboyant Brigadier General
George Armstrong Custer.* Leading the 5th Michigan, Alger participated in
most of the Michigan Brigade's engagements, from Gettysburg through the
Wilderness and Yellow Tavern to the Shenandoah Valley. On September 20,

1864, Alger resigned his commission because of ill-health. He had been a competent and dashing, but otherwise unremarkable, regimental commander. He later received brevet promotions to the volunteer ranks of brigadier and major general, which earned him the title among friends of "General Alger."

After he left the Army, Alger and his family settled in Detroit, where Alger quickly reestablished himself in the lumber business. By the mid-1880s Alger had made himself into a full-fledged Gilded Age tycoon. He controlled Alger, Smith, and Company, Michigan's largest lumbering concern. He owned timberland, sawmills, and other lumber-related property in Michigan, California, the South, and Canada, and was a director of a variety of industrial and financial corporations. Alger owned a large Detroit mansion and a private railroad car, collected art, and raised trotters; he associated with Cornelius Vanderbilt, Marshall Field, J. Pierpont Morgan, and other giants of finance and industry. Tall and distinguished in appearance, although frail in constitution as a result of wartime typhoid, Alger sported a neatly trimmed moustache and goatee and was noted for his generous gifts to charities, especially those dedicated to helping orphans.

Alger also became active in Republican politics and Union veterans' affairs. He helped form the Michigan Grand Army of the Republic (GAR), supervised the establishment of the state soldiers' home, and directed financial campaigns to aid destitute widows of Union generals. He attended GAR gatherings throughout the country. Alger's wealth and popularity among the veterans brought him influence in Michigan and upper Midwest Republican politics. He served one term as governor of Michigan, from 1885 to 1887, and in 1888 ran for the Republican presidential nomination as Michigan's favorite son. In 1889, his fellow veterans elected him GAR national commander. Alger early associated himself with the rising Ohio Republican, William McKinley. He helped secure Michigan's delegation for the Ohioan in 1896 and campaigned for McKinley among the still numerous Civil War veterans. In January 1897 President-elect McKinley rewarded Alger with the post of secretary of war.

McKinley had appointed Alger mainly for political reasons, to give recognition to the Union veterans and Midwestern Republicans, but Alger soon found himself with a war to conduct. He oversaw the mobilization and operations of the Army in the war with Spain (April-August 1898) and later directed the occupation of Cuba and Puerto Rico and the opening campaigns of the Philippine Insurrection. During his tenure in office, the Army grew from twenty-five thousand troops to a peak wartime strength of almost three hundred thousand. Alger received little credit for the quick and relatively cheap American victory, but most of the blame for the inevitable confusion of the first few weeks of hasty mobilization fell upon him, as did public denunciation for the Army's heavy losses to disease. By late 1898 Republican leaders throughout the country had decided that Alger was a political liability and were urging President McKinley to replace him. McKinley, either from loyalty or faint-heartedness, refused to ask outright for Alger's resignation. Alger, stubborn and self-righteous, did not offer it. He held out for months against the inevitable, hoping to remain until McKinley's first term ended in 1901. He finally resigned on July 18, 1899, after an ill-conceived attempt to unseat a Michigan Republican senator rendered his cabinet position untenable.

After leaving the War Department, Alger was appointed to the Senate from Michigan in 1902, to finish the term of the man he had tried to unseat in 1899, who had died. The following year, the state legislature elected Alger to a full term. He remained in the Senate until his death in January 1907.

Most accounts of the war with Spain dismiss Alger as incompetent and probably corrupt and Army administration as a study in confusion and ineptitude. Neither assessment is fully justified by the facts.

The War Department, within three months of the declaration of war in late April 1898, enlarged the Army almost tenfold and in the same period dispatched fifty thousand men on successful expeditions to Cuba, Puerto Rico, and the Philippines. The department accomplished these things in spite of equipment and supply shortages caused by years of starvation Army budgets, in spite of an initial lack of trained officers and men in both the regular service and the National Guard, and in spite of a disruptive Regular Army-National Guard dispute over organization of the wartime Volunteer Army, which forced overexpansion of the Army within too short a time.

Alger contributed to these achievements. He worked hard at his job and relied on the guidance of the very capable Adjutant General Henry Clark Corbin* to overcome his own ignorance of the changes in military tactics and technology since 1865. On matters where business experience and contacts were of value, for example, in the purchase of merchant vessels for a permanent Army Transport Service, Alger acted decisively and effectively. He also tried to short-cut overly cumbersome War Department administrative procedures. Neither contemporary investigators nor later historians ever substantiated any instance of wrongdoing by Alger for personal gain. The men who worked most closely with him respected his patriotism and devotion to the welfare of the troops.

Nevertheless, Alger fell far short of being a great secretary of war, or even a good one. The wartime successes of his department resulted primarily from the efforts of Adjutant General Corbin, the other generally competent staff bureau chiefs, and the field commanders. Alger usually rubber-stamped their advice or passed on McKinley's strategic directives to the Army chain of command. Alger displayed no interest in remedying the War Department's major structural deficiencies and, like President McKinley, preferred to make do with the existing organization. Vain and egotistical, Alger was prone to make fatuous public remarks and proved of little value as a cabinet policy advisor. He early stumbled into a debilitating feud with Commanding General of the Army Nelson Appleton Miles,* in which Miles was probably more at fault than Alger. The resulting mud-slinging by Miles, especially his agitation of the groundless "Embalmed Beef" scandal, helped give the Alger War Department its seamy contemporary reputation, a reputation that Alger's inept efforts at public defense only damaged further. Above all, Alger never seemed to be fully in control of the multifarious activities of his department: he appeared to most of his cabinet colleagues to be a small man in a big place. The postwar Dodge Commission, while praising Alger for honesty and industry, summed up the assessment of his more sympathetic contemporaries: "There was lacking in the general administration of the War Department. . .that complete grasp of the situation which was essential to the highest efficiency and discipline of the Army."

Alger's infinitely more capable successor as secretary of war, Elihu Root,* benefited from Alger's mistakes and tribulations. Alger left Root an Army which was operating effectively from day to day, which possessed adequate equipment and supplies, and which had an officer corps that had been shaken out of the pre-1898 doldrums and tempered by campaigning experience. Root, spared immediate administrative crises, could concentrate his considerable talents on colonial policy, Philippine war strategy, and long-range plans for a general staff, Army reorganization, and militia reform. Whatever his own merits or lack of them, Alger inherited an Army struggling to overcome years of neglect and inaction; Root took over an Army on the upswing and made the most of it.

BIBLIOGRAPHY

Alger, Russell Alexander. *The Spanish-American War*. New York and London: Harper and Brothers, 1901.
Baxter, Albert. *History of the City of Grand Rapids, Michigan*. New York and Grand Rapids: Munsell and Company, 1891.
Chadwick, French Ensor. *The Relations of the United States to Spain: The Spanish-American War*. 2 vols. New York: Charles Scribner's Sons, 1911.
Cosmas, Graham A. *An Army for Empire: The United States Army in the Spanish-American War*. Columbia: University of Missouri Press, 1971.

GRAHAM A. COSMAS

ALLEN, Ethan (b. Litchfield, Conn., January 10, 1738; d. Burlington, Vt., February 12, 1789), soldier, politician, writer. Allen's capture of Fort Ticonderoga was the first American victory of the Revolution.

Ethan Allen was born to Joseph Allen, a prosperous young farmer in Litchfield, Connecticut, and his wife Mary in 1738. Two years later, the family moved to the more primitive town of Cornwall, where the family increased until the death of Joseph in 1755. Allen became the head of a family of nine at the age of seventeen and so had little formal education.

He served briefly as a militia private in the French and Indian War. For five or six years he farmed successfully, bought more land, and acquired a part interest in an iron foundry at Salisbury. He sold out and, after trying his hand at some small mining ventures for two years, followed other restless Connecticut men north to Vermont, then called the New Hampshire Grants. Since New York also claimed this territory, the settlers formed a backwoods militia to fight the 'Yorkers. They called themselves the Green Mountain Boys (from the old French *Verd Mont*) and elected Ethan Allen "Colonel Commandant." He held the rough group together by his self-confidence and great size and physical prowess. The Boys routed New York forces in the summer of 1771 and from then on staged "wolf hunts" against sheriff's posses, surveying parties, and groups of would-be 'Yorker settlers. These were not true military actions, but they gave the organization cohesion and high morale.

After the American Revolution began, a Connecticut emissary went to Allen with a plan to seize Fort Ticonderoga and Crown Point between Lake Champlain and Lake George, on the main waterway between Canada and the American colonies. At once, Allen mustered a force of 230 men.

He and his Boys reached the cove across from Ticonderoga at 11:00 on the night of May 9, 1775. Boats he had expected to use were not there. Finally, at 1:00 A.M., and with only three hours left until daylight, he was able to find one large boat and one small one. Rather than postpone the attack to the following night, Allen took forty-three men across to a point a quarter of a mile from the fort. Even this required repeated trips. Leaving his second-in-command Seth Warner to bring over the main body after the attack was launched, Allen led his men to a breach in the south side of the outer wall and through it, brandishing a large sword. The gate through the inner wall was guarded by a single sentry, who leveled his flintlock at Allen at pointblank range. It failed to fire. Closely followed by Colonel Benedict Arnold,* who was present as an observer, and the Boys, Allen rushed through the gate and into the central courtyard. Another sentry lunged with a bayonet at a man standing near Allen and Arnold. Allen felled him with the flat of his sword and rushed up the stairs towards the commandant's quarters, yelling to him to come out and surrender the fort or die with every man in it. A British officer—not the commandant—came out on a landing with his britches over his arm and asked by what authority Allen presumed to make such a demand. "In the name of the Great Jehovah and the Continental Congress," was the reply. Ticonderoga, "Key to Canada," had fallen in ten minutes with no loss of life. Seth Warner seized Crown Point the next day, and Colonel Arnold, leading reinforcements from Massachusetts and sailing in a captured schooner, later rounded up a small garrison at St. John's, at the far end of Lake Champlain. In an ill-judged move, Allen subsequently attempted to occupy St. John's, but a larger force from Montreal obliged him to retreat.

As conquering heroes, Ethan Allen and Seth Warner appeared before the Continental Congress in Philadelphia and the New York Provincial Assembly in New York City to urge an invasion of Canada. After much delay, an expedition against Montreal did get underway under General Richard Montgomery.* Allen received no command but was made a "scout," with the dangerous assignment of going out to persuade Canadians and Indians to rise against the British. With his loud voice and impressive presence, Allen succeeded well and was ordered to form a regiment of Canadians. Most of the British forces defending Montreal were in strong positions at St. John's, where Montgomery besieged them. In total disregard of his orders, Ethan Allen undertook an independent attack on

Montreal itself, largely with his Canadian volunteers. As at Ticonderoga, he moved with a small portion of his forces and counted on his main body to follow. This time he planned to enter a city of nine thousand with a force of some three hundred men. Again there was difficulty in crossing a body of water by night with insufficient boats and canoes. High winds on the night of the attack made the water rough and the crossing hazardous. Allen crossed the St. Lawrence upstream with about one hundred men. The remainder, under a Major Brown, never crossed. Allen faced eighty regulars and about 250 armed townsmen. The inhabitants of Montreal were taken by surprise. In the confusion of daybreak, they did not know the true American strength, and the first reaction of the British commander was to take his regulars out of the city and withdraw. Without his main body, Allen took up a position some ten miles north of the city. He was attacked in overwhelming force during the afternoon and was forced to surrender.

Allen was put in heavy irons and kept in solitary confinement for a month aboard a ship at Montreal, with only a box to sit on. In November he was placed on a transport for England. He and thirty-three Americans who had surrendered with him were crowded into an area about twenty feet square, with two tubs for excrement, and were half-starved. Finally, a decision was made to treat Allen and his men as prisoners of war, and they were repatriated to New York for exchange.

Once freed, Allen went to General George Washington* at Valley Forge. The commander in chief received him courteously. Congress gave Allen a brevet rank of colonel, which did not guarantee a command, and a pay scale, which was not maintained. Later, Allen commanded the Vermont militia with the rank of major general.

Upon his return to his home near Bennington, Vermont, Allen found himself the most powerful political figure in the state, and he consolidated his position by drawing around himself the so-called Arlington Junta. A Declaration of Independence was adopted in January 1777, and in July of that year a constitution was adopted for the "Republic of Vermont." Vermont's struggle for admission to the United States in the face of New York's opposition was long and difficult. In his first year back from captivity, Allen made three trips to Philadelphia to win over the Congress. He gained some support from members of New England delegations but achieved no more than a stalemate. He felt bitterly frustrated.

There followed a highly controversial period in Allen's life in which he threatened to take Vermont out of the war if the nation persisted in denying it admission. To make his threat more convincing, he entered into negotiations with General Sir Frederick Haldimand, the able British governor general of Canada. Prisoners were exchanged. A truce, signed ostensibly for this purpose, lasted over a year. The Green Mountain Boys, now a veteran Continental regiment under Colonel Seth Warner, were disbanded. Haldimand concentrated approximately two thousand men near Ticonderoga and seemed about to invade Vermont if hostilities resumed. Prodded by General Washington, Congress offered to receive Vermont, but on terms the State Assembly refused. Vermont did not become a state until 1791 when it was admitted as the fourteenth American state.

In 1779 Allen published his *Narrative of Colonel Ethan Allen's Captivity*, which included an idealized version of his campaigns. It was widely acclaimed. Although he never mastered spelling or grammar, he was an effective pamphleteer and publicized the claims of Vermont against its neighboring states. His deist tract, *Reason, the Only Oracle of Man*, attacked the established church and created a sensation. For six years before his death, Allen was retired from active politics. He died of apoplexy at the age of fifty-one.

The political significance of the capture of Fort Ticonderoga was far greater than the size of the operation. The feat crystallized the war with England. Now there could be no turning back. In addition, fifty-nine serviceable cannon from Ticonderoga and Crown Point helped General Washington to drive the British from Boston. Had the Continental Congress responded with more vigor to Allen's plea for an invasion of Canada, Montreal might well have fallen. Just as success at Montreal might have spread through Canada, failure was also influential. It affected adversely the 1775–1776 campaign of Montgomery and Arnold against Quebec. French Canadians and Indians had no particular affection for either the English or the Yankees, but they were greatly influenced by who was strongest.

The extensive and degrading abuses which the British inflicted on Allen in his captivity also had far-reaching effects. His cause was championed in Parliament, and American prisoners were subsequently treated as prisoners of war.

At Valley Forge, General Washington was impressed by Allen's "fortitude and firmness," but he did not recommend him to Congress for a colonelcy and did not give him an active appointment. Allen was considered too impetuous a leader, too preoccupied with his own glory, and too untutored.

The fact that Allen held an American commission for the balance of the war puts his dickering with General Haldimand in a particularly unfavorable light. Fortunately for Allen, defeat of the British at Yorktown ended their negotiations with Vermont and saved him from becoming another Benedict Arnold. Instead, he is remembered as a stirring leader, whose action at Ticonderoga sent a wave of enthusiasm through the colonies at the outset of the struggle. His endurance as a prisoner was also a source of patriotic pride. His flamboyant actions in the Grant staved off the 'Yorkers, and his high-flown pamphlets popularized the Vermont cause. Part heroes and part legend, Ethan Allen and his Green Mountain Boys are an American tradition.

BIBLIOGRAPHY

De Puy, Henry W. *Ethan Allen and the Green Mountain Heroes of '76*. 1st ed., New York: J. C. Darby, 1854. 2d ed., Freeport, N.Y.: Books for Libraries Press, 1970.
Holbrook, Stewart H. *America's Ethan Allen*. 1st ed., Boston: Houghton Mifflin Company, 1949. 2d ed., Portland, Oreg.: Benfords and Mort, 1958.

Jellison, Charles A. *Ethan Allen: Frontier Rebel*. Syracuse, N.Y.: Syracuse University Press, 1969.

Pell, John. *Ethan Allen*. 1st ed., Boston: Houghton Mifflin Company, 1929. 2d ed., Freeport, N.Y.: Books for Libraries Press, 1972.

EDWARD A. RAYMOND

ALLEN, Henry Tureman (b. Sharpsburg, Ky., April 13, 1859; d. Buena Vista Springs, Pa., August 29, 1930), Army Officer; commander, U.S. 90th Division, World War I.

Henry T. Allen graduated from West Point in 1882 and began his career with routine frontier duty at cavalry posts in the western United States. Handsome, energetic, and ambitious, he began to cultivate and attract the attention of his superiors. In September 1884 Allen became aide de camp to General Nelson Appleton Miles,* then commanding the Department of the Columbia.

On Miles' orders, Allen soon found himself exploring Alaska's Copper, Tanana, and Koyukuk rivers. In seven grueling months, Allen's small party covered more than 2,500 miles and produced maps of these previously unsurveyed rivers as well as a wealth of mineralogical, meteorological, and sociopolitical information. His report, published in 1887, earned him international recognition and honors by several geographic societies.

In July 1887 Allen married a Chicago heiress, Jennie Dora Johnston. They spent their honeymoon abroad in St. Petersburg, where Allen, already fluent in French and German, intended to learn Russian on an extended leave of absence. Next came an assignment as a foreign language instructor at West Point. When, in 1890, the War Department decided to send out the first American military attachés, Allen applied for and received the post at St. Petersburg.

Allen's seven years as an attaché (five in St. Petersburg and two in Berlin) gave him a broad understanding of European affairs and many valuable contacts. He was never loath to exploit the contacts. During the Spanish-American War, he was able to cut short his tour in Berlin and wangle command of a cavalry troop in the invasion of Cuba. To his dismay, his unit's participation in the Santiago Campaign consisted mainly of scouting and escort duty. Worse, Allen soon caught malaria. After an extended convalescence and several brief desk jobs, he got what he wanted most: another chance to distinguish himself in combat, this time in the Philippines fighting *insurrectos*.

From early 1900 through mid-1901, Allen commanded elements of the 43d Volunteer Infantry Regiment on Samar and Leyte. His success in training and using native troops to supplement American forces led directly to his next assignment: command of the Philippine Constabulary, a quasi-military police force responsible to the newly installed civilian government. The Constabulary's officers were Americans, but the troops were Filipinos. Their mission was to sweep up the last remnants of the insurrection, to suppress brigandage and lawlessness of all types, and to provide services such as commissaries and hospitals to the civil government and its agents throughout the archipelago. The Constabulary accomplished all this and more, but not without controversy and personal cost to Allen. Some of his Army contemporaries were probably envious of his temporary rank of brigadier general as chief of Constabulary (he was still a Regular Army captain); others undoubtedly smarted from his sometimes arrogant use of power; a few even resented the fact that he was proving that native soldiers were the equal of Americans when properly trained and led. Whatever the reasons for his unpopularity in Army circles, Allen became a controversial figure and felt himself an outcast. In 1907 he left his general's star in the Philippines and went, as a major, to command two cavalry troops in Yellowstone Park.

Nevertheless, within three years Allen was back in the center of things. A position as acting chief of cavalry on the General Staff in Washington under Major General Leonard Wood* gave Allen plenty of scope for his talents and ambition, but it also embroiled him in many of the controversies that marked Wood's tenure as chief of staff. Allen had left the Philippines determined to get his star back and the General Staff assignment seemed to put that goal within reach, but such were the personal and professional animosities that swirled around Wood and his associates that by 1914 Allen was resigned to retiring as a lieutenant colonel.

When World War I broke out, Allen was preparing to leave Washington for troop duty in Georgia. Because of his contacts among Europe's diplomatic and military elite, however, he immediately became the senior military member of an official delegation sent to Europe to help bring home more than fifty thousand American civilians trapped in the war zone by travel and currency restrictions. As a military observer, Allen also visited the capitals of most of the belligerents and was present at the Battle of the Marne. His report made upon his return to Washington accurately predicted the course of the war, but his prescience was neither appreciated nor heeded. By early 1915 he was running cavalry drills at Fort Oglethorpe, Georgia, and corresponding with his friends Leonard Wood and Theodore Roosevelt* about the woeful lack of American preparedness.

Allen's unit was one of four cavalry regiments mobilized in 1916 in response to the depredations of Pancho Villa on the Texas border. Allen's participation in the Mexican Punitive Expedition, first as executive officer of the 11th Cavalry and then as John Joseph Pershing's* inspector general, brought him for the first time into close contact with Pershing. A mutual respect developed. After the U.S. entry into World War I, Allen was given the 90th Division (Texas-Oklahoma) to organize and train. He took his division to France in the spring of 1918 and commanded it with distinction, participating in both the St. Mihiel and Meuse-Argonne offensives. During the Armistice period, Pershing kept Allen in Europe as a corps commander as the American Expeditionary Forces (AEF) shrank in size with every returning troop ship.

In July 1919, after the Versailles Treaty was signed, Allen took command of the American Forces in Germany (AFG), the American contingent of the four-power occupation force that had moved into the Rhineland shortly after the Armistice and now was a fixture of the peace settlement. For the next four years from his headquarters in Coblenz, Allen exercised military governorship over 2,500 square miles of German territory and presided over a "model army" that soon stabilized at about ten thousand men. For much of this time Allen was not only the senior U.S. military official in the Rhineland, but the senior State Department representative as well. In the latter capacity he sat as a member of the four-power Inter-Allied Rhineland High Commission and, often without specific instructions from Washington, did his best to represent American interests in the Rhineland area. With the postwar policies of Britain, France, and the United States diverging, and with Franco-German tensions high over such issues as treaty violations and reparations payments, Allen found himself siding nearly as often with the Germans as with his erstwhile Allies. When the French occupied the Ruhr in retaliation for German reparations defaults, Washington decided to end its participation in the Rhineland occupation. Allen's unauthorized attempts to dissuade the French from their ill-considered move had annoyed both Paris and Washington, but by 1923 American sentiment, having repudiated President Woodrow Wilson and the League of Nations, was strongly in favor of "bringing home the boys." With the return of the AFG, Major General Henry T. Allen retired from active military service. He was sixty-four.

In retirement, Allen remained both busy and controversial. He wrote several books recounting his Rhineland experiences and in these, as well as in numerous articles and speeches, warned that in the unresolved issues of the peace settlement were the seeds of another war. He became an advocate of U.S. participation in the League of Nations and dabbled in politics, first as an organizer of veterans groups for the Democrats and finally, in 1928, as a presidential candidate. He was nominated to run with Governor Al Smith at the Democratic Convention in 1928, but he lost out on the first ballot to Senator Joseph T. Robinson of Arkansas. Allen also lent his name, and much time and energy, to a number of charities and other worthwhile causes. He divided his last years between his home in Washington and Charmian, his mountain estate sixty miles to the north. In the summers at Charmian, he wrote, compiled a lifetime's collection of papers and documents, and enjoyed his grandchildren. There, in August 1930, he died instantly of a stroke.

Three of Henry Allen's military assignments stand out as being of true historical significance: his exploration of Alaska in 1885, his work with the Philippine Constabulary from 1901 to 1907, and his dual position after World War I as commander of the American Forces in Germany and member of the Inter-Allied Rhineland High Commission.

Allen's Alaskan venture remained little known except to professional geographers. Nevertheless, his accomplishment has rightly been called one of the great explorations of North America. Few explorers have done more in less time and with such meager resources. Later, larger, and better equipped expeditions were to find his work a solid foundation on which to build.

The Philippine Constabulary is still in existence. For many years it remained largely as Allen left it, though no American officers have served in it since Philippine independence. Time vindicated Allen's basic conception of the Constabulary's organization and purpose.

Allen's influence on the course of history in the Rhineland is more difficult to measure, but there can be little doubt that he made his influence felt. His ability to partially restrain the French probably kept tensions in the Rhineland from rising even higher during his years in Coblenz. It is also possible that this restraint only contributed to the bitterness of the Ruhr crisis when it finally came. What is indisputable is that Allen represented the interests of the United States as he understood them with dignity, honesty, and honor.

Allen's activities on behalf of international cooperation and understanding after his retirement were also of more than passing importance. To rouse his countrymen from their apathy towards Europe's problems and to soften the hearts of Europeans toward each other were Allen's twin goals. That he failed does not detract from the clarity of his vision.

Perhaps the most that can be said of Allen as a writer and thinker is that he was an intelligent and articulate commentator to whom men listened with respect, if not always agreement. Much of what he wrote for publication remains of value to scholars. Of equal importance are his personal and official papers, now in the Library of Congress.

Was Allen's career an unusual one for a military professional? Army officers have always been expected to be generalists, but Allen was the military generalist *par excellence*. Few of his contemporaries could match the diversity of his experiences. His assignments frequently took him to the borderline of civil-military relations, where the code of his profession did not always provide the surest guide for action. He often made his own rules. And yet, if his career was rather atypical, in another sense it closely paralleled the history of the institution and the nation he served and loved. When Allen entered the Army, it was a tiny organization with little influence and less prestige, physically isolated from the rest of American society, and intellectually stagnant. When he retired, forty-one years and three wars later, the Army was once again in a postwar cycle of neglect, but it had become both a more professional force than he had known as a young lieutenant and one capable of exercising, for good or ill, a much more influential part in the nation's life.

BIBLIOGRAPHY

Allen, Henry T. *My Rhineland Journal*. Boston: Houghton Mifflin Company, 1923.
————. *The Rhineland Occupation*. Indianapolis, Ind.: Bobbs-Merrill Company, 1927.
Bullard, Robert L. *Fighting Generals*. Ann Arbor, Mich.: J. W. Edwards Company, 1944.
Twichell, Heath, Jr. *Allen: The Biography of an Army Officer, 1859–1930*. New Brunswick, N.J.: Rutgers University Press, 1974.

HEATH TWICHELL

ALLEN, Terry de la Mesa (b. Fort Douglas, Utah, April 1, 1888; d. El Paso, Texas, September 12, 1969), commander of 1st Infantry Division in North Africa and Italy until relieved in September 1943.

Allen was the son of Samuel Edward Allen, a career Army officer (U.S. Military Academy class of 1881), and Conchita de la Mesa Allen, the daughter of a Spanish colonel who fought for the North during the U.S. Civil War. Even though he was born in Utah, the younger Allen considered himself to be a Texan, as he spent most of his youth in Texas. In 1907 he entered West Point but had a difficult time. He failed mathematics and had to stay on a fifth year. Even five years were not enough, however, and he was dismissed after failing a gunnery course in his senior year. He then attended Catholic University of America and graduated in 1912. On November 30, 1912, he obtained a commission in the cavalry. For most of the period until the outbreak of World War I, he served in the Southwest along the Mexican border and was involved in several skirmishes. He became a first lieutenant in July 1916 and a captain in May 1917.

During World War I Allen managed to transfer to the infantry where he commanded the 3d Battalion of the 358th Infantry, 90th Division. He was wounded three times while leading this unit of Oklahomans and Texans in several battles that earned him a reputation as an aggressive leader. Before returning to the United States, he became a temporary major. His new rank became permanent in July 1920, but he did not receive another promotion until August 1935. In 1926 he graduated 203d in a class of 245 from the Command and General Staff School. He also graduated from the Army War College in 1935.

He apparently became a brigadier general in the Army of the United States in October 1940 without holding the rank of colonel. Upon promotion to major general in June 1942, Allen assumed command of the 1st Infantry Division, which he led in the North Africa Campaign and in the invasion of Sicily.

According to the plans for the invasion of Sicily, the 82d Airborne Division was supposed to drop on high ground around the Gela Beach area to prevent enemy reinforcement, while Allen and the 1st Division took Gela and the airport at Ponte Olivo. The airborne attack failed, and the beach landings could hardly be called successful. Ponte Olivo Airfield was supposed to be in Allied hands by D plus one (July 11, 1943), but everything seemed to have gone awry. George Smith Patton, Jr.* who was in charge of the landing, had a stormy interview with Allen on July 11, after which Allen described Patton as "very wrought up." The airport was taken on July 12, but Allen had more trouble a month later.

Due to inaccurate intelligence reports, Allen designated only one regiment to attack Troina, Sicily, on August 1, 1943. When the attack failed, Allen waited two days to commit more troops instead of acting immediately. As a result, it took the 1st Division a week to subdue Troina. Shortly thereafter, in September, he was relieved of command and returned to the United States where he took charge of the 104th (Timberwolf) Infantry Division.

He landed at Cherbourg with the 104th in September 1944. From there, the division proceeded in October to free the port of Antwerp and march into Holland. After 195 consecutive days of frontline combat, the 104th met the Russians in Germany on April 26, 1945. Allen thus became the only general in World War II to lead a second division into combat after being relieved of his command.

Throughout his career, Allen "had the reputation of being a hell 'raiser' and an unconventional 'hotshot operator,' " according to Mark Wayne Clark.* He frequently got into trouble. Clark further noted that "he shocked everybody—the enemy, his troops who loved him, and his superiors." To counterbalance the effect of his questionable reputation, Allen enjoyed the support of the chief of staff, General George Catlett Marshall,* whom he had impressed in 1932 at the Advanced Infantry School. It was half-seriously rumored in the Army that Allen would have been court-martialed if Marshall had not seen to his promotion to general. The chief of staff also obtained the 1st Division for Allen.

More orthodox leaders had doubts about Allen almost from the beginning of the North Africa Campaign. They questioned neither his aggressiveness nor his ability to inspire and lead troops, but they were critical of him as a disciplinarian. He seemed to repay the devotion of his troops with indulgence. On one occasion soldiers of the 1st showed their resentment of fellow soldiers who were in rear echelon service positions by roaming the streets of Oran and attacking anyone they suspected of not being an active combatant. Allen did nothing to punish them.

Despite these problems, his superiors valued his abilities. When General Dwight David Eisenhower* intended to give him command of a corps before the invasion of Sicily, General Patton asked to retain him in command of the 1st until the initial phase of the invasion was over.

Allen and Patton had been polo partners and friends before the war and became generals at the same time. Perhaps this relationship made Patton's verbal rebuke on the beach at Gela, Sicily, particularly galling to Allen. Whatever the reason, Allen resented Patton. According to General Omar Nelson Bradley,* Patton's second-in-command at that time, "By now Allen had become too much of an individualist to submerge himself without friction in the group undertakings of war. The 1st Division, under Allen's command, had become too full of self-pity and pride. To save Allen both from himself and from his brilliant record and to save the Division from the heady effects of too much success, I decided to separate them." Bradley believed the 1st had set the pace in both Tunisia and Africa, but he had doubts about Allen, who had made some questionable decisions, such as the one to attack into the Chouiqui foothills in Tunisia without purpose and at a cost of heavy casualties. His performance at Troina was, apparently, the final straw. Whatever hesitation Bradley may have felt at relieving him disappeared when he and his second-in-command, Theodore Roosevelt, Jr., answered the summons to Army Headquarters. They stormed into Bradley's office complaining that the military police had given them a ticket for failing to wear their helmets. The incident exemplified their attitude.

Tribute to his ability and successful leadership of the 104th notwithstanding, Allen's career never recovered from the blow of being relieved. Still a major general, he retired in 1946.

BIBLIOGRAPHY

Blumenson, Martin, ed. *The Patton Papers*. Boston: Houghton Mifflin, 1974.
Bradley, Omar N. *A Soldier's Story*. New York: Henry Holt, 1951.
Clark, Mark W. *Calculated Risk*. New York: Harper, 1950.

PHILIP D. JONES

ALMOND, Edward Mallory (b. Luray, Va., December 12, 1892; d. Washington, D.C., June 11, 1979), combat commander in three wars.

Edward Mallory Almond was graduated from the Virginia Military Institute in 1915 and was commissioned a second lieutenant of infantry in the U.S. Army on November 30, 1916. In World War I he commanded the 12th Machine Gun Battalion of the 4th Division in France, where he participated in the Aisne-Marne and the Meuse-Argonne offensives. For his actions in World War I, Almond was promoted to major and was awarded the Silver Star and the Purple Heart medals. He remained in Europe with the Army of Occupation until July 1919.

Upon his return to the United States, Almond was assigned to Marion Institute, Alabama, as professor of military science and tactics. Postwar reductions in the Army cost Almond his majority, and he reverted to the rank of captain until his promotion to major in 1928. He attended the Infantry School and was retained there as an automatic weapons instructor until he was selected to attend the Command and General Staff School. In 1930 he joined the 45th Infantry Regiment in the Philippine Islands, where he commanded a battalion of Filipino troops.

In 1933 Almond attended the Army War College and was then detailed to the Latin American Section of the Military Intelligence Division of the War Department General Staff. He was promoted to lieutenant colonel in 1938 and attended both the Air Corps Tactical School and the Naval War College before returning to the General Staff. In 1941 he became the assistant chief of staff (G–3) for the VI Corps, was promoted to colonel, and then became chief of staff for VI Corps.

Almond's service in World War II really began with his promotion to brigadier general and his assignment as assistant division commander of the 93d Infantry Division. In September he received his second star and command of the 92d Infantry Division. After organizing and training the division, Almond commanded it in combat in Italy in 1944 and 1945. For his World War II service, General Almond was awarded the Distinguished Service Medal, an Oak Leaf Cluster to the Silver Star, the Legion of Merit, the Bronze Star, the Air Medal, and the Army Commendation Medal with two Oak Leaf Clusters.

General Almond returned to the United States to command the 2d Infantry Division but in 1946 was ordered to Japan as assistant chief of staff (G–1) for Army Forces, Pacific. He soon became deputy chief of staff and in 1949 was assigned as chief of staff for both Army Forces, Pacific, and Far East Command. In 1950 his duties were expanded to include chief of staff, United Nations Command.

When hostilities were initiated in Korea in 1950, Almond, as the American and United Nations chief of staff, was responsible for implementing the decisions of General Douglas MacArthur,* the supreme commander, United Nations Command. In September 1950 General Almond was named commander of the X Corps for the Inchon-Seoul Campaign. He continued in command of the X Corps during the advance into North Korea, the retreat to Hungnam, and the subsequent operations in South Korea until July 1951. He was promoted to the rank of lieutenant general in February 1951. For his service in the Korean conflict, he was awarded the Distinguished Service Cross with Oak Leaf Cluster, an Oak Leaf Cluster to the Distinguished Service Medal, the Distinguished Flying Cross with two Oak Leaf Clusters, the Bronze Star with "V" device, and fifteen Oak Leaf Clusters to the Air Medal. In August 1951 General Almond was designated commandant of the Army War College, a position he held until his retirement from active service on January 1, 1953.

"Ned" Almond, as he was known, was the son of Walter Coles and Grace Pophan Almond. He married Margret Crook in 1917, and they had a son and a daughter. Both his son and his son-in-law were killed in action in World War II in Europe. After leaving the Army, General Almond became an executive of the Life Insurance Company of Alabama. He was active in numerous civic and charitable organizations, particularly the Boy Scouts of America. He was a member of the Board of Visitors of the Virginia Military Institute from 1960 to 1968, serving as president of the board in 1968.

General Almond's reputation, as any commander's, must be determined by his accomplishments as a commander in the field. He distinguished himself as a machine gun battalion commander in World War I. Between the wars he was selected to attend all the schools necessary for advancement to the higher levels of command. His performance at those schools and in command and staff assignments rightly drew the favorable attention of his superior officers. Almond impressed many observers as the embodiment of the courtly Southern soldier. Another view of Almond expressed by a contemporary stated that "when it pays to be aggressive, Ned's aggressive, and when it pays to be cautious, Ned's aggressive, and he wouldn't step two paces to the rear for the devil himself."

General George Catlett Marshall* personally selected Almond to command the 92d Infantry Division in World War II. This command was one of the most controversial of the war because the 92d was a Negro unit. From the initial organization, through its training period and deployment in the Italian campaigns, this division, the only black division committed to combat as a division, was subjected to extraordinary scrutiny by the military and the American public. As a Southern, white Regular Army officer, Almond was certainly justified in describing this command as the most difficult of his career. Almond's personal opinion of his role, and that of his division in World War II, may be deduced from the title given to the history of the 92d Division's operations in Italy: *A Fragment of Victory*.

In 1950, as chief of staff to General Douglas MacArthur, Almond was responsible for developing Operation CHROMITE, the plan for the Inchon invasion. MacArthur then named Almond to command the X Corps which was to carry out CHROMITE. Almond has described his command of the X Corps as the most rewarding assignment of his career because it afforded him the opportunity of independent command. The redeployment of the X Corps to the northeast coast of North Korea, the advance to the Yalu River, and operations in the

Chanjin (Chosen) Reservoir against Chinese "volunteers" once again made Almond a figure of controversy, but his skillfully executed withdrawal of X Corps and thousands of Korean refugees by sea from Hungnam earned him a third star. In Korea Almond made extensive use of the Marine Corps' helicopters and became a strong advocate of organic Army aviation units. He was also instrumental in instituting studies for improving tactical air support techniques based upon his Korean experiences.

General Almond's military service to his country spanned thirty-seven years and three wars. His accomplishments at each level of his career clearly indicated that he was an officer of exceptional ability. His military reputation will always be judged, however, by the accomplishments of his two major combat commands, the 92d Infantry Division in Italy and the X Corps in Korea.

BIBLIOGRAPHY

Appleman, Roy E. *South to the Naktong, North to the Yalu (June–November, 1950)*. Vol. 2. *U.S. Army in the Korean War*. Washington, D.C.: U.S. Government Printing Office, 1961.
Fisher, Ernest F., Jr. *Cassino to the Alps*. Vol. 4. *Mediterranean Theater of Operations* Subseries; *U.S. Army in World War II*. Washington, D.C.: U.S. Government Printing Office, 1977.
Goodman, Paul. *A Fragment of Victory in Italy During World War II: A Special Study*. Carlisle Barracks, Pa.: Army War College, 1952.
Lee, Ulysses. *The Employment of Negro Troops*. Vol. 8. *Special Studies* Subseries; *U.S. Army in World War II*. Washington, D.C.: U.S. Government Printing Office, 1966.
Schnabel, James F. *Policy and Direction: The First Year*. Vol. 1. *U.S. Army in the Korean War*. Washington, D.C.: U.S. Government Printing Office, 1972.

DAVID CHILDRESS

AMHERST, Jeffery, First Baron (b. Brooks Place, Riverhead, Kent, January 29, 1717; d. Montreal, Sevenoaks, Kent, August 3, 1797), British general. Amherst captured Louisbourg in 1758 and commanded the Anglo-American forces that conquered Canada in 1759–1760.

Jeffery Amherst rose to prominence in the British Army through the patronage of powerful men. The second son of a respectable Kentish lawyer, he was sent at twelve to serve as a page in the household of his neighbor, Lionel, first duke of Dorset. Dorset subsequently arranged for him to buy a commission in Colonel John Ligonier's regiment of cavalry, and in 1742 Ligonier took Amherst, then a lieutenant in the 1st Foot Guards, to Flanders as an aide de camp. Amherst continued to serve with Ligonier, distinguishing himself at Dettingen and Fontenoy, until 1746 when he gained a place on the staff of William Augustus, duke of Cumberland, the captain general of the British Army. For most of the ensuing decade he remained closely associated with Cumberland—as an aide during the campaigns of 1746 and 1747 on the Continent, as a groom of the bedchamber during the years of uneasy peace from 1748 to 1756, and, following brief tours as commissary to Hessian troops in British service, as aide once more during Cumberland's disastrous campaign in Germany in 1757.

Paradoxically, Cumberland's disgrace and recall soon brought Amherst to an independent command in America. In September 1757 William Pitt, the head of the ministry, made Ligonier commander in chief of the Army in place of Cumberland; and Ligonier, in turn, recommended Amherst to help carry out Pitt's plans for defeating France in 1758. Pitt proposed to reduce British commitments in Europe and to mount a decisive offensive in North America. He would give first priority to capturing Louisbourg (the French fortress on Cape Breton Island that guarded the Atlantic approaches to Canada) and perhaps Quebec; second, to sweeping the French from Lake Champlain and taking Montreal; and third, to reducing Fort Duquesne. In December he chose Major General James Abercromby to be commander in chief in America and Amherst to command the more than thirteen thousand regular troops destined for Louisbourg. Thus, Amherst, a colonel of infantry who had never held an independent command, was brought home from Germany, made a major general, and sent to command the most powerful expeditionary force yet assembled in the New World. He reached Halifax on May 28, 1758, just as his forces were getting underway for Louisbourg.

Amherst was determined to make the most of his opportunity to capture both Louisbourg and Quebec in the campaign of 1758. Although his forces were much superior to those at Louisbourg, the garrison was respectable, the fortifications were strong, and the harbor and adjacent coasts firmly held. To overcome these obstacles, capture Louisbourg, and still have time to attack Quebec, Amherst landed his troops within four miles of Louisbourg on the rocky and fortified shores of Garbarouse Bay. But once ashore his troops were so obstructed by terrain, weather, and illness that it took them a month to complete a siege line about the town; the garrison did not surrender until July 26. Even then, Amherst wanted to go on to Quebec—to fulfill his own and Pitt's hopes for the campaign—and only reluctantly conceded that he could not safely withdraw from Louisbourg and take Quebec before winter. Having made this decision, he sent detachments to raid the Gulf of St. Lawrence and Bay of Fundy and went himself with four thousand men to assist Abercromby, who had been defeated at Ticonderoga.

If the capture of Louisbourg did not completely satisfy Amherst, it delighted his superiors who were starved for success and who promptly chose him to command all British forces in North America. But this new command did not give him full control over the war or make his own tasks easier. William Pitt continued to decide how troops were to be raised, where they would serve, who would command, and what the plan of campaign would be. Amherst was to send four separate forces to conquer New France: one through the Ohio Valley and three into Canada via Lake Ontario, Lake Champlain, and the St. Lawrence River. Major General James Wolfe* would command the nine thousand regulars bound for the St. Lawrence; Amherst himself would command an army of provincials and regulars on Lake Champlain or Lake Ontario—an army far less dependable than the one he had taken to Louisbourg in 1758. In fact, he was so much delayed waiting for the provincials to assemble that it was late May before he could send Brigadier General John Prideaux with five thousand men to Lake Ontario, and early June before he and another eight thousand men set out from Albany for Lake Champlain.

The campaign of 1759, like that of 1758, brought Amherst success and frustration. He left Albany on June 3 determined to drive the French from Lake Champlain and to cooperate with Prideaux and Wolfe in conquering Canada. He intended to proceed as rapidly as possible without risking the kind of surprise that had ruined Abercromby's offensive in 1758. Reaching the south end of Lake George on June 21, he devoted a month to building a fort to protect his communications and vessels to carry his cannon north to Lake Champlain. Once these preparations were complete, he took less than a week to cross Lake George and capture Fort Ticonderoga. It was now the end of July, the French had offered only light resistance, and Amherst still had hopes of conquering Canada in 1759. He began at once building vessels to drive the enemy from Lake Champlain and carry his army to Montreal. But as the French continued to add to their squadron on the lake, it was another two and a half months before Amherst felt confident enough to seek and destroy that squadron. By then he knew that Prideaux and Wolfe were dead and that their armies, although successful in taking Fort Niagara and Quebec, were no longer on the offensive. Unwilling to go on without support, Amherst decided to suspend further operations until spring.

Although the French held only the upper St. Lawrence Valley, they fought on stubbornly into 1760. To end this resistance, Amherst, who had at last been given complete control of the war, called on the colonists for men, supplies, and money and adopted much of Pitt's strategy from the previous year. Amherst again proposed to send three armies converging on Canada: one across Lake Ontario and down the St. Lawrence, another across Lake Champlain, and a third up the St. Lawrence from Quebec. But he would now lead the main army from the southwest—from Lake Ontario—while Brigadier Generals William Haviland and James Murray brought smaller detachments from Ticonderoga and Quebec. As in 1759, Amherst was forced to delay the opening of the campaign while his provincials were assembling. He did not reach Lake Ontario until July 9 or embark for the St. Lawrence until August 10. By that time Murray and Haviland were also en route, and all reached Montreal at the end of the first week of September. The French, outnumbered more than six to one, promptly surrendered. The conquest of Canada was complete. Amherst would see much service after 1760—as commander in chief in America, 1760–1763, and in Britain, 1778–1782 and 1793–1795—but none of that service would contribute substantially to the fame he had won at Louisbourg and Montreal.

Amherst's success in the Seven Years' War was a triumph of his own peculiar temperament and conventional military practice. By nature ambitious and impatient, Amherst was also unusually wary, unusually careful to avoid surprise or defeat. These contradictory characteristics frequently left him frustrated: he never seemed to be able to do all he wished as soon as he wished. Yet these characteristics combined to produce the kind of persistent, careful offensives needed to overcome an enemy that skillfully used terrain and distance to offset a fundamental lack of resources. Amherst's ambition drove him to put relentless pressure on the French; and his impatience drove him to use all of each campaign—to be acutely aware of time. He prodded colonists and regulars alike to be ready in the spring; he pressed them forward while on the offensive, and he kept them in the field as long as possible in the autumn. But for all his impatience, he was extraordinarily wary of surprise: "No liklihood of the Enemys coming but I can't be too secure." Thus, he made war persistently and carefully: gaining ground, avoiding defeat, consolidating his gains, and bringing at last overwhelming force to bear on his beleaguered enemy.

Amherst's success also depended in no small measure on conventional military practice. Contemporary British theorists were unable to decide how best to wage war. In their more aggressive moods, they admired commanders like Caesar and Marlborough who sought victory through decisive engagements. In their more conservative moods, they held that the best generals won without risking battle. Amherst clearly preferred the more conservative approach, which dominated Continental thinking at midcentury and which emphasized siegecraft and maneuver as the safest way to win a war. Such an approach not only appealed to Amherst's temperament but also suited his needs in carrying out Pitt's grand strategy. At Louisbourg there was little choice: a regular siege was the only feasible way of doing what Pitt required. Thereafter, Amherst had numerous opportunities to decide how to deal with French defenses, and having to rely mainly on provincials, he uniformly preferred siegecraft to battle. Thus, he expended months bringing up artillery to drive the French from his path, fortified whatever he took, and risked no more than minor engagements with an enemy that was ever inferior. These methods were very time-consuming, but they produced a succession of victories, no defeats, and the conquest of Canada.

BIBLIOGRAPHY

Frégault, Guy. *Canada: The War of the Conquest*. Toronto: Oxford University Press, 1969.

Gipson, Lawrence Henry. *The Great War for the Empire: The Culmination 1760–1763*. New York: Alfred A. Knopf, 1954.

———. *The Great War for the Empire: The Victorious Years, 1758–1760*. New York: Alfred A. Knopf, 1949.

———. *The Triumphant Empire: New Responsibilities Within the Enlarged Empire 1763–1766*. New York: Alfred A. Knopf, 1956.

Long, J. C. *Lord Jeffery Amherst: A Soldier of the King*. New York: Macmillan Company, 1933.

Mayo, Lawrence Shaw. *Jeffery Amherst: A Biography*. New York: Longmans, Green and Company, 1916.

Webster, J. Clarence, ed. *The Journal of Jeffery Amherst Recording the Military Career of General Amherst in America from 1758 to 1763*. Toronto: Ryerson Press, 1931.

————. *Journal of William Amherst in America 1758–1760*. London: Butler and Tanner, 1927.

IRA D. GRUBER

ANDERSON, Joseph Reid (b. Botetourt County, Va., February 6, 1813; d. Isles of Shoals, N.H., September 7, 1892), military industrialist. Anderson was master of the Tredegar Iron Works, the most important manufacturing complex in the South during the Civil War.

The man who became the Confederacy's premier industrialist was born on an isolated farm in southwestern Virginia. His father had fought in the American Revolution and was the son of a Scotch-Irish immigrant. Joseph Reid Anderson received a classical education and then distinguished himself at West Point by rising to the rank of first captain of cadets and graduating near the top of the class of 1836. During his active duty of a mere fourteen months, he served in the artillery and then in the Corps of Engineers and was stationed at Fortress Monroe, Virginia, and Fort Pulaski, Georgia.

His civilian career began propitiously as a state engineer under Colonel Claudius Crozet in the construction of Virginia's Valley Turnpike, a thoroughfare destined to be significant in several Civil War campaigns. In 1841 Anderson became chief commercial agent for the Tredegar Iron Company, a modest, debt-ridden plant in Richmond—thus establishing the first link in what would become a half-century's association. Two years later he leased the complex, which he purchased outright in 1848 and reorganized in 1859 as Joseph R. Anderson and Company.

Under Anderson's energetic leadership, Tredegar Iron Works boldly expanded and rose to national prominence. In the antebellum period, the company competed for both private and public contracts, and the U.S. government was an important customer. More than twelve hundred cannon were manufactured there before the Civil War, along with a dazzling array of other iron products, including forty locomotives and an armorclad revenue cutter, the *Polk*.

While the Tredegar expanded, Anderson used black labor, even for skilled positions. This unorthodox practice led to a strike by disgruntled whites in 1847. Anderson summarily dismissed the strikers. Meanwhile, his political career blossomed as a member of the city council and as a Whig delegate in the Virginia legislature. By the mid-1850s, however, he had come to fear the rise of "Black Republicanism." He became a Democrat and later an ardent secessionist.

The prospects of war placed exceptional demands on the Tredegar works. Its products were popular throughout the Southern states, notably in South Carolina, where a Tredegar mortar opened the firing at Fort Sumter. Tredegar ordnance and ammunition largely sustained the ensuing bombardment.

A Southern patriot with prior military experience, Anderson entered the Confederate Army as a brigadier general—but with a clear understanding that he would resign if Tredegar required his managerial skills. Anderson participated in the coastal defense of North Carolina early in the war and then proceeded to Virginia as a brigade commander in the spring of 1862. As part of the "Light Division" under Ambrose Powell Hill,* Anderson and his unit fought well in the Seven Days' Battles. At Frayser's Farm on June 30, the gallant commander received a stunning blow to his head. But Tredegar's pressing needs, not the wound, led Anderson to resign his commission in mid-July. He returned to the iron works and served with distinction until the fall of Richmond in April 1865.

Although he had been a passionate Confederate, after the war, Anderson immediately became a champion of reconciliation, and he even met with President Abraham Lincoln* who came to the former Rebel capital shortly after its capture. Pardoned by President Andrew Johnson later in 1865, the master of Tredegar promptly revived his industrial plant and reorganized the works as the Tredegar Company in 1867. The Panic of 1873 brought financial distress, but prosperity marked the final years of Anderson's management.

Anderson enjoyed a lengthy, varied, and successful postwar career. In the 1870s he helped to found the Richmond Chamber of Commerce and then served as its president and longtime director. He also presided over the city council and was a two-term member of the Virginia House of Delegates. In the aggregate and over the decades, Joseph Reid Anderson had become Richmond's first citizen. His business and political leadership were only two reasons for his obvious claim to that title. Always active in St. Paul's Episcopal Church—which had been so closely tied to the Confederate high command—he participated in virtually every effort at civic improvement over a fifty-year period. A devoted family man and famous host, Anderson combined charitable instincts with a warm, affable personality, a kind demeanor, and impressive bearing. After one of the best attended funerals in the city's history, he was buried in Richmond's Hollywood Cemetery in the company of numerous other Confederate notables.

Although his record both at West Point and on the field of battle was exemplary, Anderson as a military figure is important entirely because of his Civil War leadership at Tredegar Iron Company. Wartime Tredegar manufactured 1,099 cannon—virtually the South's entire production—as well as countless stores of ammunition, a wide variety of iron products, and the equipment to launch and sustain other ordnance works from Richmond to Selma. Furthermore, under Anderson's leadership Tredegar became the hub of scientific experimentation in the Confederacy. Its pioneering contributions included the iron plate for the *Merrimac* (the CSS *Virginia*), the Williams machine gun, the first railroad battery, a submarine boat, the torpedoes and other devices used by Matthew Fontaine Maury,* and the innovative guns of John Mercer Brooke.

Anderson accomplished all of these things against seemingly insurmountable obstacles, including critical shortages of pig iron and skilled workers, and uneven governmental support. He maintained production by acquiring distant coal mines and blast furnaces, obtaining a small fleet of canal boats and even a blockade runner, and resorting to prison labor, among other expedients. To feed his 2,500 employees and their families, he sent agents throughout the Confederacy, often trading Tredegar nails for food. Although he was a genuine Southern patriot, Anderson was also a shrewd businessman. Tredegar turned a profit during each of the war years and used its blockade runner to establish a sterling account in England which materially aided its postwar revival.

On the debit side, despite Anderson's heroic efforts, Tredegar never operated at full capacity. It produced some tubes flawed by inferior materials, rolled not even one rail, and was notably lacking in long-range artillery pieces. Finally, Anderson himself must be faulted for failing to appreciate and adopt early enough the method of casting guns developed by Thomas J. Rodman. Nevertheless, Anderson's Tredegar Iron Works had no rival in the South and made an incalculable contribution to the Confederate cause.

BIBLIOGRAPHY

Bruce, Kathleen. "Economic Factors in the Manufacture of Confederate Ordnance." *Army Ordnance* 6 (1925–1926):166–73.
———. *Virginia Iron Manufacture in the Slave Era*. New York: Century Company, 1930.
Dew, Charles B. *Ironmaker to the Confederacy: Joseph R. Anderson and the Tredegar Iron Works*. New Haven, Conn.: Yale University Press, 1966.

DANIEL P. JORDAN

ANDREWS, Frank Maxwell (b. Nashville, Tenn., February 3, 1884; d. Reykjavik, Iceland, May 3, 1943), military aviation leader. Andrews was the Army aviator groomed for high command during the interwar period (1919–1930). He fought for the air force organization, the technology, and the doctrine that enabled air power to play an independent and decisive role in World War II. But his untimely death denied America the leader most qualified to command its air forces.

The first of four children of James David and Louise Adeline (Maxwell) Andrews, descendants of Thomas Andrews who arrived from London in about 1700, Frank Andrews graduated from Montgomery Bell Academy in 1901 after quarterbacking his prep school football team to an undefeated season the previous fall. The following year he entered West Point and received his commission as a second lieutenant in the cavalry upon graduation in 1906. He spent the next eleven years of his career assigned to various cavalry units in the West, Hawaii, and the Philippines. During this time his love for horses and polo led to his lifelong love, Jeanette Allen, called "Johnnie" by her many friends, daughter of Major General Henry Tureman Allen.* During his courtship Andrews grew interested in flying, but General Allen dictated that no daughter of his would marry an aviator. Frank deferred to his father-in-law for three years following his December 1914 marriage to Johnnie, but he joined the air section of the

Signal Corps in August 1917 and completed flight training (April-July 1918) at Rockwell Field in San Diego.

The young Andrews was frustrated in his attempts to fight in World War I. Instead of combat, he commanded Carlstrom and Dorr fields at Arcadia, Florida, and in October 1918 he was named supervisor of the Southeastern Air Service District headquartered at Montgomery, Alabama. He finally reached Europe in mid-1920 and replaced William ("Billy") Mitchell* as Air Service officer of the American Army of Occupation in Germany, commanded by his father-in-law, General Allen.

After three years in Germany, Andrews returned to Kelly Field, Texas, serving first as executive officer and then as commander of the Advanced Flying School. He held that post until 1927 when he entered the most important phase of his career—preparation for major command. Beginning a round of professional military schools, he attended the Air Corps Tactical School, 1927–1928, the Army Command and General Staff School, 1928–1929, and the Army War College, 1932–1933. Before War College, as a lieutenant colonel in the Office of the Chief of Air Corps (OCAC), he accepted the responsibility for the embarrassing *Mount Shasta* incident in the summer of 1931. The 2d Bomb Group, commanded by Major Herbert "Bert" Dargue, flew to sea to intercept a World War I vintage cargo ship and send it to the bottom but was unable to find the *Shasta* on August 11 because of bad weather. Three days later the bombers belatedly found the vessel, but because of improper ordnance could not sink it. The debacle highlighted Air Corps ordnance limitations and a lack of all-weather capability in the mission of coastal defense. While others were busy alibiing, Andrews replied, "What worries us most is the possibility that something is wrong with our training and our ability to attack targets at sea." Even though the incident cost him his job, he accepted the challenge to improve the Air Corps' mission capability. He vindicated the earlier setback in May 1938 when, as commander of the General Headquarters Air Force, he sent three B-17s in bad weather to intercept the Italian liner *Rex* about seven hundred miles at sea. Flight navigator, Lieutenant Curtis Emerson LeMay,* directed the planes straight to their target, enabling Major George Goddard, the father of U.S. aerial reconnaissance, to take sensational pictures of dozens of passengers waving from the crowded deck.

Major General Frank Andrews paid the price for the courage of his convictions. Following his statement to the House Military Affairs Committee in 1937, supporting Air Corps autonomy and the strategic importance of air power, he was exiled to Fort Sam Houston and reverted to his permanent rank of colonel at the end of February 1939, when his term as General Headquarters commander expired. He did not languish long; General George Catlett Marshall,* newly appointed Army chief of staff, resurrected Andrews by assigning him to the General Staff as assistant chief of staff for training and operations (G–3), the first aviator to hold that critical position. In November 1940 President Franklin D. Roosevelt personally recommended Andrews for command of the Panama

Canal Air Force. His responsibilities widened a year later to include the Caribbean Defense Command—the Achilles heel of U.S. hemispheric defense. With the Allied invasion of North Africa in November 1942, Lieutenant General Andrews assumed command of U.S. forces in the Middle East. On February 5, 1943, following the Casablanca Conference and the announcement of the forthcoming combined bomber offensive, Andrews was given supreme command of all American forces in the European Theater of Operations. He crashed in a B–24 three months later, attempting a low visibility landing at Iceland thereby fulfilling an earlier promise. Never a swivel chair air officer, he had once said: "I don't want to be one of those generals who die in bed."

No authoritative biography exists on Frank M. Andrews, and without one, the history of air power is incomplete. He possessed the perfect balance required of a military aviation leader: superior intellect, strength of character, courage, and superb pilot skills. These assets served him well as he fought for the development of air power during the interwar years. Plagued by a lack of autonomy, confined to a support mission, deprived of a four-engine bomber, and hampered by limited funds during the Great Depression, which exacerbated interservice rivalry, Andrews honed the small General Headquarters (GHQ) Air Force into an efficient fighting machine as its commander from March 1935 until February 1939. As Hugh Knerr said in 1942:

"Andrews, alone, weathered the storm and rose in rank in spite of opposition. Perhaps he will be supreme commander of the United Nations' war effort before this war is over. He deserves to be. As a military executive, he has no superior among fighting men today. He is the kind of man whom the DeGaulles, the Wavells, and the Timoshenkos can appreciate. West Point, Class of '06, eleven years in the cavalry before he joined the Air Corps, he can command an Army corps with as much skill as he can command a Flying Fortress squadron. He is 58, but when he crawls into [an] airplane, he still crawls into the cockpit."

GHQ Air Force was Frank Andrews' main legacy. A product of the 1934 Baker Board, the GHQ Air Force represented a compromise to air power enthusiasts. It was not the independent and coequal air force they sought, but nevertheless it concentrated for the first time all the air strike elements under one commander. Andrews did not waste this opportunity to develop air power. Considered a safe team player by the Army General Staff, he shocked the establishment when he gathered many of the Air Corps' "radical agitators" on his staff: Harry Burwell, Follett Bradley, George Churchill Kenney,* Joe McNarney, and Hugh Knerr. Of the twenty-three officers whom Andrews assembled at Langley Field, virtually all were believers in the "heresy" that air power could play an independent and decisive role in warfare. Under Andrews' guidance, these men accomplished the essential spade work that enabled the Army Air Forces to bear the brunt of the war against Hitler's Germany until June 1944.

BIBLIOGRAPHY

Craven, Wesley, and Cate, James, eds. *The Army Air Forces in World War II*. Vol. 1. Chicago: University of Chicago Press, 1948.
Goldberg, Alfred, ed. *A History of the United States Air Force, 1907–1957*. Princeton, N.J.: D. Van Nostrand Company, 1957.
Huie, William B. *The Fight for Air Power*. New York: L. B. Fischer, 1942.
McClendon, R. Earl. *Autonomy of the Air Arm*. Maxwell Air Force Base, Montgomery, Ala.: Air University, 1954.

DENNIS G. HALL

ARMSTRONG, John, Jr. (b. Carlisle, Pa., November 25, 1758; d. Red Hook, N.Y., April 1, 1843), soldier, politician, statesman, secretary of war.

John Armstrong, Jr., was the son of a prominent Pennsylvanian who won fame as the "Hero of Kittanning" during the French and Indian War. Young Armstrong served briefly during the Revolutionary War as the aide de camp of Brigadier General Hugh Mercer, and for most of the war as the aide de camp of Major General Horatio Gates,* rising eventually to the brevet rank of lieutenant colonel. While the Revolutionary Army was in its last encampment in 1783, Armstrong penned the controversial "Newburgh Addresses." Although these Addresses were intended to bring pressure on Congress to fulfill its promises of pensions and other benefits to the Revolutionary soldiers, they were circulated anonymously and were interpreted by George Washington,* and consequently by many historians, as a threatened mutiny. Washington crushed the incipient movement, and Armstrong, whose authorship soon became known, had to bear the onus of his authorship. He ruefully admitted many years later that the Addresses "had been a millstone hung about his neck through his life."

Following a promising career in Pennsylvania politics as secretary of the Supreme Executive Council of Pennsylvania, adjutant general of Pennsylvania, and a member of Congress under the Articles of Confederation, Armstrong married the sister of the politically powerful Chancellor Robert R. Livingston of New York and removed to that state. After a brief spell as a gentleman farmer along the Hudson River, Armstrong reentered politics in 1800 as a U.S. senator from his adopted state. The position did not please him, but during his brief tenure he impressed President Thomas Jefferson, who selected him to replace Chancellor Livingston as minister to France in 1804. Armstrong served in this capacity for six years, a stormy ministry in which he sought in vain to stem the growing rapacity of the Emperor Napoleon's policies towards American commerce. So devastating were his attacks that Napoleon briefly considered asking for Armstrong's recall. Armstrong urged his government to take stronger actions to defend American rights, and he was one of the earliest advocates of war to defend American maritime rights, preferably with both France and Great Britain.

In 1812, after war had been declared against Great Britain, Armstrong was appointed a brigadier general and was placed in charge of the defense of New York City. During this period he published a small book entitled *Hints to Young Generals by an Old Soldier* (1812), which introduced to the American military the concepts of the French military authority, Baron Antoine Henri Jomini, who had such a formative influence over American military thought during the first half of the nineteenth century. When William Eustis resigned as secretary of war, President James Madison selected Armstrong as his replacement, although with some misgivings on Madison's part, for Armstrong's pugnacious personality and penchant for controversy were well known.

Armstrong was more vigorous in conducting the affairs of the War Department than Eustis, but he nevertheless faced myriad problems of organization, supply, and manning, largely attributable to tardy legislation, a parsimonious Congress, and an apathetic public. During his tenure in office, Armstrong made some respectable contributions, but the hostility of other cabinet officers, particularly James Monroe, who viewed Armstrong as a rival for the presidency, and the lack of support and a close rapport with President Madison, reduced Armstrong's contribution to the office. When the British burned Washington, D.C., in August 1814, the responsibility was laid at Armstrong's feet by the irate citizenry of that town, and he was driven from office.

Armstrong never again held public office. He spent the remainder of his life in agricultural pursuits, occasionally taking the time out to write polemical literature lashing out at his enemies, especially James Monroe and James Wilkinson.* Late in life he published a two-volume history of the War of 1812 (*Notices of the War of 1812*). He remained active and vigorous right up to his death in 1843.

Armstrong's reputation rests primarily upon his conduct of the War Department during the War of 1812, and he has been generally considered a failure. His impact on the war and the War Department was not nearly as great as he wished nor as ineffectual as many of his detractors claimed. Under his direction, the Rules and Regulations of the Army were drawn up in 1813, a forerunner of the present elaborate Army regulations. He also gradually built up a general staff to assist him in Washington. As constituted it was essentially a housekeeping staff, but it can be reasonably considered the beginning of the sophisticated, massive staff structure of today's modern military complex. Armstrong improved the accountability but not the efficiency of the supply system, and despite his efforts to improve recruiting, the American Army had to rely upon militia for most of the war. As secretary of war, Armstrong attempted to dictate not only the strategy of the war but also the conduct of operations. His overbearing attitude led to many conflicts with his commanders, and there is little doubt that he interfered unnecessarily in their operations. He even went to the northern front in 1813 in a futile attempt to influence a successful outcome of that campaign. Perhaps his greatest failing was that he allowed weak commanders to alter his military strategy which, had it been followed and carried out, would probably have had a decisive and favorable impact upon the outcome of the war. Armstrong was a good judge of military talent, and perhaps his greatest contribution was that he recognized and advanced many outstanding young military leaders to high rank, including Winfield Scott,* Edmund Pendleton Gaines,* Alexander Macomb,* Jacob Jennings Brown,* and Andrew Jackson.* It was the judgment of the eminent historian Henry Adams that "The energy thus infused by Armstrong into the regular army lasted for half a century."

BIBLIOGRAPHY

Adams, Henry. *History of the United States During the Administrations of Jefferson and Madison.* 9 vols. New York: Charles Scribner's Sons, 1889–1891.
Armstrong, John. *Notices of the War of 1812.* 2 vols. New York: Wiley and Putnam, 1836, 1840.
Brant, Irving. *James Madison.* Vols. 4, 5, and 6. Indianapolis, Ind.: Bobbs-Merrill Company, 1953–1961.
Ingersoll, L. D. *A History of the War Department of the United States.* Washington, D.C.: Francis B. Mohun, 1879.
Risch, Erna. *Quartermaster Support of the Army: A History of the Corps, 1775–1939.* Washington, D.C.: Office of the Quartermaster General, 1962.
White, Leonard D. *The Jeffersonians: A Study in Administrative History.* New York: Macmillan Company, 1951.

C. EDWARD SKEEN

ARNOLD, Benedict (b. Norwich, Conn., January 14, 1741; d. London, England, June 12, 1801), Army officer. Arnold's name is synonymous with military treason.

Benedict Arnold was the product of an old and distinguished New England family. His great-grandfather, named Benedict, had been a governor of Rhode Island. But his father, also Benedict, failed as a merchant and was known as the town drunkard in Norwich. Arnold's mother, Hannah Waterman King, raised her energetic and athletic son with a stern hand. Declining family financial circumstances forced the decision to withdraw young Benedict from school and to apprentice him to the Lathrop brothers, family cousins who operated one of the most successful apothecary shops in eastern Connecticut.

Arnold took to the apothecary's trade and became a prosperous merchant. He purchased shares in commercial ships and, on numerous occasions, captained vessels in which he was a heavy investor. In 1767, Arnold married Margaret Mansfield, the daughter of the sheriff of New Haven, Connecticut. Before her untimely death in 1775, she bore him three sons. The first demonstrable signs of Arnold's combative character also become manifest during the New Haven years. He fought a duel with a ship captain in the Bay of Honduras over a slight matter of honor. Likewise, as one who engaged in smuggling activities, not uncommon among successful New England merchants in the late colonial period, he was active in organizing the local populace against informers to local British customs agents.

Clearly in the forefront of Connecticut citizens who advocated extreme measures in resisting king and Parliament, Arnold was anxious to attain military rank. In March 1775 he became a captain in the Governor's Second Company of Guards, a newly formed militia unit. After Lexington and Concord, Arnold marched the company to Massachusetts where it joined the forces penning up General Thomas Gage in Boston. Arnold convinced the Massachusetts Committee of Safety to entrust him with the capture of Fort Ticonderoga, one of the keys to controlling the vital Hudson Highlands corridor and an easy source of artillery for the people's army back east. Arnold rushed westward, only to confront Ethan Allen* and the Green Mountain Boys, who had been authorized by Connecticut to reduce Ticonderoga. The sorry state of British defenses made the fort's capture a foregone conclusion; yet it was marred by squabbling between Arnold, Allen, and others over such issues as command privileges, proper credit for the victory, and the post-campaign settlement of accounts.

The contention at Ticonderoga was another source of Arnold's developing reputation for belligerence, but that did not deter George Washington* from urging the Continental Congress to name Arnold a colonel in the regular service and to put him in charge of one of the two small armies that invaded Canada. His march to Quebec remains a legendary story of the human will to survive. But the final assault (under cover of a driving snowstorm late on the evening of December 30, 1775), ended in chaos after the commander in charge, Richard Montgomery,* was killed and Arnold was seriously wounded in his leg.

Named a brigadier general shortly after the battle at Quebec, Arnold supervised the hasty construction of a "fleet" of boats and prepared to defend Lake Champlain against General Guy Carleton's advancing forces. On October 11 Carleton's fleet attacked Arnold's well-chosen defensive position between Valcour Island and Lake Champlain's western shore. A furious battle ensued during which Arnold once again displayed his intrepid ability to command. The fury of Arnold's stand convinced Carleton not to press his advantage so late in the campaign season and effectively delayed the British at a time when American forces in northern New York were quite weak. Arnold's blocking action helped to set the stage for General John Burgoyne's defeat at Saratoga in 1777.

Meanwhile, Arnold became bogged down in petty disputes, including charges of slandering other officers, mismanaging public funds, and using confiscated goods for private purposes, most of which arose during the retreat from Canada. These allegations no doubt played a role in the decision of Congress to pass over Arnold for promotion to major general. In February 1777 Congress promoted five brigadiers, all Arnold's junior in service and none even close to possessing his record in accomplishments. Naturally, Arnold considered the incident a grave slap at his honor. Washington, an admirer of Arnold's battlefield grit, urged him not to act hastily. Arnold was on the verge of taking his case directly to Congress, but a British raid on Danbury, Connecticut (April 1777) intervened. Arnold rallied the local militia and drove the invaders away. The Danbury raid at last led Congress to recognize his battlefield merits and to name him major general, but without a restoration of seniority. Out of pique and disgust, Arnold resigned in late July 1777.

Fate then took a strange twist. Washington had just recommended Arnold as an officer capable of rallying revolutionary support for the Continental Army's Northern Department in its challenge to Burgoyne's invasion. Ever ready for combat, Arnold asked for a suspension of his resignation and raced northward. He led a successful relief expedition into the Mohawk Valley to free rebel forces trapped in Fort Stanwix by Colonel Barry St. Leger. But this signal achievement did not avert contention with General Horatio Gates,* who had just taken over command of the Northern Department. Gates, more cautious than Arnold, wanted to defend entrenched positions; his subordinate wanted to carry the fight to the British. At Freeman's Farm on September 19, Gates refused to send troops ahead of American lines to assist Arnold. Despite the American victory that day, Gates did not mention Arnold's important role in official reports. Heated words between the two officers resulted in Gates' decision to relieve Arnold of command of the American left wing. At the second Saratoga engagement (Bemis Heights, October 7), the sulking subordinate could not be restrained. When Arnold learned that the tide of battle was not going well, he rushed to the front, personally rallied several companies, and turned the tide. But he once again sustained a serious wound in his leg—the same that had been mangled at Quebec. Arnold refused amputation, but his well-known physical agility was gone for life.

While Gates became the hero of Saratoga, a thankful Congress restored Arnold's seniority, but that belated action did not improve his shattered health or abate the growing bitterness in his mind. The series of slights and general contention surrounding his military career led Arnold to question the merits of the Revolutionary cause. Like many other officers, he was particularly angry about civilians who profiteered from the war while he was rebuffed and accused of financial chicanery when trying to settle accounts with Congress and other civil agencies. His alienation was ripening when Washington, trying to reward Arnold in his period of physical convalescence, appointed him to command in Philadelphia in June 1778.

Washington's sense of humanity and generosity backfired. Arnold lacked the evenhandedness of a dispassionate administrator and soon made enemies all over the city. He chose to rule by pomp and circumstance and ingratiated himself with the wealthiest families, many of whom had been all but openly loyal to the British during Sir William Howe's occupation. His romance with Margaret Shippen, the youngest of neutralist Edward Shippen's three daughters, and his under-the-table business dealings irked the local republicans. Consequently, several prominent patriots mounted a campaign to get rid of Arnold and smeared him openly with a list of eight alleged abuses of authority. Arnold insisted upon a congressional investigation, which dragged on until January 1780, when a military court exonerated him on all but two charges—those of allowing a vessel in which he was a heavy investor to clear port when all others could not, and of using public wagons for private purposes. Ultimately, Congress ordered Washington to reprimand Arnold, which the commander in chief did in stern but compassionate terms.

The reprimand hurt Arnold deeply, but it was not a factor leading to initial communications with the British. The treasonous correspondence was six months old when the military court issued its decision. Far more important was Arnold's sense that human frailty had ruined the republican cause. Furthermore, in marrying Margaret Shippen (April 8, 1779), he moved closer to the British. His nineteen-year-old bride had been a favored belle among the younger British officers during their stay in Philadelphia. One in particular, Major John André, was at the center of the plot that developed. By the time Washington offered his rebuked officer the command at West Point in August 1780, Arnold was fully committed to allowing the British to seize that strategically vital fort. Only the fortuitous capture of André (September 23) and Arnold's hasty flight down the Hudson River (September 25) saved the Americans from what could have been a disastrous military blow, if Sir Henry Clinton had had the opportunity to follow up on the plans that Arnold and André had devised.

Arnold's traitorous course has biased most accounts of his life and military exploits. But that career, at least until after Saratoga, was invaluable to the success of the American War for Independence. Washington early recognized Arnold's resourcefulness and raw courage in the face of overwhelming military obstacles. The soldiers who served under Arnold clearly respected him. In battle, Arnold was a masterful tactician. But his defiant, impetuous temperament hurt him over and over again in relations with fellow officers. Rather than rising above petty disputes, he wallowed in them.

André's bravery in facing hanging as a common spy, as opposed to Arnold's seeming cupidity, made Arnold seem just that much more of a scoundrel to contemporaries. In popular lore, he quickly became the cursed general who had sold his soul to the devil for filthy lucre (the British paid him handsomely for his treason). Arnold had hoped that other disillusioned rebels would follow him and give up on the military effort, but the very name "Arnold" became a rallying cry for renewed vigor and commitment to the languishing American cause. The traitor received a commission in the Regular British Army as a brigadier general and led savage attacks against Virginia and Connecticut before he and Peggy sailed for London in 1782. In London, Arnold at first held celebrity status, even meeting with King George III. But soon the war's end led the British to treat him with circumspection. They never fully trusted him, and a few openly showed disrespect, which resulted in at least one duel.

Until his death in 1801, Arnold struggled as a merchant to bring in income for his growing family—Peggy bore him four sons and one daughter. But there was no escape from the past. Friendships were few, and he died in obscurity. The excellence of his military record simply could not outweigh his treason.

BIBLIOGRAPHY

Arnold, Isaac N. *The Life of Benedict Arnold: His Patriotism and His Treason*. Chicago: Jansen, McClurg and Company, 1880.

Flexner, James T. *The Traitor and the Spy: Benedict Arnold and John André*. New York: Harcourt, Brace, 1953. Reprint, Boston: Little, Brown and Company, 1975.

Roberts, Kenneth, ed. *March to Quebec: Journals of Members of Arnold's Expedition* ... New York: Doubleday, Doran and Company, 1938.

Van Doren, Carl C. *Secret History of the American Revolution: An Account of the Conspiracies of Benedict Arnold and Numerous Others* ... New York: Viking Press, 1941.

Wallace, Willard M. *Traitorous Hero: The Life and Fortunes of Benedict Arnold*. New York: Harper and Brothers, 1954.

JAMES KIRBY MARTIN

ARNOLD, Henry Harley (b. Gladwyne, Pa., June 25, 1886; d. Sonoma, Calif., January 15, 1950), Army Air officer. Arnold is considered the father of the modern U.S. Air Force.

Henry H. ("Hap") Arnold was one of five children born to Dr. Herbert Alonzo Arnold and Adna Louise (Harley) Arnold. Both families traced their roots to pre-Revolutionary America, and Arnold's father served briefly as a medical officer in the Spanish-American War. Henry attended public schools in Lower Merion and entered West Point in 1903 after considering medicine and the clergy as alternatives. Disappointed upon graduation at his assignment to the infantry rather than his choice of the cavalry, he was first assigned to the Philippines where he served with the 29th Infantry until his return to Governor's Island, New York, in 1909. In 1911, motivated primarily by the opportunity for promotion, Arnold took the qualifying examination for the Ordnance Department, but before learning of results, he accepted a War Department invitation to volunteer for flight training with the Wright Brothers in Dayton, Ohio. After having accumulated 3 hours and 48 minutes in the air, Arnold was designated one of the first military aviators in the United States. Assigned to College Park, Maryland, he established a world altitude record of 6,540 feet and as a consequence of this and other feats was awarded the first Mackay Trophy in 1912, presented annually thereafter for the most meritorious accomplishment in military aviation. As a result of crashes in which he was involved or witnessed or in which close friends were killed, Arnold did not fly from 1912 to 1916. His marriage in September 1913 to Eleanor A. Pool, daughter of a Philadelphia banker, was followed by reassignment to the Philippines in 1913–1916, where he served with the 13th Infantry along with fellow Lieutenant George Catlett Marshall.* Arnold volunteered for duty with the Air Service upon his return to the United States in 1916, and after several final months with the infantry at Madison Barracks, New York, he was promoted to captain and designated supply officer of the Aviation School at Rockwell Field, North Island, San Diego, California, where he returned to flying duty. On the eve of America's entrance into World War I,

Arnold was posted to Panama where he commanded the 7th Aero Squadron. With the United States' entry into the war, Arnold was recalled to Washington where he headed the information office of the Aviation Section of the Signal Corps. He rose quickly in rank and as a colonel in August 1917 became assistant director of military aeronautics with responsibility for training as well as acquisition of most American flying bases in the United States. His success in Washington prevented his acquiring the combat assignment he desired, and he did not reach France until the Armistice.

In the postwar years, Arnold, now reduced to his permanent rank (captain, promoted to major in 1921), served in a variety of assignments in California from January 1919 through the summer of 1924 and did not participate directly in the early controversy surrounding William ("Billy") Mitchell.* Arnold attended the Army Industrial College in 1925–1926, served briefly as information officer for the Air Service, and supported Mitchell with testimony at Mitchell's court-martial trial. Beginning that same year, he found time to begin authoring or co-authoring five books he would write on the subject of military aviation.

In his own words, he was "exiled" to Fort Riley, Kansas, in the aftermath of Mitchell's court-martial, but after attendance at the Command and General Staff School at Fort Leavenworth, Kansas, he served briefly at Fairfield Air Depot and Wright Field in the Dayton, Ohio, area, earning promotion to lieutenant colonel in 1931 and reassignment to California. For the next four years, he commanded March Field, Riverside, California, where he experimented with materiel and tactics associated with the transformation of the base from a training to operational one with both pursuit and bombing aircraft assigned. He worked closely with the embryonic motion picture industry, seeking publicity and support for air power. His rapport with members of the scientific community at the California Institute of Technology was to begin an association that stressed scientific assessment of air forces. While at March Field he supervised the Civilian Conservation Corps personnel assigned there and in 1934 became responsible for the western air mail zone in that ill-fated experiment.

Later that same year Arnold was chosen to lead a flight of B–10 bombers from Washington, D.C., to Juneau, Alaska, and return. This feat earned Arnold his second Mackay Trophy, contributing to his promotion to brigadier general and in March 1935, a new assignment as commander of the First Wing, General Headquarters Air Force, located at March Field. Less than a year later he was recalled to Washington as assistant chief of the Air Corps, a position he held until September 1938, when he succeeded Major General Oscar Westover, chief of the Air Corps, who was killed in a plane crash. Arnold was to head the Air Corps from this time until his retirement in March 1946.

At the threat of war, Arnold found sympathy for expansion of the air arm from President Franklin D. Roosevelt, who in the spring of 1940 following the defeat of France issued a presidential call for fifty thousand aircraft for the defense of the Western Hemisphere. Arnold's efforts to strengthen the Army Air Corps (redesignated the Army Air Forces in July 1941) resulted in congressional appropriations of over $2.1 billion for Army aviation in 1941.

De facto recognition of Arnold's role as spokesman for Army aviation was indicated by his presence at the August 1941 Atlantic Charter Conference in Argentia, Newfoundland, with Roosevelt, Churchill, and the combined British and American military staffs. From then through the end of the war, Arnold served as a member of the British-American Combined Chiefs of Staff and its American counterpart, the U.S. Joint Chiefs of Staff. Except for the Yalta Conference when he was absent because of hospitalization following a second heart attack, Arnold was the spokesman for Army aviation at wartime meetings and conferences. He enjoyed the confidence of Roosevelt, Churchill, and Marshall and at the same time earned the suspicion of American naval aviators who were concerned over Arnold's views and powers as the precursors of a separate American air arm. Arnold wisely deferred the struggle for autonomy to the postwar period. He was promoted to lieutenant general in December 1941, general in March 1943, and five star general of the Army in December 1944.

An advocate of strategic bombing, Arnold sent officers to Europe within six weeks of Pearl Harbor to develop and plan the strategy of bombing the European Continent, at the same time realizing that the bombing of Japan would have to be delayed until aircraft were developed and bases were acquired within range of such operations. Traveling extensively during the war, Arnold became familiar with the problems and difficulties of Army Air Forces units throughout the entire world.

Arnold's reputation properly rests on his having built the greatest air force the world has seen. Out of a struggling institution which at the time of the September 1938 Munich Agreement possessed but a handful of B–17s Arnold created an organization which, at its zenith, had approximately 2.5 million personnel, organized into 243 combat groups operating more than sixty-three thousand aircraft from airfields worldwide. Although neither a superb organizer nor a formulator of strategic thought, Arnold was best known as an innovator with a ready smile and a dedication to hard work. Dissatisfied with explanations, he demanded results from his staff. He had vision and an appreciation of the role of technology in air power; he solicited and received the cooperation of Dr. Theodore von Karman and other leaders of the nation's scientific community in air force experimentation and development. Concerned with the future, he rotated his most promising staff officers between staff and combat assignments, thus seeking a cadre of versatile leadership for the postwar force. Impetuous, volatile, dedicated, and outwardly friendly, Arnold was truly the father of the U.S. Air Force.

BIBLIOGRAPHY

Arnold, H. H. *Global Mission*. New York: Harper and Brothers, 1949.
Coffey, Thomas. *Hap: General of the Air Force Henry Arnold*. New York: Viking, 1982.
Copp, DeWitt S. *A Few Great Captains: The Men and Events That Shaped the Development of U.S. Air Power*. Garden City, N.Y.: Doubleday and Company, 1980.

Huston, John W. "The Wartime Leadership of Hap Arnold." In *Air Power and Warfare; Proceedings of the Eighth Military History Symposium*. Washington, D.C.: Office of Air Force History, 1979.

JOHN W. HUSTON

ATKINSON, Henry (b. Person County, N.C., 1782; d. Jefferson Barracks, Mo., June 14, 1842), frontier Army commander, Indian treaty negotiator.

Henry Atkinson was the sixth child in a successful North Carolina pioneer family. His father was a substantial farmer, local officeholder, and militia officer in eighteenth-century North Carolina. Little is known of Henry Atkinson's early life or education, but on August 9, 1808, he accepted a commission as a captain in the 3d Infantry Regiment of the U.S. Army. His first service included assignments at New Orleans and nearby posts. In 1813 he participated in General James Wilkinson's* campaign against the Spanish garrison at Mobile. Later that same year he traveled north to join General Wade Hampton's* staff as an inspector general along the New York State-Upper Canada border. In that capacity he served under General Hampton and again with General Wilkinson in two brief campaigns against the British. In 1814 he was promoted to the rank of colonel and took command of the 37th Infantry Regiment then stationed at New London, Connecticut.

When the War of 1812 ended, Atkinson was one of eight of the forty-seven infantry regimental commanders to be retained at his current rank. He received command of the newly reorganized 6th Infantry then stationed near the Canadian border. There he labored to establish a strong regiment while the troops trained and built roads for the government. In February 1819 he was ordered to move the regiment west to St. Louis where he was to lead the Missouri Expedition. As a result, the 6th Infantry traveled from Plattsburgh to St. Louis that spring. While the troops moved up the Missouri River to Council Bluffs near present Omaha, an economic depression hit the country. That, coupled with War Department difficulties with Congress, ended the Missouri Expedition. Nevertheless, the move from New York to the West placed Henry Atkinson at the center of Army activities in that region for the next two decades.

In 1819 he received command of the Ninth Military Department which included the states of Kentucky, Illinois, and Tennessee, as well as the region north and west of Missouri from the Mississippi River to the Rocky Mountains. The next year he was promoted to brigadier general, but promptly lost that rank in the army reduction of the following year. During the next several years Atkinson coordinated army road-building, fort construction, training, and dealings with the nearby Indian tribes. After the Arikara War in the summer of 1823, President James Monroe chose him as one of two commissioners appointed to conclude treaties of peace and friendship with the tribes of the upper Missouri Valley. With his fellow commissioner Benjamin O'Fallon and 450 soldiers, Atkinson set out up the Missouri River by keelboat in the summer of 1825. The party traveled upstream from Fort Atkinson at Omaha north and west until they passed the mouth of the Yellowstone River in eastern Montana. Along the way they concluded twelve treaties with sixteen bands of Indians, and, although the Senate duly ratified the agreements, they seem to have had little impact on long-range Indian-white relations in the region.

Shortly after returning to St. Louis, Atkinson received orders to choose a site for an infantry training school and to superintend its construction. This installation grew into what became Jefferson Barracks, a few miles south of St. Louis. There newly inducted infantrymen were supposed to receive their basic training, but the school operated more in theory than in fact. Continuing trouble with Midwestern Indian tribes and a pressing need to use soldiers for routine and non-military assignments kept the number of trainees small. In the spring of 1827 news of hostilities with Winnebago bands in southern Wisconsin forced Atkinson to hurry up the Mississippi with most of the troops then stationed at Jefferson Barracks. The Winnebago War proved more a scare than a real conflict, but the rapid movement of troops up the Mississippi to meet the suspected threat convinced military planners that it was wise to concentrate most of the troops at a few locations and then move them to nearby trouble spots when necessary.

During the summer of 1832 Atkinson led troops into combat for the only time in his army career. That spring dissident bands of Sac and Fox Indians had returned east of the Mississippi River into Illinois, and terrified frontier residents there fled before this Indian "invasion." Atkinson hurried troops north and then met the peaceful Sac-Fox chiefs still in Iowa to ensure their continuing neutrality. He called for militia support and then spent a frustrating summer trying to find the elusive tribesmen. His inability to locate the main body of Indians infuriated President Andrew Jackson* who sent General Winfield Scott* west to take command. Scott's troops contracted cholera and could not participate in the campaign, so Atkinson got the chance to finish the campaign. His force overtook the fleeing Indians as they tried to cross the Mississippi, and killed or captured most of those who had survived their summer of wandering through Illinois and Wisconsin. Although Atkinson completed his task and defeated the Indians, he received little but criticism for a bungled campaign, and certainly it was not one of the highlights of his military career.

The demonstrated inability of footsoldiers to pursue Indians in this campaign led Congress to establish two cavalry regiments, and these men trained at Jefferson Barracks during the mid-1830s. For the rest of that decade Atkinson had few important assignments, and most of the regulars stationed there were called for service in Florida or along the Texas border. As a result, much of the time he had little to do but to shuffle papers. On two occasions, however, he participated in the ongoing policy of Indian Removal. In 1837 he supervised the removal of the Potawatomi Indians from the northwest corner of Missouri north into Iowa. Three years later he commanded the troops which led the Winnebago west across the Mississippi from Wisconsin into Iowa. That operation was his last duty of major importance, and he died just two years later at Jefferson Barracks.

Atkinson left no stirring calls to valor and no brilliant campaigns as a legacy to the nation. Rather, his contribution was in his competent handling of basic assignments and routine duties. During his thirty-four years in the Army, he served in each major section of the nation. His career began in the South, then he moved to New England during the War of 1812, and after that conflict American expansion brought him west. From 1819 on Atkinson commanded most of the troops stationed beyond the Mississippi River. In that capacity he sought to avoid conflict with the Indians, to keep tribesmen and pioneers apart, to enforce federal laws in the Indian Country, and to protect Indians from intruding whites. Most of the time he succeeded. During his service on the frontier, he dealt with over forty tribes, who knew him as the White Beaver. He negotiated treaties, held councils, and fought in the Black Hawk War only when all other measures failed.

Troops under his command built and occupied many famous posts of that day. Fort Atkinson at Council Bluffs, Leavenworth in Kansas, and Jefferson Barracks were among the more prominent of those posts. He successfully commanded the Missouri Expedition of 1819 and the 1825 Yellowstone Expedition. After the Yellowstone Expedition he reported that, despite rumors and the claims of American fur traders, British fur traders and governments had little contact and less influence among the upper Missouri Valley Indian tribes. As the highest ranking subordinate officer in the West, Atkinson often commanded the Western Department of the Army for short periods when his superior officer was away. His careful attention to detail meant that his troops were usually well supplied and adequately trained. He repeatedly called for mounted troops for frontier service, and he thought that the Army should concentrate its few men at a couple of locations rather than scattering them widely at small, isolated posts. From the large forts the troops could move rapidly to trouble spots when needed, but at the same time they could benefit from the training offered to company- and even regimental-sized units.

Essentially a frontier policeman, manager, and successful bureaucrat, Atkinson viewed the Army as a branch of the federal government which had been charged with peacekeeping and law enforcement. He had little patience for either white or Indian lawbreakers and treated both similarly. When contending groups of Indians fought with each other, he preferred to let them settle their own quarrels, despite stated Indian Office policy to the contrary. Like most of fellow regulars, he distrusted the American militiaman, and his difficulties with the Illinois militia during the Black Hawk War reinforced this view. With the exception of the Black Hawk War, Atkinson handled every major assignment with skill, organizational competence, and strong leadership. He carried out each task quietly and without delay, and when compared to his contemporaries in the Army he has to be included among the most competent officers of that day. Describing Atkinson's career over fifty years ago, historian William J. Ghent wrote that he was "inseparably connected with the earlier period of the conquest of the frontier, and the part he bore is equaled in importance by that of no contemporary with the possible exception of William Clark.*" This characterization remains accurate.

B

BACON, Nathaniel, Jr. (b. Suffolk, England, January 2, 1647; d. Gloucester County, Va., October 26, 1676), Bacon led a controversial rebellion in colonial Virginia.

Nathaniel Bacon, Jr., was the son of Thomas Bacon of Friston Hall, Suffolk, England, thereby being cousin to Sir Francis Bacon, late lord chancellor; to Nathaniel Bacon, Sr., a member of the Virginia Council; and, by marriage, to his adversary, Sir William Berkeley,* governor of Virginia. He was educated as a fellow-commoner at St. Catherine's Hall, Cambridge, from which his father withdrew him after two years. Tutored at home, Bacon then traveled on the Continent and, in 1666, returned to St. Catherine's Hall, from which he was graduated M.A. in 1668.

In 1670 he married Elizabeth Duke whose father so objected to the union that he disinherited her. After becoming involved in an attempt to defraud a young man of his inheritance, Bacon was sent by his father to Virginia, where, with the aid of his cousins, the elder Nathaniel and Lady Berkeley, he was able to get a fresh start. He arrived in Virginia in 1674 with £1,800 capital which he used to purchase about twelve hundred acres of land on the James River. His property consisted of a cleared plantation and a house at Curles and another tract upstream at the Falls, the location of the present city of Richmond. In part because of his relationship to prominent Virginians as well as his apparent abilities, Bacon was made a member of the Governor's Council soon after his arrival in the colony.

Bacon came to Virginia during a period of unrest. The economic policies of the English government favored the English merchants to the detriment of colonial planters, who remembered the higher prices paid them when Dutch ships and merchants had access to the colonial market. Sir William Berkeley, who had been a popular governor, was now in his old age. Despite his protests to England about economic policies, Berkeley received much of the blame for the difficulties of the planters because, as a loyal official, he enforced the regulations.

Moreover, he and the remainder of the oligarchy which ran the colony profited by their position of leadership. Repeated Indian attacks, however, were to spark the conflagration known as Bacon's Rebellion.

Governor Berkeley attempted to keep the peace with the tributary Indian tribes by means of treaties. He saw these Indians both as a valuable buffer between the English and the fiercer tribes and as allies during time of war. And he believed in the obligation to live up to agreements made with them. The men of the frontier, however, saw the presence of the tributary tribes both as a threat to security and as a block to their continual need for more land.

In July 1675 the Doeg Indians raided the plantation of Thomas Mathew in order to force payment of a debt they claimed he owed them. Mathew's herdsman was killed, and retaliatory raids set off an Indian war. As Indian attacks became more frequent, the governor and council responded; their measures were defensive, however, and, at the first opportunity, the governor made peace. His plan for defense was to construct forts at the heads of rivers and to conscript five hundred men, some on horseback, to range between the forts. Frontiersmen saw this measure as ineffectual and sought permission to attack the Indians. Meeting at Jordan's Point they chose Bacon as their leader. He made a stirring speech in which he denounced the governor for both oppression and negligence and promised to destroy the Indians whether or not he had a commission. With his followers he then drove the Pamunkey Indians, a tributary tribe, into hiding. Declared a rebel, Bacon, with his armed band, eluded the governor and his troops and marched to the frontier. Arriving at the Occaneechee village near the North Carolina border, Bacon learned that the enemy Susquehannocks had forts nearby. The Occaneechee attacked and defeated the Susquehannocks; the next events, however, are unclear. Whether it was in order to get their £1,000 store of beaver or because they would not give him provisions, Bacon then attacked the Occaneechee and destroyed their village. Thus, his two victories against the Indians were against tribes that were at least nominal allies of the English.

Berkeley ordered new elections, and Bacon became one of the two members of the House of Burgesses from Henrico County. But not knowing whether he would be seated or arrested, he went to Jamestown bringing with him more than forty armed supporters. Not allowed to take his seat, Bacon fled Jamestown. He was pursued upstream and captured by Captain Thomas Gardiner who carried him back to Jamestown in irons. There Bacon apologized on his knees and asked for a pardon. Berkeley pardoned him and promised him a commission; when there were delays in granting the commission, however, Bacon became alarmed and escaped to Curles.

He then returned to Jamestown at the head of a large group of volunteers, demanding a commission which Berkeley refused to grant until persuaded to do so by the frightened burgesses. Later, when Berkeley called out the militia, he found that most of them supported Bacon. Therefore, he fled to the Eastern Shore and left Bacon in control of the mainland and temporarily in control of the waterways. Bacon then issued his "Declaration of the People" as justification for both the rebellion and his military dictatorship. In an attempt to invade the governor's stronghold on the Eastern Shore, two of Bacon's lieutenants were captured and control of the Chesapeake Bay was returned to the governor. Beginning his own offensive, Berkeley returned to Jamestown, which he fortified. Nearby, at the governor's plantation, "Green Spring," Bacon delivered his inspirational "hearts of gold" speech and then laid siege to Jamestown. Bacon prepared to defend his own troops by means of a trench dug the length of the town palisade, and he seized the wives of prominent loyalists and placed them on the ramparts as protection from attack by the governor's forces. During the siege, many of the governor's troops deserted him; Berkeley consequently decided to abandon the capital and once more retreated to the Eastern Shore. Bacon then entered the town, but, without control of the waterways, he could not defend the capital and was in danger of being trapped there. He, therefore, burned the town in order to prevent Berkeley from again having use of a fortified place on the mainland.

By now, however, Bacon was seriously ill (perhaps with typhus), and on October 26, 1676, he died at the home of a friend. His burial was in secret and the place never disclosed. His successors were neither as able nor as inspirational. As a result, when Berkeley began a series of raids against rebel strongholds, he was able to regain control of the colony before the king's commissioners arrived in January 1677.

Historians debate whether Bacon was a patriot who sought to redress the genuine grievances of the people of Virginia or an opportunist who made use of economic difficulties, Indian troubles, and the rabble for self-aggrandizement. Furthermore, historians debate whether Governor Berkeley's regime was corrupt and whether he genuinely sought the best interests of the people he governed.

Most likely there is some truth in both points of view. Although Bacon may have been genuinely concerned about the distress of the people, he was also an opportunist who confiscated the property of loyalists and attacked the tributary Indians rather than hostile tribes. By twentiety-century standards, Berkeley's regime was corrupt; however, the governor had served the colony well for many years and should not be blamed for policies set in London which he enforced. His punishment of the rebels after Bacon's Rebellion was over caused him to end his career under a cloud. Berkeley was harsh, but had he acted otherwise, he would have left the rebels in control of their property and impoverished the loyalists, including the governor himself.

Nathaniel Bacon was not the harbinger of the American Revolution. Instead, he and Bacon's Rebellion should be judged in the light of local unrest in Virginia in the late seventeenth century.

BIBLIOGRAPHY

Craven, Wesley Frank. *The Southern Colonies in the Seventeenth Century*. Baton Rouge: Louisiana State University Press, 1949.

Neville, John Davenport, comp. *Bacon's Rebellion: Abstracts of Materials in the Colonial Records Project*. Richmond, Va.: Jamestown Foundation, 1976.

Washburn, Wilcomb E. *The Governor and the Rebel: A History of Bacon's Rebellion in Virginia*. Chapel Hill, N.C.: University of North Carolina Press, 1957.
Wertenbaker, Thomas Jefferson. *Torchbearer of the Revolution: The Story of Bacon's Rebellion and Its Leader*. Princeton, N.J.: Princeton University Press, 1940.

                                                           JOHN D. NEVILLE

BAINBRIDGE, William (b. Princeton, N.J., May 7, 1774; d. Philadelphia, Pa., July 27, 1833), naval officer. Bainbridge was a controversial captain during the Age of Sail.

William Bainbridge's family had lived in New Jersey since the middle 1600s. Bainbridge went to sea as a merchant mariner in 1789, repeatedly voyaging to Europe and the West Indies before entering the U.S. Navy as a lieutenant in 1798. Later that year he was forced to surrender the schooner *Retaliation* (14 guns), the only American warship to be captured by the French in the Quasi-War. He was then ordered to take the 32-gun frigate *George Washington* on a tribute-carrying voyage to Algiers and was compelled to transport an Algerian mission to Constantinople under the Dey's flag (1800–1801). Late in October 1803 he ran the 38-gun frigate *Philadelphia* aground in Tripoli Harbor and had to endure nineteen months as the Bashaw's prisoner before he was liberated under the terms of the Tripolitan-American Treaty of 1805.

Following mercantile cruises to the West Indies, routine duty at home, and two trading voyages to Russia, Bainbridge came back in time to seize his opportunity for lasting fame when he succeeded Captain Isaac Hull* in command of the 44-gun frigate *Constitution*. Off Brazil on December 29, 1812, he hammered the frigate HMS *Java* into submission in the hardest fought large-ship action during the War of 1812. He served ably at the Boston Navy Yard from 1813 to 1815, building the 74-gun *Independence*, America's first ship-of-the-line since the Revolution, while persuading the ultra-pacifistic Bostonians to stiffen their city's resistance to such an extent that the anticipated enemy assault never occurred.

At the end of the war, he was given the opportunity to prepare a potent expedition against Algiers to end more than thirty years of Barbary harassments. Commodore Stephen Decatur,* however, with consummate selfishness and intrigue, undercut him, sailing first for the Mediterranean, winning battles, and dictating an advantageous treaty, before Bainbridge could arrive with a second squadron. This humiliation, coupled with five years of defeats and frustrations at the hands of an unfriendly Navy Department, makes it all the more remarkable that Bainbridge seconded Decatur in the latter's fatal duel with Commodore James Barron in 1820.

Bainbridge commanded the 74-gun ship-of-the-line *Columbus* in the Mediterranean during 1820–1821; it was his last sea duty. He then apparently plotted unsuccessfully with other officers to oust Isaac Hull from command of the Boston Navy Yard, a position he coveted. After serving as president of the Board of Navy Commissioners (three high-ranking officers who assisted the secretary of the navy), Bainbridge headed the Philadelphia Navy Yard. He was abruptly dismissed from that post in 1831 for clashing with Amos Kendall, close advisor to President Andrew Jackson.* Two years later he was reinstated at Philadelphia, but his painful ailments had worsened to such an extent that he turned to narcotics for relief; by the time of his death, he had become an addict.

Bainbridge had one unenviable distinction unmatched in American naval history. Within the first five years of receiving his commission, he had pulled down his flag three times: in *Retaliation, George Washington*, and *Philadelphia*. It is little wonder that he called himself the "Child of Adversity"; officers had been cashiered from the service for far less serious offenses. Instead, he was not only retained, but also twice promoted, attaining his captaincy as early as 1800, for the Navy Department realized that he had more than compensatory abilities.

Bainbridge's naval contemporaries appear to agree that he was an exemplary seaman, tactician, and strategist. His voyages in men-of-war were characterized by drilling his men incessantly at the guns, and Commodore Oliver Hazard Perry* once told him, "You brought discipline to the Navy." Few cruises in American history were better planned and executed than that of the *Constitution* to Brazil in 1812. His superb seamanship reached its apex when, in action against the *Java*, badly wounded and with his wheel shot away, Bainbridge outmaneuvered his faster adversary, three times raking her, while avoiding that calamity himself.

As a strategist, Bainbridge through his collaboration with Commodore Charles Stewart early in 1812 helped persuade President James Madison to use the fleet offensively, rather than relegating it to coastal defense. A weaker and less resolute commandant at Boston during that fear-stricken summer of 1814 could have invited the British attack which never came. Bainbridge recommended that the U.S. Navy strike at unprotected British commerce in the Pacific and Indian oceans. Using this strategy might have altered the course of the war, but the fighting ended before it could be tried.

Secretaries of the Navy often turned to Bainbridge when they needed to call upon an officer of high professional knowledge and skill. Bainbridge wrote a new signal code after the original had been lost when the 36-gun frigate *Chesapeake* was taken by HMS *Shannon*, inspected and chose sites for bases, and improved conditions at navy yards. Furthermore, he suggested alterations in ship designs, built the first post-Revolutionary ship-of-the-line, promoted better service education, and presided over the Board of Navy Commissioners. The Navy Department counted on William Bainbridge to fulfill a variety of duties during his long career.

BIBLIOGRAPHY

Dearborn, Henry A.S. *The Life of William Bainbridge, Esq., of the United States Navy.* Edited by James Barnes. Princeton, N.J.: Princeton University Press, 1931.
Forester, Cecil S. *The Age of Fighting Sail: The Story of the Naval War of 1812.* New York: Doubleday, 1956.

Guttridge, Leonard F., and Jay D. Smith. *The Commodores*. New York: Harper and Row, 1969.
Tucker, Glenn. *Dawn Like Thunder: The Barbary Wars and the Birth of the United States Navy*. Indianapolis, Ind.: Bobbs-Merrill, 1963.

                                                                            DAVID F. LONG

BAKER, Newton Diehl (b. Martinsburg, W. Va., December 3, 1871; d. Cleveland, Ohio, December 25, 1937), secretary of war, 1916–1921.

Newton D. Baker became secretary of war in March 1916, at a critical moment when traditional American military policies were being questioned seriously for the first time in almost a century. Before he left office in March 1921, he helped shape legislation to reform the armed forces to meet new realities. He was caught up in World War I and faced issues of War Department command and control, civil rights and liberties, and civil-military relations not confronted since the Civil War. To many observers his career was a paradox. A man of peace and confirmed antimilitarist, he became a celebrated war leader. He was a constructive conservative, but his public reputation at home in Cleveland, Ohio, and in the nation was that of a reformer and an architect of the "New Freedom." He died a successful corporation lawyer. Yet there was an inner consistency in his life. He was never one to shake society from the top to the bottom. He was simply a competent, humane, and compassionate man. He saw himself as a Progressive who, like his contemporaries Henry Lewis Stimson,* Charles Evans Hughes, and Woodrow Wilson abhorred extremes and entwined commitment to social and economic amelioration with profound concern for decency and order.

Baker entered the Wilson administration as part of an effort to cool a political situation that had become so heated during the preparedness debates of 1915 that it threatened the unity of the Democratic party and placed the reelection of the president in jeopardy. In February 1916 Secretary of War Lindley M. Garrison resigned to protest President Wilson's failure to support a new military manpower scheme which its supporters labeled the "Continental Army." The plan created a federally controlled reserve of four hundred thousand volunteers which threatened the traditional role of the state-controlled National Guard as the organized wartime reserve of the country. Baker had given little thought to such matters and found it easy to accept the compromises worked out in the National Defense Act of 1916. The "dual oath" imposed on the National Guard retained the "soldiers of the states" as the primary reserve force of the nation while it made them immediately available for federal service in an emergency. The voluntary Reserve Officers Training Corps (ROTC) reorganized the old military instruction programs embodied in the Morrill Land Grant Act (1862) to give systematic training and commissions to college men who completed the course of study successfully. For the first time the importance of the civilian economy in war was recognized through a rider attached to the 1916 Military Appropriations Act which created a Council of National Defense in the executive branch with an advisory commission of civilian experts attached to study problems of war supply, production, and logistics. It was no revolution, but it was more than a gesture. It was the first substantial military policy adjustment since the 1820s.

Baker would have been content to retire once the preparedness crisis was over, but the declaration of war against Germany made such an option politically impossible. Questions of unprecedented scope concerning war direction and management replaced those of long-range national military policy. The secretary of war was a cautious administrator. He chose to maintain traditional equal relationships between the General Staff and the bureau chiefs in the War Department rather than risk controversy. Predictably, he opposed every effort made during the war to lodge independent authority in civilian "super agencies" like Bernard Baruch's War Industries Board. But he could move effectively when he had to. Forced during the winter of 1917–1918 to act in haste, he reluctantly strengthened the War Department's control over industrial mobilization by concentrating procurement and logistical responsibilities in the General Staff. At the end of the war, the civilian agencies had eroded the War Department position, but in most important ways it still controlled the mobilization process.

Baker was less successful in resolving purely military command questions. From the time General John Joseph Pershing* arrived in France in June 1917, there were two American armies; one abroad and one in the United States. And it was not clear who commanded what. There was little difficulty until early 1918 when the General Staff, revitalized under the ruthless leadership of Chief of Staff Peyton Conway March* began to insist that full policy control must be lodged in Washington. Pershing declared that the commander in the field should not be restrained in any way. Baker avoided a decision on this matter and attempted to act as a facilitator between the general in France and the chief of staff at home. The war was almost over before a controversy over the ultimate size of the American Expeditionary Force (AEF) brought the secretary of war to the support of March. The issue was not settled at the time, and it remained for Henry Stimson* and General George Catlett Marshall* to resolve it twenty years later.

The greatest innovation of the war was systematic conscription. The Wilson administration had opposed even the mention of such a notion before the war. In April 1917, however, for reasons both practical and political, it executed a 360 degree change in direction. Baker rotated with the president. His conversion was particularly effective because it persuaded many of his antimilitarist associates, traditional opponents of the power of government over the individual who feared Selective Service would become a permanent policy, that such a temporary expedient might be risked in a war for democracy. Other issues, the most important of which were Army racial policy and the civil rights and liberties of drafted soldiers, were involved in the conscription decision. Little of the racism and anti-civil libertarianism which arose during the conflict can be traced to overt War Department policy, but Baker did little to control the zeal of soldiers in the training camps, in conscientious objectors' centers, or in the field. He chose to deflect and, if possible, dilute the impact of bigots and "witch-hunters" rather than confront them forthrightly. Accordingly, he was condemned by blacks and civil libertarians for the acts of subordinates and got little credit from anybody for avoiding the cruder excesses that undoubtedly would have occurred if he had done nothing at all.

Baker was always the president's man. He proved that by astutely handling his part of the Mexican crisis of 1916–1917 in such a way as to reduce public hysteria and help keep control of events in the administration's hands. Wilson's confidence in Baker grew during the war. The secretary of war proved an able diplomat. In conferences with the French and the British, he effectively protected the independence of the American reinforcement and prevented it from being absorbed piecemeal into the deteriorated Allied fighting forces. During two critical wartime trips to Europe, Baker negotiated agreements that determined American troop strength and assured the shipping necessary to move the AEF to France. When he disagreed with the president, as he did in the debates over intervention in Russia during the summer of 1918, he loyally carried out administration policy once it had been established. Near the end of the war he was prepared, if necessary, to relieve General Pershing from command of the AEF if the general continued, as he had been doing, to interfere with the efforts to secure an armistice with the Germans.

Experience at war modified Baker's views substantially. He supported Chief of Staff March's efforts to give the Regular Army its own reserves through a program of universal military service. He tried to make permanent the General Staff's control over the bureaus which had been so painfully achieved during the war. That was all well and good, but the National Defense Act of 1920, which rejected all such revolutionary changes and instead merely amended the Act of 1916, revealed that neither the Congress nor the country saw a need for such revolutionary changes at that time.

Baker retired from public office unembittered in March 1921. He threw himself into private law practice and civil, educational, and philanthropic affairs. However, in 1934 he did agree to chair the "Baker Board" which recommended operational independence for the Army Air Corps. In 1930 he assessed his war record in a letter to Frederick Palmer:

> My own responsibilities and performances in the War Department were such that it would be impossible for me to have any illusion about them. Each day of twenty-four hours had a week's work packed into it, and that there were errors and shortcomings is not only not surprising, but also inevitable. I was conscious of them at the time, as I am now, but I have been comforted by the feeling that we all did and gave our best.

Subsequent assessments of Baker's work reflect the deep national political and moral divisions of the war period itself. Critics have made clear his inadequacies as an organizer and administrator. All too often he let the soldiers have their way. He neither resolved the command conflicts between Pershing and March nor brought the bureau chiefs under effective control. He did not support civil rights and liberties in the military effectively. But Baker's strength was as an ameliorator, not a crusader. He could bring strong-minded and contentious people to subordinate, at least temporarily, their personal ambitions to higher goals. In those subtler areas of leadership Baker was gifted; he could bring out greatness in others. Finally, as secretary of war he interpreted the military to the country in such a way that the Army retained the support of segments of the American community who had grave doubts about the war. As long as Baker was at the War Department they supported the Wilson administration, admittedly half-heartedly at times, in a cause to which their commitment could easily have been lost entirely.

BIBLIOGRAPHY

Beaver, Daniel R., *Newton D. Baker and the American War Effort 1917–1919*. Lincoln: University of Nebraska Press, 1966.

Coffman, Edward M., *The Hilt of the Sword: The Career of Peyton C. March.*. Madison: University of Wisconsin Press, 1966.

————. *The War to End All Wars*. New York: Oxford University Press, 1968.

Cramer, Clarence H. *Newton D. Baker: A Biography*. Cleveland: World Publishing Company, 1961.

Palmer, Frederick. *Newton D. Baker: America at War*. 2 vols. New York: Dodd, Mead and Company, 1931.

DANIEL R. BEAVER

BANCROFT, George (b. Worcester, Mass., October 3, 1800; d. Washington, D.C., January 17, 1891), secretary of the Navy. Bancroft is known as the father of the Naval Academy.

Bancroft was the fourth son and eighth child of Aaron and Lucretia (Chandler) Bancroft. He came from old New England stock, and his father was a noted Unitarian minister. Early marked for his intellectual talents, Bancroft was graduated from Harvard in 1817 and received a Ph.D. from the University of Göttingen in 1820. He was one of the first American students to earn a nonmedical doctorate. After traveling in Europe, the young scholar returned to Harvard in 1822 as a Greek tutor. The following year he founded the noted Round Hill School in Northampton, Massachusetts. In 1830 Bancroft sold his interest in the school in order to devote his full energies to writing a *History of the United States*. The first of ten volumes appeared in 1834.

Soon after his return to the United States, Bancroft actively entered politics as a Democrat. His natural ability and growing fame thrust him into the leadership of the western or agrarian wing of the Massachusetts Democratic party. The historian developed a political alliance with Martin Van Buren who rewarded him with an appointment as collector of the port of Boston in 1838. Although removed from the post following the change of administrations in 1841, Bancroft continued his political activities and in 1844 led a pro-Van Buren Massachusetts delegation to the Democratic nominating convention. When convinced that the presidential nomination would never fall to Van Buren, Bancroft switched allegiance and helped swing the convention to Governor James K. Polk of Tennessee. Later that year Bancroft himself lost the Massachusetts gubernatorial election in a Whig landslide.

Nevertheless, Bancroft, who had lobbied for a diplomatic post in order to continue research on his *History*, received appointment as secretary of the Navy. The selection was apparently both a political gesture to the Van Buren faction and recognition of the New England Democrats. The new secretary took office on March 11, 1845. Never close, personally or politically, to President Polk, Bancroft nevertheless proved a loyal supporter of his administration.

Bancroft had two overriding concerns as secretary. The first was reduction of the Navy budget, and the second was reform of the promotion system in order to improve the efficiency of the service. In his first annual report in 1845, he proposed a cut of nearly one-third in the Navy's operating funds. Although recognizing the service's need for additional steamers, he refused to suggest either size or number. After the Senate insisted upon an estimate, Bancroft consulted his bureau chiefs. They recommended that the Navy obtain seventy-six craft of various sizes which Bancroft immediately cut to ten vessels. In fact, he evinced so little further interest in obtaining the vessels that the proposal died. Thereafter, the demands of the conflict with Mexico overwhelmed the secretary's inclinations towards retrenchment.

Bancroft's effort to revitalize the officer corps lasted longer and was more successful. In August 1845, contrary to the recommendations of a board of officers, he granted assimilated or relative rank to surgeons. In May 1847 he granted the same privileges to pursers. The granting of precedence to staff officers eased their conditions of service and improved their morale. During the summer of 1845, at the urging of the chief engineer, Bancroft instituted promotion exams and minimum entrance standards for engineers. In his annual report of that year, he pressed for promotion of line officers by merit rather than seniority and proposed a board to weed out those unable to perform their duties. He suggested elimination of 29 percent of the current captains and 48 percent of the commanders. When the proposal for merit promotion produced no congressional action, Bancroft attempted to implement it on his own but discovered that the Senate was unwilling to confirm the men selected. Despite the setback, the following year Bancroft instituted promotion examinations for naval constructors, boatswains, gunners, carpenters, and sailmakers and authorized temporary merit promotions to master for passed midshipmen.

Bancroft believed that naval school for midshipmen was an integral part of his naval reforms. The idea had been discussed for many years, but all efforts to secure adoption had foundered on a diverse combination of congressional and service antagonisms. After securing the advice of a board of senior officers, Bancroft arranged the transfer from the Army of Fort Severn at Annapolis, Maryland; ordered midshipmen not attached to ships to gather there, along with a small staff of officers; and squeezed the money needed to operate an academy from elsewhere in his budget. By early 1846 the school was well underway, and

Bancroft could now overcome fears of its cost to secure the appropriation needed to continue its operation.

Despite his interest in reforms, the secretary had to devote an increasing amount of his time and insufficient resources to the naval activities growing out of the worsening relations with Mexico which followed the annexation of Texas. Soon after entering office he diverted a small squadron under Commodore Robert Field Stockton* from a cruise to the Mediterranean to protect Texas during the period between the offer of annexation and the arrival of an army under General Zachary Taylor.* Coincidentally, the secretary ordered his Home and Pacific Squadrons to concentrate in Mexican ports so as to "discipline Mexico to acts of hostilities." He also issued the two squadrons standby orders in the event that hostilities did occur. Those to Commodore David Conner* in the Gulf of Mexico were to blockade Mexican east coast ports. Those to Commodore John D. Sloat in the Pacific, while couched in strongly cautionary terms to avoid another Monterrey incident, directed the seizure of San Francisco and other Mexican ports once war started. Later in the year Bancroft sent Stockton in the 44-gun frigate *Congress* to reinforce the Pacific force. During the fall of 1845 Bancroft selected Commodore Matthew Calbraith Perry* to succeed Conner as commander of the Home Squadron, but circumstances conspired to delay relief until the spring of 1847.

The war with Mexico erupted in May 1846. Bancroft, not a strong administrator, now had to organize the support for a war fought in two widely separated theaters. The results were not always succcessful. Both squadrons found operations hampered by erratic and often totally inadequate logistic support, while Commodore Conner's activities during the first six months of the war were hamstrung by the late arrival of the small steamers and gunboats required for operations against Mexican ports.

Bancroft exercised little control over operations in the Pacific, although the seizure of California was a major objective of the Polk administration. Nearly all the instructions sent to the commanders there either had been anticipated by the time of their arrival or else were out of date. The difficulties faced by the naval commanders in California largely grew out of personality conflicts rather than the orders dispatched from Washington. Sloat, the commander at the outbreak of the war, feared he had prematurely seized California and hastily surrendered command to Stockton. The latter proved too heavy-handed to keep California quiet and had to put down a major uprising. He then became embroiled in an unseemly dispute with Brigadier General Stephen Watts Kearny* over the political control of the conquered areas. Not until Sloat's regular replacement, Commodore W. Branford Shubrick, arrived in the spring of 1847 did the squadron acquire stable and effective leadership.

On September 9, 1846, Bancroft resigned his post to accept appointment as minister to Great Britain. Following his return from London in 1849, he devoted himself to his *History*. Six volumes appeared between 1852 and 1866. In 1865 he served as the official eulogist for Abraham Lincoln,* as he had twenty years earlier for Andrew Jackson.* In 1867 he returned to Germany to serve as minister in Berlin until 1874. Thereafter Bancroft lived in Washington where he sparkled as one of the capital's intellectual gems until his death.

Bancroft's term as secretary of the navy earned largely negative reviews within the Navy because of his stress on retrenchment and his limitations as an administrator. More recent observers have appreciated his efforts at reform and especially the establishment of the Naval Academy. While the plan of the school came from others, Bancroft brought the project to fruition.

BIBLIOGRAPHY

Bauer, K. Jack. *Surfboats and Horse Marines*. Annapolis, Md.: Naval Institute Press, 1969.
Nye, Russell B. *George Bancroft: Brahmin Rebel*. New York: Alfred A. Knopf, 1944.
Soley, James R. *Historical Sketch of the United States Naval Academy*. Washington, D.C.: U.S. Government Printing Office, 1876.
White, Leonard D. *The Jacksonians*. New York: Macmillan Company, 1954.

K. JACK BAUER

BARNETT, George (b. Lancaster, Wis., December 9, 1859; d. Washington, D.C., April 28, 1930), Marine Corps officer. Barnett was commandant of the Marine Corps, 1914–1920.

George Barnett was raised in rural Wisconsin where his father operated a stock and produce firm. In 1877 he received an appointment to the U.S. Naval Academy. Completing his studies in 1881, Barnett then spent the customary two years at sea; after his return he successfully completed examinations for commissioning. An overabundance of officers clogging the promotion ladder had resulted in a limitation on the number of Navy commissions available to Academy graduates. Seizing on this opportunity, the commandant of the Marine Corps pressed for a share of the graduates to be his new officers. Thus, the class of 1881 became the first to be offered commissions in the Marine Corps; Barnett and ten of his classmates chose the Corps.

From 1883 until his appointment to the Office of the Commandant in 1914, Barnett served in assignments typical for Marine officers of the time. Almost one-half of these years were spent at sea with Marine detachments in the fleet. During the Spanish-American War, he served as the Marine officer in the cruiser *New Orleans* and saw action in Cuban waters. Barnett also served in Marine barracks at various navy yards and as the commander of the legation guard in Peking, 1908–1910.

Barnett's service as a senior officer spans one of the most dynamic periods for institutional change in Marine Corps history. By the turn of the century, modern warship technology had made the Marine Corps' traditional mission largely superfluous. Survival was inherent in the search for a role in the Mahanian Navy. While commanding the barracks in Philadelphia, Barnett was instrumental in the development of the Advance Base Force, an organization designed to secure forward bases necessary for the replenishment of the fleet. Barnett commanded the provisional brigade which tested this concept in the Culebra maneuvers in early 1914; successes in the Caribbean most likely contributed to his selection for commandant the same year.

As commandant of the Marine Corps, 1914–1920, Barnett was the architect of unparalleled expansion for the Corps. Less than ten thousand Marines were in uniform in 1916, but more than seventy-five thousand Americans were serving as Marines by the end of World War I. Prior to this time, the Marine Corps met its expeditionary commitments, including a colonial garrison force of more than one thousand Marines in the Philippines, by pulling troops off ships and gathering them from barracks and depots. The Marines were heavily committed to support President Woodrow Wilson's foreign policy in Latin America; consequently, Barnett asked Secretary of the Navy Josephus Daniels* for an increase in authorized strength. As war loomed for the Americans, Barnett argued effectively for increasing the size of the Corps, based on both existing commitments and possible deployment of Marines to France.

Barnett's motive for getting Marines to France with the American Expeditionary Force was obvious. After recruiting under the slogan "first to fight," failure to see combat in France might have been too severe a blow to morale for the Corps to withstand. Moreover, deployment to the war in Europe provided the opportunity for a new mission for the Corps. While its traditional mission with the Navy would not change, the Marine Corps could provide forces for the advance guard of the Army when the enemy was a land power such as Germany.

The events of 1917–1918 could not have been anything but what Barnett wanted. Faced with demands for trained soldiers, the Department of War accepted Marines in increasing numbers until more than twenty-four thousand were serving in France by the end of the war. At the same time, the Marine Corps' expeditionary role continued throughout the world. The publicity earned by the Marines, described as inordinate by Army critics, was to prove useful in later years when peacetime planners sought to all but eliminate the Corps.

Despite his accomplishments, Barnett was abruptly dismissed by Daniels in 1920. Barnett's persistent pleas for expansion of the Corps and his subtle campaign for his own promotion to lieutenant general may have alienated the secretary of the Navy. Barnett was also opposed by a faction within the Corps. Led by the colorful and outspoken Colonel Smedley Darlington Butler,* this faction believed that the Office of the Commandant should be held by an officer with combat experience. Furthermore, Butler was convinced that Barnett had spitefully kept him from a combat command in France. Aided by his congressman-father, Butler worked to convince Daniels to oust Barnett. Rather than retire, Barnett accepted demotion to brigadier general and posting to a meaningless assignment. Before his retirement in 1923, his second star was restored with the help of powerful Republican friends including John Weeks, his Naval Academy roommate, who was then President Warren Harding's secretary of war.

Barnett's orchestration of Marine Corps expansion provided a precedent for subsequent conflicts. Employment as an "elite force" with the Army, while precipitating its share of acrimony, provided a sound base of public support for the Marines. Barnett's appointment and his successes in office stem in part from his personal association with the Navy and ties as a Naval Academy alumnus. As the first Marine officer to be a member of the General Board as well as the first Naval Academy graduate to be commandant, Barnett was able to make the Marine Corps more of an acceptable member of the Navy-Marine Corps team.

BIBLIOGRAPHY

Frank, Benis M. "The Relief of General Barnett." *Records of the Columbia Historical Society of Washington, D.C.* (1971–1972): 679–93.

Lejeune, John A. *Reminiscences of a Marine*. Philadelphia: Dorrance and Company, 1930.

McClellan, Edwin N. *The United States Marines in the World War*. Washington, D.C.: U.S. Government Printing Office, 1920.

Shulimson, Jack. "The First to Fight: Marine Corps Expansion, 1914–1918." *Prologue* 8 (Spring 1976): 5–16.

Thomas, Lowell. *Old Gimlet Eye: The Adventures of Smedley D. Butler*. New York: Farrar and Rinehart, 1933.

MERRILL L. BARTLETT

BARNEY, Joshua (b. Baltimore, Md., July 6, 1759; d. Pittsburgh, Pa., December 1, 1818), naval officer. Barney, prominent in the War of 1812, was typical of the capable captains born of the American merchant marine.

Barney's family had settled in Maryland in the late seventeenth century from England. His father, a wealthy planter, pressed Joshua into a respectable dry goods business. He disdained his son's desire to enter the merchantman service. When the business failed in 1771, Joshua's father placed the boy first aboard a Baltimore pilot-boat and then on the *Sidney*, engaged in the Liverpool trade, commanded by Joshua's brother-in-law, Thomas Drysdale. While bound for Nice, France, Drysdale died and Barney, only fifteen, brought the vessel to Gibraltar. After necessary repairs, he sought other business in Europe and returned home with a profit for the owners.

The American Revolution had begun shortly before Barney's return. The young merchant captain became sailing master under William Hallock, commander of the 10-gun sloop *Hornet*. Later in the Revolution, Barney served aboard the 8-gun sloop *Wasp*. Later, when only seventeen, he became executive officer aboard the 10-gun sloop *Sachem* with the rank of lieutenant. Barney was captured off the American coast while returning to port with an enemy merchantman. He was quickly exchanged by the British for several Loyalist prisoners, and he returned to duty aboard the 28-gun frigate *Virginia* in December 1777. Barney was again captured in April 1778. Once again he was promptly exchanged, but by this time the American Navy had succumbed to the British fleet.

Barney turned to privateering. While serving as first lieutenant aboard the *Saratoga*, he was captured a third time in August 1780. Joshua was sent to the Old Mill Prison in Plymouth, England. In May 1781 Barney and other prisoners scaled the walls and gained a fishing boat in which they sailed to France.

Late in December 1781 Barney returned to Philadelphia where he was reunited with his wife, Anne Bedford, whom he had married in March 1780. The state of Pennsylvania collected a number of lightly armed vessels in the Delaware Bay to protect its trade, and Barney was given command of a converted merchantman, the *Hyder-Ally*. While escorting a convoy of merchantmen, Barney sighted three British warships near Cape May. The British sloop-of-war *General Monk*, twice as powerful as Barney's ship, engaged the *Hyder-Ally* in a half-hour fight. Barney's cunning forced the British captain to sail his vessel toward the *Hyder-Ally's* side, and Barney's guns raked the *General Monk* from stem to stern. Barney took the enemy ship as a prize to Philadelphia where he was given a hero's welcome. The *General Monk*, rechristened the *General Washington* and commanded by Barney, sailed to France with a packet to the American minister, Benjamin Franklin. By the time he had returned home in March 1783, Barney had been in the Navy longer than any other American officer. The *General Washington* was decommissioned on its return to the United States in the spring of 1784, and Barney was discharged—the United States no longer had a navy. During the next decade Barney engaged in a number of private endeavors including farming and business ventures.

A new American navy was created in 1794 in response to the North African pirate attacks upon American merchantmen. When Barney's name appeared fourth on a list of senior American captains, behind that of Silas Talbot, a former lieutenant colonel in the Army, he refused to accept his commission. Instead, Barney became captain of the merchantman *Cincinnatus*. He sailed to France to collect personal debts and to present an American flag to the French National Convention. The French offered Barney a commission as captain of a French man-of-war. Although Barney declined this offer, in order to complete his personal business, he later accepted the rank of commodore in the French Navy. He served from 1796 to 1802 when he was placed on the pension list. During these years the United States and France fought an undeclared war—the Quasi-War—but Barney never had to fight his own countrymen.

In 1805 he declined appointment as the superintendent of the Washington Navy Yard. The *Chesapeake-Leopard* affair of 1807 prompted Barney to offer his service to the nation, but the pacifist President Thomas Jefferson declined to bring the United States to war. Barney, therefore, remained in Maryland farming and trading.

During the first year of the War of 1812, Barney commanded a privateer, the *Rossie*, equipped with ten 12-pounders, three long guns, and a crew of 120. While under Barney's command, *Rossie* took eighteen enemy merchantmen.

In the summer of 1813 Secretary of the Navy William Jones offered Barney command of sixteen gunboats and a sloop to guard the upper Chesapeake from

British depredations. Now an American commodore, Barney assembled a variety of vessels to defend Baltimore and the national capital. By 1814 Barney's flotilla had grown to twenty-six gunboats and nine hundred men based in Baltimore. When a large British force under Vice Admiral Alexander Cochrane attacked the Chesapeake defenses as part of the three-pronged British offensive of 1814, Barney had no choice but to burn his ships.

He took five hundred sailors, one-hundred marines, and five naval guns to Washington and left others behind to protect Baltimore. Barney's sailors were placed in the center of the American line at Bladensburg, outside of Washington. When the British fired rockets, most of the American militia fled in fear. The sailors, however, had seen rockets before, and they held their line until they ran out of powder. The majority of the American casualties (fifty out of sixty) at the Battle of Bladensburg were sailors. Barney himself was wounded in the thigh. He ordered his men to leave him on the field where he was captured by the British. This time he was treated as a senior officer. His wound was dressed by a British surgeon, and he was immediately paroled. As a token of thanks, the city of Washington presented Barney with a sword.

After the war Barney brooded on his Maryland farm because, in his mind at least, his nation had not properly rewarded him for his faithful service in two wars. Furthermore, bad investments, speculation, and prodigal living had left him in bad financial straits. He sold his farm and equipped a boat to take his wife and their possessions to Kentucky. But at Pittsburgh Barney became fatally ill. Physicians said it was a reaction to the Bladensburg wound of four years before. Barney died on December 1, 1818, and was buried in the Allegheny Cemetery.

Barney was one of the merchant seaman-naval officers spawned by colonial commerce in the eighteenth century. Contemporaries and historians have viewed his service afloat as a tribute to his personal courage, navigational skill, and quick, practical mind. Restless and unhappy on land, his true home was at sea. Barney had enough sense to know when to flee from a superior enemy force, and sufficient courage to stand and fight whenever possible. He capped his career by his stalwart service against the British outside Washington in 1814. There Barney's sailors and marines were the only bright light in the otherwise dismal American defeat which contemporaries derisively called "the Bladensburg races."

BIBLIOGRAPHY

Footner, Hulbert. *Sailor of Fortune: The Life and Adventures of Commodore Barney, USN*. New York: Harper and Row, 1940.
Lord, Walter. *The Dawn's Early Light*. New York: W. W. Norton and Company, 1972.

Muller, Claude G. *The Darkest Day: 1814, the Washington-Baltimore Campaign*. Philadelphia: J. B. Lippincott, 1963.

Paine, Ralph D. *Joshua Barney, A Forgotten Hero of Blue Water*. New York: Century Company, 1924.

EDWARD K. ECKERT

BARNWELL, John (b. Ireland, c. 1671; d. South Carolina, June [?] 1724), Carolinian army officer, colonial agent, Indian-fighter and negotiator, noted frontiersman.

A native of Dublin, Ireland, where he was a member of a good family, Barnwell emigrated to Charles Town, South Carolina, in 1701. During his early years in this proprietary colony, Barnwell received the support of some influential persons, and this support enabled him to rise to prominence. The Chief Justice befriended the young Irishman, and Governor Nathaniel Johnson appointed him deputy secretary and clerk of the council.

Because Barnwell opposed the efforts of the South Carolinian administration to exclude Dissenters from government positions, he eventually fell out of favor and lost the positions he held. After the Dissenters succeeded in gaining control of the Assembly in 1707, Barnwell received the office of comptroller of the colony. In addition to public service, Barnwell turned his attention to agricultural activities, obtained large grants of land, and established a plantation at the northern end of Port Royal Island. This plantation lay directly across from the lands held by the Yamassee Indians. In this frontier setting, Barnwell had as a neighbor and good friend the energetic provincial Indian agent, Thomas Nairne. Both men vigorously supported the idea of British colonial expansion as a necessary check to the threat of French aggression. Eventually, their expansionist views found a sympathetic hearing before high governmental circles in London and provided a basis for the formulation of British western policy in South Carolina. Barnwell's interest in South Carolinian affairs never waned. He became a member of the Commons House of Assembly and later served as a member of the Governor's Council and as a deputy surveyor-general.

In September 1711 there occurred a violent uprising of the Tuscarora Indians in North Carolina. Many white settlers lost their lives, and a number of outlying settlements were completely destroyed. Governor Edward Hyde of North Carolina appealed for aid to the authorities in Virginia and South Carolina. Officials in Charles Town decided to provide money and military assistance, and Colonel John Barnwell received appointment as commander of an expedition to bring relief to the hard-pressed inhabitants of North Carolina. Previously, Barnwell had distinguished himself in a military way as a volunteer under Colonel William Rhett fighting against the French and Spanish in Sewee Bay (1706) during Queen Anne's War. In this new military venture, Colonel Barnwell's command consisted of a small number of militia and a much larger auxiliary force of Indians.

By late January 1712 Barnwell had arrived in the area of the Tuscarora forts located on the upper Neuse and Pamlico. Although hampered by inadequate supplies and by the desertion of some of his men, Colonel Barnwell vigorously prosecuted the war against the Tuscaroras, killing many and taking others prisoner. In mid-April 1712 he concluded a peace treaty with the Indians at King Hancock's Fort on the Cotechney, a branch of the Neuse River. Barnwell sent to Charles Town for a sloop to carry his disabled men home, as well as himself, for he also had been wounded in the fighting. Meanwhile, the Indian allies proceeded homeward by land. Subsequently, Governor Edward Hyde of North Carolina and Governor Alexander Spotswood of Virginia sharply criticized this treaty and Barnwell's role in the negotiations. Back in South Carolina, however, Colonel Barnwell became a popular figure for his military successes, being known as "Tuscarora Jack." Because the peace terms concluded in April did not long prevail, Governor Hyde had to appeal again for military aid. Barnwell, recuperating from his wounds, urged that assistance be sent, and Colonel James Moore, Jr., the son of a former governor of South Carolina, received the command of this second expedition. Colonel Moore carried out his military duties with dispatch and inflicted such heavy casualties upon the Tuscaroras that by the spring of 1713 their power had been broken forever. Many of the Tuscarora Indians left North Carolina to join their kinsmen, the Iroquois in New York.

In 1715 the inhabitants of South Carolina faced a serious crisis that threatened the continued existence of the colony. The Yamassee Indians, bitterly resentful of the harsh and unjust treatment which they had long endured at the hands of Charles Town traders, and fearful of the threat of white encroachment upon their lands, finally broke out in a major rebellion. Before this conflict ended most of the Indian tribes between St. Augustine and Cape Fear as well as some in the interior had become involved. The first Yamassee attack occurred suddenly at daybreak, August 15, 1715, at Pocotaligo, in the vicinity of Port Royal. Colonel Barnwell's good friend Thomas Nairne, the Indian agent, became one of the first victims. Seized by the Yamassee, he was slowly tortured to death. The Indians boldly attacked and destroyed border settlements, killing settlers and livestock, while frightened refugees crossed into Charles Town for safety. In this critical period, Governor Charles Craven took prompt action, declared martial law, and organized the military forces of the colony by appointing James Moore, Jr., as lieutentant general, John Barnwell as colonel, and Alexander Mackey as lieutenant colonel. All these senior officers had considerable experience as Indian-fighters. The vigorous counteroffensive launched by the governor eventually succeeded, and by autumn the Yamassee had been driven far southward into the Spanish colony of Florida. Fortunately for the English colonists the Cherokee Nation, which had wavered in its sympathies, turned down Creek appeals for assistance and eventually supported the English in this major conflict.

The Yamassee War brought about a reorganization in South Carolina of the Indian trade, an economic activity that had long been a significant political and economic factor in the life of the colony. A regulation bill of June 1716 abolished private trading and provided that all animal skins had to be brought to specified "factories." Supervision of this trade was entrusted to a board of five commissioners acting under the authority of the House of Commons Assembly. John Barnwell, by now a leading political figure in the colony, received appointment as one of the five original board members.

Following the Yamassee War, popular sentiment in South Carolina crystallized in favor of the overthrow of the proprietary regime and the establishment of royal control over the colony. Failure of the proprietors to provide adequate defense measures for the colony and mounting grievances concerning many other matters led the Commons House of Assembly in December 1719 to declare itself a convention and to choose James Moore, Jr., as the provisional governor.

In the spring of 1720 Colonel Barnwell traveled to London, sent there on a special mission that had a twofold purpose. Barnwell first had the task of reconciling the London authorities to those political changes that had taken place in South Carolina, and second, he hoped to persuade the British government to develop a vigorous defense program on the frontier in order to check the aggressions of the French, Spanish, and Indians. Acting in collaboration with the local resident agent Joseph Boone, Colonel Barnwell proposed before the Board of Trade that the Crown should undertake the construction of a series of forts beginning at the mouth of the Altamaha River and ending in the lands of the Cherokee Nation on the Tennessee River. He later recommended that steps be taken for the colonization of the southern frontier along the Savannah and Altamaha rivers. Although these proposals pleased the Board of Trade, Barnwell failed to win support for this entire project from the Privy Council because of the vast expense involved. The Privy Council approved the building of only one fort, the one to be constructed along the banks of the Altamaha River. This fort would provide quarters for an English garrison on the extreme southwestern frontier.

Barnwell arrived in Charles Town in May 1721 in the company of Sir Francis Nicholson, a veteran administrator and the first appointed royal governor of South Carolina. Nicholson had the benefit of much experience in colonial service, having served either as governor or lieutenant governor over the provinces of New York, Maryland, Virginia, and Nova Scotia. Along with governor Nicholson and Colonel Barnwell came a contingent of British troops to take part in frontier fortification.

During the summer of 1721 a party of soldiers under Colonel Barnwell's command established with difficulty a small fort on the north side of the north branch of the Altamaha River. Thick heavy cyprus planks had to be used in the fort's construction because of the lack of any other type of wood nearby. The gabled blockhouse of this fort had three levels with walls pierced for cannon and muskets and loopholes provided for smaller arms. Earthworks, approximately five to six feet high, palisades, and a moat defended the fort's land side. The earthworks formed a right triangle with the blockhouse, and within this area several huts served as living quarters for the soldiers. Known as Fort King George, this construction, aside from a few warehouses of traders, constituted the first English establishment in the land later known as Georgia. Don Antonio de Benavides, the Spanish governor of Florida, considered Barnwell's activities a serious encroachment on Spanish Territory, and he made formal protests to Governor Nicholson. The English governor, however, gave no satisfaction on this point, and so the matter became the subject of dispute in various diplomatic exchanges between the courts of London and Madrid.

The subsequent English occupation of the Spanish area of Guale, later known as the English colony of Georgia, represented a logical and strategic move in the complicated international colonial rivalries of the eighteenth century. Barnwell himself, however, did not live to see this development, for he died in Beaufort, South Carolina, in June 1724 and was buried in that city.

The military career of John Barnwell during the colonial period was a distinguished one. He served effectively in Queen Anne's War, in the Tuscarora War, and in the Indian uprising of 1715. Through his long period of residence in South Carolina he gained extensive knowledge of the problems connected with the Indian, French, and Spanish frontiers of that colony. He also had the reputation of being the greatest planter of the Port Royal District.

His wide experience in holding various provincial offices gave him an understanding of the local problems which few contemporaries could match. Such a background of service proved particularly valuable when he was sent to London to represent colonial interests. Barnwell provided valuable advice for the Board of Trade, Lord Charles Townshend, the secretary of state, and General Francis Nicholson, the veteran colonial administrator who became the first royal governor of South Carolina.

Barnwell perceived the danger of French encirclement of English possessions in the southeastern part of North America long before others recognized this periolous situation. To meet the threat of French aggression Colonel Barnwell, working with his colleague Joseph Boone, presented before the Board of Trade in London in August 1720 concrete proposals for colonial defense. Barnwell pointed out that the building of a series of forts along the frontiers would preserve the advantages of Indian trade and present an important barrier to French expansion efforts. These oral representations made by Barnwell were buttressed by pertinent documentary materials.

Upon returning to South Carolina after his visit to London, Barnwell began the implementation of the policy to provide a more adequate defense for the frontiers of the new royal colony. The building of Fort King George represented a significant move in strengthening the security of the English position in the Carolinas. Further measures which might have been undertaken at this time were curtailed by Barnwell's death, but his contributions did not go unnoticed. Governor Nicholson himself highly praised the great services Barnwell had performed for his country.

BIBLIOGRAPHY

Crane, Verner W. *The Southern Frontier, 1670–1732*. Ann Arbor: University of Michigan Press, 1929; reprint edition, 1956.
Meriwether, Robert L. *The Expansion of South Carolina, 1729–1765*. Kingsport, Tenn.: Southern Publishers, 1940.
Robinson, W. Stitt. *The Southern Colonial Frontier, 1607–1763*. Albuquerque: University of New Mexico Press, 1979.
Snowden, Yates, ed. *History of South Carolina*. Vol. 1. Chicago and New York: Lewis Publishing Company, 1920

BERNARD C. WEBER

BARTON, Clara (b. North Oxford, Mass., December 25, 1821; d. Glen Echo, Md., April 12, 1912), Civil War relief worker and nurse, founder of the American National Red Cross.

Clara Barton was born into a Massachusetts family whose forebears were involved in the Salem witch trials (as the accused) and in Shays' Rebellion (as rebels). She studied in the New England public schools, and taught in them for a decade. In 1851–1852 she attended Clinton Liberal Institute, a Universalist school, in Clinton, New York, in an era when higher education for women was uncommon. From 1852 to 1854 she was instrumental in introducing public schools into Bordentown, New Jersey; from 1854 to 1857, she held a government clerkship in the Patent Office in Washington, D.C.

During the Civil War, Barton assisted and nursed wounded soldiers on the battlefields with supplies sent by friends in New England and New Jersey and transportation provided by the Quartermaster Department of the U.S. Army. She was at the battles of Cedar Mountain, Antietam, and Fredericksburg in 1862; at Morris Island in 1863; and with the troops of General Benjamin Franklin Butler* below Richmond in 1864. The two large-scale Civil War civilian relief organizations, the Sanitary Commission and the Christian Commission, were organized and dominated by men. They did not utilize women as nurses or agents at the front; Dorothea Dix's Army Nurses Corps employed women as nurses only in hospitals in the rear. Clara Barton occasionally received aid and supplies from the commissions but operated on her own as a sort of one-woman commission.

At the end of the war, Barton organized a search for information on soldiers missing in action. At the request of Secretary of War Edwin McMasters Stanton,* she joined a military expedition to Andersonville Prison in Georgia in July 1865. The following spring the Joint Committee on Reconstruction invited her to testify on her experiences in the South; she was the only woman called before this important congressional committee. That spring Congress gave her $15,000 $15,000 to continue her search for missing men: she issued a report on this work in 1869.

From 1866 to 1869 Clara Barton traveled the lecture circuit in the North, describing her battlefield experiences and her trip to Andersonville. In 1870, while vacationing in Europe, she served in the Franco-Prussian War as a volunteer in the new International Red Cross. In the city of Strassburg, she organized a relief program for destitute civilian women in the fall of 1870. In 1871 she traveled throughout eastern France distributing funds given her by the Boston French Relief Society.

While recuperating from a nervous breakdown at a health sanitarium in Dansville, New York, in 1877, Barton contacted the International Red Cross Committee in Geneva expressing her willingness to lead efforts to obtain the adherence of the United States to the Geneva Treaty (guaranteeing neutrality to relief workers in wartime). The committee accepted her offer of leadership since Reverend Henry W. Bellows, the former head of the wartime Sanitary Commission, had proved ineffectual in his ratification efforts for the committee. After years of lobbying in Washington, D.C., and around the country, Barton was successful: the U.S. Senate ratified the treaty, and President Chester Arthur signed it in March 1882. Groups that aided Barton in her effort included former soldiers (in the Grand Army of the Republic—the GAR), members of the press, feminists, and social reformers. The American National Red Cross was organized in May 1881 with Barton as its first president.

Clara Barton served as president of the American Red Cross through the 1880s and 1890s. During that time the organization functioned primarily in natural disasters and aided victims of floods in the Ohio and Mississippi River Valley, victims of tornadoes and the like. It raised funds for relief of the Americans in 1896 and sent an expedition to Turkey. Barton represented her organization at the International Conference in Geneva (1884); Carlsruhe (1887); Vienna (1897); and St. Petersburg (1902).

The American Red Cross provided nurses and services in the Spanish-American War in 1898. Barton, at the age of seventy-eight, herself went to Cuba to survey the work. Criticisms of Barton's leadership emerged at this time. In 1904, as part of the larger Progressive movement (to professionalize and improve organizations), she was forced to resign leadership of the Red Cross. She then worked for the new National First Aid Association as its president until shortly before her death in 1912 at the age of ninety.

The popular image of Clara Barton is of a woman who was the American Florence Nightingale. Considering her work as a nurse in the Civil War and her role as head of a humanitarian organization, people view her career as one of a nurturant female who aided the victims of natural and man-made disasters. It is clear, from a closer look at her life, that she was as much a frustrated would-be soldier, in a century when women had no opportunity for a career in the Army as she was a model of nurturant womanhood. Her career grew out of efforts to fashion an alternative to a strictly military career—one that enabled her to participate in three wars—where she overcame some of the prejudice against women serving at the front. She hoped that in future wars, ''there will be women there, and they will not be hindered and belittled and turned back and thwarted in their purposes.''

Barton presented herself to the American public, and was accepted by it, as a woman who hated war but felt impelled to nurse its victims. A closer look at her writings reveals a different attitude. Barton believed that woman's low status was directly tied to her noninvolvement in the war: she was frustrated because men denied women the suffrage on the basis that they did not serve in the military, and on the other hand, men denied women participation in war because they were not citizens who could vote on matters relating to war. Barton hoped that her example would help advance the cause of woman's suffrage by showing that women could take responsibility in time of war. Moreover, she also believed that women could be as brave as men under fire. Barton herself was personally fearless. In 1870, while touring a hospital of civilian wounded in Germany, she took grim satisfaction in noting that more than half the wounded were women who were stoical about their pain. After the Civil War, she supported the formation of a Women's Relief Corps, as an auxiliary to the Grand Army of the Republic, as a way for the average woman to learn more about civic responsibilities and military procedures. In her own work in Red Cross disaster relief, she particularly relished the similarity between such national emergiencies and war—both were times of crisis.

Barton's preference for things military can be traced to the influence of her father, an Army noncommissioned officer and veteran of the Indian Wars on the frontiers in the 1790s, who coached her in military lore, taught her to use red and white Indian corn to work out winning military strategy, told her tales about his own military experience, and led her to revere his military heroes, Andrew Jackson* and Napoleon. One of the proudest moments of her youth was when a doctor was impressed by her acceptance of pain after an accident and told her father that "she stood it like a soldier." Her own love of athletics and need for physical exercise contributed to her appreciation of army life. This love found expression in the Civil War and in Cuba where she lived in a tent, marched through the woods, rode over the fields, lived on military rations, and found an acceptable outlet for her endless energy.

Her view of herself as a soldier was central to her personality. In 1861 when Abraham Lincoln* called for volunteers, she half-seriously told a cousin he should not be surprised if he chanced to hear of her having enlisted. During the war she told one soldier-friend her version of a military academy for women: "I have an idea that the elevation and character and education of women has something to do even with the military world. If it were left to me to recommend the process by which a nation should be raised to the highest standard of military fame. . . .I should commence by instituting military academies for its women." During recuperation from her breakdown in the 1870s, she wished to recover and get back in step with life but wrote that "my regiment has moved and I don't know where to find it." Before her death in bed at the age of ninety her thoughts were still on war: she imagined she was back in the Civil War and compared her own pain to that of a wounded soldier and was ashamed that she complained.

In the modern debate over the future of American women in the armed forces, there is little reason to doubt that Clara Barton would approve of increased opportunities for her sex in this field, including education at military academies and a role in combat. Barton once concluded that "I see no reason why women have not the same privilege to be shot that they have to be protected, the same right to danger."

BIBLIOGRAPHY

Barton, Clara. *The Red Cross: A History*. Washington, D.C.,: American National Red Cross, 1898.
————. *The Red Cross of the Geneva Convention: What It is*. Washington, D.C.: Darby, 1978.
Barton, William E. *The Life of Clara Barton*. 2 vols. Boston: Houghton, 1922.
Henle, Ellen L. "Clara Barton: Soldier or Pacifist?" *Civil War History* 24 (June, 1978): 152–60.
James, Edward T., *et al.*, eds. *Notable American Women*. Cambridge, Mass.: Harvard University Press, 1971.

ELLEN L. LAWSON

BEAUMONT, William (b. Lebanon, Conn., November 21, 1785; d. St. Louis, Mo., April 25, 1853), military surgeon, pioneer in the study of human digestion.

William Beaumont was a member of a family that was well established in New England before the end of the seventeenth century. He attended school in Lebanon, Connecticut, but when he was twenty-one, he left his family to try his hand at farming at Champlain, New York. There he soon abandoned farming in favor of teaching school. In 1810, however, he apprenticed himself to a physician at St. Albans, Vermont, and received a license to practice medicine in that state in June 1812.

In September 1812 Beaumont joined the U.S. Army as a surgeon's mate for an infantry regiment. He served in this capacity throughout the War of 1812, seeing action during the attack on Canada in the spring of 1813, at which time he formed what would be a life-long friendship with Joseph Lovell,* who became the first surgeon general of a permanent Army Medical Department in 1818. Beaumont also helped care for the wounded from the Battle of Plattsburgh in 1814.

Resigning from the Army late in 1815, Beaumont established himself as a partner in a private practice at Plattsburgh and also went into business as a partner in a general store there. In 1816 he sold out of the store and from then on limited his interests entirely to the practice of medicine and surgery.

Beaumont was commissioned surgeon to a New York militia cavalry regiment in the spring of 1819, and the following December he applied for a commission in the U.S. Army. Giving up his private practice in Plattsburgh when he received his commission as post surgeon in 1820, Beaumont was sent to Fort Mackinac in Lake Michigan. Not long after his arrival at this post, he requested and received permission to start a private practice among the civilians of the island.

In the spring of 1822, Beaumont was called upon to care for a Canadian trapper, Alexis St. Martin, who had been wounded in the abdomen by the accidental discharge of a shotgun. Although the patient survived, the wound never completely healed. Through the opening that remained in St. Martin's side, Beaumont was able to observe the process of digestion.

Beaumont took St. Martin into his home when it appeared that no one on the island would care for him, and for two years provided him with medical care, food, clothing, and shelter, for which Beaumont never received compensation. During this period and after asking Lovell's advice on how to proceed, Beaumont began conducting a series of experiments into the mysteries of human digestion, making use of the opening into St. Martin's stomach.

Intermittently in the period 1825–1833, whenever his famous patient could be prevailed upon to stay with him, Beaumont conducted experiments with St. Martin as his guinea pig. In some of them, he attempted to determine the time necessary to digest various articles of food by tying each sample to a silk string and suspending it into the stomach through the fistula. In others, he checked the variations in the temperature of the stomach under different weather conditions. He sent samples of St. Martin's gastric fluid to some of the most prominent scientists of his day, but they were unable to ascertain its exact composition. Beaumont's attempts to collect gastric fluid when St. Martin was fasting revealed that no fluid was secreted by the empty stomach.

Once St. Martin had recovered from the effects of the accident, however, he was reluctant to remain with Beaumont, even when the surgeon was able to have his patient taken into the Army as a sergeant with a regular salary. Beaumont persuaded St. Martin to join him for brief periods at the various posts to which the surgeon was assigned, during which further experiments were run, and to have his patient accompany him for brief stays in Washington, D.C., and New York. In 1834, the Canadian returned permanently to his native land, bringing Beaumont's research to an end. Fortunately, Beaumont had already gained enough information to complete a book, *Experiments and Observations on the Gastric Juice and the Physiology of Digestion*, which was published in 1833.

During the period of his service in the Army up until this time, Beaumont's Army patients included the sick and wounded from the Black Hawk War in 1832, when the first pandemic of cholera struck the United States, as well as the ill at such posts as Forts Niagara, Crawford, and Howard.

In 1834 Beaumont was ordered on an inspection tour of five northern post hospitals and then sent to Jefferson Barracks, near St. Louis. After returning to Washington for consultations with the surgeon general in the fall of 1835, Beaumont was reassigned to the St. Louis arsenal, which became his permanent post.

In 1836 Beaumont was offered the chair of surgery in the medical school being planned for the St. Louis University. He provisionally accepted the offer, subject to the approval of the surgeon general, but the actual opening of the medical school was delayed and it appears that Beaumont never actually lectured there.

In 1838 Lovell's successor as surgeon general, Thomas Lawson, ordered Beaumont to leave St. Louis for Florida. Beaumont, who believed that Lawson had been treating him shabbily, responded to the order by resigning his commission, perhaps in the belief that by this move he could persuade Lawson to allow him to remain in St. Louis. Lawson, however, accepted his resignation, thus bringing Beaumont's career in the Army to a close.

From the time of his resignation from the Army until his death, Beaumont conducted a private practice in St. Louis, either alone or for brief periods in partnership with younger physicians. He attempted from time to time to persuade St. Martin to join him and to submit to further tests but without success. He was involved in the quarrels and feuds characteristic of the medical world of the time, but he led the life of a respected and prominent citizen of the community until his death, which resulted from a fall suffered while returning from the home of a patient.

Beaumont's pioneering work in the field of human digestion was the first large-scale, systematic study of the physiology of human digestion. Before he began his experiments, the little that was known in this field actually lay in the realm of speculation. Beaumont stood almost alone as an authority for many decades after the publication of his book. His work was praised by scientists on both sides of the Atlantic, and even today some medical historians describe Beaumont's achievement as the most important single contribution ever to have been made in the field of human digestion.

Beaumont's accomplishments were all the more unusual because of his lack of college, hospital, or medical school training. His native talent, however, was such that he recognized the opportunity presented by St. Martin's unhealed wound. He unhesitatingly sought the advice of Surgeon General Lovell, whose professional education had been unusually good for the time and, following Lovell's suggestions, turned for guidance to the scientists best able to help him.

Most of Beaumont's work was done in the most primitive surroundings, at military posts without laboratories or complicated equipment. He was even further handicapped by the state of the science of chemistry; even the best chemists of his time could not identify all the components of what Beaumont called the "gastric juice." Largely through his own observations, therefore, Beaumont established that digestion was a chemical rather than a physical process, that it was affected both by the emotions and by the nature of the food consumed, that the secretion of mucus was separate from the secretion of acid, that hydrochloric acid was not the only component of the gastric fluid, and that the walls of the stomach were capable of peristaltic motion.

Beaumont's achievements were largely the result of his own talent and determination, but he was unusually fortunate to be able to undertake his work at a time when his superior was a man who appreciated its importance and was eager to support him in every possible way.

BIBLIOGRAPHY

Ackerknecht, Erwin Heinz. *A Short History of Medicine*. New York: Ronald Press Company, ca. 1955.

Ashburne, Percy Moreau. *A History of the Medical Department of the United States Army*. Boston: Houghton Mifflin Company, 1929.

Beaumont, William. *Experiments and Observations on the Gastric Juice and the Physiology of Digestion*. Plattsburgh, N.Y.: n.p., 1833

Brown, Harvey E. *The Medical Department of the United States Army from 1775 to 1873*. Washington, D.C.: Surgeon General's Office, 1873.

Hume, Edgar Erskine. *Victories of Army Medicine: Scientific Accomplishments of the Medical Department of the United States Army*. Philadelphia: J. B. Lippincott, 1943.

Myer, Jesse S. *Life and Letters of Dr. William Beaumont*. St. Louis: C. V. Mosby Company, 1912.

MARY GILLETT

BEAUREGARD, Pierre Gustauve Toutant (b. May 28, 1818, Contreras Plantation, St. Bernard Parish, La.; d. February 18, 1893, New Orleans, La.), Army officer. Beauregard held Confederate commands at Fort Sumter, Manassas, and Shiloh during the Civil War.

The third child of a scion of Louisiana's bayou delta country, P.G.T. Beauregard attained a fame befitting his distinguished Gallic lineage. After three years at a private school in New Orleans and four in the French School in New York City, Beauregard entered West Point in March 1834. A gifted student, already well grounded in mathematics, Beauregard did well at the Military Academy, graduating second in a class of forty-five and receiving his commission as an engineer.

He spent the next eight years at various coastal posts on the Atlantic and the Gulf of Mexico, honing the engineering skills that were to be his hallmark as a soldier. As an engineer on the staff of Winfield Scott* during the Mexican War, Beauregard performed several valuable reconnaissance surveys and was twice wounded. His greatest triumph, however, was in arguing Scott into choosing the Chapultapec route into Mexico City over the objections of the rest of the staff. For this service he was brevetted to major, his second brevet commission of the war.

Until the outbreak of the Civil War, Captain Beauregard (he had been promoted in 1853) spent most of his time in his home state at a variety of activities: superintending construction of forts on the lower Mississippi, as well as that of the New Orleans Customs House; improving navigation at the mouth of the river; and dabbling in New Orleans politics. In 1858 he ran an unsuccessful campaign for mayor of that city on a reform ticket against the local Know-Nothing machine.

Thanks to his powerful Louisiana political connections (U.S. Senator John Slidell was a brother-in-law), Beauregard received the coveted post of superintendant of West Point on January 23, 1861. But because he had made no secret of his pro-Southern sentiments, Beauregard's tenure at the Academy set a record for brevity. It lasted four days.

In early March, after resigning his commission in the U.S. Army, Beauregard was commissioned a brigadier general in the Confederate Army and assigned to the command of the forces in and about Charleston, South Carolina. His command of the attack on Fort Sumter earned him overnight fame, and on June 3, 1861, the "Hero of Sumter" assumed command of the main Confederate Army in Virginia. Together with General Joseph Eggleston Johnston,* who spirited reinforcements to the field, Beauregard directed this army to victory at the First Battle of Manassas in July. His star had reached its apogee; he was promoted to full general.

Beauregard soon fell into disfavor with President Jefferson Davis,* however, and in early 1862 he was ordered to the western theater as second-in-command to General Albert Sidney Johnston.* Beauregard planned the Confederate attack on the Union Army under Ulysses Simpson Grant* at Shiloh, Tennessee, in April 1862, and he assumed command of the army after Johnston's death on the battlefield. Beauregard's retreat from the field at Shiloh and his subsequent evacuation of Corinth were skillfully conducted. Nevertheless, Davis relieved Beauregard of his command shortly thereafter for failing to secure permission before leaving the army on sick leave. Placed in command of the Department of South Carolina, Georgia, and Florida, Beauregard returned to Charleston in September. There he successfully managed the defense of the city against several Union assaults until late April 1864, when he took over command of the Department of North Carolina and Southern Virginia.

His new department included all of Virginia south of the James River, and in this command Beauregard performed his greatest service to the Confederacy. He arrived at Petersburg on May 10, brimming with plans to save Richmond and confronted by an immediate threat, the twenty thousand-man Army of the James, under General Benjamin Franklin Butler.* Beauregard's overly ambitious plan to destroy Butler's army went awry at the Battle of Drewry's Bluff on May 16, but he did succeed in immobilizing the enemy in his peninsula entrenchments, thus removing a serious threat south of the capital and freeing badly needed reinforcements for the main Confederate Army under Robert Edward Lee.* Beauregard once again rose to the occasion in mid-June. Correctly divining the shift of Grant's army to the south of Richmond, he conducted a brilliant three-day defense of Petersburg with a badly outnumbered force. His quick action held the city just long enough to enable Lee's army to arrive.

After the fall of Atlanta, Beauregard was placed in command of the Military Department of the West, a figurehead post. He spent the waning days of the war attempting to stem the surge of a Union Army under William Tecumseh Sherman,* who led his troops through Georgia and the Carolinas. On February 22, 1865, Beauregard relinquished command to General Johnston.

Following the war, Beauregard returned to New Orleans, where for the remainder of his life he figured prominently in the business and political affairs of the city and state: as president of two railroads, as adjutant general of Louisiana for ten years, as supervisor of drawings for the infamous Louisiana Lottery Company from 1877 to 1893, and, briefly, as New Orleans' commissioner of public works. Beauregard was the author of several books and articles on Civil War military affairs. His chief works include *A Report on the Defense of Charleston* (1874) and *A Commentary on the Campaign and Battle of Manassas* (1891).

As large in ego as he was small in stature, and with a touchy pride to accompany his soldierly appearance, P.G.T. Beauregard never realized his potential as a first echelon military commander. Of excellences he had more than his share: he was a confident and personally courageous leader, respected by his men. Lacking neither pugnacity nor imagination, he often demonstrated masterly defensive skills. His defense of Petersburg in 1864 with a patchwork force of about ten thousand against the better portion of two Union army corps was classic, as was his use of deception against Henry Wager Halleck* at Corinth. His engineering skills were formidable, as the disposition of his troops and guns during the defense of Charleston during 1863–1864 proved. And on more than one occasion—in Virginia in 1861 and again in northern Mississippi in early 1862—Beauregard evinced noteworthy organizational talents.

Unfortunately, Beauregard's virtues paled in comparison to his weaknesses. A better-than-average field commander, competent enough in handling situations he could see, he could not make war on a map. But how he loved to try! Undeterred by an unbroken record of overly complex battle plans that failed, Beauregard insisted upon seeing himself as a superior strategist, and he frequently pressed his ideas upon the government. What sound strategical sense he had, however, was rendered invisible by his penchant for formulating grand plans wherein fantasy and grandiose promises of victory predominated. Captivated by his study of Napoleon's campaigns and by the textbook principles of French military theorist Antoine Henri Jomini, Beauregard planned in ethereal realms, as unconcerned by the realities of his own situation and the capabilities of Confederate logistics as he was disregardful of the enemy's intentions. Even so, Beauregard had a firm grasp of the importance of the military principle of concentration, and he urged it repeatedly upon his superiors.

He might have gained a more respectful hearing for his ideas but for another, more serious, failing. For a full general, in the public eye from the very outset of the war, Beauregard displayed a shocking lack of political savvy. And like it or not, high-ranking soldiers must number this quality among their virtues to be effective. Beauregard never did. Soon after the Battle of Manassas he began to consort with the Davis administration's enemies in the Confederate Congress and to make public his distrust and disdain for the government. Too proud and vain to accept his limits as a subordinate, Beauregard swiftly earned the enmity of President Davis.

Exalting one's self at the expense of the commander in chief could have only one result: Beauregard spent the rest of the war in a series of second-rate assignments. Like many another in the large cadre of Davis-haters, Beauregard allowed his own pride, sensitivity, and suspicions to blind him to his own shortcomings. Indeed, by 1864 the relationship between the two men had become so corrosive that Beauregard dawdled about sending reinforcements from his department to Lee, a man Davis trusted.

Had he been given the chance Beauregard might have developed into an excellent commander. And perhaps the fault was not his alone. Jefferson Davis, a petulant and petty man himself on occasion, once characterized Beauregard as "forever driveling on possibilities." The characterization was unfair. To his credit, Beauregard at least *saw* possibilities. To his detriment, he never saw how how to translate vision into reality.

BIBLIOGRAPHY

Basso, Hamilton. *Beauregard: The Great Creole*. New York: Charles Scribner's Sons, 1933.
Davis, William C. *Battle at Bull Run: A History of the First Major Campaign of the Civil War*. Garden City, N.Y.: Doubleday and Company, 1977.
Roman, Alfred. *Military Operations of General Beauregard*. 2 vols. New York: Harper and Brothers, 1884.
Sword, Wiley. *Shiloh: Bloody April*. New York: William Morrow and Company, 1974.
Williams, T. Harry. *P.G.T. Beauregard: Napoleon in Gray*. Baton Rouge: Louisiana State University Press, 1954.

THOMAS E. SCHOTT

BELL, James Franklin (b. Shelbyville, Ky., January 9, 1856; d. New York City, N.Y., January 8, 1919), specialist in guerrilla warfare and military educator. Bell was one of the dominant personalities in the effort to raise the professional standards of the U.S. Army between 1898 and 1917.

The son of a small farmer and sometime captain in the Confederate Army, Bell entered the U.S. Military Academy in 1874. His West Point career was noted primarily for feats of horsemanship and high jinks, but twelve years of frontier service in the 7th Cavalry, broken only by a four-year interlude as an instructor of tactics and military art at Southern Illinois Normal University at Carbondale, Illinois, matured him. He received a thorough education in troop leading on the Plains, even though he missed the Indian Wars, and developed an intense interest in his profession. Marksmanship and physical conditioning for troops were the two fads of the 1880s and Bell participated in both reforms, trying out his ideas on his company when his superiors were absent on detached service. He also used a sand table to instruct his men in minor tactics, the first American officer to employ this pedagogical device.

His mastery of his profession attracted the attention of Colonel, later Major General, James W. Forsyth, and Brigadier General, later Major General, Wesley Merritt.* Forsyth appointed Bell the first secretary of the newly opened Cavalry and Light Artillery School. In this position and subsequently as an aide to Forsyth, Bell authored a collection of orders establishing the conditions under which units ranging in size from one troop to an entire regiment maneuvered, drew up the first set of rules guiding the conduct of maneuvers ever prepared by an American officer, and in 1895 wrote the first Army manual on the subject. Merritt in 1898 rescued Bell from the obscurity of a stateside post and made him the chief of the Office of Military Information of the Philippine Expeditionary Force.

Although Bell personally conducted all negotiations with Emilio Aguinaldo's native government and served as a key advisor to successive commanding generals, he won a Congressional Medal of Honor and advancement from captain to brigadier general because of spectacular combat leadership, first as chief of Scouts for the 2d Division commanded by Major General Arthur MacArthur* and then as the colonel commanding the 36th U.S. Volunteer Infantry, "the Suicide Club." Bell, like the American high command, believed that the dissolution of the regular Philippine Army in late 1899 signaled the end of the fighting. His first attempts to deal with the ensuing guerrilla warfare were fumbling at best. He soon, however, evolved a workable technique: the collection of detailed information about the Filipino "shadow" governments operating within the American lines, the simultaneous arrest of the members of the "shadow" governments, the garrisoning of all major towns, the concentration, if necessary, of all inhabitants within the garrisoned towns, the harassment of the guerrillas by small mutually supporting columns that would remain in the field for months, and political reforms coupled with the promise of no reprisals. Bell's application of this doctrine achieved considerable success, most notably in the surrender of Miguel Malvar, Aguinaldo's successor as head of the native government, in Batangas Province in April 1902.

Bell's return to the United States in 1903 initiated the period of his greatest influence on the Army. Bell headed the Command and General Staff School at Fort Leavenworth from July 1903 until April 1906. He revitalized the school, which had been closed during the Spanish-American War, by attracting able teachers and good students. He organized the Staff College in 1905 to allow the honor graduates from the first year of instruction to pursue advanced professional study. When Secretary of War William Howard Taft secured his appointment as chief of staff, Bell chose his own successor, Brigadier General Charles P. Hall, in order to ensure the continuation of his plans for reform.

Bell was the first American chief of staff to serve a full four-year tour (1906–1910). It was a period punctuated by domestic disaster and rumors of war. Bell coordinated all Army relief activities in the aftermath of the San Francisco earthquake of April 1906 and commanded U.S. forces during the initial phases of the second occupation of Cuba, October to December 1906. Upon his return to Washington in the midst of the San Francisco school segregation controversy, he directed the General Staff to prepare an emergency plan in the event of war with Japan. None existed. In the course of its formulation, he disagreed with the basic tenet of American Pacific strategy that Subic Bay in the Philippines should be the main American naval base in that ocean. It was an idea that the president, successive service secretaries, Admiral George Dewey,* Bell's predecessors as chief of staff, and the chiefs of engineers, artillery, and ordnance had publicly endorsed on numerous occasions. Bell argued that Subic was indefensible, and he favored Pearl Harbor in its place. An immense battle amid the bureaus ensued for over a year. Theodore Roosevelt* eventually decided in favor of Bell, but the affair damaged their relationship. Taft's strong support probably saved Bell from dismissal.

Bell used the occasion of the Japanese war scare to direct the General Staff to prepare a general mobilization plan, the first such peacetime effort in American military history. He then ordered the General Staff to compose a comprehensive long-range statement of American military needs based upon the mobilization plan. He hoped to gain congressional approval of the General Staff's goals and to enlarge the Army and National Guard by increments. Although he secured the approval of both Presidents Roosevelt and Taft, political considerations prevented them from sending the program to Congress. Bell, however, had made all the necessary preparations for the preparedness agitation launched by his successor.

From 1911 until 1914 Bell commanded the Philippine Division. His primary concern was to prepare the Corregidor garrison to withstand a siege of six months or longer. Within the limitations imposed by obsolescent equipment, he succeeded. In 1914 and 1915 he commanded the 2d (Tactical) Division mobilized on the Mexican border. At his direction Captain E. E. Booth prepared a training schedule for a mobilized division based upon the 2d Division's experiences, the first such manual in the U.S. Army. Bell sent copies at his own expense to all the senior officers in the Army. As commanding general of the Western Department, 1915–1917, he took a prominent role in the preparedness movement, thereby incurring the enmity of Woodrow Wilson. Bell played an important part in the early phases of mobilization in World War I as commanding general of the Eastern Department, but ill-health prevented him from accompanying the 77th Division, which he had trained, to France. It was a personal and professional disappointment from which he never recovered. He died while still on active duty as commanding general of the Eastern Department.

Bell's reputation with his contemporaries deservedly rested upon his work in the Philippines and at the Leavenworth schools, but his service as chief of staff was at least as important. In addition to his contributions in mobilization planning and Pacific strategy, Bell in conjunction with Major Daniel H. Boughton worked out the basic tactical doctrine, published in the *Field Service Regulations, 1910*, which the Army took into World War I. Convinced that the next major war would involve the extensive use of field fortifications, Bell encouraged tests of the impact of artillery on entrenchments and barbed wire entanglements. He played a major role in the adoption in 1906 of the machine gun as a standard part of the armament of all line regiments, and three years later he chaired the board that purchased the first Army airplane. During his second tour in the Philippines, he and John Joseph Pershing* conspired to motorize an infantry regiment on Mindanao out of surplus quartermaster funds. Bell also played an important part in the creation of the School of Musketry in 1906—predecessor of the modern Infantry School at Fort Benning—and took the initial steps leading to the establishment in 1913 of the School of Fire for field artillery at Fort Sill.

Promoted brigadier general in the regular service in 1901 and major general in 1907, Bell enjoyed the rare opportunity to influence the promotion of officers a generation his senior as well as his own contemporaries and younger soldiers. He aided the careers of, among others, five future chiefs of staff: W. W. Wotherspoon, Tasker Howard Bliss,* John J. Pershing (whom Bell wanted as chief of staff in 1914), Malin Craig,* and George Catlett Marshall.* They and the graduates of the service schools provided Bell's most enduring legacy to the Army.

BIBLIOGRAPHY

Booth, Ewing, E. *My Observations and Experiences in the United States Army*. Los Angeles: n.p., 1944.

Challener, Richard D. *Admirals, Generals, and American Foreign Policy, 1898–1914*. Princeton, N.J.: Princeton University Press, 1973.

Gates, John M. *Schoolbooks and Krags: The United States Army in the Philippines, 1898–1902*. Westport, Conn.: Greenwood Press, 1973.

Hagood, Johnson. *The Services of Supply: A Memoir of the Great War*. Boston: Houghton Mifflin Company, 1927.

Millett, Alan Reed. *The Politics of Intervention: The Military Occupation of Cuba, 1906–1909*. Columbus: Ohio State University Press, 1968.

Pogue, Forrest C. *George C. Marshall: Education of a General, 1880–1939*. New York: Viking Press, 1963.

EDGAR F. RAINES

BERKELEY, Sir William (b. at or near London, 1606; d. London, July 9, 1677), royal governor and captain general of Virginia, 1641–1652, 1660–1677.

William Berkeley was born into one of England's most celebrated families. He was the youngest son of Sir Maurice Berkeley of Burton, Somerset, and brother of John, the first Lord Berkeley of Stratton. He attended Oxford between 1623 and 1629, receiving both a B.A. and an M.A.

Intelligent, charming, and well connected, Berkeley soon became a favorite of the royal court. King Charles I knighted him in 1639, appointed him a commissioner of Canadian affairs and a member of the Privy Chamber, and in August 1641 named him governor and captain general of Virginia, a position he held for most of the remainder of his life.

Berkeley arrived in Virginia just as an unsteady truce with the surrounding Indians of the Powhatan Confederation began to break down. In April 1644, the natives launched a devastating attack on the colony, killing about five hundred of the eight thousand settlers in a single stroke. Berkeley rallied the Virginians and set in motion a powerful militia counteroffensive. He then sailed for England, ostensibly to seek aid for Virginia but more likely to offer his services to the king in the English Civil War. After campaigning with the royal forces for a few months, Berkeley returned to Virginia to find that the militia had scored a great victory over the natives. He did not participate directly in the desultory fighting that followed until 1646 when he led a daring raid which resulted in the capture and eventual death of the Indian leader, Opechancanough.* This action ended the war and endeared Berkeley to the people of Virginia.

During the thirty years of relative peace that followed the subjugation of the Powhatan Confederation, Berkeley seems to have played a major role in reshaping the Virginia militia into a more efficient combat force. By the 1660s the militia consisted of twenty regiments of infantry and twenty troops of dragoons, sixty special quick-response units located along the borders of the colony, and several detachments of frontier rangers. The colony was divided into five military districts and was ringed by eleven forts, some of them substantial structures of brick and earth.

The outbreak of the Anglo-Dutch wars presented Berkeley with the difficult problem of defending Virginia's extraordinary system of bays and rivers without a naval force. In 1667 he crammed twelve hundred militiamen aboard merchant vessels and attempted personally to lead this improvised force against a flotilla of Dutch men-of-war in the James River, but the Dutch withdrew before battle could be joined. Six years later a smaller Dutch squadron was repulsed more easily. On both occasions Virginia's amateur soldiers manned coastal batteries, patrolled the shoreline, and drove off landing parties.

Aged, infirm, and exhausted by the strain of the Dutch wars, Berkeley failed to respond effectively to Susquehannock Indian raids on Virginia's northern border in 1675 and 1676. Angry frontiersmen led by Nathaniel Bacon* set out after the raiders on their own. Following serious miscalculations by both Berkeley and Bacon, this local mutiny escalated into a full-scale civil war known as Bacon's Rebellion. In September 1676 the rebel army drove Berkeley and his loyalists across Chesapeake Bay to the Eastern Shore. From there the governor commandeered all the merchant vessels in Virginia's waters and launched a series of amphibious commando-style raids against the rebels, eventually forcing them back from the coast. Learning that Bacon had died, the governor recrossed the bay in force and soon negotiated an end to the uprising.

Berkeley had little time to enjoy his triumph. He was recalled by Charles II in early 1677 to explain the outbreak of the rebellion and died shortly after reaching England.

Berkeley's military reputation is based on two accomplishments: his leadership in defending Virginia against Indians and European invaders, and his role in the transformation of the Virginia militia.

Captain John Smith* notwithstanding, Berkeley probably was Anglo-America's first military hero. Virginians credited him with the victory over the Indians in 1646 largely, it seems, because of his willingness to lead troops into the wilderness against the enemy, a rather uncommon tactic among royal governors.

He demonstrated the same personal aggressiveness twenty years later in attempting to repel the first Dutch raid. His popularity had faded considerably by 1676, when many of the colonists were up in arms against him, but not his courage or desire to be at the head of his few followers in the maneuvers and skirmishes that punctuated the early stages of Bacon's Rebellion.

Berkeley was a gentleman administrator who never forgot that his was a dual commission: to defend Virginia as well as to govern it. Although he had no known military training or experience before coming to America, he took an unusual interest in the provincial militia, Virginia's sole means of defense. Records are sketchy for much of Berkeley's administration, but it appears that he introduced the regimental form of organization, pioneered the use of special forces such as rangers and minutemen (then called trainbandsmen), purged unreliable indentured servants from the ranks, and developed a decentralized chain of command that allowed frontier militia forces to respond quickly to an Indian incursion—a sound idea that backfired badly in 1676. Despite repeated pleas to the Crown for help, he never was able to alleviate the colony's shortage of arms and ammunition.

Such military accomplishments were of considerable importance in early Virginia but have been overshadowed by the imperial wars of the eighteenth century and the Revolution. Ironically, Berkeley, once "the Darling of the People" for his capture of Opechancanough, is best remembered today as the tyrannical villain of Bacon's Rebellion.

BIBLIOGRAPHY

Morgan, Edmund S. *American Slavery, American Freedom: The Ordeal of Colonial Virginia*. New York: W. W. Norton and Company, 1975.

Morton, Richard L. *Colonial Virginia*. Vol. 1. Chapel Hill: University of North Carolina Press, 1960.

Washburn, Wilcomb E. *The Governor and the Rebel: A History of Bacon's Rebellion in Virginia*. Chapel Hill: University of North Carolina Press, 1957.

Wertenbaker, Thomas J. *Torchbearer of the Revolution: The Story of Bacon's Rebellion and Its Leader*. Princeton, N.J.: Princeton University Press, 1940.

                                                                WILLIAM L. SHEA

BIDDLE, James (b. Philadelphia, Pa., February 18, 1783; d. Philadelphia, Pa., October 1, 1848), naval officer. Biddle was a vigorous and multi-talented captain who served in the Navy from 1800 to 1848.

James Biddle, the scion of a prominent Philadelphia family, was attracted to the Navy by the example of an uncle who had died heroically during the American Revolution. After entering the service in 1800, he was well trained by Captain Thomas Truxtun.* Assigned to the ill-fated 38-gun frigate *Philadelphia*, he endured nineteen months of imprisonment after her capture in Tripoli Harbor late in 1803. From 1805 to 1811 his time was occupied by gunboat and frigate duties, attaining his lieutenancy, and using furloughs for mercantile and diplomatic tours to China (1807–1808), Portugal, and France, the latter two in 1811.

As Jacob Jones' first lieutentant in the 18-gun sloop *Wasp*, Biddle was praised by his captain for gallantry in action while taking the sloop HMS *Frolic* on October 13, 1812. Rewarded by promotion to commander and command of his own ship, he sailed in the 18-gun sloop *Hornet* as part of the squadron of Commodore Stephen Decatur.* But during June 1813, the *Hornet* was trapped at New London, Connecticut, and could not put to sea until late the next year. Biddle's combat career reached its pinnacle in March 1815. Not only did his *Hornet* annihilate the sloop HMS *Penguin* in twenty-two minutes on March 23 off Tristan d'Acunha Island in the South Atlantic, but a few weeks later he managed by the most deft seamanship to escape capture by the ship-of-the-line HMS *Cornwallis*. Upon his arrival home Biddle learned that he had already been promoted to captain and that Congress would vote him a gold medal for his triumph.

Biddle commanded the 18-gun sloop *Ontario* from October 1817 to April 1819 off both coasts of South America, protecting American commerce from the illegal blockades and counterblockades of royalists and rebels in the Latin American wars of independence. During this cruise he dashed to Oregon, a region disputed by the United States and Great Britain, thereby helping to strengthen his country's claim to that vast area.

After almost four years without assignment, Biddle became commodore of the new West Indian Squadron assembled to end piracy in the Caribbean. His cruise in the 38-gun frigate *Macedonian* was horrifying. Off Havana yellow fever broke out in the crew; eventually about one-third of the ship's complement died.

Another leave, a quick trip to Europe, and command of the Philadelphia Navy Yard passed before Biddle was appointed commodore of the Brazilian Squadron from 1826 to 1829, operating in waters troubled by war between Argentina and Brazil. This was directly followed by another three-year tour as head of the Mediterranean Squadron, during which he signed the first Turkish-American treaty. Returning with shattered health in 1832, Biddle needed a lengthy recuperation before directing, from 1838 to 1842, the U. S. Naval Asylum in Philadelphia, a home for retired sailors, which he expanded by adding a midshipmen's school. He spent the next five years trying to cope with his family's worsening finances.

Biddle's last command added up to a grand finale. He took the 74-gun ship-of-the-line *Columbus* on a round-the-world cruise from April 1845 to March 1848, highlighted by his exchanging ratifications on the Treaty of Wanghia, the first Sino-American pact, and establishing U.S. consulates in China; a cool reception in Japan where he could open no direct negotiations; and brief duty commanding the Pacific Squadron during the Mexican War. Leaving California in the summer of 1847, he came home in March 1848. Exhausted by his strenuous voyage, he died a few months later.

Two great loves—the Navy and relatives—were the lodestars of James Biddle's life. Since he never married, the affection that would have gone to a wife and children centered instead on his younger brother Nicholas, president of the Second Bank of the United States, and his family. This relationship helped to shape James' naval career. Until the collapse of Nicholas' monetary empire late in the 1830s, James was well enough off financially to permit him the widest selection of assignments. He invariably refused navy yard commands, Philadelphia's excepted, patiently waiting through long home leaves without pay for the availability of choice overseas duty.

As a result, Biddle was unusually well traveled, rounding the world once, passing the Cape of Good Hope five times, Cape Horn, three times, and crossing the Equator on twenty occasions. He commendably fulfilled the exacting diplomatic responsibilities so often required of nineteenth-century naval officers. In this sphere, his aristocratic bearing aided him in negotiations with titled foreigners, particularly in Turkey and China. Understandably, however, his aloofness offended some of his colleagues. An officer of that day who could boast that in forty-eight years in the Navy he had "never fought a duel, never was tried by a court martial, never drank a glass of grog," could hardly expect to be universally popular among his fellows.

Service education was another of Biddle's lasting interests. His letters to his superiors are full of suggestions and admonitions as to how officers should be better trained. He stressed more than the mathematics and foreign languages which concerned almost every commander, placing much emphasis upon proper deportment and improved morality, disliking especially dueling, financial irregularity, and heavy drinking. While commodore of the Mediterranean Squadron in 1832, he proudly announced that 819 of his 1,107 total complement were accepting a small monetary payment in place of their grog ration. What is more, during his four-year tenure he turned the U.S. Naval Asylum in Philadelphia into a direct forerunner of the Naval Academy at Annapolis, by working closely with his professors in developing a better curriculum for educating midshipmen.

As Biddle was a prisoner during most of the Tripolitan-American War, 1803–1805, his battle experience was exclusively in the War of 1812, and here he served with brilliance. In 1812 he was the first to board the stricken *Frolic*, personally hauling down her flag. In 1815, although hit by splinters and shot through the neck and chin, he forced the *Penguin* to surrender. A little later, by jettisoning almost all movables and taking advantage of every errant breeze, he eluded the mighty *Cornwallis*. In performance in action, the ultimate test of a military man, Biddle scored high.

BIBLIOGRAPHY

Guttridge, Leonard F., and Jay D. Smith. *The Commodores*. New York: Harper and Row, 1969.

Johnson, Robert E. *Thence Around Cape Horn: The Story of the United States Naval Forces on Pacific Station, 1818–1923*. Annapolis, Md.: Naval Institute Press, 1963.

Paullin, Charles O. *Diplomatic Negotiations of American Naval Officers, 1778–1883*. Baltimore: Johns Hopkins University Press, 1912.

DAVID F. LONG

BILLINGS, John Shaw (b. Cotton Township, Ind., April 12, 1838; d. New York City, N.Y., March 11, 1913), military surgeon, librarian, bibliographer. Billings is a central figure in American medical scholarship.

Son of a farmer and small businessman, John Shaw Billings early showed a strong intellectual bent combined with unusual energy and determination. Joining, for a dollar, a small lending library, he formed a habit of reading; finding Latin quotations in one book, he taught himself that language with the aid of a young clergyman. He made an agreement by which his father would help him through college (B.A., Miami University, 1857) on the understanding that the whole inheritance should go to Billings' sister. Hence, he was obliged to put himself through the Medical College of Ohio, where he cared for the dissecting-rooms and suffered greatly from poverty. He received his M.D. in 1860.

One requirement for the degree was a dissertation. Billings' labors in ransacking the libraries convinced him that American repositories were poor, the volume of medical publications immense, and the indexes and catalogues untrustworthy. "It was this experience," he later declared, "which led me when a favorable opportunity offered at the close of the war, to try to establish, for the use of American physicians, a fairly complete medical library, and . . . a comprehensive catalogue and index."

Now a lecturer in anatomy at the college and a student of surgery, Billings was directed into a military career by the outbreak of the Civil War. Taking up the duties of a first lieutenant and assistant surgeon in July 1862, he endured hard field service in many of the great campaigns. After reforming a hospital at Georgetown and working in another at Philadelphia, he reported in March 1863 to Jonathan Letterman,* medical director of the Army of the Potomac. As surgeon and later as medical inspector, Billings participated in the struggles of Chancellorsville, Gettysburg, the Wilderness, Spotsylvania (where "very many of my old friends" were killed or wounded), Cold Harbor, and the opening of the siege of Petersburg. He responded to the slaughter around him, not only with high professional skill—he was an expert in the quick amputations which in those days were the chief defense against gangrene—but also with a mixture of humanity, gritty realism, and sardonic humor that was peculiarly his own. To a correspondent he wrote that he "got the butchering done in a satisfactory manner." Wielding the scalpel, organizing the movement of wounded, and later reporting on the work of others, he mastered every phase of military medicine in the field.

Billings' abilities were noted by his superiors. In August 1864 he was summoned to Washington to assist in the analysis of field reports, and in December he was assigned to the Surgeon General's Office, where he would remain until his retirement in 1895. There he handled with patience and competence a round of administrative duties, and from the fall of 1865 cared as well for the surgeon general's library, a collection of some two thousand medical books built up since the time of Joseph Lovell.* An unwontedly peaceful existence was now his. His rank increased in the glacial manner of the peacetime Army: brevetted at war's end captain, major, and lieutenant colonel, he received the rank of captain in the Regular Army in 1866; of major in 1876; and of lieutenant colonel in 1894. In 1863, while stationed in Georgetown, Billings had married Kate M. Stevens, the daughter of a former congressman from Michigan. Their family now grew large, with the successive births of six children, five of whom lived to maturity. Partly supporting his family by his pen and carrying out a daily round of often tedious duties, Billings nevertheless found time to establish a national reputation as a scholar of medicine.

Purely scientific studies interested him; he believed his own definition of a medical education as one that prepared its recipient to "study and investigate all the rest of his life." Hence, Billings studied micrography and photomicrography; investigated minute fungi, on which he published several essays; and carried out dissections, sometimes under difficulties. (His diary for 1866 noted, "March 1 . . . Worked a little at my fish's head before breakfast. . . . March 2. Cat has carried my fish head off.") And he read deeply in works of mysticism, a life-long interest that appeared to embarrass the scientist in him not at all.

But Billings' most important achievements were administrative and scholarly. In 1870 he reported on barracks and hospitals, and in 1875 on the hygiene of the U.S. Army, collating and intepreting for the surgeon general a mass of material that led him to adjudge the Army "the best fed and worst housed in the world." Billings' proposals for the reform of the Marine Hospital Serivce (1870) led to notable improvements in the organization and discipline of this forerunner of the Public Health Service. At the same time, he had begun building the library into a central repository of medical knowledge, while making its riches accessible to all. Using funds originally collected by the wartime hospitals, Billings bought widely and selectively, and by 1873 he could report that the library now contained "about 25,000 volumes," plus five thousand pamphlets. He experimented with a draft catalogue in 1876, and in 1880 he saw the government print the first volume of his *Index Catalogue*. This work was immediately hailed as a major achievement. Although a bibliography of only one library, the successive volumes so thoroughly explored so large a collection as to constitute a functional bibliography of medicine. In later years Sir William Osler called it "an exhaustive index of medical literature," adding that "there has never been issued a work so generally useful to the profession." Meanwhile, in 1879 Billings and his assistant, Robert Fletcher, had also launched the *Index Medicus*, an indispensable guide to contemporary medical literature whose publication continues to the present day.

These activities in no way exhausted Billings' energy or his ideas. A founder of the American Public Health Association (1872), Billings was elected its president in 1880, in consequence of his work for the National Board of Health during the yellow fever outbreak in Memphis. Grasping the importance of accurate statistics in public health, he trained himself in the field and took charge of vital statistics for the 1880 and 1890 censuses. His work assured him a place among the pioneers of public health in America. Meanwhile, in 1883 a new responsibility had come his way when the Army Medical Museum was placed under his control. An institution largely devoted to collecting specimens from Civil War battlefields, the museum under his guidance began to change into a storehouse of exhibits showing the human body in health and disease.

Astonishingly, during these same years Billings found time to guide the construction and shape the policies of Johns Hopkins Hospital in Baltimore. Accepted in 1876 by the board as its medical advisor, Billings provided sketches for the architect and brought his interest in sanitary engineering to bear on the problems of ventilation and heating. On the human side, he helped to define the new hospital's attitude toward the patient, medical science, and medical education. His selections for the staff, including William H. Welch and William Osler, helped to insure the unsurpassed quality demanded by the terms of the Hopkins bequest. An important side-effect of the new hospital was its influence on the Army Medical Department. George Miller Sternberg* studied bacteriology in Welch's laboratory; Walter Reed,* William Crawford Gorgas,* and Jesse W. Lazear were all Welch's pupils at one time or another. Thus, a new generation of Army surgeons, soon to carry the department to a peak of achievement never equaled before or since, benefited directly from Billings' many-sided activities.

In 1895 Billings retired from the Army. Johns Hopkins had opened in 1889; the library now contained over three hundred thousand volumes; the *Index Catalogue*, its first series of sixteen volumes complete, was an institution. Still full of energy, Billings served briefly as professor of hygiene and director of the University Hospital at the University of Pennsylvania. But in 1895 the New York State legislature had voted to form the New York Public Library by combining three existing libraries. The board of trustees of the new institution considered no one to guide the consolidation except Billings. He directed planning for the new central building and was instrumental in obtaining Andrew Carnegie's gift of $5.2 million to build sixty-five branch libraries as well. Then Billings went on to help organize and later head the Carnegie Institution of Washington. Long in ill-health, Billings died in 1913 of pneumonia following an operation and was buried with military honors at Arlington.

Billings was an able practicing surgeon but not a scientist of note. His particular genius lay in supplying the guides and institutions through which medical knowledge, and knowledge generally, were preserved and propagated. From the surgeon general's library evolved in time the National Library of Medicine; from the Army Medical Museum, the Armed Forces Institute of Pathology. The influence of Johns Hopkins Hospital and the New York Public Library need no comment. In his own lifetime, the medical profession of Europe and America honored Billings; today his name is obscured because he facilitated the work of others instead of making great discoveries himself. In this case, the judgment of contemporaries seems wiser and truer. Hailed by Welch as "our leading sanitarian during the quarter of a century from 1870 onward," Billings did much to spread the new realization that many diseases might be conquerable, and to meet the rising demand, which he heard "from people of all conditions . . . to put away these plagues which consume our children."

BIBLIOGRAPHY

Flexner, Simon, and James Thomas Flexner. *William Henry Welch and the Heroic Age of American Medicine*. New York: Viking Press, 1941.
Garrison, Fielding H. *John Shaw Billings, a Memoir*. New York: G. P. Putnam's Sons, 1915.
Henry, Robert S. *The Armed Forces Institute of Pathology: Its First Century, 1862–1962*. Washington, D.C.: Office of the Surgeon General, 1964.
Lydenberg, Henry M. *John Shaw Billings*. N.p., 1924.
Memorial Meeting in Honor of the Late Dr. John Shaw Billings, April 25, 1913. New York: 1913.

ALBERT E. COWDREY

BLACK HAWK (b. Saukenuk [Rock Island, Ill.], 1767; d. Des Moines River, Iowa, October 3, 1838), Sac and Fox war chief.

Born into the Thunder Clan of the Sac tribe, Black Hawk (Makataimeshek-iakiak) grew to maturity at Saukenuk, near the mouth of the Rock River, in northwestern Illinois. He rose to prominence among the Sacs and Foxes through his success in warfare against the Osages, Cherokees, and other tribes. Black Hawk joined his first war party at the age of fifteen, wounding an Osage warrior during a skirmish in the summer of 1782. By 1800 he could boast of personally killing over two dozen enemy warriors. His reputation as a war chief enabled him to raise war parties of over five hundred warriors to strike at Osage villages in Missouri.

Although Black Hawk never held a position as a "village" or "peace" chief, his success as a warrior enabled him to exercise considerable influence within the combined Sac and Fox tribes. Although most Sac and Fox leaders were friendly to the Americans, during the first decade of the nineteenth century Black Hawk remained tied to the British, repeatedly visiting British Indian agents and traders at Amherstburg, in Upper Canada. At first he seemed reluctant to join with Tecumseh* and the Shawnee Prophet, perhaps envisioning their growing influence as a rival to his own. However, in 1812 he led a large number of western warriors to the Lake Erie region, where they assisted the British against the Americans. Black Hawk fought in the Indian victory at Frenchtown and was present at the first siege of Fort Meigs, although he evidently took little part in the action. He also accompanied British troops in their unsuccessful attack upon Fort Stephenson, but became discouraged with their failure to take the post, and late in the summer of 1813 he returned to Illinois.

During 1814 Black Hawk led small war parties against the Illinois and Missouri frontiers, and in July 1814 he ambushed a convoy of American boats ascending the Mississippi for Prairie du Chien. In the ensuing battle, thirty-four Americans were killed or wounded and the convoy returned to St. Louis. Six weeks later, in early September, he led Sac and Fox warriors in an attack upon another convoy, defeating a force of 434 regulars and militiamen led by Major Zachary Taylor.* During the following spring, in protest against British and American peace negotiations, Black Hawk and a Sac war party raided near Fort Howard, on the Cuivre River in Missouri. The whites pursued, and the resulting Battle of the Sink Hole was the last military action of the War of 1812 in the West.

The years following the Treaty of Ghent were not happy ones for the aging Sac war chief. During the final years of the War of 1812, his leadership had been challenged by Keokuk, another Sac leader, and in the decade after the war Keokuk's influence increased. Although Black Hawk still visited the British in Canada, Keokuk cooperated with the Americans. In turn, federal officials funneled gifts and annuities to Keokuk which also enhanced his stature within the tribe.

By the late 1820s white settlement advanced into northern Illinois, and pressure mounted upon the tribe to move to Iowa. In 1829 Keokuk and the majority of the tribe complied with the government's demands, but Black Hawk refused to emigrate. When settlers moved into Saukenuk, occupying Indian houses and seizing their cornfields, bloodshed seemed imminent. In response, both the Illinois militia and regular troops converged upon the Sac village. But on June 26, 1831, when the troops reached Saukenuk, they found that Black Hawk and his followers had crossed the Mississippi into Iowa.

Short of food and embittered by their exile, Black Hawk and his people spent an unhappy winter huddled around their fires in Iowa. Unfortunately, the old chief fell under the influence of the Winnebago Prophet, a half-Sac, half-Winnebago holy man from the Rock River who assured him that other tribes would support his reoccupation of Illinois. Meanwhile, Neapope, a Sac warrior recently returned from Canada, carried false tales of British military support. Therefore, on April 5, 1832, Black Hawk led approximately eighteen hundred men, women, and children back across the Mississippi. Although he announced that he only wished to reoccupy Saukenuk and claimed he planned no military actions against the Americans, Black Hawk and his followers were well armed and ready to defend themselves.

Both state and federal officials reacted quickly to the Indians' return. General Henry Atkinson* led a force of 220 regulars from St. Louis to Fort Armstrong, in 1832 at Rock Island, while Governor John Reynolds called out the Illinois militia, sending seventeen hundred volunteers north toward the Rock River Valley. Black Hawk never reached Saukenuk, but proceeded up the Rock River to join the Winnebago Prophet at Prophetstown. There he first ignored demands by Atkinson that he surrender, and then he decided to continue up the Rock Valley, hoping to receive support from the Winnebagos and Pottawatomies. But his meetings with these tribes proved fruitless. Both refused any meaningful assistance and politely asked the Sacs and Foxes to stay away from their villages. Discouraged, by mid-May the old chief decided to return to Rock Island and surrender to Atkinson.

Tragically, his decision to surrender came too late. On May 14 when a small party of Sac warriors attempted to negotiate surrender terms, they were fired upon by a large force of Illinois militia. The resulting Battle of Stillman's Run was an Indian victory, but it ended any chance for a peaceful settlement. Fleeing before superior forces, the hapless Sacs and Foxes rode north into Wisconsin. Hoping to safely recross the Mississippi, Black Hawk and his people turned west along the Wisconsin River, fighting a series of rearguard actions. Meanwhile, other Sac warriors, accompanied by a few dissident Kickapoos and Pottawatomies attacked several isolated settlements in northern Illinois.

On July 21, following the Battle of Wisconsin Heights, Black Hawk and his people successfully eluded capture, and by August 1 they had reached the Mississippi, just below the mouth of the Bad Axe River. There their attempts to surrender again were ignored, and as the Indians attempted to cross the Mississippi, Atkinson's forces fired upon them from the bank. Meanwhile, the *Warrior*, a gunboat from Prairie du Chien, caught the Sacs and Foxes in midstream, raking their flimsy rafts with its six-pounder. When the Battle of the Bad Axe ended, most of the Indians were dead, either from gunshot wounds or drowning. Those survivors who reached the western bank were later attacked by the Sioux, who killed sixty-eight of the refugees and captured most of the others.

Black Hawk survived the battle and surrendered to American officials in Wisconsin. He was taken to Jefferson Barracks near St. Louis where he was imprisoned during the winter of 1832–1833. In April 1833, Black Hawk, the Winnebago Prophet, and several other Indians were sent east to visit President Andrew Jackson* and to see the power and numbers of the American nation. After an audience with the president and a tour through Washington, New York, and other Eastern cities, Black Hawk returned to Iowa, where he lived quietly until his death.

Although Black Hawk's reputation rests upon his leadership in the Black Hawk War, most of his military career came almost two decades before these tragic events. Indeed, his early success against enemy tribesmen and against the Americans in the War of 1812 gave him the stature to attract followers in his opposition to removal. Yet the events following the old chief's return to Illinois in the spring of 1832 have emerged from history as the "Black Hawk War," and he is most widely known for his leadership in this conflict. Black Hawk undoubtedly led the Indians, but whether the military events in the summer of 1832 constitute a "war" remains open to question. With the exception of the Seminole campaigns in Florida, the Black Hawk War was the last major Indian-white military confrontation east of the Mississippi. It was much romanticized by many of its white participants. Black Hawk's image as a formidable opponent also increased accordingly.

Such an assessment does not mean that Black Hawk was not an important Indian military leader. Throughout his career he remained the leading Sac and Fox war chief, and his role in the western theater of the War of 1812 was a major one. In many ways he epitomizes the reluctance of many traditional Indians to cooperate with the government and their determination to defend their homeland.

BIBLIOGRAPHY

Black Hawk. *Life of Black Hawk: Ma-Ka-Tai-Me-She-Kia-Kiak*. Edited by Donald Jackson. Urbana: University of Illinois Press, 1964.
Hagan, William T. *The Sac and Fox Indians*. Norman: University of Oklahoma Press, 1958.
Josephy, Alvin M., Jr. *The Patriot Chiefs*. New York: Viking Press, 1961.
Nichols, Roger. *General Henry Atkinson: A Western Military Career*. Norman: University of Oklahoma Press, 1965.
Stevens, Frank E. *The Black Hawk War Including a Review of Black Hawk's Life*. Chicago: F. E. Stevens, 1903.
Wakefield, John. *A History of the War Between the United States and the Sac and Fox Nation of Indians, and Parts of Other Disaffected Tribes of Indians in the Years 1827-31-32*. Jacksonville, Ill.: C. Goudy, 1834.
Whitney, Ellen, comp. and ed. *The Black Hawk War, 1831-1832*. Springfield: Illinois State Historical Library, 1970-1975.

R. DAVID EDMUNDS

BLACK KETTLE (b. ca. 1801; d. on the Washita River, Indian Territory, November 27, 1868), peacemaker chief of the Southern Cheyennes.

Black Kettle was the son of a Sutai warrior, Swift Hawk Lying Down. The Sutai at one time lived near the Cheyennes and fought them but eventually made a lasting peace and became one of the Cheyenne tribal divisions. The Sutai made many important contributions to the Cheyenne way of life, including the sundance and the buffalo hat medicine. Very little is known about the Cheyennes prior to the eighteenth century, but they appear to have lived near the upper reaches of the Mississippi River until pressure from the Sioux, the need for more adequate food supplies, and a desire for horses caused them to migrate southwestward, preceded by their allies the Arapahoes. By the 1830s, the Cheyennes were living between the Platte and Arkansas rivers and were at war with the Utes, Kiowas, and Comanches, who regarded these lands as their own. During these hostilities, young Black Kettle rose to prominence as a warrior but was among the leaders who arranged a lasting peace with the Kiowas and Comanches in the 1840s. In 1850 he was elected a chief of the Southern Cheyennes.

Unfortunately for the Cheyennes, their new range was directly astride the great trails to Sante Fe, California, and Oregon, and the rush of miners and settlers brought them into frequent contact with the whites. From the first, Black Kettle espoused the cause of peace with the whites and was among the leaders of his tribe that supported the Treaty of Fort Laramie, Wyoming, September 17, 1851. By the provisions of this agreement, the Cheyennes and Arapahoes had their lands clearly delineated, and they were in legal possession of a vast area ranging from southeastern Wyoming to southern Colorado.

The Fort Laramie Treaty did not, however, solve the problems created by the continued influx of miners and settlers who had little if any regard for Indian land claims. When tens of thousands of miners pushed across the Plains towards Pike's Peak in 1859, serious friction was inevitable. In order to preserve peace and prevent a future slaughter of the Southern Cheyennes and Arapahoes, agents of the Bureau of Indian Affairs prevailed on a few chiefs, among them Black Kettle, to sign the Treaty of Fort Wise, Colorado, on February 18, 1861. The Indians surrendered a magnificent domain at Fort Wise in exchange for a sandy triangle in southeastern Colorado. Black Kettle was now regarded by many whites as headchief of the Southern Cheyennes but this was not the case, and many of his tribe were unwilling to abide by the treaty. Nevertheless, an uneasy peace was maintained until 1864. In the spring of that year, isolated skirmishes broke out between parties of Indians and Colorado troops as a result of alleged cattle thefts. By summer a full-scale war was in progress, though it is clear that most of the Cheyennes did not want war and that the real impetus for conflict came from Colorado authorities.

Black Kettle sought to make peace and eventually led a delegation of chiefs to meet with Governor John Evans of Colorado Territory and other officials at Camp Weld, near Denver, on September 28, 1864. Evans refused to make peace, but extensive talks convinced the Indians that if they proceeded with their people to Camp Lyon, Colorado, and encamped they would not be attacked and that the details of a peace would be arranged. By early November 1864 Black Kettle, a number of other chiefs, and about six hundred of their followers were encamped on Sand Creek some thirty-five miles northeast of Fort Lyon. The chiefs had held a number of talks with officers at the post, received some rations from them, and had been given assurances that word would soon come from Denver as to future arrangements. The stage was thus set for tragedy.

Early on the morning of November 29, without warning, a force of more than seven hundred men of the 1st and 3rd Colorado Cavalry Regiments, under the command of Colonel John M. Chivington, struck the Indian camp. Despite the fact that Black Kettle raised the American flag and a white flag, Indian men, women, and children were shot down and their bodies horribly mutilated. Black Kettle and his wife escaped, though she suffered nine bullet wounds. While Chivington boasted that he had slain five hundred Indians, more reliable sources reported the number at about 150.

The aftermath of the Sand Creek Massacre was an Indian war of unprecedented proportions on the Great Plains. Survivors of the massacre carried the news to northern kinsmen and to the Kiowas and Comanches. The result was the outbreak of hostilities from Montana to Texas that did not end until a questionable peace treaty was signed with the Southern Plains tribes on October 14, 1865, at the mouth of the Little Arkansas River. Prominent among those affixing their marks to the treaty was Black Kettle.

This treaty provided for cession by the Cheyennes of their lands in Colorado, and in return they accepted a reserve lying partly in Kansas and partly in Texas. Unfortunately, these provisions could not be carried out. Texas held title to its public lands, and Kansas refused even to consider an Indian reservation within its borders. Thus, the Southern Cheyennes were left without a home of any kind.

For many months sporadic warfare characterized Indian-white relations on the Great Plains, and it was not until an Indian Peace Commission met with representatives of the Southern Plains tribes at Medicine Lodge, Kansas, in October 1867 and new treaties were agreed to that a measure of peace was restored. Black Kettle was instrumental in persuading some of his tribesmen to accept the new agreement, but he could not speak for the more warlike members of his tribe whose memories of Sand Creek were still fresh.

Medicine Lodge assigned reservations in Indian Territory (later the state of Oklahoma) to the Southern Cheyennes and Arapahoes, the Kiowas, Comanches, and Kiowa-Apaches. For a brief time, peace prevailed. Providing reservations was one thing, but persuading the Indians to remove to them was quite another and Black Kettle's influence was waning. In August 1868 raiding parties from a number of Cheyenne camps, including Black Kettle's, struck at white settlers living in the Saline and Solomon River valleys of Kansas. More than a dozen men and women were killed, and a number of children were taken prisoner. Within a short time further raids occurred, and General Philip Henry Sheridan,* commanding the Military Division of the Missouri, decided to undertake a winter campaign designed to punish those guilty of depredations and to drive the Southern Plains tribes into their reservations.

At dawn, on November 27, 1868, Lieutenant Colonel George Armstrong Custer,* with eleven companies of the 7th Cavalry Regiment, struck an Indian village on the upper reaches of the Washita River in Indian Territory. After a furious fight, Custer burned the village, and captured fifty-three women and children and nine hundred ponies. He claimed that he and his troopers had killed 103 Indian men. While this claim was exaggerated, both Black Kettle and his wife were among the dead. Twenty-one of Custer's soldiers were also killed in the Battle of the Washita.

Sheridan's forces accomplished their objective. The Indians were roundly defeated. By late spring of 1869 the Southern Plains tribes were on their reservations, and their days of freedom were at an end. Sheridan gave Black Kettle no credit for his efforts to keep the peace and referred to him as a worthless and worn-out old cypher.

Black Kettle was among the first of the Plains Indian leaders to realize the futility of armed resistance to white occupation and settlement of tribal lands. He realized that peace was the only hope of preserving his tribe's way of life, and he pursued that goal at the cost of respect among many of his own people and certainly among the whites. Less than a generation later few, if any, Indian leaders would have disagreed with him.

Black Kettle failed to achieve a lasting peace, but to his everlasting credit he tried at the cost of his life. He was not the first and certainly will not be the last to pursue the dream of peace and discover that dream elusive.

BIBLIOGRAPHY

Berthrong, Donald J. *The Southern Cheyennes*. Norman: University of Oklahoma Press, 1963.
Grinnel, George. *The Cheyenne Indians*. New Haven, Conn.: Yale University Press, 1924.
Hoig, Stan. *The Sand Creek Massacre*. Norman: University of Oklahoma Press, 1961.
Leckie, William H. *The Military Conquest of the Southern Plains*. Norman: University of Oklahoma Press, 1963.

WILLIAM H. LECKIE

BLISS, Tasker Howard (b. Lewisburg, Pa., December 31, 1853; d. Washington, D.C., November 9, 1930), military diplomat, educator, staff officer, chief of staff. Bliss was the founding president of the Army War College and one of the five American commissioners at the Paris Peace Conference of 1919.

Tasker H. Bliss was the son of a Baptist clergyman, a professor at Lewisburg Academy, forerunner of Bucknell University. His father, George Ripley Bliss, was a nationally respected expert in classical languages who trained his son in Greek and Latin. The combination of a large family and a small income led to Bliss's interest in the service academies.

Graduating from the Military Academy eighth in the class of 1875, Bliss joined the 1st Artillery in Savannah, Georgia, but he was destined to spend very little time with his regiment. In 1876 he returned to West Point for four years' service as an instructor of modern languages. While there, his interest in military history brought him to the attention of Major General John McAlister Schofield,* the superintendent.

After another three years of regimental duty, Bliss attended the Artillery School at Fortress Monroe, graduating with honors in 1884 and serving the following year on the school's staff. His growing intellectual reputation led to Bliss's appointment to the fledgling Naval War College in 1885, where for three years he lectured on military science. In connection with the duty, he was sent to Europe to study the military education systems of Britain, France, and Germany.

When Schofield became commanding general of the Army in 1888, he chose Bliss as an aide de camp. Appointed inspector of small arms and artillery target practice, Bliss became involved in the Army's cult of target shooting, but more to his taste were the efforts of the coast artillery to adjust to the new technology of rifled weapons and indirect fire. During this period, he also secured a transfer to the Commissary Bureau, which brought with it promotion to captain.

In 1897, Bliss went to Spain as military attaché. When war broke out, Bliss was ordered home to serve on the staff of General James H. Wilson,* commanding the 1st Corps at Chickamagua Park, Georgia. A division under Wilson served in the brief Puerto Rican Campaign, where Bliss distinguished himself by attempting to negotiate the surrender of the Spanish troops opposing Wilson's force.

January 1, 1899, found Bliss serving as collector of customs for Cuba and the port of Havana. Over the next three and one-half years, Bliss worked hard to eliminate the atmosphere of casual corruption that had permeated the Customs House under Spain. He trained Cubans to replace the American personnel, while at the same time rebuilding the Customs House to improve its sanitation. His knowledge of tariffs had to be acquired on the job, but the War Department's respect of his newfound knowledge made his opinions important in the revision of American tariffs on Cuban products. After the American withdrawal, Bliss returned to negotiate a treaty of reciprocity with the Cuban government.

His outstanding work in Cuba earned Bliss his first star in 1902. He reported to Washington, D.C., for service on the Army War College Board, which Secretary of War Elihu Root* was using as a *de facto* general staff. When the General Staff Corps came into being on August 15, 1903, Bliss became president of the Army War College. For the first year, it was a school without students, while Bliss prepared his faculty for what he considered the proper role of the institution. He sought a college in the Latin sense, a group of men working together on matters of common concern. Thus, Bliss's War College served as the planning arm of the General Staff, with the students forming committees to study the likely campaigns in various geographic areas, under the supervision of General Staff officers. A plan consisted largely of the orders for the first few days of a campaign; when complete, it was filed for possible future use. It was one of these War College plans that was used during the second occupation of Cuba in 1906.

By that time, Bliss was in the Philippines. He left Washington in 1905, as part of Secretary of War William Howard Taft's diplomatic mission to Japan. In late 1905 Bliss arrived in the Moro Province as military governor. He served briefly, in 1909, as commanding general of the Philippine Division.

Bliss returned to Washington in 1909 for another four months' duty as president of the War College, followed by command of the Department of California. The Mexican Revolution made this another assignment with diplomatic overtones. It was followed by two years as the head of the Department of the East, until in 1913 Bliss went back to border duty, commanding the Southern Department.

In 1915 Bliss became assistant chief of staff and a major general, in charge of the Mobile Army Division, where he once again had a hand in war plans. Still in this position when the United States entered World War I, Bliss was not particularly successful in dealing with the problems of mobilization. He did, however, play a large role in shaping American strategy to concentrate the war effort in France. With Chief of Staff Hugh Lenox Scott's* departure for Russia in May 1917, Bliss became acting chief of staff, succeeding to the position on September 23, 1917. Bliss remained chief officially until May 18, 1918, though most of that time he was out of the country.

Bliss reached retirement age at the end of 1917, but the Congress continued him on active duty, while also making him a brevet full general. In January 1918 he arrived in Europe to take up new duties as the American military representative on the Supreme War Council, a body recently formed to bring unity to Allied strategy. In this position, Bliss worked to concentrate Allied efforts on the defeat of the German armies in France, opposing tangential efforts for strategic reasons and always worrying that the Allies were fighting an imperialistic war to divide up the world.

President Woodrow Wilson chose Bliss as one of the five American commissioners heading the delegation to the Paris Peace Conference of 1919. Although Bliss was an ardent supporter of Wilson's Fourteen Points, he felt that the president ignored him during the conference. Bliss did influence the technical military portions of the German treaty, and perhaps he modified the conference's policy toward Soviet Russia by strongly and eloquently opposing schemes for large-scale military intervention.

Bliss returned to the United States to face retirement, but he continued to be active in many areas. He served two terms as governor of the Soldiers' Home in Washington, D.C., and he helped to found the Council on Foreign Relations in New York City. In numerous speeches and articles until his death, he continued to advocate American membership in the League of Nations, as well as the cause closest to his heart, international disarmament.

There are many officers whose careers demonstrate the changing nature of the Army between 1877 and 1917: Leonard Wood,* Robert Lee Bullard,* and Henry Tureman Allen* are three good examples. Bliss's career certainly illustrates the new duties of the Army that came with world power: he served as an educator, colonial administrator, diplomat, and staff officer. Bliss was probably the leading strategic thinker in the Army from 1903 through World War I. But his career is more than just a representation of these changes; Bliss played a major role in the creation of the modern American Army.

As a young lieutenant and captain, he was active in the Army's professional society, the Military Service Institution, and he was one of the organizers of the Army and Navy Club in Washington, D.C. His duties as an aide to the commanding general involved him in the technological modernization of the artillery, as well as the changes in drill techniques necessary to adjust to that modernization.

Of special importance are the three years Bliss spent in Washington as one of the organizers of the General Staff. The Army War College Board began the efforts to create long-range policies in such areas as mobilization planning and education, as well as preparing the way for the General Staff Corps. As president of the Army War College, Bliss chose to make the institution a functioning part of the General Staff, writing the first comprehensive group of contingency plans for the Army. These plans may appear primitive when compared to the products of the European general staffs, but in view of America's political isolation, they were generally appropriate. Another of his duties, as its chief planner, was to represent the army in the sessions of the Joint Army and Navy Board. Bliss reformed the Army's educational system, creating a progressive structure beginning with post schools for junior officers and culminating in the Army War College. Thus, Bliss shaped the Army's organization to deal with its new tasks as the army of a great power, but also, more than any other officer, he prepared the Army intellectually to face this new situation.

During the Great War, Bliss's service on the Supreme War Council was of great importance to the American war effort. Enjoying the respect and trust of his colleagues, Bliss quickly became a reconciler of differences, a task that suited his personality. At the same time, however, he helped to achieve two major American goals, the acceptance of an Allied supreme commander in France and the concentration of Allied effort on the defeat of the German armies in France.

A reflective man greatly influenced by his study of Greek and Roman history, Bliss saw the destructiveness of modern war as a threat to the entire progress of Western civilization. As he wrote in 1921, "a war of the nations in arms is in reality one of life and death. . . . [Thus] for the first time in modern history, we are confronted by a war of a nature which threatens the continuity, if not the existence, of our civilization." Thus, Tasker Bliss, because of his knowledge of warfare and its role in history, became a leading advocate of the League of Nations and of disarmament, two means to limit the need for war.

BIBLIOGRAPHY

Challener, Richard D. *Admirals, Generals and American Foreign Policy, 1898–1914.* Princeton, N.J.: Princeton University Press, 1973.

Coffman, Edward M. *The War to End All Wars: The American Military Experience in World War I.* New York: Oxford University Press, 1968.

Millett, Allan R. *The General: Robert L. Bullard and Officership in the United States Army, 1881–1925.* Westport, Conn.: Greenwood Press, 1975.

Palmer, Frederick. *Bliss, Peacemaker: The Life and Letters of General Tasker Howard Bliss.* Freeport, N.Y.: Books for Libraries Press (reprint edition), 1970.

Trask, David F. *The United States in the Supreme War Council: American War Aims and Inter-Allied Strategy, 1917–1918.* Middletown, Conn.: Wesleyan University Press, 1961.

THOMAS R. ENGLISH

BOMFORD, George (b. New York City, N.Y., 1780 or 1782; d. Boston, Mass., March 25, 1848), chief of ordnance. Bomford is the inventor of the type of cannon known as the columbiad.

The facts of George Bomford's early life are much in dispute. Born in 1780 or 1782 on Long Island or in New York City, he was reputedly the son of either an officer in the Continental Army or an officer in the British Army. The official date of his admission to West Point is listed as October 24, 1804, although Joseph Swift noted his presence there as early as the spring of 1803. Bomford was graduated from the U.S. Military Academy and was promoted to second lieutenant in the Corps of Engineers on July 1, 1805. He was first assigned to the fortifications of the inner harbor of New York City, where he served as assistant engineer until 1808. By then a captain, he performed similar work on the defenses of Chesapeake Bay and its tributaries during the years 1808–1810. Having served his apprenticeship, Bomford took charge of the fortifications on Governor's Island, New York City, from 1810 until the outbreak of the War of 1812. There he supervised the completion of Castle Williams, the prototype of American coastal forts prior to the Civil War.

During his tour at Castle Williams, Bomford designed a new type of cannon which he called the columbiad. Before this time American ordnance had consisted either of guns that fired a solid projectile nearly horizontally, or howitzers and mortars that hurled explosive shells along a much higher trajectory. Bomford's design, which some authorities consider to be the first major American contribution to ordnance developments, combined the characteristics of both gun and howitzer. Intermediate in length between the two, the columbiad could fire solid shot and explosive shells horizontally or at high angles. Little is known about this gun, and few, if any, have survived beyond a single specimen at West Point. Even the source of the weapon's name is obscure. Presumably, it was derived from Joel Barlow's epic poem ''The Columbiad,'' although alternative theories have been advanced.

At the beginning of the War of 1812, Bomford joined Colonel Decius Wadsworth* in the newly created Ordnance Department. Previously, ordnance items had been purchased from private suppliers through contracts supervised by the secretary of war. The new department now assumed the responsibility of providing ordnance stores of all varieties for the Army. Some it manufactured, others it contracted out, and all it inspected. In addition, the department issued ordnance regulations for the Army, and armed and equipped the militia. Wadsworth became the first commissary general of ordnance and Bomford his deputy. Promoted to major shortly after the conflict began, Bomford spent most of the war years at an ordnance depot at Albany, New York. There he supervised the construction of gun carriages, the repair of small arms, and the manufacture of ammunition. In 1814 he tested a breech-loading rifle invented by John H. Hall and strongly urged its adoption by the Army.

The end of hostilities brought a reorganization of the Ordnance Department. Wadsworth became chief of a new Ordnance Corps, while Bomford, promoted to lieutenant colonel, was retained as his assistant. In addition to its other duties, the Ordnance Department now assumed responsibility for the supervision of the nation's armories and arsenals. Strong advocates of the uniformity system, which in 1815 meant only similarity in construction, Wadsworth and Bomford drew up a new system of regulations for the armories at Springfield, Massachusetts, and Harper's Ferry, Virginia. As Wadsworth's deputy, Bomford was responsible for improving the efficiency of the armories. Thus, he was able to exert a strong influence on armory policy.

In the Army reorganization of 1821, the Ordnance Corps was abolished, although the Ordnance Department remained. Ordnance Corps officers were recommissioned in the artillery, then detailed to ordnance duty. Bomford became lieutenant colonel of the 1st Artillery Regiment and replaced Wadsworth as head of the Ordnance Department a few months before Wadsworth's death in November 1821. Following the course charted by Wadsworth, he continued to promote the uniformity system at the Springfield and Harper's Ferry armories. Operations at Harper's Ferry were especially significant because John H. Hall, a strong proponent of the uniformity system, had recently established a rifle factory there with Bomford's assistance.

Throughout the 1820s Bomford and the Ordnance Department struggled to operate with officers detailed from the artillery for brief periods. By the time these men had become proficient in ordnance duties, they were required to return to their original branch. This unsatisfactory state of affairs was rectified in 1832 when Congress reestablished the Ordnance Corps with Bomford, now promoted to colonel, as its chief. The limited activity of the previous ten years had produced a large backlog of ordnance projects that required attention. Artillery, both field and garrison, needed standardization, while a new regiment of dragoons required outfitting. Bomford directed the attention of the Ordnance Corps toward these problems, but immediate solutions were not forthcoming.

Although he continued to monitor John Hall's progress in small arms manufacture at Harper's Ferry, Bomford reserved most of his concern for artillery matters. As a member of the Ordnance Board appointed in 1832, he worked diligently to establish a system for American field artillery. These efforts proved unsuccessful, primarily because of the failure of the purchasing agent to acquire suitable foreign equipment for comparison. More successful were Bomford's efforts to improve the large-caliber weapons emplaced in the nation's coastal fortifications. His original design, the columbiad of 1811, had long been obsolete, but Bomford retained his faith in the concept of a heavy shell-gun. A series of experimental pieces, the first cast as early as 1838, ultimately led to Bomford's "new columbiad" of 1844.

Bomford's new design rested upon a series of experiments he had conducted to measure the pressures generated at various points within a gun tube at the moment of firing. These experiments produced a series of values that could be plotted to yield a functional curve of firing pressures. Utilizing the results, Bomford refined his design into a weapon standardized in eight- and ten-inch models in 1844. Chambered like a howitzer, but with a tube length more like a gun, the "new columbiad" fired both solid shot and explosive shells out to ranges approaching five thousand yards. It quickly replaced seacoast howitzers in the American inventory.

In 1842 Bomford assumed the title of inspector of arsenals, ordnance, arms and munitions of war, in addition to remaining chief of ordnance. He continued his experiments in the casting of heavy guns, but left the day-to-day operations of the Ordnance Department in the hands of his deputy, Lieutenant Colonel George Talcott. Private affairs also clouded his final years. Disastrous speculation in real estate and the failure of his cotton mill on Rock Creek ultimately forced him to sell his famous estate "Kalorama" in the District of Columbia to settle his debts. Not long thereafter, he died at Boston on March 25, 1848, while on a trip to vist a cannon foundry.

Bomford's place in American military history rests upon two important achievements in the field of ordnance. The first was his effort to introduce greater uniformity in the production of small arms at the national armories. The second was his exprimental work in the design and production of improved heavy cannon for the nation's seacoast fortifications.

From the time of his first association with Colonel Decius Wadsworth during the War of 1812, Bomford diligently applied the older man's dictum of "Uniformity, Simplicity, and Solidarity." Beginning in 1815 and continuing until his death, Bomford labored to bring greater efficiency to the manufacture of small arms at Springfield and Harper's Ferry. Frustrated by indifferent management at Harper's Ferry, he established inventor John H. Hall there in a semi-independent operation. Bomford had been a proponent of Hall's breech-loader since 1814, and Hall's goal of totally interchangeable parts appealed strongly to him. Hall resented the small size of the contracts he received, but the contracts gradually led to more sophisticated production machinery and greater uniformity of product. Absolute interchangeability was not attained by the armories in Bomford's lifetime, but his sustained support of Hall contributed greatly to the ultimate success of the uniformity system.

As for his work in the design of heavy guns, Bomford was not so much the originator of new ideas as he was the developer. He was not the first to fire shells horizontally, but his columbiad seems to have been the first weapon specifically designed for that purpose. It thus predates the far more famous Paixhans shell-gun produced in France a decade later. Similarly, cannon makers had long been accustomed to casting their guns thicker at the breech than at the muzzle, but it was Bomford who verified the conventional wisdom experimentally. Bomford's attempt to measure firing pressures resulted in the improved columbiad of 1844, the most scientifically designed heavy weapon of its time. Although later experiments proved Bomford's figures to be systematically in error, his pioneer efforts laid the foundation for the work of later designers, such as Thomas J. Rodman.

BIBLIOGRAPHY

Comparato, Frank E. *Age of Great Guns*. Harrisburg, Pa.: Stackpole Company, 1965.
Ellery, Harrison, ed. *The Memoirs of Gen. Joseph Gardner Swift, LL.D., U.S.A.* Worcester, Mass.: F. S. Blanchard and Company, 1890.
Lewis, Emanuel Raymond. *Seacoast Fortifications of the United States: An Introductory History*. Washington, D.C.: Smithsonian Institution Press, 1970.

Rodenbough, Theo F., and William J. Haskin, eds. *The Army of the United States.* Reprint edition, New York: Argonaut Press, 1966 [originally published 1896].

Smith, Merritt Roe. *Harpers Ferry Armory and the New Technology: The Challenge of Change.* Ithaca, N.Y.: Cornell University Press, 1977.

WILLIAM GLENN ROBERTSON

BOUQUET, Henry (b. Rolle, Switzerland, 1719; d. Pensacola, Fla., September 2, 1765), British General. Bouquet is noted for successful wilderness campaigns during the French and Indian War.

Henry Bouquet was a Swiss Huguenot, the son of Isaac B. Bouquet, a hotel owner in Rolle, and Madeleine Rolaz, of a Swiss noble family. Many of Bouquet's paternal and maternal relatives were professional soldiers.

At age seventeen, Bouquet joined as an ensign in a professional Swiss regiment in the service of the Dutch Republic, remaining with that unit for three years. He then joined the Swiss Regiment in service to His Royal Majesty of Sardinia as a second lieutenant, receiving his promotion to lieutenant and remaining with the regiment until 1748. Later that year, Bouquet accepted a commission as lieutenant colonel in the Regiment of Swiss Guards, in the service of William IV, prince of Orange, and leader of the Dutch Republic. While stationed at the Hague, he studied military arts with professors Hemslerhuis, Konig, and Allemand.

In 1755, following the defeat of General Edward Braddock,* the British Parliament authorized the recruiting of Protestant German and Swiss officers for service in America. Bouquet was commissioned a lieutenant colonel in the Royal American Regiment (RAR) on January 3, 1756, and arrived in New York seven months later.

After brief duty at Saratoga, the 1st Battalion, RAR, under Bouquet went into winter quarters in Philadelphia. To acquire adequate quarters for his battalion, Bouquet dealt with Benjamin Franklin, then head of the Governor's Council, and they formed a lasting friendship.

In March 1757, Bouquet received command of the troops in the South and embarked with five companies of the 1st Battalion for Charleston, South Carolina. He found the Southern colonies poorly defended, without adequate militia and supplies, and their forts in disrepair. In trying to overcome these weaknesses, Bouquet annoyed Governor William Lyttelton of South Carolina, who asked for his recall, adding that Bouquet was unfit because he had entered into partnership with other foreign officers to acquire two plantations in South Carolina. Despite this criticism Bouquet received his promotion to colonel in December 1757.

Returning to Pennsylvania in 1758, Bouquet became second-in-command, under Brigadier General John Forbes,* of the expedition against Fort Duquesne. Due to Forbes' illness (he was to die in March 1759), Bouquet was largely responsible for organizing the campaign: amassing supplies, opening a new road, building or strengthening fortifications at intervals along the route from Fort Loudoun to Loyalhanna (later Fort Ligonier), all despite adverse weather and political dissension over the route.

The planned British campaign of 1758 included attacks on Louisbourg, the forts of the Great Lakes and in New York (Carillon or Ticonderoga), and Fort Duquesne. Three hundred and fifty Royal Americans, twelve hundred Highlanders, twenty-six hundred Virginians under Colonel George Washington* and Colonel William Byrd, twenty-seven hundred Pennsylvanians, and one thousand wagoners, sutlers, and army followers, comprised Forbes' expedition against Duquesne. Of the total, eight hundred were detached to garrison the forts.

The defeat of Major James Grant, with eight hundred men, in front of Fort Duquesne on September 14, 1758, was followed by a moderate success by the garrison at Loyalhanna against a sortie from Duquesne. Intelligence then arrived that the French had weakened the garrison at Duquesne following their defeat at Fort Frontenac. Forbes ordered a quick march and attack. Under British pressure, Captain de Ligneris, commanding at Fort Duquesne, destroyed the outpost and escaped with his garrison on the night of November 24, 1758. Forbes took command the following day, and renamed the place Pittsburgh.

From 1759 through 1762 Bouquet under the command of Generals Robert Monckton and John Stanwix, was responsible for rebuilding and strengthening the forts in western Pennsylvania. Throughout this period, Indian hostilities along the frontier increased.

On June 22, 1763, during the Conspiracy of Chief Pontiac*, Fort Pitt, garrisoned by 250 men under Captain Simon Ecuyer, was invested by more than four hundred Indians. Sir Jeffery Amherst* ordered Bouquet to relieve Fort Pitt and other garrisons. On July 13, 1763, Bouquet left Carlisle with a force of 350 Highlanders and 150 Royal Americans. On August 5, near Bushey Run, he was surprised by the Delawares, Shawnees, Wyandots, and Mingoes who lifted the siege at Fort Pitt to meet him. The following day, Bouquet feinted a retreat, drew the Indians into the open, and the Highlanders, lying in ambush, drove them off with heavy casualties. Bouquet lost 110 killed or wounded, but relieved Fort Pitt without further difficulty.

To complete the pacification of the Indians, in the fall of 1764 Bouquet led an expedition of Pennsylvanians and Virginians into the Muskingum Valley in Ohio. This bloodless campaign achieved the submission of the warring tribes and the Indians' release of hundreds of prisoners.

In 1765 Bouquet was raised to brigadier general, in command of the southern district of North America. He arrived at district headquarters in Pensacola, Florida, but was stricken with yellow fever and died on September 2, 1765.

Henry Bouquet was a trained, experienced European professional military officer. He utilized his extensive theoretical education and practical background as a basis from which to examine the military situation in America and to offer many suggestions for improvements in arms, equipment, training, and strategy. He was the first European officer to successfully adapt traditional military discipline and tactics to wilderness warfare.

As early as March 1757 Bouquet provided John Campbell,* Lord Loudoun, commander in chief of the British forces in North America, with a plan for an expedition against Fort Duquesne, based on cutting a road west through Pennsylvania, and building stockaded forts every thirty miles, to provide a secure line of communication and supply. At Loudoun's request, Bouquet amplified this plan with details of logistics, supplies, and troop requirements. This was in essence the strategy that proved successful the following year.

In 1758 Bouquet outlined the need to train frontier soldiers to shoot, take positions, and load while lying behind a log or running for a new position. Earlier recognition and use of training in these skills to adapt to the Indian style of warfare by officers such as Braddock might have brought about successes such as the one Bouquet had at Bushey Run.

Having observed the Indian preference for a flank attack on a column, Bouquet developed a plan of march for seven columns, double file, with light troops and cavalry on the flank, which could be used even in dense undergrowth and from which a line of battle could be formed in two minutes at need. This line of march was employed on the expedition to relieve Fort Pitt in 1763. It enabled Bouquet to gather his forces after the initial ambush, move to the most defensible ground, and devise the stratagem which drew the Indians from their cover, thus allowing a concerted attack by the Highlanders, which overpowered the enemy.

Bouquet's victory at Bushey Run was the first defeat of the Indians at an ambush of their choosing. As such, it increased the confidence of the colonial and regular troops, proved conclusively that the adaptations he recommended would work, and forced the Indians to become more cautious in their attacks on the armies.

Bouquet's victory, coupled with his successful expedition to the Muskingum Valley the following year, opened the Pennsylvania frontier to settlement. Without the Western settlements which were initiated following these campaigns, the United States would not have had justification for its claims to the Western lands during the treaty negotiations following the American Revolution.

BIBLIOGRAPHY

Leach, Douglas E. *Arms for Empire: A Military History of the British Colonies in North America, 1607–1763*. New York: Macmillan Company, 1973.
O'Meara, Walter. *Guns at the Forks*. Englewood Cliffs, N.J.: Prentice-Hall, 1965.
Stevens, Sylvester K., and Donald H. Kent, eds. *The Papers of Colonel Henry Bouquet*. Series 21649, 21651, 21655. Harrisburg: Pennsylvania Historical Commission, 1942–1943.
———, Donald H. Kent, and Autumn L. Leonard, eds. *The Papers of Henry Bouquet*. 2 vols. Harrisburg: Pennsylvania Historical and Museum Commission, 1951–1972.

COLLIER C. HARRIS, JR.

BRADDOCK, Edward (b. London, winter of 1694–1695; d. near Great Meadows, Pa., July 13, 1755), British general. Braddock's defeat by the French and

Indians underscored the problems of campaigning in the North American wilderness.

Edward Braddock followed in the footsteps of his father, a lieutenant colonel of the Coldstream Guards who served as a major general during the closing years of his long but unremarkable career. The younger Braddock joined the Coldstream as an ensign in 1710 and six years later became a lieutenant, but not until 1736 did he obtain a captaincy in the regiment. His father's rank helped him little. The family was of the lesser gentry and had little social or political influence, a decided disadvantage in the long years of peace that Britain experienced after 1720. Braddock had to rely on talent, longevity, and luck.

The War of the Austrian Succession opened the way for more rapid advancement. In 1743 Braddock became second major of the Coldstream Guards and in 1745 first major and then lieutenant colonel of the regiment. He saw little action in the war, however. During the summer of 1745 he inspected the defenses of Ostend. That fall he served briefly under the Duke of Cumberland against the Jacobite rebels, and the following year he commanded a Coldstream battalion to Flanders where it garrisoned Flushing (Vlissingen). The battalion wintered at Bois-le-Duc and returned home after the peace of 1748.

Having no prospect of further promotion in the Coldstream Guards, Braddock sought opportunity elsewhere in the postwar Army. Early in 1753 he succeeded in securing the colonelcy of the 14th Regiment of Foot, which he soon joined on station at Gibraltar. He was commissioned a major general in April 1754 and in September was called home to assume the greatest responsibility of his career. The Duke of Cumberland had chosen him to take command of the king's forces in North America and clear the Western frontier of French encroachments. Reaching England in November, Braddock sailed for Virginia late the next month in advance of two regiments of the Irish establishment assigned to him, the 44th and 48th Foot.

To send a stout general of sixty with limited combat experience to conduct offensive operations in the American backwoods may have been ill-advised. Braddock, however, was a no-nonsense disciplinarian capable of making soldiers of the dregs he would find in his Irish regiments and the raw provincials to be recruited in America. An honest and efficient administrator, he could also organize the large logistical effort needed at minimum cost. He was not expected to fight a war, only to reduce a few French outposts. His strategy was outlined for him in Cumberland's instructions. Marching from Virginia, Braddock was to take Fort Duquesne at the forks of the Ohio and proceed against Niagara. As circumstances permitted, operations were also to be undertaken against outposts in the Champlain Valley and Nova Scotia.

Braddock reached Virginia in February 1755 and, after a stay in Williamsburg, established his headquarters at Alexandria. He expected confusion but found worse. Recruits were few and, in Braddock's opinion, mediocre. Horses, wagons, and provisions were expensive and elusive. Little money could be extracted from the suspicious and tightfisted colonial assemblies. Indian auxiliaries, despite the assurances and advice of some self-styled experts, never appeared in large numbers. Accurate information about the western country also proved almost impossible to obtain. Braddock was in America several weeks before learning that more than a few miles of mountains lay between him and Fort Duquesne.

In April, however, men and provisions began moving to the advanced base at Fort Cumberland (now Cumberland, Maryland), and in early June, after much bullying of colonial officials, Braddock had a force of about eighteen hundred regulars and five hundred provincials ready to march. At a conference of colonial governors held in Alexandria, he also arranged for forces raised in the northern colonies to move against Niagara, Lake Champlain, and Nova Scotia.

On June 7 Braddock's little army commenced its 110-mile march to Fort Duquesne. Strict security was maintained according to European practice by deploying camp guards, flankers, and advanced parties. So effective were these measures that enemy raiders from Duquesne were able to pick off only occasional stragglers. But progress was slow. The heavy loads of provisions needed for survival in the uninhabited wilderness and the large artillery train that Braddock thought necessary to reduce French fortifications overtaxed men and horses on the steep mountain grades. Engineers toiled daily to cut a roadway through the forest and to bridge the many steams. Anxious to speed the march before Duquesne was further reinforced, Braddock decided at Little Meadows, Maryland, on June 17 to divide his army. He pushed ahead with a picked force of about fourteen hundred regulars and provincials and thirteen cannon, the rest to follow under Colonel Thomas Dunbar as best they could.

A dangerous double crossing of the Monongahela River carefully executed on July 9 brought the forward detachment within eight miles of Duquesne. "Every one. . . ," wrote an eyewitness, "hugg'd themselves with joy at our Good Luck in having surmounted our greatest Difficultys, & too hastily Concluded the Enemy never wou'd dare to Oppose us." Proceeding in normal line of march, the detachment suddenly encountered a force of about 250 French and 650 Indians rushing through the woods. The Indians promptly flanked Braddock's column on both sides and began a deadly fire from the trees. Retreating, the advance guard got entangled with troops coming to their support. Within a short time the regulars became a panic-stricken mob. No officer could persuade them to form and charge the unseen enemy. While attempting to do so, Braddock had four or five horses shot under him and was severely wounded in his arm and chest.

After two hours of butchery, the survivors retreated. Unpursued by the enemy, they marched all night and the next day to reach Dunbar's camp about fifty miles to the rear. A total of 63 officers and 914 soldiers were killed or wounded in action. Braddock died four days after the battle and was buried in the roadway over which his retreating army was to pass the next morning in order to obliterate any signs that would enable the Indians to find his body.

"So much for English Genrals skill in bush fighting," concluded one Virginian five weeks after the disaster at the Monongahela. Most colonists, while acknowledging Braddock's bravery, judged him a brutal man, too haughty and narrow-minded to exchange the rigid linear tactics that worked so well on the fields of Flanders for the Indian-style tactics that frontiersmen believed essential for fighting in the North American woods. The colonists had reason to be bitter. The demoralized remnants of Braddock's army marched to winter quarters at Philadelphia in August, leaving the frontier almost undefended.

The colonists' view of Braddock was not entirely justified. He showed his quick temper to contractors and officials who disappointed him, but he treated his troops well and was quite friendly with many Americans, notably young George Washington* whom he made an aide de camp. Nor were Braddock's European tactics inappropriate. Despite logistical and Indian problems not wholly of his own making, he nearly succeeded with those tactics. Only a moment's carelessness bred of overconfidence after weeks of vigilance and the chance timing of an impetuous enemy attack thwarted him. He dealt well with expected dangers, poorly with unexpected ones.

If Braddock could have kept his regulars in formation, their superior numbers, firepower, and discipline would undoubtedly have carried the day, but once allowed to break under the shock of the enemy onslaught, they were at great disadvantage. Indians were ever the best fighters in disorder. Few Europeans or Americans from east of the mountains could hope to match, much less defeat, Indians at their own game, as Indians could seldom hope to prevail against European organization. Only flawless security and disciplined fire and maneuver could have saved Braddock's army.

In the long war that followed Braddock's defeat, British commanders were to succeed where he had failed, not by revolutionizing their mode of warfare but by better applying European methods to North American conditions. European light infantry tactics were to be employed to enable troops to maneuver better in rough American terrain without sacrificing security and cohesion. Better handling of the intricacies of Indian diplomacy and recruitment of backwoods hunters were to make available the scouts and screening forces that Braddock had wished for but lacked. Waterways and blockhouses were to be used to avoid long logistical trains such as had hindered Braddock on his march and in battle. Strategy was to be altered to pursue easier routes and to strike at more vital places.

With better luck Braddock might have won his battle, but many problems of wilderness warfare would have been obscured. His ill-luck left a legacy of valuable insights to both British and American soldiers.

BIBLIOGRAPHY

Gipson, Lawrence Henry. *The Great War for the Empire: The Years of Defeat, 1754–1757. The British Empire Before the American Revolution* Vol. 6. New York: Alfred A. Knopf, 1946.

Kopperman, Paul E. *Braddock at the Monongahela.* Pittsburgh, Pa.: University of Pittsburgh Press, 1977.

McCardell, Lee. *Ill-Starred General: Braddock of the Coldstream Guards*. Pittsburgh, Pa.: University of Pittsburgh Press, 1958.

Sargent, Winthrop. *The History of an Expedition Against Fort Du Quesne in 1755; Under Major-General Edward Braddock, Generalissimo of H. B. M. Forces in America*. Philadelphia: J. B. Lippincott, 1856.

Shy, John. *Toward Lexington: The Role of the British Army in the Coming of the American Revolution*. Princeton, N.J.: Princeton University Press, 1965.

PHILANDER D. CHASE

BRADLEY, Omar Nelson (b. Clark, Mo., February 12, 1893; d. New York City, N.Y., April 8, 1981), military commander; the "GI's General" in World War II.

Omar Nelson Bradley was born on February 12, 1893, in Clark, Missouri. Upon the death of his father, John Smith Bradley, a schoolmaster, in 1908, Bradley and his mother, Sarah Elizabeth Bradley, a seamstress, moved to Moberly, Missouri. Bradley won a congressional appointment to the U.S. Military Academy at West Point in 1911. He graduated forty-fourth in the class of 1915, the class upon which general's stars later fell in profusion.

While serving in various posts in the United States and Hawaii, Bradley came under the eye of General George Catlett Marshall* when Bradley became chief of the Weapons Section while Marshall was assistant commandant of the Infantry School at Fort Benning, Georgia. As Marshall organized the Army, he made Bradley assistant secretary of the General Staff and, in February 1941, commandant of the Infantry School. The commandant's position brought to Bradley the first general's star of the class of 1915. Marshall then gave Bradley stateside command experience with the 82d Infantry (later Airborne) and then the 28th Infantry Division. Bradley received his second star.

From Marshall, Bradley moved into the orbit of Dwight David Eisenhower,* the man who would lead Marshall's organization in Europe. Marshall suggested that Bradley be Eisenhower's "eyes in North Africa." Eisenhower agreed, and Bradley landed in Algiers on February 24, 1943, to assist his former West Point classmate. Eisenhower shortly ordered General George Smith Patton, Jr.,* to assume command of II Corps in the theater, and Bradley and Patton would be together for most of the war. Patton, not comfortable with Bradley's "looking over his shoulder," had Bradley appointed his assistant corps commander. When Patton left the command to prepare for the invasion of Sicily, Bradley led the II Corps to a successful conclusion of the North African Campaign. Bradley then led II Corps in the invasion on July 10, 1943, of Sicily. After slapping some soldiers during the campaign cost Patton his chance to command the American ground forces for Overlord, the invasion of Normandy, France, Brad-Bradley in October 1943 got the assignment. The assignment would culminate in a command that comprised 1.3 million troops, the largest American field command in history, and Bradley would have Patton as one of his Army commanders. Bradley's First Army landed in France on June 6, 1944. After failing at one attempt, the First Army broke through at St. Lô on July 26. Bradley then assumed overall command of American ground forces in the Twelfth Army Group. In this capacity, Bradley would confront Britain's Field Marshal Bernard L. Montgomery.

Bradley and Montgomery had disagreements over command and strategy. Montgomery wanted to continue as overall ground commander and to concentrate on a single thrust into Germany instead of a broad advance. Bradley agreed with Eisenhower's decisions of no overall ground commander and of a broad advance. Tactically, he felt that Montgomery's failure to move quickly to affect a linkup between the Canadians and elements of Patton's army had resulted in the escape through Falaise of too many Germans.

Bradley restrained Patton from going beyond Montgomery's orders in closing the gap at Falaise, but he gave Patton permission to prepare an offensive in late December while allowing Courtney Hicks Hodges'* First Army to continue its offensive. Even though the front stalemated, Bradley did not shift forces to build up the Ardennes area which had been depleted for troop building in the other areas. The subsequent German thrust on December 16, 1944, through the Ardennes Forest made a shambles of American optimism as it was initially quite successful. Although this Battle of the Bulge was settled within a short time, the Allied victory was a costly one. One cost was an estrangement between Eisenhower and Bradley, brought about by Eisenhower's giving Montgomery command of part of Bradley's forces.

Although Eisenhower's plans for the drive into Germany assigned the leading role to Montgomery's forces, Bradley exploited his own successes to cross the Rhine before Montgomery. Eisenhower then decided to have Bradley's forces link up with the Russians. During the last week of April, the First and Ninth Armies met the Russians at the Elbe River while Patton moved south and took Czechoslovakia. Eisenhower decided not to mount a drive on Berlin or Prague, and the European war ended in May.

After the war ended, Bradley became Veterans Administrator, where he tried to ease the return for millions of veterans. On February 7, 1948, he became chief of staff. On January 16, 1949, he became the first chairman of the Joint Chiefs of Staff, earning a fifth star in September 1950. Bradley's years on the Joint Chiefs of Staff were hectic ones, as both internal fights and actions by other nations created a constant sense of crisis. From the Berlin Blockade to the formation of the North Atlantic Treaty Organization to the rearmament of Western Europe, from the flush deck carrier to the funding of NSC 68, from reliance on nuclear deterrents to reliance on a deterrent of nuclear and conventional readiness, from agreement to a ground war in Asia to a clarification that the involvement had to be limited, from an unsuccessful attempt to stop a landing at Inchon, to defense of the president's removal of the American commander in Korea—Bradley was at his post.

On August 15, 1953, Bradley left full-time active service, forty-two years after his entry into West Point. After that time, he served in a variety of public and private positions and was frequently called upon for military advice. He died in New York City on April 8, 1981.

Although not nearly as colorful as many of his contemporaries, the general who seemed so democratic, self-effacing, and concerned that he became the "GI's General" was in fact as controversial as his more flamboyant peers. Bradley's professional life involved him directly with Marshall, Eisenhower, Montgomery, Patton, and Douglas MacArthur,* as well as many others. Much of American military history revolves around the decisions of these men and those whom they opposed. The period from the beginning of World War II was a critical turning point for the United States, including the military. During the war Bradley was at the center of decisions that did not lose the war and may indeed have helped to win it. But there remains intense debate both over many of those decisions and over their consequences for the postwar world. After the war, military technology seemed to have robbed the United States of any time to decide whether or not a conflict would involve this nation, and yet, to many the atomic bomb promised security on the cheap. Many felt that communism was a mortal threat, but did not want to pay for defense and thus sacrifice the good life to higher taxes, especially after fifteen years of Depression and then war.

The Army's position was especially precarious, for the Army now seemed obsolete in a world which, if it went to war, would destroy itself in a nuclear holocaust. The Korean War did bring enormously increased defense spending as well as acceptance of the notion of a limited war, but the policy of containment as well as the emphasis on European defense brought new division in the wake of President Harry S. Truman's firing of MacArthur.

Bradley's imprint during all these years was that of a stabilizer. He was not a bloodless patsy above bureaucratic battles. There is no study in depth of Bradley, although Charles Whiting's highly critical *Bradley* is an effective beginning. All the same we do know some things. Bradley used Patton as well as any commander could have; he helped to shape much of the strategy in Europe by personal influence and by allowing his commanders tactical flexibility, often turning a potential liability into an asset; despite differences with Montgomery, he avoided an open break; he commanded at various levels throughout the war and, despite the Ardennes scare, suffered no great defeats and at times capitalized on opportunities for tactical success. After the war, he, like Eisenhower before him, kept some semblance of an army in being during a perilous period in which the Army fought for its existence, discovered limited war, and saw its most famous general fired. Through all of this, Bradley's personal prestige remained high and this in turn helped the Army.

Omar N. Bradley was a lieutenant colonel at the beginning of 1941; four years later he was a five star general. Most of the advancement came for leadership of men in combat. Whatever the mix of motivation or wisdom of various decisions, Bradley did much more than hold his own in the company of giants. If he had done nothing more, this alone would merit his full inclusion in the ranks of those commanders.

BIBLIOGRAPHY

Ambrose, Stephen E. *The Supreme Commander*. Garden City, N.Y.: Doubleday and Company, 1970.

Bradley, Omar N. *A Solider's Story*. New York: Holt, Rinehart and Winston, and London: Eyre and Spottiswoods, 1951.

————, and Blair, Clay, Jr. *A General's Life*. New York: Simon and Schuster, 1983.

Manchester, William. *American Caesar*. Boston, Toronto: Little, Brown and Company, 1978.

Pogue, Forrest C. *The Supreme Command: U.S. Army in World War II*. Edited by Kent Roberts Greenfield. Washington, D.C.: Office of the Chief of Military History, U.S. Department of the Army, 1954.

Whiting, Charles. *Bradley*. New York: Ballantine Books, 1971.

JOSEPH P. HOBBS

BRAGG, Braxton (b. Warren, N.C., March 22, 1817; d. Galveston, Tex., September 26, 1876), Army officer. Bragg commanded the Army of the Tennessee, the principal Confederate field army in the western theater during the Civil War.

Braxton Bragg was born into the family of a moderately successful North Carolina contractor, Thomas Bragg, who had been able to acquire more than twenty slaves. Bragg's father did all in his power to instill ambition into his sons, and young Braxton received his early education at Warrenton Male Academy. Although a fine horseman, Bragg showed little interest in the recreational activities pursued by his peers as they took time away from more serious duties. He entered the U.S. Military Academy at West Point, New York, in 1833 at the age of sixteen. He proved to be an excellent student, graduating number five in a class of fifty.

Commissioned second lieutenant, 3d Artillery, as of July 1, 1837, he served in the frustrating Florida War against the Seminole Indians at various times from 1838 to 1843. Early in his military career, he developed a quarrelsome character, often tangling with his peers, superiors, and even himself, as the following anecdote illustrates. Ulysses Simpson Grant,* in his *Memoirs*, recalled a story about Bragg when he was both company commander and the company quartermaster: "As commander of the company he made a requisition upon the quartermaster—himself—for something he wanted. As quartermaster he declined to fill the requisition, and endorsed on the back his reasons for so doing. As company commander he responded to this, urging that his requisition called for nothing but what he was entitled to, and that it was the duty of the quartermaster to fill it. As quartermaster he still persisted that he was right." He then referred the matter to his commanding officer, who remarked: "My God, Mr. Bragg, you have quarreled with every officer in the army, and now you are quarreling with yourself.'' During the Mexican War, Bragg fought with distinction during the defense of Fort Brown, Texas (May 3–9, 1846), and the battles of Monterrey, Mexico (September 21–23, 1846), and Buena Vista (February 22–23, 1847). For his battlefield performance, he was brevetted captain, major, and lieutenant colonel. After the war, Bragg served on garrison duty at Jefferson Barracks, Missouri, and on frontier duty before declining promotion to major, 1st Cavalry, as of March 3, 1855, and resigning from the U.S. Army as of January 3, 1856.

Bragg purchased and operated a sugar plantation in Louisiana in 1856, and, on the eve of the Civil War, he owned 109 slaves and had a net profit of $30,000. He was also elected a commissioner of the Board of Public Works in Louisiana, serving in that office from 1859 to 1861.

With the outbreak of the Civil War, Bragg accepted an appointment as brigadier general, Confederate States Army, as of February 23, 1861, and was assigned to the command of coastal defenses between Pensacola and Mobile. Promoted to major general, he commanded a corps in the Army of the Mississippi (later named the Army of the Tennessee). As a subordinate of Albert Sidney Johnston* and Pierre Gustauve Toutant Beauregard* during the Battle of Shiloh (April 6–7, 1862), Bragg conducted an aggressive attack on the first day of the battle that brought initial success to the Confederate forces. After the Confederate retreat from Shiloh, Bragg was promoted to general to rank from April 6 and placed in command of the army on June 27.

In late August, Bragg moved his army into central Kentucky in what began as a brilliant campaign. The purpose of the move was to bring Kentucky into the Confederacy, but Bragg soon became bogged down in politics, allowing the Union forces to escape from a precarious position. After the indecisive Battle of Perryville, Kentucky, on October 8, Bragg withdrew into Tennessee. On December 31, Bragg attacked a Union force led by Major General William Starke Rosecrans* at Murfreesboro, Tennessee, inflicting heavy casualties. Bragg, however, did not exploit his immediate tactical successes, and on January 3, 1863, withdrew his forces from the field. Subject to severe criticism for his withdrawal, Bragg was able to retain his command because of his friendship with Confederate President Jefferson Davis.* But during the next six months Bragg became involved in a series of bitter disputes with his subordinates, and his army was curiously inactive. He neither sought out the enemy nor prepared adequate defensive positions. Defensive positions were of particular importance because Bragg's army was growing smaller as it sent reinforcements to Mississippi while the opposing Union force was growing stronger. Consequently, William Rosecrans,* in a brilliant summer campaign, maneuvered Bragg out of Chattanooga on September 9, 1863.

Reinforced by a corps under James B. Longstreet,* Bragg attacked Rosecrans south of Chattanooga in the Battle of Chickamauga, September 19–20. Only the heroic stand of Major General George Henry Thomas* prevented the destruction of the Union forces. Even so, Bragg missed an opportunity by not again attacking the disorganized enemy forces, and, instead, he besieged Chattanooga. Perhaps overconfident because of a seemingly impregnable defensive position, Bragg detached Longstreet for a campaign against Union forces in east Tennessee. As a result, General Grant was able to defeat Bragg decisively in the Battle of Chattanooga, November 23–25, and shortly thereafter, Bragg was relieved of his command.

After his defeat at Chattanooga, Bragg never again held an important field command. He spent most of the remainder of the war as a military advisor to Davis with the impressive, but ineffective, title of general in chief. He was captured by Union forces in Georgia on May 9, 1865, while accompanying Davis in his flight from Richmond. After the war, Bragg served as a commissioner of public works in Alabama, and at the time of his death in Galveston, Texas, he was chief engineer of the Gulf, Colorado, and Sante Fe Railroad.

Bragg is perhaps the most harshly criticized Confederate commander of the Civil War. Yet, at the beginning of the war, few had doubts about his military abilities. A genuine hero of the Mexican War, he appeared to be one of the more distinguished officers to support the Southern cause. And he was without doubt an excellent organizer and disciplinarian. Although his sternness was not always an asset in dealing with volunteer troops, he built the Army of the Tennessee into an efficient and effective fighting force.

At crucial moments, however, Bragg's nerve failed him and he was unable to make decisions, thereby greatly weakening his effectiveness as a commander. This trait during his campaign in Kentucky during 1862 after an impressive start cost the Confederacy dearly in missed opportunities. After tactical success against Rosecrans at Murfreesboro, Bragg failed to renew the battle even though he was in a favorable situation, and his notable victory over Rosecrans at Chickamauga was canceled by an unwillingness to follow up his success. By settling for a siege of Union forces in Chattanooga, Bragg missed one of the real opportunities that the Confederacy had to strike a severely damaging blow at the Union.

To make matters worse, Bragg had a series of recurring illnesses that were probably psychosomatic. Under intense pressure, he became ill. His rigid thought patterns and inability to make decisions support the contention of mental illness. In modern terms, the evidence suggests that Bragg had a mental and physical breakdown during the summer of 1863. It had a real, if unmeasurable, impact on Bragg's performance and was probably reflected in his relationships with his officers.

Bragg's inability to get along with his subordinates was seriously debilitating. He was constantly involved in prolonged (and often petty) arguments with his officers. These disputes destroyed command unity in the Army of the Tennessee which was so essential for success. While he was a good planner and organizer, he did not work in a vacuum. His indecision on the field coupled with his quarrelsome nature makes credible the harsh criticisms of Bragg by both his contemporaries and later historians.

BIBLIOGRAPHY

Connelly, Thomas L. *Army of the Heartland: The Army of Tennessee. 1861–62.* Baton
    Rouge: Louisiana State University Press, 1967.
————. *Autumn of Glory: The Army of Tennessee, 1862–65.* Baton Rouge: Louisiana
    State University Press, 1971.
Horn, Stanley F. *The Army of Tennessee: A History.* New York: Bobbs-Merrill Company,
    1941.
McWhiney, Grady. *Braxton Bragg and Confederate Defeat.* Vol. 1. New York: Columbia
    University Press, 1969.
Tucker, Glenn. *Chickamauga.* Indianapolis, Ind.: Bobbs-Merrill Company, 1961.

DAVID L. WILSON

BRANT, Joseph (b. Ohio River country, 1742; d. Ontario, Canada, November 24, 1807), Mohawk leader and soldier.

Joseph Brant was the son of Nickus Brant, a full-blooded Mohawk and chief of the Wolf clan, and an obscure Shawnee woman. Accounts of Brant's nativity vary somewhat, but he probably was born while his parents were camped near the Ohio River during a hunting expedition. Joseph's father died while he was an infant, and his mother later remarried. Because of his father's death and his mother not being a Mohawk, Joseph did not seem destined to greatness among his people. The circumstances surrounding the life of Thayendanega, Joseph's Indian name, were profoundly altered in 1755.

In 1755, Molly Brant, one of Joseph's sisters, moved into Sir William Johnson's* home and lived with him as his common-law wife. Johnson was a wealthy and powerful trader and representative of the British government among the Iroquois, and young Brant immediately enjoyed increased status among his contemporaries because of his new patron.

Johnson's impact upon Brant's life was significant. In 1755, for example, he took Brant off to war with him and the thirteen-year-old boy witnessed the Battle of Lake George, the battle that catapulted Johnson into prominence across the American colonies and in London. As William Johnson's political and economic fortunes improved during the 1750s, Brant's future as a principal leader of the Mohawks was assured. Upon the urging and with the support of Johnson, Brant enrolled in Moor's Indian Charity School in 1761. For two years, Brant attended the school located in Lebanon, Connecticut, which was operated by Eleazar Wheelock. Brant proved to be an apt student, but he departed in 1763, served in the war against Pontiac,* and then settled among his Mohawks in New York.

In 1764, Brant married, became an Anglican, and settled into a comfortable routine befitting of a promising young man. Over the next ten years, Brant assisted Reverend John Stuart in his missionary work among the Iroquois, translated religious material into Mohawk, and gradually asserted himself as one of the major leaders of his nation.

Sir William Johnson died in 1774, and he was succeeded as superintendent of Indian affairs by his son-in-law Guy Johnson. The new superintendent appointed Brant to serve as his secretary, thereby strengthening his influence among the Iroquois, and, at the same time, guaranteeing Brant's rise to eminence. Indicative of his mounting prestige, Brant was elevated to the status of a "Pine Tree Chief" among the Iroquois in 1774. A "Pine Tree Chief" was a man chosen for his wisdom, honor, and bravery and wielded great influence in Iroquois councils. At the age of thirty-two, Brant was firmly entrenched as a leader of the Mohawk Nation.

As the political situation in the American colonies deteriorated in the mid-1770s, Brant labored diligently to keep the Iroquois League loyal to Great Britain. He was commissioned a captain in the king's forces in 1775, and he journeyed to England that autumn. Brant was received and entertained by the elite of London society, sat for a portrait done by George Romney, and deepened his commitment to Great Britain.

Upon returning to America in the spring of 1776, Brant actively supported Great Britain as a soldier during the American Revolution. In 1777 he participated in the assault on Fort Schuyler in western New York, and fought in the Battle of Oriskany. Then, in 1778, he led a series of raids in the vicinity of Lake Oswego and directed the attack on Cherry Valley in New York.

When the American Revolution ended, the Mohawks found most of their lands controlled by the United States, and they reluctantly began to relocate in Canada. Brant, having decided to seek compensation for the losses the Mohawks had suffered, again traveled to England. His 1785 visit to England proved to be both pleasant and productive. Brant was enthusiastically received in London's social milieu that season, and, while enjoying the city's amenities, he obtained land grants for his Mohawks along Grand River in Ontario, Canada. As a special recognition of his service to Great Britain, he was granted an estate near the entrance to Burlington Bay on the western shore of Lake Ontario. Upon Brant's return to Canada, the Mohawks took possession of the Grand River lands and eventually established the village of Brantford which became their capital.

After assessing the defeat of the Indian forces at Fallen Timbers in 1794, Brant became an advocate of peace with the United States. He also spent energy protecting the Ontario land claims of the Mohawks from encroachment by land speculators. Brant was frequently plagued, in his latter years, by the political machinations of his old adversary Red Jacket, an influential Seneca leader, who sought to discredit him among Indian councils.

Despite the disappointments he encountered toward the end of his life, Brant lived comfortably on his estate in Ontario and frequently traveled abroad. On November 24, 1807, Brant died, and he was taken to the Grand River Cemetery in Brantford, Ontario, where he was buried.

Since the American Revolution, Brant's fame has centered mainly on his reputation as a soldier. He was a courageous and resourceful adversary who often exhibited compassion for his enemies when a situation warranted such action. No other Indian leader eclipsed Brant's wartime feats; consequently, his military exploits are well remembered.

In actuality, however, Brant's military accomplishments during the American Revolution were relatively modest. From the viewpoint of royal authorities, Brant served a more important function during the Revolution. He was responsible for retaining the loyalty of several of the Iroquois tribes to Great Britain, and his role as a statesman proved more valuable than his military leadership.

Brant again demonstrated remarkable political acumen as he led his defeated nation after it settled Canada. The 1780s and 1790s were times of difficult adjustment for the proud Mohawk people. During this painful transition, Brant supplied firm and wise guidance to a dispirited yet resilient Mohawk tribe. Brant was a fine soldier, but he was an outstanding political figure and a skilled diplomat who served his people with distinction and devotion.

BIBLIOGRAPHY

Flexner, James Thomas. *Mohawk Baronet, Sir William Johnson of New York*. New York: Harper and Brothers, Publishers, 1959.
Hamilton, Milton W. *Sir William Johnson, Colonial American, 1715-1763*. Port Washington, N.Y.: Kennikat Press, 1976.
Wallace, Anthony F.C. *The Death and Rebirth of the Seneca*. New York: Alfred A. Knopf, 1970.

                                                                                                        LARRY G. BOWMAN

BRERETON, Lewis Hyde (b. Pittsburgh, Pa., June 21, 1890; d. Washington, D.C. July 19, 1967), senior U.S. Army Air Force commander in World War II. Brereton was a central figure in controversies, including destruction of Douglas MacArthur's* air units at Clark Field on December 8, Ploesti, Operation "Cobra" and Arnhem.

Brereton, the son of a mining engineer, initially hoping to enter the Army, obtained a Naval Academy appointment and upon graduation in 1911 transferred to the Army's Coast Artillery. Soon afterward, he became one of the first U.S. Army aviators and entered the Signal Corps' air service. After tours in the Philippines, Philadelphia, and Washington, D.C., Brereton went to France with the American Expeditionary Force's (AEF's) first contingent of eight aviation officers. Following service with the French near Verdun, he took command of the 12th Aero Squadron, an observation unit, in March 1918. After downing four German planes, for which he received the distinguished Service Cross, Brereton was himself shot down while commanding a corps observation squadron at St. Mihiel. In July 1918 he became I Corps chief of aviation and ended the war as a lieutenant colonel and G-3 of the AEF air service. After the war, he remained close to William "Billy" Mitchell,* helping draft a study in 1919 which challenged the Army General Staff's rejection of an aviation coast defense role. After service in the Army of Occupation in Washington, and a tour as attaché in Paris, 1920–1922, Brereton returned to the United States, reverting to major, at which grade he remained until 1935.

Between the world wars, his assignments included a tour as a Bombardment Group commander (the 2nd); teaching at both the Air Tactical School and at

Fort Leavenworth; and command of air units in Panama. In 1926 Brereton served as defense counsel and witness in the Mitchell court-martial, and in the years that followed, like other Mitchell supporters, was frequently snubbed. Brereton divorced twice and married three times) was tough and profane. His penchant for late hours and drinking fostered an image of a soldier suffering through the tedium of peace. To friends, he was known as "Looey, dot dope," a name taken from Milt Gross's stories, consistent with his description of anyone who had been shot down as a "dope."

As the Army Air Forces expanded, Brereton was promoted to brigadier general in 1939 and to major general in 1941. Late that year, he was ordered from Tampa, where he headed the Third Air Force, to command the U.S. air buildup in the Philippines, which was increasing due to growing tension with Japan.

On December 8, 1941, in spite of several hours' warning, the Japanese destroyed nearly half of the modern combat aircraft in the Philippines in a single attack at Clark Field. By December 10, only 35 of MacArthur's 145 frontline aircraft were operational. Massed without camouflage and protective revetments, many of the B-17s still unpainted, the planes were caught while refueling. The Clark Field affair was swallowed up in the swirl of disasters that beset the Allies in the Pacific from Pearl Harbor to the fall of the Philippines.

His forces gone, Brereton was sent south in January 1942 to command the air units of the American-British-Dutch-Australian (ABDA) command, bracing for a Japanese onslaught already ahead of its own schedule. When ABDA collapsed, Brereton headed the Tenth Air Force in India, under Joseph Warren Stilwell's* command, assembling bits and pieces from ABDA remnants and a sporadic flow of supplies from the United States. Brereton and Stilwell clashed when Brereton launched unauthorized attacks against Rangoon and Port Blair.

In June 1942, as the Japanese push on India slowed and Rommel's threat to Egypt mounted, Brereton was ordered to the Middle East with the Tenth's remaining B-17s and much of its transport planes. There, he formed the Ninth Air Force, aiding the British in North Africa and then supporting Anglo-American operations in Tunisia, Sicily, and Italy. While in North Africa, units under Brereton's command hit Ploesti in August 1943, in which B-24 heavy bombers tried to smash Germany's main source of natural petroleum with a surprise, low-level attack. While the basic plan was an Air Staff product, Brereton was also involved in its shaping, waving aside the objections of many pilots, when he decided that the attack should proceed from distant bases and go in low. Many problems—bomb failures, navigation errors, unexpectedly strong and alert fighter and antiaircraft defenses—led to disaster. A quarter of the attackers failed to return, and damage fell far short of expectations.

A month after Ploesti, Brereton went to England to command the Ninth Tactical Air Force. His try for autonomy there was blocked by the newly appointed chief of the U.S. Strategic Air Forces, Carl A. Spaatz,* and there were problems with General Omar Nelson Bradley,* commander of U.S. ground forces in the invasion, who objected to Brereton's refusal to joint ground-air training exercises before D-Day (June 6, 1944). After the invasion, the Anglo-American-Canadian forces were penned up in the beachhead area by the Germans for almost two months. Bradley asked for a heavy bomber strike (code name: Operation COBRA) to aid the breakout. Two strikes, on August 24 and August 25, plastered German positions, but also killed General Lesley James McNair* and a hundred U.S. troops, and stunned many survivors. While errors in planning and execution were not all Brereton's fault, his argument that ground troops lacked aggressiveness did not explain his decision to mount the second attack with a bomb run perpendicular to the front, in spite of objections from other air commanders and Bradley.

Brereton, promoted to lieutenant general in the spring of 1944, was appointed head of the 1st Allied Airborne Army soon afterward, a move designed to strengthen coordination between troop carrier and airborne elements. Brereton's role in the MARKET-GARDEN disaster was marginal, since he was newly appointed and operations were controlled by XVIII Airborne Corps. Brereton spent much time in late 1944 and early 1945 in planning for contingencies and in preparing the airborne phase of the big Rhine crossing in the North scheduled for the spring of 1945. He also entered into debates with a number of Allied commanders, including Lieutenant General Sir Frederick Browning, XVIII Airborne Corps commander, and Field Marshal Bernard Law Montgomery, all the while receiving prods from General Henry Harley Arnold,* chief of the Army Air Force, who had long urged Generals George Catlett Marshall* and Dwight David Eisenhower* to mount a major airborne assault.

After the war, Brereton faded from public view. After commanding the Third Air Force once again and then moving on to a series of marginal assignments, he retired in 1948. A brief flurry of notice in the press followed the publication of his diaries.

It may be that Brereton gained much by being a pioneer aviator and by loyalty to Mitchell as his cause. The pattern of bad luck and/or misjudgment that dogged his career during World War II certainly offers a rich possibility for speculation and research by psychohistorians and dramatists as well as military historians. Considering his visibility at so many crucial junctures of World War II and his senior rank, it seems strange that he faded so quickly from view, especially since he commanded the largest airborne force in history. The Clark Field Affair, reexamined from time to time as a command error by Douglas MacArthur, upon close scrutiny appears as much a product of Brereton's misjudgment. MacArthur ordered the B-17s to be dispersed, and Brereton gained a delay to allow young officers to attend a party in Manila. "Hap" Arnold thought Brereton the main culprit and waved aside MacArthur's attempt to take the blame. Unhappily, key documents were later found missing from the relevant files. Brereton's acidity and his clashes with principals in all his commands obviously did not stand him in good stead in the postwar period. Yet no one suggested that he was not aggressive. There is some suggestion of a Captain Queeg syndrome in the case of Brereton.

BIBLIOGRAPHY

Arnold, Henry H. *Global Mission*. New York: Harper and Brothers, 1949.

Brereton, Lewis H. *The Brereton Diaries*. New York: William Morrow, 1946.

Craven, Wesley Frank, and James Lea Cate. *The Army Air Forces in World War II*. Vol. 1. Chicago: University of Chicago Press, 1948.

DuPre, Flint O. *U.S. Air Force Biographical Dictionary*. New York: Franklin Watts, 1965.

Huie, William Bradford. *The Fight for Air Power*. New York: L. B. Fischer, 1942.

ROGER BEAUMONT

BROWN, Jacob Jennings (b. Bucks County, Pa., May 9, 1775; d. Washington, D.C., February 24, 1828), hero of the War of 1812; general in chief of the U.S. Army, 1821–1828.

Jacob Jennings Brown was born into a Quaker family whose ancestors were among the first settlers in Bucks County, Pennsylvania. His father was a prosperous farmer who lost his money in commercial ventures, forcing young Brown to seek his own living at the age of eighteen in 1793. After teaching school for three years in Crosswicks, New Jersey, Brown worked two years surveying land near Cincinnati, Ohio. Finally, in 1798 after moving to New York City, he opened a select school, studied law, and found time to write several articles for local newspapers. Brown's articles attracted the favorable attention of Alexander Hamilton. When Hamilton was made acting inspector general of the army raised to fight the French in 1799, Brown served as Hamilton's secretary.

Later in the year when the war scare with France abated, Brown moved to northern New York where he purchased a large tract of land on Lake Ontario and founded Brownsville. He was very successful and in 1809 was given the command of a militia regiment—a testament to his political and financial success, not his military knowledge. Although he was a novice, Brown's energetic command improved upon many of the deficiencies within his unit, and in 1811 he was promoted to the rank of brigadier general of militia. When the War of 1812 began, Brown was given the responsibility for protecting a two hundred-mile stretch of northern border beginning at Oswego, New York, and continuing to Lake St. Francis. Brown's force consisted of a mixed group of regulars augmented by local militia. With this small command, he successfully defended Ogdensburg from an attack by the British on October 4, 1812.

When the British attempted to capture the American base at Sackets Harbor, Brown was placed in charge of its defense. With a force of only four hundred regulars and five hundred militia, he had to defend against a superior British force of approximately nine hundred regulars. Placing his militia on the frontline, supported by the regulars in the rear, Brown prepared for the British attack on May 29, 1813. Although the American militia panicked, the regulars, despite heavy losses, stood their ground. Brown was able, therefore, to rally part of the militia and to harass the British flank, forcing its withdrawal to awaiting ships.

Brown was named brigadier general of the Regular Army on July 19, 1813, and was one of the brigade commanders in General James Wilkinson's* ill-fated attack against Montreal in November. On January 24, 1814, Brown was promoted to the rank of major general and placed in command of the frontier of western New York. Assisted by two excellent subordinates, Brigadier Generals Winfield Scott* and Eleazer Wheelock Ripley,* Brown prepared his defense. Recognizing Scott's abilities as an organizer and administrator, Brown placed Scott in charge of training the undisciplined men—men listed as regulars by the War Department.

Having determined that his forces were ready for action, Brown crossed the Niagara River on the night of July 2–3 and took Fort Erie without a fight. Moving north toward the Chippewa River, Brown's advance units under Scott were attacked by the British on July 4. Before Brown could bring up the rest of his command, Scott had driven the attackers from the field. Learning that the promised naval support would not be forthcoming, Brown realized that he could not continue the campaign, but he decided to remain in Canada.

On July 25, 1814, Brown defeated a British attack at Lundy's Lane, successfully assaulting the British position and capturing their guns. Twice wounded in the battle and lacking logistical and naval support, he was forced to fall back to Fort Erie, which was then besieged by the British. Despite his wounds and a severe fever, he successfully defended Fort Erie from a British assault on August 15 and then led a sortie on September 17 that forced the British to lift their siege operations. Feeling that the British had been severely weakened by their losses during the campaign, Brown requested support so that he could destroy the enemy. The ever cautious General George Izard,* Brown's superior, failed to take advantage of the situation and went into winter quarters after a series of skirmishes. Izard subsequently resigned his command and Brown replaced him. The war ended before the spring campaign could begin in 1815.

At the end of the war, Brown became the commander of the northern division of the U.S. Army and on March 10, 1821, he was named general in chief of the Army of the United States, a position he held until his death in 1828. Despite ill-health due to his wounds, Brown was active in formulating the defense plans for the northern boundary of the United States and the establishment of Army control on the western frontier.

Brown's reputation rests upon his successful command of troops in the Niagara Campaign in the War of 1812. Although overshadowed by the reputation of Winfield Scott, Brown was one of the most successful combat commanders in American military service. According to Fletcher Pratt, "there was some secret of leadership in Brown's presence and manner that made green country boys fight like the devil." Had he been provided the support he had been promised, his successes in the 1814 campaign might have been decisive.

After the war, the effects of the wounds received at Lundy's Lane and the fever contracted at Fort Erie diminished his energy. Moreover, Brown possessed few of the technical skills necessary for successful peacetime command and would have preferred to retire to Brownsville, New York. Feeling that it was his patriotic duty, he assumed the command of the northern division first, then the entire U.S. Army. Without Brown's close support and cooperation, the effectiveness of John Caldwell Calhoun* as secretary of war would have been diminished. Brown's energetic support for orderly Western defense practices and his championship of the Military Academy at West Point were important factors in American military development before the Civil War.

BIBLIOGRAPHY

Adams, Henry. *History of the United States during the Administration of James Madison.* Vols. 7 and 8. New York: Albert and Charles Boni, 1930.

Cruikshank, Ernest A. *Documentary History of the Campaigns upon the Niagara Frontier in 1813 and 1814.* 9 vols. Welland, Ontario: Lundy's Lane Historical Society, n.d.

Mahon, John K. *The War of 1812.* Gainesville: University of Florida Press, 1972.

Pratt, Fletcher, *Eleven Generals.* New York: William Sloan Associates, 1936.

Prucha, Francis Paul. *The Sword of the Republic: The United States Army on the Frontier.* Toronto: Macmillan Company, 1969.

Weigley, Russell F. *History of the United States Army.* New York: Macmillan Company, 1967.

Wiltse, Charles M. *John C. Calhoun: Nationalist.* Indianapolis, Ind.: Bobbs-Merrill Company, 1944.

JACK W. THACKER

BUCHANAN, Franklin (b. Baltimore, Md., September 17, 1800; d. Easton, Md., May 11, 1874), naval officer. Buchanan was a Confederate admiral and first captain of the *Virginia (Merrimack)*.

The son of a prominent Maryland physician, Buchanan enjoyed a comfortable life as a child. In January 1815 he received his commission as midshipman in the U.S. Navy. Buchanan served initially under Oliver Hazard Perry.* Subsequent duties took him to the Mediterranean, China, and the West Indies. Buchanan was promoted to lieutenant in 1825 and to commander in 1841. In 1845 Secretary of the Navy George Bancroft* chose Buchanan to be the first superintendent of the new U.S. Naval Academy at Annapolis, Maryland, an institution for which Buchanan had to draw up plans of organization.

With the outbreak of the Mexican War, Buchanan petitioned for active sea duty and received command of the 20-gun sloop *Germantown* in March 1847. During the war Buchanan served under David Conner* and Matthew Calbraith Perry,* participating in the capture of Vera Cruz and other Mexican towns. Buchanan later commanded Commodore Perry's flagship in Perry's expedition to Japan in 1852. After his promotion to captain in 1855, Buchanan commanded the Washington Navy Yard.

In April 1861 Buchanan resigned his commission, thinking that Maryland would soon secede from the Union and join the Confederate States of America. He soon concluded that his native state would not secede, and he attempted to have his resignation nullified. Secretary of the Navy Gideon Welles* had already accepted the resignation, however, and so Buchanan was without employment for several months. In August 1861 he decided to join the Confederacy and traveled to Richmond to offer his services.

On September 5, 1861, Confederate Secretary of the Navy Stephen Russell Mallory* issued Buchanan a captain's commission. Following brief duty improving coastal defenses and river fortifications in Virginia, Buchanan assumed the position of chief of the Office of Orders and Detail in the Navy Department. Buchanan, in this capacity, made all assignments of personnel, helped to formulate naval policy, and acted as advisor to Secretary Mallory. In order to circumvent the seniority system and place Buchanan in command of the new ironclad *Virginia* (formerly the USS *Merrimack*) Mallory on February 24, 1862, appointed Buchanan as flag officer in command of the naval defenses on the James River. Moving to Gosport Navy Yard, Buchanan made the *Virginia* his flagship.

Buchanan hoped to participate with Major General John B. Magruder in a joint land-sea attack on the Federal forces at Newport News. When Magruder rejected this idea, Buchanan decided to strike at the Federal base without the Army's assistance. He took the *Virginia* into Hampton Roads on March 8, 1862, to attack the Federal squadron there. The *Virginia*'s first target was the frigate *Cumberland*. After exchanging broadsides with this adversary, Buchanan rammed her. The *Cumberland* began sinking and threatened to take the *Virginia* down with her as the Confederate ironclad's ram was stuck in her hull. Fortunately for Buchanan, the ram broke off, and his ship was freed to continue her attack. He turned the *Virginia* toward the frigate *Congress,* whose captain ran her aground to avoid the *Virginia*'s ram. An hour's pounding by the *Virginia* set the *Congress* afire and killed and wounded dozens of her men. The Federal captain then struck his colors and surrendered. Because Federal shore batteries and rifle fire prevented Buchanan from receiving the surrender, he ordered his gunners to destroy the *Congress*. While supervising this destruction, Buchanan was wounded in the thigh by a rifle bullet. Subsequently, he yielded command to Lieutenant Catesby ap Roger Jones.

Buchanan's wound kept him out of the action on the following day between the *Virginia* and the Federal ironclad *Monitor*. He convalesced at Norfolk and later at Greensboro, North Carolina. On August 21, 1862, the Confederate Congress confirmed Buchanan's appointment as admiral. He thus became the ranking officer in the Confederate Navy. In September 1862 Mallory assigned Buchanan to command the naval forces in Mobile Bay, Alabama. Several ironclads were being constructed at Selma, Alabama, for use in the bay, and the Confederate high command hoped Buchanan would be able to raise the blockade there and possibly attack New Orleans and the lower Mississippi River. Work on Buchanan's ironclads proceeded very slowly. Only one, the *Tennessee*, was ever fully completed. While Buchanan awaited his ironclads, he was busy trying to procure men, supplies, and equipment for them.

By early 1864 the *Tennessee* was almost ready for combat. Buchanan moved his flag aboard in May and made plans to attack the blockading fleet. Since the odds facing his small squadron of one ironclad and three wooden gunboats were too great, Buchanan canceled the attack. On August 5, 1864, a Federal fleet under Admiral David Glasgow Farragut* ran past Fort Morgan into Mobile Bay. Buchanan watched helplessly as his gunboats were disabled, captured, or run aground. He then ordered the *Tennessee* to attack the Federals. Buchanan hoped to surprise the enemy, do what damage he could to them, and then beach the *Tennessee* near Fort Morgan as a stationary battery. The odds were against Buchanan in his attack. His ship was too slow to be effective as a ram and was hopelessly outgunned by the Federals. Buchanan was wounded, and the *Tennessee* was disabled by Federal fire. Finally, he ordered his ship surrendered. Buchanan was held prisoner at Fort Lafayette, New York, until February 1865, when he was exchanged. He was reassigned to Mobile but did not reach the city before its surrender. Buchanan was included in the surrender of Lieutenant General Richard Taylor and his Department of Alabama, Mississippi, and East Louisiana in May 1865.

After the war Buchanan returned to his home in Maryland. He served for one year as president of Maryland Agricultural College (later the University of Maryland). He retired to his home and remained there for the rest of his life.

With the exception of his role in the founding of the Naval Academy, an assessment of Buchanan's career must focus on his services in the Confederate Navy. Although his tenure at Annapolis was brief, Buchanan's contributions there are important. He established the Academy's curriculum and its internal operations once he had transformed Fort Severn into a midshipman's school. Buchanan was a stern disciplinarian, and this attitude helped get the Academy off to a successful start.

In his administration of the Office of Orders and Detail in the Confederate Navy Department, Buchanan ran his office with imagination and efficiency. He recognized talented and efficient officers and was able to tactfully place them in important commands over more senior officers of mediocre abilities. Buchanan supervised the publication of the Confederacy's *Navy Regulations*, which was adapted from the regulations of the old Navy. He made a beginning at establishing a merit system of promotion to replace the seniority system, although much of his work in this regard was undone by his successors.

Buchanan was a temperance man and demanded the same of his subordinates. He also expected his subordinates to match his efficiency, physical courage, and hard work. Incompetency and laziness were not tolerated under him. Buchanan was a fighter and became one of the Confederacy's most aggressive naval officers. Even though he was a stern disciplinarian, Buchanan's aggressiveness and personal courage made him respected and admired by those around him.

Under Buchanan's command, the *Virginia* won one of the Confederacy's few naval victories in the actions of March 8, 1862. His wound prevented him from participating in the famous battle with the *Monitor*, but his handpicked officers and spirit of aggressiveness served the *Virginia* well in that engagement. Buchanan displayed a great deal of energy and resourcefulness at Mobile in completing work on and arming the ironclads at that city. Probably no other officer could have accomplished as much as he did in that command. He enjoyed good relations with the army command at Mobile and fostered a spirit of cooperation between the services that was lacking in other areas. Buchanan's decision to attack Farragut's fleet after it had entered Mobile Bay may be subject to criticism because of the obvious futility of the attack. It probably would have been better for him to have anchored near Fort Morgan and used the *Tennessee* as a floating battery. To act in such a passive manner, however, was foreign to Buchanan's personality; he always preferred taking the fight to the enemy.

BIBLIOGRAPHY

Lewis, Charles L. *Admiral Franklin Buchanan, Fearless Man of Action*. Baltimore: Norman, Remington, 1929.

Still, William N., Jr. *Iron Afloat: The Story of the Confederate Armorclads*. Nashville, Tenn.: Vanderbilt University Press, 1971.

Wells, Tom H. *The Confederate Navy: A Study in Organization*. University: University of Alabama Press, 1971.

ARTHUR W. BERGERON, JR.

BUELL, Don Carlos (b. near Marietta, Ohio, March 23, 1818; d. near Paradise, Ky., November 19, 1898), Army officer. Buell held various Union commands during the Civil War.

Born of Welsh descent, Buell was taken to Lawrenceburg, Indiana, after his father died, and he spent most of his boyhood in the home of an uncle. In 1837 he entered the U.S. Military Academy at West Point, graduating in 1841 and ranking thirty-second in a class of fifty-two. Posted to the 3d Infantry Regiment as a second lieutenant, he served in the Seminole and Mexican Wars, and was brevetted captain for gallant and meritorious conduct at the Battle of Monterey in 1846. The next year he was brevetted major for gallant conduct at the battles of Contreras and Churubusco and was severely wounded at Churubusco.

Buell then transferred from line to staff, working as an adjutant general and serving at the headquarters of several military departments from Washington, D.C., to the frontier. When the Civil War began, the forty-three-year-old lieutenant colonel was in San Francisco as adjutant general of the Department of the Pacific. Commissioned a brigadier general of volunteers on May 17, 1861, Buell helped to organize and train the fledgling Army of the Potomac. Soon General George Brinton McClellan* picked him to organize and train the Union forces in Kentucky. Arriving at Louisville in November, he assumed command of the newly formed Army of the Ohio with instructions to lead his forces into east Tennessee and on to Knoxville. Buell was keenly aware of the lack of roads and rail facilities in east Tennessee. He recommended an alternative, appreciated by neither McClellan nor President Abraham Lincoln,* of striking south by the Cumberland and Tennessee rivers and into Nashville.

In mid-February 1862, aided by the advance of General Ulysses Simpson Grant* on Forts Henry and Donelson which was, with minor variations, the essential strategy earlier recommended by Buell himself, his Army of the Ohio occupied Bowling Green, Kentucky. With the Confederate defensive perimeter pierced at the rivers, forces under General Albert Sidney Johnston* fell back rapidly, enabling Buell to reach Nashville on February 24, without meeting any opposition. On March 11, President Lincoln placed Buell under the command of General Henry Wager Halleck,* who headed the new Department of the Mississippi. Halleck ordered Buell to advance on Savannah, Tennessee, in order to join forces with the troops moving south up the Tennessee River. Halleck said nothing about hurrying, and as late as April 4, Grant advised Buell that there was no need for haste.

Marching slowly, Buell's lead division did not arrive on the Tennessee River until April 6, the day of the Confederate attack at Shiloh, Tennessee. The division helped to boost Union morale when it crossed the river and began taking position on the Federal left late in the first day of battle. During the night two more divisions came up, and on the morning of April 7 Buell's fresh forces attacked the enemy, contributing significantly to the eventual Union triumph. Neither Buell nor Grant made an effort to pursue the Confederates when they abandoned the field.

Now a major general of volunteers, promoted on March 21, 1862, Buell took part in the advance on the rail junction town of Corinth, Mississippi. After the Confederates abandoned Corinth, Halleck detached Buell with four divisions to march on Chattanooga, repairing the Memphis and Charleston Railroad as he proceeded. Harassed by enemy cavalry raids and delayed by the tedious repair work, Buell never reached Chattanooga. Generals Braxton Bragg* and Edmund Kirby Smith* had launched a two-pronged invasion of Kentucky that compelled Buell to leave a small force to cover Nashville and retreat to protect his supply line from Louisville.

In mid-September, north of Bowling Green, Buell found that Bragg was between him and Louisville. Buell chose not to attack on ground selected by his enemy. Bragg then marched away northeastward toward Bardstown and Frankfort, leaving open the road to Louisville, which Buell reached on September 25. On the last day of September, Buell was ordered to turn over his command to General George Henry Thomas,* but Thomas was unwilling to accept and Buell was reinstated the next day.

With reinforcements bringing his army's strength to sixty thousand, Buell moved southeastward on October 1, looking for the Confederate forces. The climax came at Perryville on October 8, when Buell's army, searching for waterholes along Doctor's Creek, stumbled into a portion of Bragg's command. The Confederates attacked boldly, Bragg not realizing that the Federals had more than three times as many troops at hand as he did (about fifty-five thousand to sixteen thousand). Despite the numerical disparity, the battle was indecisive tactically. Buell, badly shaken when thrown from a horse the previous day, and not aware that his army had been fighting until about 4:00 in the afternoon of October 8, failed to use his superior forces effectively. That night Bragg discovered that the Federals were united while his own command was still scattered. The Confederates retreated toward east Tennessee and Buell followed, but slowly, finally breaking off the pursuit altogether. As a result, he was relieved from command on October 24, and was succeeded by General William Starke Rosecrans.*

In November 1862 a military commission was convened to investigate Buell's conduct. The general's explanation for failing to pursue the Confederates was that his army could not subsist off the country. The commission reported the facts without making a recommendation. After awaiting orders for a year, Buell was discharged as a major general of volunteers. Thereupon he immediately resigned his commission in the Regular Army on June 1, 1864. Although General Grant later recommended that he be restored to duty, no action was taken. Following the war Buell settled in Kentucky, engaging in mining and serving for a time as a pension agent.

Buell's pre-Civil War reputation seemed to indicate a brilliant future. He was bearded and of medium stature, and the expression about his eyes conveyed determination. A man of high principle, he was personally courageous and a good organizer and disciplinarian. But he lacked a magnetic strength of personality that could inspire the volunteer troops he led. This unfavorable image would undoubtedly have improved if he had been successful in battle. Unfortunately, Buell's Civil War career is marked by deliberation and caution. He lacked aggressiveness.

When his own plan for an advance up the Cumberland and Tennessee rivers was put into effect by Grant, eventually becoming a spectacular success, Buell wrote General McClellan that, while the move was right in its strategical bearing, it had been begun without adequate appreciation of the problems involved or preparations to cope with them. The result, he said, was to place his own army in a "hazardous" position if he tried to support Grant.

Buell's role in the Battle of Shiloh, where he believed that he had arrived just in time to save Grant's army from disaster, is a moot point. It seems likely that Grant, with his shortened and more compact line on good defensive terrain, could have held his last position on the evening of April 6 without Buell's help. Whether or not Buell saved Grant's army, he was too slow in arriving at Savannah. He was not told to hurry, but the dalliance that Buell demonstrated in marching from Nashville to Savannah, particularly in crossing Duck River, should not be tolerated as a general principle. There is no evidence to support the more sinister charge that he was slow because he hoped Grant would be defeated.

Later, in Kentucky, Buell allowed Bragg to steal a march on him and was fortunate when the Confederate general inexplicably abandoned his commanding position on Buell's line of retreat. Buell fought the Battle of Perryville badly and then again, as at Shiloh, showed little inclination to press a pursuit of the enemy. In the final analysis, Buell's good qualities seemed to be overshadowed by his pedantic approach to campaigning.

BIBLIOGRAPHY

Foote, Shelby. *The Civil War: A Narrative*. Vol. 1. New York: Random House, 1958.
McDonough, James. *Shiloh—in Hell Before Night*. Knoxville: University of Tennessee Press, 1977.
Ropes, J. C., and William R. Livermore. *The Story of the Civil War*. New York: Putnam, 1913.

JAMES LEE MCDONOUGH

BULLARD, Robert Lee (b. Yongesborough, Ala., January 15, 1861; d. New York City, N.Y., September 11, 1947), lieutenant general, U.S. Army. Bullard became one of the most successful field commanders of the Army during World War I.

Tall, slender and athletic in appearance, Robert L. Bullard served forty-four years in the U.S. Army, commanded every type of combat unit from platoon to field army, and fought foes from the Apaches in the Southwest to Germans on the Western Front. Once when asked to describe his career, he answered that "my job as an officer was to make my men fight." A fellow officer thought that Bullard's "outstanding characteristic as a soldier was a constant drive to get into the thick of things—always to go to the sound of the guns and get into the fight, no matter where the fight was taking place . . . and he always got there." Another, however, recalled that Bullard's aggressiveness applied only to military operations: "His common sense and simplicity, the stories he told so well, his keen sense of humor and warmth of friendship endeared him to all who were privileged to know him."

The eleventh of twelve children and second son of Daniel Bullard and Susan Mizell, Bullard was born on his father's farm in Lee County, Alabama. Christened William Robert, he changed his name to Robert Lee after the Civil War. His father, descended from English mariners, came from North Carolina. Bullard's mother was of French Huguenot ancestry. Daniel and Susan Bullard were pioneer settlers in eastern Alabama, where Daniel raised cotton, sold cotton gins, and speculated in land. The family was part of an industrious, ambitious, education-oriented rural elite that supported its own church and school. Bullard showed such academic promise as a boy that he attended the Agricultural and Mechanical College of Alabama (now Auburn University) for one year and then won a competitive appointment to the U.S. Military Academy, which he entered in 1881. His motive for going to West Point was to finish college without going into debt.

Bullard's academic record at West Point was undistinguished, and he finished twenty-seventh of thirty-nine in the class of 1885. Like other graduates of low standing, he was assigned to the infantry. Joining the 10th Infantry in New Mexico, Bullard spent most of the next thirteen years with his regiment. In 1886 he participated in the campaign against Geronimo.* In 1888 he married Rose Douglass Brabson, the daughter of a Tennessee congressman and stepdaughter of an Army surgeon. They had four children. Weary of frontier duty and disturbed by his stagnant career, Bullard, still a first lieutenant at thirty-seven, arranged a transfer to the Subsistence Department in 1898.

When the war with Spain began, Bullard accepted command of a black Alabama infantry regiment, an assignment for which he lobbied vigorously. As colonel of the 3d Alabama Volunteers, he earned a deserved reputation as an effective troop trainer and disciplinarian. Bullard was then appointed colonel of the 39th U.S. Volunteer Infantry regiment, a unit raised to fight in the Philippine Insurrection. Bullard commanded this regiment in combat in southern Luzon in 1900 and 1901. The regiment was noted for its aggressiveness and determination—the qualities of its colonel. When his regiment mustered out, Bullard stayed in the Philippines as a commissary but arranged a transfer back to the infantry in 1902 at his regular rank of major, thus "jumping" more than a hundred of his peers in seniority. To answer his critics, he volunteered for more combat service against the Moros on Mindanao, where he served as a battalion commander and district governor until 1904.

Between 1904 and 1917, Bullard enhanced his reputation with varied service. Between 1906 and 1909, he was an official in the Provisional Government of Cuba; in 1910 he went to Mexico to search for Japanese naval bases. He instructed the California and Hawaiian National Guard. Graduating from the Army War College in 1912 and promoted to colonel, he took command of the 26th Infantry. Bullard turned his unit into a combat-ready part of the 2d Division, a force organized for possible intervention in Mexico. In 1915 Bullard's regiment helped pacify the lower Rio Grande Valley, which was plagued with Anglo-Mexican guerrilla war. In 1916 Bullard commanded a brigade of National Guard regiments from Louisiana, South Dakota, and Oklahoma. The guardsmen found Bullard a demanding but personable officer.

When the United States entered World War I, Bullard first commanded an officer training camp, but he was reassigned in June 1917 to the 2d Brigade of the 1st Division, sent to France to boost French morale. He was finally promoted to brigadier general, a rank for which he had lobbied for fifteen years. In France General John Joseph Pershing* made Bullard commandant of the American Expeditionary Force's (AEF's) infantry officer and specialist schools, a post he held until December 1917. Pershing then returned Bullard to the 1st Division to replace a commander who did not meet Pershing's standards for personal leadership. Under Bullard's command, the 1st Division staged the successful attack on Cantigny (May 28–31, 1918) that demonstrated to the Germans and Allies the AEF's offensive ability. An able division commander, Bullard made many inspection trips to the frontlines and was popular and respected by his men. He also gathered an exceptional group of officers, including three future chiefs of staff and many future generals. Because he spoke French and knew European history, Bullard also got along well with his French superiors.

In July 1918 Bullard assumed command of the III Corps, which took over a sector along the Vesle River during the Aisne-Marne counteroffensive. Until early September 1918, the III Corps attacked the German defenses but advanced only after the Germans retreated to the Aisne. The III Corps then moved to the Meuse-Argonne sector where Pershing's First Army attacked on September 26. The progress of the offensive was disappointing, but the III Corps did well enough to convince Pershing to assign Bullard to command the new Second Army. This force saw serious combat for only two days before the Armistice, but would have mounted an offensive on Metz if the war had continued. Promoted to lieutenant general, Bullard received the Distinguished Service Medal and several foreign decorations for his service in France.

Bullard's last assignment before his compulsory retirement at sixty-four in 1925 was as commanding general of the II Corps Area at Fort Jay, Governors Island, New York. He had no major impact on military policy, but he publicized military affairs by writing articles, making speeches, and stimulating interest in the ROTC, the Reserve, and the National Guard. He continued this work as president of the National Security League and by writing articles on military affairs for the Hearst newspaper chain. His memoir, *Personalities and Reminiscences of the War* (1925), was a candid analysis of the AEF. His other books, *Fighting Generals* (1944) and *American Soldiers Also Fought* (1936), were anecdotal narratives about World War I designed to counter claims that the AEF played no major role in the Allied victory. Bullard was also active in New York society and veterans' organizations during his retirement. The general died of a cerebral hemorrhage in 1947 and is buried at West Point.

Little known outside the Army and the veterans of World War I, Bullard served during the Army's transition from a frontier constabulary to a modern force of citizen-soldiers, commanded by professional officers and designed for war with other industrialized world powers. Like most of his contemporaries in the AEF, Bullard served in relative anonymity, a characteristic of the professionalized Army officer corps of his era. Bullard was an accomplished officer who built his reputation on his ability as a field commander, his loyalty to both superiors and subordinates, and his thorough knowledge of tactics, logistics, administration, communications, and unit organization. He was especially effective in building troop morale. Although he remained skeptical of academic military education and the virtues of centralized management, he supported the wide-ranging military reforms of his era since he appreciated the value of staff planning, merit promotion, and continuing military education.

Throughout his career, Bullard cultivated the image of Alabama "country boy" and "Old Army" Indian-fighter, but he was a sophisticated, cosmopolitan officer who consistently demonstrated his intelligence, adaptability, and industriousness in a variety of challenging assignments. His personal motto was "wherever you are, do as much as you can." In his later years, Bullard became a nativist, isolationist, philosophical conservative, and critic of the New Deal. His post-retirement literary career, however, did not reflect those personal qualities that made him a successful officer. Instead, he successfully responded to a series of demanding changes in the U.S. Army and proved over a period of twenty years (1898–1918) that he could command American field forces of growing size and complexity. Like other officers of his Army, Bullard helped define the role of modern American general.

BIBLIOGRAPHY

Chase, Joseph Cummings. *Soldiers All: Portraits and Sketches of the Men of the A.E.F.* New York: George H. Doran Company, 1920.
Millett, Allan R. *The General: Robert L. Bullard and Officership in the United States Army, 1881–1925.* Westport, Conn.: Greenwood Press, 1975.

ALLAN R. MILLETT

BURKE, Arleigh Albert (b. Boulder, Colo., October 19, 1901), naval officer. Burke served a record three terms as chief of naval operations from 1955 to 1961.

Arleigh Burke, who was of Swedish descent (his grandfather's name was Björkgren), was raised in the hard-working rural environment of post-frontier Colorado. His interest in a military career developed early, and in 1919 he won appointment to the Naval Academy. Industrious and ambitious, he overcame the handicap of a modest education in Boulder and was graduated seventieth in a class of 412 in 1923. His early career was characteristic of that of junior naval officers in the interwar period. After five years at sea in the battleship *Arizona*, Burke chose a career specialty. He studied ordnance explosives at the Navy Postgraduate School in Annapolis and then earned an M.S.E. degree in chemical engineering from the University of Michigan in 1931, thereby joining the prestigious "Gun Club" of the Bureau of Ordnance. Burke's service in destroyers began in 1937, following a series of ordnance-related assignments. In 1939, as a lieutenant commander, he took command of the *Mugford* and led his ship to the coveted Destroyer Gunnery Trophy for that year.

The attack on Pearl Harbor found Burke serving as a gun mount inspector at the Naval Gun Factory in Washington. He immediately applied for sea duty, but his request was not granted until January 1943, when he was sent to command a destroyer division in the Solomon Islands. His innovative concepts for use of destroyers in night actions, as well as his impressive performance as commander of Destroyer Squadron 23 in the battles of Empress Augusta Bay and Cape St. George in November 1943, established Burke as a top tactician and combat commander, and won him the Distinguished Service Medal, the Navy Cross, and the Legion of Merit. In March 1944 Captain Burke became chief of staff to Vice Admiral Marc Andrew Mitscher,* commander, Fast Carrier Task Force

58, and in that post coordinated the operations of the largest naval striking force in history in the battles of the Philippine Sea, Leyte Gulf, and Okinawa.

Burke's subsequent career was closely linked with the Navy's struggle to preserve itself as a modern fighting force in the face of the unification of the armed forces, rapid technological change, and the Cold War between the United States and the Soviet Union. A year-long tour as Mitscher's postwar chief of staff introduced Burke to these problems, as he helped to organize the Navy's first postwar striking fleet. After Mitscher's death in 1947, Burke was appointed to the General Board, the group of officers that advised the secretary of the Navy on high policy questions. In this post he prepared a major report on the Navy's future role in national security, which was the most comprehensive and influential study of its kind produced during this period. In 1949 Burke became head of the Organizational Reseach and Policy Division of the Office of the Chief of Naval Operations, which developed the Navy's position on the National Security Act Amendments of 1949 and then coordinated the Navy's presentations during the controversial B-36 investigation and unification and strategy hearings. Temporarily removed from the flag officer selection list as a result of his role in the so-called Admirals' Revolt, Burke was reinstated by President Harry Truman and became a rear admiral in 1950.

When the Korean War broke out, Burke was immediately dispatched to serve as deputy chief of staff to the commander, U.S. Naval Forces, Far East, and in July 1951 began six months of service on the United Nations Truce Negotiating Team. This experience, which he found intensely frustrating, sharpened his understanding of the Communist threat facing the United States, and helped shape his emerging strategic philosophy. After his return to Washington, Burke served for two years as director of the Navy's Strategic Plans Division, tackling such problems as the Navy's place in the American rearmament program begun in 1950, and the implications of the Eisenhower administration's "New Look" at U.S. defense policy taken in 1953.

In June 1955, while Rear Admiral Burke was serving as commander, Destroyer Force, Atlantic Fleet, President Dwight David Eisenhower* promoted him to chief of naval operations (CNO) over ninety-two more senior admirals. He was reappointed to the Navy's top uniformed post in 1957 and again in 1959. After retiring from the Navy in 1961, Burke served on the board of directors of a number of large corporations and public service organizations, until his second retirement in the early 1970s.

Arleigh Burke is best known for his exploits in destroyers and his service with Admiral Mitscher during World War II, but his greatest historical significance lies in his contributions to postwar naval strategic planning and policymaking. As chief of naval operations, Burke was committed above all to improving the combat capability of the U.S. Navy and applied his technological training, his operational experience, as well as his considerable leadership abilities to this task. President Eisenhower had appointed him as CNO in hopes that he would speed up the Navy's assimilation of new technology, appoint younger, more vigorous officers to positions of responsibility, and provide inspiration to a somewhat demoralized fleet. All three expectations were realized.

Burke was particularly effective in bringing new technology into the navy. He accelerated programs for construction of nuclear-powered submarines and surface ships and, building on the work of preceding CNOs, brought guided missiles into widespread use through the fleet. He also promoted innovations in aircraft design, communications systems, and antisubmarine warfare. His proudest accomplishment as CNO was his sponsorship in 1955 of the fleet ballistic missile development program which produced the Polaris submarine-launched nuclear deterrent system.

Taking office at a time when the Navy's role in national defense was eclipsed by public emphasis on nuclear weapons and massive retaliation, Burke focused attention on the unique characteristics and capabilities of naval forces. He identified limited war as the primary task facing the Navy of the future. Furthermore, Burke prepared the service to confront that challenge, with emphasis on the need for a balanced, versatile fleet.

The value of Burke's efforts to prepare the Navy for limited conflicts was proven during the 1958 crises in Lebanon and the Taiwan Straits and subsequent tensions in Berlin and the Congo. The Navy that undertook the quarantine of Cuba in the 1962 missile crisis owed much of its success to Burke's preparations. Burke was less successful in his opposition to increased centralization of American defense organization. His fight to maintain an independent, modern Navy and introduce greater flexibility into defense planning received a series of setbacks with the 1958 amendments to the National Security Act, the 1960 establishment of a centralized, joint targeting agency for strategic nuclear weapons, and the introduction in 1961 under the Kennedy administration of Robert Strange McNamara's* Planning, Programming, and Budgeting System.

Despite such setbacks, Arleigh Burke was an able and even inspiring spokesman for his generation of naval officers. His efforts to maintain the strength of American sea power established a standard for naval leadership in the post-World War II era.

BIBLIOGRAPHY

Davis, Vincent. *The Admirals Lobby*. Chapel Hill: University of North Carolina Press, 1967.

Hewlett, Richard G., and Francis Duncan. *Nuclear Navy, 1946–1962*. Chicago: University of Chicago Press, 1974.

Jones, Ken, and Hubert Kelley, Jr. *Admiral Arleigh (31–Knot) Burke, the Story of a Fighting Sailor*. Philadelphia: Chilton Books, 1962.

Kinnard, Douglas. *President Eisenhower and Strategy Management, A Study in Defense Politics*. Lexington: University of Kentucky Press, 1977.

Rosenberg, David Alan. "Arleigh Albert Burke." In *The Chiefs of U.S. Naval Operations*. Edited by Robert William Love, Jr., Annapolis, Md.: Naval Institute Press, 1980.

DAVID ALAN ROSENBERG

BURNSIDE, Ambrose Everett (b. Liberty, Ind., May 23, 1824; d. Bristol, R.I., September 13, 1881), Army officer. Burnside commanded the Union's Army of the Potomac at the Battle of Fredericksburg in the Civil War.

Of Scottish ancestry, Ambrose E. Burnside was born in a log cabin in Liberty, Indiana, well educated at a local seminary, and, when family fortunes declined, apprenticed to a tailor. But when his father became a state senator, young Burnside secured an appointment to the U.S. Military Academy. In 1847 he graduated eighteenth at West Point in a class of thirty-eight. The Mexican War ended just as he arrived in Mexico City to join his artillery battery.

Routine Army assignments then followed, heightened only by his marriage in 1852 to Mary Richmond Bishop. Burnside invented a breech-loading rifle while in the Army and resigned from the service in 1853 in hopes of manufacturing it in Rhode Island. When this enterprise was unsuccessful, he fell on hard days. He was taken in by an old friend, George Brinton McClellan,* vice-president of the Illinois Central Railroad, who also provided him with a job, first in the Land Department and then as treasurer of the railway.

Burnside's fortunes began to climb, aided by his winning personality, engaging manners, and friendly mien. He stood six feet tall, had flashing eyes, prominent sideburns, a large face, and a small head. He possessed an open, brigandish air that appealed to most people, but his congenial appearance and good manners concealed a shallow intellect and mecurially emotional temperament.

When the Civil War erupted, Burnside—who had been a major general of Rhode Island militia—was named colonel of the 1st Rhode Island Infantry Regiment and then brigade commander by President Abraham Lincoln,* who was impressed with his fine martial bearing. But at the First Battle of Bull Run, on July 21, 1861, Burnside's attacks, along with most of the other Federal blows, were parried, and he was seen riding to the rear at great speed, ostensibly to find reinforcements. Despite this lackluster performance, he was promoted to brigadier general of volunteers on August 6.

Burnside was then selected to lead—along with the Union Navy's Flag Officer Louis Goldsborough—an amphibious force against the Carolina littoral. After organizing this force at Annapolis, Maryland, Burnside and the fleet, against light opposition, in early 1862 defeated Confederate forces in Pamlico and Albemarle Sounds, and at Roanoke Island, New Bern, Beaufort, and Fort Macon. This gained Burnside national acclaim in the North and a major generalcy of volunteers on March 18, 1862. Then, most of his troops were sent in July and August to Virginia to participate in the ill-fated Second Manassas Campaign under John Pope.* Because he ranked Pope, Burnside remained at Fredericksburg, away from the battlefield, thereby not exercising direct command of his soldiers in the engagement.

With McClellan back in command of the Army of the Potomac in early September 1862, Burnside was named right wing commander, his force comprising his own IX Corps, under Jacob D. Cox, and the I Corps, under Joseph Hooker.* At South Mountain, on September 14, Burnside's two corps were

sharply engaged in striving to drive Confederates under Robert Edward Lee*
from Turner's and Fox's Gaps. But it was only after McClellan arrived and
assumed personal command that the Federals drove back the graycoats and seized
the vital passes.

At Antietam—the bloodiest single-day's battle of the Civil War—Burnside's
right wing was split, his I Corps being assigned to the extreme right flank of
the Army and the IX Corps—which Burnside refused to command in person
even though he stationed himself with it—to the left flank. All of McClellan's
ensuing orders were grandly passed on by Burnside to Cox without Burnside
following through to see that they were executed effectively. The result was
that, when McClellan told Burnside on September 16, the evening before the
battle began, that the IX Corps would most likely be directed to assail the
Confederate right wing early the following day, Burnside inexplicably failed to
see that the corps was deployed in attack positions. His belated, piecemeal attacks
on the forenoon of the next day were readily repulsed by the Southerners. Finally,
much later in the afternoon, Burnside's troops captured the so-called Burnside
Bridge, and then mounted a delayed attack on the enemy near Sharpsburg. But
it was too late. Burnside's procrastination enabled unbloodied Confederate troops
under Ambrose Powell Hill* to arrive on the field from Harper's Ferry and crush
Burnside's left flank. Had Burnside attacked earlier, as McClellan had ordered,
it is difficult to reject the belief that the Confederates would have suffered an
overwhelming defeat, for Burnside's delays enabled Lee to shift most of his
troops from his right to check the Federal attacks on his left and center.

When McClellan did not follow up his strategic victory at Antietam as swiftly
as Lincoln wished, he was relieved of his command on November 5, 1862, and
replaced by Burnside, the least competent of the Army's corps or wing commanders. Twice before he had been offered the command and both times had
declined it, saying that only McClellan could command so large an army. At
last, peremptorily ordered to take the command, he thought that he had no
alternative but to accept it, although he admitted he was not fit for the high
position.

Burnside advanced east of the Blue Ridge Mountains and was reinforced to
approximately 122,000 men as against Lee's 78,000. Moving with celerity to
the north bank of the Rappahannock River opposite Fredericksburg in December,
Burnside, through a careless misunderstanding with General in Chief Henry
Wager Halleck,* did not have pontoon bridges prepositioned there to enable him
to cross his army promptly. After considering several plans at length, he determined to cross directly at Fredericksburg and launch frontal assaults across an
open plain against the Confederates who were firmly ensconced in near-impreg-
nable positions.

After encountering hostile opposition in crossing the Rappahannock, Burnside
issued vague orders for an attack on December 13 by his left wing under William
B. Franklin. Despite a temporary lodgment in the enemy lines by a division
under George Gordon Meade,* this unsupported Union advance was checked

by Lee. Then, in one of the greatest blunders of the war, Burnside—in a blue funk—ordered sixteen separate, piecemeal assaults against the Confederates who were posted five deep along a sunken road behind a stonewall, and who were backed by powerful artillery on Marye's Heights behind. It was slaughter for the blueclads. Not one Union regiment got within one hundred yards of the stonewall. Burnside was reduced almost to a raving madman at the end of the battle and was barely restrained by several of his senior generals from placing himself at the head of his old IX Corps and renewing the suicidal attacks on the morrow. He had suffered casualties of some 12,653 in contrast to Lee's losses of 4,756.

In January 1863, after the ill-advised "Mud March" up the Rappahannock had to be recalled, and after he had tried to remove several high-ranking officers, Burnside was replaced in command of the Army of the Potomac by his rival, "Fighting Joe" Hooker. Although at the time uncharacteristically blaming others for his fiasco at Fredericksburg, Burnside later admitted that all was his fault and acknowledged the wisdom of the president in removing him from command.

After a leave of absence, Burnside headed the Department of the Ohio from March 25 to December 12, 1863. There he encountered problems in civil affairs when he ordered the arrest of a "Copperhead," former Ohio Congressman Clement L. Vallandigham, who was a fiery anti-administration agitator. But Burnside's forces did score some military successes. They repelled and captured many of John Hunt Morgan's raiders; they took Cumberland Gap and occupied eastern Tennessee; and, in perhaps his finest military achievement of the war, Burnside and his troops successfully defended Knoxville in a siege by Confederate General James Longstreet,* repelling Longstreet's attacks.

In the 1864 Overland Campaign of Meade and Ulysses Simpson Grant* against Lee, Burnside again commanded his old IX Corps. He did poorly in the battles of the Wilderness, Spotsylvania Court House, and Petersburg. The battle at Petersburg was the scene of the promising but ill-conducted operation in which the detonation of a huge mine was followed by a humiliating repulse of Burnside's troops in the resulting Battle of the Crater. Burnside properly received the chief criticism for this debacle, and he was finally allowed to leave the Army.

Burnside's post-Civil War career was highlighted by an almost unbroken series of achievements gained in part by his character, personal gifts, and integrity. He was a director of the Illinois Central Railroad, president of the Cincinnati and Martinsville Railroad in 1865, president of the Indianapolis and Vincennes Railroad Company, president of the Rhode Island Locomotive Works, and director of the Narragansett Steamship Company in 1867. He was a three-time governor of Rhode Island from 1866 to 1869 and capped his civilian career by serving as U.S. senator from Rhode Island from 1874 until his death in 1881.

Ambrose Burnside's personal magnetism won a multitude of friends, and not until a keen observer got to know him for some time under the stress of high command did it become apparent that he lacked the grasp and intellectual capacity to command more than a brigade efficaciously. Though personally brave, he lacked the mental and moral courage to alter his strategy and tactics when these were shown to be faulty. In this respect, when his plan of battle and his execution of it were patently in error, he could merely repeat unthinkingly his orders. This approach led to such a crushing defeat as that suffered at Fredericksburg—perhaps the most one-sided contest of the war. But, on his behalf, it must be said that he did not seek the command of the Army of the Potomac; he had twice declined it until it was forced upon him.

In the operations along the Carolina coast, Burnside received too much credit for accomplishments against small enemy forces, for in reality most of the Federal victories there were won by the Navy. Furthermore, Burnside performed most ineptly at Antietam. In the Fredericksburg Campaign, Burnside was too precipitous when the situation demanded caution and too timid when he should have been energetic. He was unimaginative and a slow thinker, especially in the heat of battle, and the heavy weight of responsibility paralyzed him from innovative action. Consequently, he played right into Lee's hands at Fredericksburg, doing precisely what his adversary wished him to do.

Only in his command of the Department of the Ohio did Burnside show much military talent, and he was entitled to all of the credit he received for his skillful defense of Knoxville. But he came a cropper again in Grant's Overland Campaign in Virginia, again showing little ability as a corps commander in a swiftly changing situation involving large forces. However, Burnside's business and management talents, and his political acumen in the post-Appomattox years earned him encomiums that were unalloyed.

BIBLIOGRAPHY

Catton, Bruce. *The Army of the Potomac: Glory Road*. Garden City, N.Y.: Doubleday and Company, 1952.

Hassler, Warren W., Jr. *Commanders of the Army of the Potomac*. Baton Rouge: Louisiana State University Press, 1962.

Palfrey, Francis W. *The Battles of Antietam and Fredericksburg*. New York: Charles Scribner's Sons, 1882.

Whan, Vorin E. *Fiasco at Fredericksburg*. University Park: Pennsylvania State University Press, 1961.

Williams, T. Harry. *Lincoln and His Generals*. New York: Alfred A. Knopf, 1952.

WARREN W. HASSLER, JR.

BUTLER, Benjamin Franklin (b. Deerfield, N.H., November 5, 1818; d. Washington, D.C., January 11, 1893), Civil War Army commander and military governor.

Benjamin Franklin Butler was of Scotch-Irish stock, his ancestors settling in New England in the late seventeenth century. His father was a captain of dragoons in the War of 1812, afterward a trader and privateer in South America. During Butler's youth, his widowed mother moved to Lowell, Massachusetts, where, following his graduation from Waterville College in 1838, he taught school and read law. He was admitted to the Lowell bar in 1840 and in time expanded his practice to Boston.

Butler acquired a reputation as a clever criminal lawyer who specialized in defending the working class. By the late 1840s he was prominent in Massachusetts politics. As a Jacksonian Democrat, he won election to the State House of Representatives in 1852 and, six years later, to the State Senate. Butler had been politically successful despite an unprepossessing appearance: obese, with a pudgy, ravaged face and bulging eyes, he resembled a dissipated toad. Militarily as well as politically ambitious, he became a colonel of Massachusetts militia in 1852 and was elected a brigadier general in 1857. In 1860 he was a delegate to the Democratic National Convention, where he voted to nominate Jefferson Davis* for president. Later, he joined bolters from the Baltimore convention in nominating John C. Breckinridge. When civil war broke out, however, he betrayed no reservations about fighting against his presidential choices, now high Confederate officials.

When his militia was mustered into Federal service, Butler became one of the Union's earliest heroes. Late in April 1861 his troops came to the relief of Washington and on May 13 occupied secessionist Baltimore, a move that secured Maryland for the Union. Three days later he was nominated a major general of volunteers. His unauthorized entry into Baltimore, however, rankled General Winfield Scott,* who relegated him to the command of Fortress Monroe, Virginia. In that garrison command Butler won notice by articulating the ''contraband'' theory under which fugitive slaves were regarded as spoils of war.

Butler's first combat effort ended in a minor debacle at Big Bethel early in June. Ten weeks later he recouped prestige by leading a combined Army-Navy force in capturing fortifications along Hatteras Inlet, off the North Carolina coast. The prominence accorded this feat (magnified by recent Union setbacks in other theaters) gained him command of a fifteen-thousand-man expedition to seize New Orleans, the Confederacy's most vital port. Thanks to the firepower of a fleet under David Glasgow Farragut,* Butler's soldiers occupied the Crescent City on May 1, 1862, and he became its military governor.

His seven-month rule over the Department of the Gulf aroused admiration in the North and enmity in the South. By threatening to treat as a prostitute any woman who insulted or harassed his troops, he incensed Southern opinion and won a local reputation as ''Beast.'' Butler's treatment of those who incited opposition to his regime—culminating in the hanging of a citizen who desecrated the Stars and Stripes—prompted Jefferson Davis to declare his former supporter an outlaw liable to execution if captured. His efforts to prove that local foreign consuls were providing material support to the Confederacy in violation of neutrality laws embarrassed several European nations, whose officials pressured President Abraham Lincoln* to relieve him. And his commercial dealings in New Orleans stirred charges of corruption—plus an accusation that he filched silverware from the home in which he had established headquarters. Some crimes, including his theft of tableware, were later proved ficticious. Nevertheless, the taint of scandal (and the nickname "Spoons") clung to him ever afterward. It is known that Butler purchased goods cheaply from Southern merchants and sold them dearly in the North. Conceivably, he also profited from the sale of property confiscated from locals. Associates and relatives, including his brother Andrew, engaged in corrupt business practices in the city with Butler's knowledge. As military governor, Butler deserves credit for improving municipal sanitation and instituting relief programs, for reducing the city's susceptibility to yellow fever, and for easing the chaotic state of its currency. Still, his more provocative policies, especially those inimical to consular officials, occasioned his relief in December 1862.

By now Butler had converted to Republican principles, despite maintaining an identity as a War Democrat. Speaking engagements in the North while on inactive service in 1863 were so well received that he considered seeking the 1864 presidential nomination. His popularity led Salmon P. Chase to offer him a vice-presidential berth, provided he promoted the Treasury secretary as the Republican nominee for president. Lincoln, seeking reelection, tendered Butler the same position. The general rejected both, announcing a desire to retake the field. In public he disavowed presidential ambitions; in private he supervised the efforts of agents in Washington to secure him the top position on a major party's ticket.

He was furnished a means of advancing his candidacy when in November 1863 Lincoln, seeking to woo Democrats, named him commander of the Department of Virginia and North Carolina, headquartered at Fortress Monroe. As leader of the forty thousand-man Army of the James, the largest field force in the war to be commanded by a nonprofessional soldier, Butler enjoyed several opportunities to win military renown. But his winter and spring attempts to capture Richmond failed through ill luck, the unrealistic strategy of General in Chief Ulysses Simpson Grant,* and the incapacity of Butler's corps leaders. His June 9 and 15, 1864, offensives against Petersburg, the supply conduit to the Confederate capital, also met defeat. Soon afterward, Grant and the Army of the Potomac reached the Petersburg front and Butler had no further chance to distinguish himself in independent operations. His army's partial success at Fort Harrison and New Market Heights on September 29 (largely due to the valor of its black units) marked the last of his effective military performances.

In December Butler accompanied sixty-five hundred troops sent by Grant to capture Fort Fisher, guarding Wilmington, North Carolina, the Confederacy's last open seaport. His failure to coordinate operations with the fleet of Admiral David Dixon Porter,* and his irresolution under pressure, led to the project's defeat. After landing a few troops near the fort, Butler declared his objective impregnable. He disobeyed orders by retreating and returning to Virginia. Angered by his withdrawal, Grant requested his relief. Lincoln, no longer in need of Butler's good-will, complied. On January 7, 1865, the general was packed off to Massachusetts to await orders—eight days before a second expedition, under one of his subordinates, seized Fort Fisher and closed Wilmington.

Though never returned to duty, Butler flourished in postwar life. From 1867 to 1875 he served as a Republican congressman from Massachusetts, helping manage the impeachment trial of Andrew Johnson. In 1878 he regained his House seat as a member of the Greenback party but served only one term. Elected governor of his state, as a Democrat, in 1882, he ensured the end of his public office career by his controversial policies and stormy relations with the legislature. He was the Antimonopoly and Greenback candidate for president in 1884 but in the general election received fewer than two hundred thousand votes. He devoted his remaining years to his law firm and to writing *Butler's Book*, an acerbic volume of memoirs published a few months before his death.

Butler was the most prominent political general in the Civil War, perhaps in American history. As a soldier, he displayed certain strengths: a commonsensical approach to tactics that sometimes yielded surprising success; a strategic acuity denied many professional soldiers (he perceived the importance of Petersburg, for example, months before Grant or Lee); an enlightened attitude toward the employment of black soldiers, whose cause he championed from 1862 on; an innovative view of hospital care and camp sanitation; a propensity to experiment with weaponry, including the Gatling gun, railroad-mounted ordnance, and chemical warfare; a talent for the purely administrative side of army command; and skill at negotiating prisoner of war exchanges.

As a politico in uniform, Butler allowed personality flaws to limit and sometimes negate his military talents. He occasionally permitted political ambition to dictate strategy. He was prejudiced against Regular Army officers, especially West Pointers; in turn, he lacked their confidence and respect (one called him "as helpless as a child on the field of battle and as visionary as an opium eater in council"). More than once, he insulted subordinates who did not share his ideological views. He trampled legality and ignored military ethics in formulating some administrative policies. And in Virginia as well as Louisiana he was unable to rise above suspicion of war profiteering. In short, Butler exhibited the best and worst qualities which a political figure elevated to high military command can possess.

BIBLIOGRAPHY

Holzman, Robert S. *Stormy Ben Butler*. New York: Macmillan Company, 1954.
Parton, James. *General Butler in New Orleans*. Boston: Ticknor and Fields, 1866.
Trefousse, Hans L. *Ben Butler: The South Called Him Beast!* New York: Twayne Publishers, 1957.
West, Richard S., Jr. *Lincoln's Scapegoat General: A Life of Benjamin F. Butler, 1818–1893*. Boston: Houghton Mifflin Company, 1965

EDWARD G. LONGACRE

BUTLER, Smedley Darlington (b. West Chester, Pa., July 30, 1881; d. Philadelphia, Pa., June 21, 1940), Marine Corps officer. Butler was prominent in most of the U.S. military interventions in the Caribbean, Central America, and Far East from 1898 through the 1920s, and was an outspoken anti-imperialist and ardent convert to the peace movement of the 1930s.

Smedley Darlington Butler's ancestors included three locally prominent Pennsylvania Quaker families, the Smedleys, the Darlingtons, and the Butlers, with American roots tracing back to the early eighteenth century. His two grandfathers were presidents of the two principal banks in West Chester, and one of them, Congressman Smedley Darlington, represented the same district that his son-in-law, Thomas S. Butler, took over from 1896 until his death in 1928. Smedley D. Butler's career in the Marine Corps, beginning in 1898, was thus full of political significance from the outset, particularly as his father Thomas S. served on the House Naval Affairs Committee continuously and was chairman from 1919 onwards.

Butler enlisted as a sixteen-year-old second lieutenant, two years underage, was initiated to expeditionary duty with the Guantánamo Battalion in the Cuban war, and did a stint as junior marine officer on the USS *New York*. In 1899 he shipped out to the Philippines, and in 1900, he won his first combat laurels in the Boxer Uprising in China, being brevetted to captain before his nineteenth birthday. He was twice wounded, at Tientsin and Peking.

In 1903 and 1904 he took part in interventions in Honduras and Panama, and in early Advance Base Force combined exercises with the fleet at Culebra off Puerto Rico. From 1905 to 1907 he was posted in the Philippines at Olongapo, doing garrison duty and mounting feeble Advance Base fortifications against anticipated Japanese attack.

His first field grade command was the mobile Panama Battalion, 1909–1914, based in the Canal Zone on alert for expeditionary duty up either coast of Central America. He led the battalion in interventions in Nicaragua in 1909 and 1910, and in the crucial 1912 campaign that definitively established the long-term American client state. With substantial experience and high reputation for aggressiveness and imagination in colonial warfare, he was selected by diplomat John Lind and the U.S. naval command off Vera Cruz in 1914 to plan a thousand-man commando "flying column" to penetrate to Mexico City and kidnap President Victoriano Huerta, thereby securing the capital in advance of coalescing revolutionary armies. While the plan was never executed, Butler and his marines were ready at the railway station in Vera Cruz through the summer of 1914.

In 1915 he and his longtime mentor, Colonel Littleton W. T. Waller, the two master bushwhackers of the Marine Corps in their era, oversaw the U.S. intervention and occupation of Haiti. Butler, after an energetic pacification campaign in which he won his second Congressional Medal of Honor, established the *Gendarmerie d'Haiti* and served as its first commandant until 1918. The gendarmerie was a prototype for subsequent marine-sponsored constabularies in the Dominican Republic and Nicaragua.

During World War I, he commanded the major embarkation camp in Europe, Camp Pontanezen at Brest, France, and was promoted to brigadier general at age thirty-seven, retaining that rank after the war partly in recognition of the monumental achievement of having converted the mudhole at Brest into an efficient transit point for a million troops. As commander of the marine base at Quantico from 1920 to 1924, under the aegis of his close friend Commandant John Archer Lejeune,* he staged a number of publicity spectacles to keep the Corps in the news and safeguard it against congressional budget cuts. Most notable was the 1922 month-long expedition to Gettysburg where the marines reenacted the Civil War battle before President Warren Harding and one hundred thousand spectators.

In 1924 he took a two-year leave from the Marines to lead an anticrime push as director of public safety in Philadelphia, focusing particularly on Prohibition enforcement and police corruption. This was the most extreme and widely publicized attempt to militarize a big-city American police force according to the contemporary Progressive reform ideal whereby urban law enforcement was to be wrested from the control of ward heelers and machine politics. Over the next decade Butler was a leading public spokesman for paramilitary police reform featuring state and federal constabularies as a means of breaking syndicated crime linked to urban politics. Back in the Marines in 1926, he court-martialed his second-in-command at San Diego for public drunkenness. The result was the famous "Cocktail Trial," one of the more bizarre Prohibition era incidents, especially as regards military subculture.

Butler's last overseas expedition was to China, 1927–1929, where he commanded five thousand marines in Shanghai and Tientsin. Butler spent most of his time in command of the brigade at Tientsin as diplomatic and military counterweight to Japanese Kwantung Army forces, which were at this time just beginning to assert themselves in aggressive military insubordination that presently culminated in full-scale Japanese invasion.

Upon returning to the United States, he resumed an active public speaking and writing sideline that, given his characteristic outspokenness, got him into trouble with his superiors in the Hoover administration. In December 1929 he told how marines had rigged mock elections in Nicaragua in 1912 and manipulated Haitian client politicians. Partly as a result, he was passed over for the commandancy in 1930, although he was the ranking major general in the Corps and the most famous fighting marine of his day. He retired in 1931 and devoted himself to increasingly radical criticisms of American imperialism, drawing the explicit analogy between underworld gangsterism at home and international gangsterism on behalf of Wall Street overseas: "I spent most of my time being a high-class muscle man for Big Business, for Wall Street and for the bankers. In short, I was a racketeer for capitalism."

In 1934 Butler exposed an alleged fascist plot, whereby Wall Street interests involved with American Legion political manipulations on the one hand and the American Liberty League on the other were ostensibly bent on organizing a veterans movement to topple President Franklin Roosevelt. Butler's plot was ridiculed in the right-wing press, but was partly substantiated by an attenuated congressional inquiry.

From 1935 onward, he was in the vanguard of the peace movement among veterans organizations, particularly the Veterans of Foreign Wars which supported a series of antiwar resolutions and gestures. He also campaigned vigorously on behalf of the united-front League Against War and Fascism at a time when the league had a substantial Communist membership, and he did a sympathetic interview for *New Masses* magazine. He spoke on the same platforms with Vito Marcantonio, Earl Browder, Roger Baldwin, James Ford, and other prominent leftists at antiwar and soldiers' bonus rallies.

Butler's career encompassed the full cycle from strident and adventuristic overseas military imperialism in which the marines fought as colonial light infantry in a succession of punitive campaigns, such as China in 1900, to the mediatory, indecisive, and closely tethered interventions characteristic of formal empire in retreat, as in his essentially political role in China, 1927–1929. In his 1930s recantation, he drew logical conclusions from extensive personal experience in military and paramilitary affairs, casting aside the patriotic rhetoric and specious legalism that had justified a long series of U.S. overseas military expeditions. His critical reassessment of his career and of ongoing uses of official coercion at home and overseas provided a compelling judgment according to high moral standards and a rigorous soldier's code of honor. As a well-known popularizer of military life through his many lectures, articles, boys adventure stories, and marine publicity stunts, and as a longtime insider in high-level civilian and military politics, his apostasy amounted to a unique and valuable perspective on American militarism.

BIBLIOGRAPHY

Archer, Jules. *The Plot to Seize the White House*. New York: 1973.
Butler, Smedley D. *Old Gimlet Eye: The Adventures of Smedley D. Butler as Told to Lowell Thomas*. New York: 1933.
————. *War Is a Racket*. New York: 1935. Reprinted in John Whitclay Chambers, ed. *Three Generals on War*. New York: 1973.
————, and Arthur J. Burks. *Walter Garvin in Mexico*. Philadelphia: 1927.
Lejeune, John A. *The Reminiscences of a Marine*. Philadelphia: 1930.
Vandegrift, Alexander A. *Once a Marine: The Memoirs of General A. A. Vandegrift*. As told to Robert B. Asprey. New York: 1964

HANS SCHMIDT

BYRD, Richard Evelyn (b. Winchester, Va., October 25, 1888; d. Boston, Mass., March 11, 1957), pioneer aviator and naval explorer. Byrd was the leader of five expeditions to Antarctica.

Richard Evelyn Byrd was born into an aristocratic Virginia family. At the age of twelve, he was invited by a friend to visit the Philippines. While there he accompanied an American constabulary unit sent out from Manila to suppress guerrilla forces in the interior. Byrd thrived on this dangerous mission, and it set the tone for the rest of his life in which he would display incomparable zest for excitement and adventure. The young man traveled around the world on his trip back to the United States.

When Byrd returned to Virginia, he was sent to Shenandoah Military Academy, then attended Virginia Military Institute for two years, and finally studied at the University of Virginia for one year. In 1908 he entered the U.S. Naval Academy where he was an average student but a superb athlete, and captained the gymnastics team during his first class year. Byrd graduated on June 7, 1912, ranking 62d in a class of 155.

The newly commissioned ensign was sent out to the fleet where he served in various battleships before a recurrence of an old gymnastics injury forced him to retire in March 1916. Two months later, he was recalled to active duty to serve as the administrator of naval militia in Rhode Island. After the United States entered World War I, Byrd served in the Bureau of Navigation and headed a commission on training camps. In 1918 he worked out an agreement with the naval medical examining board to let him try one more month of active service in which he went to Pensacola and entered pilot's training. He was so successful as a flyer that he was permitted to remain on active duty.

Later that same year, Byrd was ordered to Halifax, Nova Scotia, as commander of the Navy's Aviation Force in Canada. When the war ended, he became engrossed in plans to make a solo flight across the Atlantic. In 1921 Byrd was scheduled to cross from England to America in a newly purchased Navy dirigible. At the last moment, someone took his place. In this case, however, the disappointment was a blessing because the airship exploded and crashed on its maiden voyage, killing most of its passengers.

In the postwar years, the ingenious aviator invented two indispensable tools for his later explorations—the aerial sextant and the wind-drift instruments. In 1925 Byrd organized the naval aviation unit which went with the MacMillan Mission to the North Polar regions. The following year, he and Floyd Bennett won worldwide acclaim for making the first flight over the North Pole. As a result of this achievement, Byrd was promoted to commander on the retired list and was awarded the Medal of Honor and the Distinguished Service Medal.

In June 1927 Byrd and three companions in their airplane "America" crossed the Atlantic from New York to France in thirty-nine hours and fifty-six minutes. Despite having reached Paris, the four aviators were forced by fog and miserable weather to head back toward the French coast and to land in the water one hundred yards short of their goal. Byrd recounted all the details of these air adventures in his first book, *Skyward*.

In the fall of 1928 Byrd started out on his South Pole Expedition. He had spent months soliciting private donations of money from wealthy men such as Edsel Ford and John D. Rockefeller, Jr., and making all the logistical preparations for his hazardous journey into unknown reaches. Upon arriving at Antarctica, he and his company set up a command base, which they called "Little America."

From there, on November 29, 1929, Byrd and three other men flew over the South Pole. During the next two years, Byrd and his companions discovered and named vast areas of land and mapped approximately 150,000 square miles of Antarctica. When he returned to the United States, he was promoted to rear admiral on the retired list and was awarded a special medal by Congress. The following year, he wrote his second book, *Little America*, which gave a complete description of his first Antarctic adventure.

From 1933 to 1935 Byrd led his second expedition to the South Pole. This was a much larger venture, with live radio broadcasts originating from their base on the shores of the Ross Sea. During this trip, Byrd broke his cardinal rule of following the "buddy system." For some unexplained reason, the admiral decided to go into the vast polar unknown alone and he spent five solitary months in a shack on the Ross Ice Shelf making meteorological observations. During this ordeal, he almost lost his life by breathing carbon monoxide and was seriously ill from its poison when he was rescued.

Byrd's third expedition to Antarctica was financed by the U.S. government under the U.S. Antarctic Service established by President Franklin D. Roosevelt. In 1937 Byrd and his band of men again reached the southernmost continent, discovering and surveying many new mountains, islands, and an important peninsula.

During World War II, the Antarctic project was abandoned, as all effort had to be directed toward winning the struggle against the Axis powers. During the conflict, Admiral Byrd studied sites in the Pacific for use as Allied bases. In 1946 Byrd resumed his polar expedition, which was called Operation "Highjump." His group consisted of thirteen ships and 4,700 men. Byrd flew over the South Pole and photographed from the air countless spaces which had previously been blank spots on the maps of Antarctica.

In 1954 Byrd was appointed officer-in-charge of U.S. Antarctic programs for the International Geophysical Year of 1957–1958. In 1955 the United States sent an expedition called Operation "Deepfreeze," under Byrd's leadership, to the Antarctic. Admiral Byrd remained active in his exploring work until early 1957 when he returned to Boston in poor health. He died there on March 11, 1957.

> Go where he may, he cannot hope to find
> The truth, the beauty, pictured in his mind.

These two lines of poetry which headed the entry on Byrd in the 1912 *Lucky Bag*, the Naval Academy's yearbook, eloquently sum up the eminent explorer's life. Byrd was driven by a consuming passion to discover, study, and understand new and uncharted places. He never hesitated to tread unexplored paths, and in the early years of aviation he became one of the world's foremost aviators. His flying, in turn, prompted him to invent invaluable navigation instruments which advanced the art of aviation by many years.

He was extraordinarily gifted in organizing successful expeditions to both polar regions. Byrd's five expeditions to the South Pole provided scientists with a storehouse of information concerning the continent of Antarctica, and they furnished the impetus for most of the exploratory and scientific work done in the antipodes during the twentieth century. Furthermore, Byrd brought representatives of many nations of the world into a scientific community in which they worked in harmony together in the polar regions for the well-being and advancement of all mankind.

Richard Byrd stands alone as the last great independent explorer who ventured into mysterious and unknown areas of the world.

BIBLIOGRAPHY

Betrand, Kenneth J. *Americans in Antarctica, 1775–1948*. New York: American Geographical Society, 1971.
Byrd, Richard E. *Alone*. New York: G. P. Putnam's Sons, 1930.
———. *Little America: Aerial Exploration in the Antarctic, the Flight to the South Pole*. New York: G. P. Putnam's Sons, 1930.
———. *Skyward*. New York: G. P. Putnam's Sons, 1928.
Hoyt, Edwin P. *The Last Explorer: The Adventures of Admiral Byrd*. New York: John Day Company, 1968.

PEGGY HAMILTON MOONEY

C

CALHOUN, John Caldwell (b. Long Canes Settlement, S.C., March 18, 1782; d. Washington, D.C., March 31, 1850), politician and political theorist. As secretary of war, Calhoun was known as the "Hamilton of the War Department."

John C. Calhoun was born in the Ninety-Six District of South Carolina in 1782, a son of the Revolution and a father of the Civil War. His father Patrick was a well-known upcountry farmer, provincial legislator, former surveyor, and sometime Indian-fighter. Patrick died when John was thirteen and just beginning his formal schooling at the hands of Moses Waddell. Left by himself for several months with the run of Waddell's substantial library, the boy so took to reading history and metaphysics that he fell "alarmingly" ill and had to be sent home. He did not see Waddell's academy again until he was eighteen. Apparently none the worse for this hiatus, the young Calhoun so distinguished himself that he was packed off eventually to Yale. There, New England Federalism was virtually the school religion, but it was a religion whose precepts, Calhoun found, merely sharpened his own nationalistic brand of Republicanism.

He returned briefly to South Carolina after graduation in 1804 but set off for the North once more to read law at Tapping Reeve's School in Litchfield, Connecticut. One year here was enough for the talented and ambitious young man, and he attended to his plans for a political life with dispatch: he returned to South Carolina, made a good and convenient marriage to his cousin, completed his legal training, and within one year of opening his practice in Abbeville, was elected to the state legislature. Two years later, he was elected to the U.S. House of Representatives and given a seat on the Foreign Relations Committee.

For several years, the United States had been extremely sensitive to real and imagined threats from its old enemy, Great Britain. Anxious to assert its rights in the Atlantic world and less tolerant toward British presumptions as time went by, a war crisis was building up in 1812. The House of Representatives was the cockpit of this nationalistic fever, fed by new men like Calhoun, elected from the less established western and southern districts. Calhoun quickly became one of the leaders of this faction, known as the "War Hawks." From his seat on the Foreign Relations Committee and in his Washington boardinghouse, Calhoun took a hand with his bellicose colleagues in bringing the country to a war with Britain in the summer of 1812. One of his boardinghouse messmates, Secretary of State James Monroe, wrote the war manifesto, and Calhoun delivered the message to Congress.

Calhoun did not join the Army during the war, but he entertained vagrant thoughts about it, ruling them out in the end because he thought himself too valuable in the capital. Throughout the war, he was a bulwark in Congress for the Madison administration's war policies and in fact was often more warlike than the armies in the field. Calhoun and the Kentuckian Henry Clay often misunderstood that their rhetoric, so useful for plunging the country into war once more, could not be translated into the power of battle, and their sanguine estimates of a quick and decisive war proved woefully incorrect. The United States barely escaped losing the war, but Calhoun's soaring confidence in the military power of democracy never waned.

Calhoun's leading role during the war made him a candidate for an office with the new administration of James Monroe after President James Madison retired in 1816. But Calhoun's selection was long in coming; Monroe considered seven other aspirants for secretary of war before choosing the South Carolinian. The appointment was a propitious one, both for Calhoun and the War Department, which then was a morass of paper and inefficiency, governing a mere shadow of an army. Calhoun had received something of a military education in Congress during the war, but he never betrayed a particular liking for things military; a campaign biography once held that he had never read a book on the art of war. For all that, Calhoun had no difficulty in applying his natural talents to the problems that faced him, and, with energy and imagination, he set off on an eight-year tenure such as the War Department had never seen.

Within the first year of his administration, Calhoun had established a system of fiscal accountability for the governance of War Department disbursements (no real system had ever existed); launched expeditions up the Missouri River toward Yellowstone and up the Mississippi to Minnesota to interdict incursions by British fur traders; and extinguished all Indian land claims east of the Mississippi in his capacity as overlord of Indian affairs. Neither did the Army itself escape Calhoun's attention. The war had taught Calhoun the dangers of relying upon a militia for national defense. Although the militia was an article of republican faith, Calhoun declared a preference for a professional army after the European style and sought to ensure one. He interested himself in the welfare of the Army as well, fighting for increased pay, attacking the practice of flogging and using soldiers for contract labor, and defending the Army from further cuts. To effect further his insistence upon a truly professional army, Calhoun became West Point's chief patron and established the army's first "postgraduate" school, the Artillery School of Practice at Fortress Monroe. Finally, he oversaw the beginnings of the second system of American coastal fortifications and the nationwide construction projects to put the system into place.

But these and other reforms did not often survive partisan wrangling. Calhoun was still a politician, and he had not been in the War Department six months before writing a campaign biography for the presidential race he planned in 1824. In this ambition, for perhaps the first time in his life, Calhoun tasted failure. During the acrimonious presidential campaign, which lasted nearly four years, Calhoun's War Department was held hostage by his opponents in Congress, and in the end Calhoun had to accept the consolation of the vice-presidency under John Quincy Adams.

Calhoun continued in this office when Andrew Jackson* was elected in 1828. In the interim, Calhoun's nationalist stance was replaced by a fervent sectionalism that was brought on by the tariff question and his own disappointed ambitions for the presidency. It was the beginning of Calhoun's opposition to what he would have called "the despotism of the central government." While still vice-president, Calhoun wrote a defense of his native state's position on the tariff entitled "The South Carolina Exposition and Protest," in which he argued closely for the right of a state to "nullify" national laws that acted contrary to any state's interests. This tract, and South Carolina's increasing resistance to the Jackson administration, finally drove Calhoun to resign the vice-presidency.

Afterward, Calhoun returned to the Senate where he would finish his career, leaving only in 1844-1845 to serve as secretary of state. During this time his ardent sectionalism produced two more tracts remarkable in the history of political theory in the United States, the "Disquisition on Government" and the "Discourse on the Constitution and Government of the United States." Both works are said by scholars to be the most creative writing on the theory of democratic government after the writings of Thomas Jefferson. The foundation of Calhoun's argument was that majorities often overturned the rights of minorities and that minorities (in Calhoun's mind, these were the states) must somehow concur in the policies affecting them or exercise a check on their effects. This being the case, he wrote, democracy must have a constitution that allows states a defense against laws that treat them unjustly. Less theoretically, during his last twenty years Calhoun was a major contributor to the debate over slavery, defending that institution as a so-called positive good. If the Southern states could be said to have had an ideological rationale for their secession and rebellion during the Civil War, Calhoun's elegantly phrased theories had provided it. Ever the palladin of Southern sectionalism, Calhoun's career from the late 1820s to his death during the debates over the Compromise of 1850 constituted a complete rejection of his youthful and exuberant flirtation with nationalism.

In an 1843 campaign biography that was approved by Calhoun, his time in the War Department covered only a few pages. His later writings barely mention the eight years he spent there. No doubt these were years of frustration for Calhoun (even though greater frustrations lay ahead), and no doubt too he did not wish to call attention to his earlier incarnation as an unbridled nationalist. His War Department years thus were not the centerpiece of a life filled with political excitement, but for the War Department and the Army that it supervised, Calhoun's period as secretary of war was of considerable import.

Calhoun would have agreed with James Monroe, who said at the end of the War of 1812, "the late war formed an epoch, we cannot go back." For Calhoun, this meant that the time had come for America to depend less upon the skills of military amateurs and turn its energies to the development of a professional army. Calhoun knew well the antimilitary traditions of his republic, and he launched an imaginative campaign to overturn them by endearing the Army to its nation. At a time when constitutional objections were being raised by those who opposed using national monies for internal improvements, Calhoun and President Monroe used soldiers on construction projects that Congress would not approve, thereby circumventing advocates of "strict construction" of the Constitution. His "Report on Internal Improvements" in 1819 suggested the extent to which he once was willing to interpret the Constitution on the grounds of national need, and stood in direct contrast to his later, more conservative views. The expeditions he launched to explore the Trans-Mississippi West were clearly the most popular of his efforts, even though most failed in execution. All these enterprises, Calhoun believed, would contribute to the Army's standing, and for a time at least career officers such as Jacob Jennings Brown* and Winfield Scott* were encouraged.

The officer corps came under Calhoun's special protection at the same time, and he set himself to protecting the corps from the periodic demobilizations with which the nation already had become enamored. In 1822 Calhoun put forward a plan for an "expansible army," which was meant to keep the military art alive until war once again required a mobilization—an early version of preparedness. In aid of this objective, Calhoun took up the still struggling West Point as a special concern. He saw to the importation (by Sylvanus Thayer* and others) of a large collection of foreign military treatises and provided for their translation into English, creating a body of technical military knowledge that would sustain the American Army to the eve of the Civil War. As superintendent of West Point, Thayer enjoyed Calhoun's support in his own campaign to improve both the instruction and the facilities of the Academy, and was aided by Calhoun in preventing unwonted political interference in the school's programs and appointments. Finally, Calhoun built upon the Army staff reforms begun by his predecessor, William H. Crawford, by attempting to centralize the so-called General Staff in Washington. With mixed success, Calhoun created offices in the War Department for the surgeon general (Joseph Lovell*), the quartermaster general (Thomas Jesup), and, for the first time, a commissary general. So began the "bureau system" that dominated American military organization to the turn of the century.

Before Calhoun the War Department had never been directed by a first-class mind. No candidate for the presidency had ever come forward from the War Department, an honor that belonged to the State Department and Treasury until then. While other cabinet departments had improved their management steadily since their establishment, the War Department had suffered under a sad line of mediocrities. But not even Calhoun could ensure the beginning of a new tradition. It would be three decades before another secretary of war as talented as Calhoun would take over the War Department.

BIBLIOGRAPHY

Current, Richard. *John C. Calhoun*. New York: Washington Square Press, 1963.

Weigley, Russell F. *History of the United States Army*. New York: Macmillan Company, 1967.

Wiltse, Charles. *John C. Calhoun, Nationalist*. Indianapolis, Ind.: Bobbs-Merrill, 1944.

———*John C. Calhoun, Nullifier*. Indianapolis, Ind.: Bobbs-Merrill, 1949.

ROGER J. SPILLER

CAMPBELL, John, Fourth Earl of Loudoun (b. Loudoun Castle, Galston, Ayrshire, May 5, 1705; d. Loudoun Castle, April 27, 1782), commander in chief of British forces in North America during the French and Indian War, 1756–1758.

Loudoun's career in the British Army was founded as much on family, wealth, and political connections as on military merit. A direct descendant of two Scottish noble families, he succeeded his father in the peerage and family estates when only twenty-six; by the time he was thirty-five, he was a representative peer of Scotland, a fellow of the Royal Society, and governor of Sterling Castle. Although he had entered the Army at the relatively advanced age of twenty-two, he rose steadily through the elite Scots Greys and Scots Guards to become a captain and lieutenant colonel in 1739 and an aide de camp to King George II immediately after the Battle of Dettingen in 1743. His subsequent service against the Jacobite rebels in 1745–1746 (he twice raised a regiment of Highlanders) confirmed his ties with the king and his son, William Augustus, duke of Cumberland, the captain general of the British Army, 1745–1757. In 1749 when Loudoun's Highland regiment was disbanded, he was promptly compensated with the colonelcy of another regiment; and in 1755 at the outbreak of war with France, he was promoted to major general.

Just as Loudoun's advancement in the Army depended heavily on family and politics, so too did his selection in early 1756 to be commander in chief of British forces in North America. In choosing Loudoun, the government sought not merely to please its friends in Scotland but especially to win support in America for a war that was becoming ever more costly. Since fighting began in the summer of 1754, the government had drifted from a strategy of defending its frontiers against the French and Indians toward one of conquering Canada. To carry out this ambitious, expensive strategy without asking too much of

Parliament and British taxpayers, the government hoped to persuade the colonists to bear much of the cost of the war and to accept a British commander in chief. Thus, the government chose Loudoun perhaps as much for his wealth, title, and political experience as for his ties to the royal family and reputation as a respectable officer.

In drafting his instructions and making plans, the government sought to give him great power without alienating the colonists. It clearly intended Loudoun to be the supreme military authority in America. Yet to avoid offending royal governors and colonial assemblies, it left his authority over governors ambiguous and it required that he ask rather than order assemblies to obey him. Similarly, the government expected him to persuade the colonists to furnish recruits, provisions, and quarters for his army. Yet it also decided to begin recruiting in England and Scotland, to reimburse the colonists for expenses incurred in raising provincial troops in 1755, and to pay a British contractor to supply regular and provincial forces in America.

When at last Loudoun reached New York in late July 1756, he found the war going badly and the colonists determined to avoid serving under British officers. His predecessor, Governor William Shirley* of Massachusetts, had drawn up elaborate plans for an offensive against Canada but, knowing he was to be superseded, had done little to carry them out. Shirley had also neglected to make clear that a detachment at Fort Oswego on Lake Ontario was in danger of being captured. When Oswego fell, Loudoun blamed Shirley, charged him with profiteering, and began a prolonged, destructive controversy. More serious than the loss of Oswego and the quarrel with Shirley was the colonial assemblies' insistence on raising men exclusively for service in provincial units under their own provincial officers. The assemblies were determined to retain control over their troops and to spare their officers the indignity of being commanded by every regular captain. Loudoun, who had expected to rely heavily on colonial recruits to fill his regular units and to use provincial troops sparingly, was able to take command of provincials only by agreeing to keep regular and provincial units separate and by allowing provincial officers to rank after regular majors.

Moreover, his subsequent efforts to defend New York were thwarted repeatedly by the colonists' preoccupation with profits, interests, and rights. When he undertook to repair the forts on the frontiers of New York, to construct new barracks, storehouses, and hospitals, and to establish rudimentary transportation and intelligence services, he became the victim of extortionate prices. When he called upon the militia of New York and neighboring colonies to keep the French from going around his outposts and down the Hudson, he ran afoul of extreme provincialism: New York alone sent troops. And when in desperation he offered to buy supplies for any troops serving with him, he created suspicions that he was merely trying to deprive the assemblies of control over their men.

Nowhere did Loudoun encounter more trouble and opposition than in getting recruits and quarters for his regulars. He had no doubt that colonists preferred serving in provincial units. In the autumn of 1756 he also discovered that the colonial assemblies would no longer raise men for service in the Regular Army: colonists were too concerned with defending their homes and controlling their own military affairs to pay soldiers serving with regular units on distant campaigns. Nor were they any more willing to furnish quarters. When Loudoun demanded shelter, fuel, and refreshments for his men (at the colonists' expense), the colonists balked; and he had to use force or threats of force to quarter his men in New York and Pennsylvania. These experiences persuaded him that he would in the future have to recruit regulars in Britain and build barracks for them in America.

Loudoun was also sure that to defeat the French he would have to rely mainly on regular forces. Well before the campaign of 1756 ended in a statemate on the frontiers of New York, he began drafting a plan to end the war in 1757. Assuming that victory depended on the destruction of the main French army and that that Army would have to fight to defend its principal base at Quebec, he decided to attack Quebec by sea. He would ask the colonies to provide provincials enough to defend the upper Hudson and to raid the frontiers of Canada. He would then combine most of his regular forces with troops, ships, and artillery from the British Isles for an expedition to the St. Lawrence. This plan, approved in general terms by the government, showed clearly that neither he nor the government any longer depended on colonial forces to win the war in America.

To carry out his plan while the weather was favorable and the St. Lawrence open, Loudoun intended to embark as early as possible in the spring of 1757. But he was so obstructed by his government (which was slow to approve plans and assemble the necessary forces), by assemblies preoccupied with their rights, by foul winds, and by French squadrons that he decided eventually to modify and then to cancel his plans. Indeed, by the time he had gathered all of his forces at Halifax on July 9, the French had assembled a powerful fleet at Louisbourg on Cape Breton Island. Loudoun chose to postpone an attack on Quebec until he had taken Louisbourg and destroyed the French fleet. But preparing for a siege of Louisbourg consumed another four weeks, and by then a council of war concluded that it was too late to besiege Louisbourg successfully in 1757. Loudoun returned to New York and was recalled early in 1758. With the exception of a brief command in Portugal (1762–1763), he would spend the remainder of his days on his estates in Scotland, enjoying military preferment but no further active service.

Loudoun's performance as commander in chief in America has frequently been judged a failure. He certainly failed to persuade the colonists to support the war as enthusiastically and dutifully as the British government hoped, and he also failed to carry out his own plans for ending the war in 1757. But these failures can by no means be attributed primarily to Loudoun. No British commander could have persuaded the colonists to provide all the men and supplies and quarters that the British government expected, and none could have persuaded the colonists to place provincial units under British officers. Nor does it seem likely that anyone could have taken Louisbourg or Quebec in 1757 without more timely support from both sides of the Atlantic. Loudoun was not a resolute field commander: he preferred taking counsel and gathering intelligence to making decisions. But on the whole he seems to have been more unlucky than culpable—unlucky in what he was sent to do, in the nature of the support he received, and in the fleeting chance he had had to prove himself.

What Loudoun did accomplish was long obscured by the failure of 1757. While no model administrator (he devoted too much energy to details, personalities, and petty controversies), he did work steadily and successfully to build an army capable of defeating the French—an army of regulars that was independent of the colonists, an army recruited in England, supplied by English contractors, served by horses and wagons and teamsters under long-term government contracts, and trained, when possible, in the tactics of irregular warfare. Such an army was a burden to English taxpayers, but it was the kind of army needed to conquer Canada. Indeed, the army that Loudoun raised would at length find and destroy French forces at Louisbourg, Quebec, and Montreal.

BIBLIOGRAPHY

Frégault, Guy. *Canada: The War of the Conquest*. Toronto: Oxford University Press, 1969.
Gipson, Lawrence Henry. *The Great War for the Empire. The Years of Defeat, 1754–1757*. New York: Alfred A. Knopf, 1946.
———. *The Great War for the Empire. The Victorious Years, 1758–1760*. New York: Alfred A. Knopf, 1949.
Pargellis, Stanley McCrory. *Lord Loudoun in North America*. New Haven, Conn.: Yale University Press, 1933. [Archon Books, 1968.]
———. *Military Affairs in North America 1748–1765 Selected Documents from the Cumberland Papers in Windsor Castle*. New York: D. Appleton-Century Company, 1936. [Archon Books, 1969.]
Schutz, John A. *William Shirley King's Governor of Massachusetts*. Chapel Hill: University of North Carolina Press, 1961.

IRA D. GRUBER

CANBY, Edward Richard Sprigg (b. Piatt's Landing, Ky., November 9, 1817; d. Siskiyou County, Calif., April 11, 1873), Army officer. Canby repulsed the Confederate invasion of New Mexico and commanded the Union's Military Division of West Mississippi during the Civil War.

Edward Canby's father, Israel, a physician, emigrated to Kentucky from Maryland in 1814. Two years later he married Elizabeth Piatt, the daughter of a Kentuckian with extensive landholdings. Within a year of Edward's birth, the family moved across the Ohio River to Madison, Indiana, and then in 1830 to Crawfordsville, Indiana. Edward Canby attended Wabash College and entered West Point with the class of 1839; he graduated thirtieth in a class of thirty-one. Upon graduation he was posted second lieutenant to the 2d Infantry Regiment which was engaged in the Second Seminole War.

Shortly after the outbreak of the Mexican War, Canby was brevetted captain and made assistant adjutant of the second brigade of the 2d Infantry. He won two brevets (to major and lieutenant colonel) while participating in campaigns in Mexico under Winfield Scott.* Canby was cited for "gallant and meritorious conduct" for his behavior at the battles of Contreras and Churubusco.

After the Mexican War, Canby continued to attract favorable attention from his superiors and to gain experience in military administration. For two years (1849–1851) he served in the Adjutant General's Office of the Tenth Military Department in California. Subsequently, he was dispatched to conduct an inspection of the military posts on the Arkansas and Red rivers. He submitted an admirable report of this inspection in April 1855 and was then ordered to Carlisle Barracks, Pennsylvania, as major of the 10th Infantry. While serving with that regiment, he participated in the "Mormon War" (1857–1858) in Utah Territory, under Colonel Albert Sidney Johnston.* When the Civil War began, Canby was in command of Fort Defiance, New Mexico Territory, and had just concluded a frustrating and futile campaign against the Navaho Indians.

In July 1861 Canby was placed in command of the Department of New Mexico and received promotion to colonel of the 19th Infantry. Beset by Indian problems and the lack of men and supplies, he faced the Confederate invasion of the territory that began in February 1862, and was led by his old second-in-command in the Navaho Campaign, Henry Sibley. Canby's successful and cautious defense of New Mexico Territory was generally one characterized by scorching the earth and drawing the invading Confederates away from their supply base. However, Canby did attack at Valverde (February 21, 1862) and suffered a defeat. He chose to stay at Fort Craig athwart the Confederate line of retreat as the Southerners advanced northward. On March 28, 1862, Union forces under one of Canby's subordinates scored a victory at Glorieta—the "Gettysburg of the West." Canby had not authorized the battle, but the defeat at Glorieta forced the Confederates to retreat from New Mexico into Texas. Canby and his soldiers followed Sibley's retreating Southerners, but he refused to engage the Confederates. These tactics drew charges of cowardice and even accusations of treason from some of Canby's officers and men. These charges were unjustified, and a grateful nation accepted Canby as one of its heroes of 1862, although not of the same order as Ulysses Simpson Grant* or George Brinton McClellan.*

By his own request Canby was transferred on May 13, 1862, to the East, where for eighteen months he was engaged in important administrative duties. Now a brigadier general of volunteers, he had the fullest confidence of Secretary of War Edwin McMasters Stanton.* Canby served as the commanding general of New York City for the four months immediately following the draft riots. The city fathers had demanded a man of "iron will" to reestablish order.

On May 7, 1864, he received promotion to the rank of major general of volunteers and four days later took command of the Military Division of West Mississippi, which encompassed an area as far south as the Dry Tortugas and as far north as Missouri and included the Indian Territory and the Gulf Coast to

West Florida. His chief duty was to keep the Mississippi open. Some of the officers under General William Tecumseh Sherman* feared that Canby might conduct operations that would detract or be detrimental to Sherman's campaign in Georgia; nothing of this sort happened. On the contrary, the Sherman-Canby relationship was a model of harmony. Canby cooperated with Admiral David Glasgow Farragut* in the reduction of the Mobile Bay forts in September 1864. Mobile did not fall until April 12, 1865. At the time Grant criticized Canby for taking so long to achieve the city's final surrender. However, in his *Memoirs*, Grant remembered things differently and credited Canby's slowness to inexperience in leading large forces in battle, especially against a fortified town. Canby negotiated the surrender of General Richard E. Taylor's Confederate troops and the submission of the last organized Confederate field force, that of General Edmund Kirby Smith.*

After the Civil War, Canby continued to command troops in Louisiana, but he ran afoul of General Philip Henry Sheridan,* his new superior officer who commanded the Military Division of the Gulf. When Canby could not carry out touchy Reconstruction duties to Sheridan's satisfaction, he left the Gulf area in May of 1866 and reported to the War Department in Washington, D.C. There he headed a commission that decided special war claims brought to the War Department. Later, Canby specialized in Reconstruction duty, serving as commanding officer in three of the five Military Districts created by the congressional Reconstruction Act of March 2, 1867. These posts called for men with the tact and administrative ability that Canby possessed in abundance. He served in the Second Military District (the Carolinas), August 1867-August 1868; the Fifth Military District (Texas), November 1868-April 1869; and the First Military District (Virginia), April 1869-January 1870.

In 1870 Canby accepted command of the Department of Columbia in the Far West. In this capacity, and while conducting peace negotiations with Captain Jack, chief of the Modoc Indians, Canby was attacked and killed. He was the only Regular Army general to be killed in the Indian Wars.

If Canby is popularly remembered for any accomplishment, it is his repulse of the Confederate invasion of New Mexico. Drawing on his organizational talents, Canby marshaled regulars and volunteers into an effective force and used Fabian tactics, rather than slashing offensive operations, to make his campaign a victorious one. Canby's practice of destroying all supplies in front of the advancing Confederates probably weakened Sibley's forces. Yet Canby was not present at nor did he order the engagement at Glorieta that forced the Confederates to abandon New Mexico. It is an overstatement to call him the sole savior of the Southwest, but he set the tone of the campaign by not risking a large engagement when outnumbered, and he did not throw away the fruits of victory by endangering his army after the Southerners retreated from Glorieta. The Confederates never attempted another full-scale invasion of New Mexico.

While serving at the War Department in the Civil War, Canby acted on cases relating to political prisoners, including Clement L. Vallandigham, a former Ohio congressman who became the war's most famous "copperhead." The general also sat on a board of officers that revised and collated the Articles of War. These services pointed to the fact that Canby was highly respected by his contemporaries for his ability and prudence as an administrator.

It was his ability as an administrator that earned Canby the chance to command the Military Division of West Mississippi, and his capture of Mobile is one of the war's neglected campaigns. Canby took charge of his sprawling division following the failure of Nathaniel Banks' Red River Expedition, bringing order and raising morale in a disorganized and dispirited command. Canby cooperated effectively with Admiral Farragut in reducing Mobile's forts, and it is to Canby's credit that simultaneously he adhered to Grant's orders to launch raids against Selma and Montgomery, Alabama, further weakening the interior of the Confederacy.

During Reconstruction Canby's ability as an administrator came to the fore once again. He had been cultivating an interest in law since the Mexican War, and these studies helped him deal with the extraordinary problems of martial law and military government in the Southern states.

There is an irony in Canby's death. During his career, Canby had made no enemies in his profession, and his conduct had been marked, above all, by caution. Although forewarned that there would be trouble, Canby went unarmed to parley with Captain Jack. At the conference the Modoc drew a pistol and killed the general, ruining President Grant's "Peace Policy" and eventually bringing stern retribution to the Modocs, who were relocated to a reservation in Indian Territory (Oklahoma).

BIBLIOGRAPHY

Colton, Roy C. *The Civil War in the Western Territories: Arizona, Colorado, New Mexico, and Utah*. Norman: University of Oklahoma Press, 1959.

Hall, Martin H. *Sibley's New Mexico Campaign*. Austin: University of Texas Press, 1960.

Heyman, Max L., Jr. *Prudent Soldier: A Biography of Major General E.R.S. Canby, 1817–1873*. Glendale, Calif.: Arthur H. Clark Company, 1959.

Utley, Robert M. *Frontier Regulars: The U.S. Army and the Indian, 1866–1890*. New York: Macmillan Company, 1973.

————. *Frontiersmen in Blue: The United States Army and the Indian, 1848–1865*. New York: Macmillan Company, 1967.

RONALD RIDGLEY

CARLSON, Evans Fordyce (b. Sidney, N.Y., February 26, 1896; d. Portland, Oreg., May 27, 1947), Marine Corps officer. Carlson helped to organize the Marine Raiders during World War II.

Evans Carlson, the son of a Congregationalist minister, grew up in small towns in Vermont and Massachusetts. He left home at age fourteen, enlisted in the Army at sixteen, and served three years in Hawaii and the Philippines. Discharged in 1915, he was recalled to duty during the Mexican troubles in

1916. During World War I, he was commissioned, promoted to captain, and sent to France with the 87th Division but arrived too late to fight. In 1919 he resigned his commission and worked as a salesman for a fruit packing company until 1922, when he decided to reenter military service. Although he could have returned to the Army as a second lieutenant, he chose not to do so because he would be outranked by his former associates. Instead, he enlisted as a private in the Marine Corps.

Carlson was commissioned a second lieutenant of marines in December 1922. During the next fifteen years, his most significant assignments were two tours in China (1927–1929 and 1933–1935), which led him to study the Chinese language, service with the *Guardia Nacional* in Nicaragua (1930), where he participated in fighting against rebel guerrillas, and duty with President Franklin D. Roosevelt's guard at Warm Springs, Georgia (1935), where he developed a personal friendship with the president.

Returning to China as a captain in 1937, Carlson became an observer with the Communist Eighth Route Army which was then fighting the Japanese. For months he lived with the Communists, marching more than two thousand miles with them and participating in several guerrilla forays behind Japanese lines. Profoundly impressed by the Communists' dedication and "spiritual strength," he praised them highly to the press and, at the same time, criticized America for its continued sale of war materials to Japan. The Navy Department warned him that his statements were indiscreet, whereupon, in April 1939, he resigned from the service so that he could write and speak freely.

Carlson spent the next two years writing and lecturing. Repeatedly, he urged more American aid for China and warned of the danger of selling scrap metal and other war materials to Japan. In 1940, he published two books: *The Chinese Army*, a technical work that attracted little notice, and *Twin Stars of China*, a more popular book relating his personal experiences and lauding the Eighth Route Army.

In May 1941, convinced that war was imminent, he reentered the Marine Corps and was soon promoted to lieutenant colonel. Early in 1942, he organized the 2d Marine Raider Battalion, with Major James Roosevelt, the president's son, as executive officer, and in August 1942 he led two hundred of his men in a hit-and-run raid on Makin Atoll. Landing from submarines, the Raiders wiped out the Japanese garrison of about eighty-five men and destroyed radio stations, fuel, and supplies. Although the military value of the raid was negligible, it served to boost homefront morale at a critical time. On Guadalcanal, in November 1942, he and his Raiders executed one of the great combat patrols of the war. In a thirty-day incursion behind enemy lines, they marched 150 miles over difficult jungle terrain, fought more than a dozen actions, and killed nearly five hundred Japanese while suffering only thirty-five casualties.

After Guadalcanal, Carlson became second-in-command of the newly formed 1st Raider Regiment but was soon sent home with malaria. While convalescing, he served as technical advisor for Universal Studios, which produced a film, entitled *Gung Ho!*, about the Makin raid. Later, he was present as an observer during the assault on Tarawa (1943) and served on the staff of the 4th Marine Division during the campaigns in the Marshalls and Marianas Islands. In June 1944, on Saipan, he rushed out under fire to rescue a wounded radioman and was himself seriously wounded. Nine months later he returned to duty as a colonel and deputy chief of staff, V Amphibious Corps, but his wounds had not healed. In June 1945 he returned to the United States, and in July 1946 he was retired for wounds and disability with the rank of brigadier general. His decorations included the Legion of Merit (Saipan), three Navy Crosses (Nicaragua, Makin, and Guadalcanal), and two Purple Hearts.

After his retirement, Carlson was active in attempting to redirect U.S. foreign policy. He deplored the growing rift with the Soviet Union, favored sharing our atomic secrets with the world, opposed support for Chiang Kai-Shek, and defended the Communists as the "only democratic force" in China. He became vice-chairman of the Progressive Citizens of America, forerunner of the Progressive party which in 1948 supported Henry A. Wallace for the presidency. In 1946 he considered becoming a candidate for the U.S. Senate, as a progressive Democrat, but was prevented from doing so by a heart attack. A subsequent heart attack was fatal.

Carlson of the Raiders was a deeply religious, bible-quoting idealist of acute social consciousness and intense convictions. As the first foreign military officer to serve with the Eighth Route Army, he was one of the best informed and most influential observers of the Chinese Communists before World War II. His idealistic portrayal of them in his writings, as well as in confidential letters to President Roosevelt, exerted considerable influence on their behalf.

Carlson met and admired many of the Communist leaders, including Mao Tse-tung, whom he thought completely selfless, and Chu Teh, commander of the Eighth Route Army, whom he described as combining the best qualities of Robert Edward Lee,* Abraham Lincoln,* and Ulysses Simpson Grant.* He was most impressed, however, by the courage, endurance, loyalty, and high ethical standards of the individual Chinese soldier. Carlson believed that the explanation for these qualities lay in a process which he called "ethical indoctrination" and which he defined as the creation, in each soldier, of "the desire to do what is right." The process involved high moral standards, social equality between officers and men, group cooperation, open discussions of strategy, and the political education of troops so that they understood why they fought.

During the war, Carlson patterned his Raider Battalion after the Eighth Route Army and applied the principles of "ethical indoctrination." As a rallying cry for the Raiders, he introduced "Gung Ho!," his adaptation of a Chinese slogan meaning "working together." Carlson's men were handpicked volunteers, and his officers were carefully chosen for their initiative and democratic outlook. He abolished officers' privileges and required officers to live and eat with their troops. He instituted group meetings where his men discussed such topics as "democracy" or the kind of society they wanted after the war. Before each battle, Carlson discussed his plans with his men and invited suggestions and, afterward, encouraged self-criticism. Carlson's men were intensely loyal to him and believed him to be tireless and fearless. His biographer, Michael Blankfort, an ex-Raider, recalled that

> He marched with a full pack like the rest of us, but when we rested he stood up studying a map or talking with the company commanders or he walked off to do a little scouting of his own. We never heard him say he was tired, so how could we complain. . . . When the man who leads you has no fear, you feel safe. We loved him because so few of us were killed.

Despite his success in battle, Carlson's methods and political views were unpopular with many senior Marine Corps officers. It is significant that after Guadalcanal he never again directly commanded troops in combat and that by 1944 all the Raider battalions had been converted to regular Marine infantry units.

After Carlson's death, Senator Joseph R. McCarthy condemned him as a member of the international Communist conspiracy. Those who knew him, however, including Communists, knew that McCarthy was wrong. Agnes Smedley, a radical journalist who spent years with the Chinese Communists, reported that Carlson joined the Eighth Route Army with such an "air of utter simplicity" that she first thought it a cunning disguise. Afterward, she wrote that he knew nothing of the basic principles that motivated Communists. Instead, his reactions reminded her of the *Battle Hymn of the Republic*, particularly the line, "As He died to make men holy, let us die to make men free." Smedley was correct in her assessment. Carlson was nonidealogical and knew nothing about abstract doctrine. His observations, however, convinced him that the Communists were self-sacrificing patriots while the Nationalists were controlled by corrupt bureaucrats. Carlson's primary impulse was humanitarian concern for the Chinese people. He was an egalitarian democrat who believed in the brotherhood of man.

BIBLIOGRAPHY

Blankfort, Michael. *The Big Yankee: The Life of Carlson of the Raiders*. Boston: Little, Brown, and Company, 1947.
Hough, Frank, W., et al. *Pearl Harbor to Guadalcanal*. Washington, D.C.: U.S. Government Printing Office, 1958.
Moskin, J. Robert. *The U.S. Marine Corps Story*. New York: McGraw-Hill Book Company, 1977.
Shewmaker, Kenneth E. *Americans and Chinese Communists, 1927–1945: A Persuading Encounter*. Ithaca, N.Y.: Cornell University Press, 1971.
Smedley, Agnes. *Battle Hymn of China*. New York: Alfred A. Knopf, 1943.

NORMAN V. COOPER

CASEY, Silas (b. East Greenwich, R.I., July 12, 1807; d. Brooklyn, N.Y., January 22, 1882), Union general. Writer on tactics.

Silas Casey was a lineal descendant of Joseph Wanton, governor of Rhode Island in the late colonial period. Young Silas spent his boyhood years in the East Greenwich homestead of his grandfather and father. He received his early education in local schools and entered West Point when he was fifteen. One contemporary said candidly: "The records of the Military Academy show that his boyhood was not free from wild escapades, one of which led to his being seriously disciplined by the authorities." Casey graduated near the bottom of his class in 1826 and was commissioned second lieutenant in the 2d Infantry.

Casey was stationed with the 2d Infantry at several posts, including Fort Towson, Sackets Harbor, and Buffalo. He was promoted to first lieutenant in 1836 and to captain in 1839. Casey served with his regiment in Florida for five years during the Second Seminole War. In April 1842 he distinguished himself during a successful attack made by the 2d Infantry and two other regiments on a small band of Indians led by the Mikasuki chief Halleck Tustenuggee. When Casey left Florida with his regiment, he was thirty-five years old. He had been a strong and athletic young man, but his health was affected for the rest of his life by his years in Florida.

Casey was often praised for his conduct during Winfield Scott's* campaign of the Mexican War. Casey was brevetted for Contreras and Churubusco, and was commended in Persifor F. Smith's official report of the action. Casey played a prominent role in the last major engagement of the Mexican War, the storming of Chapultepec. In the attack on the Mexico City fortress, the Americans used two small columns, storming parties made up of volunteers and picked officers. Captain Casey led the column that advanced in front of John Anthony Quitman's* division on the Tacubaya Road. He was severely wounded early in the assault, and the advance of his column was checked. Quitman reported that the "gallant Capt. Casey" had been wounded "directly before the [Mexican] batteries." The assault eventually succeeded, and Casey won another brevet.

Casey drew various assignments between the Mexican and Civil wars. He was stationed at Benicia, California, between 1849 and 1852, and commanded the escort of Captain William H. Warren's topographical party, accompanying the expedition north into the Oregon Territory. In the mid-1850s Casey served on three different boards of officers, including one that examined breech-loading arms and one that reviewed William Joseph Hardee's* manual of infantry tactics. When the 9th Infantry was created in 1855, Casey was made its lieutenant colonel and was promoted to colonel in October 1861. He held various commands in the Washington Territory between 1856 and 1861.

After the outbreak of the Civil War, Casey was appointed brigadier general of volunteers. During the first fall and winter of the war, he organized and trained troops as they came into Washington, D.C., from the Northern states. Several years after the Civil War, Richard B. Irwin praised Casey's work in organizing new regiments into provisional brigades and training them in the "dry nursery" of the Washington defenses. Irwin said Casey "was exactly fitted" for this assignment.

The first edition of Casey's *Infantry Tactics* was published in 1862. After the Civil War began, the federal government wanted a tactical manual to replace the one adopted in 1855, which had been prepared by William J. Hardee. The Northern government wanted to avoid the embarrassment of using a tactical manual that was associated with a man who was now a Confederate general. The War Department turned to Casey to prepare an alternative manual. Casey's manual appeared in 1862 and was republished without revision in 1865.

Casey's *Tactics* was very similar to Hardee's manual. It was based in large part on the same French source used by Hardee. Like Hardee's work, Casey's *Tactics* attempted to compensate attacking infantry for the increase in firepower that defenders had gained from the adoption of the rifle. In the preface to his manual, Casey acknowledged some of the tactical changes made since the adoption of the rifle, including the use of the two-rank formation in place of three and the decision "to increase the rapidity of the gait." Hardee's *Tactics* had increased, from Winfield Scott's musket tactics, the step rates at which infantry would advance against defenders. Casey retained Hardee's step rates and virtually all of Hardee's system. Casey also prepared a tactical manual for the black troops of the North, which was endorsed and published by the War Department in 1863. This manual also followed, with a few changes, Hardee's tactical system.

Casey's only Civil War field service was as a division commander during the Peninsula Campaign. When George Brinton McClellan* brought the Army of the Potomac near Richmond in late May 1862, Casey's division was posted across the Williamsburg Stage Road west of Seven Pines. Casey's line was strengthened by abatis, rifle pits, a redoubt, and a picket line well in front of the division. The Confederate attack on May 31 overran the division, and Casey lost more than fourteen hundred casualties. McClellan was harshly critical of Casey's division in a telegram sent to Secretary of War Edwin McMasters Stanton* on June 1. Casey and several other officers associated with the division took exception to McClellan's remarks, and a controversy ensued. McClellan later modified his comments. Many of the division's units fought well at Seven Pines; the division's greatest weakness was that eight of its thirteen regiments were green. Casey was brevetted for the battle and promoted to major general of volunteers. During the Seven Days' battle, Casey commanded the troops at the White House Landing supply base.

Casey saw no further combat service after the Peninsula Campaign. He returned to the Washington defenses, where he continued the work of organizing and training new troops. He sat on the Fitz-John Porter* court of inquiry and on the later court-martial, which ordered Porter cashiered. From May 1863 until July 1865 Casey presided over the board that examined candidates for commissions as officers of black troops. He was given his last brevet on March 13, 1865, for his wartime service, and he mustered out of the volunteer service in August 1865. After the war Casey was stationed at Fort Wayne, Detroit, until April 1867, and was later appointed commissioner to examine the war claims of Ohio.

Casey continued his interest in tactical theory after the Civil War ended. He contributed articles on tactics to the *Army and Navy Journal*, arguing for a new tactical system that would emphasize simplicity of maneuver and would take into account the use of entrenchments that had recently developed in America. Casey also advocated a unified system of tactics for all three arms of the service, an idea that was eventually adopted. Casey's *Tactics* was replaced in 1867 by a new manual prepared by Emory Upton.* Two years later John McAllister Schofield* presided over a board of officers convened to prepare an assimilated tactical system for all three arms of the service. Casey revised his *Tactics* and submitted the work to the Schofield Board. The Schofield Board rejected Casey's work and returned his manuscript to his son. Upton's work was eventually adopted as the infantry tactics in the assimilated system. Casey died at his home in Brooklyn in January 1882.

Casey is best known for the *Tactics* he prepared during the Civil War. His manual made a modest contribution to tactical theory. His preface to the manual showed some awareness of the importance that the adoption of the rifle would have for infantry tactics. Casey retained virtually all of the Hardee system, but he did introduce a few changes. A more efficient deployment from column to line would help attackers overcome some of the advantages that the rifle gave defenders, and Casey's manual offered a system of deploying a battalion from column to line which was somewhat simpler than Hardee's. Casey also gave the division column, a small column of two companies, more emphasis than Hardee had. Hardee's *Tactics* was a two-volume manual; the largest unit it treated was the battalion. Casey's work was in three volumes; his third volume provided a tactics for brigade and larger units.

Most of Casey's *Tactics* was identical to Hardee's work, and neither manual adequately compensated attackers for the increased firepower that the rifle gave defenders. Casey's *Tactics*, like Hardee's, relied primarily on increased step rates to speed up assaults and overcome the new advantage of the defensive. Casey used essentially the same close order formations found in the manuals of Hardee and Scott. Casey's manual, for example, had ranks deploy at the same close distance used by both Scott and Hardee. Casey's ideas about skirmisher tactics were also traditional. When the War Department endorsed Casey's *Tactics* in 1862, it suspended his original skirmisher system, and Casey had to replace it with another one. By the end of the Civil War, the need for an alternative to the Hardee-Casey tactical system was evident.

Although never a successful field general, Silas Casey was well respected by his contemporaries. The Civil War did not prove to be the opportunity for him that it was for many other Old Army officers. Casey saw action only once during the war, a brief appearance at Seven Pines. By the time of the Peninsula Campaign, Casey was fifty-five years old and in poor health. He was best remembered for his *Tactics*, but the manual lacked originality and proved inadequate in the face of the rifled firepower and entrenchments of the Civil War. Casey's greatest contribution to the Federal war effort was his work in organizing and training new regiments as they arrived in Washington. Silas Casey was an intelligent man, a brave soldier, and, above all, a dedicated career officer.

BIBLIOGRAPHY

Casey, Silas. *Infantry Tactics*. 3 vols. New York: D. Van Nostrand, 1862.
Hardee, William J. *Rifle and Light Infantry Tactics*. 2 vols. Philadelphia: Lippincott, Grambo, and Company, 1855.
Johnson, Robert U., and Buel, Clarence C., eds. *Battles and Leaders of the Civil War*. Vol. 2. New York: Thomas Y. Yoseloff, 1956.
McWhinney, Grady, and Jamieson, Perry D. *Attack and Die: Civil War Military Tactics and the Southern Heritage*. University, Alabama: University of Alabama Press, 1982.

                                                                        PERRY JAMIESON

CHAFFEE, Adna Romanza, Jr. (b. Junction City, Kans., September 23, 1884; d. Boston, Mass., August 22, 1941), cavalry officer. Chaffee became instrumental in the development of the U.S. Army's mechanized forces before World War II.

Adna R. Chaffee, Jr., was the third of four children, and the only son, of Adna Romanza Chaffee and Anna Frances Rockwell Chaffee. The elder Chaffee was a distinguished Army officer who rose from the enlisted ranks during the Civil War to become chief of staff of the Army from 1904 to 1906.

As the family moved from post to post, young Adna attended a succession of public schools until he was fourteen and enrolled in St. Luke's School for Boys at Wayne, Pennsylvania. His boyhood, especially on the Western military posts, was filled with outdoor activities. Chaffee became an expert horseman at an early age and remained an avid equestrian until his death. When he entered West Point in 1902, his active youth and military family background had prepared him better than most of his classmates for the rigors of the Military Academy. At the Academy he was active in athletics and assumed successive leadership roles in the Corps of Cadets as a corporal, sergeant, and lieutenant. Chaffee graduated thirty-first out of seventy-eight in the class of 1906.

For the eleven years between graduation and World War I, Chaffee served exclusively as a cavalryman. He had troop duty with the 15th Cavalry during 1906 and 1907 in the Army of Cuban Pacification and later during 1914 and 1915 with the 7th Cavalry in the Philippines. As a student officer at the Mounted Service School at Fort Riley, from 1907 to 1909, he studied the basic tactics of mounted combat and learned to command cavalry troops and squadrons. After organizing and commanding the mounted detachment which supported staff and students at the Army War College during 1910 and 1911, Chaffee went as a member of the American team competing in the International Horse Show in London during the coronation week of George V. Chaffee, the youngest member of the American team, had gained the reputation as one of the Army's finest horsemen. That reputation was enhanced when following the London competition he remained overseas to attend the one-year course at Saumur, the supreme French Army school of horsemanship. Upon completion of the Saumur course, Chaffee returned to Fort Riley for a year as instructor at the Mounted Service School. Following his Philippines service, he went back to West Point as senior cavalry instructor in the Tactical Department, a post he held from early 1916 until after the United States entered the war.

During the war, Chaffee gave up horses, riding competitions, and the cavalry to become a General Staff officer, thus considerably broadening his professional horizons, responsibilities, and potential. He began the war a captain of cavalry; when it ended, he was a full colonel (although a temporary, wartime rank) and operations officer of an army corps engaged in a major offensive.

In August 1917 he joined the 81st Division, then in training at Camp Jackson, South Carolina, as the division adjutant. He served as acting chief of staff of the division before going to France early in 1918. Upon arriving overseas, he went directly to the General Staff College at Langres, where he was a student from March through May 1918. He stayed on through August 1918 as an instructor. After leaving Langres, he served briefly as assistant operations officer (G–3) of the IV Corps, G–3 of the 81st Division, G–3 of the VII Corps, and during the last ten days before the Armistice as G–3 of the III Corps. For his service at the Staff College and with the III Corps the War Department awarded Chaffee the Distinguished Service Medal in part for acting ''with sound judgement and wide comprehension of existing conditions in the discharge of the grave responsibilities connected with his office during the closing days of the Meuse-Argonne offensive.'' Chaffee remained with the corps on occupation duty in the Rhineland through July 1919 when he returned to the United States to become an instructor at the School of the Line and Staff School at Fort Leavenworth.

Like most of his contemporaries, when Chaffee returned from overseas in August 1919 he lost his temporary wartime rank, reverting to his permanent rank of captain. Within one year, however, he was promoted to major, but it took until 1929 to reach lieutenant colonel and until 1935 to return to his wartime rank of colonel. Chaffee taught at Leavenworth for one year, until May 1920 when he served briefly with the 3d Cavalry. In August 1920 he resumed his General Staff career as the intelligence officer of the IV Corps Area in Atlanta. Leaving that post the next year, he became the operations officer of the 1st Cavalry Division at Fort Bliss, Texas, a post he retained until July 1924 when he again became a student. During 1924–1925 Chaffee was at the Army War College finishing his formal military education. Upon graduation he returned to troop duty for two years as a squadron commander with the 3d Cavalry at Fort Myer, Virginia.

The most significant phase of Chaffee's career began on July 1, 1927, when he joined the Operations and Training Division on the War Department General Staff. At this juncture Chaffee became intimately involved with the development of mechanization policy in the Army.

In 1927 Secretary of War Dwight Davis, impressed with the maneuvers of a British experimental mechanized force he had witnessed, ordered the General Staff to organize a similar American unit. Davis wanted a service test of equipment, organization, and doctrine that would enable the Army to formulate a long-term policy on mechanization. Chaffee supervised the General Staff's efforts to organize the force, observed the unit's training and exercises, and at the conclusion of maneuvers prepared the final report outlining future action. He recommended a permanent mechanized force, independent of existing branches, composed of tanks, mobile artillery, and motorized infantry that was capable of great tactical and strategic mobility. In 1930 the War Department organized, along the lines Chaffee outlined, a permanent mechanized force. Chaffee joined this new organization as its executive officer. But within a year General Douglas MacArthur,* then Army chief of staff, disbanded the mechanized force and ordered all branches of the service to mechanize as far as practical. The infantry would use tanks for close support; the cavalry would employ armored, mechanized vehicles to accomplish its traditional roles of reconnaissance, pursuit, and exploitation.

In June 1931 Chaffee became executive officer of the first regiment mechanized, the 1st Cavalry. By the end of that year, the regiment began arriving at its permanent post, Fort Knox, Kentucky, where Chaffee also served as post executive officer. As post executive, he worked hard to improve the buildings, quarters, roads, and public works at Fort Knox. As regimental executive he planned and supervised the exercises and maneuvers in which the regiment tested and perfected tactics, equipment, and doctrine. Chaffee eventually commanded the 1st Cavalry (Mechanized) from February through June 1934. He returned to the General Staff in July 1934, this time as chief of the Budget and Legislative Planning Branch, a post he retained for the next four years. From that well-placed position Chaffee worked to increase the funds available for mechanization. The mechanization of a second regiment, the 13th Cavalry, in 1936 was testament to his success. He returned to Fort Knox in June 1938 to command the 1st Cavalry. On November 1, 1938, the Army promoted Chaffee to brigadier general and gave him command of the 7th Cavalry Brigade (Mechanized) which consisted of both mechanized regiments. He led the brigade in important maneuvers at Plattsburgh, New York, in 1939 and near Alexandria, Louisiana, in 1940.

Experience in these maneuvers and the example of the German panzer units in Europe had convinced Chaffee, other mechanized cavalry officers, leaders of the infantry tank units, as well as important War Department officials, that American tank and mechanized forces required rapid expansion and that this would best be accomplished by formation of a new, independent organization. On July 10, 1940, the War Department organized the Armored Force, which encompassed all former mechanized cavalry and infantry tank units in addition to supporting infantry, artillery, and engineers. Chaffee was the first commander of the Armored Force which initially consisted of two armored divisions and a separate tank battalion. Over the course of the next year, Chaffee worked to mold these disparate elements into an administratively and operationally unified force. He was rewarded with promotion to major general on October 2, 1940, and a second Distinguished Service Medal. Chaffee died of cancer in August 1941 at Massachusetts General Hospital before the success of his efforts on behalf of mechanization became fully apparent.

As a General Staff officer and unit commander, Adna Chaffee played a crucial role in the development of American mechanized and armored units. In the late 1920s and early 1930s while on the General Staff he stimulated, then kept alive, War Department interest in mechanization. Earlier than most cavalry officers, Chaffee recognized that the horse was no longer a significant factor on the battlefield and that consequently the cavalry had to utilize mechanized vehicles to perform its traditional roles. When he commanded the 1st Cavalry Regiment and the 7th Cavalry Brigade, Chaffee made important original contributions to the formulation of tactical doctrine and organization of mechanized forces. While emphasizing cavalry mobility, he nonetheless made clear that infantry, artillery, and other support units were required to add striking power. The combat command concept of tactical command and control, which enabled any number of units to be attached to a single headquarters depending on the requirements of the assigned mission, was also an original idea of Chaffee's. The mobility, flexibility, striking power, and combined arms organization emphasized by Chaffee as a mechanized cavalry and armored force commander characterized the operations of the American armored divisions employed during World War II. This doctrinal legacy and his administrative ability in organizing the armored force and preparing it for the wartime expansion from two to sixteen divisions earned Chaffee the title father of the American armored force.

BIBLIOGRAPHY

Gillie, Mildred H. *Forging the Thunderbolt: A History of the Development of the Armored Force*. Harrisburg, Pa.: Military Service Publishing Company, 1947.
Nenninger, Timothy K. "The Development of American Armor." *Armor* (January-February, March-April, May-June, and September-October, 1969).
Robinett, Paul M. "Adna Romanza Chaffee." In *Dictionary of American Biography: Supplement Three*. Edited by Edward T. James. New York: Charles Scribner's Sons, 1973.

TIMOTHY K. NENNINGER

CHAUNCEY, Isaac (b. Black Rock, Fairfield County, Conn., February 20, 1772; d. Washington, D.C., January 27, 1840), naval officer. Chauncey is noted for his command on the Great Lakes in the War of 1812.

Little is known of Chauncey's early life. His father, Wolcott Chauncey, was a prominent farmer whose ancestor was the second president of Harvard. At an early age Isaac wished to go to sea. He rose to command his own vessel, the *Jenny*, by the time he was nineteen, and once he singlehandedly brought the vessel into port while all other officers and men were sick with yellow fever.

In June 1799 Chauncey was appointed first lieutenant and superintendent of construction of the 44-gun frigate *President*. Chauncey's commission had been backdated by Congress to September 17, 1798, so that he would be one of the senior lieutenants in the Navy. Mutual interests cemented Chauncey's friendship with the captain of the *President*, Thomas Truxton.* After the Quasi-War with France had ended, Chauncey continued active service as a first lieutenant aboard the *President*. The frigate was sent to the Mediterranean under Captain Richard Dale. Upon his return to the United States in 1802, Chauncey was given his own command, the 36-gun frigate, *New York*, which he sailed to the Mediterranean. Subsequent to that cruise, Chauncey was appointed captain of the 28-gun frigate *John Adams* which was refitting to take supplies to the Mediterranean fleet. During the preparations Chauncey was dispatched to New York City to make the necessary purchases of supplies and to locate superior craftsmen to work for the Navy. There Chauncey married Catherine Sickles. Two of their sons would become officers in the U.S. Navy.

When Chauncey returned to the Mediterranean, the commanding officer, Commodore Edward Preble,* accepted Chauncey as a volunteer to be master commandant of his flagship, the 44-gun frigate *Constitution*, prior to the fierce battle at Tripoli in August 1804. Reassigned to the *John Adams*, Chauncey returned to the United States where he was promoted to captain on April 24, 1806, and given permission to leave the Navy on furlough for merchant service. As captain of the ship *Beaver* owned by John Jacob Astor, Chauncey sailed to China. There he had a confrontation with the Royal Navy, whose ship-of-war, *Lion*, demanded that Chauncey permit members of his crew to be impressed into British service. Chauncey refused to muster his crew or produce the requested papers of citizenship, whereupon the British captain took control of the *Beaver*. Still refusing to cooperate, Chauncey informed the English captain that the *Beaver* was now a prize, and he demanded international adjudication. Quite clearly, the British captain had exceeded his instructions. He released the *Beaver* and its entire crew. Chauncey was one of the few American merchant captains willing to twist the lion's tail. After a profitable voyage, Chauncey returned to the United States where he reclaimed his naval rank and became commanding officer of the New York Navy Yard.

Proper supervision of a naval yard was every bit as important to the young nation as command of warships. Navy Yard commanders were responsible for handling a sizable amount of money for properly administering and supervising the construction and repair of naval vessels. Clearly, this was a job in which Chauncey excelled. He demanded strict accountability and careful supervision. His expertise in New York City was rewarded in August 1812, when he was appointed to superintend the construction of a Great Lakes fleet.

At the time of Chauncey's appointment, the only American vessel on the Lakes was the 16-gun brig *Oneida* which almost was unsailable. The British fleet on the Lakes was composed of six small vessels. Headquartering himself at Sackets Harbor on the eastern end of Lake Ontario, Chauncey created a fleet with little material save huge stands of green timber. He supervised the construction of a naval hospital and navy yard, enlisted workmen and sailors, and transported every type of supply imaginable to the remote northern frontier. President James Madison and Secretary of the Navy William Jones considered the Great Lakes to be the most important post in the Navy. Jones gave Chauncey a free hand over money and materials. Chauncey's shipbuilding and enlistment programs can only be called brilliant. The sailors, although given a bonus, disliked the primitive shore conditions with pine bough huts and the prevalence of disease. Chauncey convinced three experienced shipbuilders to come north and design the American vessels. These men, Henry Eckford on Lake Ontario, and the brothers Adam and Noah Brown on Lake Erie, put together a seaworthy, green-timbered fleet in remarkably little time. On Lake Erie, Oliver Hazard Perry* and the Browns had independent command, and were supplied from Pittsburgh via the Allegheny River. Nonetheless, Chauncey technically was the commanding officer on the Lakes, and he received some credit and the largest share of prize money for Perry's victory on Lake Erie on September 10, 1813. Despite Chauncey's brilliance as a naval administrator, he fell short as a strategist and a fighting captain. Although by the summer of 1813 Chauncey's fleet would be superior to the British fleet on Lake Ontario, he continued to overestimate his foe's strength. He refused to commit his fleet to a major action—the outcome of which everyone knew could decide the outcome of the entire war. While Secretary Jones never lost his confidence in Chauncey, in October 1814 he referred to the naval war on Lake Ontario as "a warfare of Dockyards and arsenals." When offered a chance to seize the strategically crucial port of Kingston in April 1813, Chauncey decided to attack the less important and weaker York (modern Toronto). On September 28, 1813, after learning of Perry's victory, Chauncey challenged Sir James Yeo near Burlington. The British commander quickly discovered that the American fleet outgunned his own, and he fled after only one pass.

Chauncey's other major shortcoming was a myopic concern for naval parity with the Army. Despite an appeal for aid by General Jacob Jennings Brown* on the northern Niagara frontier, Chauncey refused to cooperate fully with the Army. Brown desired naval support when he crossed into Canada in the summer of 1814. After first pleading illness, Chauncey later delayed due to what he called a lack of material, and he formally asked for "some Brevet rank" so that he would be of equal rank to the Army commander when "acting on shore." Chauncey permitted Brown to fight alone. His failure to respond was a key factor in the American inability to maintain its land forces in Canada after the summer of 1814. President James Madison became so disgusted with Chauncey's inactivity that he ordered Stephen Decatur* to take command on the Lakes in late 1814. The president later rescinded the order when he learned that Chauncey's fleet had finally sailed. No decisive battle, however, was fought on Lake Ontario. The nineteenth-century naval strategist, Alfred Thayer Mahan,* maintained that Yeo and Chauncey never wished to force the ultimate test since each "was deeply impressed with the importance of preserving his own fleet, in order not to sacrifice control of the lake."

Following the War of 1812, Chauncey first went to New Hampshire as commander of the Portsmouth Navy Yard where he supervised completion of the 74-gun ship-of-the-line *Washington*. He took the *Washington* as his own flagship when he commanded the Mediterranean Squadron from 1816 to 1818. Because he had difficulty controlling the squadron, Chauncy accepted shore duty for the rest of his life. For most of his remaining twenty-two years, he served on the Board of Navy Commissioners in Washington, D.C. This board was responsible for running the nonpolitical aspects of the Navy, including shipbuilding, supply, personnel, and strategy. From 1825 to 1832 Chauncey again commanded the New York Navy Yard. He died in Washington in 1840.

Chauncey was a heavy, large man, and it was unfortunate for him that his naval career required seaboard service. His competent administration of naval yards was every bit as important as the contributions of the more aggressive captains. His excellence on land, especially on the northern frontier during the War of 1812, was not balanced by a similar genius at sea. That failure, however, at most produced a draw on Lake Ontario, and Chauncey's reputation remains secure today because of his superior contribution in the area of early naval administration.

BIBLIOGRAPHY

Eckert, Edward K. *The Navy Department in the War of 1812*. Gainesville: University of
    Florida Press, 1973.
Forester, Cecil S. *The Age of Fighting Sail, the Story of the Naval War of 1812*. Garden
    City, N.Y.: Doubleday and Company, 1956.
Mahan, Alfred Thayer. *Sea Power in Its Relation to the War of 1812*. 2 vols. Boston:
    Little, Brown and Company, 1905.
Mahon, John K. *The War of 1812*. Gainesville: University of Florida Press, 1972.
Pratt, Fletcher. *Preble's Boys, Commodore Preble and the Birth of American Sea Power*.
    New York: William Sloane Associates, 1950.

                                                                 EDWARD K. ECKERT

CHENNAULT, Claire Lee (b. Commerce, Tex., September 6, 1893; d. Washington, D.C., July 27, 1958), air tactician and commander of the Fourteenth Air Force in China during World War II.

Born in Texas but raised in rural northeast Louisiana, Claire Lee Chennault attended local schools, Louisiana State University, and Louisiana Normal School. Between 1908 and 1913, he held a variety of teaching positions in the South, ranging from English instructor at a business college in Biloxi, Mississippi, to assistant director of physical training at the YMCA in Louisville, Kentucky. American entry into World War I found Chennault married, with three children, and working in a tire factory in Akron, Ohio.

Chennault entered Officers' Training School, Fort Benjamin Harrison, Indiana, in August 1917. Emerging ninety days later as a lieutenant in the Infantry Reserve, he transferred with alacrity to the Aviation Section of the Signal Corps. Initially refused flight training because of age and marital status, Chennault overcame all objections and earned his wings before discharge in April 1920.

The enthusiastic aviator secured a regular commission in the newly organized Air Service in the fall of 1920. Various assignments followed over the next seventeen years, including commander of the 19th Pursuit Squadron in Hawaii, 1923–1926, and instructor at the Air Corps Tactical School, Maxwell Field, Alabama, during the early 1930s. One of those individuals who always seemed to be marching to the beat of a different drummer, Chennault championed fighters at a time when most contemporaries believed that the future lay with bombers. The taciturn Louisianian wrote treatises on pursuit tactics (*The Role of Defensive Pursuit*, 1935), led an acrobatic team to demonstrate some of his theories, and found rewards few and far between. He retired as a captain in April 1937, partially deaf and totally frustrated.

Chennault's career entered a new phase when he went to China in May 1937 as aviation advisor to the Nationalist government of Chiang Kai-shek. He barely had time to initiate a reform program before the Sino-Japanese War broke out in September. Chennault helped to direct Chinese air units and on occasion led them into battle. When Chiang's understrength forces fell victim to the powerful Japanese air armada, Chennault retreated with the government into the interior and opened a flight training school in Kunming. He shared with Nationalist leaders the dark days of 1938–1939, a time when China seemed bereft of friends and hope. His loyalty would be long remembered.

American assistance began flowing to China in 1940. The following year Chennault assumed leadership of the American Volunteer Group (AVG), or "Flying Tigers," an aspect of President Franklin D. Roosevelt's efforts to stiffen Nationalist resistance against Japan. Surmounting numerous obstacles, Chennault had the AVG ready for action on the eve of Pearl Harbor. Over the next seven months, the "Flying Tigers" gained a reputation as the most effective Allied fighter group in the Far East, destroying some three thousand enemy planes at a cost of twelve aircraft and four pilots lost in aerial combat. During a period of despair, when news from abroad sounded like a litany of disaster, the success of Chennault's young flyers in their shark-nosed P-40s gave hope to Americans. For many, the craggy-faced, square-jawed leader of the AVG seemed the very symbol of determined resistance.

Recalled to active duty in April 1942, Chennault took command of the China Air Task Force (July 1942) and, later, the Fourteenth Air Force (March 1943). Logistics was the cross that Chennault had to bear during the war years. His supply lines stretched twelve thousand miles by sea from the East Coast of the United States, through the Panama Canal and across the Pacific to ports on India's west coast; then, fifteen hundred miles by rail, with frequent transshipments, across the Indian subcontinent to Upper Assam; next, five hundred miles by air over the forbidding Himalayas ("The Hump"); and finally, three hundred miles by truck on a tortuous mountain road to forward air bases in east China. And even the meager supplies that did reach the China-Burma-India theater— which held lowest priority in Allied global planning—became the focal point for competing strategy and interests.

Chennault's air units made the best of limited resources and accomplished a great deal against the Japanese. In three years of operations, American flyers claimed some 2,600 enemy aircraft destroyed and 2,230,000 tons of shipping sunk or damaged. Chennault's military career ended on a sour note, however. The acerbic warrior had made too many enemies in high places, notably the Army's influential chief of staff, George Catlett Marshall.* Refused a third star and command of all air forces in the China theater, an embittered Chennault retired shortly before Japan surrendered.

Chennault returned to the Far East in 1946 and established Civil Air Transport (CAT), a contract cargo carrier, in partnership with Whiting Willauer. At the height of the Chinese civil war, 1948–1949, CAT frequently acted as a paramilitary adjunct of the Nationalist Air Force. A vehement anti-Communist, Chennault became a leading public advocate of American support for Chiang Kai-shek. When resistance on the mainland collapsed, he joined the remnants of the Nationalist regime in exile on Formosa. After the Central Intelligence Agency purchased CAT in 1950, marking the beginning of the CIA's extensive network of air proprietaries, Chennault remained active with the airline under a management contract until ill-health forced retirement in 1955. Congress, by special legislation, promoted Chennault to lieutenant general shortly before he died of lung cancer.

Chennault married Nell Thompson on December 25, 1911. Eight children followed. Divorced in 1946, he married Anna Chan on December 2, 1947. This union produced two daughters.

Chennault's controversy with Joseph Warren Stilwell,* commander of the China-Burma-India theater, provided a continuing leitmotif for military, political, and diplomatic aspects of the war in Asia. Two more abrasive personalities could hardly be found. Chennault was belligerent, blunt, and outspoken, and Stilwell shared many of the same qualities. Chennault's ability to inspire loyalty among subordinates was matched only by his capacity to irritate superiors. For his part, "Vinegar Joe" Stilwell was hardly the type of individual to suffer insubordination—or the presumption of insubordination—in silence. At issue was the proper strategy to employ against Japan. Chennault, with the full support of Chiang Kai-shek, coveted the theater's limited resources in order to fight an air war; Stilwell wanted to open a land supply route to China and fight on the ground. Stilwell, according to Chennault, completely lacked appreciation for air power. Chennault, according to Stilwell, had a grossly inflated concept of the ability of air power to affect the course of the war. Compounding these difficulties was the festering problem of command structure. Both Stilwell and Chief of Staff Marshall were incensed by Chennault's direct access (with permission) to

President Roosevelt and his close relationship—too close, they thought—with Chiang Kai-shek.

Roosevelt, following the Trident Conference of May 1943, ordered an emphasis on air power in the China-Burma-India theater; however, supplies were never fully adequate to implement this decision. After Japan's successful offensive in 1944 against Fourteenth Air Force bases in east China, Chennault's influence faded in Washington. At the same time, the Joint Chiefs of Staff decided to bypass Formosa as a base for the final assault against Japan; China thus would remain a backwater until the end of hostilities.

Chennault never lacked detractors, either during the war or after. Critics have emphasized his tendency for dramatic overstatement, especially on the topic of air power, and have viewed with suspicion his unswerving loyalty to the Nationalist cause. Defenders of the controversial airman have been equally vocal. George E. Stratemeyer, for one, has written: "Claire Chennault was an honest, forceful and great air tactician. He deserves much more than our Republic gave him."

BIBLIOGRAPHY

Chennault, Claire Lee. *Way of a Fighter*. New York: Putnam, 1949.

Craven, Wesley Frank, and James Lea Cate, eds. *The Army Air Forces in World War II*. 7 vols. Chicago: University of Chicago Press, 1948–1958.

Romanus, Charles, and Sunderland, Riley. *Stilwell's Command Problems*. Washington, D.C.: U.S. Department of the Army, 1956.

———. *Stilwell's Mission to China*. Washington, D.C.: U.S. Department of the Army, 1953.

———. *Time Runs Out on CBI*. Washington, D.C.: U.S. Department of the Army, 1959.

Schaller, Michael. *The U.S. Crusade in China, 1938–1945*. New York: Columbia University Press, 1979.

Tuchman, Barbara. *Stilwell and the American Experience in China, 1911–45*. New York: Macmillan Company, 1972.

Young, Arthur N. *China and the Helping Hand, 1937–1945*. Cambridge, Mass.: Harvard University Press, 1967.

WILLIAM M. LEARY, JR.

CHURCH, Benjamin (b. Plymouth or Duxbury, Plymouth Colony [now Massachusetts], 1639; d. Little Compton, R.I., January 17, 1718), New England Indian-fighter. Church has been called "the Miles Standish* of the second generation."

Benjamin Church was the son of a Puritan carpenter, and he himself is said to have followed the same craft. In 1667 he married Alice Southworth, daughter of the treasurer of Plymouth Colony. Throughout his long life, Church exemplified the upward mobility of colonial society by his acquisition of land and his shouldering of public responsibilities. In 1670 he was made a freeman of the town of Duxbury. Shortly thereafter, he became one of the twenty-nine proprietors of Sakonnet, forty miles southwest of Plymouth, and was in the process of establishing his home there when the Indian uprising known as King Philip's War broke out in 1675. In later years he served as a deputy in the colony legislature and held other important civil posts as well. A devout Puritan, Church also was a founder of the Congregational church in Little Compton (formerly Sakonnet), the town where he resided from 1705 until his death in 1718.

Church served conspicuously and successfully as a captain in King Philip's War (1675–1676). Active in the July campaign of 1675, he also was present as a member of General Josiah Winslow's staff at the Great Swamp Fight of December 19, 1675, when an intercolonial army attacked and destroyed the principal stronghold of the powerful Narragansett tribe. Had Church's plea to preserve rather than destroy the Indian dwellings and stores of corn been heeded, some English lives which were lost during the subsequent difficult withdrawal might have been saved. The following summer Church was given command of an independent company of volunteers, whites and allied Indians together. Making good use of his Indians' special abilities in the woods, and employing imaginative, innovative tactics, Church proved highly successful in a series of forays against hostile groups. His service in King Philip's War culminated in his entrapment and elimination of Sachem Philip, for whom Church showed no compassion, followed by his daring capture of one of Philip's principal lieutenants, Annawon, for whom Church came to feel much respect. These exploits as an independent commander made Church's name famous throughout New England.

Early in King William's War (1689–1697), the government of Massachusetts solicited Church's services against the hostile Indians in Maine and the French in Acadia. Commissioned a major by Plymouth Colony, he participated in four successive expeditions northward up the coast, utilizing, as before, his effective combination of Indian and white volunteers. On the first of these ventures, in 1689, Church successfully defended the threatened settlement of Falmouth (now Portland, Maine). The following year he overran an Indian village and rescued a number of white captives. In 1692 he destroyed an Indian fort on the Kennebec River opposite the present Waterville, Maine, and returned with considerable plunder. Finally, in 1696, he led an expedition to Acadia, where he destroyed a French settlement and captured an uncompleted French fort, taking some prisoners. These various exploits failed to win for Church the gratitude of the Massachusetts government, and he returned home disgruntled.

Queen Anne's War (1702–1713) against the French and Indians brought Church out of retirement for one last military operation. Commissioned a colonel at Boston on May 4, 1704, he led an expedition up the coast of Maine, using whaleboats for advancing up rivers. Now in his sixties and decidedly corpulent, the old Indian-fighter, when on foot in the woods, required the constant presence of an aide to help him clamber over natural obstacles. The expedition continued on to the French base at Port Royal (now Annapolis Royal, Novia Scotia), but it failed to force the surrender of the fort there. At the agricultural settlement of Les Mines, Church had his men breach the dikes so as to flood the fields. He finally returned to Boston with about a hundred prisoners and much plunder, only to encounter public criticism for the apparently needless killing of a group of Frenchmen in one of the villages he had attacked. Nevertheless, Church did receive an official vote of gratitude from the Massachusetts legislature.

In 1705 Church established his residence at Little Compton. There, in collaboration with his son Thomas, he compiled his memoirs, under the title *Entertaining Passages Relating to Philip's War. . . . As Also of Expeditions More lately Made Against the Common Enemy, and Indian Rebels, in the Eastern Parts of New-England*, which were published at Boston in 1716. Shortly after suffering a fall from his horse, Church died on January 17, 1718, and was buried in the cemetery of the Congregational church at Little Compton. He was survived by his wife and seven children.

Church undoubtedly had an inflated view of his own military exploits, but there is no denying that he was a remarkable commander, especially in King Philip's War where he first established his reputation. Unlike many Indian-fighters, Church liked and respected Indians, an attitude that was reciprocated by many Indians who knew him. On numerous occasions he showed humanity toward them and took a genuine interest in their welfare. Even former enemies found Church to be a remarkably lenient conqueror who used his influence when he could to prevent their being executed or sold into foreign slavery. His practice of sparing captured enemy warriors if they would agree to join his company was novel and courageous, providing him with able recruits. It seems never to have occurred to Church that this was, from the Indian perspective, dishonorable.

Church is most notable as an innovative field commander, in some respects anticipating the style and methods of the famous eighteenth-century ranger, Robert Rogers.* He was a bold leader who inspired his soldiers by his own example of confidence and courage, but sometimes he antagonized his more cautious and less imaginative superiors by his frank criticism of their policies and decisions. While campaigning against elusive bands of Indians he scorned his colleagues' penchant for building forts, preferring instead to go on the offensive whenever possible. He quickly perceived that standard drill-book formations and tactics were not generally effective in wilderness warfare. Therefore, borrowing from the Indians themselves, he developed his own procedures, which proved to be highly effective. When advancing on foot through a wooded area, Church's company of Indian and white volunteers habitually went in a loose, spread-out formation so that the enemy could not easily determine the full strength of the group or suddenly inflict heavy casualties. They moved with stealth, always seeking to exploit the advantage of surprise. One maneuver that sometimes proved effective was to envelop an enemy force by a rapid advance of both flanks. Conversely, Church occasionally made good use of ambush to trap unwary Indians.

Church's highly acclaimed success in King Philip's War, when he still had the zest of youth, was not matched by his performance in the later, more extensive, and difficult operations of King William's War and Queen Anne's War, which suggests that the complexity of higher command was beyond his capability. He was, after all, an amateur at war. But Church's early success and fame as an amateur, and his ready resort to innovative tactics under wilderness conditions, marked the beginning of what was to become a pervasive American military tradition—the woods-wise frontiersman as a more effective fighter in the New World environment than the formally trained European regular soldier.

BIBLIOGRAPHY

Bodge, George M. *Soldiers in King Philip's War.* 3d ed. Boston: Printed for the Author, 1906.
Church, Thomas. *Entertaining Passages Relating to Philip's War Which Began in the Month of June, 1675.* Edited by Henry Martyn Dexter. Boston: John Kimball Wiggin, 1865. (See also the 1975 edition by Alan and Mary Simpson.)
———. *The History of the Eastern Expeditions of 1689, 1690, 1692, 1696, and 1704 Against the Indians and French.* Edited by Henry Martyn Dexter. Boston: J. K. Wiggin and Wm. Parsons Lunt, 1867.
Leach, Douglas Edward. *Flintlock and Tomahawk: New England in King Philip's War.* 1st ed., New York: Macmillan Company, 1958. 2d ed., New York: W. W. Norton, 1966.

DOUGLAS EDWARD LEACH

CLARK, George Rogers (b. November 19, 1752, near Charlottesville, Va.; d. February 13, 1818, near Louisville, Ky.), Revolutionary War military officer, frontier surveyor. Clark is considered the "Conqueror of the Old Northwest."

George Rogers Clark's parents were tobacco planters of Scottish ancestry; his younger brother William* later achieved fame for his work with Meriwether Lewis* in 1804. Young George's formal education was not extensive. At the age of eleven, he and William joined classmates James Madison and John Tyler at Donald Robertson's School, but George could not master French, Latin, or Greek and within eight months he left the institution. His moderate interest in history, geography, and natural phenomena eventually yielded to a fascination for land surveying, and at age nineteen, in 1772, Clark left for the Virginia mountains to perfect his skills.

Embarking upon an adventure along the Ohio River in 1772, Clark joined a company of Virginians and explored the interior of Kentucky. He gained his first military experience in 1774, when he took part in an expedition organized by Lord Dunmore, and he received his first command during that operation as captain of a Virginia militia company.

Early in 1775 Clark returned to Kentucky, ostensibly to survey land for the Ohio Company. He feared competition from Illinois and North Carolina surveyors, but his greatest anxieties concerned British designs upon the area: if the Crown's forces obtained control of centrally located Kentucky, every part of the frontier would become vulnerable to redcoat attack. Consequently, Clark formulated a plan to make Kentucky secure. He requested Patrick Henry, Virginia's governor, to authorize the appropriation of a loan of £500 so that he could purchase gunpowder to defend Kentucky, but he also insisted that Virginia make a commitment to govern that area on a permanent basis. After initial hesitation, the Old Dominion agreed to incorporate Washington, Montgomery, and Kentucky counties into Virginia, commissioned Clark a major with authority to raise a militia company, and supplied him with the necessary troops.

During 1776 and early 1777, Clark and his soldiers fought at three stockades in Kentucky against forces which British Commander Henry Hamilton at Detroit sent from Illinois and Michigan in an effort to secure British control in Kentucky. Shortly thereafter, Clark developed a daring plan to make permanent Kentucky's security by obtaining sufficient manpower to destroy British control in Illinois and Michigan. Early in 1777, the Virginia legislature approved an expedition to seize Kaskaskia, Illinois, and promoted Clark to the rank of lieutenant colonel. The government granted him £1,200 in depreciated currency, authorized him to secure provisions, and permitted him to raise militia. The soldiers were to be publicly informed that their sole objective was the destruction of British power in Kentucky; in fact, Clark was authorized to lead his troops to Kaskaskia—and then Detroit.

On May 12, 1778, Clark led 175 Virginians to Louisville. Then, in July, he revealed the expedition's real objective and pushed into Illinois. The few hundred French inhabitants of that province were located principally at Kaskaskia, Prairie du Rocher, Cahokia, and Vincennes. After traveling 120 miles in six days on flatboats, Clark's men reached the Tennessee River. Hiding their crafts, the frontiersmen marched through prairies and forests for an additional 120 miles, reaching Kaskaskia on July 4, 1778. The Chevalier de Rocheblave, a veteran French officer in British service, had just evacuated the fort. Without firing a shot, Clark's men in fifteen minutes captured Kaskaskia by surprise. After securing the loyalty of the French inhabitants of that town, Clark sent detachments to secure other prairie villages. Although his force was now depleted, Clark insisted upon yet another march. His men moved east to Vincennes, where the British had neglected to post regular troops at Fort Sackville, and for a second time Clark was victorious without firing a shot. On July 20, 1778, the French inhabitants of Vincennes took an oath of allegiance to Virginia, thus completing Clark's conquest of Illinois.

The Virginia legislature was unable to reimburse Clark for cash payments he had made to secure provisions during the Illinois Campaign. What is more, the assembly did not authorize an attack upon Detroit, Clark's final objective. Consequently, on October 7 British Commander Henry Hamilton, discovering that Vincennes lacked protection, organized a counterattack to recover that fort. The situation was now in delicate balance; victory would be awarded to the fleet of foot.

Clark took the initiative. He prepared a winter march to recapture Vincennes. Without assistance from Virginia, he boldly moved out of Kaskaskia on February 6 accompanied by about 150 men and marched east once again to Vincennes.

During the 180-mile trek, an untimely thaw caused rivers to overflow and low-lands to flood; the patriots suffered from physical hardships, fatigue, and other miseries. Clark and his men encountered the Wabash, swollen to a width of five miles, three feet deep at the shallowest. His freezing and starving soldiers built canoes, pushed ahead, slogged through water shoulder deep, and finally reached Fort Sackville. Clark's morale remained high throughout the march. Late in February, the patriots, with drums beating and flags flying, entered Vincennes at dusk, deliberately creating the illusion of a large, powerful invading army. Hamilton was stunned as Clark stormed the solidly constructed fort all night and into the following morning. At daybreak on February 25, 1779, Clark demanded Hamilton's surrender, whereupon the British commander, exhausted and de-moralized after the thirty-six-hour battle, yielded his garrison.

The battle of February 24, 1779, was the turning point of the war in the Illinois country. Unfortunately for Clark, however, Virginia did not support his proposed operations for 1779 and 1780 against Detroit. Finally, in 1781, Clark persuaded Virginia Governor Thomas Jefferson to promote him to the rank of brigadier general, equip him with two thousand soldiers, and authorize an assault against the British outpost in Michigan. Clark encountered a variety of difficulties on his march and was unable to achieve his objective. His final action—a punitive expedition against the pro-British Shawnee at Chillicothe and five other towns, all of which he destroyed—was one of the last military operations of the American Revolutionary War.

Clark retired at age thirty with a pittance from the Virginia legislature. Nor did he receive recognition from European diplomats assembled in Paris for the peace negotiations; his conquest of Illinois was dismissed as an "ephemeral raid." However, Benjamin Franklin successfully argued for the American claim to Illinois, and on September 3, 1783, the U.S. government legally obtained possession of the entire area. Clark's name was not mentioned in the Treaty of Paris.

Eventually returning to live with his parents in Louisville, Clark contended with creditors who learned upon the death of Clark's father in 1799 that the family fortune had become severely depleted: the "Conqueror of the Old North-west" inherited only two slaves. In 1803 Clark retired to a cabin in Clarksville, Indiana, on the falls of the Ohio River. After suffering a paralytic stroke in 1808, in addition to the amputation of a leg, the Virginia legislature finally awarded Clark a pension of $400 per month. A second stroke destroyed Clark's mind in 1813, the year in which Fort Clark, the site of Peoria, was constructed in his honor. He died later at the age of sixty-six. In 1928, the U.S. government appropriated $1 million for a memorial to Clark at Vincennes.

Clark's reputation as a military leader rests chiefly upon the success of his exploits during the American Revolution. A lean, strong six footer with red hair and piercing black eyes, Clark was a born leader of men. Canny, magnetic, and fearless, he evoked unswerving loyalty from his soldiers. Once allegedly engaged to the sister of a Spanish official stationed in New Orleans, Clark never married. He drank heavily upon occasion, although he did not let his fondness for spirits interfere with his military operations. His enemies and subsequently some historians made much of his addiction to liquor, but upon balance it is probably fair to say that the lack of cooperation which he experienced in his dealings with the Virginia legislature hindered his efforts during the Revolution more profoundly than alcohol. Unfortunately, after the war Clark became involved in a variety of activities which cast into serious doubt his integrity and from which his reputation has never fully recovered.

During the summer of 1786 Virginia authorized him to conduct a punitive expedition into Kentucky and Illinois, where the British, still occupying Detroit in violation of the treaty, continued to provoke the Indians. At Vincennes, several of Clark's men mutinied, and Clark was forced to negotiate a peace, leaving only a small garrison at the fort. Governor Edmund Randolph of Virginia chose to believe that Clark was responsible for the mutiny, having presumably, while intoxicated, caused friction between townspeople and troops in Vincennes. Historians have subsequently noted that these allegations were primarily inspired by ex-Brigadier General James Wilkinson,* a notoriously unreliable double agent. Wilkinson made the most of Clark's misfortune at Vincennes in part because Clark was expected to obtain an important public appointment in Kentucky which Wilkinson coveted. Clark was held in public contempt, and his services to state and nation came to an end.

A second series of episodes further clouded Clark's reputation. At the age of thirty-five, destitute and publicly dishonored, Clark tried to pay his debts by offering to help Spain establish a colony in Louisiana. Five years later, Clark volunteered his services to the French government to help reclaim Louisiana, but Washington blocked the scheme. In 1798 Clark joined the French Army as a general and supported an effort to reconquer Louisiana for France. When American military officers demanded that Clark surrender his appointment, he refused, taking shelter in St. Louis instead.

Although these events detracted from Clark's record of service to his country and marred his reputation as a man of honor, historians in recent years have treated such unfortunate episodes as aberrational. His work during the Revolution has not been forgotten, and, recently, a leading scholar of the American Revolution offered a summation of his career in which Clark was described as "an architect of the United States."

BIBLIOGRAPHY

Bakeless, John. *Background to Glory: The Life of George Rogers Clark*. Philadelphia and New York: J. B. Lippincott Company, 1957.

Harrison, J. H. *George Rogers Clark and the War in the West*. Lexington: University of Kentucky Press, 1976.

Havinghurst, Walter. *George Rogers Clark, Soldier in the West*. New York: McGraw-Hill, 1952.

James, James Alton. *The Life of George Rogers Clark*. Chicago: University of Chicago Press, 1928.

Thwaites, Reuben Gold. *How George Rogers Clark Won the Northwest and Other Essays*. Freeport, N.Y.: Books for Libraries Press, 1968.

RICHARD J. HARGROVE, JR.

CLARK, Mark Wayne (b. May 1, 1896, Madison Barracks, N.Y.; d. Charleston, S.C., April 17, 1984), soldier, statesman, author, educator.

Mark Wayne Clark, a 1917 graduate of the U.S. Military Academy, was rapidly promoted and sent to France for World War I. In France he commanded a battalion of the 11th Infantry Regiment and served on the staff of the First Army. After the war he served with the Third Army on occupation duty in Belgium and Germany.

Upon his return to the United States, Clark was sent on the Chautauqua circuit as a speaker. He then was assigned to the Office of the Assistant Secretary of War. In 1925 he graduated from the Infantry School, was assigned to the 30th Infantry Regiment, and from 1929 to 1933 was an instructor with the Indiana National Guard. In 1935 Clark, now a major, was assigned to duty with the Civilian Conservation Corps. Upon graduation from the Army War College, he was posted to Fort Lewis, Washington, and in 1940 was appointed an instructor at the Army War College and promoted to lieutenant colonel. Within months he was ordered to the General Headquarters of the Army to serve as assistant chief of staff for operations. In August 1941 he was promoted to the grade of brigadier general. In early 1942 he was assigned to Army Ground Forces, first as deputy chief of staff and then as chief of staff.

In June 1942 Clark went to Great Britain as commander of Army Ground Forces in Europe, and in October, after promotion to major general, he was named deputy commander in chief of Allied Forces in North Africa. In January 1943 Clark, now a lieutenant general, assumed command of the Fifth Army, which in September 1943 landed in Italy to begin its long and bloody approach march towards Rome, which fell to Clark in June 1944. In December Clark assumed command of the 15th Army Group in Italy, a position he occupied until the cessation of hostilities in Europe. In March 1945 Clark received his fourth star, and in June he was appointed U.S. commander in chief of Occupation Forces in Austria and U.S. high commissioner of Austria. In 1947 Clark assumed command of the Sixth Army and in 1949 became chief of Army Field Forces. In May, 1952 General Clark was sent to Korea as commander in chief, United Nations Command, and U.S. commander in chief, Far East Command. In October 1953 General Clark returned from Korea and retired from active duty to become the president of The Citadel in March 1954. He held this position until July 1965 when he became president emeritus.

As a military commander General Clark's reputation of necessity is based upon his role as commander of two of the more controversial operations in American military history: the Italian campaigns of World War II and the final years of the Korean conflict. Clark's selection for both of these commands was obviously the result of the favorable impressions created by years of diligent work in school, command, and staff assignments. He was promoted from lieutenant colonel to brigadier general in thirteen months, bypassing the rank of colonel, before America entered World War II. His close relationship with both Generals George Catlett Marshall* and Dwight David Eisenhower,* combined with his diplomatic demeanor, made him the ideal choice to establish the American logistical and training program in the European theater. General Clark managed to escape the coils of staff work prior to the invasion of North Africa by leading a clandestine mission to negotiate with French officers in North Africa.

In 1943 Clark was given command of the Fifth Army for the conquest of Italy, which Winston Churchill described as "the soft underbelly of the Axis." Clark's experiences in Italy proved Mr. Churchill wrong, and Rome fell, for only the second time in history, to Clark's forces two days before the Normandy invasion in June 1944. The long and bloody Italian Campaign from Salerno, by way of Cassino, Anzio, and Rome, to the Alps is still one of the more misunderstood operations of World War II. Clark, in his book *Calculated Risk*, relates that after Normandy, Italy was the "forgotten front." He aptly compares his army's role to that of guards and tackles in football who block and tie up the enemy's line, an unglamorous but vital function. Clark's achievements earned for him command of the 15th Army Group and a fourth star, but he was still in Italy, and the primary focus of the war had long since shifted to the North.

Clark's postwar experiences as high commissioner of Austria enhanced his reputation as a soldier-diplomat, and in 1947 he was named as deputy to the U.S. secretary of state to participate in the London and Moscow conferences of the Council of Foreign Ministers. Here Clark demonstrated his abilities in negotiation with the Communists. This experience would be invaluable to him a few years later in Korea.

In 1952 General Clark, as commander in chief of United Nations Command in Korea, found himself once again fighting a determined enemy on a mountainous peninsula. As had been the case in Italy, he was given limited resources to achieve a limited objective. Clark remained committed to the concept of victory, but again, as in Italy, military considerations were secondary. Denied the means to achieve victory by his government and ordered to negotiate an armistice with the Communists, Clark put aside his own personal feelings and called upon his past experiences to attempt to reach a fair and honorable truce in Korea. In that endeavor Clark was successful, but as he stated, "In carrying out the instructions of my government, I gained the unenviable distinction of being the first United States Army commander in history to sign an armistice without victory."

General Clark requested retirement from active service in October 1953. In 1954 his second book, *From the Danube to the Yalu*, was published. He accepted the position of president of The Citadel, and during a tenure of eleven years he guided the academic and military training of 4,046 graduates of that institution.

General Clark has in his lifetime earned repute as a soldier, diplomat, author, and college president. Few Americans have had the opportunity to make the contributions to this nation that General Clark has had, and fewer still have been as successful.

BIBLIOGRAPHY

Blumenson, Martin. *Salerno to Cassino*. Vol. 3: *Mediterranean Theater of Operations* Subseries; *U.S. Army in World War II*. Washington, D.C.: U.S. Government Printing Office, 1969.
Clark, Mark W. *Calculated Risk*. New York: Harper and Brothers, 1950.
————. *From the Danube to the Yalu*. New York: Harper and Brothers, 1954.
Fisher, Ernest F., Jr. *Cassino to the Alps*. Vol. 4: *Mediterranean Theater of Operations* Subseries; *U.S. Army in World War II*. Washington, D.C.: U.S. Government Printing Office, 1977.
Hermes, Walter G. *Truce Tent and Fighting Front*. Vol. 4: *U.S. Army in the Korean War*. Washington, D.C.: U.S. Government Printing Office, 1966.

DAVID CHILDRESS

CLARK, William (b. Caroline County, Va., August 1, 1770; d. St. Louis, Mo., September 1, 1838), explorer, territorial governor, Indian superintendent. Clark was one of the nation's greatest explorers and Indian superintendents.

Clark belonged to an old Virginia family. His ancestors migrated from Scotland to Jamestown in the late seventeenth century. Although born in Virginia, William moved with his family to a new plantation at the Falls of the Ohio (Louisville) in Kentucky in 1785, when he was only fourteen years old. At that time the Kentuckians were carrying on desultory warfare with the hostile Indians living north of the Ohio, and young Clark participated as a militiaman in a number of filibustering expeditions against these tribes in the 1780s and early 1790s. In 1794 he fought as a second lieutenant in the Regular Army under General Anthony Wayne* in the famous Battle of Fallen Timbers. Clark remained in the Army until July 1, 1796, when he resigned his commission as a first lieutenant in order to return home and manage the family plantation in Kentucky.

It was while in Kentucky managing the family plantation that Clark received and quickly accepted the invitation of Meriwether Lewis,* then a captain in the 1st U.S. Infantry Regiment, to join him in leading a military expedition to explore a commercially feasible route from the mouth of the Missouri River across the continent to the Pacific Ocean. Clark had become acquainted with Meriwether Lewis a few months before his resignation from the Army, and perhaps earlier. In late 1795 or early 1796 Ensign Lewis was assigned to the "Chosen Rifle Company" which Clark commanded. The two men maintained at least occasional contact in the ensuing years.

Clark joined Lewis in October 1803 with several young recruits for the expedition as Lewis descended the Ohio River from Pittsburgh in a keelboat. The expedition spent the winter of 1803–1804 at Camp Wood River, Illinois, opposite the mouth of the Missouri, preparing for the journey. While there, Clark was primarily in charge of the camp and the training of the men. Although promised a captaincy in the Corps of Engineers, when it arrived just before the expedition's departure up the Missouri, Clark's commission was as a second lieutenant in the Corps of Artillerists. Nevertheless, on the expedition Clark was treated as a captain—equal in every respect to Lewis. Of the two officers Clark was the more expert waterman, and whenever the Corps of Discovery was traveling by water, he usually stayed with the boats while Lewis walked on shore. He was also the expedition's cartographer and made nearly all of the expedition's maps. A big, bluff, warm-hearted redhead, Clark was the more skilled of the two officers in dealing with the Indians, and he enjoyed a closer relationship with the enlisted members of the party than Lewis.

Following the return of the expedition, as part of the reward for his services, in 1807 Clark became principal Indian agent for Louisiana Territory and brigadier general of its militia. His main duties were to keep the Indians of the Missouri and upper Mississippi at peace and to protect the frontiers of Louisiana in case of Indian attack. To strengthen the defenses of the territory, Clark helped Acting Governor Frederick Bates reorganize its militia, and in 1808 he and Governor Lewis arranged for the establishment of two new frontier military posts—one on the Lower Missouri and one on the upper Mississippi. Through his agents and spies, Clark gathered and relayed to the governors of Louisiana and Illinois, as well as the secretary of war, information on the intentions and activities of the tribes in and near those territories.

As Louisiana's principal Indian agent, Clark received, counseled, and sometimes made agreements with many different delegations of Indians that visited St. Louis. He also escorted a number of delegations of chiefs and principal men to Washington so that they might see the evidence of the great wealth and power of the United States and confer with important federal officials.

In June 1813 Clark became governor of Missouri Territory (as Louisiana was renamed the year before), in which capacity he also served as *ex-officio* superintendent of Indian affairs and commander in chief of the territorial militia. Clark estimated the Indian population under his authority at that time at about sixty-four thousand. There were an additional one hundred thousand or more Indians living farther to the west and north over whom he had only nominal control. Clark became governor of Missouri when the United States was in the middle of the War in 1812, and one of his principal responsibilities was to protect the territory from attack by the hostile tribes of the upper Mississippi. To this end, he had gunboats constructed to patrol the Mississippi above St. Louis, he relocated several hundred friendly Sauk and Fox Indians away from the war zone, and he ordered the erection of a chain of blockhouses along the north side of the Missouri River. In the spring of 1814, then, he led a force of regulars and volunteers up the Mississippi and seized Prairie du Chien, Wisconsin, from the British and their Indian allies, but the Americans were able to hold it for only a short time. He also sent agents to the tribes of the upper Missouri to try to induce those Indians to send war parties out against the pro-British tribes on the upper Mississippi.

After the war, Clark was one of the three commissioners appointed by President James Madison to conclude peace treaties with those hostile tribes. That accomplished, his chief concern was to keep all the tribes friendly and promote trade with them both for the economic benefits to be enjoyed by the American traders and as a means of controlling the Indians.

Soon after the admission of Missouri to the Union as a state, in May 1822 Clark became superintendent of Indian affairs at St. Louis, a post newly created by Congress. In this position he continued to have responsibility for the tribes of the Missouri and upper Mississippi. While trying to keep the Western tribes at peace, during the ensuing decade and a half Clark was mainly concerned with the removal of Indians living east of the Mississippi River and in Missouri to reservations in present eastern Kansas. As the Indians moved westward, the importance of Clark's post gradually declined. His administrative powers were somewhat reduced by the terms of the Indian Administration Act of 1834, and the area of his jurisdiction was made smaller by the creation of Wisconsin Territory in 1836. By this time Clark was in failing health. On August 1, 1838, he celebrated his sixty-eighth birthday, and one month later he died.

Clark's fame depends first and foremost on his achievements as co-leader of the Lewis and Clark Expedition. His early experience growing up on the Virginia and Kentucky frontiers and participating as a junior officer in campaigns against the Indians of the Old Northwest equipped him superbly for joint command of the Corps of Discovery. His steadfastness of character, calm determination, unusual understanding of the Indians, and concern for the welfare of his men, together with his frontier experience, all contributed significantly to the success of that historic enterprise. His genial, extroverted, and humane qualities complemented ideally Lewis's intense, introspective nature.

Besides being a great explorer, Clark was one of the United States' most able and successful Indian agents and superintendents. He enjoyed to a remarkable degree the trust and confidence of thousands of Indians living on the upper Mississippi and on the Missouri and its tributaries. By his advice and wise counsel he contributed greatly to reducing the violent resistance of the Indians living in those vast areas to the inexorable push of the whites into their country. Although not a policymaking official, because of his vast experience and great integrity his superiors frequently asked Clark for advice and help in formulating measures for the management of Indian affairs. The recommendations which he and Governor Lewis Cass of Michigan Territory made in 1828, for example, significantly influenced the framing of the sweeping Indian reorganization and intercourse acts which Congress passed in 1834.

While serving his government ably and conscientiously, Clark sought also to promote the best interests of the Indians as he understood them. In the judgment of his contemporaries, he succeeded exceptionally well in doing so. In 1833,

Pierre Menard, the Kaskaskia merchant-trader and Indian subagent, wrote Clark upon resigning his commission in the Indian Department: "The poor remnant (in this region at least) of those who once covered the greatest portion of our quarter of the Globe, are more indebted to your active and humane exertions, for the comparative happiness which they have in prospect, than to any other individual within my knowledge." Although Clark's attitude toward and treatment of the Indians may be considered by modern standards to have been paternalistic and patronizing, by the standards of his own time and place they were enlightened, fair, and often humane.

BIBLIOGRAPHY

Bakeless, John. *Lewis and Clark: Partners in Discovery*. New York: William Morrow and Company, 1947.

Jackson, Donald, ed. *The Letters of the Lewis and Clark Expedition*. Urbana: University of Illinois Press, 1962.

Osgood, Ernest S., ed. *The Field Notes of Captain William Clark, 1803–1805*. New Haven, Conn.: Yale University Press, 1964.

Steffen, Jerome O. *William Clark: Jeffersonian Man on the Frontier*. Norman: University of Oklahoma Press, 1977.

Thwaites, Reuben G., ed. *The Original Journals of the Lewis and Clark Expedition, 1804–1806*. 7 vols. and atlas. New York: Dodd, Mead, 1904–1905.

JOHN L. LOOS

CLAY, Lucius DuBignon (b. Marietta, Ga., April 23, 1897; d. Chatham, Mass., April 16, 1978), engineer, administrator, military governor.

Lucius D. Clay was a descendant of Senator Henry Clay, the Great Compromisor, and the sixth and youngest child of U.S. Senator Alexander Stephens Clay. During his father's tenure Clay served as a page in the Senate.

Clay entered West Point in 1915, graduating in 1918. (The curriculum had been curtailed because of the ongoing World War.) In a class of 137 he graduated near the top academically, but near the bottom in conduct. Although his first choice was the field artillery, Clay was sent to the engineers. Rapidly promoted to captain because of a dearth of officers in the Corps of Engineers, he reverted to first lieutenant after the war and remained in that rank for seventeen years. His career, until the advent of the Franklin Roosevelt administration, was lackluster at best, there being little scope in the interwar years for Clay's special talents.

The many projects launched under the New Deal allowed Clay to begin to demonstrate his fine administrative talents. On the Works Project Administration (WPA) and the Civilian Conservation Corps (CCC) he worked closely with presidential aide Harry Hopkins. For four years he was also the Corps of Engineers spokesman to Congress. In 1937 Clay served as chief engineer under General Douglas MacArthur* in the Philippines; from 1938 to 1940 he was in charge of the construction of Denison Dam on the Red River in Texas.

Lieutenant Colonel Clay's next assignment was that of assistant administrator of the Civil Aeronautics Authority (CAA), with responsibility for the Defense Airport Program, which included enlarging and improving 277 airports and building 197 new ones. His first wartime post was a mission to Brazil to secure additional air bases, rather than the preferred combat assignment. In March 1942, now the youngest brigadier general in the Army, Clay became assistant chief of staff for Materials, Service of Supply (SOS), later becoming director of materials, Army Service Forces after SOS was reorganized. In brief, Clay was now responsible for the basic details of Army war production—schedules, priorities, deliveries, shortages, allocations. While it was not the assignment Clay had wanted, it was one well suited to his administrative and bureaucratic talents, as well as his personality. In the sometimes intensely jealous atmosphere of wartime Washington as administered by Roosevelt, Clay built a reputation for ability and fairness.

Shortly after D-Day General Dwight David Eisenhower* sent for Clay to help clear the wartorn port of Cherbourg, which was vital to the Allied flow of supplies. In one day the flow doubled; in ten it tripled; and in three weeks the port was functioning very well. Clay received the Bronze Star for this accomplishment, but his escape from Washington proved short-lived. In December 1944, recognizing Clay's administrative abilities, Director of War Mobilization and Reconversion James Byrnes made Clay his deputy, virtually making the general the "third most powerful" man in America after the president and Byrnes.

Clay still hoped for a combat assignment in 1945, but when he was called to a meeting with Roosevelt in March he emerged as Eisenhower's deputy for military government, a position he again owed to Byrnes. Under Eisenhower, and then under General Joseph Taggart McNarney,* Clay had overall responsibility for the maintenance of daily life in U.S.-occupied Germany. Questions of food, housing, health, government, currency, industry, religion, restoring wartime plunder, refugees, denazification all came to him. In addition, he was responsible for the redeployment of troops to the Pacific and then for demobilization; in March 1947 he succeeded McNarney, with whom he did not always get along, as military governor and theater commander (CINCEUR), a unique post for an engineer.

Working at first without firm instructions or interdepartmental consultations, and then from the sometimes impractical and overly restrictive occupation directive JCS 1067, Clay had to rely heavily on his own discretion. However, he quickly established a good working relationship with his political advisor, Robert Murphy of the State Department, and he never lost sight of his own fundamental beliefs about his mission. Paramount among these beliefs were the necessities of keeping the military government separate from the Army Command, of fostering an eventual civilian takeover of the occupation and within Germany itself, and of recreating a viable German state.

Clay also served as the U.S. representative on the Allied Kommandatura, the body responsible for overall Allied occupation policy. Here Clay ran into almost as much friction with the French, who vigorously resisted any effort to reestablish centralized functions within Germany, as he did with the increasingly hostile Soviets.

Early in 1948 Clay began to detect a definite change in Soviet attitudes, and he warned Washington to expect some sort of action, although probably short of war. This expected pressure came in Berlin, as the Soviets restricted and then shut down access to the city in June. Although an early effort to run a train through failed (the troops referred to themselves as "Clay's Pigeons"), Clay remained convinced that the blockade was a bluff that should be called. His superiors in Washington did not agree. Acting on his own initiative as CINCEUR, Clay ordered an airlift begun, and then he convinced President Harry Truman of the necessity and ability to keep Berlin supplied. Operations "VITTLES," the Berlin Airlift, bore out Clay's confidence, bringing in over 2 million tons of food and supplies. In May 1949 the Berlin Blockade was lifted. Clay left Germany on May 15, 1949, and retired from the Army.

Clay remained very active, however. From 1950 to 1962 he was chairman of the board and chief executive of the Continental Can Company; after reaching the mandatory retirement age there, he went on to be a senior partner with the investment banking firm of Lehman Brothers from 1963 to 1973. More significant, perhaps, was his appointment by President John F. Kennedy in 1961 during the Berlin crisis as his personal representative in Berlin, a living symbol of the continuing U.S. commitment to that city.

Clay was also active in the Republican party. In 1952 he was among those who convinced General Eisenhower to seek the presidential nomination; from 1965 to 1968 he chaired the party's National Finance Committee. In addition, he served on numerous civic groups, including the Red Cross and the Public Development Corporation of New York City, which he founded and headed in 1966 at the behest of Mayor John Lindsay.

Lucius D. Clay was among the first of a new breed of professional soldiers— those who built their careers on demanding administrative assignments, some of which shaded across civil-military boundaries, rather than on combat experience. Indeed, Clay's talents for this role were exemplary, especially his ability to take charge of chaotic situations and bring about working order. As World War II was very much a managerial war, Clay's rise during the "Battle of Washington" was not unusual.

His application of these talents to the occupation of Germany was even more demanding, given the dearth and then limitation of instructions. However, by keeping his ultimate goals firmly in mind, and influenced by the experience of his native South during Reconstruction, Clay not only helped rehabilitate a devastated country, but also helped create a new nation. Here Clay had to branch out into the field of diplomacy as well, in an especially trying period as the Cold War rapidly got worse. Perhaps more aggressive than his superiors in Washington, Clay reflected the position of the man on the spot, as well as his usual inclination to get to the heart of the matter.

The ultimate accolade paid to Lucius Clay was the farewell he received from the German people in 1949. Rarely, if ever, has a military governor been so highly and warmly regarded by an occupied people.

BIBLIOGRAPHY

Clay, Lucius D. *Decision in Germany*. Garden City, N.Y.: Doubleday and Company, 1950.
Coles, Harry L., and Albert K. Weinberg. *Civil Affairs: Soldiers Become Governors*. Washington, D.C.: Office of the Chief of Military History, 1964.
Coll, Blanche D., et al. *The Corps of Engineers: Troops and Equipment*. Washington, D.C.: Office of the Chief of Military History, 1958.
Fine, Lenore, and Jesse Remington. *The Corps of Engineers: Construction in the United States*. Washington, D.C.: Office of the Chief of Military History, 1972.
Gimbel, John. *The American Occupation of Germany: Politics and the Military, 1945–1949*. Stanford, Calif.: Stanford University Press, 1968.
Kuklick, Bruce. *American Policy and the Division of Germany*. Ithaca, N.Y.: Cornell University Press, 1972.
Millett, John D. *The Organization and Role of the Army Service Forces*. Washington, D.C.: Office of the Chief of Military History, 1954.
Murphy, Robert. *Diplomat Among Warriors*. Garden City, N.Y.: Doubleday and Company, 1964.
Smith, Jean Edward, ed. *The Papers of General Lucius D. Clay: Germany, 1945–1949*. 2 vols. Bloomington: Indiana University Press, 1974.

MARK M. LOWENTHAL

CLINCH, Duncan Lamont (b. Nash County, N.C., April 6, 1787; d. Savannah, Ga., November 27, 1849), Army officer, politician.

Duncan Clinch was born to parents of good standing in Nash County, North Carolina. If he was christened with a middle name, it was Lamon, but this was altered in time to Lamont. Clinch's father, Joseph John, commanded a regiment of volunteers for local service in the American Revolution, and following that conflict he became a prominent citizen in Nash County. Good family enabled Duncan to obtain a commission as first lieutenant in 1808 without either military experience or a college education. This was possible because on April 12, 1808, Congress had authorized a threefold increase of the Army, and there was no way to officer such an increase except by looking to the sons of "respectable and substantial" families. The catalyst for Army enlargement was the humiliation which Britain's frigate *Leopard* had inflicted on the U.S. frigate *Chesapeake* on June 22, 1807. The very sovereignty of the new nation seemed threatened, and the American people were willing to fight.

Clinch's first task as a commissioned officer was to serve as paymaster of the 3d Infantry Regiment stationed in New Orleans. He performed this duty well enough to be promoted to captain on October 27, 1810. Unfortunately, now he had to leave the pleasant post at New Orleans and go to Baton Rouge. There, although he exercised his first independent command, the post was dull and the work simply routine. Nevertheless, Clinch stuck through that and other boring assignments, a tenacity that paid off during the War of 1812. On August 5, 1813, he became lieutenant colonel of a new regiment of infantry, the 43d, without ever having had to serve as a major. Since his regiment was to be recruited from North Carolina, he went back home.

Within a year Clinch was removed from the 43d and ordered northward toward the active theater of war to join the 10th Infantry. He and the regiment found themselves at Camp Lake Erie, near Buffalo, New York, in an area that had been laid waste by British and Indians in late 1813 and early 1814. Although Clinch commanded a brigade there, the fighting in that region was finished. Indeed, when the war ended, Clinch had experienced no combat.

Clinch went back to Tarboro, North Carolina, to await orders, and although the Army was sharply cut back in size following the war, he retained a commission in it without reduction in rank. He was given command of the 4th Infantry Regiment which late in 1815 was moved to the troubled border between Georgia and Spanish Florida. At Fort Hawkins the health of the Army was generally bad, but Clinch so effectively enforced camp sanitation and chose his camp sites that his regiment was scarcely affected. Thus, he began to gain a reputation for caring for his men better than most other officers.

Clinch and his command transferred from Fort Hawkins to Fort Gaines and then to Camp Crawford on the Apalachicola River closer than before to the trouble on the border. It happened that the simplest supply route for the American installations on the Apalachicola was up the river from the Gulf of Mexico and, of course, through Spanish Territory. Major General Edmund Pendleton Gaines,* commander of the Army in the Southeast, secured permission to use this route from the Spanish government, but this did not make the route secure. The river could be interdicted by the heavy guns of what was known as the Negro Fort, in Spanish Territory. The British had turned this fort over to the Indians and Negroes after the War of 1812, and the recipients had promised not to transfer it to any other nation. In 1816 blacks garrisoned the fort and let it be known that they would allow no American vessels to pass.

Gaines ordered Colonel Clinch to take two companies, 116 men, and to start down the river from U.S. territory in boats, to join with a naval flotilla coming up the river from the Gulf. The campaign ended when the naval gunners on July 26, 1816, lobbed a lucky hot shot into the fort, which happened to land squarely in the middle of an open powder magazine. The fort and its occupants were blown sky high. With not a man lost in Clinch's command, his reputation for taking care of his soldiers rose higher than before.

In 1817, Duncan Clinch was back on the East Coast. He became commander of the Eastern Section of the Seventh Military District with headquarters at Fernandina on Amelia Island. He also had occasion to confer with President James Monroe, who came south on an inspection tour. Monroe sometimes seemed to act on the advice of Clinch on certain military matters.

On April 20, 1819, Clinch was promoted to colonel. In eleven years he had climbed from first lieutenant to colonel, a high rank he attained very close to his thirty-second birthday. This was rapid advancement for that time. In December 1819 Colonel Clinch married Eliza Bayard McIntosh, the daughter of a wealthy and influential Georgia family. Two years later the colonel established his official residence in Camden County, Georgia. In 1821 he also became commandant of the troops in Florida, newly acquired from Spain, with headquarters at Pensacola. He and his growing family lived for five years at Pensacola, and he was responsible for building part of the first road which ran from Pensacola to St. Augustine.

On April 20, 1829, for ten years of faithful service in the grade of colonel, Clinch received the brevet rank of brigadier general. In the ensuing years the new general was transferred here and there in the Southeast. In 1833 the headquarters of the 4th Infantry was Mobile, and the Clinch home was there. But Clinch was sent to Florida because of the growing chance of conflict with the Indians. The 1820s and early 1830s were bad for the Florida Indians. They would not live within the conditions which the United States wanted to impose upon them after it took over Florida. Clinch had had to travel among them a great deal to attempt to persuade or to intimidate them to accept American terms. From this tense duty he was summoned back to Mobile upon the death of his wife on April 15, 1835. Eliza Bayard Clinch died at the age of thirty-four, leaving eight motherless children. Her husband traveled with them to St. Marys, Georgia, where the children were to live with their McIntosh grandparents.

Clinch returned at once to Florida where he established his headquarters at St. Augustine. He was fortunate to be in Florida when the Second Seminole War broke out in December 1835, for his reputation as a general stemmed altogether from that conflict. The Indians annihilated Major Francis L. Dade's column of more than one hundred men, and at Fort King murdered the Indian agent on December 28, 1835. General Clinch did not know of these catastrophes when he started two hundred regular soldiers and five hundred volunteers from the Florida militia toward the Cove of the Withlacoochee River, where it was presumed that the Indian warriors were concentrated. His point of departure was Fort Drane which sat on a small portion of three thousand acres which he owned and which was about twenty-five miles from the Withlacoochee River.

Clinch's small army arrived at the north bank of the river after a slow march but now had to cross to the south side to get to the Cove. The only means to make the crossing was one leaky Indian canoe, in which the commander began to send his regulars across five at a time. This took place on December 31, 1835, and when all the regulars were on the south side, large numbers of Indians, firing from the forest, attacked them. For one reason or another, the volunteers never got across to help the soldiers who were under attack; hence, for a time it was uncertain whether or not the beleaguered troops could be saved. In the end, however, most of them recrossed the river, but four had been killed and fifty-nine wounded. Clinch saw no course open to him but to march his battered army back to Fort Drane.

This was the one action that might be referred to as a battle in the twenty-eight years during which Clinch served in the Army. It made him well known, but by no means universally acclaimed. Bitter disputes over their conduct went on for years between the regulars and the irregulars as to who was at fault. The controversy over Clinch's generalship continued for the rest of his life, and became especially active when in the 1840s he ran for public office. His Whig supporters gave him the honorific name of "Old Withlacoochee," but the Democratic opponents presented him to the voters as a blunderer who had split his army with a wide river between the parts, and who had been turned back by a meager force of savages.

After the Battle of the Withlacoochee, General Clinch remained in the Army only nine months. Major General Winfield Scott* arrived to take command in Florida. He placed Clinch in command of one of the three columns which he expected to converge upon the Indians, and he praised Clinch for his handling of that command. But Scott's entire campaign was a failure, and Clinch, who had been preparing to retire from the Army for some time, insisted upon being released. Although at first refused, he was finally allowed to resign effective September 21, 1836.

For the rest of his life he was known as general, although his permanent rank was colonel. Sometimes his career touched the military establishment: he had to appear and testify before a court of inquiry that attempted to weigh the performance of two of the senior major generals in the service, Scott and Gaines. Clinch would say nothing against either of these men, but he was hard on Lewis Cass, who had been secretary of war in 1835 and 1836. He was invited to serve on the Board of Visitors for the U.S. Military Academy, and he did so serve one time. His oldest daughter, Eliza, married Robert Anderson, a career officer, who happened to be in command at Fort Sumter when the confederates fired on it in 1861. Duncan L. Clinch, Jr., offered himself during the Mexican War and received a commission as captain without prior military experience, but he did not remain in the service long after the war. In April 1841 Congress appropriated $25,756.25 to pay Clinch for property losses during the Florida war.

Duncan L. Clinch married three times, but all of his eight children were by his first wife. He served part of one term, 1843–1844, as Whig congressman from Georgia. Then in 1847 he became Whig candidate for governor, but he lost the election by 1,239 votes. One reason for his loss was that he had never been an effective public speaker, whereas his opponent was eloquent. The end of his life came on November 27, 1849. It was widely noticed throughout the United States, but only in Georgia was he given the honors of a military hero.

Duncan L. Clinch did not come close to equaling the military distinction of such contemporaries as Winfield Scott, Edmund Pendleton Gaines, and Thomas S. Jesup. They had a chance to gain acclaim through combat during the War of 1812 whereas, he, through no fault of his own, did not. His principal contribution to the Army was to serve in it faithfully and efficiently for twenty-eight years at a time when many officers left the service. His career suggests the unprofessional character of the Army in the era before the Military Academy began to supply most Army officers. He, like many other civilians, was able to obtain a commission without any military experience at all, and in his case without any higher education. In addition, even while in the service he was able to be on leave often enough to slowly build up an impressive fortune. At his death his estate was valued at more than $2 million, a princely sum in those days. In that quarter there were fine opportunities to buy land which would appreciate in value, and this Clinch did, especially in Florida.

The enlisted men who served with Duncan Clinch admired him because he was careful of their lives and health, and was sensitive to their suffering. Moreover, during the few times when he was under fire, the men testified to his cool courage. He left a permanent example in the Regular Army of the value of humane treatment of enlisted men, regardless of their origins.

BIBLIOGRAPHY

Bemrose, John. *Reminiscences of the Second Seminole War*. Edited by John K. Mahon. Gainesville: University of Florida Press, 1966.
Mahon, John K. *History of the Second Seminole War*. Gainesville: University of Florida Press, 1965.
Patrick, Rembert W. *Aristocrat in Uniform: General Duncan L. Clinch*. Gainesville: University of Florida Press, 1963.
Sprague, John T. *The Origin, Progress and Conclusion of the Florida War*. Gainesville: University of Florida Press, 1964.

JOHN K. MAHON

COLLINS, Joseph Lawton (b. New Orleans, La., May 1, 1896), World War II division and corps commander; chief of staff, U.S. Army.

Joseph Lawton Collins, son of an Irish-born father, entered the U.S. Military Academy in June 1913 at the age of seventeen. He graduated in April 1917, ranked thirty-fifth in a class of 139. He was commissioned a second lieutenant of artillery, and his first assignment was with the 22d Infantry at Fort Hamilton, New York. Despite stateside assignments in a time of war, Collins won rapid promotions. In less than four months he was a temporary captain; he won his major's leaves in September 1918 when he returned to the 22d Infantry as supply officer.

Collins then spent twenty-six months in Germany, initially commanding a battalion of the 18th Infantry at Coblenz and then serving as assistant chief of staff, G–3, American Forces in Germany. He was promoted to permanent captain in June 1919, a rank he reverted to from temporary major in the following March. He returned to the United States in the summer of 1921 for a four-year assignment as instructor in the Chemistry Department of the U.S. Military Academy. In fact, Collins' career from 1921 to 1933 was entirely devoted to education— student in the Company Officers Course at the Infantry School and in the Field Artillery School's Officers Advanced Course; Infantry School instructor; and student at the two-year Command and General Staff School, Fort Leavenworth. This twelve-year academic stint ended in 1933 with assignment to the 23d Brigade (Philippine Scouts), followed by duty as assistant chief of staff, Intelligence, in the Philippine Division. He was promoted to major in 1932.

Collins returned to the United States in June 1936. He graduated from the Army Industrial College in 1937 and from the Army War College in 1938. From July 1938 until the approaching war forced the institution to close in June 1940, Collins taught at the Army War College. He then served as assistant secretary of the War Department General Staff, with promotion to lieutenant colonel coming in June 1940. The following January found Collins in Alabama as chief of staff of the VII Corps.

Five days after Pearl Harbor, the VII Corps received orders to move to California. Collins soon learned that he was to be chief of staff of the Hawaiian Department, a position which he held from December 1941 until May 1942 and which earned him temporary promotion to brigadier general and a Distinguished Service Medal.

On May 6, 1942, Collins assumed command of the 25th Infantry Division. He took his unit to Guadalcanal the following December where it relieved the 1st Marine Division. Major General Collins also commanded the 25th in the New Georgia Campaign. While in the Pacific, he earned a second Distinguished Service Medal, the Silver Star, and the Legion of Merit. He also picked up the nickname "Lightning Joe," a reference to the lightning bolt depicted on the shoulder patch of the 25th Infantry Division. December 1943 saw his transfer to the European Theater of Operations where, in the following February, Collins assumed command of the VII Corps in England preparing for the invasion of Normandy.

The VII Corps landed on Utah Beach on D-Day, June 6, 1944. Collins came ashore on D plus 1 and led his corps in the capture of the port of Cherbourg. He continued to lead the VII Corps throughout the European fighting until the April 1945 linkup with the Russians on the Elbe River. In the course of the European Campaign, Collins won his third Distinguished Service Medal, his second Silver Star and Legion of Merit, and a Bronze Star Medal. His foreign decorations included the Legion of Honor and Croix de Guerre with Palm (France); Companion Order of Battle (Great Britain); two presentations of the Order of Suvarov (USSR); and the Grand Officer Order of Leopold II and the Croix de Guerre with Palm (Belgium). By April 1945 he had received the three stars of a lieutenant general.

Collins became deputy commanding general and chief of staff, Headquarters, Army Ground Forces, Washington, D.C., in August 1945. Three and one-half months later he became director of information, U.S. Army, followed in June 1946 by assignment as chief of public information. His appointment as deputy chief of staff, U.S. Army, in September 1947 was followed by service as vice chief of staff in November 1948. On August 16, 1949, Joseph Lawton Collins became the eighteenth chief of staff of the U.S. Army. He had been promoted to general in January 1948.

Collins served as chief of staff until August 14, 1953. These four years encompassed the Korean War, a period made more difficult by the disconcerting disagreement between President Harry S. Truman and General Douglas MacArthur.* Service as chief of staff won for Collins his fourth Distinguished Service Medal.

President Dwight David Eisenhower* requested Collins, upon termination of his four-year term as Army chief of staff, to remain on active duty as the U.S. Representative on the Military Committee and Standing Group of NATO. Then in October 1954, Eisenhower asked Collins to interrupt this duty in order to serve as special representative of the United States in Vietnam with personal rank of ambassador. Collins was to recommend a program of assistance aimed at reinforcing the political and economic stability of President Diem's government, as well as improving the internal security of the country. This thankless assignment was beset by endless difficulties. At its termination a year and a half later, Collins remarked to President Eisenhower and Secretary of State John Foster Dulles that he hoped he had not let them down. Dulles replied that when Collins went to Vietnam there was a 10-percent chance of saving that country from communism. "You have raised that figure to at least 50 percent." Collins returned to his NATO assignment until March 31, 1956, when he retired from military service.

In April 1957 General J. Lawton Collins joined Charles Pfizer and Company as vice-chairman of its international division. He held that position until retirement in April 1969. Meanwhile, he had served as vice-chairman and director of the President's Committee for Hungarian Refugee Relief, chairman of the Foreign Student Service Council of Greater Washington, and member of the Board of Trustees of the Institute for International Educators.

The 1917 and 1918 edition of the *Howitzer*, the yearbook of the U.S. Military Academy, said this about the attitude and characteristics of Cadet Lieutenant Joe Collins: "first, concentration and decision, second, rapid and hearty action." The writers of yearbook blurbs seldom are so prescient. This description aptly describes Collins' entire military career. He was short, feisty, and ruggedly handsome. His confidence and enthusiasm were unbounded; he seldom seemed discouraged. General Omar Nelson Bradley* called Collins one of the most outstanding field commanders in Europe and certainly the most aggressive. Having picked the "nervy and ambitious" Collins as corps commander for Operation "COBRA" in France, Bradley told Collins that he had given him all possible support, except his pistol. Collins held out his hand for the pistol.

Bradley also wrote of Collins' "unerring tactical judgment with just enough bravado to make every advance a triumph." To his energy, Bradley continued, "he added boundless self-confidence. Such self-confidence is tolerable only when right, and Collins, happily, almost always was."

This was the man who led the U.S. Army VII Corps from Normandy to the

Elbe, the corps that spearheaded the First Army's breakthrough at St. Lô, blocked the German counterattack at Mortain, and broke through the Siegfried Line and captured Aachen. Later, the VII Corps drove to the Rhine, captured Cologne, and led the First Army attack that enveloped the Ruhr. Collins' admirers were not restricted to fellow Americans; Bernard L. Montgomery said that he was the First Army's most aggressive corps commander.

Collins' postwar positions as deputy chief of staff and vice chief of staff essentially were the same—principal assistant to the chief of staff, U.S. Army. He was, in fact, the author of the headquarters reorganization plan that prompted this change. Combining these jobs with his tour as chief of staff meant that J. Lawton Collins served almost six years in the two top positions of Army leadership.

In addition to his prowess as a combat commander, Collins was an educator, a superb administrator, a diplomat, and a humanitarian. His literary bent resulted in two fine books—*War in Peacetime* and *Lightning Joe, An Autobiography*.

J. Lawton Collins—Lightning Joe—has been called a soldier's general. He was also a general's general which, parodoxically, might be an even greater accolade.

BIBLIOGRAPHY

Blumenson, Martin. *Breakout and Pursuit: U.S. Army in World War II*. Washington, D.C.: U.S. Government Printing Office, 1961.

Collins, J. Lawton. *Lightning Joe, An Autobiography*. Baton Rouge: Louisiana State University Press, 1979.

———. *War in Peacetime, The History and Lessons of Korea*. Boston: Houghton Mifflin Company, 1969.

Harrison, Gordon A. *Cross Channel Attack: U.S. Army in World War II*. Washington, D.C.: U.S. Government Printing Office, 1951.

MacDonald, Charles B. *The Last Offensive: U.S. Army in World War II*. Washington, D.C.: U.S. Government Printing Office, 1973.

———. *The Siegfried Line Campaign: U.S. Army in World War II*. Washington, D.C.: U.S. Government Printing Office, 1963.

BROOKS E. KLEBER

CONNER, David (b. Harrisburg, Pa., 1792; d. Philadelphia, Pa., March 20, 1856), naval officer. Conner was commander of the Home Squadron during the Mexican War.

Conner was descended from Irish immigrants who arrived in the Wyoming Valley of Pennsylvania in the middle of the eighteenth century. His parents David and Abigail Rhodes Conner fled the area after the Wyoming Valley Massacre in 1778 and settled in Harrisburg. Following the death of his father, young Conner in 1806 moved to Philadelphia to join his brother Edward, a West Indies merchant. While working in a counting house, Conner studied French and mathematics and made a voyage to the West Indies.

He applied for a midshipman's warrant, received it on January 16, 1809, and joined the 44-gun frigate *President* (Captain William Bainbridge*) for a cruise along the coast. Conner secured leave in 1810 to serve as mate to Bainbridge during an abortive merchant voyage to St. Petersburg in which the vessel was seized by a Danish privateer.

In August 1811 Conner reported on board the 18-gun sloop-of-war *Hornet* (Master Commandant James Lawrence*). In July 1812, as an acting lieutenant, Conner served as prize master for the former British privateer *Dolphin* but she was recaptured before reaching port. Exchanged soon afterwards, the young officer rejoined the *Hornet*. He served as third lieutenant during her successful February 24, 1813, fight with the British brig *Peacock*. Conner commanded the boats charged with rescuing the crew of the sinking British vessel as well as the abortive efforts to salvage her. He barely escaped when the battered hulk suddenly sank. Conner received a silver medal from Congress for his part in the victory.

When Master Commandant James Biddle* assumed command of the *Hornet* later in the year, Conner, a lieutenant since July 24, 1813, became first lieutenant. After being blockaded in New London, Connecticut, and New York, the sloop finally slipped to sea in mid-November 1814 to join the squadron of Commodore Stephen Decatur.* On January 22, 1815, the *Hornet* met and defeated the British brig *Penguin* off Tristan da Cunha Island. Conner received two wounds. One, a grapeshot in the hip, proved nearly fatal, forced him to use crutches for the next two years, and caused him to suffer from tic douloureux for the rest of his life. His valor during the battle earned him another congressional silver medal.

During 1817–1818 Conner served as Biddle's first lieutenant on the 18-gun sloop-of-war *Ontario* during her voyage around Cape Horn to take formal possession of Oregon. Two years of shore duty at the Philadelphia Navy Yard followed. The young lieutenant then received his first command, the 12-gun schooner *Dolphin*. He sailed the schooner to the Pacific where in 1821–1823 she served in Commodore Charles Stewart's squadron of observation during the Chilean War for Independence.

Shortly after his return from the Pacific, Conner on March 3, 1825, received his promotion to master commandant. He remained on waiting orders in Philadelphia where he married Susan Dillwyn Physick, the daughter of the distinguished surgeon Philip Syng Physick. The following year Conner commanded the 18-gun sloop-of-war *Erie* in the West India Squadron under Commodore Charles G. Ridgeley. He went to sea again in August 1834 as commander of the 18-gun sloop-of-war *John Adams*, assigned to Commodore Daniel T. Patterson's Mediterranean Squadron. On March 3, 1835, Conner was promoted to captain.

Nothing is known of Conner's activities during the next six years, but on July 29, 1841, he assumed office as one of the three Navy commissioners. He moved to chief of the Bureau of Construction, Equipment, and Repair on September 1, 1842, when the bureau system went into effect. He deftly transferred functions from the Board of Naval Commissioners, organized the bureau, and administered it until forced to withdraw by ill-health in January 1843. Ten months later, he replaced Commodore Stewart as commanding officer of the Home Squadron. A cautious diplomat and a firm believer that the difficulties with Mexico could be resolved peaceably, Conner acted circumspectly during the difficult period preceding the outbreak of fighting.

As soon as he realized that the American forces in the disputed territory along the Rio Grande were in danger of attack, Conner hastened northward from Vera Cruz with the bulk of his squadron. They arrived in time to hear the distant boom of cannon at the Battle of Palo Alto. After assisting the army of Brigadier General Zachary Taylor* across the Rio Grande, Conner's squadron clamped a blockade on the Mexican coast. Its operations throughout the summer and fall of 1846 were hampered by a shortage of vessels, supplies, and the need to establish a floating base at Anton Lizardo, near Vera Cruz. Offensive operations required a large number of small craft capable of operating inside the shallow bars that obstructed the mouths of the Mexican rivers, but the vessels were slow to arrive.

Nevertheless, on August 7 Conner led a small force against Alvarado, but he suspended the attack when the weather turned bad; a second attack on October 15 accomplished little more when one of his two small steamers could not cross the bar. Conner dispatched his second-in-command, Commodore Matthew Calbraith Perry,* on an expedition up the Grijalva River against Villahermosa on October 23–24. Although Perry seized the town, he lacked the strength to hold it. Conner himself led the next assault, the seizure of Tampico on November 14. That attack was a preliminary to the Vera Cruz Expedition led by Major General Winfield Scott.* On December 21, Conner's vessels seized the Laguna de Terminos in Yucatan.

Although due for replacement during the summer of 1846, the Polk administration refused to recall Conner who, despite his long separation from his family and deteriorating health, refused to request relief until Scott's army safely reached shore. The landing of Scott's army below Vera Cruz on March 9, 1847, was Conner's most important action during the war. He proposed the landing point at Collado Beach; provided the transportation for many of the assault troops on his warships; and supplied the crews for the landing craft. In less than five hours, nearly ten thousand men went ashore without a loss. While Scott's men lay siege to Vera Cruz, Perry arrived with orders for Conner to transfer command, which he did on March 21. That surrender of command in the midst of an operation cost Conner much of the popular credit which he deserved.

Some of his contemporaries charged Conner with being overly cautious. But he had to conduct his operations without suitable vessels and with no assurance of replacement for any that might be lost. Moreover, he firmly believed that Mexico would not fight a long war and that a negotiated peace was possible at any time.

His return to Philadelphia in May 1847 was greeted by a celebration, and the Order of the Cincinnati bestowed an honorary membership. President James K.

Polk offered him charge of the Bureau of Construction, Equipment, and Repair as a further recognition of his services, but Conner's poor health prevented his acceptance. After a recuperation in Florida, Conner assumed command of the Philadelphia Navy Yard in October 1849. He gave it up the following June, apparently because of ill-health. Placed on the Reserve List in 1855, he died the following year in Philadelphia.

Conner was fond of music, a good dancer, and something of a dandy. He was a leading opponent of flogging, which he called "a remnant of a barbarous age." He had a reputation as a very capable but somewhat aloof officer, demanding but considerate of his juniors; a man untouched by scandal and unafraid to hold his own opinion; a cautious but extremely capable seaman; a man more respected than loved by his contemporaries.

BIBLIOGRAPHY

Bauer, K. Jack. *The Mexican War, 1846–1848*. New York: Macmillan Company, 1974.
————. *Surfboats and Horse Marines*. Annapolis, Md.: Naval Institute Press, 1959.
Callahan, Edward W. *List of Officers of the Navy of the United States and the Marine Corps*. New York: L. R. Hamersly and Company, 1901.
Smith, Justin H. *The War with Mexico*. 2 vols. New York: Macmillan Company, 1919.

K. JACK BAUER

CONNER, Fox (b. Slate Springs, Miss., November 2, 1874; d. Washington, D.C., October 13, 1951), Army staff officer.

Fox Conner was born and raised in Calhoun County, Mississippi, and entered the U.S. Military Academy in 1894. Although he graduated high in his class, he did not upon graduation get to join the cavalry as he wished. Instead, he was commissioned in the field artillery and posted to Fort Adams, Rhode Island. His new regimental commander assigned Conner responsibilities to ensure that he developed into a creditable artillerist, but Conner continued to try for a transfer to the cavalry until 1899.

Conner did not participate in the Cuban Campaign, but he did join the occupation forces there in early 1899, and was stationed at Camp Columbia in Havana. While there, Conner passed his first promotion examination as an artillery man, but, said his judges, there was considerable room for increased technical knowledge of artillery and military engineering. Having acquired some administrative skill and some facility with Spanish, Conner returned to the United States in 1900 to a posting with the artillery unit at Washington Barracks.

By the time Conner appeared before his next promotion board in June 1901, he had considerably improved in his technical fields. At the lyceum library at Washington Barracks, Conner continued his study of Spanish and field artillery. His superiors were beginning to note his potential for assignment to the bureaus of the War Department as well as his capability as an officer of the line.

In November 1901 Captain Conner was given command of the newly formed 123d Company of Coast Artillery at Fort Hamilton, New York. The duties were routine, but Conner had changed his marital status and so he was kept quite busy. The routine of garrison life he used to his best advantage by studying both drill regulations and other subjects, such as "troops in campaign." He was developing a taste for the theories of warfare. His commander noted this interest, and Conner was recommended in 1903 for the General Service and Staff College at Fort Leavenworth. Two years later, the chief of artillery approved Conner's appointment.

By this time, Conner had become a serious soldier and a technically proficient artillerist. Even before he went to Staff College, he had submitted a design for an improved handle for the elevating hand wheels of mortar carriages. By the time he arrived in Leavenworth, Conner had worked hard on his French and could now converse in two languages. He was allowed to skip the first year of schooling at the General Service School and enroll directly in the Staff College year. Predictions for his success at Leavenworth came true: the Staff College recommended him for the faculties of Leavenworth itself, West Point, and the Army War College as well as for numerous staff appointments.

The job he received was post adjutant at Fort Riley, Kansas. There, he was able to take a direct hand in artillery training, and his performance led to his recommendation for the Army General Staff in Washington. Duty on the General Staff included teaching at the War College and service with the 3d Division of the staff, with responsibility for artillery tactical doctrine. Still, the General Staff was not to Conner's liking. He was challenged by the tactical problems he occasionally faced, but he detested having to deal with contemporaries and seniors who were his students at the War College. For all that, his superiors noted that Conner had a particular flair for military research, the conduct of tactical problems, and staff rides. For himself, Conner used his time to develop his fluency in French and German, participating in numerous staff rides in Massachusetts, Pennsylvania, and Virginia, and helping revise the 1911 Field Artillery Regulations.

It was at this time, too, that Conner became involved in the blossoming preparedness movement and was one of several officers on the staff who examined the history of the preparedness of the United States. In a series of letters on this subject, Conner concluded that Congress should be held accountable for taking "the reasonable and necessary measures to fulfill the duties imposed on it by the Constitution." Such a statement served as the perfect introduction to the General Staff's 1912 proposal for the Land Organization of the United States.

In 1912 Conner was selected to be the first American officer to be assigned to a French Artillery Regiment (the 22d). Passing up an offer to become the artillery instructor at West Point, Conner traveled to France, expecting a second year abroad after service with the regiment at the *École Superieure de Guerre*. This plan was foiled, however, when the "Manchu Act" forced Conner's return to the United States (he had spent too much time as a General Staff officer). After three months' duty in Washington on the Field Artillery Board, Conner returned to Fort Riley, where he took command of a battery of the 6th Field Artillery in early 1913.

Conner's regiment moved to the Texas border the following year. The next two years were busy ones for Conner. His competence in artillery was such that he was literally on the move perpetually, from the School of Fire at Fort Sill, to Washington and a seat on the Field Artillery Board, and back to the Southwest. But for a bout with appendicitis, Conner would have been posted to France as an observer in November 1915. By June of the following year, he had finally made it back to France, whose dominant geographical feature was now the trenchlines of the Western Front.

When the United States entered the war, Conner was in a position to be of real value to the Army as a whole. He was made coordinator of the visit of General Joseph Joffre's French Commission to the United States, and while back in the country General John Joseph Pershing* personally chose Conner to be a member of the Advance Staff of the American Expeditionary Force (AEF). Returning to France on the SS *Baltic*, Conner worked under John McAuley Palmer* as a member of the Operations Section mapping the strategy for the employment of an American force in its own sector of the Allied Front, one of the most difficult questions of the early American involvement. The French had particularly insisted upon integrating American troops with their own, disposing them along the front as circumstances required. Pershing and his men mightily— and successfully—resisted any such proposal, insuring in the end that American troops would fight as units. It was a campaign that would last the rest of the war.

Once back in France, Conner continued on the Operations Staff and eventually took charge after Palmer fell ill. Conner fit well as Pershing's man. He was a demanding chief whose meticulous attention to the planning of AEF operations set high standards for all the American staffs and, not least, impressed the French. In one form or another, nearly every major American action of the war came under Conner's view and influence.

Conner's influence continued after the war as well. He was detailed to write the AEF's after-action report. There he discussed the structure of future Army divisions and indeed, the future shape of the Army itself. His arguments were so consistent with Pershing's own views that Pershing used them verbatim as his recommendation to the secretary of war on the National Defense Act of 1920.

From 1921 to 1925 the new Brigadier General Conner commanded a brigade in Panama. For all that he had done until now, this period perhaps saw Conner's most significant achievement. Believing that Versailles had sown the seeds for another war, he determined to seek out and groom a future wartime leader from among his junior officers. The officer he chose, on George Smith Patton's* recommendation, was Dwight David Eisenhower.* Together, the brigadier general and the captain studied the American battles of World War I, conducted three intensive readings of Karl von Clausewitz' *On War*, and discussed the organizational difficulties of the coalition war on the Western Front, a kind of war that Conner thought would be fought in the future. It was a remarkable tutelage with demonstrable results.

Conner's subsequent career was not quite so dramatic. He returned to Washington in 1925 and served as the deputy chief of staff. The battles during these years were over the budget. He argued constantly for centralized control over budget proposals for the General Staff and disapproved of other Army agencies arguing their own cases before congressional committees. He was particularly outraged at the obstreperous officers of the Air Service. In 1928, he left Washington for the last time, and, having been promoted to major general, held commands in Hawaii and New England before retiring in 1938, disappointed that he never achieved the pinnacle for the career staff officer, chief of staff of the Army.

Conner was a "good soldier" in more ways than one. From the beginning of his career, he had disappointments and bore them to the end. When his dissatisfactions overtook him, he would turn to his own pursuits of language and the literature of war, particularly military history. In a branch he did not choose, Conner became a tactical and technical expert in great demand. His intelligence and drive marked him for the staff eventually, and he was never able to escape from it to command troops in wartime. Although it was clear that he thought staff work was a lower order of enterprise for a soldier, he nevertheless made himself so valuable that he rose to high rank without the cachet of combat command. He had a significant influence over the National Defense Act of 1920 by formulating Pershing's own position on the future of the Army. His greatest contribution, however, may have been his influence over the young Eisenhower. Conner was a fiercely loyal subordinate, a superb if stern and demanding teacher, and a meticulous planner; and while Fox Conner is generally unknown to the public, Army professionals like Pershing, George Catlett Marshall,* Patton, and Eisenhower revered Conner and his work.

BIBLIOGRAPHY

Conner, Virginia. *What Father Forbad*. Philadelphia: Dorrance, 1951.
Eisenhower, Dwight D. *At Ease: Stories I Tell to Friends*. New York: Doubleday, 1967.
Pogue, Forrest. *George C. Marshall: Education of a General, 1880–1939*. New York: Viking Press, 1963.

ROBERT FRANK

CONWAY, Thomas (b. February 27, 1735, Ireland; d. ca. 1800), Revolutionary War military officer, supposed co-conspirator in the Conway Cabal.

Very little is known about Thomas Conway's early life. He was born in Ireland during 1735, but removed to France at an early age and received his education there. Conway, a Roman Catholic, was barred automatically from the British Army, and had no alternative but to join a European fighting force if he desired a military career. He joined the French Army, campaigning in Germany during the years 1760–1761. In 1772, he was promoted to the rank of colonel.

During 1776 Conway's reputation as an infantry leader attracted the attention of Silas Deane, American minister to France, who highly recommended him and others for commissions in George Washington's* army. In a letter written on November 29, 1776, Deane noted Conway's advancement by merit, and his fame as one of the most skilled disciplinarians in Europe. Consequently, Conway obtained an appointment to the U.S. Army, left Bordeaux in April 1777, and arrived the following month in North America. He quickly obtained command of a brigade of Pennsylvania troops that happened to be open in Lord Stirling's division, and served with distinction at Brandywine and Germantown. His brigade was considered among the best instructed and disciplined in the Army, and was chosen to lead the attack at Germantown. Afterward, General John Sullivan* observed that Conway's men had "remarkably distinguished themselves," and the Marquis de Lafayette* predicted that Conway was so "brave, intelligent and active" that he would rise rapidly in the Army.

In September 1777, when Baron Johann de Kalb received a promotion to the rank of major general, Conway demanded similar recognition. Not only had Conway outranked de Kalb in Europe, but also Deane had specifically promised Conway equal status with his French Army peers. Unfortunately for Conway, Washington disapproved the promotion, calling the French officer a mediocre braggart. Certainly Conway was voluble, speaking and writing imprudently about his fellow officers and superiors. However, there is also sufficient evidence to conclude that he was at least a competent soldier and probably also possessed superior talents. But Washington's decision was influenced by demands for preferment from older officers whom the commander in chief believed worthier. Conway thereupon offered his resignation and early in October 1777 wrote a letter to General Horatio Gates*—now lost—in which he apparently criticized Washington's generalship. Analogous behavior in Europe was not unusual among French officers, but in the United States Conway's letter caused a sensation. Henry Laurens, president of the Continental Congress, later copied parts of the letter for Washington's information, including a flattering reference to the victor of Saratoga ("what pity there is but one Gates!") and unflattering contrasting remarks concerning Washington (". . . the more I see this army the less I think it fit for general action under its actual chiefs and actual discipline. I speak to you sincerely and freely, and wish I could serve under you.")

On October 27, 1777, James Wilkinson,* an unreliable aide to Gates, held a conversation about that letter with Major William McWilliams, aide to Lord Stirling, at Reading, Pennsylvania, while Wilkinson, en route to Congress with news of Saratoga, was apparently in an intoxicated condition. During the course of the conversation, Wilkinson may have embroidered the substance of the letter, which he had perused in Gates' correspondence file, and which McWilliams transmitted to Stirling, who told Washington on November 8. The following day, in a stinging note, Washington informed Conway that he had been made cognizant of Conway's statement to Gates that "Heaven has been determined to save your country, or a weak general and bad counsellors would have ruined it.'' Very sensitive to criticism, Washington regarded the sentence as a deliberate insult. Henry Laurens later confirmed that the copy of the letter which he examined did not contain the offensive sentence, but John Fitzgerald, one of Washington's aides, noted that ''in substance it contained that and ten times more.'' As Bernard Knollenberg and Paul David Nelson, two scholars of the Conway cabal, have observed, it is curious in the light of Fitzgerald's comment that Laurens' extracts for Washington were comparatively innocuous. As Laurens persuaded Conway not to publish the original (returned to him by Gates who called it ''perfectly harmless'' but feared its publication might aid the British cause), its contents will probably never be known.

Gates replied to Washington on December 8 in high dudgeon, pleading with him to disclose the source of the leak, fearing for Army security, and betraying not the least apprehension concerning the possible unmasking of a ''conspiracy,'' as it was later called. Although Washington should have double checked his sources before writing to Gates, it is interesting to note that Gates did not deny the accuracy of Washington's transcription at that stage, although he did so later.

It was in such a climate of distrust, nurtured by Washington's defeats at Brandywine and Germantown in contrast to Gates' victory at Saratoga, that Congress determined on December 13 to decline Conway's preferred resignation. Instead, it promoted him to major general and in addition created for him the new position of inspector general of the U.S. Army—an appointment that would involve the close cooperation of Washington. It also organized a new board of war and appointed Conway's correspondent, General Gates, to it along with Thomas Mifflin and Timothy Pickering. Congress was presumably still ignorant of Washington's recent contretemps with Conway and Gates. However, interpreting those appointments as deliberate affronts to the commander in chief rather than rewards for outstanding service, Washington and his staff concluded that Conway had joined a widening conspiracy whose object was the replacement of Washington by Gates. In a letter dated February 28, 1778, Washington told Patrick Henry that ''General Conway, I know, was a very active and malignant partisan'' in those plans. However, of all the congressmen and others suspected by Washington and his family of treason against the commander, only Benjamin Rush actually called for Washington's replacement—perhaps by Conway—and he was apparently alone in doing so. Although Gates acted suspiciously and Conway wrote imprudently, there is no evidence to prove that a ''Conway Cabal'' to unseat Washington existed. In truth, Congress most probably desired merely to reward Conway, an able soldier, when it promoted him.

Washington, however, was unpersuaded that such was the case. He deluged Conway, who had also written an impertinent letter to him, with criticism, joined by John Laurens, Alexander Hamilton, Nathanael Greene,* and others. And on January 23, Washington's suspicions deepened when Congress appointed Lafayette, Conway, and John Stark to command a new invasion of Canada. Although such a plan had long been approved in principle, and even though Lafayette and Conway were Catholics identified with France who would be expected to gain support in Quebec, Washington chose to view the decision as yet another example of congressional infringement of his authority (and also an attempt to alienate Lafayette from Washington and lure him to the conspiracy). Lafayette, who had once praised Conway, asserted that Congress was behaving disrespectfully to his chief, and he threatened to return to Europe with other soldiers, thus thwarting the proposed Franco-American alliance. Consequently, Congress appointed de Kalb to replace Conway.

Meanwhile, in February Lafayette journeyed to Albany, where he saw Conway "looking as if he had good intentions; but we know a great deal upon that subject." He feared Conway schemed to replace him, and he complained bitterly to Gates that Conway did not deserve it, that among other things he was not even French. Partly because Lafayette had devoted two months lobbying against Conway instead of organizing the expedition, he found the situation at Albany "quite impossible"—as Conway had written—and on February 26 Congress discontinued the invasion. There was even less reason to suspect a plot in the appointment of Conway to the Canadian Campaign than the November 9 letter or the December 13 promotion, for it would have placed Conway outside the country, far from Washington's army.

In March confidence in Washington returned, and in April the agony of Valley Forge came to an end. On April 28, Conway submitted a formal resignation, which, to his surprise, was accepted. Although he subsequently wrote Gates several letters asking him to gain preferment for him, nothing materialized. On July 4 Conway was seriously wounded in a pistol duel with General John Cadwalader concerning allegations stemming from the supposed conspiracy. Believing himself near death on July 23, Conway wrote to Washington an apology for any offense he might have committed against the commander in chief. It hardly constituted a confession of treason against Washington.

On balance, it would appear that the Conway Cabal was nothing more than a delusion in the mind of Washington, based upon a series of highly questionable assumptions during a time of considerable stress. No evidence has been brought forward in two hundred years to support the allegations of Washington, Lafayette, and others that a deliberate conspiracy to depose the commander in chief existed. That Conway was indiscreet, harsh, and possibly entirely wrongheaded in his appraisal of Washington to Gates may not be doubted. Nor was there an absence of strong criticism of Washington at the time. But the Conway Cabal was more myth than reality.

Conway subsequently returned to France, rejoined its army, and after posting in Flanders during 1779 became commander of a French regiment in Pondicherry, India. In 1784 he was promoted to marechal de camp and achieved the position of governor general of the French colony in the subcontinent in 1787. Honored as a commander of the Order of St. Louis in December 1787, Conway returned to France in 1793. As a royalist, he was compelled to flee, and he died, probably in 1800, in exile. Conway, also known as the Comte de Conway, married the daughter of Marechal Baron de Copley.

BIBLIOGRAPHY

Alden, John R. *The American Revolution 1775–1783*. New York: Harper and Row, 1954.

Burnett, Edmund C. *The Continental Congress*. New York: W. W. Norton, 1941.

Gottschalk, Louis. *Lafayette Joins the American Army*. Chicago: University of Chicago Press, 1937.

Higginbotham, Don. *The War of American Independence: Military Attitudes, Policies and Practice, 1763–1789*. New York: Macmillan Company, 1971.

Knollenberg, Bernard. *Washington and the Revolution, A Reappraisal: Gates, Conway and the Continental Congress*. New York: Macmillan Company, 1940.

Nelson, Paul David. *General Horatio Gates: A Biography*. Baton Rouge: Louisiana State University Press, 1976.

RICHARD J. HARGROVE, JR.

COOKE, Philip St. George (b. Loudoun County, Va., June 31, 1809; d. Detroit, Mich., March 20, 1895), Army officer and Indian-fighter; author of the Army cavalry textbook.

Philip St. George Cooke was the son of Stephen and Catherine Cooke. Stephen, a naval surgeon in the American Revolution, had been captured by the British and taken to St. George, Bermuda, where he met and married Catherine Esten, the daughter of a British official. After the war Dr. Cooke continued his practice in Bermuda, then returned to the mainland, settling in Alexandria, Virginia, in 1791. Ten years later they moved to Leesburg, where Philip St. George was born. (There is a possibility that the Philip was added to his name at West Point, but this is unclear.) For two years Philip lived with his brother, John Rogers Cooke, in Martinsburg (later to be a part of West Virginia), to attend school. At the age of fourteen, Philip's career was determined for life when he enrolled at West Point, where he met Jefferson Davis,* Robert Edward Lee,* Albert Sidney Johnston,* and Joseph Eggleston Johnston,* all to be leaders of the Confederacy. Cooke's West Point record was not especially noteworthy, except for his age—Cooke was some four years younger than virtually all of his classmates. He left the Point in 1827 with a commission as second lieutenant, 6th Infantry, Jefferson Barracks, Missouri, beginning a long career on the Western frontier.

Lieutenant Cooke's first expedition placed him in dangerous Indian Country. For several years merchants of various nationalities had been hauling freight from western Missouri into Mexican territory, sometimes as far as Chihuahua. Because they were often attacked, in 1829 Major Bennet Riley was ordered to escort the traders through Kiowa and Comanche country of present-day Kansas and Colorado to the Mexican border. Riley's mission succeeded except that the Indians waited until the escort had turned back and then attacked the merchants in Mexican territory. Future merchants learned to travel in sufficient numbers that they could reasonably protect themselves. Congress never again asked the Army to escort the merchants, but Cooke had his first experience with the Western tribes.

Shortly after this exposure to Indian warfare, Cooke took leave and met and married Rachel Hertzog, daughter of a Philadelphia merchant. Rachel was to spend most of her life on Army posts, and their son and all three daughters were born at forts near the frontier.

Cooke next fought the Indians in 1832 when he volunteered for the Black Hawk War, participating in the fray at Bad Axe River in Michigan. At the close of the war Cooke, with six years in the infantry, asked for and received an assignment to the newly organized 1st Dragoons. Promoted to first lieutenant, Cooke had found his home. For combat on the Western Plains Cooke was convinced that mounted men were absolutely essential, and in time he was to become the nation's authority on that method of warfare. He spent many months on recruiting duty, often returning to Jefferson Barracks or Fort Leavenworth to train the raw farm boys whom he had enlisted. In 1835 he became captain, usually serving as commander of companies engaged in minor patrol duty on the frontier or leading punitive expeditions against the Indians.

During one of his missions, Captain Cooke acquired the permanent hatred of a number of Texans. In 1843 the Republic of Texas authorized a band of men under Jacob Snively to prey on the Santa Fe merchants to acquire their goods and animals. The U.S. government looked upon this as piracy, and Cooke was ordered to disarm the Texans and get them off the trail. The Texans killed some Mexicans guarding the wagons, but Cooke captured Snively's men, disarmed them, and sent them back to Texas without weapons. As a result, some of the Texans were killed by Indians. In consequence, Cooke earned a positive reputation among the Mexicans, but for years bore the enmity of many Texans.

On occasion Cooke journeyed to South Pass in the Rockies to halt Indian disputes, and in 1845 he escorted emigrant wagons that far to protect them from Indians along the Oregon Trail. In ninety-nine days he and his command traveled twenty-two hundred miles. Few men saw as much of the frontier or knew its residents as well as Captain Cooke.

When the war broke out between Mexico and the United States in 1846, Cooke's experience was immediately sought by Colonel Stephen Watts Kearny,* under whom Cooke had frequently served. Assuming that he would help conquer California, Cooke was delighted. Instead, he received a strange and, to this day, not absolutely clear assignment. With only twelve dragoons Cooke preceded Kearny's Army of the West down the Santa Fe Trail, escorting a merchant, J. Wiley Magoffin, to the Mexican capital for secret discussions with the governor of New Mexico. Some agreements and bribes apparently were exchanged, for the American Army entered Santa Fe without the Mexican troops firing a shot. Kearny's army was now free to move on to California, but not with Cooke. Now a lieutenant colonel of volunteers, Cooke was given command of an independent battalion of some four hundred Mormons, who had enlisted in Iowa for the advanced clothing allowance that would help Brigham Young's desperate band get across the Middle West and into the promised land of Utah. Almost totally lacking military experience, the men were a trial to Cooke, just as his severe discipline tested the Mormons. But they survived and learned to respect one another. With sixty days of rations they covered two thousand miles in ninety days, carving out a new and permanent route to southern California and proving the feasibility of hauling wagons to the Pacific.

Loyal to Kearny, the proper commander of the American troops in California, Cooke took an active part in the John Charles Frémont* affair. He considered Frémont a traitor, helped escort him back to Washington for court-martial, and was on the witness stand for a week in that tense and highly political affair. Unhappy with having to participate in the trial, Cooke was even more disappointed that he could not rejoin his command until after the war had ended.

From 1848 until 1861 Cooke continued his peacetime duties: commanding frontier posts, recruiting, patrolling, impressing Indians. (He reached the rank of colonel in 1858.) But his duty was not always peaceful. He fought the Navajos with Kit Carson and put down the Sioux in the Platte country. In the wake of burnings and terror, he brought law into Kansas Territory, maintaining an uneasy truce among John Brown's abolitionists, slaveholders, and guerillas and bandits of all types. The following year he escorted the governor of the new territory of Utah to his post, in the face of strong Mormon opposition, but diplomatically avoided hostilities until the U.S. government was installed. Meanwhile, Cooke produced a considerable body of military writing, primary among these being elaborations of his journal and, at the request of the War Department, a new study of cavalry tactics, completed in 1860 and adopted almost immediately by the Army.

When the Civil War broke out, Cooke faced the problem of so many regulars— whether his loyalty to the national government or to his state was supreme. Although Cooke publicly confirmed his support of the national government, many officers looked upon him suspiciously. It undoubtedly handicapped his Civil War career, for two sons-in-law (including the famous General James Ewell Brown Stuart*) and his own son chose to go with their state of Virginia into the Confederacy. (In time Cooke's command was to battle with troops led by his son and Stuart.)

Cooke's war career was limited to some minor campaigning in Virginia under General George Brinton McClellan* and some fairly peaceful military government and board duty. He was brevetted major general in 1865, commanded several military districts after the war, and retired in Detroit in 1873.

Philip St. George Cooke's years on the Western Plains corresponded closely to those decades of American expansion when the settlement line moved rapidly west, Indians were fought, and international disputes and border questions were commonplace. Cooke took part in all these affairs and earned company and field grade reputations second to none. A fair, firm man, he also had his share of controversy, some of it lingering all his life, but his skills as a cavalry officer were never questioned. In modern parlance the thin, six foot-four inch Cooke was all "G.I."

Cooke was the beau sabre of American history, the cavalry leader ideal. Through thousands of hours of campaigning, he learned the best methods of mounted warfare and gained recognition for this skill when his government asked him to prepare the textbook for that kind of combat. Yet ironically, while Cooke was perfecting these tactics, America's greatest war made them—and Cooke— obsolete. Like most of his West Point classmates, he could ably command a battalion or a regiment, but the massive numbers of troops and quantities of material of the Civil War armies were beyond their grasp. But Cooke must be remembered for much more: he opened the wagon—and railroad—route to the Pacific, making the Gadsden Purchase a necessity; he gained the respect of the Mormons and helped place them without serious bloodshed into the American family; he brought peace to a divided California and a terrible Kansas; and he once more offered himself to his country in its darkest hour, even though it tore his family apart. Philip St. George Cooke was the ideal frontier soldier.

BIBLIOGRAPHY

Cooke, Philip St. George. *The Conquest of New Mexico and California*. New York: G. P. Putnam's Sons, 1878.
———. *Scenes and Adventures in the Army*. Philadelphia: Lindsay and Blakiston, 1857.
Young, Otis E., Jr. *The West of Philip St. George Cooke*. Glendale, Calif.: Arthur H. Clark, 1955.

THOMAS L. KARNES

CORBIN, Henry Clark (b. Clermont County, Ohio, September 15, 1842; d. New York City, N.Y., September 8, 1909), Civil War and Indian Wars Army officer, adjutant general of the Army. Corbin largely directed the mobilization of the Army for the Spanish-American War and assisted Elihu Root* in Army reform and reorganization.

Henry C. Corbin was the son of Ohio pioneers of Welsh, Irish, and Pennsylvania Dutch ancestry. He grew up on his family's farm near Cincinnati and was educated in public grammar schools and at a private academy. As a young man, he taught school to support himself while he read law with a local attorney.

Corbin's Army service began in the Civil War. In August 1862 he obtained a second lieutenancy in the 79th Ohio Volunteer Infantry by recruiting a portion of a company at his own expense, with little support beyond his own powers of persuasion. Corbin possessed no previous military training or experience. During a year of service with his regiment in the Army of the Ohio and the Department of the Cumberland, he managed to teach himself the rudiments of soldiering by poring over manuals and treatises and asking questions of the few regular officers he met. Corbin was promoted to first lieutenant in May 1863 and eventually became adjutant of his battalion.

On November 14, 1863, after passing a qualifying examination, Corbin received a major's commission in the newly raised 14th U.S. Colored Infantry. He spent the rest of the war with this regiment, much of the time guarding railroads and chasing guerrillas in Kentucky and Tennessee. In late 1864 he participated in the campaign and Battle of Nashville. Corbin rose to the rank of lieutenant colonel of his regiment in March 1864 and to colonel in September 1865. Mustered out of the Volunteer Army in March 1866, Corbin received brevet promotions to brigadier general of volunteers and later to major and lieutenant colonel in the regular service for gallantry in action at Decatur, Alabama, and in the Battle of Nashville.

In May 1866, on the recommendation of his wartime commanders, the War Department offered Corbin a second lieutenancy in the 17th U.S. Infantry. Corbin initially refused this commission and returned to Clermont County to resume law studies. He soon reconsidered, reportedly at the personal insistence of General Ulysses Simpson Grant,* a fellow Clermont County native. On September 3, 1866 Corbin joined the 17th Infantry at Fort Gratiot, Michigan. In July of the following year, he transferred to the 38th Infantry as a captain, and in 1869 he moved to the 24th Infantry in the same rank.

Corbin spent fourteen years as an infantry officer, ten of them in continuous service on the southwestern frontier. He did occupation duty in Austin, Texas, during Reconstruction; he took part in the Mexican border deployment against Maximillian; and he marched, scouted, and fought Indians throughout much of Texas, New Mexico, and Arizona. During Mexican border troubles in the mid-1870s, Corbin performed the delicate task of keeping revolutionary general and future dictator Porfirio Diaz from too blatantly violating U.S. neutrality. In April 1876 Corbin went to Washington to testify on the border situation before a House of Representatives committee, receiving his first taste of politics in the national capital.

In Corbin's career, politics and the military profession became inextricably intertwined after 1876. Corbin's regiment sent him to Columbus Barracks, Ohio, in October of that year on recruiting duty, which was then a customary way of rewarding an officer for long, hard frontier service. At Columbus, Corbin became acquainted with Republican presidential candidate Rutherford B. Hayes and, through Hayes, with other rising Ohio politicians, including James A. Garfield and William McKinley. Corbin's political friends were impressed in part by his appearance. A newspaper writer said of him: "He adorned his uniform, and he and his aguillettes were mutually enhanced. An inch or so over six feet, finely proportioned, [he was] the ideal of a soldier, in figure and bearing." On closer acquaintance, the politicians found Corbin to be competent, tactful, and discreet, bluntly honest in giving private advice on sensitive matters and reliably close-mouthed in public.

Corbin remained at Columbus Barracks from October 1876 to March 1877, except for two months in command of troops at Aiken, South Carolina, during the turmoil accompanying the overthrow of Republican rule in that state. In March 1877 Corbin accompanied President-elect Hayes to Washington as his aide. Corbin spent most of the next three years in Washington, until May 1877, as Hayes' aide and thereafter on recruiting service. He left the capital temporarily to serve as Brigadier General Alfred H. Terry's* aide de camp in the Nez Perce Campaign and then to act as secretary of the commission negotiating Canadian border difficulties caused by Sitting Bull's* activities.

On June 16, 1880, Corbin received a promotion to major and a transfer to the Adjutant General's Office, which was then the real center of Army administration. Initially assigned to duty in Washington as an assistant adjutant general, he remained a member of the White House inner circle under both Hayes and Garfield. He also displayed ability to organize large parades and ceremonies, a task he undertook in addition to his regular duties. He arranged Garfield's inaugural parade and is credited with originating the practice of selling tickets to the inaugural ball to finance the festivities. In 1881 he directed the Yorktown Centennial ceremony. Later in his career, he conducted inaugural ceremonies for Presidents Grover Cleveland, Benjamin Harrison, and McKinley and managed a seventy thousand-man parade for the dedication of Grant's Tomb in New York City.

Corbin left Washington in September 1882 to become assistant adjutant general, Department of the South. A year later, he was transferred to the Division of the Missouri, where he served as assistant adjutant general until March 1891. During this tour of duty, Corbin participated in operations against hostile Indians in 1885 and again in January 1891 in the aftermath of Wounded Knee. He was promoted to lieutenant colonel in June 1889. During a tour as assistant adjutant general of the Department of Arizona (March 1891-December 1892), Corbin distinguished himself in quelling a minor outbreak among the Moqui Indians; he employed quiet diplomacy backed by a show of force to disarm the hostiles without bloodshed. Corbin returned to Washington as assistant in the Adjutant General's Office in December 1892 and became principal assistant in November of the following year. He held this position until October 1895, when he moved to New York as adjutant general, Department of the East. Promoted to full colonel in May 1896, Corbin came back to the War Department again in September 1897 as principal assistant to the adjutant general. On February 25, 1898, as senior colonel of his bureau, he became adjutant general of the Army, with the rank of brigadier general.

During his five years as adjutant general, Corbin made himself chief of staff of the Army in everything but name. His authority resulted in part from the inherent strength of his bureau, which, besides being the principal recordkeeping office of the Army, transmitted all communications from the secretary of war and the commanding general to the other staff bureaus and the field and department commands. It also had charge of mobilizing militia and volunteers in war and contained the Army's embryonic intelligence service. To this advantage, Corbin added tireless energy, decisiveness, and an ability to explain military problems to politicians, including his old Ohio friend, President William McKinley. With over a decade of infantry service behind him, Corbin, unlike most other Washington bureau chiefs, possessed the confidence of line officers. This confidence, combined with tact and an ability to view Army problems from an overall perspective, enabled him to mediate between the perennially feuding line and staff. In addition, Commanding General of the Army Nelson Appleton Miles,* by his erratic political behavior, alienated both McKinley and Secretary of War Russell Alexander Alger,* causing them to rely even more completely on Corbin as advisor and executive agent. As a result, Corbin more than any other individual coordinated the Army's mobilization for the Spanish-American War. His office drafted Army legislation, directed the organization and concentration of almost three hundred thousand regulars and volunteers, and brought a degree of unity of effort to the supply bureaus.

The replacement of the floundering Alger by Elihu Root in August 1899 did nothing to reduce Corbin's influence. The new secretary of war also found in Corbin an able, reliable assistant. In 1900 Root secured Corbin's promotion to major general, to strengthen his authority over the other bureau chiefs. Corbin in turn loyally supported Root's campaigns for Army reorganization, National Guard reform, and creation of a general staff. Colonel William H. Carter, Root's closest advisor on staff reform, was one of Corbin's assistants. Corbin used his influence with Congress and made public speeches on behalf of the reforms. He also helped Root on other matters. In 1901, for example, Root sent Corbin on special assignment to the Philippines, to help reconcile Army commanders there to the establishment of civil government.

In 1903 the newly created General Staff absorbed many functions of the Adjutant General's Office. Corbin, at his own request, returned to line duty as a major general in command of the Department of the East, enlarged in January of the following year into the Division of the Atlantic. While commanding this geographical division, Corbin conducted the first major Army-National Guard peacetime field maneuvers at Manassas in September 1904. In November 1904 he assumed command of the Division of the Philippines, where he supervised the mopping up of remaining rebels, helped settle the garrison in permanent posts, and established cordial relations with the civilian colonial government. Returning to the United States in March 1906, he was promoted to lieutenant general in April and commanded the Northern Division until his retirement on September 15. Corbin died on September 8, 1909, at Roosevelt Hospital in New York City and was buried at Arlington Cemetery.

Henry C. Corbin is probably the least known and least written about of major nineteenth-century American military leaders. This neglect results in part from his own monumental discretion, which left few documentary records of his activities. It also reflects the longstanding preference of military historians for operational over administrative and logistic subjects.

Corbin was both a political soldier and a capable administrator. Early in his career, he acquired powerful friends among the Ohio Republican leaders. Yet he apparently rarely used his backers directly to advance himself. He rose in the Army primarily through his own ability and through the workings of seniority, holding his political backers in reserve, in effect, to protect his rights when necessary. He displayed scrupulous respect for the integrity of the officer corps, especially in matters of promotion, and at times risked alienating his political friends to protect it. When McKinley in 1898 offered Corbin a commission as major general of volunteers, to reward his Spanish-American War services, Corbin gratefully declined. He urged that the few vacancies in that grade be "given to the gallant and more deserving officers serving with troops in the field." The following year, he argued privately but strenuously against the meteoric promotion of Leonard Wood* and blocked politically inspired efforts to award Theodore Roosevelt* the Medal of Honor.

Corbin aligned himself and his office with the Army followers of Emory Upton.* While he was adjutant general, the Army bills emerging from his office bore the Uptonian stamp, including provisions for three battalion regiments and an expansible enlisted force. Corbin used his considerable influence over officer assignments to place Army "Young Turks" like Carter in key positions. He both supported and understood the intent of the Root reforms. In 1905 Corbin declined an offer of the post of chief of staff as a short preretirement sinecure. He reminded then Secretary of War William Howard Taft that the position was intended for a young, vigorous general officer able to serve for at least four years and engage actively in military administration and war planning. Corbin, while not a vanguard theorist, was an influential facilitator of the modernization of the U.S. Army. He was also an early example of the administrator/politician generals who increasingly have dominated twentieth-century high command.

BIBLIOGRAPHY

Alger, Russell Alexander. *The Spanish-American War*. New York and London: Harper and Brothers, 1901.
Chadwick, French E. *The Relations of the United States to Spain: The Spanish-American War*. 2 vols. New York: Charles Scribner's Sons, 1911.
Cosmas, Graham A. *An Army for Empire: The United States Army in the Spanish-American War*. Columbia: University of Missouri Press, 1971.
Dunn, Arthur W. *From Harrison to Harding*. 2 vols. New York and London: G. P. Putnam's Sons, 1922.
Leech, Margaret. *In the Days of McKinley*. New York: Harper and Brothers, 1959.

GRAHAM A. COSMAS

CRAIG, Malin (b. St. Joseph, Mo., August 5, 1875, d. Washington, D.C., July 25, 1945), Army officer; chief of staff, 1935–1939.

Malin Craig, the son of a career Army officer, spent his formative years on various military posts on the Western Plains. Desiring to follow the career of his father, he sought and, in 1894, received an appointment to the U.S. Military Academy. While at West Point he fashioned only a mediocre academic record, but performed very well on the football field, where his abilities as a drop-kicker became legendary. In the spring of 1898 the Spanish-American War erupted, creating a need for junior officers; thus, Craig's class was graduated a month early. Although commissioned in the infantry, he was immediately transferred to the cavalry before being sent to Cuba; from that time on, he always considered himself a "cavalry" man. During the war with Spain, the young officer participated in the Santiago Campaign. Less than two years later, he was off to another foreign land. This time it was to China as part of the Relief Expedition during the Boxer Rebellion. In 1901 he returned home where he married Genevieve Woodruff of Berkeley, California. From that union was to come one son, Malin. Shortly after his marriage, Craig was sent to the Philippines where for three years he was actively involved in putting down the Philippine Insurrection. This tour included service as aide de camp to General James Franklin Bell.*

Having completed five very rewarding years in the field, Lieutenant Craig returned to the states where he attended several service schools, including the Infantry and Cavalry School (1904), Staff College (1905), and the Army War College (1910). It was at these schools that he began to display, for the first time, real ability in the realm of strategy and tactics. These skills, along with his ever-present administrative talents, led to an instructorship at the Army War College in 1911. There followed several assignments at Western posts before going to the Mexican border in 1915 where he again became aide de camp to General Bell. He then joined the staff of the General Service School at Fort Leavenworth, Kansas, in 1916.

When the United States entered World War I in 1917, Craig, then a forty-one year old major, was serving in Washington in the Office of the Chief of Staff. He immediately requested overseas duty and that fall sailed for France as chief of staff of the 41st Division. He subsequently became chief of staff of the I Army Corps. Active involvement in the Second Battle of the Marne and the Saint-Mihiel and Meuse-Argonne offensives provided a wealth of experience as well as numerous decorations. Promotions came rapidly during that period, and near war's end he became a brigadier general. Following hostilities, Craig remained in Germany where he served as chief of staff for the Third Army, the Army of Occupation.

In the 1920s and early 1930s Craig filled a number of key posts such as director of the Army War College, assistant chief of staff, G–3, of the Army General Staff, chief of cavalry and commandant of the Army War College. It was while serving in the commandant post in the fall of 1935 that the quiet, low-keyed major general was unexpectedly selected by President Franklin D. Roosevelt to replace General Douglas MacArthur* as Army chief of staff. That appointment, which carried with it promotion to general, shocked the Washington political and military establishments because Craig had not even been among those mentioned for the post. Many generals had been campaigning vigorously behind the scenes for the position, but Craig had done nothing to put himself forward. In all probability it was this low profile that made him so appealing to the president.

From October 1935 until his retirement in August 1939, Craig served in the Army's top post of chief of staff. His 1939 retirement, after forty-one years of active duty, was short-lived, however. In 1941, with war on the horizon he was recalled to active duty to head the War Department's Personnel Board, a body responsible for selecting individuals who were to receive direct commissions in the Army. He headed the board until shortly before his death in Washington, D.C., on July 25, 1945.

When Craig assumed the chief of staff position in the fall of 1935 the U.S. Army was an ill-equipped, poorly trained force of 147,000 officers and enlisted men. The Army had felt the full brunt of the Great Depression as the Hoover and Roosevelt administrations slashed their budgets severely. Compounding the economic difficulties was the strong isolationist mood that gripped the country and made any additional outlay for military purposes highly unlikely. Under such circumstances, General Craig held little hope of receiving the funds needed to significantly increase Army strength. He therefore came to the conclusion that the next best thing was to develop the machinery necessary to quickly and efficiently mobilize an effective fighting force.

According to Craig, the biggest problem facing him was the "lack of realism in military plans." The mobilization plan then in effect had as its goals the inducting, equipping, and training of a one million man army three months after mobilization began, a two million man force six months after M-Day, and four million combat-ready soldiers one year after M-Day. Under the plan the first increment of troops was to be one million, whether or not that many were needed.

Craig immediately put his war planners to work evaluating the current mobilization plans, and they came to the same conclusion he had: the manpower, training, and supply requirements could not be met in time of emergency. Unfortunately, during his first eighteen months as chief, Craig's efforts to make headway in mobilization planning were stymied because he could not convince Secretary of War George Dern of the need for revision. After Dern's death in the summer of 1936, however, the new secretary, Harry Woodring, was more amenable. Consequently, on December 16, 1936, Craig directed the General Staff to begin development of a new mobilization plan that came to be known as the "Protective Mobilization Plan" (PMP). Under his leadership, the plan was pushed to completion by early 1939.

The PMP introduced a new concept in basic mobilization planning. Whereas the earlier plans called for a million man force by the end of three months, the PMP provided for a well-trained, well-equipped four hundred thousand man "Initial Protective Force" (IPF). This force, comprised of Regular Army and National Guard units would be ready for action one month after M-Day. If that group proved insufficient, there could then be mobilized a six hundred thousand man "Protective Mobilization Force" (PMF), to be ready eight months after mobilization day. From that point on 150,000 men could be provided monthly until four million troops were ready.

Compared with previous mobilization plans, the PMP seemed to be a step backward, but the goals of the earlier plans were clearly unattainable. The soundness of the PMP became quite apparent immediately before and immediately after American entrance into World War II because it served as the basis for the large-scale mobilization of that period. That the U.S. Army was able to mobilize as quickly and efficiently as it did was primarily due to General Craig's success in providing a realistic and workable mobilization plan. For that accomplishment Craig can truly be called the father of World War II mobilization planning.

Craig was also largely responsible for a number of other significant accomplishments such as acquisition of much of the armament and equipment necessary for the one million man Protection Mobilization Force; adoption of the Garand, M–1, semi-automatic rifle to replace the old Springfield; development of the first antitank guns; reorganization of cavalry and infantry divisions in such a way as to provide more flexibility; development of new tanks; and the largest peacetime field exercise ever held up to that time.

Unquestionably, Craig's effectiveness as chief of staff was hindered by an unfortunate feud that disrupted the War Department in the late 1930s. Secretary of War Harry Woodring and Assistant Secretary of War Louis Johnson were involved in a running battle as Johnson attempted to run the department, and Craig was continually caught in the middle of their dispute. In view of the obstacles of feuding, Depression, and isolationism that he faced, Craig's accomplishments as chief of staff are even more impressive.

BIBLIOGRAPHY

Frye, William. *Marshall: Citizen Soldier*. Indianapolis, Ind.: Bobbs-Merrill Company, 1947.

Kreidberg, Marvin A., and Merton G. Henry. *History of Military Mobilization in the United States Army, 1775–1945*. Washington, D.C.: U.S. Government Printing Office, 1955.

McFarland, Keith D. *Harry H. Woodring: A Political Biography of FDR's Controversial Secretary of War*. Lawrence: University Press of Kansas, 1975.

Pogue, Forrest C. *George C. Marshall: Education of a General, 1880–1939*. New York: Viking Press, 1963.

KEITH D. MCFARLAND

CRAZY HORSE (b. ca. 1845; d. Fort Robinson, Nebr., September 6, 1877), Oglala Sioux war leader. Crazy Horse defeated General George Crook* on the Rosebud River and General George Armstrong Custer* on the Little Big Horn in June 1876.

Crazy Horse grew up at a time when the Sioux nation was at the peak of its power. The buffalo were unlimited for these lords of the Plains, who had horses and guns from Europe to hunt and kill with, but who as yet had not had to face the challenge of the white miners, the Army, and the settlers. Crazy Horse rode before he walked, killed his first buffalo before he was ten, went on his first horse-stealing expedition against the Crows before he was a teenager, and led his first war-party himself before he was in his twenties. Like his fellow warriors, he was completely undisciplined; his concern was personal prestige in a fight, not "victory" for the Sioux over the Crows. Unlike his fellows, he did not enjoy bragging about his accomplishments and became noteworthy at an early age precisely because of this unusual behavior. By all accounts, he was absolutely fearless, probably as a result of a vision he had when he was about fifteen years old which promised him that he would never be killed by a bullet. Over the next two decades, he had eleven horses killed under him in fights with other Indians or with soldiers, but was never hit himself.

Immediately upon the conclusion of the Civil War, the whites began to challenge the Sioux for control of the Northern Great Plains. The Army attempted to open a trail (the Bozeman Trail) to the silver and gold mines in Montana. The Sioux, under the general direction of Red Cloud* and reinforced by the Cheyennes (with whom Crazy Horse always had a special relationship because he had relatives among them) and the Arapahoes, laid siege to the soldiers' forts. Crazy Horse led small raids against the soldiers' supply camps and harassed the troopers whenever they emerged from Fort Phil Kearny. Captain William J. Fetterman, anxious to teach the Indians a lesson, decided to drive them away. Red Cloud set up an ambush; young Crazy Horse lured Fetterman and his eighty troopers (he had said, "With eighty men, I can ride through the entire Sioux nation") into a ravine. The oldest trick in Plains warfare worked with spectacular success—Fetterman and all his men were massacred. Shortly thereafter, the whites withdrew from the high Plains country, leaving it to the Sioux, according to the Treaty of 1868, "for as long as the grass shall grow."

In the years following the great victory in the Red Cloud War, Crazy Horse turned his attention to domestic affairs. He ran off with No Water's wife, Black Buffalo Woman; after No Water stole her back, Crazy Horse married Black Shawl, with whom he lived happily until his death. They had one daughter, whom Crazy Horse named They Are Afraid of Her. He hunted, fought the Crows, visited with the Cheyennes, and occasionally skirmished with white soldiers. In the summer of 1873 he turned back a surveying party that was being guarded by General Custer and the U.S. 7th Cavalry, after a sharp little fight at Pompey's Pillar, Montana, on the Yellowstone River.

In 1875 the government tried to buy the Black Hills of South Dakota from the Sioux (Custer had discovered gold there), but the Sioux refused to sell. The government thereupon declared that all Sioux not on a reservation by January 1, 1876, would be considered hostile and shot on sight—in other words, Montana, Wyoming, and the Dakotas were now a free fire zone. Instead of browbeating the Sioux into submission, however, the order led hundreds of Sioux families to leave the reservations to join Crazy Horse, Sitting Bull,* and the other wild Indians of Montana in an act of defiance.

The Army came after the Sioux from the west, south, and east. General George Crook* commanded the column coming from the south, and the Indians were ready. It was the largest encampment of Indians ever seen on the Great Plains; their numbers gave them confidence. In addition, Sitting Bull,* a Hunkpapa Sioux medicine man, had a vision that promised them a great victory. Best of all, the Sioux had Crazy Horse to lead them in battle. When his scouts reported that Crook was approaching, Crazy Horse took about half his men (around two thousand warriors) to attack Crook before Crook could attack the big village. On the morning of June 17, 1876, he found Crook on the Rosebud River. An all-day fight ensued. The Sioux attacked with a ferocity not previously seen on the Plains. On two occasions, Crook's column was saved only by his Crow allies. At the end of the day Crook withdrew. He fell back to his base camp and played no further role in the campaign.

An even greater victory lay ahead for Crazy Horse. On June 25, 1876, George Custer and the 7th Cavalry rode down on the Sioux village, beside the Little Big Horn River in southeastern Montana, and the most famous white versus Indian battle in the history of the Continent took place. Custer ordered Major Marcus Reno and half of the 7th Cavalry to attack the southern end of the village, while he swung around to hit it from the north. But Reno did not attack, primarily because he was so badly outnumbered and his men were exhausted after three days and nights of marching across broken country. When Custer turned to make his assault, he was met by Gall and the Hunkpapa Sioux, who prevented him from crossing the river to reach the village. Custer fell back, towards the high bluffs behind him, in what had become a retreat.

Crazy Horse, meanwhile, had gathered together a force of about one thousand warriors (all counts of Indians in battle are estimates at best), mainly Oglalas but including many Cheyennes. He led them through the village, away from the sound of the guns, past the scene of the Gall-Custer fight, behind some bluffs, and then forded the river. Turning to the south, he reached the high ground, Custer's objective, moments before Custer got there. With a whoop, Crazy Horse's warriors rode down on Custer's men, who now had Gall in front of them, Crazy Horse behind. Within twenty minutes it was over—Custer and his entire command were wiped out.

Inevitably, the Army came gunning after Crazy Horse after that. General Nelson Appleton Miles* kept the pressure on all through the winter of 1876–1877. Worse, the buffalo were just about gone, and with them the Sioux' source of supply. In the spring of 1877 Crazy Horse surrendered the small remaining band that still followed him. He had been promised his own reservation, but instead he was forced to live on Red Cloud's Reservation at Fort Robinson, Nebraska. Red Cloud was jealous of the young upstart who was so much admired by the warriors and urged Crook to send Crazy Horse off in captivity. Fearful that Crazy Horse might go back on the warpath, Crook ordered his arrest. When they attempted to put Crazy Horse into a ball and chain, however, he broke loose and made a dash for freedom. But Little Big Man grabbed his arms, and the guard ran him through with his bayonet. He died that night.

Crazy Horse was remarkable for his courage—even among the Sioux he was held in awe because of his fearlessness—but, more importantly, he was unique among American Indian leaders in that he managed to learn and apply some of the principles of war as practiced by the whites, such as flanking, maneuvering, concentration of force, surprise, and firepower.

BIBLIOGRAPHY

Ambrose, Stephen E. *Crazy Horse and Custer: The Parallel Lives of Two American Warriors*. New York: Doubleday, 1975.

Brown, Dee. *Fort Phil Kearny: An American Saga*. New York: Alfred A. Knopf, 1962.

Hyde, George E. *Red Cloud's Folk: A History of the Oglala Sioux Indians*. Norman: University of Oklahoma Press, 1937.

Sandoz, Mari. *Crazy Horse: The Strange Man of the Oglalas*. Lincoln, Nebr.: University of Nebraska Press, 1942.

Stewart, Edgar I. *Custer's Luck*. Norman: University of Oklahoma Press, 1955.

STEPHEN E. AMBROSE

CROOK, George (b. Taylorsville, Ohio, September 8, 1828; d. Chicago, Ill., March 21, 1890), Army officer. Crook was a noted Union general in the Civil War and very prominent in the Indian Wars after 1865.

George Crook was the son of a prosperous farming family that had originally emigrated to the American colonies from Scotland in the late seventeenth century. During the War of 1812, Crook's father had fought in defense of Fort McHenry. Crook attended school in Dayton, Ohio, and entered West Point on July 1, 1848. He compiled an unenviable academic record at the Military Academy, and in July 1852 he was graduated thirty-eighth in a class of forty-three. Crook was the lowest ranking cadet ever to achieve the rank of major general, U.S. Army. Even as a cadet Crook reflected the laconic, taciturn, and stoical personality that became so well known to his staff and the press in later years.

Crook spent most of the pre-Civil War years of his career fighting hostile Indians in California and Oregon. The rapid settlement of California brought about by gold strikes and a booming economy created conflict between the gold seekers and the Indians. Crook began his life-long study of Indians, their environment, cultures, languages, and ways of warfare. Crook, the cadet who had been at the bottom of his French class at West Point, learned some of the West Coast Indian languages. He preferred field duty to garrison life and was appalled at the drunkenness and dullness of many of his fellow officers. While fighting the Pit River Indians in 1857, Crook was wounded and carried the arrowhead to his grave.

Crook saw extensive action during the Civil War. In September 1862 he was promoted to brigadier general of volunteers and after commanding a division at Antietam (September 1862), he served in West Virginia for several months. In 1863 he took part in the Tullahoma Campaign (June 1863) and fought at Chickamauga (September 1863). Subsequently, he engaged in a brisk chase of Confederate cavalry under General Joseph Wheeler.* In 1864 Crook was assigned to command first the Department of West Virginia and later the VIII Corps in the Army of the Shenandoah under General Philip Henry Sheridan.* Crook and his corps performed in exemplary fashion in the important battles of Winchester and Fisher's Hill (September 1864), but in October they were routed out of their positions at Cedar Creek by a Confederate attack planned by General Jubal

Anderson Early.* In February 1865 Crook was captured by Confederate raiders and spent some time in Richmond's Libby Prison. After being exchanged, he assumed command of the Cavalry Corps of the Army of the Potomac. By the end of the war, he had been cited for gallant and meritorious service on several occasions and had been promoted to major general of volunteers and brevet major general in the Regular Army.

As a lieutenant colonel in the regulars, Crook returned west in 1866. He continued to build his reputation as an innovative Indian campaigner in Idaho, Oregon, and California, but he earned his greatest laurels when pitted against the Apaches of the Southwest. As commanding general of the Department of Arizona from 1871 to 1875, Crook utilized Apache auxiliaries, established a famous logistics service using mule pack trains, and brought peace to that troubled territory. For his brilliant work he was promoted to the rank of brigadier general in 1873. In addition to his organized innovations, a great part of Crook's success with the Apaches lay in his attempt to deal openly and honestly with them.

In 1875 Crook became commanding general of the Department of the Platte and was a principal architect of the vigorous and unrelenting campaign that finally broke the back of Sioux and Northern Cheyenne military resistance. He personally commanded his force of thirteen hundred soldiers and Indian allies against a slightly larger force of hostiles led by Crazy Horse,* the astute warchief of the Oglala Sioux. In a controversial battle at the Rosebud River in Montana on June 17, 1876, Crook and his troops were handled roughly by Crazy Horse and the Sioux, but held the battlefield at the end of the fight. Eight days later at the Little Big Horn, the same warriors destroyed a large portion of the 7th Cavalry under Lieutenant Colonel George Armstrong Custer.* After the 1876 campaign, Crook made it a central part of his policy to protect the Indians from corrupt Indian agents and hostile frontiersmen, and to deal equitably with the various tribes.

Corrupt government agents, a corrosive factional strife between the Indian Bureau and the Army, and white encroachment on Indian lands had undone much of Crook's earlier work in the Southwest. In 1882 Crook was reassigned to the Department of Arizona. The hostile Chiricahua, led by the chiefs Geronimo,* Chato, and Nana, presented the Army with a serious problem. Enlisting Western Apache auxiliaries and taking a few soldiers, Crook plunged into the Sierra Madre of Mexico and successfully apprehended the hostiles in 1883. For two years Indian affairs in the Southwest were peaceful under Crook's stern and watchful eyes. Disgruntled with reservation life, Geronimo and some Chiricahuas left the reservation in 1885. In the spring of 1886 Crook and a handful of men again crossed into Mexico and convinced the hostiles to surrender, but the chary Geronimo again fled. Because of his evenhanded treatment of the Chiricahua and the Western Apaches, Crook was the target of vilification in the frontier press. Furthermore, General Sheridan doubted the wisdom of Crook's using Apaches to fight other Apaches. Other generals, especially Nelson Appleton Miles,* were critical of Crook's tactics. Relations between Crook and Sheridan reached the breaking point, and Crook asked to be relieved of command in Arizona. Crook was reassigned to the Department of the Platte until May 1888. Promoted to major general, Crook moved to Chicago and assumed command of the Division of the Missouri in 1888. Although he was far removed from the frontier, Crook continued to work for Indian rights. Crook never retired, and nearing his thirty-eighth year of active duty, he died in Chicago.

Following important service in the Civil War, General Crook became a central figure in the military history of the American West. He and other soldiers faced the turmoil caused by thousands of settlers spilling into the Indian lands of the Trans-Mississippi. Crook believed that pacification of the West depended upon two factors, military success and equitable treatment of the Indians, whom he believed were often unjustly treated. Crook concluded that white injustice to the Indians lay at the bottom of most of the Indian wars.

To ensure military success against the Indians, Crook stressed innovation and mobility. He scrapped the cumbersome supply wagon trains and developed the mule pack train to such a degree of proficiency that his methods were still utilized in World War II. The soldiers of the Regular Army were seldom able to meet the unique and rigorous demands of fighting the Indians, and, whenever possible, Crook enlisted Indian auxiliaries and scouts. Crook knew that using Indian auxiliaries often demoralized the hostiles, hastened surrender, and saved countless lives. Using mule pack trains and Indian allies, Crook's forces achieved a mobile striking ability denied to traditional army units. His most phenomenal success with his methods came against the Apaches of the Southwest who had defied and defeated the Europeans since the sixteenth century.

Crook realized that winning battles was only a part of maintaining peace between the Indians and settlers. He believed that the only guarantee for any peace was an honest, humane, and consistent Indian policy. Through his long association with the Indians in many parts of the West, he learned that deceitful and corrupt government officials, both civilian and military, caused the terrible wars that resulted in so many deaths. Crook's views on Indian management rankled the Indian Bureau and many residents of the Western states. The use of Indian auxiliaries earned him the animosity of many fellow officers, including General Philip Sheridan (once Crook's friend) and General Nelson Miles, who subsequently found himself forced to use Crook's methods when all else had failed.

The Indians perhaps gave the greatest testimony to the validity of the work of General Crook. He won the friendship and respect of many Indians and their chiefs at the same time he was being abused in the frontier press. Towards the end of his life, Crook became a severe critic of government Indian policy and took his crusade for Indian rights to the public; the shy, quiet general addressed audiences on behalf of the Indians. By the time of his death, the sixty-one-year-old Crook could look back on a career that embraced the settlement of the last American frontier.

BIBLIOGRAPHY

Bourke, John G. *On the Border with Crook*. New York: Charles Scribner's Sons, 1891.
King, Charles. *Campaigning with Crook*. New York: Harper and Brothers, 1890.
Schmitt, Martin, ed. *General George Crook: His Autobiography*. Norman: University of Oklahoma Press, 1960.
Thrapp, Dan L. *The Conquest of Apacheria*. Norman: University of Oklahoma Press, 1967.
Utley, Robert M. *Frontier Regulars: The United States Army and the Indian, 1866–1891*. New York: Macmillan Company, 1973.

JOSEPH C. PORTER

CULLUM, George Washington (b. New York City, N.Y., February 25, 1809; d. New York City, N.Y., February 29, 1892), military engineer, writer. Cullum's lasting achievement was his monumental *Biographical Register of the Officers and Graduates of the U.S. Military Academy* (2d ed., New York, 1867).

George Cullum was the son of Arthur and Harriet Cullum, who moved to Meadville, Pennsylvania, when he was a young boy. Cullum was appointed to the U.S. Military Academy in 1829 and graduated in 1833, third in a class of forty-three. Even as a cadet he demonstrated a keen interest in engineering, military history, and Unitarianism. While still a second lieutenant, he designed the Unitarian church for his friends in Meadville, and his expressed objectives— "durability, economy, simplicity and harmony of parts"—were achieved sufficiently to have the building listed today in the National Register of Historic Places. He also left the Military Academy with strong feelings against "our rebellious Southern brethren" who had supported South Carolina in the Nullification Crisis in 1832, a prejudice he would never outlive.

Upon graduation Cullum served as assistant engineer in the construction of Fort Adams near Newport, Rhode Island, and for the next twenty years he was involved in the design or construction of harbor defenses at Annapolis, Boston, New York, New Bedford, and Charleston. He did not see service in the field during the Mexican War but remained, as he put it, "in honorable exile" at Fort Warren, near Boston, and at West Point, where he supervised construction of a pontoon train of thirty-six India Rubber boats for the army of General Zachary Taylor.* Although rubber pontoons had already been used during the Seminole War (1835), Cullum's pontoon train impressed foreign officers as "the most perfect pontoon train that was ever used in the civilized world," and his professional paper, *Military Bridges with India Rubber Pontoons* (1849) established him as an early authority on the subject.

In 1848 Captain Cullum reported to West Point to teach practical military engineering. Aside from his expressed conviction that what the cadets most needed was "a well digested and complete course on the science and art of war," we know little of his activities as an instructor at the Military Academy. His correspondence during the years before the Civil War, particularly with his good friend, Captain Henry Wager Halleck,* reveals a lively interest in fortification, military literature, and army politics, and soon after the firing upon Fort Sumter in April 1861, Cullum began work on a translation from the French of Duparcq's *Elements of Military Art and History* (New York, 1863), which in his judgment was "the best book" to help prepare the volunteer armies for war. The first months of the war he spent as aide de camp to Winfield Scott,* commander in chief of all Union armies. He also was one of three Army officers apppointed to the Sanitary Commission when it was formed in 1861.

After Scott's retirement in November of that year, Cullum, by now a brigadier general, became Halleck's chief of staff when Halleck was named commander of the Department of the Missouri. In this capacity Cullum served his good friend loyally and with distinction, arranging for the logistical support for Major General Ulysses Simpson Grant* during the Fort Donelson campaign and coordinating the actions between the Army and Navy in the early operations on the Cumberland, Tennessee, and Mississippi rivers. Later he organized the Union defenses at Cairo, Illinois, and Bird's Point, Columbus, Island Number 10 and New Madrid, Missouri. Cullum was chief engineer of the three armies that Halleck commanded in the siege operations at Corinth, Mississippi (April 29-June 10, 1862), and when Halleck was called to Washington later in 1862 to become general in chief, Cullum accompanied his old friend as chief of staff. Early in 1864 Grant replaced Halleck, who was demoted to chief of staff, and Cullum subsequently was named superintendent of the Military Academy, the last to hold that office while West Point was solely the responsibility of the Corps of Engineers. Evidently, the two years he spent there were a success, for none other than Sylvanus Thayer* wrote that Cullum's administration confirmed "the hopes and expectations I conceived when I heard of his appointment, which made my heart bound with joy." From 1866 until his retirement in 1874, Cullum performed various engineering duties. In 1875 he married Halleck's widow; when she died a few years later he left a quarter of a million dollars from Halleck's fortune to West Point to build Cullum Memorial Hall!

His last labors were primarily literary. He wrote biographical and historical articles, produced a lengthy work on the *Campaigns of the War of 1812* (New York, 1879), and compiled his *Biographical Register of the Officers and Graduates of the U.S. Military Academy*. He also found time to serve as vice-president of the American Geographical Society for nearly two years. In 1881 he was a delegate to the Conference of the Association for the Reform and Codification of the Law of Nations in Cologne, Germany. He died at his home on Fifth Avenue after a period of failing health at the age of eighty-three.

Cullum did not lead armies, nor was he ever in the public eye. He was, however, one of the most respected and efficient of that elite Corps of Engineers that labored anonymously on the coastal defenses along the Eastern Seaboard before the Civil War. During the war Lincoln "on more than one occasion" sought his advice: it is probable that Cullum played a part in Halleck's rapid rise in 1862, for Halleck wrote privately that "I owe you . . . very much, my dear Cullum for what you have done for me and hope that I may . . . render you a good turn." Cullum emerged from the Civil War with his reputation intact, although he probably suffered by hitching his wagon to a falling star. It was Grant's army after 1865, a fact which Cullum referred to more than once in his correspondence, and Grant, it was believed, took no particular shining to engineers.

As an educator Cullum was conventional. His greatest contribution to West Point probably was not the time spent there as superintendent or even his several bequests that included Cullum Memorial Hall, but his *Biographical Register*. This work gave a full summary of the career of every West Point graduate (and was brought up to date at ten-year intervals after 1890 in supplementary volumes provided for in his will). This labor of love was the product of exhaustive research, unmatched personal knowledge, and voluminous correspondence. Cullum, however, suffered the defects of his qualities. If his passionate devotion to the Military Academy is apparent on every page, making future generations of West Pointers conscious of their heritage, Cullum never forgave those who had resigned to fight for the "wrong" cause. The career of his friend Robert Edward Lee,* with whom he used to exchange playful letters while both were second lieutenants, is included, but Lee's record as well as the records of every graduate who had joined the Confederacy ends abruptly with the terse comment: "Joined in the Rebellion of 1861–65 against the United States."

BIBLIOGRAPHY

Ambrose, Stephen E. *Duty, Honor, Country: A History of West Point*. Baltimore: Johns Hopkins University Press, 1966.

Cullum, George W. *Biographical Register of the Officers and Graduates of the U.S. Military Academy*. 3d ed. 3 vols. Boston and New York: Houghton Mifflin and Company, 1891.

Warner, Ezra J. *Generals in Blue: Lives of the Union Commanders*. Baton Rouge: Louisiana State University Press, 1964.

JAY LUVAAS

CUSTER, George Armstrong (b. New Rumley, Ohio, Dec. 5, 1839; d. Little Big Horn River, Montana, June 25, 1876), Army officer.

Although the son of an Ohio blacksmith, Custer spent much of his childhood in the home of a half-sister in Monroe, Michigan. He received an appointment to West Point in 1857 and graduated four years later as the goat of his thirty-four member class. In his last year at the academy he displayed the inclination to disregard military rules that later would win him both fame and death when, as officer of the guard, he failed to stop a fight between cadets. Courtmartialed and found guilty, he was saved from punishment by the urgent need for officers to command the rapidly expanding army.

Appointed a second lieutenant in the 2d Cavalry, Custer participated in the campaigning around Washington and came to the attention of General George B. McClellan,* who appointed him as an aide on his staff in June 1862. After

McClellan's replacement Custer moved onto the staff of General Alfred Pleasonton, who assumed command of the Army of the Potomac's cavalry corps in June 1863. In an effort to bring more aggressive leadership to the moribund Union cavalry, Pleasonton secured brigadier's stars in the volunteers for three of his young aides; Wesley Merritt,* Elon Farnsworth, and Custer. The latter was but twenty-three at the time of his promotion.

At Gettysburg, in his first test as a brigade commander, Custer proved the soundness of his promotion by distinguishing himself in the great cavalry battle on July 3. A tenacious, fierce fighter, Custer was utterly fearless but was as careless with the lives of other men as he was with his own. But as the Union army leaders grew more concerned with results than casualties Custer's reputation would continue to rise. When Philip Sheridan* took command of the Army of the Potomac's cavalry in the spring of 1864 he recognized in Custer a kindred spirit and soon came to regard him as one of his most trusted officers. Custer impressed Sheridan with aggressive performances at Yellow Tavern in May, where one of his men killed Jeb Stuart,* and at Trevillian Station in June, where he extricated his men from a Confederate trap.

In the Shenandoah campaign Custer was given command of the 3d Cavalry Division and promoted to brevet major general of volunteers. Sheridan often gave Custer's division the advance and the "Boy General" repeatedly won distinction as Jubal Early's* Confederates were swept from the valley. Even the glory of the Shenandoah was soon overshadowed as Custer's division took a prominent part in cutting off Lee's army in the Appomattox campaign. Custer, always in the front, received the Confederate flag of truce. During the last six months of the war, Custer's division had captured 111 pieces of artillery, 65 battle flags, and nearly 10,000 Confederate soldiers. An appreciative Sheridan purchased the table on which the surrender terms were written and presented them to Custer's wife, declaring that "there is scarcely an individual in our service who has contributed more to bring this about than your very gallant husband." Along with the praise came promotions to brevet brigadier and brevet major general in the regulars and major general of volunteers.

With the disbandment of the volunteer army Custer returned to his regular rank of captain in the 5th Cavalry, but in the army reorganization of 1866 he was commissioned lieutenant colonel of the new 7th Cavalry. Custer held that rank until his death, but since the regiment's colonel remained on detached duty Custer actually commanded the 7th.

Custer saw his first Indian fighting in the unsuccessful 1867 campaign against the southern Cheyennes and their allies led by General W. S. Hancock.* The dismal campaign ended with Custer found guilty by court-martial for being absent from duty to visit his wife. Custer, who felt he was being made a scapegoat for the failure of the ill-planned campaign, was suspended from the army for a year. Sheridan, who replaced Hancock as commander of the Department of the Missouri soon after the court martial, was in complete agreement with Custer on the trial and soon recalled Custer to duty against the Cheyennes. Custer's regiment formed the major strike force of Sheridan's winter campaign of 1868–1869, and on November 27 the Seventh destroyed the village of Black Kettle* on the Washita River in Indian Territory. It was an important victory over a band of Indians that the government had clearly branded as hostiles, but the deaths of numerous Indian women and children and the abandonment of a seventeen-man detachment of the 7th on the field clouded the battle in controversy.

Custer served in Kansas and then on Reconstruction duty in Kentucky before being ordered to the northern plains in 1873. He participated in the 1873 Yellowstone expedition, where he got his first taste of battling the Sioux, and the following year led a 1,200 man expedition to explore the Black Hills of South Dakota. Custer's expedition discovered gold in the Black Hills and the ensuing influx of prospectors helped bring on war with the non-reservation Sioux.

Custer was to have commanded the expedition ordered out in 1876 to force the hostiles onto their reservations, but his testimony before Congress concerning fraud in the management of post sutlerships and Indian traderships won him President Grant's enmity. He was stripped of his command and only the intercession of Generals Alfred Terry* and Sheridan permitted him to accompany the expedition in command of his regiment. The campaign's plan called for three columns to move into the hostile country from different directions: General George Crook* to move north from Fort Fetterman in central Wyoming; Colonel John Gibbon* to move east down the Yellowstone River from Forts Ellis and Shaw in Montana; and General Terry to move west from Fort Abraham Lincoln on the Missouri River. It was hoped that these movements would disconcert the hostiles and drive them into one of the columns.

Unknown to the others, Crook was defeated by Crazy Horse* at the Rosebud on June 17 and forced to retire to his supply base. Meanwhile, Terry's column joined Gibbon on June 21, and a plan was devised whereby Custer would follow an Indian trail up Rosebud Creek while Gibbon moved up the Big Horn and Little Big Horn rivers. Terry would go with Gibbon and the two columns would meet on the Little Big Horn.

Custer, with 655 men, marched rapidly up Rosebud Creek and then crossed to the Little Big Horn where he discovered a large hostile encampment on the morning of June 25. Custer planned to wait another day to give Gibbon's column time to close in, but, discovered by Indian scouts, he decided to attack immediately before the hostiles could escape. Without knowing the size of the enemy force he unwisely divided his command into four parts: Captain Frederick Benteen with three companies was sent off to the left to block the Indians' escape; Major Marcus Reno with three companies was sent up the center to attack the Indian village; Captain Thomas McDougall was detailed with a company to guard the pack train; and Custer with five companies was to support Reno's attack by striking the village from the right. The Indian fighting force, variously estimated at from 1,500 to 5,000, proved larger than anyone had dreamed possible. Reno's attack was repulsed with heavy losses, and he sought safety on some bluffs above the Little Big Horn where he was soon reinforced by Benteen and McDougall. Custer and his five companies, some 212 men, were surrounded and killed. Terry and Gibbon arrived on June 27 and rescued Reno's men. Much of the blame for the disaster must be placed on Custer, whose rashness and overconfidence led him to split his command in the face of a numerically superior army so that it was defeated in detail. It can be argued in his defense, however, that his attack was justified under the circumstances since no one expected the Indians to be so numerous or so willing to stand and fight.

"Custer's Last Stand" has overshadowed the rest of Custer's career and has become one of the best-known battles in American history despite its lack of military importance. Custer quickly emerged as the symbolic hero of the Army in the West and was lionized throughout the following fifty years. Recent shifts in the popular mood regarding the plight of the Indians have led to Custer, still ever the symbol, becoming identified as a villainous figure. Despite this shift in popular opinion, Custer and his last battle continue to fascinate the public.

While still alive Custer nurtured this public fascination. He realized the usefulness of dramatic flair to impress soldiers and civilians alike, and so during the Civil War sported a uniform of black velvet trimmed with gold braid. On the western plains he adopted the fringed buckskin suit of the frontiersman, but kept the crimson scarf and shoulder-length, reddish-blonde hair from his Civil War days. Custer was one of the most flamboyant officers ever to serve in the Army, and most observers failed to understand him, blinded by either the gallant cavalier or the eccentric egomaniac. Those who served with him in the Civil War tended to remember him with "a pistol in his boot, jangling spurs on his heels, and a ponderous claymore swinging at his side—a wild daredevil of a general, and a prince of advance-guards, quick to see and act." But to many who rode with him on the western plains he was "an incarnate fiend" and a "complete example of a petty tyrant," who spared neither man nor beast in his search for glory. Sheridan, who perhaps knew him best, fondly remembered that "if there was any poetry or romance in war Custer could develop it." He saw in Custer the aggressiveness and blind courage so essential in an effective cavalry officer. But Sheridan also recognized the volatile side of Custer's character, feeling him "too impetuous, without deliberation; he thought himself invincible and having a charmed life." According to Sheridan, Custer was a man-child who "was as boyish as he was brave and always needed someone to restrain him." At Little Big Horn there was no one to offer a restraining hand.

BIBLIOGRAPHY

Custer, Elizabeth B. *Boots and Saddles, or Life in Dakota with General Custer*. New York: Harper & Brothers, 1885.

Custer, George Armstrong. *My Life on the Plains or, Personal Experiences with Indians*, Edgar I. Stewart, ed. Norman: University of Oklahoma Press, 1962.

Graham, W. A. *The Custer Myth: A Source Book of Custeriana*. New York: Bonanza Books, 1957.

Jackson, Donald. *Custer's Gold: The United States Cavalry Expedition of 1874*. New Haven: Yale University Press, 1966.

Merington, Marguerite, ed. *The Custer Story: The Life and Intimate Letters of General George A. Custer and His Wife Elizabeth*. New York: Devin-Adair, 1950.
Monaghan, Jay. *Custer: The Life of General George Armstrong Custer*. Boston: Little Brown, 1959.
Stewart, Edgar I. *Custer's Luck*. Norman: University of Oklahoma Press, 1955.
Utley, Robert M., ed. *Life in Custer's Cavalry: Diaries and Letters of Albert and Jennie Barnitz 1867–1868*. New Haven: Yale University Press, 1977.

PAUL A. HUTTON

D

DAHLGREN, John Adolphus Bernard (b. Philadelphia, Pa., November 13, 1809; d. Washington, D.C., July 12, 1870), naval officer. Dahlgren is best known for inventing the heavy naval cannon used in the Civil War.

John A.B. Dahlgren was the eldest son of a Swedish immigrant to the United States and his American wife. He secured an appointment as an acting midshipman in the Navy in 1824 and made cruises with the Brazilian and Mediterranean squadrons. After promotion to passed midshipman in 1832, he served with distinction with the U.S. Coast Survey from 1834 to 1837 until failing eyesight forced him to take an extended sick leave of four years. After returning to active duty in 1842, Dahlgren, who had been promoted to lieutenant in 1837, spent another cruise in the Mediterranean as aide to the squadron commander. At the outbreak of the Mexican War, he requested sea duty but was sent instead to the Washington Navy Yard in 1847 as an assistant inspector of ordnance in charge of rocket manufacture.

During his fifteen years at that post, Dahlgren modernized the Navy's heavy and light cannon and established a position as the service's leading authority on ordnance. First, he constructed a firing range to determine the accuracy of the Navy's principal cannon. Next, in 1849, he designed and won departmental approval for a new howitzer for use on small boats and by shore parties. In 1850 and 1851 Dahlgren submitted plans for more powerful smoothbore cannon of 9-inch and 11-inch caliber. Despite initial resistance from senior officers Dahlgren eventually won approval for the guns. These cannon (which the British disparagingly nicknamed "soda-water-bottles" because of their distinctive shape) were a significant departure from the previous types because they were designed to fire only shell projectiles filled with explosives rather than solid-shot. They were also much heavier in weight and larger in caliber than earlier guns. These cannon were used extensively throughout the Civil War by both Union and Confederate forces, and they were found to be highly effective in firing solid-shot at Confederate ironclads, although Dahlgren had not intended them for that purpose. Due to the lack of replacements, these guns served as the main battery weapons for the Navy until the early 1890s. In the late 1850s, Dahlgren experimented with rifled cannon, but the conservatism of the ordnance bureau chief prevented much progress. Dahlgren was promoted to commander in 1855.

At the outbreak of the Civil War, Dahlgren quickly won the appreciation of the Federal government by fortifying the strategically important Washington Navy Yard. President Abraham Lincoln* liked Dahlgren, and the officer became his confidant. As soon as Dahlgren could be spared from the navy yard, he was elevated to command of the Bureau of Ordnance in July 1862 with the rank of acting rear admiral and permanent captain. A year later, the resignation of the commander of the South Atlantic Squadron, Rear Admiral Samuel Francis Du Pont,* and the death of Rear Admiral Andrew Hull Foote,* Du Pont's appointed successor, opened the way for Dahlgren to take command, despite the fact that he had not been on sea duty for many years. Under his control, the squadron failed in its second attempt to take Charleston, South Carolina. For the remainder of the war, the squadron's duty consisted primarily of maintaining the blockade.

Dahlgren commanded the Pacific Squadron from 1866 to 1868 and then returned to Washington as chief of the Bureau of Ordnance in July 1868. He found the duty distasteful because the lack of funds prevented making improvements or experimentation. With the change in presidential administration in 1869, he arranged to take command of the Washington Navy Yard where he died in the summer of 1870.

John Dahlgren influenced American naval ordnance development through his cannon designs and advocacy of a system of mounting guns, his establishment of facilities for developing and testing weapons, and his role as a career model for line officers who specialized in ordnance work.

In designing the famous ''soda-water-bottle'' shaped cannon in 1850 and 1851, Dahlgren consciously applied the concepts of the French artillerist Henri Paixhans who had popularized the shell-gun. Dahlgren advocated replacing the usual mixed battery of shot and shell cannon with his 9–inch and 11–inch guns. He thought that the use of the larger caliber explosive projectiles and the faster rate of fire would greatly increase the firepower of any warship.

The U.S. Navy began to adopt Dahlgren's system during the 1850s by mounting his cannon on the new screw frigates. During the Civil War, the guns proved to be effective against both wooden and armorclad ships. A 15–inch Dahlgren gun built for use on monitors against Confederate ironclads was, according to many contemporaries, the best naval cannon ever mounted for operational use. Dahlgren's heavy cannon marked the apex of development of the cast iron, smoothbore naval gun. Artillerists had begun to turn to wrought iron and steel rifles for sufficient firepower to combat ironclads. Dahlgren's guns were obsolescent by the time he died in 1870.

Army ordnance officers, particularly Captain Thomas Rodman, also developed heavy cast iron, smoothbore cannon during the 1840s and 1850s for coastal defense, but their approach to cannon design differed from Dahlgren's. Rodman utilized measurements of explosive pressure behind the projectile as the basis for his design, while Dahlgren conjectured where the greatest pressure would be and placed more metal there to withstand it. Dahlgren unfairly accused Rodman of stealing his ideas, but nothing came of the dispute except bad feelings. Dahlgren also disparaged and refused to use a novel method of fabricating cast iron guns that Rodman developed.

Dahlgren's second major contribution was the establishment of facilities for ordnance development and testing. The Washington Navy Yard had been center of the Navy's effort in this area for twenty years prior to Dahlgren's arrival; however, his achievements enhanced it status. Furthermore, he built a firing range and other facilities there for experiments and production, and these eventually developed into the Naval Gun Factory in the 1880s.

Dahlgren's third important contribution was the creation of a small corps of line officers who specialized in ordnance work while they were on shore duty. Unlike the Army, which had a group of staff officers to handle such matters, the Navy entrusted ordnance development, procurement, and administration to men who rotated between sea and shore billets. Dahlgren's career showed that a line officer could specialize and not jeopardize his opportunity for sea command. Furthermore, his achievements illustrated the importance of training a group of experts in this highly sophisticated technology. Prior to the Civil War, line officers with general experience commanded the Bureau of Ordnance; after the war, only one such officer became bureau chief. All of the others had served extensive apprenticeships in ordnance shore duty.

BIBLIOGRAPHY

Bruce, Robert V. *Lincoln and the Tools of War*. Indianapolis: Bobbs-Merrill Company, 1957.
Dahlgren, John A.B. *Shells and Shell-Guns*. Philadelphia: King Baird, 1856.
Dahlgren, Sarah M.V. *Memoirs of John A. Dahlgren, Rear Admiral, United States Navy, by His Widow*. 2 vols. Boston: J. R. Osgood and Company, 1882.
Ripley, Warren. *Artillery and Ammunition of the Civil War*. New York: Van Nostrand Reinhold Company, 1970.

RICHARD D. GLASOW

DANIELS, Josephus (b. Washington, N.C., May 18, 1862; d. Raleigh, N.C., January 15, 1948), secretary of the Navy. Daniels is best known as secretary of the Navy in President Woodrow Wilson's cabinet during World War I.

During the first phase of his career, Daniels built a national reputation as one of the leading journalists in the South. In 1885 he acquired a newspaper in Raleigh, North Carolina, and gradually built it into the Raleigh *News and Observer*. This publication became a principal outlet for the views of Southern liberals during the era of Populism and Progressivism. Daniels became a devoted follower of William Jennings Bryan; he championed many of the Great Commoner's causes in the *News and Observer*, including Prohibition and regulation of railroads. Despite close ties with Bryan, Daniels became one of Woodrow Wilson's earliest supporters for the presidency in 1912, an act that led to his appointment as secretary of the Navy when Wilson—a former professor and president of Princeton University—entered the White House. Unlike Bryan, Daniels proved sufficiently flexible to maintain a good relationship with President Wilson, the basis for his longevity in the Navy Department (1913-1921).

Daniels soon aroused the enmity of many naval professionals and their civilian associates. The secretary's prohibitionist views led to an order that aroused deep irritation in the officer corps—elimination of the traditional wine mess on board ship. Moreover, during the early years of his incumbency, he opposed two pet projects of the naval reformers—creation of a general staff for the Navy comparable to the one granted the Army in 1903, and expansion of the battlefleet to make it comparable to the greatest navies in the world. An advocate of fiscal economy and an opponent of militarism, Daniels gave much more attention to the well-being of enlisted personnel, particularly to their education, than to the dreams of reformers such as his principal naval subordinate, Rear Admiral Bradley Allen Fiske.*

A confrontation developed between Daniels and the reformers when Fiske led a campaign in 1914–1915 to force a bill through Congress that would establish a powerful chief of naval operations. The secretary interpreted this initiative as an attempt to "Prussianize" the Navy. Daniels agreed to establish the Office of Chief of Naval Operations (CNO), but he managed to confine the powers of that office sufficiently to preclude undue interference with the legitimate functions of the civilian secretary. The struggle between Daniels and Fiske led to a significant improvement in the administration of the Navy without compromise of civilian control. To serve as the first CNO, Daniels selected Captain William S. Benson, an officer who was not affiliated with the reformers. Benson proved both loyal and efficient, and he helped to shape the office of CNO into an effective institution.

The beginning of World War I gradually led President Wilson toward a remarkable change of direction in naval policy. The president attempted to mediate the European struggle, but his efforts ended in failure. This outcome led him by degrees to a decision to strengthen the Navy. He realized that force was necessary to underpin important diplomatic initiatives. He also recognized the existence of political pressure to accommodate the demands of many people in the country who advocated military and naval "preparedness," given the unstable international situation. After the president publicly called for a navy equal to the best foreign establishment, the Navy Department drafted appropriate legislation, and the result was the Naval Act of 1916. Daniels was helpful in shepherding the law through Congress. It provided for construction of sixty capital ships by 1925, if the program was completed. It authorized construction of sixteen battleships and cruisers by 1919 along with 146 lesser vessels. As in the case of the decision to create a chief of naval operations, the Wilson administration took action that had long been a principal objective of navalists—the creation of a powerful battlefleet capable of holding its own against any other navy.

When the United States finally entered World War I in April 1917, high officials serving in the Navy Department debated the proper combat role of the fleet. The European Allies believed that the prime naval challenge was to counter Germany's submarine offensive against world shipping, the very enterprise that became the occasion for the American intervention. Because the Allies lacked sufficient antisubmarine craft, they urged the United States to suspend construction of capital ships and to build antisubmarine vessels such as destroyers. Admiral Benson opposed this change, arguing that the building program of 1916 should continue. As a result, the United States could prepare itself to wage naval warfare by itself, should Germany defeat the Allies, a disaster that seemed quite conceivable during the dark months of 1917. A different opinion came from the American admiral sent to London to establish naval liaison with the world's principal sea power. Rear Admiral William Sowden Sims* strongly supported the views of the British Admiralty. That organization insisted that failure to press construction of antisubmarine craft would insure the triumph of the Central Powers. Although both president Wilson and Secretary Daniels entertained lively suspicions of Great Britain and considered Sims unduly pro-British, they eventually recognized the necessity of suspending the capital-ship program, and the Navy Department fell into line.

During 1917–1918 Daniels presided over a massive naval contribution to the victory over the Central Powers. Units of the Navy reinforced the antisubmarine forces of the Allies and helped contain the German U-boats. Escort vessels succeeded in protecting the ships carrying more than two million troops and essential supplies to Europe. This extraordinary achievement, inconceivable without the assistance of the Navy, decided the war in favor of the Allied and associated powers.

Daniels accompanied President Wilson to the Paris Peace Conference of 1919 and took part in what has become known as "the naval battle of Paris," an angry Anglo-American wrangle over postwar naval dispositions. Before going to Europe, the president proposed resumption of the building program that had been suspended during the period of belligerency. His purpose was not to encourage a naval armaments race but to use the nation's potential naval power as a crucial bargaining chip in efforts to negotiate a new international order. If the nations gathered in Paris acquiesced in a league of nations capable of maintaining peace and sponsoring fundamental international reforms, the president would not complete his building program. Despite the urgings of British statesmen, the United States refused to accept a naval position inferior to that of the Royal Navy. The president contended for an American Navy equal to that of Great Britain; each country would be expected to make comparable contributions to an international navy capable of enforcing the decisions of the league. The question of postwar naval relationships was not settled in Paris, but discussions there led directly to the Washington Naval Conference held during the administration of President Warren G. Harding. Wilson and Daniels deserve recognition as early contributors to the naval disarmament treaty negotiated in 1921-1922.

After Daniels returned to the United States, he became involved in a sweeping congressional investigation of the Navy's performance during the late war. Admiral Sims precipitated the inquiry; he made many criticisms of the Navy Department, most of them designed to support the allegation that it had not rallied efficiently to the support of the Allies during the great emergency of 1917. Daniels managed the defense of the administration's naval policies skillfully, and the sea service escaped serious damage to its reputation.

After leaving the Navy Department in 1921, Daniels resumed his journalistic career in North Carolina, but he returned to government in 1933, when President Franklin D. Roosevelt named him ambassador to Mexico. Daniels played a leading role in the application of the "Good Neighbor Policy," helping to avoid a serious break with Mexico after that country expropriated American-owned oil properties in 1938. During the last years of his life, he found time to write a five-volume set of memoirs, two volumes of which chronicled his years in the Navy Department.

Historians used to depreciate the service of Josephus Daniels as secretary of the Navy. His old antagonists, the naval reformers and their partisans, contributed most of the early writings on naval activity during World War I, not the least among them Admiral Sims himself, who received the Pulitzer Prize for his *Victory at Sea* (1920), and the admiral's son-in-law, Elting E. Morison, who offered a brilliant study entitled *Admiral Sims and the Modern American Navy* (1942). Daniels' critics cultivated the view that the tar heel editor had been an expediential politician who knew nothing of naval requirements. Naval success came during the war, they held, because professionals such as Sims were able to counter the serious errors of the Wilson administration.

Historians of more recent vintage advance a less negative interpretation. Daniels' actions as secretary of the Navy appear steeped in irony. A Bryanite who was strongly inclined toward pacifism, he proved loyal to President Wilson and willing to support dramatic new departures during World War I. Daniels presided over accomplishments that naval reformers such as Fiske and Sims had urged for many years, and he deserves credit for them. Experience confirms the wisdom of Daniels' stubborn resistance to encroachments on civilian control of military decisions. His concern for the well-being of enlisted personnel also wears well. Finally, no one seriously contests the claim that the Navy under Daniels made a vital contribution to the victory of 1918 or rejects the judgment that the Wilson administration built the foundations of the great naval force that waged World War II against the Axis powers.

BIBLIOGRAPHY

Braisted, William R. *The United States Navy in the Pacific, 1909–1922.* Austin: University of Texas Press, 1971.

Cronon, E. David, ed. *The Cabinet Diaries of Josephus Daniels, 1913–1921.* Lincoln: University of Nebraska Press, 1963.

Daniels, Josephus. *The Wilson Era*. 2 vols. Chapel Hill: University of North Carolina Press, 1944–1946.

Morison, Elting E. *Admiral Sims and the Modern American Navy*. Boston: Houghton Mifflin Company, 1942.

Trask, David F. *Captains & Cabinets: Anglo-American Naval Relations, 1917–1918*. Columbia: University of Missouri Press, 1972.

DAVID F. TRASK

DAVIS, Benjamin Oliver, Jr. (b. Washington, D.C., December 18, 1912), first black lieutenant general, leader in military and civil aviation.

Benjamin O. Davis, Jr., grew up in a military environment. His early years were spent with his two sisters and parents at his father's (Brigadier General Benjamin O. Davis, Sr.*) stations at Tuskegee and Cleveland. The younger Davis was an excellent student and at an early age displayed his leadership qualities. In his senior year, he was elected president of his graduating class at Cleveland's Central High School. After one year at Western Reserve University, he transferred to the University of Chicago (1930–1932) where he majored in math with the goal of becoming a teacher or a mining engineer. However, the Army was never far from his thoughts, and he began to consider a military career. With this in mind, his father convinced Congressman Oscar DePriest (R-Ill) to nominate him to West Point. He passed the entrance examination and entered the Military Academy in the fall of 1932.

Davis' experiences at the Academy put to the test his determination to become an officer. During his first year, none of the cadets spoke to him. When he demonstrated that he could take the "silence", a few cadets became more friendly. In his senior year at the Academy, he received basic training in flying. In 1936 he graduated thirty-fifth in his class of 276. He was only the fourth black to graduate from the Academy and the first in the twentieth century.

Racial practices shaped the early years of Lieutenant Davis' military career. His request to enter the Air Corps was denied because it did not accept blacks. Instead, Davis was sent to the 24th Infantry, an all-black regiment, then stationed at Fort Benning, Georgia. In 1938 Davis returned to Tuskegee, as Professor of Military Science and Tactics. In the next two years he was promoted to first lieutenant (1939) and then to captain (1940). His first assignment as captain was to act as an aide to his father, who was then commanding the 2d Cavalry Brigade, Fort Riley, Kansas.

In 1941, when the War Department reluctantly made the decision to allow blacks into the Air Corps, Davis was asked to participate in the first flight training class. He graduated from this program in 1942, was promoted from captain to major to lieutenant colonel in the course of two weeks, and then was assigned command of the first black air unit, the 99th Pursuit Squadron. The unit moved to North Africa in April 1943 and flew its first combat mission in June. Lieutenant Colonel Davis returned to the United States later in the year to head the 332d Fighter Group and to testify as to the combat-effectiveness of the 99th. During the remainder of the war, Davis continued to command the 332d, was promoted to colonel (1944), flew sixty combat missions, and was awarded the Distinguished Flying Cross (pinned on by his father) and the Silver Star. At the end of the war he was withdrawn from combat and assigned command of the racially troubled 477th Composite Group.

In the first years of the postwar era, Colonel Davis was an important person in the Army Air Force's attempt to deal with the race issue. Davis tried to resolve some of the racial problems faced by the 477th but found little support from higher echelons. He testified before the Gillem Board and called for integration on a gradual basis; he noted that the "attitude that there is no place for the Negro officer still exists in the Army." Although Davis was eligible for advanced schooling, the Air Force felt it could not spare him because of his expertise on the race issue. When integration finally began in 1948, he helped draft desegregation plans and then was assigned to the Air War College. After graduation, he was promoted to the permanent rank of colonel. When the Korean War started, he was ordered to the Pentagon to serve as chief of the Fighter Branch, deputy for operations.

Over the next fifteen years, Davis moved up in rank and received a variety of commands in trouble spots. In 1954 he was promoted to brigadier general; in 1959 to major general; and in 1965 to lieutenant general. He was assigned to Formosa during the first Quemoy crisis; to Germany in the mid–1960s; and to the Philippines during the Vietnam War. At the end of the decade he became deputy commander, U.S. Strike Force.

In 1970 Davis retired from the Air Force and began his second career, this time as a civil servant. It was a tumultous year. In February he was appointed director of public safety in Cleveland, Ohio. In June he was named to the President's Commission on Campus Unrest. The next month he resigned his post in Cleveland, stating that he was not receiving the support he needed. In September he was appointed director of civil aviation security in the Department of Transportation. His function was to coordinate the programs designed to end the air hijacking incidents. Over the next few years, he advanced in the Department of Transportation, eventually becoming assistant secretary of transportation for safety and consumer affairs. In 1978 General Davis followed in his father's footsteps when he became a member of the Battle Monuments Commission.

General Davis has had two careers, both connected with aviation. In his first career as an Air Force officer, he commanded a number of segregated and integrated units in a variety of hot spots. As a civilian, he has worked effectively to end air hijacking and to reassure the public of the safety of aviation. His career has spanned an era of great change in race relations.

When Benjamin Davis, Jr., graduated from West Point, no career in the Air Corps was possible. Segregation determined his command assignments. Five years later political pressure opened avenues previously blocked to him because of his race, and Davis' abilities carried him to the top. As he said, "I'm ambitious. I like a challenge." The Air Force continually provided one. During World War

II he commanded the three black Air Force units; he was under constant pressure for them to prove their capabilities and at the same time to deal with racial disturbances arising from the discriminatory policies of the Air Force. After the war he helped develop and execute the plans for integration. In the 1950s he was sent to command units that were under the threat of attack from China. In the next decade he led the Thirteenth Air Force, which was then involved in the middle of the Vietnam War. Those working under him thought very highly of his capabilities. "He epitomizes the finest type of Air Force officer we ever had," one said. By 1970, when General Davis turned fifty-eight, he had already served in the Air Force for over thirty years; had reached the rank of lieutenant general, something no black had ever done before; and had held almost every possible command. New challenges outside the Air Force now beckoned.

The first year of Davis' civilian service was filled with tumult and trial. He found the racial and political situation in Cleveland much more difficult to handle than the ordered ways of the Air Force. Although nearly everyone praised him for what he was doing, he still felt uneasy. Within a few months he began to feel that Mayor Carl Stokes was not supporting him fully. Rather than be forced out on a limb, he resigned. Several months later he returned to government service, at the request of President Richard Nixon, to head the sky marshal program. It apparently was a much simpler situation than trying to control Cleveland, and he was quite successful at it. Within a year the measures that were adopted under his recommendations helped bring the vast majority of air hijackings in the United States to an end.

General Benjamin O. Davis, Jr., found that the racism and discrimination that had blocked his father's advancement were less of a hindrance to his own career. He began his professional advancement at a time when barriers created by segregation were being removed and his talents could be fully displayed. His thirty-four year career in the military and his subsequent civilian positions have demonstrated that this is a talented individual, a good administrator, and a forceful personality. He has ably followed in his father's footsteps.

BIBLIOGRAPHY

Brown, Wesley A. "Eleven Men of West Point." *Negro History Bulletin* 19, no. 7 (April 1956): 153.
Gropman, Alan L. *The Air Force Integrates, 1945–1964*. Washington, D.C.: U.S. Government Printing Office, 1978.
Osur, Alan M. *Blacks in the Army Air Forces During World War II*. Washington, D.C.: U.S. Government Printing Office, 1977.

MARVIN E. FLETCHER

DAVIS, Benjamin Oliver, Sr. (b. Washington, D.C., May 28, 1880; d. Chicago, Ill., November 26, 1970), first black general. Davis had a significant influence on the Army's radical policies during and immediately after World War II.

Benjamin Davis' family was part of black middle-class society in Washington, D.C. His father, Louis, worked as a messenger for the U.S. Department of the Interior. As a youth Davis was fascinated by stories of the Civil War that he heard from his relatives and by the military exercises of the black battalion of the District National Guard. When he entered high school, he became a member of the school's military organization and later joined the Guard. In high school he took business courses and competed in baseball and football. After graduation he attended Howard University for one year.

Davis' participation in the Spanish-American War marked the beginning of his offical military career. Against his parents' wishes, he helped recruit a company for the 8th U.S. Volunteer Infantry; in return he was appointed a first lieutenant in that regiment. The 8th never saw any combat, but spent the year of its existence at different training camps. It was during this year that Davis became acquainted with John C. Proctor, a former noncommissioned officer in the 9th Cavalry, who intrigued Davis with his stories of life in the Regular Army.

These experiences whetted his appetite for a career as an Army officer. Louis Davis sought an appointment to West Point for his son, but he was turned down because of his race. Seeking another route to a commission, in 1899 Davis joined the 9th Cavalry. During his two years as an enlisted man, he quickly rose from private to post sergeant-major. In 1901, against the advice of his fellow soldiers, he took and passed the examination for a commission. His first assignment as a second lieutenant was to the 10th Cavalry.

Davis rose slowly through the officer ranks and had very few opportunities to command troops. He was appointed first lieutenant in 1905, captain in 1915, major in 1917, and lieutenant colonel in 1920; in 1930 he became the first black to achieve the rank of colonel. His duty assignments included service with his regiment in the Philippines and on the Mexican border; as professor of military science and tactics at Tuskegee Institute (1920–1924, 1931–1937), and Wilberforce University (1905–1909, 1915–1917, 1929–1931, 1937–1938); as instructor to the 372d Infantry, Ohio National Guard (1924–1929), and the 369th Infantry, New York National Guard (1938–1940); and as military attaché to Liberia (1909–1912). All of these assignments were designed to prevent a situation wherein Davis might be in a position to command white troops or officers. Because of racial constraints, the Army often had difficulty finding an assignment for Davis. Nevertheless, it was a comfortable career, especially during the Depression.

The most significant opportunity in Benjamin Davis' life came shortly before he reached retirement age. One week prior to the 1940 presidential election, Franklin Roosevelt appointed Davis to the rank of brigadier general. His first command was the 2d Cavalry Division, Fort Riley, Kansas. In June 1941 he reached retirement age, but immediately was reactivated and reported to the inspector general in Washington. For the next five years he headed a special section that dealt "with matters pertaining to the various colored units in the service." In the course of those duties, he traveled around the United States inspecting camps, investigating racial disturbances, and trying to improve the morale of the black soldiers. He made two trips to Europe (1942, 1944–1945) and carried out many of the same functions there. In 1944 he convinced the Army to try a limited form of integration. For these activities, he received the Distinguished Service Medal (1944) and the Bronze Star (1945).

Davis returned home in November 1945 and became involved in planning for the postwar utilization of black manpower. He testified before the Gillem Board on this issue but was not completely satisfied by the final report. Later he became special assistant to the secretary of the Army. In July 1948 Davis retired, having served fifty years. He was honored with a special ceremony at the White House.

Davis spent the next twenty years living in Washington and serving on a few government boards. He represented the United States in Liberia in 1951 and served on the Battle Monuments Commission. After the death of his wife in 1966, he moved to Chicago. He lived there with his youngest daughter, Elnora Davis McLendon, until his death in 1970.

The length of Benjamin O. Davis, Sr.'s service as an enlisted man and officer has few parallels in the history of the U.S. Army. Only in his last ten years of service, however, did Davis make an impact on the military. In many ways, the first forty years were preparation for the last ten.

Denied the opportunity to attend the Army's postgraduate school system or to command large bodies of troops, Davis learned other skills. Through working in a segregated society and institution, Davis learned to balance his opposition to racism with the need to get ahead. As he wrote to his wife-to-be, Sadie Overton, in 1919, "The United States is a great country but unfortunately it possesses many little folks who in many instances have only one thing upon which they are given rank and position—The fact that they are white men." Davis also learned the ways of foreign countries during his tour in Liberia and in the several summers he spent in France in the early 1930s. His longevity and diplomacy earned him the respect of many of the white officer corps.

When Davis was appointed head of the special branch in the Inspector General's Department in 1941, he used his personal skills to try to mitigate the stings of racism. For the next seven years he acted as an ombudsman for the black soldiers. Because of his diplomatic manner and Army background, he had more credibility with the War Department than civilians like William Hastie or Truman Gibson, who advised the secretary of war on racial problems. From within the system he did his best to make the Army accept blacks as human beings and to reduce the policy of segregation and discrimination. His one great victory occurred during World War II when he convinced the European Theater of Operations leadership that an attempt should be made to integrate some of the combat forces. The experiment was judged a great success by most people. Davis felt that this attempt at integration was the most important thing "since the enactment of the constitutional amendments following emancipation."

Benjamin O. Davis, Sr., worked in a segregated army but helped mitigate the effects of this system on the average black soldier. He sought equal treatment, something he himself was denied until the last years of his career. In his quiet way, this old soldier advanced the cause of equality a great deal during his fifty years of service. As Secretary of the Army Kenneth Royall wrote in 1948, "His long record of outstanding service has been an inspiration to many, both in the military service and in civilian life".

BIBLIOGRAPHY

Lee, Ulysses. *The Employment of Negro Troops*. Washington, D.C.: U.S. Government Printing Office, 1966.

MARVIN E. FLETCHER

DAVIS, Jefferson (b. Christian County [now Todd County], Ky., June 3, 1808; d. New Orleans, La., December 6, 1889), Army officer, secretary of war; president of the Confederate States of America.

Jefferson Davis was born in a log cabin in what is now Fairview, Kentucky, the tenth child of Samuel Emory and Jane (Cook) Davis. Of Welsh stock, Jefferson's father, a farmer, had served in the Revolutionary War on the patriot side. His mother was Scotch-Irish. Samuel took his family to Louisiana in 1810 and in 1811 to frontier-like Mississippi near Woodville, Wilkinson County, where he prospered moderately on his cotton farm. The eldest son, Joseph, a successful planter, took a paternal interest in young Jefferson. The youth attended St. Thomas' College in Kentucky, then Jefferson College near Natchez, Mississippi, and later the Wilkinson County Academy.

In 1823 Davis entered Transylvania University at Lexington, but he left before graduating to accept an appointment to West Point in 1824. He was graduated from the Military Academy in 1828, twenty-third in a class of thirty-two, and entered the Army as a second lieutenant of infantry. A number of future Confederate generals attended "the Point" with Davis, including Albert Sidney Johnston,* Leonidas Polk,* Joseph Eggleston Johnston,* and Robert Edward Lee.*

Davis spent the early months of his career in Wisconsin at Forts Crawford and Winnebago and at Fort Gibson in what is now Oklahoma, among other posts. He served in the Black Hawk War of 1832, was appointed to the dragoons in 1833, and was named first lieutenant in 1834. While at Fort Crawford he fell in love with Sarah Knox Taylor, daughter of the post commander, Colonel Zachary Taylor.* Despite her father's disapproval, they were married in 1835, shortly after Davis had resigned from the Army.

Returning to Mississippi, Davis became a planter, first at his brother's plantation and later at his own "Briarfield" below Vicksburg. He was an avid reader, mainly in politics and history, and his interest in current politics grew. Established as a country gentleman, he was accepted as a member of the planter aristocracy. To his slaves he apparently was benevolent and patriarchal. His first marriage ended tragically when Sarah died of malaria in 1835. He married the youthful

Varina Howell of Natchez in 1845, and that same year he was elected to the U.S. House of Representatives from Mississippi as a Democrat.

Davis supported the annexation of Texas and in 1846 voted in favor of the Mexican War. He resigned from the House to accept command of a volunteer regiment, the "Mississippi Rifles." Davis later emphasized his part in the Mexican War, which included service with his former father-in-law, General Taylor, at Monterrey and Buena Vista, where his stand possibly saved Taylor from defeat. Certainly Davis' Mexican War experience expanded his military knowledge and his belief in his own military capacity.

In 1847 Davis left the volunteer service and was appointed to the U.S. Senate from Mississippi to fill a vacancy. He supported President James K. Polk and championed the right of slavery to expand into the territories. Elected to a full term in 1850, he resigned his seat in 1851 to run unsuccessfully as Democratic candidate for governor of Mississippi.

President Franklin Pierce appointed Davis secretary of war in 1853, and he served until 1857. Serving in this post was one of the peaks of his career. Even Davis' critics agree that he was a highly creditable administrator. He introduced camels into the West, improved infantry tactics, substituted iron for wood in gun carriages, advocated improved coastal defenses, and, as he wrote, "secured rifled muskets and rifles and the use of Minié balls." He urged construction of a "military railway" across the continent and supervised the surveys of possible rail routes.

Davis returned to the Senate in 1857 and defended the South in the mounting crisis over slavery, slavery expansion, and states' rights. Often considered radical in his views by Northerners, he was in fact moderate in comparison with the Southern "fire-eaters." Plagued by ill-health, Davis still put forth his views with vigor and thus received public attention. He railed against the abolitionists, pointing out what he saw as the dangers of an abolitionist presidency, and inveighed against Stephen A. Douglas' idea of popular sovereignty and Abraham Lincoln's opposition to slavery expansion into the territories. Yet Davis basically disapproved of secession. In the split of the Democratic party in 1860, he supported John C. Breckinridge, the Southern Democratic candidate for president.

When Mississippi seceded in 1861, Davis, in a sorrowful address on January 21, withdrew from the Senate, expressing pain and regret at the breaking of the nation. He believed that secession meant war. He apparently expected to be named military commander of the South but was appointed major general of the Mississippi state troops.

On February 9, 1861, the Convention of the Confederate States of America elected Davis as provisional president of the newly formed nation, a post he reluctantly accepted. He arrived in Montgomery, Alabama, first capital of the Confederacy, on February 16, and orator William Lowndes Yancey proclaimed, "The man and the hour have met."

On the portico of the state capitol Davis delivered a calm, dignified inaugural address on February 18. He did not mention slavery but emphasized what he saw as the justice of the task before the Confederacy. Davis then tackled perhaps the most awesome job in American political history, for the Civil War began in April. In May the Confederate capital was moved to Richmond, Virginia. On October 16 Davis was elected president of the Confederate States of America without opposition.

Unprepared for war, the Confederacy, led by Davis, managed to survive for four years against a formidable opponent. An army and a navy were created that would have done credit to any nation. Davis often used his military ability effectively, but was criticized for meddling too much, for protecting inept commanders such as Braxton Bragg,* and for quarreling with others, among them Joseph Johnston and Pierre Gustauve Toutant Beauregard.* Yet, to Davis' credit, a number of great Confederate captains emerged. His cabinet personnel did change frequently (he had six secretaries of war), and relations with Congress were never completely harmonious. Some complained that Davis was a dictator, and others that he was not dictatorial enough to win the war.

Davis of necessity played a major role in both the mistakes and triumphs of the Confederacy. His embargo of cotton surprisingly proved ineffective; neither Davis nor the Confederate Navy could thwart the strangling Federal blockade. Davis and his government failed to obtain much desired foreign recognition and intervention. He struggled to give equal attention to the entire Confederacy, as shown by his trips into the Western states during the conflict and his correspondence with the state governors. Confederate financial woes, for which he was often blamed, including inflation, were probably incurable. To compound his concerns, there arose a vocal opposition from many sources: politicians, extreme states' rightists, his own vice-president Alexander Stephens, and many Southern newspaper editors.

As the military fortunes of the Confederacy declined and as public morale weakened, Davis refused to admit the obvious. Near the end he reluctantly approved the use of slaves as soldiers but resisted Federal pressure for surrender at the Hampton Roads Conference early in 1865. He was the rock upon which the tottering Confederacy stood, along with its military heroes and soldiers.

On April 2, 1865, Davis and part of his cabinet left Richmond, as the fall of the Confederacy was imminent. Largely out of touch with what scattered forces were left in the field, Davis and his shadow government traveled slowly through Virginia and North and South Carolina. His last cabinet meeting was held at Washington, Georgia. On May 10, near Irwinville, Georgia, he was captured.

Manacled for a time, Davis was confined at Fortress Monroe, Virginia, for two years. His indictment for treason in May of 1866 came to nothing, and he was never brought to trial.

After his release on May 1, 1867, Davis was president of a life insurance company and devoted himself to writing his *Rise and Fall of the Confederate Government*. He refused to take part in politics. In financial straits, in 1877 he was given a home, "Beauvoir," near Biloxi, Mississippi, by an admirer. Davis died in New Orleans at the age of eighty-one and was buried in Hollywood Cemetery, Richmond, Virginia.

In any appraisal of Davis, complete objectivity becomes almost an impossibility. Davis' actions, particularly during the Civil War, are inextricably interwoven with those of Abraham Lincoln,* the Confederate military leaders, and the whole panorama of the Confederacy. He remains one of the most controversial figures in U.S. history. Davis was the leader of the "Lost Cause," and his post and personality make him vulnerable for the role of "whipping boy." Robert E. Lee is often seen as the folk hero of the South, while Davis is the villain of the piece, although he did regain some popularity after the Civil War and was viewed almost as a martyr by some Southerners.

While a few biographers defend Davis uncritically, the view of participants, historians, and others has been generally anti-Davis in one degree or another, and he suffers from an overdrawn comparison to Lincoln. Some critics credit Davis with an overweaning ego, particularly as to things military. He is seen as inflexible, uncompromising, stubborn, possessed of an imperious temper, austere, aloof and grim, argumentative, and overly prone to defend his friends and keep them in position. In the military realm he is accused of interfering too much, as in the Atlanta Campaign, of not concentrating his armies, or of concentrating them too much. These criticisms stem in part from a desire to explain or even to expiate the Southern defeat.

It is true that Davis could not deal successfully with politicians or make the most effective use of them. Yet few will deprecate his integrity, his loyalty to principles, his sense of honor, his unselfish sensitivity, his self-controlled courage, his dedication to the cause of the Confederacy, and his willingness to take on the overwhelming tasks assigned him. High strung and nervous, he could act decisively and displayed growth as Confederate president. Many credit him with holding together the Confederacy and being instrumental in making it last as long as it did.

Actually, Davis was the logical choice to head the Confederacy, and he bore admirably the responsibilities thrust upon him. Despite his faults and considering the impossible burdens of his office, Jefferson Davis remains an eminent American, an essentially noble leader, deeply imbued with the spirit of his time and region, steadfast to his principles, and of great worth to his two nations.

BIBLIOGRAPHY

Davis, Jefferson. *The Rise and Fall of the Confederate Government*. 2 vols. New York: D. Appleton and Company, 1891.
Eaton, Clement. *Jefferson Davis*. New York: Free Press, 1977.
Escott, Paul D. *After Secession: Jefferson Davis and the Failure of Confederate Nationalism*. Baton Rouge: Louisiana State University Press, 1978.
Patrick, Rembert W. *Jefferson Davis and His Cabinet*. Baton Rouge: Louisiana State University Press, 1944.

Strode, Hudson, *Jefferson Davis*. 3 vols. New York: Harcourt, Brace, 1955–1969.
Wiley, Bell I. *The Road to Appomattox*. Memphis: Memphis State College Press, 1956.

E. B. LONG

DAWLEY, Ernest Joseph (Mike) (b. Antigo, Wisc., February 17, 1886; d. Carmel Valley, Calif., September 8, 1973), Army officer. Dawley was the American ground forces commander at Salerno and was relieved for incompetence, perhaps unjustifiably.

General Dawley's career began in 1910, when he graduated from the U.S. Military Academy with a commission in the field artillery. Unassuming as a cadet, he had made little impression on most of his peers at the Academy, but after being commissioned he quickly established a reputation as an artillery expert and a superior staff officer while serving in the Philippines, Mexico, and France. Dawley began to gain recognition shortly after graduating, while on maneuvers in the Philippines. At that time, he nearly rode down an "enemy" officer, impressing George Catlett Marshall,* then a divisional chief of staff, by his dash. Afterwards, he acquired combat experience as a junior officer by participating in General John Joseph Pershing's* 1916 punitive expedition into Mexico, and one month after the United States entered World War I, he was promoted to captain and posted to France in May 1917. He remained in Europe for two and a half years, until September 1919. During that time he served with distinction, and, by actual combat performance in a variety of assignments and in situations of exceptional stress, he became recognized as an outstanding staff officer and artillery expert.

After arriving in France, Dawley attended the French Artillery School at Fontainbleau before becoming executive officer of the newly organized American Artillery School at Saumur (September 1917). Subsequently, he served with two field artillery regiments (2d Division, 12th Field Artillery; 4th Division, 16th Field Artillery) and successfully held a number of increasingly important staff positions as artillery expert for First Army Headquarters, Second Army Headquarters, and the American Expeditionary Force General Staff. At First Army Headquarters, Dawley planned the artillery operations for the St. Mihiel and Meuse-Argonne offensives, working closely with George C. Marshall, the chief of staff. Marshall was particularly impressed by the fact that Dawley never succumbed to stress but, on the contrary, performed a valuable service during moments of crisis by relieving tension with his dry humor. While in France, Dawley was cited for gallantry (Silver Star) and was promoted to colonel. But most important, he gained extensive experience handling large formations (up to and including the level of field army) in combat, although only as a staff officer and not as actual commander. He greatly impressed Marshall, not only by his expertise as an artillery and staff officer, but also by his even disposition and exceptional ability to cope with stress.

During the twenty years of the interwar era, Dawley's wartime performance was recognized in a variety of assignments. He was appointed military advisor to the American Mission to the Paris Peace Conference, instructor in the Tactical

Department at the Military Academy, and staff officer in the Office of the Chief of Field Artillery. He graduated from Field Artillery School, the Command and General Staff School, and the Army War College.

Dawley was a fifty-three-year-old colonel when World War II broke out. A senior field artillery officer with a solid reputation and extensive experience and training, he was marked for high command and rose rapidly in rank and authority. In October 1940 he was promoted to brigadier general and took command of the field artillery of General Joseph Warren Stillwell's* 7th Division; in June 1941 he became a major general and was given command of the 40th Division; in April 1942 he took command of VI Corps; and in April 1943 he led VI Corps into the Mediterranean, where it was assigned to Mark Wayne Clark's* Fifth Army and began preparing to invade the Italian mainland. On September 9, 1943, the Fifth Army landed at Salerno; after only twelve days of combat, on September 20, Dawley was relieved of his command at the request of General Clark. He reverted to his permanent rank of colonel, was returned to the United States, and was assigned to a field artillery training center. However, in February 1944 he became commandant of the Tank Destroyer School (Fort Hood, Texas); afterwards, he regained the rank of brigadier general and was given command first of the Tank Destroyer Center (June 1944) and then (March 1945) of the Ground Force Reinforcement Command, European Theater of Operations, in Paris. Dawley retired in 1947 as a brigadier general but was promoted to major general in 1948.

Dawley's historical reputation is based on his role in the Battle of Salerno. Allied headquarters had given this extremely risky amphibious assault ("Avalanche") only a 50–50 chance of success, and some wanted to cancel it. General Dwight David Eisenhower,* the Supreme Allied commander, agreed that the Fifth Army would have a "very bad time" and that it would be "touch and go" as to whether it would be driven "back into the sea." But he insisted that Allied sea and air power would offset initial deficiencies in ground strength and enable the Fifth Army to secure a lodgment.

The predicted near-disaster occurred. On September 13, four days after the Fifth Army landed, counterattacking German panzer and panzer grenadier units annihilated elements of the 36th Infantry Division under General Fred L. Walker, broke through the American lines, and for a time threatened to overrun the beachhead and destroy the Fifth Army. General Clark decided that Dawley's leadership was partly responsible for the near calamity. Hasty visits to the battlefield convinced both General Eisenhower and General Harold Alexander (commanding the 15th Army Group), neither of whom knew Dawley well, that he should be relieved, as Clark recommended, because he had mishandled his forces and was "extremely nervous and indecisive" under conditions of "extraordinary battle stress" to the point that he "ceases to function as a commander."

But Dawley's relief greatly surprised General Walker, who had worked closely with him throughout the battle. Many officers outside the battle zone were equally surprised, for glaring contradictions existed between Dawley's reputation and the reasons given for his relief. Those who knew Dawley well, like General Marshall, who had served with him during World War I, and General Lesley James McNair,* Army Ground Forces commander, generally considered him an exceptional officer, unshakable under pressure and experienced at skillfully conducting operations of large bodies of troops in combat, at least as a staff officer. Nevertheless, Dawley was charged with exposing his forces to attack by disposing them poorly and by becoming indecisive and nervous under pressure.

In fact, unique circumstances apparently created this impression. Not only did both corps and Army headquarters lack combat experience, but also Dawley had had to assume command prematurely with only a skeleton staff, leaving him unable to delegate authority adequately for several days. Laboring under this unusual burden, Dawley was already greatly fatigued by the time the crisis began. What is more, the Army commander, who had no experience handling large formations of troops in combat, and who only reluctantly sought Dawley's advice, despite his experience, had immediately become excessively involved in the details of Dawley's operations, ultimately even placing very small units in line personally. Under heavy German attack in an exceptionally hazardous operation, with a commander who continually interfered with his formations, plans, and authority while simultaneously criticizing him for not effectively conducting operations, it is not surprising that the exhausted and harassed Dawley appeared nervous and indecisive to outside observers.

Neither was Dawley primarily responsible for the vulnerable position of his troops. The Army commander had insisted on including the inexperienced 36th Division in AVALANCHE. Then, despite Dawley's protests, he had simultaneously reduced its strength and forced Dawley to extend its front to an incredible thirty-five miles. This simultaneously absorbed all of Dawley's reserves and made him susceptible to attack nearly everywhere. Dawley was left with a green and understrength (seven effective battalions) division holding a greatly extended and imbalanced front, and the Germans quickly effected their breakthrough on a particularly vulnerable sector of it.

Thus, evidence indicates that questionable leadership by the Army commander, and not the stress of the battle per se, was primarily responsible both for the failures of Dawley's forces and for his shaken appearance when Eisenhower and Alexander saw him. Consequently, although the singular pressures Dawley experienced at Salerno may have required his temporary relief at that time, his permanent relief from combat command seems to have been unjustified solely on the basis of the events that occurred there. In sum, Dawley's abilities as a commander cannot be definitely ascertained, since he seems to have never had a real opportunity to develop or demonstrate them.

BIBLIOGRAPHY

Ambrose, Stephen E. *The Supreme Commander*. Garden City, N.Y.: Doubleday and Company, 1970.

Blumenson, Martin. *Salerno to Cassiono*. Washington, D.C.: U.S. Department of the Army, 1969.

Chandler, Alfred D., Jr. *The Papers of Dwight David Eisenhower: The War Years.* 5 vols. Baltimore: Johns Hopkins University Press, 1970.

Eisenhower, Dwight David. *Crusade in Europe.* New York: Doubleday and Company, 1948.

Jackson, William F. G. *The Battle for Italy.* London: B. T. Batsford, 1967.

Marshall, George C. *Memoirs of My Services in the World War.* Boston: Houghton-Mifflin Company, 1971.

Mason, David. *Salerno: Foothold in Europe.* New York: Ballantine Books, 1972.

PAUL V. JOLIET

DEAN, William Frishe (b. Carlyle, Ill., August 1, 1899; d. Berkeley, Calif., August 26, 1981), Korean War division commander and the most famous prisoner of war of that conflict.

Dean was the son of Charles Watts and Elizabeth Frishe Dean. His father practiced dentistry in Carlyle, Illinois, but the family moved to California after William's graduation from high school. Dean's youthful military ambitions were frustrated when he failed to gain entrance to West Point and again when his mother prevented him from enlisting during World War I. He did belong briefly to the Students' Army Training Corps at the University of California (Berkeley), from which he graduated in 1922. He was commissioned as a second lieutenant in the Infantry Reserve in 1921 and entered the Regular Army on October 18, 1923. Dean married Mildred Dern on August 25, 1926; they had two children: William F., Jr., and Marjorie June (Mrs. Robert B.C. Williams).

Dean received some choice assignments before World War II. In 1936 he attended the Command and General Staff School; in 1938–1940, he enrolled in the Army Industrial College and the Army War College; and in 1940–1942, he was assistant secretary of the War Department General Staff. He was promoted to captain in 1936, major in 1940, lieutenant colonel in 1941, and colonel and brigadier general in 1942. In 1943 he attained the temporary rank of major general. He served first as executive officer and then as chief of the Requirements Division, Army Ground Forces, in 1942–1944. He was next appointed assistant division commander of the 44th Infantry Division, which arrived in France during the summer of 1944. He served as division commander from December 1944 until the end of the war.

After World War II, Dean served as director of the command class at the Command and General Staff School and later as assistant commandant. In October 1947 he became military governor of South Korea. In 1948 Dean took over the 7th Infantry Division during its relocation from Korea to Japan. In 1949 he served briefly as chief of staff of the Eighth Army in Japan; in October of that year he became the commanding general of the 24th Infantry Division, part of the Eighth Army. The 24th Division, like all of the Eighth Army, was in the postwar doldrums; it was soft, underequipped, and undermanned. The Eighth Army was just beginning to rehabilitate itself when the Korean War began.

Dean received orders on June 30, 1950, to move his division to Korea as the leading element of the Eighth Army. He sent a small task force to delay the enemy while the rest of his division prepared to enter the peninsula. Dean himself arrived in Korea on July 3. Inadequate communications made it difficult for him to contact his task force; indeed, throughout their campaign, Dean and his men would be plagued by communications problems, despite the efforts of Signal corpsmen. The task force was defeated, but it had bought precious time for the establishment of a position at Pyongtaek which blocked the road to Taejon. When the Americans abandoned this position on July 6 the 24th Division's left flank was exposed. Dean was angry because of the unwarranted retreat from Pyongtaek, but he gallantly shouldered much of the responsibility for it himself on the grounds that he had perhaps not made his intentions clear.

Dean now prepared for the defense of Taejon. He did not intend to fight for the city indefinitely, but only long enough to allow the 1st Cavalry Division to arrive in Yongdong, to the southeast, as part of the Eighth Army's attempt to protect its port of entry at Pusan. On July 18 the commanding general of the Eighth Army, Lieutenant General Walton Harris Walker,* asked Dean to defend Taejon until July 20, although Dean could abandon the city earlier if absolutely necessary. In response, Dean changed his plans and postponed withdrawal. Dean further decided to stay with the frontline troops in the city because poor communications made it difficult for him to direct the battle from his headquarters in Yongdong. The low morale and inexperience of his men also made his presence in Taejon essential.

The battle for Taejon took place on July 19–20. Dean's division—already damaged by the delaying actions of the previous two weeks and forced to cover an abnormally wide frontage—immediately began to suffer encirclement. At first, Dean was unaware of the situation because of poor communications and because he had lent his reconnaissance unit to a subordinate commander—a decision he was later to bemoan. As the division's plight became more obvious, Dean reverted in frustration to the role of combat soldier. He personally went tank-hunting to prove to his men that the enemy's T–34s could be destroyed by the newly arrived 3.5 inch bazooka. Dean's personal success with the bazooka could not save Taejon, however, and so he turned his attention to organizing a breakout column. As he left Taejon, he took a wrong turn and got cut off from his scattered division.

On the night of July 20–21, Dean and some other Americans attempted to find their way back to the Eighth Army's lines. Dean fell down a slope while fetching water for the wounded; he suffered a broken shoulder and was separated from the other American refugees. For thirty-six days he wandered alone trying to reach safety, losing sixty pounds in the process. On August 25, he was captured by the North Koreans. The American government did not know whether Dean was alive, but in recognition of his delaying action and of his personal bravery in Taejon, he was awarded the Congressional Medal of Honor on September 30—the first given for service in the Korean conflict.

Dean's years as a prisoner of war (POW) now began. The North Koreans tried to force him to denounce the United Nations' war in Korea. Ill and exhausted, he suffered the threat of torture and death. As his captors explained, they could do as they pleased with him because no one in the outside world knew he was alive. Dean refused to cooperate, but he did make one important mistake: he wrote a letter to General Walker suggesting that United Nations' bombers should concentrate on military targets. His captors were delighted because Dean's words could be construed as a criticism of the United Nations' bombing of civilians. Dean agonized over this, but in fact nothing further was ever heard of the letter. Fearing that he might make similar mistakes, Dean unsuccessfully attempted to commit suicide. On December 19, 1951, the Communists revealed that Dean was among their POWs; after that, he was treated much better and slowly regained his health. On May 23, 1952, while still in captivity, he was promoted to major general in the Regular Army. He was released on September 4, 1953, soon after the Armistice; with typical modesty, he was astonished to learn that he had been a hero in the United States ever since his disappearance. Remembering his own ordeal, he urged clemency for those American POWs who had "confessed" to germ warfare charges.

On January 1, 1954, Dean became deputy commanding general, Sixth Army, at the Presidio in California. He retired on October 31, 1955, and lived in California until his death in 1981.

Dean has been criticized for his campaign in Korea because generals are supposed to manage their battles instead of performing personal heroics. But his communications were inadequate, and he was therefore obliged to stay in Taejon. Furthermore, one of a commander's duties is to lead his troops in person when extraordinary circumstances—such as low morale—make that necessary. Dean certainly made some mistakes in his campaign, but he did as well as could be expected, given the difficult tasks he was asked to perform. To Dean's credit he accepted more than his fair share of personal responsibility for the defeat of the 24th Division. He was called a hero because in those days of defeat and frustration, the American government and public needed a hero but he fully deserved the honor nevertheless.

In his memoirs, Dean painted a disturbing picture of communism close up, and he strongly suggested that the American people should be better educated as to the nature of the Communist menace. On the other hand, his kind words for the Communist newspaperman Wilfred Burchett (who interviewed him in prison), his appeals for clemency for the "confessing" POWs, and some other aspects of his mental life during and after captivity, were all symptomatic of the soul-searching and ambivalence that many Americans experienced during the Korean "war in peacetime." Dean's memoirs are most important, however, as a warm and inspiring chronicle of human suffering and endurance.

BIBLIOGRAPHY

Appleman, Roy E. *United States Army in the Korean War: South to the Naktong, North to the Yalu (June-November 1950)*. Washington, D.C.: U.S. Government Printing Office, 1961.

Collins, J. Lawton. *War in Peacetime: The History and Lessons of Korea*. Boston: Houghton Mifflin Company, 1969.

Dean, William F., and William L. Worden. *General Dean's Story*. New York: Viking Press, 1954.

Fehrenbach, T. R. *This Kind of War*. New York: Macmillan Company, 1963.

Higgins, Marguerite. *War in Korea*. Garden City, N.Y.: Doubleday, 1951.

Leckie, Robert. *Conflict: The History of the Korean War, 1950–1953*. New York: G.P. Putnam's Sons, 1962.

KARL G. LAREW

DEARBORN, Henry (b. Hampton, N.H., February 23, 1751; d. Roxbury, Mass., June 6, 1829), soldier, legislator, cabinet member, diplomat.

Henry Dearborn, the son of Simon and Sarah Marston Dearborn, began his professional career with the study of medicine. In 1772 he began practice as a physician at Nottingham Square, New Hampshire, but gave up the medical profession with the coming of the Revolutionary War in 1775. At the news of fighting at Lexington, Dearborn formed a company of sixty volunteers and marched them to Cambridge, Massachusetts. Although they covered the fifty-five miles in less than twenty hours, they arrived too late to join the excitement. Shortly after returning home, Dearborn accepted a captaincy in Colonel John Stark's regiment and set about recruiting a company. On June 17, 1775, his regiment was stationed at a rail-fence, securing the left flank of positions on Breed's Hill. When attacks against that flank failed, the battle developed into a series of costly frontal attacks known to all school boys as the Battle of Bunker Hill. In mid-September 1775 Dearborn left Cambridge in command of a company of New Hampshire musketmen who had volunteered for Benedict Arnold's* expedition to Quebec. At one point on the march, he became seriously ill and had to be left behind in the lodging of a French settler, but he rejoined the Army in time to take part in the assault on Quebec. Dearborn was captured in the action, confined for a time at Quebec, paroled in May 1776, and formally exchanged in March 1777.

Upon his exchange, he was appointed major of the 3d New Hampshire Regiment, commanded by Colonel Alexander Scammell, and promoted to lieutenant colonel a week later. He fought at Ticonderoga and Freeman's Farm against General John Burgoyne, passed the winter of 1777–1778 at Valley Forge, and took part in the Battle of Monmouth. In the summer of 1779 his regiment joined General John Sullivan's* army in the Wyoming Valley Campaign against the Six Nations. In January 1781 the regiment was disbanded, and Dearborn joined the 1st New Hampshire Regiment under Colonel Joseph Cilley. In July of that year General George Washington* appointed Dearborn to his staff as deputy quartermaster general, and in that capacity Dearborn accompanied the forces to Yorktown where he witnessed the surrender of General Charles Cornwallis. The next spring he was given command of his regiment and retained it until the New Hampshire regiments were consolidated in early 1783. Dearborn was discharged on March 1, 1783. His first wife had died in 1778, and he had remarried the next year. After the war he joined his new family in Exeter, New Hampshire.

Little is known of his activities immediately after the war except that he was involved in the formation of the New Hampshire Society of Cincinnati and was its vice-president. In the summer of 1785 he moved to Maine (then a district of Massachusetts). There he engaged primarily in lumbering and land speculation. He built a house on the west bank of the Kennebec River (in the present town of Gardiner) where he lived for seventeen years. A prominent citizen of that community, he became a brigadier general and later a major general of militia. In 1789 he was appointed U.S. marshal for the District of Maine. From 1793 to 1797 he represented his district as a Republican in Congress where he made little mark except for his adherence to the rising Republican party, his advocacy of economy in military expenditures, and his opposition to the Jay Treaty. Although he lost his seat in the elections of 1796, he continued active in Massachusetts politics, gaining election in 1798 to the State House of Representatives. Dearborn once again entered the national stage in Thomas Jefferson's cabinet.

On February 18, 1801, the day after the deadlocked presidential election was decided in Jefferson's favor, the president-elect addressed a letter to Dearborn asking him to take the post of secretary of war. He accepted immediately. (For a time he also filled the position of secretary of the navy.) During his first year in office, the general peace in Europe allowed the administration to let the Army decline in size. In 1802 the authorized strength was reduced commensurably. In his years as secretary, Dearborn introduced Whitney's muskets and new gun carriages, and established the first properly equipped light artillery. Beginning in 1806, and increasingly after the *Chesapeake-Leopard* crisis in 1807, he worked to build the nation's defenses. Work on fortifications that had been stopped as an economy measure during the period of relative peace was begun again. The Army was enlarged, and arms production was increased. Dearborn, who was also responsible for Indian affairs, obtained treaties ceding millions of acres to the United States, much of this along the Mississippi, providing first a buffer between the Indians and foreign forces, and later jumping off points from which to secure the new Louisiana Purchase. His policies kept the Indians at peace (though unrest did increase after 1805). To counteract the influence of foreign traders and secure Indian good-will, he greatly expanded the government system of Indian trading factories. He also encouraged government and privately sponsored projects to teach the Indians agriculture and the basic arts of white civilization.

At the end of Jefferson's second term, Dearborn asked for and was granted the post of collector of customs at Boston, where he settled. Three years later, in 1812, he reluctantly accepted an appointment as the senior major general. He was placed in command of what was expected to be the most important theater of war—the northeast sector from the Niagara River to the New England coast. After conferences with William Eustis, the secretary of war, he established headquarters at Albany and went to Boston to superintend recruiting and to organize the defense of the New England coast. His stay there, prolonged by gubernatorial refusal to call up the militia, delayed planning and preparations for the long-discussed invasion of Canada—the only part of the British Empire vulnerable to attack by the United States. The only major campaign launched in 1812 was Hull's from Detroit. Unfortunately, Hull's plans fell into the hands of the British who were not only able to counter them, but also to capture Detroit in the process. The year ended with another American defeat at Queenston on the Niagara River, a futile march to the Canadian border late in the year, and a return to winter quarters.

In 1813 John Armstrong, Jr.,* the new secretary of war, decided to abandon attempts to capture Montreal directly and ordered an attack on Kingston at the eastern end of Lake Ontario. Dearborn, however, secured his permission to attack first York (Toronto) and then Fort George. He captured York on April 27, 1813, though with heavy losses, and took Fort George a month later, but in both cases he allowed the British Army to escape. Dearborn then became so ill that command passed for a time to Morgan Lewis. The campaign was aborted completely when the British made a surprise attack on the exposed American base of Sackets Harbor (May 28) and very nearly succeeded in capturing it. With the season's campaign in shambles, Dearborn was relieved of command on July 6, 1813. En route home Dearborn wrote both President James Madison and Secretary of War Armstrong asking for a court of inquiry. Madison gently put him off, and Dearborn finally let the matter rest.

Upon his arrival in New York, Dearborn was given command of the defenses of the city and was later appointed president of the court-martial that tried and condemned General William Hull*—his former subordinate who had lost Detroit. Dearborn at first objected that the appointment was improper but later accepted it. (Hull made no move to challenge his fitness then, but in 1824 launched a scurrilous attack on the general.) General Dearborn was honorably discharged from the Army on June 15, 1815. President Madison nominated him once more for secretary of war, but the nomination met stiff resistance and was withdrawn. In 1815 Dearborn returned to Roxbury, Massachusetts, entered retirement, and emerged only twice, first in 1817 when he was an unsuccessful candidate for governor of Massachusetts, and finally from 1822 to 1824, as U.S. minister to Portugal.

Dearborn's reputation is usually measured by his War of 1812 service; however, recent scholarship has demonstrated his important role as Jefferson's secretary of war. Of necessity, the new administration that took office in 1801 pursued twin Republican goals: economy and security. The latter goal, however, included security of both the republic and the republican forms that seemed threatened by monarchical Federalists. These goals were served by what Jefferson called a ''chaste reformation'' of the Army—a program that would ultimately Republicanize the Army, a program that was largely directed by Dearborn.

The major instrument of this reform was the Military Peace Establishment

Act of 1802. A reorganization of the staff provided a means of breaking the Federalist domination and control of the Army. The force, in size and structure, that Dearborn requested allowed the administration to eliminate a majority of the most ardent Federalist officers, many of whom had persisted in a vociferous oppposition to the new government. At the same time, the act created new positions—military and civil—within the military establishment to which Republicans could immediately be appointed. Death, discharge, and resignation created added vacancies to which men of Republican persuasion were assigned. By 1806 more than half of the officer corps bore the Jefferson-Dearborn stamp.

The U.S. Military Academy was created by the same act in 1802 to provide a rudimentary education to the Republican youth (whose station in life often foreclosed other schooling opportunities) needed as officers of the new, more Republican army. The Army even took on a more republican look—short hair and common trousers became standard fare while stylish shoe-buckles were dispensed with. The success of Dearborn's efforts as secretary of war prompted Jefferson to write that Dearborn's service had "given me the most complete and unqualified satisfaction."

Dearborn's reputation as the Army senior major general during the War of 1812 suffers by comparison with his earlier performance. "In time of peace," he had written, "a Tolerable portion of common understanding with some practical knowledge and pure intentions, may suffice." (That, he felt, he had demonstrated.) He noted, however, that war required talents "superior to any I have ever laid claim to." Historians have judged his evalauation to be correct.

As a battalion and regimental commander during the Revolution, Dearborn proved an adequate (even brave and resourceful) leader. He was commended for his action at the battles of Freeman's Farm and Monmouth. But of equal importance was the fact that he never commanded more than three hundred men in action and had obtained no experience in either tactical or strategic planning. He did obtain some staff experience as deputy quartermaster general, a position that gave him some contact with the larger problems of Army administration. Neither the command nor the staff experience, however, was adequate preparation for the responsibilities he was asked to assume during the War of 1812.

Dearborn, better at following a plan than at conceiving one, could not provide the forceful leadership the theater needed. He must shoulder much of the blame for the failure of the campaigns of 1812 and 1813. Even when enemy posts were captured, Dearborn repeatedly allowed the British Army to escape his grasp. Yet, on Dearborn's behalf, it should be pointed out that throughout his years in command, and particularly in the critical early stage, he personally had to handle the administration of his army. The Ordnance and Quartermaster Departments were undermanned and poorly run; Dearborn could make them function, even fitfully, only with the greatest effort on his part.

The country's unpreparedness for war, inadequate administrative support, Dearborn's poor generalship, and the refusal of militiamen to enter Canada at crucial times, all contributed to the disastrous campaign of 1812. With little better success the next year, Dearborn was quite rightly dismissed from command and reassigned to less demanding duty.

BIBLIOGRAPHY

Brown, Lloyd A., and Howard H. Peckham, eds. *Revolutionary War Journals of Henry Dearborn, 1775–1783*. Chicago: Caxton Club, 1939.
Cunningham, Noble E. *The Process of Government Under Jefferson*. Princeton, N.J.: Princeton University Press, 1978.
Jacobs, James Ripley. *The Beginning of the US Army, 1783–1812*. Princeton, N.J.: Princeton University Press, 1947.
Prucha, Francis Paul. *The Sword of the Republic, The United States Army on the Frontier, 1783–1846*. New York: Macmillan Company, 1969.

THEODORE J. CRACKEL

DECATUR, Stephen (b. Sinepuxent, Md., January 5, 1779; d. Washington, D.C., March 23, 1820), naval officer. Decatur is recognized for his success over the Barbary pirates in the early 1800s.

Decatur was the son of a seafaring family. His father, Stephen Decatur, Sr., was a merchant captain and privateer. During the Quasi-War with France (1798–1800), the elder Decatur was commissioned a U.S. Navy captain in command of the 36–gun frigate *Philadelphia*. Stephen, Jr., was born on the Eastern Shore of Maryland, but his formative years were spent in Philadelphia where he attended the Episcopal Academy and matriculated for a year at the University of Pennsylvania. The young man was first employed in the offices of the shipping firm of Gurney and Smith. The lure of the sea, however, spurred Decatur to sign on in 1797 as a midshipman aboard the new 44–gun frigate *United States* (Captain John Barry).

After the war with France, Decatur, then a lieutenant, sailed in the Caribbean and to the Mediterranean where a U.S. fleet was patrolling the western waters guarding against North African pirates. In 1803 Decatur served as a second in a duel for Midshipman Joseph Bainbridge, who killed the secretary to the British governor of Malta. The international repercussions abated only when the two Americans were sent home. Returning to the Mediterranean, Lieutenant Decatur commanded the *Enterprise*, a 12–gun schooner. The commodore of the Mediterranean fleet at that time was Edward Preble,* the foremost teacher of the young naval captains who would later serve in the war of 1812.

The U.S. 38–gun frigate *Philadelphia* had been taken by the Tripolitan pirates while stranded on a sandbar. Preble was determined either to regain or to destroy the vessel before it could be used by the pirates. The frigate was protected by the fortifications in the harbor of Tripoli. Decatur suggested a plan in which he and an American crew would sail a recently captured Tripolitan ketch into the harbor, lay it aside the *Philadelphia*, and then set the frigate afire. On February 16, 1804, the ketch drew alongside the *Philadelphia*, but the ruse was detected. Decatur's men swiftly took control and set combustibles aboard the frigate. As the ketch fled with all Americans, save one, unhurt, the Tripolitan forts ineffectively fired. This act, which the British Admiral Lord Nelson called "the most bold and daring act of the age," gained Decatur promotion to captain and everlasting fame in American naval history. Six months later (August 3, 1804), Decatur, in command of a small force of gunboats, boarded and took a larger enemy vessel in the harbor of Tripoli. Later, however, Preble was ordered home when the Jefferson administration decided to pay the tribute rather than fight. As captain of the 44–gun frigate *Constitution*, Decatur returned to America where his heroic exploits had already been proclaimed.

On March 8, 1806, Decatur married Susan Wheeler of Norfolk, Virginia. There he supervised construction of several gunboats until 1808 when he was ordered to sit on a court convened to judge Commodore James Barron's conduct during the disgraceful *Chesapeake-Leopard* affair. The commission found Barron guilty of neglect and sentenced him to five years' suspension without pay.

With the outbreak of the War of 1812, Decatur was given command of the frigate *United States*. His ship was part of a fleet under Commodore John Rodgers.* While sailing in the mid-Atlantic, Rodgers reaped no great harvest of English merchantmen, but he did temporarily lure the British fleet from American waters. This action enabled many American merchantmen to return home safely.

In October 1812 Decatur sailed alone. On October 25, five hundred miles west of the Canary Islands, the *United States* spotted the British 38–gun frigate *Macedonian*. Decatur held off from the British frigate and used the *United States'* long-range guns effectively. Superior American seamanship and gunnery forced the British vessel to surrender. The human losses were lopsided—seven Americans wounded and five killed to the *Macedonian*'s 105 casualties. The following spring, the *United States* and the refitted *Macedonian* tried to make it to sea from New London. Traitors on shore had set up blue lights to warn the British fleet, and the two vessels returned to the Connecticut port where they remained for the rest of the war. Decatur and his crew were transferred to the best of the 44–gun frigates, the *President*, in New York City. It was not until the war was nearly over that Decatur attempted to get the *President* through the British blockade. On the stormy night of January 14, 1815, the ship attempted to sail out on a strong tide. A sandbar damaged the ship and delayed her passage until daylight. The British fleet spotted the American frigate and gave chase. The HMS *Endymion* (40 guns), supported by three other ships, pounded the *President*. The *Endymion* tried to close, but her sails were shot away. The British vessel was relieved by the *Pomone* (38 guns) and the *Tenedos* (38 guns). With the odds so against him, Decatur surrendered. A court of inquiry excused Decatur's actions, even though some critics thought he had surrendered too soon. However, his fellow captains credited him with the *Endymion*, which he probably would have captured if the ship had not been supported. The American people greeted the paroled Decatur as a conquering hero, and he was given his choice of assignments after the war.

Decatur chose the new 74–gun ship-of-the-line *Washington* as his flagship for a squadron to return to the Mediterranean. His mission was to end the pirate menace once and for all. Reaching Gibraltar in June 1815, Decatur's strong fleet passed into the sea and surprised the pirate princes. Swiftly capturing two Algerine vessels, including the national flagship *Meshouda* (46 guns), Decatur sailed his fleet into the Bay of Algiers and demanded peace without tribute. The Dey of Algiers initially refused, but finally capitulated when Decatur threatened to land and seize the city. The American fleet then sailed to Tunis where similar threats gained not only peace, but also a $46,000 indemnity to the United States for past losses. Decatur enjoyed similar success at Tripoli. Later, when the Algerine fleet asked his destination, Decatur summed up the new American power with his answer, "American ships sail where they please."

Dinners and celebrations again awaited Decatur's return. At a dinner in his honor in Norfolk, Decatur offered his oft-quoted toast, "Our country! In her intercourse with foreign nations may she always be in the right; but our country, right or wrong." Prize money had made Decatur a wealthy man. He was assigned to the highest position in the peacetime Navy, a land-bound job on the three-man Board of Navy Commissioners.

On October 10, 1818, Decatur was second to his friend Oliver Hazard Perry* in a duel with Captain Heath of the Marine Corps whose second was naval Captain Jesse D. Elliott. Elliott and Perry had been enemies since the Battle of Lake Erie. Perry, like Decatur, was young, brave, handsome, daring, and energetic—a romantic hero to the young nation. Elliott, under the shadow of disgrace, fell in with another disgraced captain, James Barron. Decatur had sat on Barron's court-martial ten years earlier. Since Barron's five-year suspension had now passed, Elliott convinced Barron, who by virtue of time was on the senior captains' list, to apply for a sea command. Decatur particularly opposed Barron's petition because Barron had remained in England throughout the War of 1812. As long as Decatur lived, Barron's honor and position could never be regained. Barron challenged Decatur to duel. At Bladensburg, Maryland, just a short distance from the national capital, the two met on the morning of March 22, 1820. Each man's bullet struck the other in his hip. Barron's wound was in his thigh and he lived. Decatur, however, was mortally wounded when Barron's shot deflected into his groin. In excruciating pain, the young hero died at his home the following day. Although Decatur's funeral was attended by thousands including the president, the chief justice, and other high government officials, it was not held with official honors because Decatur had died as the result of a duel, and dueling was illegal.

Decatur is in the first rank of American naval captains. A man of action, he was sometimes foolhardy in his bravery. Despite his insistence upon discipline and training, he was beloved by his men. Never much of a navigator, Decatur required battle efficiency and competent gunnery. He knew that the ultimate challenge to the Navy would be to use the fleet in battle. He, therefore, prepared the foundation for the American naval tradition of going after the jugular of the enemy. The best example of his success is his firm dealing with the pirates in 1815 which ended a generation of American tribute and disgrace. Decatur's place is secure as the foremost American naval hero of the Age of Sail.

BIBLIOGRAPHY

Anthony, Irvin. *Decatur*. New York: Charles Scribner's Sons, 1931.
Forester, Cecil S. *The Age of Fighting Sail, The Story of the Naval War of 1812*. New York: Doubleday and Company, 1956.
Guttridge, Leonard F., and Jay D. Smith. *The Commodores: The U.S. Navy in the Age of Sail*. New York: Harper and Row, 1969.
Lewis, Charles L. *The Romantic Decatur*. Philadelphia: University of Pennsylvania Press, 1937.
Pratt, Fletcher. *Preble's Boys, Commodore Preble and the Birth of American Sea Power*. New York: William Sloane Associates, 1950.
Tucker, Glenn. *Dawn Like Thunder: The Barbary Wars and the Birth of the U.S. Navy*. Indianapolis: Bobbs-Merrill Company, 1963.

EDWARD K. ECKERT

DEVERS, Jacob Loucks (b. York, Pa., September 8, 1887; d. October 15, 1979), Army officer, military administrator, and World War II commander.

Jacob L. Devers was the eldest of four children born to Ella and Philip Devers, a York jeweler. After distinguishing himself as a leader in his high school class, he enrolled to study engineering at Lehigh University. At the last moment he decided instead to attend the U.S. Military Academy when he received an appointment there in the fall of 1905. He graduated in 1909 (thirty-ninth out of a class of 103) and began his forty-year military career as a field artillery officer. Following two assignments in the Western United States, he returned to West Point in 1912 as a mathematics instructor and became an excellent polo player as well as coaching basketball and baseball in his spare time.

He was stationed in Hawaii when the United States entered World War I. In December 1917 he was posted to Fort Sill, Oklahoma, and served there in various positions related to artillery training throughout the war. Gravely disappointed that he had not been sent to France during the conflict (in fact, he felt it had ruined his career), he received some solace by being ordered to Europe in May 1919, attending a French artillery school, and then serving in the Army of Occupation in Germany for several months.

During the interwar years, he was given assignments primarily at West Point, Fort Sill, and Washington, D.C., and he devoted a good deal of his seemingly boundless energy seeking improvements in artillery techniques and tactics. Like many officers at midcareer, he attended the Command and General Staff School at Fort Leavenworth, Kansas (graduating with distinction) and the Army War College in Washington. His efforts were rewarded during this third tour of duty at the Military Academy (between 1936 and 1939), when he was promoted to the permanent rank of colonel.

When World War II broke out in Europe, Devers was serving as chief of staff in the Panama Department. In May 1940 President Franklin D. Roosevelt named him the senior Army member of a military board to locate suitable bases in the bases-for-destroyers deal with Great Britain. He accomplished this taxing assignment by flying and sailing from Newfoundland to Trinidad in almost every imaginable type of air and naval craft. After a short tour of duty in Washington, in October 1940 he became commander of the 9th Division at Fort Bragg, North Carolina. During Brigadier General Devers' nine-month stay, the number of personnel handled at Fort Bragg rose dramatically, and he was responsible for directing an extensive building program along with streamlining training procedures for draftees and National Guard troops.

His ability to get things done led General George Catlett Marshall,* the acting Army chief of staff, in July 1941 to select Devers to head the armored forces training center at Fort Knox, Kentucky. With the situation in Europe and Asia becoming more ominous, the armored forces were also expanding rapidly and undergoing numerous changes. Devers' dynamism and his advocacy of improved techniques in mobile warfare and weaponry went a long way in shaping the armored units into a modern force considered capable of fighting the vaunted Wehrmacht on equal terms.

In May 1943, with America's presence in the European theatre growing and with the untimely death of Lieutenant General Maxwell Andrews* in an airplane crash, Devers was named overall commander of American forces in Europe. From his headquarters in London, he was responsible for much of the organizing and training of U.S. divisions which were arriving in Britain for the projected cross-Channel attack.

Nevertheless, Devers, now fifty-six years old and a lieutenant general, still longed for a combat command. Originally, he hoped the Normandy invasion would provide him with the chance, but at the end of 1943 he was named deputy supreme commander in the Mediterranean theater instead. In July 1944, however, he was finally given an opportunity to command Army formations in the field. He was appointed head of 6th Army Group, which was being formed to direct U.S. and French units once they had invaded southern France, advanced northward, and established contact with General Dwight David Eisenhower's* forces as Eisenhower pushed across France. The junction was effected much sooner than expected, and Devers took over active command on September 15.

While not gaining the notoriety of the other army groups in the West, Devers' group did participate in a number of important operations, including the clearing of Alsace and the reduction of the Colmar pocket in early 1945. On March 26, 1945, his twelve American and eleven French divisions proceeded to cross the Rhine River and started moving across central and southern Germany and into Austria at a rapid rate. Nuremberg fell on April 20, and Hitler's retreat at Berchtesgarten on May 4. On May 6, Devers, representing the Allies, accepted the surrender of German forces in western Austria.

With the war in Europe over, Devers was named commanding general of Army Ground Forces, a job which, after the defeat of Japan, consisted of the almost thankless tasks of training and administrating the army units that remained. He served in this capacity until his retirement in 1949. After assuming several civilian and military advisory positions in the 1950s, he lived for a number of years in Washington.

In assessing Devers' long and illustrious military career, four personal characteristics stand out: his enthusiasm, energy, dependability, and devotion to the armed services and country he loved. These traits are quite evident in the way he handled the many tasks he was asked to perform.

His most significant contribution was his appreciation of the possibilities of twentieth-century warfare and his good fortune to serve in positions that allowed him to make many of these possibilities become a reality. He was fascinated by innovative ideas. At Fort Sill in the 1920s, for instance, he developed techniques that allowed artillery units to fire for effect much sooner than had been the case previously. While at Fort Knox, he fostered the increased use and development of self-propelled artillery, more and better medium tanks, and improved tank engines, suspension systems, and design. He also advocated extensive air support for mobile formations, thus calling for tactics that resembled those used by Germany's *blitzkrieg* forces. And even though certain of his ideas were never implemented, others that were initially turned down, such as the attachment of tank destroyer battalions to divisions, became accepted practice by the end of the war.

Devers was further impressed by the possibilities of air power. Not only did he understand its application for armored warfare; he also appreciated how it could be utilized in amphibious and airborne operations. After the war his belief in the importance of air power continued, and he strongly backed guided missile and atomic research for both land and aerial weapons.

In addition, Devers was an outstanding organizer, and his hard work and dedication produced impressive results. At Fort Bragg and again at Fort Knox, he oversaw important construction projects, expanded greatly the number of troops being trained, and improved training methods. His organizational ability also allowed him to deal successfully with the myriad of duties he performed in 1943 in Great Britain and later in Italy, where he was overall commander of U.S. forces. And his last active military assignment, as head of Army Ground Forces (later Army Field Forces), was singularly suited to his administrative talents.

Despite his reputation as an administrator, Devers always wanted to be considered a fighting man. While his command of 6th Army Group in 1944 and 1945 was not as distinguished as it might have been (he was decisive, but at times impulsive and inaccurate in the evaluations he sent to his superiors), it was sufficient to earn him the acclaim of his fellow citizens at war's end. He rightly deserved the fourth star he received in March 1945.

Another contribution made by General Devers (and one too often overlooked) was his effectiveness in dealing with the other services and with foreign leaders.

Whether he dealt with naval representatives in Panama, air force commanders in Italy, or British or French generals in Europe, his firm, yet fairminded, approach to problems gained him their respect.

Although not as flamboyant as some of the other American generals, he enjoyed good relations with the press. No doubt, part of the reason stemmed from his infectious smile, almost boyish appearance, and amiable manner. But besides being likeable, the reporters also recognized that General Devers was an extremely competent, thoroughly professional military leader. His competence and professionalism are well exemplified in his understanding of how technology could be applied effectively to modern warfare.

BIBLIOGRAPHY

Blumenson, Martin, ed. *The Patton Papers*. 2 vols. Boston: Houghton Mifflin Company, 1972–1974.
Chandler, Alfred D., Jr., ed. *The Papers of Dwight David Eisenhower: The War Years*. Vols. 3–4. Baltimore: Johns Hopkins University Press, 1970.
Lattre de Tassigny, Jean de. *The History of the First French Army*. Translated by Malcolm Barnes. London: Allen and Unwin, 1952.
MacDonald, Charles B. *The Last Offensive. (United States Army in World War II. European Theater of Operations.)* Washington, D.C.: U.S. Government Printing Office, 1973.
Pogue, Forrest C. *George C. Marshall: Organizer of Victory*. New York: Viking Press, 1973.
Seventh U.S. Army. *Report of Operations in France and Germany 1944–1945*. 3 vols. Heidelberg: Aloys Gräf, 1946.

ALAN WILT

DEWEY, George (b. Montpelier, Vt., December 26, 1837; d. Washington, D.C., January 16, 1917), naval officer. Dewey is renowned as the victor at Manila Bay during the Spanish-American War, and for his service as president for seventeen years of the Navy's General Board.

Dewey claimed descent from a French Huguenot family that settled briefly in Kent, England, before Thomas Duee emigrated to Massachusetts in 1634. Dewey's father, Julius Yemans Dewey, was a prominent physician who built a small fortune as president of the National Life Insurance Company. Dewey won appointment to the Naval Academy in 1854 and ranked fifth among the fifteen graduates in 1858. After a cruise with the European Squadron in the steam frigate *Wabash*, Dewey passed his final examination and on April 19, 1861, was the third in his class to receive his commission as lieutenant.

Because of the scarcity of naval officers at the outbreak of the Civil War, Dewey won the billet of executive officer in the steam frigate *Mississippi* shortly before the old side-wheeler joined the blockading squadron under David Glasgow Farragut* in Gulf waters. Dewey later claimed that his service under Farragut was far better training than any schooling he had received at Annapolis, and he always regarded Farragut as the model naval officer—"urbane, decisive, and indomitable.'' As Melancthon Smith, the *Mississippi*'s skipper, suffered from poor night vision, he trusted Dewey to navigate his ship during the dash by Farragut's squadron on April 24, 1862, past Forts Jackson and St. Philip, the defenders of New Orleans. The following year, when Farragut attempted a similar run past Port Hudson, the *Mississippi*'s inept civilian pilot grounded her on a mud bank, but Dewey won high praise for his cool-headed direction of the small boats that removed the crew from the stranded ship under heavy enemy fire. Subsequently, Dewey served as executive officer in the steam frigate *Colorado* during the attack led by David Dixon Porter* on Fort Fisher in 1865. Dewey emerged from the war with the rank of lieutenant commander.

After a tour with the revived European Squadron in the sloop-of-war *Kearsarge*, Dewey returned to the United States to marry Susan Boardman Goodwin, the daughter of the former New Hampshire governor, and to serve five years at the Naval Academy under a reforming superintendent, David D. Porter. Susan Dewey died in 1872, just five days after giving birth to a son, George Goodwin Dewey.

Dewey's naval service during the three decades after the Civil War was honorable but without special distinction. He was saddened by the Navy's postwar decline, but he was not sufficiently moved to join such reformers as Stephen Bleeker Luce,* Alfred Thayer Mahan,* and Bradley Allen Fiske* to demand improvements. Among his duties during the 1870s and 1880s, Dewey led a survey of the waters of the Gulf of California on the third-class sloop *Narragansett*, acted as lighthouse inspector with an office in Boston (1875–1877), and was secretary of the Lighthouse Board in Washington (1878–1882).

Dewey employed political influence in 1889 to win appointment as chief of the Bureau of Equipment; in this post he was much concerned with providing coal for the "New Navy" of steam and steel. From Equipment he moved in 1893 to the presidency of the Lighthouse Board and two years later to the presidency of the then prestigious Board of Inspection and Survey. It was in the latter capacity that he observed the trials of the early battleships *Texas, Maine, Iowa, Indiana,* and *Massachusetts.* In 1896, at the age of fifty-nine, he was finally promoted to the rank of commodore, which rank entitled him to command a squadron and to fly a single starred pendant. The following year, encouraged by Assistant Secretary of the Navy Theodore Roosevelt,* Dewey again employed political influence to achieve position, command of the Asiatic Station.

Dewey raised his pendant at Yokohama in January 1898 as the United States moved toward war with Spain. He was already assembling the scattered ships of the Asiatic command when, ten days after the sinking of the *Maine*, Roosevelt cabled the commodore the famous order: "Keep full of coal. In event of declaration of war with Spain, your duty will be to see that the Spanish Squadron does not leave the Asiatic Coast, and then offensive operations in the Philippines.'' Dewey had his squadron concentrated at Mirs Bay near Hong Kong when on April 24 the Navy Department directed him to use his "utmost endeavors...to capture or destroy" the Spanish Squadron in the Philippines.

The four cruisers and two gunboats that Dewey, in the manner of Farragut, led into Manila Bay in the early hours of May 1 were far superior in tonnage, guns, and general fighting efficiency to the pathetic squadron of the Spanish commander, Rear Admiral Don Patricio Montojo. Once Dewey spotted the Spanish ships drawn up in crescent formation before the old arsenal at Cavite, he led his force into battle standing on the unprotected bridge of the protected cruiser *Olympia*, his flagship. Firing at ranges of two thousand to three thousand yards, Dewey's squadron passed the Spanish thrice to the west and twice to the east before withdrawing to the center of the bay at 7:30 A.M. for breakfast and to count ammunition. At 11:16 Dewey returned to complete the destruction of Montojo's remaining vessels.

Dewey thereafter occupied and controlled Manila Bay, awaiting the arrival from the United States of Army units sufficient to hold Manila. During the summer, Dewey encouraged the Philippine insurgents under Emilio Aguinaldo to rise against Spanish rule and assumed a stern attitude toward the German Vice Admiral von Diederichs, who for unexplained reasons assembled his squadron in the bay. Dewey also engaged in secret negotiations with the Spanish governor general that paved the way for the city's surrender on August 12 after only token resistance to attacks by the American Army and Navy. Dewey was deeply impressed by the strategic importance of Subig Bay to the north of Manila, but he was ambivalent as to whether the United States should retain the Philippines. In recognition of his war achievements, Congress in 1899 bestowed on Dewey the rank of Admiral of the Navy with proviso that he could not be retired except by his own request.

Dewey returned to the United States in the summer of 1899 at the height of his extraordinary popularity. His public image was shortly dimmed, however, by circumstances attending his marriage to a wealthy Washington socialite, Mildred MacLean Hazen, and by his rather awkward bid for the presidency.

From 1900 until his death in 1917 Dewey served as the first (and only) president of the General Board of the Navy, the senior body established by Secretary of the Navy John D. Long to advise on high-level naval policy. In 1902–1903 Dewey commanded the widely publicized fleet maneuvers in the Caribbean, which have been regarded as a warning to Germany during the second Venezuelan Crisis. And in 1903 he assumed the chairmanship of the new Joint Army and Navy Board, the predecessor of the Joint Chiefs of Staff.

During his last eighteen years George Dewey was the unchallenged elder statesman of the U.S. Navy with a public reputation comparable to that of his great foreign contemporaries: John Arbuthnot Fisher of Britain, Alfred von Tirpitz of Germany, and Marquis Heihachiro Togo of Japan. It was his spectacular victory at Manila Bay that catapulted Dewey to first place in the Navy. Although accomplished with exemplary dispatch in the heroic manner of a Farragut, his May Day victory was really a foregone conclusion given the overwhelming superiority of the American squadron over the Spanish. Indeed, the battle was significant chiefly for its political consequences. But for Manila Bay, it is hardly likely that the United States would have acquired the Philippines or so rapidly assumed a major role in East Asian affairs.

Dewey's contributions to the Navy as leader of the General Board, although largely unknown to the public, were probably as significant to the Navy as was his victory at Manila Bay. Under his direction, the General Board debated strategies for war against Germany (Plan Black) and Japan (Plan Orange), proposed the 1903 building program to complete a fleet of forty-eight battleships by 1920, recommended the development of naval bases commanding a naval route from the Atlantic seaboard via the Caribbean and an isthmian canal to the Pacific and China, and generally supported the maintenance of a single battlefleet concentrated in the Atlantic. Dewey supported the all-big-gun *Dreadnought*-type battleship in opposition to the more conservative Alfred Thayer Mahan, and he fought hard for a naval base at Subig Bay against General Leonard Wood* and Army strategists, who wanted to concentrate Philippine defense at Manila.

Dewey sought with considerable success to hold himself above naval factional politics. His success is demonstrated by the fact that he was idolized by both Secretary of the Navy Josephus Daniels* and Daniels' bitter critic, Rear Admiral Bradley Fiske. During the preparedness campaign prior to the United States' entry into World War I, Dewey publicly defended the Navy's efficiency against the critics of the Wilson administration even as he supported the General Board's program for a Navy second to none. Far more than to brilliance or to intellectual originality, Dewey's success must be attributed to a combination of fortuitous accident, extraordinary dignity, sound common sense, and skillful personal diplomacy during nearly three decades of practically unbroken tenure on the Washington scene.

BIBLIOGRAPHY

Dewey, George. *Autobiography of George Dewey, Admiral of the Navy*. New York: Charles Scribner's Sons, 1916.

Sargent, Nathan. *Admiral Dewey and the Manila Campaign*. Washington, D.C.: Naval Historical Foundation, 1947.

Spector, Ronald. *Admiral of the New Navy: The Life and Career of George Dewey*. Baton Rouge: Louisiana State University Press, 1974.

West, Richard S. *Admirals of Empire: The Combined Story of George Dewey, Alfred Thayer Mahan, Winfield Scott Schley, and William Thomas Sampson*. Indianapolis: Bobbs-Merrill Company, 1948.

WILLIAM R. BRAISTED

DICKMAN, Joseph Theodore (b. Dayton, Ohio, October 6, 1857; d. Washington, D.C., October 23, 1927), Army officer. Dickman was one of the outstanding field commanders in the American Expeditionary Force (AEF) during World War I.

Joseph Dickman was born into a family of German ancestry. His father served as a captain in the Ohio Volunteer Infantry during the Civil War and early interested him in a military career. In 1876 Dickman was appointed to the U.S. Military Academy at West Point, New York. Because of his mischievous and full-spirited nature, he had difficulty in adjusting to the military's strict discipline. He accumulated a large number of demerits and was suspended from the Academy for one year "for interfering with and striking a new cadet." Returning to West Point, chastised by the suspension, Dickman graduated in 1881 and was commissioned a second lieutenant in the cavalry.

For the next two decades Dickman served principally in the West, participating in campaigns against Indians, bandits, and Mexican revolutionaries. He also attended the Infantry and Cavalry School at Fort Leavenworth, Kansas, where he was an honor graduate in 1883, and was an instructor at the school from 1895 to 1898. In his spare hours, he doggedly studied foreign languages and military history and thoroughly versed himself in the writings of European strategists and tacticians. During the Spanish-American War, Dickman served on the staff of General Joseph Wheeler* in the Santiago Campaign. In 1899 he commanded an infantry regiment in operations against insurgents on the island of Panay in the Philippines and a year later saw action in China during the Boxer Rebellion.

In the early years of the new century, Dickman had a variety of assignments. He served successively as an instructor at the Infantry and Cavalry School, an original member of the newly created War Department General Staff, a regimental officer, inspector general of the Department of Mindanao, Philippine Islands, inspector general of the Department of Missouri and the Central Division, a detached officer assigned to various uniform, equipment, and organizational boards, and commanding officer of the 2d Cavalry. In the process, he rose steadily in rank; he was promoted to major in 1906, lieutenant colonel in 1912, colonel in 1914, and brigadier general in 1917. During these years, Dickman was recognized as one of the Army's outstanding tacticians and an officer of wide accomplishment. His students at Fort Leavenworth long remembered the emphasis he placed upon effective use of terrain in his classes on tactics, and in 1905, while assigned to the General Staff, he prepared the first American edition of the *Field Service Regulations*. Modeled after the German Army regulations, this "military bible" ultimately became the comprehensive guide to the organization, administration, and tactics governing the Army in the field.

Six months after the United States entered World War I in April 1917, Dickman, now quite portly and serving as commander of the 85th Division, was given command of the 3d Division. He determinedly guided the division through its training phase at Camp Greene, North Carolina, and in May 1918 took it to France. Before the end of the month, he and part of the division were moving into the line in the Chateau-Thierry sector. In July Dickman's 3d Division played a crucial role in repulsing the last major German offensive of the war. Impressed with his efficient handling of the division, General John Joseph Pershing,* commander of the AEF, gave Dickman command of IV Corps. Commanding the corps from August 18 to October 12 and the I Corps from then until after the Armistice, he ably performed in the St. Mihiel and Meuse-Argonne offensives.

On November 15, 1918, Dickman was named commander of the Third Army, the American force assigned to the occupation of Germany. It was a short-lived assignment. French arrogance and harshness toward German civilians angered Dickman, and in April 1919 he was replaced because of his strained relations with the French and French wonderings that he was pro-German. For a brief time afterward Dickman, who had been recently promoted to major general in the Regular Army, presided over a board of directors charged with developing and setting forth the lessons of the war. He then was appointed commander of the Southern Department and the VIII Corps Area, a post he held until his retirement in October 1921.

Dickman lived the remainder of his life in Washington, D.C., devoting much of his time to the writing of his memoir, *The Great Crusade*, a straightforward narrative of his experiences during World War I. Its bald descriptions of military operations aptly reflect the professionalism that was the essence of Dickman's career.

Dickman's place in American military history rests upon his service in France in 1918. Rushed into the line at the end of May to help prop up the wavering French, Dickman and units of his eager but green 3d Division made an initial good showing in stopping the Germans at the Marne River crossings at Chateau-Thierry. The real test, however, came in the Second Battle of the Marne. The Germans planned to enlarge the Marne salient, and Dickman's men, who were guarding the south bank of the Marne east of Chateau-Thierry, stood directly in the path of one prong of the German onslaught. Dickman's French superior ordered him to defend the Marne "with one foot in the water." But Dickman wisely judged the instructions as suicidal and ignored them. Instead, he thinned out his frontline and, calling upon his unparalleled soldier's eye for ground, prepared a defense in depth. In this way the bulk of his men were largely unscathed by the German preparatory artillery fire and ready to meet the German attack, which was launched in the dawn hours of July 15.

The French troops on Dickman's right gave way before the Germans, threatening his flank. But Dickman held firm. The 38th Infantry echeloned backward to protect the flank and, using rifle fire with deadly effect, stood off two German divisions. Elsewhere, Dickman's stalwart infantry also fought like fiends, battling the Germans to a standstill in vicious little melees. The day ended with no Germans south of the Marne in Dickman's sector "except the dead" and the German offensive blunted. There could be no doubt after Dickman's stand on the Marne that the American reinforcement ensured an Allied triumph in the war.

According to Coffman Dickman's actions in the Second Battle of the Marne proved him to be "a practical, hard-fighting, hard-driving field commander." Pershing rewarded him with the command of the IV Corps, which was being assembled to assist in the reduction of the St. Mihiel salient. Entrusted with pinching in the east side of the salient, Dickman's corps made good progress on the morning of September 12, the first day of the attack. By the afternoon, however, it was clear that the advance from both sides of the salient was not fast enough to prevent the Germans from evacuating large numbers of troops. As a result, the bag of prisoners was disappointing, although Dickman, still a cavalryman at heart, found some satisfaction in the part mounted troops played in the offensive, the only time they were used by the AEF in battle.

In the mid-October shakeup of field commanders that followed the stalling of Pershing's offensive in the Meuse-Argonne sector, Dickman took over the I Corps. Situated on the extreme left of the sector, it had encountered the greatest difficulties and was the lagging portion of the advance. Over the next two weeks, Dickman carried out local attacks to obtain better positions for the jump-off for the final push against the Germans in the Meuse-Argonne. It came on November 1, and two days later the enemy was in full retreat with the victorious Americans in pursuit. For Dickman, however, the euphoria of the breakthrough was marred by the infamous Sedan incident. Misinterpreting instructions from Pershing's headquarters, the American 1st Division marched directly across the front of Dickman's corps and into the advance of the French upon Sedan. A "master of military punctillo," Dickman was choleric over this tactical atrocity and thereafter was characteristically bitter and unforgiving toward the division's commander, Brigadier General Frank Parker. Not only had the division's action interfered with his battlefield tactics, but, at least in Dickman's opinion, it had also given the French a bad opinion of himself and the American Army.

Dickman came out of World War I with a deserved reputation as a skilled military technician second to none among AEF field commanders. Although he had embarked upon his military career at a time when the U.S. Army was little more than a frontier constabulary, he had successfully met the challenge of command in modern war. In this respect, Dickman epitomizes the experience of the American Army officer corps during the nation's emergence as a world power.

BIBLIOGRAPHY

Bullard, Robert L. *Fighting Generals*. Ann Arbor, Mich.: J. W. Edwards, 1944.
Coffman, Edward M. *The War to End All Wars; The American Military Experience in World War I*. New York: Oxford University Press, 1968.
Dickman, Joseph T. *The Great Crusade; A Narrative of the World War*. New York: D. Appleton and Company, 1927.
Nelson, Keith L. *Victors Divided; America and the Allies in Germany, 1918–1923*. Berkeley: University of California Press, 1975.
Stallings, Laurence. *The Doughboys; The Story of the AEF, 1917–1918*. New York: Harper and Row, 1963.
Vandiver, Frank E. *Black Jack: The Life and Times of John J. Pershing*. 2 vols. College Station: Texas A&M University Press, 1977.

JOHN KENNEDY OHL

DODGE, Henry (b. Vincennes, Ind., October 12, 1782; d. Burlington, Iowa, June 19, 1867), frontiersman, politician, soldier, Territory of Wisconsin governor and delegate to Congress, U.S. senator.

Henry Dodge was born into an American frontier family at Vincennes, Indiana. His father was a veteran of the American Revolution and his mother was from Kentucky. He spent his boyhood in Kentucky and the Illinois country. In 1796 the Dodges settled in Spanish Louisiana in the District of Ste. Genevieve where Henry learned farming, lead mining, and trading. He married Christina McDonald.

Succeeding his father in 1805, he became sheriff of the district, an office he continued to hold for sixteen years. For reasons unclear, Dodge prepared to join Aaron Burr on his Western expedition, but returned when he heard of Burr's arrest. In 1813 he became marshal of the Territory of Missouri. He rose in the ranks of the Missouri militia to major general and during the War of 1812 led troops to the relief of the settlement at Boone Lick.

Dodge moved in 1827 with his family of nine children and his slaves to the lead fields of the upper Mississippi Valley, settling first at Galena and then on Winnebago lands near Dodgeville, Wisconsin. He was soon regarded as a leader on the mining frontier, and he quickly seized every opportunity to work for the miners' claims to the land against both the federal government and the Indians. In 1827 when a crisis developed over Winnebago resentment of white lead miner encroachment into their lands, Dodge commanded a militia cavalry in support of the regulars under General Henry Atkinson.* The Winnebago surrendered without resistance. Dodge built a stockade and established a substantial mining and refining operation employing some 230 workers. An Indian agent warned him of trespassing but to no avail.

The return back east across the Mississippi River in 1832 of more than a thousand of the Sauk and Fox Indians who had been evicted from their homes the year before as a consequence of the Indian Removal policy precipitated the Black Hawk War. State militia and federal troops were soon involved. Dodge, with a commission as colonel in the territorial militia, recruited a body of mounted volunteer rangers to protect the mining region. The Dodge volunteers were involved in a minor skirmish in southwestern Wisconsin in which eleven Indians were killed. This much publicized encounter, called the Battle of Pecatonica, encouraged the whites. Three militia brigades were on a supply mission a few weeks later when they got word of the location of Black Hawk's fugitive band attempting escape. Dodge and General James D. Henry's brigades took up the pursuit and engaged Black Hawk in the Battle of Wisconsin Heights, a prelude to the final battle of the war. Although Black Hawk gained a temporary reprieve when Dodge and Henry chose to recuperate for a day, the war was soon ended.

Realizing that foot soldieers were not able to deal with Indian problems on the Great Plains and concerned with the increasing restlessness of the Indians in the upper Mississippi Valley, of which the Winnebago outbreak and the Black Hawk War were symptomatic, Congress created a battalion of volunteer mounted rangers to handle the situation. While yet engaged in the Black Hawk War,

Dodge received a presidential appointment as major to command the rangers. In 1833 his companies of rangers endeavored to keep the Illinois-Wisconsin frontier quiet, escorted Santa Fe traders, and attempted to deal with problems of Indians removed into the Oklahoma area. The militia unit, however, because of its one-year enlistments and the magnitude of its mission, was simply inadequate and ineffective.

Congress correctly assessed the situation and replaced the rangers the next year with a professional dragoon regiment. Again Dodge, with a new commission as colonel, was placed in command. In 1834 he led the dragoons on their first expedition, through eastern and southern Oklahoma. Although insufficient supplies made it impossible to cover the area in his orders, and even though some one-third of his officers and men died of disease, the expedition was considered successful. The tribes were friendly with the dragoons and even gave them some food; Dodge had learned considerably about intertribal relations, and the dragoons had learned a great deal about campaigning on the Plains.

The regiment was split into three squadrons. Dodge led his contingent the following summer from eastern Kansas, along the Platte and South Platte rivers to the Rockies, and returned down the valley of the Arkansas River and along the Santa Fe Trail. The extended march into distant Indian country was successful. As before, there were no clashes, and the Indians seemed favorably impressed.

When the territory of Wisconsin, including Iowa, Minnesota, and parts of the Dakotas, was created in 1836, Dodge was appointed its first governor. He was intimately acquainted with the problems of living on the frontier and widely regarded as a leader. He was reappointed in 1839. Although he was replaced in 1841 when the Whigs came to power in the national government, he was elected to serve as the territory's delegate to Congress. With the return of a Democrat to the presidency in 1845, Dodge was again appointed territorial governor. Wisconsin became a state in 1848, and Dodge was elected one of its first U.S. senators. In 1851 he was reelected to a full term. His senatorial career coincided with the decline of the Democratic party in the state. At the expiration of that term in 1857, Dodge retired from public life and moved to Burlington, Iowa.

Henry Dodge had limited service as a Missouri militia officer in the War of 1812, but the experience marked him as a leader to whom his fellow frontiersmen would turn in times of crisis as they were aleady doing for nonmilitary situations. With the Winnebago outbreak in 1827, Dodge was chosen by his fellow miners to lead them against that threat.

Months later, when the Black Hawk War flared up, Dodge emerged once more as a military leader. His stature was considerably enhanced by the overdrawn significance of the engagement at Pecatonica. Even though they were closely related, the morale implications of Pecatonica were more significant than the military consequences.

Dodge made his first substantial contribution in the events that brought the war to a close. Black Hawk's* fugitive band had eluded capture by the federal troops and state militia. When the supply brigades under Dodge and General Henry learned of Black Hawk's probable location, they pursued the Indians and gave them battle at Wisconsin Heights. Although Dodge and Henry did not follow through and Black Hawk's doom was momentarily postponed, General Atkinson and the brigades brought the pursuit to a close several days later at the Bad Axe Massacre. The Dodge and Henry proponents have long contended the relative importance of each to this final campaign. Evidence is rather conclusive that Dodge took the initiative in the decision to pursue Black Hawk rather than to return directly to Atkinson as their orders had specified. This gave Atkinson the break he needed to bring the campaign to a successful conclusion.

The short-lived ranger battalion under Dodge's command accomplished little. It performed patrol and peacekeeping functions over widely scattered areas, but it was simply unequal in makeup and size to its assignment. This is in no way a discredit to Dodge. The ranger experience had demonstrated the weakness of the volunteer service concept and the necessity of regular mounted regiments.

When Congress recognized this and created the regular dragoon regiment, Dodge was raised in rank and placed in command. The rangers were the connecting link between two important periods of the military establishment. Dodge's ability and the more favorable circumstances of his new command proved the worth of the new concept which assured continuity to what eventually became the cavalry.

Dodge's appointment as chief executive of the Territory of Wisconsin, although he was also to be commander in chief of the militia and superintendent of Indian affairs in his new capacity, essentially ended his military career. His abilities as a natural leader and his cumulative experiences served him well in his several positions of military responsibility at local, territorial, and national levels.

BIBLIOGRAPHY

Pelzer, Louis. *Henry Dodge*. Iowa City: State Historical Society of Iowa, 1910.

Prucha, Francis Paul. *The Sword of the Republic: The United States Army on the Frontier, 1783–1846*. New York: Macmillan, 1977.

Whitney, Ellen M. comp. and ed. *The Black Hawk War, 1831–1832*. Vol. 1, *Illinois Volunteers*, 1970; Vol. 2, *Letters and Papers*, Part 1: *April 30, 1831–June 23, 1832*, 1973; Vol. 2, *Letters and Papers*, Part 2, *June 24, 1832–October 14, 1834*, 1975. Springfield: Illinois State Historical Library.

DWIGHT L. SMITH

DONIPHAN, Alexander William (b. Mason Couny, Ky., July 9, 1808; d. Richmond, Mo., August 8, 1887), lawyer; Doniphan was a commander of the expedition that wrested the American Southwest from the Mexicans in 1846.

Alexander W. Doniphan was born into the family of Joseph Doniphan and Anne Smith, both Virginians. Joseph had gone to Kentucky with one of Daniel

Boone's parties and had taught school there for perhaps a year, then returned to
Virginia sometime before 1779 to enlist in the Continental Army. He was present
at Yorktown for the surrender of Lord Charles Cornwallis. After the Revolution,
he married Anne Smith and returned with her to Kentucky in about 1790. When
Joseph died in 1813, Anne decided that Alexander needed an education that she
could not provide and sent the boy to school in nearby Augusta, Kentucky,
where he resided with his elder brother, George. His tutor, Richard Keene, was
a graduate of Trinity College and a fugitive of the Irish rebellion of 1798. Keene's
influence proved very great to the boy; Keene forced him to study the major
poets and the classics, developing in him a zest for oratory and a concern for
political liberty. At age fourteen Alexander enrolled in the new Methodist academy, Augusta College, from which he graduated at age eighteen with distinction
in the classics. His mother encouraged him to study the law and helped him to
find a place in the office of Martin Marshall of Augusta in the manner of the
times. Marshall required the lad to continue his study of the classics for six more
months; then Doniphan studied U.S. and English history with emphasis on Anglo-
Saxon legal history before turning to law texts. After three years of this work,
Doniphan was admitted to the bar of both Kentucky and Ohio.

In 1830 Doniphan moved to Lexington, Missouri, and began the practice of
law, his chief occupation for the next thirty years. He acquired an outstanding
reputation in unpopular causes and served as defense attorney in virtually every
major criminal case tried in western Missouri during those decades. The demand
for his services undoubtedly was based as much on his renowned eloquence as
on his knowledge of the law.

Some of Doniphan's law practice came about as a result of the large migration
of Mormons into western Missouri; in one instance Doniphan defended a church
leader charged with conspiracy to commit the murder of the state governor. Even
though most of the region disliked the Mormons and sought revenge, Doniphan
got the accused off with a punishment of only five minutes in jail.

In 1833 Doniphan moved from Lexington to Liberty and made that his home
for the rest of his life. It was there that in 1837 he met and married Elizabeth
Jane Thornton, described by a friend as a very intelligent, cultured lady. The
couple had two sons, both of whom died in accidents while yet young. And it
was from Liberty that Doniphan was elected three times to serve in the Missouri
State General Assembly.

During the so-called Mormon War of 1838, Doniphan was appointed commanding officer of the 1st Brigade of Missouri militia. His reputation as a
responsible state leader was enhanced greatly by his conduct in this affair.
Ordered by his commander to put to death some Mormon leaders, including
Joseph Smith, Doniphan refused, calling the proposed action murder. Although
he took a very unpopular stand and at the same time disobeyed a direct military
order, Doniphan saved the lives of the men and added considerably to the public
estimate of his courage and integrity.

Missourians remembered these characteristics, and in 1846 when war broke out with Mexico, Doniphan received the recognition of his neighbors and the state. The War Department created the Army of the West at Fort Leavenworth, using Colonel Stephen Watts Kearny's* 1st Dragoons as the nucleus, fleshed out with eight companies representing as many counties in Missouri. These companies combined into a unit classified as the 1st Regiment of Missouri Volunteers. Into the Clay County company Alexander Doniphan enlisted as private. Shortly thereafter, Kearny ordered the troops to elect their own field grade officers. Assembled on the parade grounds at the fort, the Missouri volunteers were addressed by the candidates before conducting the balloting. Aided by his appearance, oratory, military experience, and some free meals provided by residents of Liberty, the six foot-four inch Doniphan was the overwhelming choice for commander of the regiment with the rank of colonel in the volunteers.

Under the overall command of Colonel Kearny, the Army of the West left Fort Leavenworth for Santa Fe, New Mexico, in June 1846. This portion of the campaign was uneventful in a military sense. But with the army spread out for many miles over the Santa Fe Trail, Doniphan's portion—roughly half of the men—gradually changed from an undisciplined mob of boys, farmers, German immigrants, and unemployed into a tough military unit. Five weeks and 850 miles later, Doniphan and his regiment entered Santa Fe, accepting it from the Mexicans without a fight. At this point, Kearny, now a brigadier general, critically divided the Army of the West. His own mission was to take California from the Mexican government, leaving Doniphan the combined tasks of capturing the rest of New Mexico, subduing Navajos, Utes, and Zuñis and invading northern Mexico at least to Chihuahua, where he was "to link up with General Wool." All of this was to be done with less than nine hundred volunteers completely cut off from their government during the entire campaign.

In the heart of enemy country, Doniphan's own command was now weakened by the necessity of coercing the three tribes into accepting the jurisdiction of the United States and, more importantly, keeping the Utes and Navajos from kidnapping Mexicans and running off their livestock. Some of the Missourians struggled nearly one thousand miles, often in blizzard conditions, to track down the tribes, who fled as far as Canyon de Chelly in what is now Arizona. By this prodigious feat, Doniphan brought temporary peace among the Southwestern tribes and could feel that his right flank and rear were protected before he plunged into old Mexico.

Already beaten up by weather and the effect of long marches, Doniphan's regiment started toward Mexico. On Christmas Day 1846 they were attacked at El Paso by about twelve hundred Mexican dragoons. The Mexican forces seriously underestimated the morale of the Americans; their bold cavalry charge was sharply turned away by Doniphan's defensive tactics. The Mexicans lost forty to fifty killed and 150 wounded; the Americans lost only seven wounded.

Doniphan occupied El Paso with certain feelings of insecurity, but he took the proper steps to gain the friendship of the Mexicans before he dared resume his march south. He gradually realized that the natives feared the American occupying force less than they did their neighbors, the Apaches, who behaved toward them just as did the Navajos and Utes further north. Thus, Doniphan used more of his precious time and supplies pursuing the Apaches to teach them to let the citizens of El Paso alone. Only then did he dare resume his march to Chihuahua, another 270 miles of pitiless desert away.

Just north of Chihuahua along the Sacramento River, the Mexicans set up their last defense against the Missouri Volunteers. Through superior artillery tactics, the Americans drove the Mexicans from their entrenchments and opened the door to Chihuahua and the entire Mexican northwest. Incredibly, three hundred Mexicans but only two Americans were killed. Doniphan's orders had been to help Brigadier General John Ellis Wool* capture Chihuahua, then await further instructions. Without help or even knowledge of Wool's whereabouts, Doniphan had taken the province and the city. Some of his men wanted to continue on to Mexico City, but most were ready to go home. Their one-year enlistments had ended. They were completely isolated and unsupported in a foreign land; they were ragged, filthy, and broke. A messenger to General Zachary Taylor* finally cleared matters; Doniphan learned for the first time of Winfield Scott's* campaign aimed at Mexico City; the war in the north was nearly over, and Doniphan was to join Taylor prior to letting his men go home. Three more weeks of desert marching brough Doniphan to Taylor, who had not moved since his victory at Buena Vista in February. Some men reenlisted, but the majority made one more long march to Matamoros and then took ship to New Orleans and home.

After the war Doniphan resumed his law practice. In 1861 he went to Washington to represent Missouri in an attempt to prevent civil war; then he was offered command of the Missouri state guard but declined because the death of his two sons had undermined the health of his wife. He continued law practice in Liberty until his death.

Alexander Doniphan represented the finest type of American pioneer and civilian soldier, helping to bring law and stability to his state in the most trying of times. Pressed into military duty, he exhibited great leadership and skill in commanding the Missouri Volunteers. Virtually unaided by their government, they fought their way across thirty-six hundred miles of prairie and desert, land as unknown and unfriendly as the Mexicans and Indians whom they fought. Doniphan's military victories were complete and unquestioned; just as important was his judicious manner of managing the conquered, not only adding vast terrain to the American nation, but also bringing the first taste of American law to thousands of people who would now be citizens and wards of the United States.

BIBLIOGRAPHY

Bauer, K. Jack. *The Mexican War, 1846–1848*. New York: Macmillan, 1974.

Connelley, William E. *Doniphan's Expedition*. Topeka, Kans.: By the author, 1907.

George, Isaac. *Heroes and Incidents of the Mexican War*. Greensburg, Pa.: Review Publishing Company, 1903.

Hughes, John T. *Doniphan's Expedition*. Cincinnati: J. A. and U. P. James, 1848.
Karnes, Thomas L. *William Gilpin, Western Nationalist*. Austin: University of Texas, 1970.

THOMAS L. KARNES

DONOVAN, William Joseph (b. Buffalo, N.Y., January 1, 1883; d. Washington, D.C., February 8, 1959), World War I combat hero, lawyer, World War II strategic intelligence chief. Donovan is considered the father of American intelligence by some.

William "Wild Bill" Donovan was born into an Irish immigrant family in New York. His father was a railroad man. A devout Roman Catholic, William attended church schools until entering Niagara University for three years before transferring to Columbia College where he continued in the law school of Columbia University. At Columbia he was a contemporary of Franklin D. Roosevelt, although they moved in separate circles, and he was quarterback of the football team. He received the LL.B. degree in 1907 and returned to Buffalo at the age of twenty-four to practice law.

By 1912 Donovan had formed his own law firm (specializing in corporate law) and was instrumental in organizing the Buffalo Cavalry Troop I in the New York National Guard. In this unit he saw duty during the Depew railroad strike and along the Texas border as part of John Joseph Pershing's* expedition against Pancho Villa. On July 15, 1914, he married Ruth Rumsey, a member of an old and wealthy Buffalo family. The first of many overseas missions began in 1915 when he went to Poland as a representative of the Rockefeller Foundation's American War Relief Commission.

With the U.S. entry into World War I, Donovan joined the 69th Regiment of the 27th New York National Guard Division. Although this unit continued to call itself the Old 69th, it became the 165th Infantry of the 42d Rainbow Division. Some accounts claim that the strenuous training program which he developed as battalion major for the 165th gave him the nickname "Wild Bill"; other accounts indicate that the name came from his football days or from the Mexican Campaign. At any rate the nickname was widely known by the end of the war.

Donovan emerged from World War I as a national hero, having seen action at Champagne-Marne, St.-Mihiel, and Argonne. Wounded twice, he was promoted to colonel and given command of the regiment. He was the first to receive the triple honors of Congressional Medal of Honor, Distinguished Service Cross, and Distinguished Service Medal, along with numerous foreign decorations. In 1957 when he received the National Security Medal, he became the first to hold all four decorations. The poet Joyce Kilmer was also a member of the 165th and was killed while with Donovan.

Mustered out in 1919, Donovan and his wife traveled privately to Japan, which resulted in a brief official trip to Siberia to evaluate the Kolchak government. He returned to Buffalo as an attorney and entered Republican politics. In 1922 he was appointed U.S. district attorney for western New York. He developed a reputation as a crime-fighter, cracking down on narcotics, burglary rings, both labor and corporations, and vigorously enforcing the Volstead Act. In 1924 he was the Republican nominee for lieutenant governor. He lost the election but did considerably better than his running mate who lost to Al Smith.

Following his defeat in 1924, Donovan moved to Washington, D.C., where President Calvin Coolidge appointed him head of the Justice Department's Criminal Division. The next year he became assistant attorney general, leading the important Anti-Trust Division. In 1928 he became chairman of a commission on studying the problem of water rights related to the Rio Grande River. As a leader in the Republican party, Donovan was a strong supporter of Herbert Hoover. With Hoover's election as president in 1928, many assumed that Donovan would become attorney general. He did not receive the appointment, perhaps because he was both a "wet" and a Catholic, two major issues in the 1928 election.

In 1929 Donovan returned to private life and opened a law office in New York City. During the Depression, he worked with the American Legion on behalf of unemployed veterans. He made an unsuccessful bid for the New York governorship in 1932, which was a bad year for Republicans generally. The 1930s saw considerable foreign travel for Donovan, as he was fascinated by events in Europe. He amazed foreign affairs experts in 1935 by gaining an audience with Mussolini and receiving unprecedented permission to observe the Italian Army action in Ethiopia. The following year he traveled to Spain to see the civil war.

The advent of hostilities in Europe saw President Franklin Roosevelt rely increasingly on Donovan for foreign intelligence. In 1940 he went on a series of secret missions for the president, including Africa, South America, the Middle East, and the Pacific, as well as Europe. He covered some twenty-five thousand miles, and his confidential reports to Roosevelt convinced the president, despite their political differences, of Donovan's great worth. On March 26, 1941, Donovan made a report to the nation, over national radio, on the dangers of Nazism. On July 11, Roosevelt appointed him to head the new Office of the Coordinator of Information (COI), with a staff of 250 experts in various fields.

After the United States entered World War II, Roosevelt created the Office of Strategic Services (OSS) with Donovan in charge. The public information component of the old COI became a separate agency, the Office of War Information, under playwright Robert Sherwood. As OSS chief, Donovan reported to the Joint Chiefs of Staff.

The American intelligence and counterintelligence posture at the beginning of the war was extremely limited, and most of the successes later achieved must be credited to Donovan and his fledgling OSS. Except for Latin America and the Far Eastern Command, Donovan's mandate included the entire world. In addition to responsibility for gathering and evaluating strategic intelligence, the OSS also planned and executed special operations and services. Donovan, by virtue of his personality and his leadership, must be credited with the broad definition of "strategic services" which came to encompass counterintelligence, sabotage, and espionage, as well as behind-the-lines operations with partisans, propaganda, and psychological warfare. He was made brigadier general in 1943 and major general the following year.

The basic organization of the OSS included secret intelligence (operatives in the field), morale operations (propaganda), and research and analysis (intelligence estimates and analyses), as well as documentation and map components. Donovan recruited into the OSS a wide variety of people, including a number of well-known personalities. These familiar names, along with their romantic exploits, are no doubt in part responsible for the reputation the OSS achieved— not that there was any ambivalance in the American mind as to the techniques used. "Oh So Secret" was a popular nickname for the organization.

Looking forward to the end of the war, Donovan proposed to Roosevelt that a peacetime agency similar to OSS be developed. Roosevelt died before approving the plan, and President Harry Truman disbanded the OSS immediately after the Japanese surrender. After serving briefly as assistant chief counsel for the prosecutor at the Nuremberg trials, Donovan returned to private law practice in New York where he continued to lobby for a central intelligence agency.

Eventually, much of what Donovan had recommended was achieved by the National Security Act of 1947 which established the Central Intelligence Agency as a separate organization. Although Donovan was not chosen to head the new CIA, as some had expected, his influence was undoubtedly felt in it since many OSS personnel joined the CIA, notably Allen Dulles and Richard Helms who served as CIA directors.

In 1946 Donovan sought but did not get the Republican nomination for U.S. senator from New York. In 1953, at the age of seventy, he was appointed ambassador to Thailand; he served until 1954. Throughout this period he was an elder statesman in the legal field, and as late as 1956 he visited Europe to work for refugees from the Hungarian rebellion, for whom he raised $1.5 million. He received the National Security Medal in 1957. He suffered a stroke in 1956 and upon his death in 1959 was buried in Arlington Cemetery with full military honors.

Although Donovan established a solid reputation for himself as a soldier in World War I, he is best known as head of the OSS in World War II. The OSS suffered its share of failures and was criticized for wastefulness and costly errors, but by comparison to any wartime intelligence effort and especially to other contemporary agencies, the OSS must be rated a significant success. Donovan's role is almost unanimously appreciated by historians. Although Donovan personally regretted that he was not appointed to head the new CIA, it may be fortunate for his standing in history that he was not. His position rests securely on the now romantic days of World War II, and the subsequent criticisms of intelligence agencies, especially the CIA, beginning in the late 1960s have not sullied that reputation. The role, techniques, and even desirability of intelligence and counterintelligence continue to be debated, but "Wild Bill" Donovan remains an American hero.

BIBLIOGRAPHY

Alsop, Stewart, and Thomas Braden. *Sub Rosa; O.S.S. and American Espionage*. New York: Reynal and Hitchcock, 1948.
Duffy, Francis P. *Father Duffy's Story*. New York: George H. Doran Company, 1919.
Ford, Corey. *Donovan of OSS*. Boston: Little, Brown, and Company, 1970.
Ransom, Harry Howe. *The Intelligence Establishment*. Cambridge, Mass.: Harvard University Press, 1970.
Rowan, Richard Wilmer, and Robert G. Deindorfer. *Secret Service; Thirty-Three Centuries of Espionage*. New York: Hawthorn Books, 1967.
Seth, Ronald. *Encyclopedia of Espionage*. Garden City, N.Y.: Doubleday and Company, 1972.
Smith, R. Harris. *OSS: The Secret History of America's First Central Intelligence Agency*. Berkeley: University of California Press, 1972.
Wilhelm, Maria. *The Fighting Irishman: The Story of "Wild Bill" Donovan*. New York: Hawthorn Books, 1964.

ROY TALBERT

DOOLITTLE, James Harold (b. Alameda, Calif., December 14, 1896), aviation pioneer; World War II aviation commander. Doolittle is most famous for his aviation exploits and his leadership of the first bombing attack against Japan during World War II (April 18, 1942) for which he was awarded the Congressional Medal of Honor.

James Harold Doolittle was a product of the waning days of the American frontier. He was born in California and moved to Nome, Alaska, in 1900. There, the tough, combative personality that was to mark Doolittle throughout his life began to take shape, as the small Jimmy (as he came to be called) was forced to defend himself against an assortment of school bullies. This personality was further developed after 1908 when the Doolittles returned to California where Jimmy became an excellent amateur boxer, winning the Pacific Coast amateur flyweight championship in 1912.

Young Doolittle first showed interest in flying during his days in California. At age fifteen, he constructed a glider from plans that appeared in *Popular Mechanics*. When the glider failed to fly, he attempted to build a powered aircraft. The failure of this second aviation project marked the close of Doolittle's early interest in flying.

Under the influence of his mother and Josephine "Jo" Daniels, the woman he would later marry, James abandoned some of his riskier interests and began to study mining engineering, matriculating first at Los Angeles Junior College and then at the University of California. Still one year from graduation when the United States entered World War I, Doolittle enlisted in the Aviation Section of the U.S. Army Signal Corps. Although he completed pilot training soon after he enlisted, he was not assigned to a combat unit before the war ended.

Following the war, Doolittle remained in the Army and soon began a series of epoch-making flights that established his fame as one of America's pioneer aviators. The first of these flights was his record-setting, transcontinental flight in September 1922; he crossed the United States from near Jacksonville, Florida, to Rockwell Field at San Diego, California, in twenty hours and thirty minutes.

Later in 1922, Doolittle began advanced technical training in aeronautics at the Air Corps Engineering School, McCook Field, Ohio. Shortly after completing this school, he entered graduate school at the Massachusetts Institute of Technology (MIT) and received a doctoral degree in aeronautical engineering in June 1925.

Following his work at MIT, Doolittle learned to fly seaplanes and in October 1925 won the internationally renowned Schneider Cup seaplane race, setting a new world seaplane speed record of 232.573 miles per hour. Four years later, Doolittle established another aviation milestone when he made the first flight in which the pilot took off, flew his aircraft, and landed without seeing outside the cockpit.

Shortly after this first instrument flight, Doolittle resigned from the Army to head Shell Oil Company's aviation products department. But his activities in civilian life kept him immersed in aviation developments. He set several new aviation records, served on the Baker Board (1934), and twice toured Europe in the late 1930s where he observed at first hand the buildup of Nazi air power. He also led Shell Oil into a pioneering developmental effort that produced the first practical 100–octane gasoline which was so important in ensuring the top performance of U.S. and British combat aircraft during World War II.

On July 1, 1940, as World War II expanded, Doolittle was recalled to active duty in the U.S. Army Air Corps as a major. Following the Japanese attack on Pearl Harbor, he became involved in planning the daring attack on Japan that was carried out on April 18, 1942, by sixteen B–25s launched from the deck of the carrier *Hornet*. Lieutenant Colonel Doolittle led the raid; he was promoted to brigadier general and awarded the Congressional Medal of Honor for his leadership.

Doolittle's next major assignment was as commander of the Twelfth Air Force, the principal U.S. air component supporting the 1942 Allied invasion of North Africa. In February 1943 Doolittle, now a major general, became commander of the Northwest African Strategic Air Force of General Carl Andrew Spaatz's* Northwest African Air Forces. Following the Allied victory in North Africa, Doolittle led elements of the Allied air force in operations against Pantelleria, Sicily, and Italy. In November 1943 he assumed command of the Fifteenth Air Force in Italy while continuing to command the Northwest African Strategic Air Force.

Within two months, Doolittle was involved in a major command shuffle that resulted from the decision to make General Dwight David Eisenhower* the supreme Allied commander in Europe. General Spaatz was named to command the U.S. Strategic Air Forces in Europe under the Supreme Commander Eisenhower. Spaatz wished to keep his staff intact and decided to take Doolittle with him to command the Eighth Air Force in England; Doolittle assumed command of the Eighth as 1943 came to a close. He led the Eighth through some of the most important aerial campaigns of the war, including efforts to destroy the German fighter aircraft industry, attacks on V-weapons facilities, aerial assaults designed to isolate and soften up the Normandy area, and attacks on the German synthetic oil industry.

These campaigns played an important role in the defeat of Germany. When the war in Europe ended, Doolittle, a lieutenant general since March 1944, was ordered to the Pacific to establish the Eighth there for operations against Japan. Before the Eighth became operational, the war ended, and Doolittle returned to the United States in September 1945.

General Doolittle remained in the Army until the spring of 1946 when he returned to work for Shell Oil. Thereafter, he continued his involvement in government aviation activities. In 1946 he chaired the Board on Officer-Enlisted Men Relationships (the Doolittle Board). Two years later he became a member of the National Advisory Committee for Aeronautics and served as its chairman from 1956 until it became the National Aeronautics and Space Administration in 1958. In 1951 General Hoyt Sanford Vandenberg,* chief of staff of the Air Force, used Doolittle as a special advisor in an Air Force effort to establish a new organizational structure for its research and development program. Four years later, the Air Force again called Doolittle into its service, this time as chairman of the Air Force Science Advisory Board. In 1957 and 1958 he was a member of the president's Science Advisory Committee. In addition to these major positions, Doolittle served in several other important advisory roles for the federal government. He also remained very active as a manager in the aerospace industry.

During World War II General Jimmy Doolittle played an important part in establishing the role of aviation in modern warfare. His national fame, his skill as an aviator, and his detailed, technical knowledge of aircraft contributed to his success.

He was a commander who led from the front much as George Smith Patton, Jr.* and Erwin Rommel did. He demonstrated his leadership and his personal mastery of the aircraft as an instrument of war in the daring raid on Tokyo which pushed crews and aircraft to the limits of their performance. The dramatic uplift which the raid gave to American spirits during the dark days of 1942 was heightened by Doolittle's national reputation as an aviation pioneer. With leaders such as Doolittle, how could the nation lose the war? In addition to raising American morale, there is some indication that the Tokyo raid may have contributed to Japan's decision to expand its defensive perimeter in the Pacific, a decision that led to the crucial Japanese defeat at Midway.

Later, on the other side of the world, Doolittle's "out-front" leadership helped to hold aircrews together through some of the most difficult and important aerial offensives of the war. His personal energy and ability to deal effectively with superiors and Allies were just as important as his personal leadership, for they were key factors in the planning, organizing, and directing of the air offensives against Germany. These offensives made major contributions to the Allied victory in Europe and supported postwar efforts to establish the Air Force as a separate service from the Army.

Even after the war when Doolittle returned to civilian life, he continued to be a powerful and influential friend of the nation's air service. His support of a more independent air service had been publicly known since his service on the Baker Board. After the war he served in high government posts under two presidents and was involved in several special, advisory roles with the Air Force. His leadership helped establish the United States as a leader in modern civil and military aviation.

BIBLIOGRAPHY

Glines, Carroll V. *Doolittle's Tokyo Raiders*. Princeton, N.J.: D. Van Nostrand Company, 1964.
———. *Jimmy Doolittle: Daredevil Aviator and Scientist*. Air Force Academy Series, Carroll V. Glines, ed. New York: Macmillan Company, 1972.
Reynolds, Quentin. *The Amazing Mr. Doolittle: A Biography of Lieutenant General James H. Doolittle*. New York: Appleton-Century-Crofts, 1953.
Thomas, Lowell, and Edward Jablonski. *Doolittle: A Biography*. Garden City, N.Y.: Doubleday and Company, 1976.

DONALD R. BAUCOM

DRUM, Hugh Aloysius (b. Fort Brady, Mich., September 19, 1879; d. New York City, N.Y., October 3, 1951), Army officer. Often in the middle of controversy, at the outbreak of World War II, Drum was the most experienced general on active service in the U.S. Army.

Hugh Drum was the fourth generation of his family to serve in the Regular Army. When his father, a captain, fell at San Juan Hill in 1898, Drum left Boston College to accept a direct commission offered by President William McKinley to sons of officers killed in action. In the Philippines, Drum won a brevet captaincy and a Silver Star with the 25th Infantry against the Moros, where he became a protegé of Colonel Frank Baldwin, as well as a friend of John Joseph Pershing.* Two more tours in the Philippines followed, interspersed with duty in New York and Colorado. In 1911 Drum graduated with honors from the School of the Line, and in 1912 he graduated from the General Staff College, where, over the years, he served at every level. His article on the storming of stone cities brought him to the attention of Frederick Funston,* who took him along as an aide de camp during the Vera Cruz affair of 1914. After U.S. forces withdrew from Mexico, Drum worked on border defense plans. In 1917, he sailed with Pershing and the advanced party of the American Expeditionary Force (AEF) as one of two unassigned staff captains, the other being George Smith Patton, Jr.* After observing the British and French armies and conducting a port survey, Drum presided over expansion of First Army staff from two to over two thousand, as well as planning for St.-Mihiel and Meuse-Argonne. At this time, Drum's G–3 was Lieutenant Colonel George Catlett Marshall.* In the last days of the war, Drum amended Marshall's order issued in the name of the Army commander, ordering a push toward Sedan. Drum's amendment decreed that boundaries were to be disregarded, which produced confusion. Drum was also criticized for the confusion that beset the rear areas of the AEF during the Meuse-Argonne.

After the war, as one of the two youngest wartime generals, he was initially passed over for promotion to general in the Regular Army. He served as commandant at Fort Leavenworth, and, later, as a National Guard advisor and a regional Coast Artillery commander.

In 1922 Drum was promoted to brigadier general and a year later became G–3 on the General Staff. At this point, Drum became involved in bureaucratic battling within the Army over the issue of a separate air force. Eventually seen as a principal foe by air power advocates—at the Mitchell court-martial he appeared as a prosecution witness—Drum was named in a bill proposed in Congress (which did not pass) to suspend William ("Billy") Mitchell's* opponents from rank and command. Later, he headed the Drum Board in 1933 and then served on the Baker Board in 1935, which led to a General Headquarters Air Force directly under the General Staff, the first step on the long road to Air Force autonomy. After commanding the 1st Division, 1926–1930, Drum served as inspector general and was involved in investigating West Point athletics. Promoted to major general, he commanded V Corps, 1931–1933. As Deputy chief of staff to Douglas MacArthur,* 1933–1935, he worked on the Civilian Conservation Corps (CCC) program updating of doctrine and equipment, in addition to being involved in air policy review. When MacArthur retired in 1935, many expected Drum to succeed him, but Malin Craig* was named chief of staff instead. President Franklin Roosevelt told James Farley, postmaster general (who like many American Catholics hoped for Drum's appointment) that Drum was a MacArthur man, and, as such, not a viable candidate. Drum then commanded in Hawaii, where he vigorously updated defenses. At that time, he asked Patton to put in a good word with Pershing for help in becoming chief of staff. His hopes were dashed again in 1938 when Roosevelt selected Marshall. Drum served as a corps commander in Chicago and then in New York, only slightly comforted by promotion to lieutenant general in 1939, and the assumption of command of the First Army.

As the war in Europe intensified, Drum became vocal, speaking regularly in public, demanding greater preparedness, defending the draft, dramatizing equipment shortages on maneuvers—and criticizing those in higher places for such deficiencies. In 1940, after France fell and the U.S. Army grew, Drum was visible as the only general with service as a general in World War I and as a vigorous leader in the large maneuvers held in 1940–1941—even though at one point he was captured by Patton's forces. After Pearl Harbor, his hopes of commanding a European Expeditionary Force mounted when he was called to Washington. Early in January 1942 he attended a series of meetings with Secretary of War Henry Lewis Stimson;* Marshall, the chief of staff; Dwight David Eisenhower,* representing the War Plans Division; and General Henry Harley Arnold,* commander of the Army Air Forces. Drum, an expert on European topography, was startled to find that he was being offered an assignment in China, and one of unclear proportions—the role which Joseph Warren Stilwell,* Marshall's favorite all along, ultimately filled. Drum correctly saw the situation as uncertain but expressed his concern in terms of talent being wasted. In a heated meeting, Marshall accused him of putting his career before the needs of the nation in a crisis, a view that Stimson came to share. When Drum had second thoughts and asked for the assignment, Stimson rejected him. After heading the Eastern Defense Command, Drum retired in 1943 at age sixty-five and succeeded Al Smith as president of the Empire State Building Corporation. In that year, Drum openly supported Republican Presidential candidate Thomas E. Dewey and two years later was Dewey's choice to block General William Joseph Donovan's* path to nomination for the Senate, which led to a compromise candidate. Drum died of a heart attack in his office on October 3, 1951.

Drum, heavily decorated by the United States and several foreign countries, held a dozen honorary degrees and was very active socially. He was quoted in 1940 as saying that his most prized honor was the Laetare Medal, awarded by Notre Dame to outstanding members of the Catholic laity.

Drum was a tireless worker, a quick thinker, an effective speaker and writer, and had evident command presence. Some saw his self-assuredness as arrogance. The almost-but-not-quite nature of his career, however, offers several problems for students of the U.S. Army. Drum was something more of a military intellectual than the average officer, and competent, if egoistic. He was not alone in playing small-politics, self-consciously building associations, and maneuvering in the system. With the exception of the Drum Board, his name is not associated with any major change, theory, or innovation. At the time, his failure to make chief of staff was seen as conspiratorial in origin, for example, the West Point clique blocking a nongraduate, (which did not hold up in view of the president's choice of Virginia Military Institute graduate Marshall), and the forces of anti-Catholicism and the influence of Freemasons—which the president and most of the senior commanders in World War II were. The intensity of the rivalry between such factions is difficult to gauge through documentary sources, and a case that Drum was denied reward because he was a Catholic cannot be made without depending mainly on circumstantial evidence. There is somewhat more evidence to suggest that Marshall manipulated the situation in January 1942 in order to get his candidate sent to China. It is not clear whether he intentionally set up Drum, whom he knew well, to overextend himself, by dangling the plum of

commanding a new AEF. More distance and perspective are needed, farther
from the afterglow and hagiography that surrounds Marshall. A biography of
Drum based on his papers and interviews would give a reasonable degree of
surety. It does seem strange that in view of Marshall's tolerance of eccentricity
in other cases, he chose to put the most experienced and very able general in
the Army on the shelf. Truly, more research needs to be done.

BIBLIOGRAPHY

Busch, N. F. "General Drum: Nation's Number One Field Soldier."*Life* 10 (June 15,
    1941), pp. 82–84.
Davis, Burke. *The Billy Mitchell Affair*. New York: Random House, 1967.
Eliot, George Fielding. Portrait. *Scribner's Magazine* 105 (February 1939), pp. 5–9.
Hunter, Liggett. *A.E.F.: Ten Years Ago in France*. New York: Dodd, Mead and Com-
    pany, 1927.
Obituaries, *New York Times*, October 4, 1951; *Newsweek*, October 15, 1951; *Time*,
    October 15, 1951.

                                                              ROGER BEAUMONT

DUANE, William (b. near Lake Champlain, N.Y., May 17, 1760; d. Philadelphia, Pa., November 24, 1835), journalist, political pundit, Army officer,
military writer.

William Duane was born in New York State of Irish Catholic parents; upon
his father's death in 1765, he went with his mother to Ireland where he spent
his youth. At the age of nineteen he offended his family by marrying a Protestant—Catherine Corcoran—and was disinherited. To support himself he learned
the printer's trade, and in 1787 he went to India where, through successful
speculation, he acquired a modest fortune and established a newspaper, *The
Indian World*. His denunciations of the methods of the East India Company,
and his championing of a group of army officers and local troops in their grievances with the company and home government, led to his arrest and deportation
to England. In the process, he suffered the confiscation of his property. In London
he served as parliamentary reporter for the *General Advertiser* and vainly sought
restitution of his estate.

In 1795 he gave up the case, left England in disgust, returned to America,
and took up residence in Philadelphia. There he associated himself with Benjamin
Franklin Bache on the newspaper *Aurora*. In September 1798, when Bache died,
Duane succeeded to the editorship and immediately made the *Aurora* a key organ
of Thomas Jefferson's Republican party. His genius in controversy, the intensity
of his convictions, and his virile style of writing made him one of the most
effective political journalists of his time. In the spring of 1799 he was arrested
by the Federalists then in power and charged with sedition. Although he was
indicted, his trial was twice postponed; Jefferson dismissed the charge when he
assumed the presidency in 1801. While the seat of government had been located
at Philadelphia, the *Aurora* had enjoyed a decided advantage in access to government news, ensuring the paper an extensive readership. When the government

moved to Washington, that advantage (and much of that readership) evaporated. Hopes of gaining at least some of the printing and stationery business in 1801 from the new Republican administration (which Duane had done so much to promote) miscarried, ultimately creating financial difficulties for the editor. Publication of a small tome, *The Mississippi Question* (1803), did nothing to improve his situation. Jefferson did what he could for his faithful supporter: he promoted his literary efforts, sought subscribers for him, and ultimately (1808) appointed him a lieutenant colonel in the Army. Prior to this appointment, Duane had begun writing the first of several military works, the *American Military Library* (1809). Most of his time in the Army was devoted to the preparation of a series of military manuals which, despite his service ties, were published privately. The *Library*, his first work, was written "with the sole view of exciting military study [and] a military spirit" among the people. Duane had begun the work in 1807 as war clouds gathered over the *Chesapeake-Leopard* affair. The strongly anglophobic Duane urged war, and his writing became a contribution to the readiness effort. The secretary of war, Henry Dearborn,* kept track of his work and in March 1808 strongly urged him to finish it quickly. Duane's appointment as the second-in-command of the new Regiment of Riflemen provided him with both the time and income necessary to complete that effort and a successor, a *Military Dictionary* (1810). The *Library* was published in two volumes with an additional set of lithograph plates. The first volume contained a historical examination of the art of war, an outline of a tactical doctrine supposedly adapted to American conditions, his translation of the current French tactical system, and other materials drawn from European sources. The final volume contained an elaboration on the doctrinal designs he had proposed, with a section devoted to each branch—infantry, engineers, cavalry, and artillery. As the possibility of war with England declined, and with his finances partially restored (through his military pay and the sale of his books), Duane resigned from the Army and returned full time to the *Aurora*. Once home he undertook a new project, *An Epitome of the Arts and Sciences* (1811), a brief work that advertised itself as a "useful and polite education" in the arts and sciences.

As the prospects for war once again heightened, Duane returned to his earlier efforts. An appointment as a colonel in the Adjutant General's Department (March 18, 1813-June 15, 1815) provided the opportunity once again to pursue his military writing full-time. His *Handbook for Infantry* (1812) was adopted by the War Department in 1813. It is probably no coincidence that Duane returned to active duty in the Adjutant General's Office just one day before his new manual was adopted for Army-wide use. He spent the rest of the war producing nine editions of his infantry manual, a *Handbook for Riflemen* (1813), and a *Handbook for Cavalry* (1814).

After the war Duane returned to the *Aurora* which he edited until 1822. He retired that year and made a trip to South America, recording his observations in *A Visit to Colombia in the Years 1822 & 1823* (1826). On his return he became the prothonotary of the supreme court of Pennsylvania, a position he held until his death.

Duane is best known as a political journalist and avid supporter of the Jeffersonian Republicans. His efforts in the field of military writing, however, deserve some note. Observing that there had been "a disposition to discourage the acquisition of military knowledge, particularly in the militia," Duane took it upon himself to write his first work, *The American Military Library* (1809). While widely circulated in both military and civilian circles, and considered by the Army, neither this work nor his next book—the *Military Dictionary* (1810)—was adopted officially. Perhaps the heavy European influence on his thought made them unacceptable. Nevertheless, the *Library* did make one important contribution. Duane was among the first Americans to discover the yet uncompleted early work of Antoine Henri Jomini—*Traité des grandes operations militaires* (8 vols., 1804–1810)—and to bring it to public attention. Of course, the works of Jomini that were most influential in America were still years in the future (his interpretation of Napoleon), but Duane's early recognition of his genius indicates the care with which he approached the subject.

Of Duane's later books only one, the *Handbook of Infantry* (1812), was officially adopted by the Army—its first manual of modern doctrine and its first new drill manual since Baron Frederic William von Steuben's* *Blue Book*. Although the tactical doctrine that Duane promoted had little long-term impact, it seems likely that Winfield Scott* and Jacob Jennings Brown* used Duane's *Infantry* in 1814 to train the new regiments which at Chippewa and Lundy's Lane garnered what little glory the regulars attained in that war. Nevertheless, Scott at least was not completely satisfied with the new manual and immediately after the war (1815) headed a panel that revised the infantry system completely.

BIBLIOGRAPHY

Malone, Dumas. *Jefferson and His Time*. 5 vols. Boston: Little, Brown and Company, 1948–1974.
Steward, Donald H. *The Opposition Press of the Federalist Period*. Albany: State University of New York Press, 1969.
The very important correspondence between Duane and Jefferson will ultimately appear in *The Papers of Thomas Jefferson*, edited by Julian P. Boyd, projected 50 vols. Princeton, N.J.: Princeton University Press, 1950–.

THEODORE J. CRACKEL

DU PONT, Samuel Francis (b. Bergen Point, N.J., September 27, 1803; d. Philadelphia, Pa., June 23, 1865), naval officer. Du Pont commanded the South Atlantic Blockading Squadron and the attacks on Port Royal and Charleston during the Civil War.

Scion of a famous American munitions-making family, Samuel Francis Du Pont was born on September 27, 1803, in Bergen Point, New Jersey, where his French emigré father Victor and aristocratic mother Gabrielle Josephine de Pelleport had fled from the excesses of the French Revolution. After unsuccessful business ventures in northern New Jersey, Victor moved his family to Wilmington, Delaware, and joined other family members in the establishment of a very successful powder mill. Young Francis was sent to nearby Germantown, Pennsylvania, to attend an exclusive boarding school in 1812. The War of 1812 coincided with the formative years of Du Pont's education and undoubtedly stirred him. Moreover, his father's firm sold powder to the fledgling U.S. Navy in its battle against the British fleet, making the war a major topic in the Du Pont household. Francis longed to become a naval officer. His influential grandfather Pierre Samuel Du Pont de Nemours, an intimate of Benjamin Franklin and Thomas Jefferson, interceded on his behalf, winning Francis a presidential appointment to the U.S. Navy.

In the days before the creation of the U.S. Naval Academy, midshipmen were appointed directly to sea duty, and in 1817 Du Pont boarded the 74–gun ship-of-the-line *Franklin* for his first cruise. Before becoming a regular officer, however, he needed to undergo years of schooling as a sailing master under a variety of tough commanding officers, including Commodores Charles Stewart (1817–1818) and John Rodgers* (1824–1826). By the time Du Pont received his commission as lieutenant in April 1826, he had served in the line-of-battle ships *North Carolina* and *Franklin*, and the frigates *Constitution* and *Congress*. Only a brief return to Mount Airy College in Germantown in 1820 to complete his studies interrupted this intensive education at sea. During the 1830s, an uneventful decade for the U.S. Navy, Du Pont performed his duties quietly, secured command of his first ship, the 10–gun schooner *Grampus*, in 1836, and weathered a short controversy with aging Commodore Isaac Hull* over employment of staterooms on the ship-of-the-line *Ohio* for personal family use.

Promoted as commander on October 28, 1842, Du Pont entered upon one of the more exciting periods of his professional life. He visited the Orient in 1843 and served on the board to create a U.S. Naval Academy in 1845. He commanded the *Congress* during the Pacific Ocean cruise of Commodore Robert Field Stockton* and the 18–gun sloop-of-war *Cyane* in California waters during the Mexican War. Du Pont saw considerable action in this short conflict, directing landing operations at San Diego in July 1846, blockading lower California in September, fighting at San Gabriel in January 1847, attacking Mazatlan in November, and rescuing some trapped U.S. Marines at Guaymas.

Du Pont found the post-Mexican War period anticlimactic. Between 1849 and 1855 he served on various boards to improve the service and was superintendent of the new Naval Academy. Such duty enabled him to recover from ill-health and attend his invalid wife. Promotion to captain in 1855 stirred a new phase in Du Pont's career. As a member of the Naval Efficiency Board, he pressed hard for the retirement of inefficient and incompetent officers, drawing criticism from fellow officers and their friends in political circles. The next year, in command of the big warship *Minnesota*, Du Pont carried U.S. Minister William B. Reed on a mission to negotiate a more favorable commercial treaty with

China. While on duty in Chinese waters, Du Pont intently observed the combined Anglo-French operation against some Chinese fortifications on the Po Hai River. Next, the *Minnesota* made ceremonial visits and showed the American flag in Japan, Hong Kong, Malaya, India, and South Africa. This trip gave Du Pont the reputation as something of a diplomat, and when he returned to the United States, the Navy Department selected him to accompany a Japanese mission around the United States.

When the American Civil War started Du Pont commanded the quiet Philadelphia Naval Yard, close to his Brandywine Creek estate and infirm wife. However, over forty years of flawless service recommended the senior officer for important naval command against rebel forces. On June 20, 1861, the Navy ordered Du Pont to serve as senior member of a top strategy board in Washington, where he established close working relations with dynamic Assistant Secretary of the Navy Gustavus Vasa Fox.* Several months later Du Pont visited New York City to scrounge for any vessel capable of joining a South Atlantic Blockading Squadron, assembled to strangle the Confederacy. In September he assumed command of the squadron from which he launched the two most spectacular amphibious operations on the Atlantic coast during the Civil War. The first operation at Port Royal was immensely successful, but the other against Charleston led to defeat and resignation.

Fox and Du Pont considered Port Royal a key target since seizure would allow the blockading squadron to use it as a base of operations. Naturally, command of the amphibious assault fell to Du Pont, who won a surprisingly easy victory on November 7, 1861. Capture of Port Royal was a deceptive battle, however, since it reflected only overwhelming naval firepower over outgunned Confederate forts. No one really reflected on this at the time, as victory-starved Northerners turned Du Pont into a naval hero and urged Abraham Lincoln* to unleash him against the great Rebel stronghold at Charleston. Meanwhile, Du Pont continued blockade duty, searching for badly needed coal depots for his steam-powered warships. Soon, public and political pressure in Washington and the obvious success of Confederate blockade runners emanating from Charleston convinced the Lincoln government to attack the South Carolina harbor. Once again Navy leaders expected Du Pont to command the operation, urging a quick preparation to avoid sharing the glories with the U.S. Army. Fox and Secretary of the Navy Gideon Welles* ordered Du Pont to employ powerful new ironclad monitors against the Confederate batteries, even though he doubted the ability of these shallow-draft, floating gun platforms to reduce heavily defended earthworks. As Du Pont suspected, Charleston's excellent artillery checked his monitors and forced a withdrawal on April 7, 1863.

Although Du Pont had not really lost at Charleston and in fact had captured the powerful Rebel ironclad, the *Atlanta*, his failure to provide Lincoln's administration with a tangible, politically useful victory, led to Du Pont's replacement as commander of the South Atlantic Blockading Squadron on July 6, 1863. Moreover, his own intemperate comments to Secretary Welles precluded reassignment to another responsible command. His active war duty was over, blemished by one unsuccessful amphibious operation against insurmountable odds. Not surprisingly, he remained bitter, participating in vindictive debates with various political factions and department leaders, especially Welles, who charged him with neglect at Charleston. For the remainder of the war, congressional investigators, administration spokesmen, and even an occasional fellow officer criticized Du Pont specifically while discussing the general limitations of armored warships and naval strategy. The entire controversy over naval operations during the war remained unsettled when on June 23, 1865, a thoroughly exhausted and unwell Du Pont died in Philadelphia.

Du Pont's Civil War career exemplified the political, strategic, and technological complications confronting most commanders both at sea and in the field during a conflict that simultaneously featured traditional methods and untested new weaponry. During the fighting, both senior Army and Navy officers were buffeted by the Lincoln administration's uncertain strategic plans or political opportunism, while at the same time searching for the correct application of modern weapons to old-fashioned tactics. In Du Pont's case all these problems coincided at Charleston, permanently affecting both his immediate reputation and larger historical image. Until his disastrous repulse by heavy Rebel guns, Du Pont's career had never suffered even a momentary setback. Indeed, he had contributed successfully to improvement of the Navy's ships, tactical doctrine, discipline, and efficiency in the years before the Civil War. In addition, he had performed a wide range of diplomatic functions and military operations without difficulty. The early success at Port Royal reinforced his position as the perfect model for a successful naval officer and possibly blinded him to the requirements to alter radically his thinking about similar operations against Charleston. Certainly, tremendous pressure from Washington to use unreliable monitors and to win a politically popular victory complicated Du Pont's preparation for the attack on Charleston, but still he failed to display the ability of a good battle commander to adjust quickly to innovations, changed conditions, pressures from civilian administrators, and the unexpected. Du Pont was a solid naval officer but not a great commander.

BIBLIOGRAPHY

Du Pont, H. A. *Rear-Admiral Samuel Francis Du Pont, United States Navy: A Biography.* New York: National Americana Society, 1926.

Hayes, John D., ed. *Samuel Francis Du Pont: A Selection from His Civil War Letters.* 3 vols. Ithaca, N.Y.: Cornell University Press, 1969.

Niven, John. *Gideon Welles: Lincoln's Secretary of the Navy.* New York: Oxford University Press, 1973.

Reed, Rowena. *Combined Operations in the Civil War.* Annapolis, Md.: Naval Institute Press, 1978.

West, Richard S., Jr. *Mr. Lincoln's Navy.* New York: Longmans, Green and Company, 1957.

JEFFERY M. DORWART

E

EADS, James Buchanan (b. Lawrenceburg, Ind., May 23, 1820; d. Nassau, Commonwealth of the Bahamas, March 8, 1887), civil engineer. Eads is known for constructing ironclad gunboats for the Union during the Civil War.

James Buchanan Eads moved with his family to St. Louis, Missouri, in 1833. He did not attend school, but while working as a store clerk he read widely, especially scientific works. Always fond of machinery, at age twenty-two Eads devised a diving bell that allowed a man to salvage materials from sunken steamboats. Using his invention as his investment, Eads convinced a St. Louis shipbuilding firm to accept him as a partner, construct his diving bell, and install it upon a salvage ship. The enterprise reaped huge profits. Enlarging upon his plan, Eads constructed a fleet of diving bell ships and associated salvage equipment. He retired at the age of thirty-seven after making a fortune.

At the outbreak of the Civil War, Eads wrote to his friend, U.S. Attorney General Edward Bates, that something should be done to secure the Mississippi River and its tributaries from the Confederates. Bates replied that Eads should be prepared to come to Washington and assist in developing a plan to secure the Mississippi. In Washington, Eads proposed converting a number of existing riverboats into armored gun platforms.

Union leaders decided that several riverboats would be purchased by the War Department and converted into timber-armored gunboats. The War Department had jurisdiction over inland waters. In addition, based upon plans developed by the Navy's Chief of the Bureau of Construction John Lenthall and Naval Constructor Samuel M. Pook, a number of ironclad, steam-powered gunboats were to be built in the West. On July 18, 1861, bids based on engine and hull specifications were advertised. Although not a shipyard owner, James Eads offered to build and deliver four to sixteen ships in sixty-five days at $89,600 each. His offer was either a brilliant stroke of good business skill or a foolish mistake. It was an offer the War Department could hardly refuse. His bid was accepted with the stipulation that Eads pay $600 per ship for every day beyond sixty-five that the ships were not ready. In return, the government offered to pay Eads in installments based on the percentage of completion.

Eads began work immediately and mobilized the shipbuilding facilities that were lying idle because of the war. Four of the ironclads were built at Carondelet outside St. Louis. Three of the ships were built at Mound City, Illinois, on the Ohio River north of Cairo. The first two ships were delivered on time, but due to bureaucratic red tape, the government defaulted in its installment payments to Eads. Although he was eventually paid, he was forced to mortgage his personal fortune in order to build the ironclads. The first of the seven identical sisterships, the USS *Carondelet*, was launched on October 12, 1861. The other six sisters were also named after river towns: the *Cairo, Pittsburgh, Louisville, Cincinnati, Mound City*, and *St. Louis* (later renamed *Baron Dekalb*).

Known variously as the "Eads gunboats," "Pook gunboats," or "City-class gunboats," the *Cairo*-class ironclads arrived in time to supplement the converted timberclads *Lexington, Tyler*, and *Conestoga* and the ironclad *Essex* in the first drives against Confederate forces in Missouri, Kentucky, and Tennessee. Comprising the Mississippi Flotilla, the band of timberclads and ironclads formed the nucleus of what would become the powerful Mississippi Squadron under the U.S. Navy. The *Cairo*-class ships were an unusual combination of both Navy and riverboat technology. One hundred seventy-five feet in length and fifty-one feet in width, the 512–ton ships drew only six feet of water. They were armored with two and a half inches of charcoal iron plate spiked to the forward shield, and slanted at 45° to repel shot. Vertical lengths of railroad rails protected the four port and four starboard broadside guns. Behind the armor were twenty-six inches of timber backing. Three large guns usually pierced the forward shield, and two small chase guns pierced the unarmored after bulkhead. The guns were mixed, using what could be found between the Army and the Navy in the West. The boilers were cramped below the waterline to help protect them from shot. A twenty-two foot diameter centerwheel drove the ships at about six knots, and the boilers consumed about one ton of coal an hour. The ships were clumsy and slow, but they were effective. Following the construction of the seven *Cairo*-class ships, Eads sold a redesigned snagboat to the War Department. The thousand-ton snagboat was converted to an ironclad on the pattern of the *Cairo*-classs ships and became the *Benton*, flagship of the Mississippi Flotilla.

Next Eads began work on his own designs. The *Cairos* had bought the Union some precious time and had secured the upper Mississippi River. He obtained a contract to build two novel river gunboats that would become the *Neosho* and the *Osage*. These ships, while still having the required shallow draft, boasted a single turret based upon the design of John Ericsson.* The ships had a sternwheel drive, and the paddleboxes were lightly armored. These sternwheel monitors arrived after the bulk of the heavy river fighting had been done, but they saw some action later in the war.

The ultimate ironclads built by Eads were the *Milwaukee*-class monitors: clearly, the most technologically advanced machines built in America to that time. The *Kickapoo* and the *Winnebago* each mounted two turrets built on Ericsson's pattern. The *Milwaukee* and the *Chickasaw* each mounted one Ericsson turret and one turret especially designed by Eads. Eads' plans were carefully formulated to avoid many of the problems that had become a regular part of the Ericsson units favored by the Navy Department and used in all other monitors. Eads' turrets rotated on a ball-bearing race set into the keel of the ship. The weight was evenly distributed over a large, flat area rather than on the single spindle shaft that was so vulnerable to bending in the Ericsson units. After the guns were fired, they were run in, the ports were closed, and the two-gun platform was lowered into the hull of the ship for muzzle reloading. The gunner stayed in the turret and resighted the guns towards the next target. On command, the guns were raised, run forward, and the ports were opened, all as a continuous steam-powered mechanical operation. Although more complicated than the damage-prone Ericsson turrets, there is no evidence that the Eads design was inferior in any way. The *Milwaukee*-class monitors also bore decks of solid iron plate four inches thick. Iron rolling mills on the Eastern Seaboard were not capable of shaping thick armor plates, and all of the Ericsson-designed monitors were made up of laminated courses of one-inch iron. The superior *Milwaukee*-class ships did not arrive on the scene early enough to see any action on the rivers. Despite the danger of operating high-pressure fresh water boilers in saltwater, the *Chickasaw* and the *Winnebago* were steamed along the Gulf of Mexico to help Admiral David Glasgow Farragut* in his attack on Mobile Bay in August 1864. The *Chickasaw* played an important part in forcing the surrender of the Confederate ironclad *Tennessee*.

After the Civil War, Eads designed several large projects, the most important of which was the Brooklyn Bridge in New York. In 1883 the Brooklyn Bridge became the first all-steel bridge. A tribute to fine engineering, the Eads Bridge is still in daily use.

Eads' greatest contribution to the Union war effort was his expertise. By mobilizing a great many timber yards, iron works, and engine builders, and by capitalizing on an idle labor force, Eads was able to build the seven *Cairo*-class ships in a remarkably short time. The timing was critical. The first three Eads gunboats, the *Cincinnati, Carondelet*, and *St. Louis*, arrived in time to assist Flag Officer Andrew Hull Foote* in his successful attack on Fort Henry on the Cumberland River in February 1862. Although Fort Henry was not formidable, the ships built by Eads performed to expectation and their novel appearance and easy-won success sparked the public's imagination and allayed fear in the North. Undoubtably, the success at Fort Henry gave the Eads gunboats a higher reputation than they deserved.

Looking retrospectively at the *Cairo*-class, though economical and quickly built, they did not work very well. They had been designed by the Navy to fight other ships head-on. When the Confederates deemphasized their floating forces and tried to block the Mississippi with fortifications, the *Cairo*-class was out of its element but did its best to adapt. The armor was perforated; the ships were rammed and were sunk. Several of them were sunk by mines. But built by Eads to hardy riverboat standards, all except the *Cairo* lived to fight another day. Six of the seven Eads gunboats survived the Civil War. The class has been dubbed "the workhorses of the Mississippi Squadron." Individually, they were not often victorious, but as a group they formed the necessary power at a time when force was badly needed. The seven *Cairo*-class ships, along with Eads' *Benton*, and the *Lexington, Tyler, Conestoga*, and *Essex* had so completely done their work in securing the upper Mississippi River and beginning the southward movement toward Vicksburg that few, if indeed any, of the more elaborate and expensive ironclads built after them in the West had much left to accomplish.

BIBLIOGRAPHY

Bearss, Edwin C. *Hardluck Ironclad.* Baton Rouge: Louisiana State University Press, 1966.
Dorsey, Florence. *The Story of James B. Eads and the Mississippi River.* New York: Rinehart, 1947.
Eads, James B. "Recollections of Foote and the Gun-Boats." In *Battles and Leaders of the Civil War.* Edited by Roy F. Nichols. Vol. 1. New York: Thomas Yoseloff, 1956.
Milligan, John D. *Gunboats Down the Mississippi.* Annapolis, Md.: Naval Institute Press, 1965.

DANA M. WEGNER

EAKER, Ira Clarence (b. Field Creek, Tex., April 13, 1896), Army officer, World War II air commander, air power pioneer and advocate.

Born in Texas' Hill Country, Ira C. Eaker entered the U.S. Army in 1917, after having graduated from Southeastern Normal College in Durant, Oklahoma. He began his military career as an infantry officer, but soon transferred to the Air Corps, served as a flight instructor, and became a rated pilot in September 1918.

During the interwar period, he held a number of interesting flying and administrative positions. His flying assignments allowed him to participate in three highly significant events in aviation history. In 1926–1927 he piloted one of the planes involved in a Pan-American Goodwill Flight; in 1929 he and others, including Major Carl Andrew Spaatz,* set a world endurance record of nearly 151 hours aloft with the use of air refueling; and in 1936, with his plane hooded over (except for refueling stops), he flew the first transcontinental instrument flight.

Eaker's administrative assignments included service as an executive officer in the Philippines and an adjutant at Mitchell Field, New York. He also served four tours of duty in Washington, where he learned to know intimately many of the Air Corps officers who, like himself, were eventually to lead the American air effort during World War II.

During this time, Captain Eaker (he became a major in 1935) also took advantage of opportunities to further his formal education. In addition to attending the Air Corps Tactical School at Maxwell Field, Alabama, and the Command and General Staff School at Fort Leavenworth, Kansas, he studied at the University of the Philippines (1920–1921), Columbia Law School (1922–1923), and the University of Southern California (1932–1933), where he received a degree in journalism.

Eaker put his journalistic training to good use, for he soon became well known as a writer and a speaker on topics related to air power. In 1936 he and Brigadier General Henry Harley ("Hap") Arnold,* who was to head the Army Air Forces throughout World War II, published their first book together. Entitled *This Flying Game*, the work was a popular account which chronicled the history of flight and extolled its virtues from both a military and a civilian standpoint. Their collaborative efforts continued and resulted in two additional widely read works, *Winged Warfare* (1941) and *Army Flyer* (1942), which were especially timely as the United States started mobilizing for war.

Eaker was heavily involved in the Air Corps' prewar expansion. Among his duties, he was sent to England to observe the Royal Air Force in action, and in November 1940 he assumed command of the 20th Pursuit Group at Hamilton Field, California. During 1941 he was transferred to Mitchell Field and was stationed there at the time the United States entered the war.

At this point his illustrious combat career began. His wartime service consisted of two main parts: from 1942 to the end of 1943, he headed the U.S. bombing effort in Great Britain; and from 1944 to April 1945, he commanded the Allied Air Forces in the Mediterranean theater. Both of these assignments were extremely challenging and required a good deal of ability and energy as well as diplomacy to balance off the desires of the Air Force against those of the other services and the various countries involved.

Near war's end, Eaker, now a lieutenant general, was named deputy commander of the Army Air Forces in Washington. He remained in this important administrative post until 1947, when, after thirty years of service, he retired at the relatively young age of fifty-one.

Since that time he has actively continued to espouse the cause of air power, first, as an executive for the Hughes and Douglas aircraft corporations; and second, through numerous speaking engagements and writing activities. In 1962 he became so concerned about what he considered to be America's inadequate defense posture that he began writing for the *Los Angeles Times* syndicate a weekly column called "Viewpoint."

Foremost among General Eaker's many accomplishments was his record as a combat commander in World War II. His first task was to organize and forge the U.S. bomber force in Great Britain into a formidable instrument of war. The American strategic air arm began to take shape in February 1942 when Eaker, as head of VIII Bomber Command, and his small staff arrived in England. They quickly assimilated the Royal Air Force's (RAF's) experience and know-how into their own thinking, and by May the Americans were ready to start ferrying Eighth Air Force formations across the Atlantic. Eaker and the other U.S. commanders insisted that their B–17 Fortresses be used primarily for precision daylight raids, since this was the mission for which the aircrews were being trained and the aircraft equipped. The British, though skeptical of daylight bombing, allowed the Americans to have their way, for they agreed that, whatever the method, air power was of overriding importance in winning the war. They, therefore, coordinated their efforts closely to gain the maximum effect possible. When the first American bombing raid took place at Rouen in northern France on August 17, Eaker himself flew one of the aircraft (it was one of his dicta that a leader should lead by example).

From this point on, the American bombing commitment started to expand, though not as rapidly as U.S. and British leaders would have liked. In fact, at one point the lack of spectacular results prompted Prime Minister Winston Churchill to advocate switching the Americans over to night attacks. But at the Casablanca Conference in January 1943, Eaker persuaded Churchill to let the United States continue daylight bombing. At the same time, the Americans discontinued the "drain-off" of bomber strength from England to support the North African Campaign, and this move assured that air attacks against Western Europe and Germany could now be stepped up.

In February General Eaker was named commander of the entire Eighth Air Force, and by midyear, with an increasing number of aircrews, bombers, and spare parts becoming available, the British and Americans were able to commence their Combined Bomber Offensive. While there were some difficulties, especially over the need for a suitable fighter escort, Eaker was well aware of the problems and worked hard to overcome them. In addition, his insistence on procuring the most advanced equipment available, such as the Norden bombsight and H_2X radar, began to yield impressive results.

At the end of 1942 General Arnold selected Eaker to take command of the Mediterranean Allied Air Forces. It was a most demanding and complex assignment. He had to move the command organization forward from North Africa to Italy as Europe became the center of operations. He had to coordinate the efforts of his strategic bombers with the B–17s and B–24 Liberators that were being flown against German targets from England. He had to support, with tactical as well as strategic aircraft, ground operations in Italy, and in 1944 this support was expanded for a number of months to include the southern France Campaign as well.

He was further committed to keeping the sea lanes open, airdropping aid to partisans in the Balkans and personally leading the first of five shuttle missions (codenamed "Frantic Joe") to Soviet-held bases in Eastern Europe. This latter enterprise, which occurred during the summer of 1944, started well but never lived up to its great promise. Almost all of these tasks were cooperative ventures, undertaken with America's British, French, and other allies, and their success was attributable in large part to Eaker's expertise and experience.

Besides his command contributions, several other aspects of Eaker's varied career stand out. One was his participation in a number of events that dramatized and signaled the coming of age of aviation, events such as the Latin American tour, the *Questionmark* endurance record, and the first transcontinental instrument flight during the 1920s and 1930s. These were followed by several other "firsts" during World War II, including his taking part in the first American bombing raid against the Continent and the first shuttle mission to Eastern Europe.

His second noteworthy contribution has been his devotion to the cause of air power. Throughout his military career and afterwards, his many books, articles, columns, and speeches have stood as ample evidence of his belief in its importance. In effect, General Eaker has dedicated his life to explaining and promoting its significance to a sometimes receptive, sometimes more skeptical, American public.

BIBLIOGRAPHY

Arnold, Henry H., and Ira C. Eaker. *Army Flyer*. New York: Harper and Brothers, 1942.
———. *This Flying Game*. 3d ed. New York: Funk and Wagnalls, 1943.
———. *Winged Warfare*. New York: Harper and Brothers, 1941.
Craven, Wesley F., and James L. Cate, eds. *The Army Air Forces in World War II*. Vols. 1–3. Chicago: University of Chicago Press, 1948–1951.
Eaker, Ira C. "Soviet Leaders and People." *Aerospace Historian* 25 (Summer 1978): 74–77.
Webster, Sir Charles K., and Frankland, Noble. *The Strategic Air Offensive Against Germany, 1939–1945*. (*United Kingdom Military Series*.) Vols. 1–3. London: Her Majesty's Stationery Office, 1961.

ALAN WILT

EARLY, Jubal Anderson (b. Franklin County, Va., November 3, 1816; d. Lynchburg, Va., March 2, 1894), Army officer. Early was a division and corps commander in the Confederacy's Army of Northern Virginia.

Although "Old Jube" Early graduated from the U.S. Military Academy at West Point (in 1837, eighteenth in a class of fifty), he never intended to become a career soldier. The third of ten children, he lived and studied around his western Virginia home until he was sixteen and his mother died. Since West Point provided a suitable and respectable change of scene for the grief-stricken youth, his father secured an appointment for him in 1833.

Early's short-lived service as an artillery officer was undistinguished: garrison duty at Fortress Monroe in 1837, brief service in the Seminole War of 1837–1838, and then resignation of his commission on July 31, 1838. Eighteen months later, he successfully passed the bar and began practicing law at Rocky Mount, Virginia. Politically the staunchest of Whigs, Early won a seat in the Virginia House in 1841 but was soundly defeated for reelection. In 1842 he was appointed commonwealth attorney, a post he held for the next ten years. Only his voluntary service in the Mexican War and two more unsuccessful runs for office (for delegate to the state constitutional convention in 1850 and for the legislature in

1853) interrupted Early's moderately prosperous law business before the Civil War.

Appointed a major in the 1st Virginia Volunteers on January 7, 1847, Early went with it to northern Mexico. Zachary Taylor* had already fought his great battles. Only occupation duty and a two-month stint as military governor of Monterrey remained for Early—this, and a severe case of rheumatism that stooped his back for life.

Mustered out in April 1848, Early returned to Virginia. In 1861 he served as a delegate to the state convention where he vehemently opposed and voted against secession. At the onset of hostilities, however, he volunteered for Confederate service and was appointed colonel of the 24th Virginia Infantry. Commanding a brigade at First Manassas, Early performed well enough to earn a promotion to brigadier general.

For the next two years Early showed steady growth as a soldier. Wounded at Williamsburg in May 1862, he was forced to relinquish his brigade. By July he had another. In the corps of Thomas Jonathan "Stonewall" Jackson* he served with distinction in the Second Manassas Campaign. His sterling performance at Sharpsburg—a savage counterattack at a critical moment on the left of the Confederate line and skillful performance as a stand-in for his wounded division commander—earned him the commendation of Robert Edward Lee,* Jackson, and James Ewell Brown Stuart.* But no promotion. This would come on January 17, 1863, after another timely counterpunch on the right at Fredricksburg the previous month.

Now commanding a division, Early held Fredricksburg despite having an inferior force and receiving garbled orders while Lee crushed Joseph Hooker* at Chancellorsville in May 1863. At Gettysburg Early's division saw action late on July 1 and participated in the fruitless dusk assault on Culp's Hill the next day. Twice during the next several months Early assumed temporary corps command, first replacing Richard Stoddert Ewell* during the Mine Run Campaign of late 1863 and then replacing Ambrose Powell Hill* during the Wilderness Campaign. Promoted to lieutenant general, on May 31, 1864, Early took over command of the II Corps after Cold Harbor and Ewell's retirement.

Ordered to the Shenandoah Valley in June 1864, Early's fourteen thousand-man army chased one Federal force from the lower Valley and another from Harper's Ferry, and advanced on Washington, defeating a third Union force under Lewis Wallace* at Monocacy, Maryland, on July 9, 1864. Encountering VI Corps veterans from the army of Ulysses Simpson Grant* on the capital's outskirts, Early skirmished and then retired to Virginia.

Early remained in the Valley, disrupting communications and launching a series of destructive cavalry forays, one of which burned the town of Chambersburg, Pennsylvania, until confronted by a formidable Federal force under Philip Henry Sheridan* in September. Early then sustained a series of crippling defeats: at Winchester, at Fisher's Hill, and, on October 19, 1864, at Cedar Creek. In March, 1865 George Armstrong Custer* obliterated what was left of

Early's force at Waynesborough. Bowing to public outcry, Lee reluctantly relieved Early of command.

After Appomattox, Early fled to Mexico and from there to Canada where he stayed until 1869, when he returned to his law practice in Lynchburg, Virginia. In 1877 he began a long, lucrative association with the Louisiana Lottery Company as a director. Prominent in the formation of the Southern Historical Society in 1869, Early served as its president and guiding spirit until his death. As a champion of Lee and Jefferson Davis* and a bitter, unforgiving critic of James B. Longstreet,* Early contributed prolifically to the Society's *Papers* and to a wide range of journals, newspapers, and magazines. His apologetic but scrupulously accurate *Autobiography*, published posthumously in 1912, is still regarded as a model of its kind and perhaps his finest achievement. Early was unreconstructed to the last. He died a bachelor.

Of men's affections Jubal Early earned very little. Sarcastic, outspoken, profane, irreligious, and caustic, Early was a born scrapper, both on and off the battlefield. Little love was lost between Early and his subordinates, but his superiors—Lee, Jackson, and Ewell—all recognized his considerable talents as a soldier. Early fought as hard as any general in the Army of Northern Virginia. Not really a professional soldier, despite his West Point education, he learned the art of war quickly and grew in stature as the war progressed.

Unfortunately for the Confederacy this growth was uneven. Until Gettysburg, Early's star had risen steadily; afterwards, with the notable exception of his campaign in the Valley and march on Washington it shone with its former brilliance only sporadically. On many fields until then, he had exhibited the kind of aggressiveness and pluck in battle clearly distinguishing a warrior of self-reliant grit. Early specialized in timely, tactically decisive counterattacks. At First Manassas the arrival of his brigade on the left of Pierre Gustave Toutant Beauregard* turned the tide of battle. Early performed even more spectacularly at Sharpsburg by pitching into Hooker's corps and repulsing it just as Lee's left was being overrun. A similar slashing counterpunch corked a breech on Lee's right at Fredericksburg. By the time of Chancellorsville, Lee had enough confidence in him to entrust Early with protecting his rear at Fredericksburg. Early accomplished this job admirably, despite an almost disastrous mixup in orders that caused him to abandon his position temporarily.

Early also had talents as a planner: on his own in the Valley, he carried out operations during the summer of 1864 that strategically accomplished all that Lee could have hoped. In addition to gathering vast quantities of stores, he established the Valley as a second front, preserved Lee's supply source, and kept communications open to the West. And his basic plan of attack at Cedar Creek, so successful at first, miscarried only because of Early's failure to press his advantage, though his subordinates warned that such delay courted disaster. This curious hesitancy was also evident at Gettysburg. It was Early rather than Ewell who remonstrated so strongly with Lee against further attacks on the Union right on July 1, an attack that had it been delivered might have proven decisive.

Several shortcomings limited Early as a commander. His natural aggressiveness sometimes degenerated into recklessness and impetuosity, as at Williamsburg in 1862. By late 1864 Early's self confidence had actually become a liability: he underestimated Sheridan—to his cost. Indeed, almost all of Early's weaknesses came into play during that final inglorious campaign. His tendency to commit his forces piecemeal—a tactic that had succeeded at Monocacy—ruined him at Winchester where he lost almost 40 percent of his twelve thousand-man force. Several times before the Battle of Fisher's Hill on September 22, 1864, Early had proven a poor judge of terrain. (He had gotten hopelessly lost at Malvern Hill; had launched an ill-fated, badly coordinated attack without proper reconnaissance at Bethesda Church on May 30, 1864; and had once, in December 1863, muffed an opportunity to bag a sizable enemy cavalry unit by dispatching his own troopers in the wrong direction.) This time, however, he disposed his small force so badly—in a line much too long to defend—that Sheridan easily routed it.

For a commander of combined arms, Early also evinced severe deficiencies in his employment of cavalry. He never respected the mounted force anyway, and so he neglected its training and alienated its commanders. Inefficiencies in the cavalry contributed heavily to the Fisher's Hill defeat: Early had invited disaster by dismounting a lackluster unit and using it as an anchor for his flank. And at Cedar Creek a month later, Early irreparably weakened himself by detaching a large portion of his cavalry.

A superb brigadier and an excellent division commander, Early faltered only in corps command—and then only on occasion. Lee, it should be noted, always thought highly of his abilities, and more often than not Early justified the confidence of his superiors. The last six months of the Civil War enhanced the reputations of very few Confederate commanders, and Early's miserable showing against Sheridan in the Valley has clouded his reputation, perhaps unfairly. It can be argued that no Confederate general could have succeeded there against the kind of power that was brought to bear. Until then, Jubal Early ranked among the finest soldiers in the Army of Northern Virginia. It is an accolade he still deserves.

BIBLIOGRAPHY

Bushong, Millard K. *Old Jube: A Biography of General Jubal A. Early*. Boyce, Va.: Carr Publishing Company, 1955.
Early, Jubal A. *Autobiographical Sketch and Narrative of the War Between the States*. Philadelphia: J. B. Lippincott Company, 1912.
Freeman, Douglas S. *Lee's Lieutenants: A Study in Command*. 3 vols. New York: Charles Scribner's Sons, 1942–1944.
Vandiver, Frank L. *Jubal's Raid: General Early's Famous Attack on Washington in 1864*. New York: McGraw-Hill Book Company, 1960.

THOMAS E. SCHOTT

EICHELBERGER, Robert Lawrence (b. Urbana, Ohio, March 9, 1886; d. Asheville, N.C., September 26, 1961), Army officer; commander, U.S. Eighth

Army in the Pacific, 1944–1945. Eichelberger's crowning achievement was his role in the liberation of the Philippines.

The youngest of five children of a prominent lawyer who was a Union veteran, and a former Southern girl who could remember the ravages of the Vicksburg Campaign, Robert Eichelberger grew up on a farm near Urbana, Ohio. After two years at Ohio State University, he entered the U.S. Military Academy at West Point in 1905, graduating sixty-eighth in a class of 103 in 1909. Twenty-seven of his classmates ultimately became general officers.

Lieutenant Eichelberger's first assignment was with the 10th Infantry at Fort Benjamin Harrison, Indiana. He accompanied his regiment to Texas in 1911 when it was part of the Maneuver Division hastily assembled to keep a watchful eye on Mexico. Six months later the 10th was sent to Panama, where Eichelberger met and married Emma Gudger, daughter of the chief justice of the Canal Zone. Miss Em, as she was affectionately called, became his life-long companion, confidante, and ardent champion. In 1915 Eichelberger served on patrol duty on the Mexican border with the 22d Infantry. The following year he became professor of military science and tactics at Kemper Military School in Boonville, Missouri. After a brief stint as instructor at the Third Officers' Training Camp in Camp Pike, Arkansas, Captain Eichelberger joined the War Department General Staff in Washington.

There he served Major General William Sidney Graves* as executive assistant to the chief of staff, and when General Graves left to command the American Expeditionary Force sent to Siberia in 1918 as part of a joint allied military action, Eichelberger, now a major, went along as assistant chief of staff and later as chief intelligence officer. For Eichelberger the Siberian experience was a crash course in leadership; he admired Graves for his integrity, courage, and honesty, and he learned much from the candid discussions that animated their daily walks. Eichelberger also learned to respect the Japanese soldier while distrusting the militarism and motives of the Japanese leaders. "Some of the biggest liars and crooks in the world are assembled here," he confided to Miss Em, "and they are all knocking us. . . . It is a great life for a poker player."

After leaving Siberia in 1920, Eichelberger continued in military intelligence in China, the Philippines, and with the War Department. During the Washington Disarmament Conference in 1922, he was the liaison officer with the Chinese delegation, and in 1924 he transferred to the Adjutant General's Department. His name was at the top of the 1926 list of "Distinguished Graduates" of the Command and General Staff School at Fort Leavenworth, where he remained for three more years as an instructor, and in 1930 Eichelberger graduated from the Army War College. From 1931 to 1935 he served at the Military Academy as adjutant and secretary of the Academic Board, after which he spent three years as secretary to the War Department General Staff, first under General Douglas MacArthur* and then General Malin Craig.* When war clouds darkened over Europe, he transferred back to the infantry. After attending the Infantry

School at Fort Benning, Colonel Eichelberger assumed command of the 30th Infantry at the Presidio of San Francisco.

In October 1940 Eichelberger was promoted to brigadier general and soon afterwards was named superintendent of the Military Academy, where his reforms brought greater realism to training—and greater success to the football team. He successfully fought to preserve the four-year course of instruction in the face of demands to accelerate the program to meet wartime needs.

Soon after the Japanese attacked Pearl Harbor, Eichelberger was given command of the 77th Division, which was being organized at Fort Jackson, South Carolina. The smart performance of his troops in a demonstration staged for the benefit of Sir Winston Churchill helped to persuade Britain's wartime leader of the ability of the United States to raise an army capable of pulling its weight in Europe. In June Eichelberger was given command of I Corps, which was being trained in amphibious warfare; by late August 1942 he and part of his staff reached Australia, where MacArthur was organizing his counteroffensive against the Japanese in New Guinea.

Ordered "to take Buna, or not come back alive," Eichelberger assumed command of the American forces that were bogged down in the New Guinea jungle, and by January 1943 he had won the first Allied victory over the enemy in the Pacific. In April 1944 Eichelberger commanded RECKLESS Task Force in the seizure of Hollandia; two months later he was sent to straighten out the nasty situation on the island of Biak, where another American offensive was stalled. His success in these operations contributed to his selection as commander of the newly formed Eighth Army, and in the Philippines the "Amphibious Eighth" planned and executed fifty-two landing operations. While the Sixth Army bore the brunt of the early fighting on Leyte and the conquest of Luzon, elements from the Eighth Army did participate in the dash for Manila in February 1945. After the war Eichelberger's Eighth army was charged with the military occupation of Japan.

Eichelberger spent three years in Japan supervising the demobilization of the Japanese Army, the processing of some 6 million repatriots, the destruction of military supplies and equipment, the trial of Japanese war criminals, and the execution of MacArthur's policies in maintaining order and reshaping Japanese society. He retired from the Army on December 31, 1948, to write his recollections of the war, *Our Jungle Road to Tokyo*. In 1950 he was awarded his fourth star. General Eichelberger spent most of his retirement years in Asheville, where Miss Em felt most at home.

Eichelberger's first triumph, in his own estimation at least, was his greatest. At Buna, he first demonstrated his skill as a combat leader. Before his arrival, the American forces had become bogged down in the swamps and were falling victim to the mosquitoes and the Japanese. His arrival, according to his Australian superior, "was a very pure breath of fresh air." He quickly reorganized his forces, improved supplies, and provided dynamic leadership that infused his troops with new life. For many years Buna served as a case study of the modern corps commander in the leadership course at the U.S. Army Command and General Staff College, Fort Leavenworth.

At Hollandia, where MacArthur's strategy achieved a tactical surprise, Eichelberger's speedy construction of bases and airfields necessary to support forthcoming operations was regarded as "a logistical miracle," and at Biak he put life into a sagging offensive to capture a vital site for heavy bomber fields.

Eichelberger's most spectacular achievement was the part played by his new Eighth Army in the liberation of the Philippines. MacArthur considered the Visayan operations "a model of what a light but aggressive command can accomplish in rapid exploitation," and General George Catlett Marshall* wrote of the "lightening speed" of the amphibious thrusts at Panay, Cebu, and Mindanao.

Although his Eighth Army seldom got the recognition Eichelberger craved, it was slated for a leading role in the projected invasion of Japan, and MacArthur's appreciation is a matter of record. "No army of this war," he proclaimed, "has achieved greater glory and distinction."

BIBLIOGRAPHY

Eichelberger, Robert L. *Our Jungle Road to Tokyo*. New York: Viking Press, 1950.
Fleming, Thomas J. *West Point: The Men and Times of the United States Military Academy*. New York: William Morrow and Company, 1969.
James, D. Clayton. *The Years of MacArthur*. 2 vols. Boston: Houghton Mifflin Company, 1975.
Luvaas, Jay, ed. *Dear Miss Em: General Eichelberger's War in the Pacific, 1942–1945*. Westport, Conn.: Greenwood Press, 1972.
Milner, Samuel. *Victory in Papua*. Washington, D.C.: Office of the Chief of Military History, 1957.
Smith, Robert Ross. *The Approach to the Philippines*. Washington, D.C.: Office of the Chief of Military History, 1953.
———. *Triumph in the Philippines*. Washington, D.C.: Office of the Chief of Military History, 1963.

JAY LUVAAS

EISENHOWER, Dwight David (b. Denison, Tex., October 14, 1890; d. Washington, D.C., March 28, 1969), general of the Army; thirty-fourth president of the United States.

"Ike" Eisenhower was descended from German immigrants ("Pennsylvania Dutch") who had moved west after the Civil War. When he was one year old, his father, a semiskilled worker, moved the family to Abilene, Kansas, where Ike grew up. Although the family lived on the "wrong side of the tracks," his mother Ada, a strong-willed, intelligent woman, filled Ike and his five brothers with ambition, often saying that America was full of opportunity for those who would seize it.

Ike seized it. He passed a competitive examination that gained him admittance to West Point in 1911; he graduated in 1915 with a good, if not outstanding, record. The next year he courted and won the hand of Mamie Dowd; they remained happily married for fifty-three years. Unfortunately for Eisenhower's career, however, he did not get to France to command men in combat in World War I, which had a depressing effect on both his promotion rate and his ego. He spent the interwar years on various staff assignments, especially in Washington, or attending the postgraduate schools of the Army, where he always stood first in his class. On the eve of World War II he was fifty years old, still a lieutenant colonel, unknown to the public. But Douglas MacArthur* thought him the best officer in the army, and General John Joseph Pershing* had recommended him to Chief of Staff George Catlett Marshall.*

Four days after Pearl Harbor, Marshall called Eisenhower to Washington, to serve as his chief planner in the War Plans Division (later the Operations Division). There Ike, working under Marshall's guidance, sketched out the strategy the United States would follow in World War II, basically a holding, defensive action in the Pacific, with an all-out offensive in Europe, capped by an invasion of Nazi-occupied France and a drive on into Germany. Marshall then selected Ike as the ideal officer to execute the plan. In May 1942 Ike went to England to take command of the American Army in the European Theater of Operations.

The Eisenhower-Marshall strategy of an immediate invasion of France, however, was vetoed by the British, who persuaded President Franklin D. Roosevelt of the wisdom of an Allied invasion of French North Africa instead. Eisenhower, already on the spot, was given the command. In November 1942 he launched the first Allied offensive as Anglo-American forces under his command captured Algiers, Casablanca, and Oran. By May 1943, following a temporary setback at Kasserine Pass, Eisenhower's forces had destroyed all Axis resistance in North Africa. In July Ike commanded the invasion of Sicily, and in September his forces hit the beaches of Salerno, on the Italian mainland. Although they did not reach Rome before winter, Ike had managed to drive the Axis from the Mediterranean. In the process he had welded together a team of British and American officers, unequaled in the annals of warfare for its cooperation.

In January 1944 Eisenhower left the Mediterranean to go to London, where he took command of Operation OVERLORD, the long-postponed invasion of France. His response to that challenge, especially the tough decision he had to make on June 5 about whether or not weather conditions would permit the invasion, is one of the most famous stories of the war. A period of stagnation followed the success of OVERLORD, as the Germans pinned down Ike's men in Normandy, but on August 1 the Americans broke through and General George Smith Patton, Jr.'s* Third Army began the process of running the Germans out of France. By October France had been liberated, but the war was not over, according to Ike's senior British officer on the Continent, Field Marshall Bernard L. Montgomery, because of Ike's cautious strategy. Instead of advancing into Germany on a broad front, Monty advocated a single narrow thrust along the North German Plain on into Berlin. Ike refused, on military as well as political grounds, and insisted on advancing with all armies abreast. After hurling back the German last-ditch counterattack of December 1944 (Battle of the Bulge), Eisenhower's forces drove into Germany, crossed the Rhine in March 1945, and by early May brought all resistance to an end. Eisenhower emerged from the war as one of the great generals of modern times and one of the two or three most popular Americans of his age.

His popularity was so great that he was inevitably a candidate for the presidency. But in 1948, after a short hitch as chief of staff, he retired from the Army, turned down offers from both parties for the nomination, and instead took up duties as president of Columbia University. In 1950 he returned to active duty when President Harry S.Truman made him the first commander of the National Atlantic Treaty Organization (NATO) forces, which were just being formed. In 1952 the Republicans convinced him that it was his duty to run for the presidency, which he did with great success, winning a decisive victory in November, the first for a Republican since 1928.

As President, Eisenhower's emphasis was on peace and a balanced budget. He had been elected on a violent anti-Communist platform that denounced Truman's policy of containment and called instead for the liberation of Communist-enslaved countries. But that was rhetoric; in practice, Ike's policy was also containment, which was shown immediately in Korea, where he negotiated a cease-fire and armistice with the Chinese without liberating North Korea, much less China. The next year, 1954, Eisenhower spurned numerous opportunities to enter the war in Vietnam on the French side. And in 1956, when the Hungarian revolt offered him a chance to drive the Russians from at least one Central European satellite, he stayed out. Similarly, he turned down opportunities to get involved in a shooting war with China over the islands of Quemoy and Matsu.

Ike insisted on peace because he believed that war, or an all-out arms race, would bankrupt the United States. A fiscal conservative, he was the last president to have a balanced budget (inflation averaged one and one quarter percent per year during his eight years in power), brought about by extensive cuts he made in the Department of Defense. He cut the Army, Navy, and Air Force, and refused to spend money on missile development or the building of nuclear weapons at anything like the rate demanded by the Pentagon and by hawkish Democratic senators, led by John Kennedy and Lyndon Johnson. Instead, Ike introduced the "New Look," which relied on the nuclear bomb to deter the Russians from any aggressive adventures. Reporters called the policy "More bang for a buck," while three Army chiefs of staff denounced it as an "all-or-nothing" posture and resigned in protest against Ike's cuts in the Army budget. Eisenhower continued to hold down the expenditures, based on his knowledge—gained from the CIA's U–2 flights—that the United States was comfortably ahead of the Russians in military affairs.

In November 1956 Eisenhower was reelected in a landslide. In his second term he continued to pursue peace and a balanced budget. He turned his back on the civil rights revolution, which was just getting underway, although he did set a crucial precedent in 1957, when he sent U.S. Army paratroopers to Little

Rock, Arkansas, and federalized the Arkansas National Guard to enforce a desegregation court order. In general, however, his was never a reform administration. What was important about his eight years in power was that the Republicans accepted the New Deal reforms, such as social security. His best known innovation was the interstate highway system.

Ike responded to Fidel Castro's coming to power in Cuba with equanimity, saw no reason to panic when the Russians tried to force the West out of Berlin, and shrugged off Russian threats after Francis Gary Powers' U–2 was shot down deep inside the Soviet Union in 1960. This opened him to charges of having neglected the nation's defenses. In the 1960 presidential campaign, John Kennedy made a major issue out of the so-called missile gap and bomber gap, and defeated Richard Nixon in a tightly contested race. In his farewell address, Ike warned the nation about the influence, sought or unsought, of the military-industrial complex. He retired to his farm in Gettysburg, Pennsylvania, where he wrote and enjoyed the role of elder statesman.

Although never a battlefield commander, Ike was nevertheless a great general, perhaps the best of his century. His breadth of view and strategic vision were unmatched. He had, as MacArthur once said and Churchill repeated, the gift of being able to see the whole problem. He was especially good at getting the best out of his subordinates, be they staff officers or field commanders. And he had the ability to make a decision and make it stick.

Eisenhower was never a war president. Indeed, his proudest boast was that for eight years he kept the peace; his next boast was that he balanced the budget. His critics called him a do-nothing president, but by the end of the 1960s many of those critics would like to have seen Ike back in office.

BIBLIOGRAPHY

Ambrose, Stephen E. *The Supreme Commander: The War Years of Dwight D. Eisenhower*. New York: Doubleday, 1970.

Chandler, Aldred D., Jr., and Stephen E. Ambrose, eds. *The Papers of Dwight David Eisenhower: The War Years*. 5 vols. Baltimore: Johns Hopkins University Press, 1970.

Eisenhower, Dwight D. *Crusade in Europe*. New York: Doubleday, 1948.

————. *The White House Years*. 2 vols. New York: Doubleday, 1963 and 1965.

Parmet, Herbert S. *Eisenhower and the American Crusades*. New York: Macmillan Company, 1972.

Pogue, Forrest C. *The Supreme Command*. In *United States Army in World War II*. Edited by Kent Roberts Greenfield. Washington, D.C.: U.S. Department of the Army, 1954.

STEPHEN E. AMBROSE

ELLIS, Earl (b. Iuka, Kan., December 19, 1880; d. Koror, Palau Islands, Western Caroline Island Group in the Central Pacific, May 12, 1923), Marine Corps officer. Ellis was one of the Marine Corps' early articulators of amphibious doctrine.

Earl "Pete" Ellis was one of eight children of Augustus W. and Katherine E. Ellis. His maternal grandfather, Andrew Axline, a Presbyterian minister, led a group of parishioners, including Ellis' parents, from Iowa to "dry" Kansas in 1877. These pioneers founded the town of Iuka (named after a Civil War battle) in Pratt County, "where they could raise their children free from the influence of liquor." Augustus Ellis joined his father, John, in the family real estate business in the city of Pratt, not far from Iuka. Young Earl Ellis attended the Pratt public schools and graduated from the local high school in 1900. With his parents' consent, Earl Ellis enlisted in the Marine Corps that September in Chicago.

The motivation underlying Ellis' decision to join the Corps remains a matter of speculation. Youthful rebellion against the narrow strictures of his upbringing may have been a reason for his enlistment. Moreover, the romantic appeal of the sea, faraway places, and patriotism probably all played their part.

In any event, Ellis did very well as a Marine enlisted man. Promoted rapidly, he became a corporal in February 1901, a scant five months after his enlistment. The Marine Corps further recognized the young corporal's ability later in the year when it commissioned Ellis as a second lieutenant on December 21, 1901.

Ellis' early assignments conformed to the usual pattern for a career Marine officer of that period. He completed his officer training at the Boston Navy Yard in 1902, and then joined the 1st Marine Brigade in the Philippines. In 1903 Lieutenant Ellis became one of the officers of the Marine guard serving in the battleship *Kentucky*, flagship of the Asiatic Fleet. He received his promotion to first lieutenant in 1904.

Beginning with a second tour in the Philippines in 1908, Ellis became identified with the Marine Corps Advance Base Force, which was the forerunner of the modern Fleet Marine Force. In the event of war, the Navy's General Board had assigned to the Marine Corps the task of seizing and defending advanced bases in support of the fleet. In 1908 the emphasis was on defense of such a base, and the only existing Marine Advance Base Force was the Marine brigade in the Philippines. Captain Ellis, promoted to that rank in December 1908, served as the Advance Base officer and was responsible for the defenses of Grande Island in Subic Bay. Despite occasional eccentric behavior and heavy drinking, Ellis impressed his immediate superiors in the Philippines, Major John Archer Lejeune* and Lieutenant Colonel Joseph Henry Pendleton,* both of whom praised the young captain for his ability and devotion to duty.

Returning from the Philippines in 1911 with a reputation for brilliance, Ellis attended the Naval War College at Newport, Rhode Island. After completing the course, he remained at the Naval War College as a member of the permanent staff until September 1913. While at the college, Ellis wrote a seminal study on advance base theory.

After leaving the War College, Ellis served as the intelligence officer of the Advance Base Brigade which carried out the first major advance base maneuver in conjunction with the Atlantic Fleet. Ellis made a reconnaissance of the island of Culebra, near Puerto Rico, where the brigade landed in January 1914 and set up extensive defenses.

With the successful completion of the exercise, Ellis, at the request of the Navy, was sent to Guam, where he supervised the establishment of the permanent defenses on that island. While on Guam, Ellis suffered the first of his physical and emotional collapses which were to reoccur periodically throughout the remainder of his career. After being hospitalized, Ellis returned from Guam in December 1915, in apparent good health and still enjoying the confidence of senior Marine officers.

From early 1916 until mid–1917 Ellis remained at Headquarters, Marine Corps in Washington as the personal aide to the commandant, Major General George Barnett,* who, as a colonel, had commanded the Advance Base Brigade on Culebra. Ellis and two other junior officers made up the nucleus of the Headquarters planning staff under the direction of the assistant to the commandant, Colonel Lejeune. This staff was largely responsible for the development of plans for the expansion of the Marine Corps which occurred during this period in response to the growing possibility of American involvement in World War I. The pressures on the small staff increased even more after the American entry into the war in April 1917. Overwork, an excess of alcohol, and nervous exhaustion all took their toll on Ellis, who had been promoted to major. During this period, he suffered two relapses, one in 1916 and a more serious breakdown in 1917. Upon releasing Ellis from the hospital after the last collapse, his doctor blamed the sick officer's condition partially on the close confinement of office work and recommended that he be reassigned to more active duty.

Obeying his new orders, Ellis made a liaison visit to France to study Allied training procedures and then returned to Washington in early 1918. In May 1918, at his request, he returned to France, becoming the adjutant of the 4th Marine Brigade, which formed part of the U.S. 2d Division under General Lejeune's command. Serving with distinction, Ellis was credited with developing a plan that resulted in driving the German lines back some thirty kilometers in October 1918, during the Battle of Blanc Mont Ridge. After the Armistice, the Marine Brigade moved into Germany and finally returned to the United States in August 1919.

Upon his return, Ellis continued his unorthodox career. Almost immediately, he combined a leave home to Pratt with a secret mission to Mexico, where he visited the oilfields in Tampico. Coming back to Washington, he suffered another emotional breakdown. Following a three-month sick leave, Ellis, in April 1920, became the intelligence officer of the 2d Marine Brigade stationed in the Dominican Republic. In December 1920 General Lejeune decided to assign Ellis to the newly created Operations and Training Section at Headquarters, Marine Corps. Prompted by renewed attention to the potential threat of war with Japan in the Pacific, the Marine Corps commandant ordered Ellis to revise Marine Corps war plans. Working day and night, Ellis developed the important Operation Plan 712, entitled "Advanced Base Operations in Micronesia," which foreshadowed the Marine campaign in the Central Pacific during World War II. During the writing of the plan, he suffered several relapses and began checking himself into the hospital every morning. Nevertheless, he completed his work by the end of May 1921. General Lejeune approved the plan in July.

Following the completion of the Micronesia Plan, Ellis' career took a most bizarre turn. He convinced Marine and naval authorities to send him on a sensitive intelligence mission to determine the extent of Japanese fortifications, if any, in the mandated islands that Japan had recently acquired from a defeated Germany. Traveling as a tool manufacturing representative, Ellis, recently promoted to lieutenant colonel, obtained a visa from the Japanese consul general in Sydney, Australia. Unable to find a direct steamer to the Carolines, Ellis went via the Philippines to Yokohama, Japan, in hopes of finding passage to the Pacific Islands. While in Japan, Ellis collapsed from nephritis, a kidney disease, and from alcohol poisoning. Confined to the U.S. Naval Hospital at Yokohama, Ellis escaped from the hospital on the night of October 6, 1922, when he learned that the American authorities in Japan planned to send him home. The American officials were not to learn about Ellis' whereabouts until the Japanese informed them that Ellis had died on the island of Koror in May 1923.

The circumstances surrounding Ellis' death caused much speculation that the Japanese may have killed him. These suspicions were strengthened when a U.S. sailor, Chief Pharmacist Lawrence Zembsh, who was sent to the Carolines to pick up Ellis' ashes, returned in a catatonic state. Zembsh continued to suffer from amnesia until his death in September 1923, during the earthquake that destroyed the U.S. Naval Hospital in Yokohama. Nevertheless, the evidence, including interviews conducted with the inhabitants of Koror following World War II, would indicate that Ellis died a natural death, although the Japanese were suspicious of him and had him watched and followed. General Lejeune's assessment in a letter to Ellis' brother Ralph was probably correct: "I am personally of the opinion that Earl's death was due to disease, which probably was aggravated by intemperance. Of course, there are rumors, but there is no evidence that these rumors are true."

Ellis made important contributions to the development of American war planning for the Pacific and the articulation of amphibious doctrine. His writings on the Advance Base Force reflected the evolutionary change in Marine Corps and naval thought from an emphasis on the defense of the advanced base to the seizure of such a base in an amphibious assault.

In his 1913 study of the advanced base, Ellis provided a synthesis of existing advance base doctrine developed by the Navy's General Board, the Naval War College, and the Marine Corps Advance Base School, which had been founded in 1910. He focused on the need of the Marine Corps to secure bases in time of war in support of the fleet and to deny the same to the enemy as well as the location and defense of such bases. Although Ellis stressed the defensive aspect of the advance base mission, he implied that it could also be offensive. He observed that "In a war with Japan, the U.S. would assume the strategic offensive. The U.S. Navy must proceed to the Far East and gain command of the sea."

Although writing on other aspects of advance base work, it was not until his Micronesia Plan in 1921 that Ellis addressed the full ramifications of seizing advanced bases defended by a determined enemy. He predicted that the Japanese would probably initiate the war and that an American counteroffensive would require the capture of the Japanese-controlled islands in the Central Pacific. He described at considerable length the geography and physical characteristics of Micronesia and then detailed the organization, tactics, air, and naval gunfire that would be required to take these islands. Ellis made a distinction between the assault forces with its infantry and field artillery and what he called the Base Defense Force of heavy artillery, antiaircraft guns, and technical troops which would come in later and hold the base.

Ellis was in the forefront of those Marine planners during the 1920s and 1930s who were responsible for making the terms "Marines" and "amphibious assault" synonymous.

BIBLIOGRAPHY

Heinl, Robert D., Jr. *Soldiers of the Sea: The U.S. Marine Corps, 1775–1962*. Annapolis, Md.: Naval Institute Press, 1962.
Hough, Frank O., et al. *Pearl Harbor to Guadalcanal*. Washington, D.C.: U.S. Government Printing Office, 1958.
Isely, Jeter A., and Philip A. Crowl. *The U.S. Marines and Amphibious War*. Princeton, N.J.: Princeton University Press, 1951.
Millet, Allan R. *Semper Fidelis: The History of the U.S. Marine Corps*. New York: Free Press, 1980.
Reber, John J. "Pete Ellis: Amphibious Warfare Prophet." U.S. Naval Institute *Proceedings* 103 (November 1977): 53–64.

                                                      JACK SHULIMSON

ERICSSON, John (b. Langbanshyttan, Province of Wermland, Sweden, July 31, 1803; d. New York City, N.Y., March 8, 1889), engineer, inventor. Ericsson is best known as the designer of the USS *Monitor* in the American Civil War and as a pioneer in screw ship propulsion.

John Ericsson was the youngest of three children of a Swedish mineowner and his wife, who was of Flemish-Scotch descent. He received an excellent education at home from tutors until his early teens when he worked on the construction of the Gota Canal. He displayed an early proficiency for mechanical work and entered the Swedish Army at age seventeen where he served as a topographical engineer.

In 1827, at age twenty-four, Ericsson went to England and spent twelve years there working as a mechanical engineer, principally on the design and construction of steam-powered machinery, such as a locomotive and a fire engine. During his last four years there, he designed a screw propeller, which he patented in

1836. The Lords of the Admiralty saw a demonstration of his screw but were not interested.

Ericsson immigrated to the United States in 1839 at the urging of Navy Captain Robert Field Stockton* who had enlisted his assistance in the design and construction of a war steamer. When Stockton encountered resistance from the Navy for his proposals, Ericsson turned to commercial work and successfully applied his propeller to a large number of ships and boats. Stockton's political maneuvering won approval for the warship in 1841, and Ericsson planned and supervised the construction of the USS *Princeton*, which was commissioned in 1844. It was the first warship equipped with a screw propeller and engines mounted below the waterline where they could be safe from enemy shot. The vessel also mounted a main battery of two powerful 12–inch wrought-iron smoothbore guns, one designed by Ericsson and the other by Stockton. The latter gun exploded on February 28, 1844, during a cruise for government officials and killed five men, including the secretary of state and the secretary of the Navy. Although Ericsson was not directly involved, the incident clouded his reputation and his relationship with the Navy until the Civil War. During the interim, he applied his screw propeller to foreign and domestic merchant ships and European men-of-war. Ericsson also tried to perfect the caloric engine, which he believed would transfer heat more efficiently by using air instead of steam as the working fluid. Application of the concept in the ship *Ericsson* was unsuccessful; however, the use of the principle in small stationary engines ashore worked well.

Soon after the outbreak of the Civil War, the U.S. Navy bought Ericsson's revolutionary design for an armored, turreted, and mastless warship with low freeboard to counter an ironclad under construction by the Confederacy. The USS *Monitor*, which Ericsson and his associates designed and built in a remarkably short time, fought the CSS *Virginia* (ex-*Merrimack*) in a legendary sea battle in Hampton Roads, Virginia, in March 1862. Ericsson became an instant hero. The *Monitor* became the prototype of four classes of turreted Union warships built during the war and the namesake for a ship type employed all over the world. Ericsson's friction-brake gun carriage was also widely adopted at home and overseas; however, his 13–inch wrought-iron heavy gun did not meet the Navy's specifications and was rejected.

After the war, Ericsson supplied the engines for the USS *Madawaska*, one of a new class of commerce raiders; however, the ship could not match the performance of the *Wampanoag*, whose machinery had been designed by naval Chief Engineer Benjamin Franklin Isherwood.* *Madawaska* was refitted with conventional engines in 1869 and renamed *Tennessee*. In 1869 Ericsson designed and constructed thirty gunboats for the Spanish government for Cuban service, and he proposed to the U.S. Navy adoption of a torpedo propelled by compressed air supplied through a rubber hose. Extensive tests during the 1870s showed the impracticality of this concept. His armored, semisubmerged torpedoboat, *Destroyer*, built in the late 1870s and early 1880s, received the same cold reception from the Navy when it failed to live up to Ericsson's claims. During the last few years of his life, Ericsson lived quietly in New York City and worked on experimental devices such as methods to harness solar energy.

Ericsson's fame rests principally on his design and construction of the USS *Monitor*. Ironclads were not uncommon at the time, for other navies, such as the French and British, had sizable numbers of them either in commission or under construction. However, the battle between the *Monitor* and the *Virginia* was the landmark, first combat between two such ships, and it captured the public imagination. The triumph of armor over ordnance in that encounter accelerated the contest between naval constructors and ordnance designers. Ericsson's monitor design long survived the Civil War, as navies built coastal defense ships of similar type well into the twentieth century.

Ericsson's turret design was not the one widely adopted by modern navies. His contemporary, Captain Cowper P. Coles of the British Navy, independently invented the popular concept of supporting the weight of the turret on the outside rim and protecting the base of the turret with a raised shield on the deck. Ericsson, on the other hand, placed the weight on a spindle in the center of the turret and did not protect the base in his initial plan. However, both men share credit for popularizing the concept and proving its utility and feasibility.

Ericsson's other major innovation for the U.S. Navy was the screw steamer USS *Princeton* in the early 1840s. He incorporated into the vessel novel features that were universally adopted later, including the screw propeller and location of the machinery below the waterline. His design of the wrought-iron, banded, 12–inch "Oregon" gun has been viewed as a precursor to a pattern of construction used by the British in the late 1850s, but the similarity is only superficial.

Ericsson's unsuccessful proposals for a self-propelled torpedo and the torpedoboat in the 1870s should be viewed within the context of the period. Torpedo warfare was in its infancy, and no type of torpedo or mine had established clear superiority in battle. His concepts were just as rational and possible as any other when first proposed.

In a broader sense, Ericsson was one of the leading marine engineers and inventors of his age and an important popularizer of the screw propeller, which he admitted was not a new idea when he patented his design in 1836.

BIBLIOGRAPHY

Baxter, James P. *The Introduction of the Ironclad Warship*. Cambridge, Mass.: Harvard
    University Press, 1933.
Brodie, Bernard. *Sea Power in the Machine Age*. Princeton, N.J.: Princeton University
    Press, 1941.
Church, William C. *The Life of John Ericsson*. 2 vols. New York: Charles Scribner's
    Sons, 1890.
White, Ruth. *Yankee from Sweden: The Dream and the Reality in the Days of John
    Ericsson*. New York: Henry Holt and Company, 1960.

                                                            RICHARD D. GLASOW

EVANS, Robley Dunglison (b. Floyd County, Va., August 18, 1846; d. Washington, D.C., January 3, 1912), naval officer. "Fighting Bob" Evans culminated his varied career by commanding the Great White Fleet at the outset of its round-the-world voyage in 1907.

Robley Evans was born in the mountains of Virginia. His father died when the boy was ten, and the family moved to Fairfax Courthouse, Virginia. Evans lived in Washington with an uncle who helped him gain admission to the Naval Academy in 1860 by establishing residency in the congressional district of Representative William H. Hooper of Salt Lake City, Utah.

In spite of family pressure, Evans remained loyal to the Union in the Civil War and was commissioned acting ensign in 1863 at the age of seventeen. He served as a watch officer aboard the steam frigate *Powhatan* in the North Atlantic Blockading Squadron and on January 15, 1865, commanded a company of marines in a land assault in the second attack on Fort Fisher. He was so severely wounded in the attack that a medical board ordered him placed on the retired list, a decision he successfully appealed. He was promoted to the rank of lieutenant in 1866 and was placed on ordnance duty at the Washington Navy Yard in early 1867.

Obtaining a seagoing post aboard the *Piscataqua*, the new flagship of the Asiatic Squadron, Evans enjoyed a Far Eastern odyssey of visits in China, Japan, and the Philippines. In Hong Kong, in 1868, he was promoted to lieutenant commander.

On his return in 1870, Evans was ordered to the Ordnance Department of the Washington Navy Yard where he served for less than a year. He was married to Charlotte Taylor, the sister of his classmate, Henry Clay Taylor, in July 1871. Evans next served as an instructor at the Naval Academy for two years.

In 1873 Evans reported to Captain C. H. Wells as navigator aboard the sloop-of-war *Shenandoah* of the Mediterranean fleet. In 1874 he was transferred to the screw sloop *Congress* as executive officer under Captain Earl English and sailed along the West African coast in the Mediterranean.

In 1877 Evans gained command of the teaching ship *Saratoga*, an old sailing sloop-of-war. His satisfying duty was to enlist and train sailors for naval service. He was promoted to commander in 1878 and left the *Saratoga* in 1881 to become an equipment officer at the Washington Navy Yard. Secretary of the Navy William Hunt assigned him to the newly formed Naval Advisory Board in 1882 under Admiral John Rodgers, Jr.* The board's chief task was to make recommendations for rebuilding the depleted and deteriorated Navy.

Evans became an inspector and disbursing officer for the Fifth Lighthouse District (Baltimore) in 1882. In 1885 he became chief steel inspector for the Navy Department. From 1887 to 1889 Evans was naval secretary to the Lighthouse Board in Washington. He also traveled regularly to New York to assist in the supervision of the construction of the Navy's new steel ships.

A leave of absence in 1890 was followed by an appointment in August 1891 to command the gunboat *Yorktown* in the North Atlantic Squadron. Evans and the *Yorktown* were ordered to Valparaiso, Chile, in the midst of a diplomatic crisis touched off by the murder of two American sailors from the *Baltimore* and the right of asylum for political refugees in the American legation. Evans skillfully handled the serious problems arising from both of these circumstances. He kept his crew ready for military action over several tense months and finally was able to conduct most of the refugees to safety. Soon after his return to San Francisco, he was given command of five ships on a grueling six-month cruise to police the sealing areas of the North Pacific and Bering Sea.

Captain Evans (promoted to that rank in 1893) gained a significant compliment when, as a junior captain, he was put in command of the fine new armored cruiser *New York* in the summer of 1894. As skipper of the *New York*, he represented the United States in the celebrations honoring the opening of the North Sea Kiel Canal in Germany in 1895. In July of that year he reported to Admiral F. M. Bunce for duty as flagship of the North Atlantic Squadron; Bunce was the third admiral in *New York* in less than two years. In October Evans was assigned to Philadelphia to fit out and take command of the first American battleship, the *Indiana*. On the eve of the war with Spain, in March 1898, he was given command of the fine battleship *Iowa* under Admiral William Thomas Sampson* of the North Atlantic Station.

During the war with Spain, Evans served with Sampson at the initial blockade of Havana, Cuba, the cruise and bombardment of Puerto Rico, and on May 18 he was sent to join Commodore Winfield Scott Schley* at Cienfuegos. On May 31 he participated with Schley in the unsuccessful long-range shelling of the *Colon* at Santiago. The *Iowa* was the first to draw searchlight duty in the month-long blockade of Admiral Cervera's ships in Santiago. In the battle against Cervera's fleet on July 3, the *Iowa* fired on and received fire from almost every Spanish ship. Evans' work was central to the exceptional victory, and he was made rear admiral in February 1901.

In 1902, Evans was given command of the Asiatic Fleet and toured the Yangtze region of China. He was actively in favor of the creation of the Navy League in 1903 and served on both the Lighthouse Board and General Board of the Navy.

In 1907, President Theodore Roosevelt* chose Evans to serve as commander of the cream of the American fleet, sixteen white-painted battleships, which he would take on a world cruise. The round-the-world trip was typical of T.R.'s grand gestures, but it also had practical implications. During the cruise, communications and maintenance, coaling procedures, and gunnery training could all be put to the test. The sailors and officers would be tested as well as the ships; the fleet had never sailed in such strength for such a distance before (eventually it traveled forty-six thousand miles). Evans took the Great White Fleet from Hampton Roads, Virginia, on December 16, 1907, and called at ports in Brazil, Chile, and Peru. He fell ill at Magdalena Bay, Mexico, and in San Francisco he relinquished the fleet to Admiral Charles S. Sperry, who commanded the white ships on the remainder of the voyage. By invitation, the fleet made port calls in New Zealand, Australia, the Philippines, Japan, and China, then sailed through the Indian Ocean, the Suez Canal, the Mediterranean Sea, and, after making stops in Europe, eventually returned to Hampton Roads on February 22, 1909. In the meantime, Evans had retired from the Navy in August 1908.

At every stage of his career, Evans earned distinction by his actions. In the Civil War he suffered severe wounds as he bravely led his marine detachment. As chief steel inspector, he helped establish new standards for American steel. During the Chilean crisis, his diplomatic talents were tested as much as his leadership skills, and "Fighting Bob" became a favorite figure in the press. At the Battle of Santiago, the *Iowa* inflicted damage to almost every Spanish vessel and destroyed two torpedoboats as they attempted to streak out into the open sea.

Actually, one of Evans' most demanding tasks may have been during the six months he spent on patrol duty in the Bering Sea. He covered more than twenty-five thousand miles and supervised the seizure and inspection of every British or Canadian vessel in the area under delicate international conditions. He could finally report the end of seal poaching there. Evans was commended for his work by both the secretary of the Navy and the president, who noted Evans' achievements in his State of the Union message.

As a fleet admiral, Evans continued to emphasize technical improvements and practice drill procedures, and actively assisted in the development of new loading machinery used in gunnery. All of these things were tested under trying conditions during the voyage of the White Fleet. It may have been one of Evans' great personal and professional disappointments that illness prevented him from completing that cruise at the close of his career. Later, however, he was critical of President Roosevelt and indicated that the cruise may have been made only to satisfy T.R.'s desire for prestige and publicity. Nevertheless, Evans had not turned down command of the White Fleet when he might have done so for reasons of health, and he had struggled mightily to make the first half of the voyage a success.

BIBLIOGRAPHY

Evans, Robley D. *An Admiral's Log: Being Continued Reflections of Naval Life*. New York: D. Appleton and Company, 1910.
———. *A Sailor's Log: Recollections of Forty Years of Naval Life*. New York: D. Appleton and Company, 1901.
Falk, Robert A. *Fighting Bob Evans*. New York: J. Cape and H. Smith, 1931.
Hart, Robert A. *The Great White Fleet: Its Voyage Around the World, 1907–1909*. Boston: Little, Brown and Company, 1965.
Herrick, Walter R. *The American Naval Revolution*. Baton Rouge: Louisiana State University Press, 1966.

PHILIP Y. NICHOLSON

EWELL, Richard Stoddert (b. Georgetown, D.C., February 8, 1817; d. "Spring Hill," Maury County, Tenn., January 25, 1872), Army officer. Ewell served as a division and corps commander in the Confederacy's Army of Northern Virginia.

Richard Stoddert Ewell moved to Virginia during his early years when his father returned the family to his native Prince William County at "Stony Lonesome." Despite the middle name he bore (derived from his grandfather, Benjamin Stoddert,* first secretary of the Navy), he entered the U.S. Military Academy at West Point in 1836 without dreams of military grandeur. Upon graduation as brevet second lieutenant in July 1840, he ranked thirteenth in a class of forty-two.

Following the advice of his brother Benjamin (also a West Point alumnus), Ewell applied for assignment with the 1st Dragoons. He served briefly at Carlisle Barracks before being assigned to the frontier as second lieutenant in November 1840. Fort Wayne, Indian Territory, and Fort Scott, Kansas Territory, were his principal posts for the next six years, with sporadic duties on the Santa Fe and Oregon Trails under Captain Philip St. George Cooke* and Colonel Stephen Watts Kearny.* Two tours of recruiting service and a month on the Coast Survey interrupted his frontier duties before the Mexican War. Meanwhile, Ewell had been promoted to first lieutenant in 1845.

Ewell accompanied the army of General Winfield Scott* from Vera Cruz to Chapultepec in 1847. During the campaign his brother Thomas was mortally wounded at Cerro Gordo. Ewell himself was subsequently brevetted captain for gallantry at Contreras and Churubusco. Ewell's first exposure to fire had occurred only days earlier while reconnoitering the Pedregal with Captain Robert Edward Lee,* whom he assessed as "one of the most talented men connected with this army."

Following the war, Ewell rendered recruiting service in the East. He returned to the frontier in 1850 with captain's bars that had been awarded to him the previous year. During the 1850s Ewell was garrisoned at Los Lunas, New Mexico, and Fort Buchanan, Arizona, and he campaigned against the Apaches and suffered a wound while fighting them in 1859. In 1860 he was reassigned to Fort Bliss, Texas.

Captain Ewell was in Virginia in April 1861, convalescing from one of several maladies that vexed him throughout his life. The week after Virginia seceded from the Union, he tendered his resignation from the U.S. Army as "a painful sense of duty." By early May he was a lieutenant colonel in the Confederate Army and was drilling cavalry recruits at Ashland. He transferred to Fairfax Courthouse where he was wounded in a skirmish on June 1.

The Confederate government recognized Ewell's experience by promoting him to brigadier general in mid-June. He commanded a brigade at Manassas where he was confused by a series of conflicting orders; his men marched and countermarched twenty miles that day without seeing action. Yet the Confederate high command displayed further confidence in his abilities as Congress confirmed him a major general with division command in January 1862.

General Thomas Jonathan "Stonewall" Jackson* summoned Ewell to the

Shenandoah Valley in April. After some preliminaries, the pair marched north-ward to victory at Front Royal and, under Ewell's initiative, pressed toward Winchester where General Nathaniel Banks was crushed two days later. The Confederates then withdrew to evade the combined forces of Generals John Charles Frémont* and James Shields. The Valley Campaign reached its finale in June at Cross Keys and Port Republic, and Ewell's leadership was conspicuous in these twin victories. He participated in the final charge and personally served an artillery piece.

Hastening to Richmond, the Valley Army joined Lee for the Seven Days' Battles. Ewell's division made a significant contribution at Gaines' Mill and provided support at Malvern Hill. The Jackson-Ewell combination was reacti-vated in July to stymie the approaching army under General John Pope.* After clashing at Cedar Mountain with Banks, Jackson was joined by the remainder of Lee's army. During this Second Manassas Campaign, Ewell was severely wounded at Groveton on August 28. His right leg was amputated. Thereafter he endured nine months of laborious recovery and subsequently used a wooden leg.

After Jackson's mortal wounding at Chancellorsville, Lee reorganized his army and designated Ewell to command the II Corps. In conjunction he was promoted to lieutenant general. But when Ewell assumed command at Fredericksburg on May 29 he was a changed man. Formerly a bachelor and a skeptic who was fiery and profane, he returned as a Christian husband who possessed a civil tongue. Physically, he alternated his riding between horseback and a carriage to accommodate his more fragile constitution, accentuated by his artificial leg.

Lee launched his army northward, and Ewell raised its spirits by capturing Winchester, displaying a tactical brilliance reminiscent of Jackson. When the divided Confederate forces concentrated in Pennsylvania, Ewell moved toward Gettysburg on July 1 to reinforce the embattled corps of General Ambrose Powell Hill* and joined the fighting. Ewell entered the town in late afternoon as the routed but reinforced Union army was regrouping on the formidable heights of Cemetery Hill. The Southerners were disorganized and exhausted, and Ewell remembered Lee's advice to avoid a general engagement with a large force until the entire army was concentrated; Lee's discretionary orders were to capture Cemetery Hill "if practicable." Ignorant of Federal numbers on Cemetery and nearby Culp's Hills, Ewell terminated combat. The next day Ewell's corps made uncoordinated efforts with inadequate artillery support to capture Cemetery and Culp's Hills. The futile attack was renewed on Culp's Hill on July 3. After Union forces repulsed the attack led by George Edward Pickett,* Lee's army retreated back into Virginia.

In November, during the Bristoe Campaign, Ewell's troops were roughly handled at Rappahannock Bridge. He absented himself from the Mine Run Campaign due to illness, and his health wavered during the winter. However, Ewell showed rekindled radiance in the defensive action at Morton's Ford in February 1864.

Ewell's corps fought next in the Wilderness. On the second day (May 6, 1864), a golden opportunity eluded Ewell when he failed to attack the exposed Union right. Days later at Spotsylvania, Lee removed vital artillery which nearly doomed Ewell's defense of the crucial "mule shoe." By the time the vying armies repositioned themselves at North Anna River and Totopotomoy Creek, Ewell's declining health forced him to turn over the corps to General Jubal Anderson Early.* On May 31 Early became lieutenant general and corps commander. The protesting Ewell was assigned the less strenuous duty of directing the Department of Richmond.

In the war's final year, Ewell lost his bid for active service under General Joseph Eggleston Johnston* and declined an offer as chief of the cavalry bureau. In April 1865 he was given the unenviable task of evacuating Richmond and destroying its vital stores. On April 5 the men in Ewell's department joined Lee's retreating army. The following day Ewell's troops were severed from the main army at Sayler's Creek, and after desperate fighting he surrendered and afterwards suffered several months' imprisonment at Fort Warren, Massachusetts. His remaining years passed quietly as a gentleman farmer at "Spring Hill" in Maury County, Tennessee.

Douglas Southall Freeman described the five foot-ten and a half inch Ewell as a "strange, unlovely bird" whom admiring soldiers called "Old Bald Head." Unfortunately, this positive estimation of Ewell waned in the Confederates' quest for Gettysburg scapegoats. Only Ewell's action on July 2 deserves partial censure; the erroneous timing of his attack on the third day was typical of the era when couriers delivered communiques, and the first day's "orders" were discretionary ones concerning a foe of unknown strength and position. Hindsight provided "lost opportunities" for Confederates who ignored brilliant Federal actions that secured victory.

Ewell played an important role in the Valley Campaign. It was Ewell's proposal on May 18, 1862, that he cooperate with Jackson in lieu of Richmond's restraining orders. His continued initiative throughout the campaign contributed vastly to its success.

A man who abhorred the horrors of war, Ewell nonetheless mastered tactics and demonstrated a grasp of strategic problems. His emphatic concern over Tennessee in early 1862 and Vicksburg in 1863 indicates that he was not preoccupied with his own theater of war. And his advocacy of Negro regiments in July 1862 preceded the Confederacy's belated effort, prompted by desperation and lassitude, to enlist black soldiers in 1865. However, it is a comment on the condition of the Confederacy that an officer in Ewell's physical condition was retained as a corps commander in a major field army. Despite his ailments, Ewell was a masterful brigade and division commander, but he was enfeebled when he assumed his greatest burden. Perhaps disfavor was inevitable for the man who had the dubious honor of being "Stonewall" Jackson's successor.

BIBLIOGRAPHY

Coddington, Edwin B. *The Gettysburg Campaign: A Study in Command*. New York: Charles Scribner's Sons, 1968.

Freeman, Douglas Southall. *Lee's Lieutenants: A Study in Command*. 3 vols. New York: Charles Scribner's Sons, 1942–1944.

Hamlin, Percy Gatling. *The Making of a Soldier: Letters of General R. S. Ewell*. Richmond, Va.: Whittet and Shepperson, 1935.

———. *"Old Bald Head" (General R. S. Ewell): The Portrait of a Soldier*. Strasburg, Va.: Shenandoah Publishing House, 1940.

Tanner, Robert G. *Stonewall in the Valley: Thomas J. "Stonewall" Jackson's Shenandoah Valley Campaign, Spring 1862*. Garden City, N.Y.: Doubleday and Company, 1976.

DAVID F. RIGGS

F

FARRAGUT, David Glasgow (b. Campbell's Station, near Knoxville, Tenn., July 5, 1801; d. Portsmouth, N.H., August 14, 1870), naval officer. Farragut was the most successful officer of the Union Navy during the Civil War (1861–1865).

Originally named James Glasgow Farragut, the U.S. Navy's future first admiral became the ward of Master Commandant David Porter in 1808 after the lad's mother died of yellow fever. Two years later the boy accepted an appointment as a midshipman. Out of devotion to his benefactor, he changed his name from James to David. Porter assumed command of the 32-gun frigate *Essex*, and young Farragut learned the routine of a man-of-war under his tutelage. During the War of 1812, *Essex* successfully operated against British merchantmen in the Atlantic and preyed on English whalers in the Pacific. Porter showed his confidence in Farragut by giving him command of a prize. Porter's intrepidity and seamanship ever served as an inspiration to Farragut.

After the war with England, Farragut had a variety of assignments. In 1815 he was sent to the 74-gun ship-of-the-line *Independence*, flagship of a squadron formed under Commodore William Bainbridge* to defend American rights against pirates in the Mediterranean. He later served in Porter's ''mosquito fleet'' fighting piracy in the West Indies. There he fell ill with yellow fever which badly impaired his health. In 1823 the young officer married Susan C. Marchant of Norfolk, Virginia. In ill-health, she became an invalid for life. In 1825 Farragut got his promotion to lieutenant. After a cruise to Europe and duties at Norfolk, in 1828 he reported to the 18-gun sloop-of-war *Vandalia*, being fitted out for service along the coast of South America. A year later serious trouble with his eyes compelled him to return home; he was inactive until 1832. In the spring of 1833, once more in *Vandalia*, Farragut sailed for South America.

After his return, almost four years ashore elapsed before Farragut embarked in the 38-gun frigate *Constellation* at Pensacola, Florida. Next, he was selected to command the 20-gun sloop *Erie* to the coast of Mexico. This mission enabled him to observe operations of French warships against Mexico. His reports to Washington concluded that properly used men-of-war could be extremely effective against shore fortifications. In 1839 Farragut returned to Norfolk and remained there until his wife died in 1840. He welcomed orders in 1841 assigning him to the *Delaware*, and while that 86-gun ship-of-the-line was being refitted for service on the Brazil Station, was promoted to commander (September 1841). On the Brazil Station, Farragut was placed in command of the 16-gun sloop *Decatur* and brought her back to Norfolk in 1843. That December he married and remained devoted to another Norfolk girl, Virginia Loyall. In 1845 he became second-in-command of the Norfolk Navy Yard. Much to his disappointment, Farragut saw no important action in the Mexican War (1846–1848).

During the early 1850s, Farragut filled administrative assignments in Washington and Norfolk. In 1854 he helped establish and then commanded the Mare Island Navy Yard near San Francisco, California. Farragut received his captain's commission in September 1855. After returning east, he took command of the new screw sloop-of-war *Brooklyn* in January 1859. In *Brooklyn*, Farragut became familiar with the type of vessels that would be the capital ships of the Union Navy during the Civil War.

Following the Confederate attack on Fort Sumter, the state of Virginia seceded, forcing Farragut to choose between his nation and his adopted state. Without hesitation, he elected to remain loyal to the Old Flag that he had served for half a century. Farragut sailed from Norfolk to New York and requested active duty in defense of the Union. He remained involuntarily idle for most of the first year of the Civil War.

In the autumn of 1861, President Abraham Lincoln* and his advisors began planning a seaborne attack on New Orleans to match a drive down the Mississippi River by Union forces. Farragut was selected to lead the thrust from the sea. He had extraordinary successes against the forts below New Orleans (April 1862) and the defenses of Mobile, Alabama (August 1864). In addition, forces under his command had operated against Vicksburg, Mississippi (1862–1863). While he was near Vicksburg, Congress created the rank of rear admiral, and Farragut was the senior of the four officers who got the new title (July 1862). He was given the newly created rank of vice admiral (December 1864) and was further elevated to admiral in July 1866.

The admiral was placed in command of the European Squadron in 1867. With his flag in the five thousand-ton screw frigate *Franklin*, Farragut began a triumphal cruise in the waters of the Old World. Europe's royalty welcomed and entertained him. He returned home in November 1868. The admiral died in Portsmouth Navy Yard on August 14, 1870.

In late 1861 Farragut was chosen to lead the attack on New Orleans. He sailed for the Gulf of Mexico in February 1862. After reaching Ship Island, Mississippi, he labored for almost two months getting his deep-draft warships in position to attack the downriver forts that protected the Crescent City. On April 18, a flotilla of mortar schooners opened fire on the Southern works and kept up the barrage for six days. When this cannonade failed to make the Confederates surrender, Farragut demonstrated his decisiveness, ordering his steamers to dash upstream by the Rebel guns. On April 24 his warships ran the gauntlet past the batteries and found New Orleans helpless. The city surrendered on April 25, and the forts struck their colors on April 28. The capture of New Orleans meant that the Confederacy had lost its largest city—the home of many banks, industries, and shipbuilding facilities.

Subsequently, Farragut pushed up the Mississippi to meet the gunboats of the Western Flotilla. Farragut twice ascended the river from New Orleans to Vicksburg. On his second run, he actually ran past the Vicksburg batteries and joined the Western Flotilla, but his actions contributed no lasting benefit to the Union cause. The unexpected foray of the Confederate ironclad *Arkansas* forced Farragut to retire below Vicksburg, leaving a few gunboats to guard Baton Rouge. After responding to a Confederate strike on Baton Rouge, Farragut returned to blockade duty in the Gulf.

In the autumn, Farragut went back up the Mississippi to help the Army wrest the last stretch of the river—from above Vicksburg to below Port Hudson—from Confederate hands. Meanwhile, Major General Ulysses Simpson Grant* and Rear Admiral David Dixon Porter* (Farragut's foster brother) were laboring to take Vicksburg. Farragut decided to run past Port Hudson with or without Army support. On the night of March 14, 1863, Farragut led a flotilla of seven ships upriver. Each of his heavier ships was lashed to the inboard or fort side of a gunboat. Thus, while the gunboat protected the smaller warship from the Southern guns, her consort's masked machinery was available to provide additional propulsion. The *Albatross* was paired with the *Hartford*, Farragut's flagship, which led the Union advance. Despite a fearful cannonade and a hairbreath escape from grounding, these two ships fought their way upstream; but, for various reasons, none of the others were able to follow. Nevertheless, the two successful Union ships blockaded the mouth of the Red River and cut the communications line which was feeding Vicksburg and Port Hudson, as well as the army of Robert Edward Lee* in the East. In May vessels of David Dixon Porter's squadron moved south of Vicksburg, and Farragut returned to New Orleans. Port Hudson surrendered in July.

Ordered north for a rest, Farragut reached New York in August 1863, devoting the remainder of the year to regaining his strength. *Hartford* then departed for the Gulf and anchored in Pensacola Harbor in January 1864. The admiral devoted ensuing months to overseeing the blockade of his part of the Gulf coast while awaiting troops and ironclads to reduce Forts Morgan and Gaines which guarded the entrance to Mobile Bay.

On August 5 Farragut's squadron of eighteen ships fought its way into Mobile Bay. In this operation, Farragut again tied a gunboat to the port or lee side of each of his heavier wooden ships. The guns of the forts, a large group of submerged torpedoes (or, in modern terms, a minefield) which narrowed the deep-water channel, and the Confederate squadron led by the ironclad ram *Ten-nessee* awaited the Federal fleet. Southern vessels were under the command of Admiral Franklin Buchanan.* Eager to engage the South's most powerful ship, the monitor *Tecumseh* headed straight for *Tennessee*, but struck a torpedo and sank. *Brooklyn*, the Union's leading wooden ship, began backing to clear the torpedoes and thus threw the entire column into confusion. In *Hartford*, Far-ragut—lashed to the rigging so that he might see the action from above the smoke of battle—boldly directed his ships to steer right through the minefield. "Damn the torpedoes," he was quoted, "full speed ahead." The flagship, followed by the rest of the fleet, raced past *Brooklyn* through the mines; fortu-nately for Farragut and his ships, no more torpedoes exploded. A wild melee ensued in which several Federal ships rammed the *Tennessee* and forced her to strike her colors. This victory left the Union squadron in control of the waters approaching Mobile and closed the South's last important Gulf port.

The many virtues that were happily blended in Farragut's personality enabled him to become a master of his profession. His excellent grasp of the strategic realities of the Civil War enlightened the planning and execution of his operations on the Gulf and on the Mississippi. His tactical skill and decisiveness enabled him to lead his squadron through the unpredictability of battle to victory against dedicated opponents—especially at Mobile. Farragut's signal accomplishments were over land fortifications, which he considered vulnerable, and his attitudes toward shore forts and batteries had been developing since the time of his observations on the Mexican coast. All of these factors combined to make Farragut the most noteworthy American naval officer between the heroes of 1812 and World War II.

BIBLIOGRAPHY

Anderson, Bern. *By Sea and by River: The Naval History of the Civil War*. New York: Alfred A. Knopf, 1962.
Jones, Virgil C. *The Civil War at Sea*. 3 vols. New York: Holt, Rinehart, and Winston, 1960–1962.
Lewis, Charles A. *David Glasgow Farragut: Admiral in the Making*. Annapolis, Md.: U.S. Naval Institute, 1941.
———. *David Glasgow Farragut: Our First Admiral*. Annapolis, Md.: U.S. Naval Institute, 1943.
Mahan, Alfred Thayer. *Admiral Farragut*. New York: University Society, 1905.
———. *The Gulf and Inland Waters*. New York: Charles Scribner's Sons, 1883.

JAMES L. MOONEY

FISKE, Bradley Allen (b. Lyons, N.Y., June 13, 1854; d. New York City, N.Y., April 6, 1942), naval officer. Fiske is considered the greatest naval inventor of his age and creator of the Office of Chief of Naval Operations.

The son of an Episcopalian minister of English descent, Fiske rejected a career in the law or ministry in favor of that of naval officer. Following attendance at the Naval Academy from 1870 to 1874, he served in the Navy for forty-one years.

As a junior officer he served a three-year tour afloat, had equipment duty in New York, and then did shipboard experimental work. Following a second three-year tour at sea, he took a year's leave of absence to study electricity and write a textbook on that subject. He then supervised the installation of ordnance on the protected cruiser *Atlanta*. As a lieutenant he helped conduct the acceptance trials of the "dynamite cruiser" *Vesuvius* (1888–1889); in 1890 he was detailed to "electric light duty new ships, Philadelphia." After another year's leave to sell some of his inventions to other navies (1891–1892), he was billeted in the protected cruiser *San Francisco* (1893–1894). In 1895 he worked on an electric turret-turning mechanism for the Bureau of Ordnance and also attended the Naval War College before being attached as navigator and executive officer to the gunboat *Petrel* (1896), which saw action in the Battle of Manila Bay during the Spanish-American War. As the executive officer of the monitor *Monadnock* and then of the gunboat *Yorktown*, he supported Filipinos fighting against Spain and then the U.S. Army against Filipino insurgents.

As a lieutenant comander, Fiske was billeted as inspector of ordnance at the E. W. Bliss Company, New York (1900–1902), and as executive officer of the battleship *Massachusetts*. As a commander he took a second course at the Naval War College before serving as inspector of ordnance at the William Cramp works at Philadelphia and at the New York Shipbuilding Company, New York (1903–1904). He also was a member of a board that recommended the adoption of radio for naval communications. In 1906 Fiske commanded both the protected cruiser *Minneapolis* and the monitor *Arkansas*, the latter while it served as an Academy school ship. When promoted to captain in 1907, he was offered command of a battleship of the Great White Fleet, slated to circle the globe. Because his wife—Josephine Harper, of the publishing family, whom he had married in 1882—was ill, he was excused from command and given duty as recruiting officer in New York City and then captain of the League Island (Philadelphia) Navy Yard. He commanded the armored cruiser *Tennessee*, and then a cruiser division of the Pacific Fleet (1907–1910). In 1910 he served as a member of the General Board of the Navy; in 1911 he was promoted to rear admiral and began an eleven-year tour as president of the U.S. Naval Institute, a record that still stands.

In 1911, Rear Admiral Fiske commanded Cruiser Division Five of the Atlantic Fleet. Subsequently, he commanded Battleship Division Three and then Battleship Division One of the Atlantic Fleet. While with the latter he was second-in-command. He was next detailed as aide for inspections to Secretary of the Navy George von L. Meyer (1911), who was succeeded in 1913 by Josephus Daniels.* At odds with Daniels, Fiske resigned as aide for operations and served his last year on active duty in rustication at the Naval War College (1915–1916). He then spent twenty-six years in retirement.

In 1876, at the age of twenty-two years, there awakened in Fiske the spirit of investigation that made him the most innovative, inventive, and scientific-minded naval officer of his generation. Using private industry to help him because the Navy had no research and development program, he devised electrical and gunfire control systems that metamorphosed the ships of the "New Navy" into efficient vessels with improved habitability.

Between 1876 and 1883 Fiske invented an electric log, a sounding machine, an insulator that reduced voltage leaks from electrical wires, and an electric primer for firing guns. He provided electric motors that turned gun turrets with precision and powered hoists for powder, shells, and coal ashes, and began work on an electric range finder. In 1886 he fixed a telescope to the sight bar of a gun and, by using electric motors to train and elevate guns, showed the possibility of achieving continuous aim battery fire.

Between 1888 and 1896 Fiske built an electric range finder, an electric ship-steering mechanism, and an electric position finder, and devised the rudiments of a gunnery plotting room. In addition, he installed the first telephones in a warship and invented an engine order telegraph, helm angle indicator, a flashing light for signaling, a speed and direction indicator, and the stadimeter—the basic elements in the pre-electronic gear in a pilot house.

From a platform he built forty feet up the mast of the *Petrel*, stadimeter in hand, Fiske communicated the ranges of enemy ships to his own gunners in the Battle of Manila Bay, thus becoming the first man to direct a ship's firing from aloft. He subsequently invented a radio system that permitted the wireless control of such distant objects as torpedoes and missiles, a turret range finder, a control tower fitted with a periscope, and a super-heater that greatly increased a torpedo's range. He also increased a torpedo's accuracy by adding a turbine drive and a more powerful gyroscope to it. His system for blowing a whistle to alert a crew when watertight doors were to be closed in an emergency is still in use, as is his telescope pivoted at eye level and supported on a frame by a counterweight, and after-steering. In addition, he obtained a patent for a torpedo plane (1912), invented "check fire," and was the first admiral in full uniform to fly in an aircraft. In 1913 he created the administrative framework for a naval aviation program, and with Elmer Sperry, in 1914, he devised a fire control system that permitted continuous aim battery fire.

Fiske held that a naval officer had two careers, one as a "scientific person" and one as a "line officer," the line officer being one who correlated the military and engineering arts. He advocated the creation of a naval general staff and also advised that the military, diplomatic, political, and economic policies of the nation should be formed into a coherent whole in a national security council. The General Board established in 1900, he argued, could only advise the secretary and lacked executive authority. When Daniels spurned his ideas about a general staff, in 1915 he and various friends wrote the legislation creating the Office of Chief of Naval Operations and granted the chief a staff to write war plans. Daniels had the bill modified so as to retain civil supremacy. Nevertheless, a military man was finally made responsible for the military end of the naval service. Moreover, Fiske's administrative plan for having the naval bureaus prepare for war was adopted soon after he left his office, and he also felt rewarded when Congress established a council of national defense.

During his long years in retirement, Fiske spoke and wrote in favor of keeping America's powder dry. Following the death of Alfred Thayer Mahan* in 1914, Fiske was considered the greatest American writer on sea and air power, for he wrote six books and sixty-five articles during his lifetime.

BIBLIOGRAPHY

Coletta, Paolo E. *Admiral Bradley A. Fiske and the American Navy*. Lawrence: Regents Press of Kansas, 1979.
Fiske, Bradley A. *From Midshipman to Rear-Admiral*. New York: Century Company, 1919.
————. *The Navy as a Fighting Machine*. New York: Charles Scribner's Sons, 1918.
Morison, Elting E. *Admiral Sims and the Modern American Navy*. Boston: Houghton Mifflin Company, 1942.

PAOLO E. COLETTA

FLETCHER, Frank Jack (b. Marshalltown, Iowa, April 29, 1885; d. Bethesda, Md., April 25, 1973), naval officer. Fletcher was carrier task force commander in the Battles of the Coral Sea and Midway in World War II.

Appointed from Iowa, Frank Jack Fletcher entered the U.S. Naval Academy in 1902 and graduated in 1906. His first command (1910) was the destroyer *Dale* in the Asiatic Torpedo Flotilla. In 1914 while serving as an aide to his uncle, Rear Admiral Frank Friday Fletcher, he earned the Medal of Honor for gallant service during the occupation of Vera Cruz. As a lieutenant commander, Fletcher saw active service during World War I as captain of the destroyer *Benham*, operating on convoy escort and patrol duty in British and French waters, and received the Navy Cross. Subsequently, he remained with destroyers, then commanded a submarine tender and the susbmarine base at Cavite, Philippine Islands.

In 1929 Fletcher attended the Naval War College, received his promotion to captain (1930), and was posted to the Army War College. These assignments prepared him to become, in 1931, chief of staff of the Asiatic Fleet under Admiral Montgomery M. Taylor. His tour coincided with the Japanese invasion of Manchuria and the fighting in Shanghai. In 1933 Fletcher joined the Navy Department as aide to the secretary of the navy, Claude A. Swanson. After sea duty (1936–1937) as captain of the battleship *New Mexico*, he returned to the Navy Department and later served as assistant chief, Bureau of Navigation. Attaining flag rank in November 1939, Rear Admiral Fletcher proceeded to the Pacific, first as commander of Cruiser Division Three. Then in June 1940 he took over the four heavy cruisers of Cruiser Division Six, the post he held when war broke out on December 7, 1941.

Fletcher's first major assignment was command of Task Force 14 with the aircraft carrier *Saratoga*. His mission was to reinforce the Wake Island garrison. Ordered to reach Wake on December 24, Fletcher was recalled on the morning of December 23 because Wake had fallen to Japanese atack. On December 31, 1941, he received the administrative posts of commander, Cruisers, Scouting Force, Pacific Fleet, and also commander, Cruiser Division Four. In early January 1942 Fletcher formed Task Force 17 around the carrier *Yorktown* and later that month escorted a convoy bound for Samoa. On February 1, 1942, Task Force 17, in concert with forces led by Vice Admiral William Fredrick Halsey, Jr.,* executed air strikes against Japanese bases in the Marshall and Gilbert islands.

In late February 1942 Fletcher took Task Force 17 into the South Pacific and joined Vice Admiral Wilson Brown's Task Force 11 in the Coral Sea. Together on March 10 they launched an air attack on Japanese ships at Lae and Salamaua in New Guinea. After Brown's departure, Fletcher remained on patrol in the Coral Sea area guarding the line of communication between the Hawaiian Islands and Australia. Meanwhile on April 19, he became commander, Cruisers, Pacific Fleet. Coming under his control in May was Task Force 11 (Rear Admiral Aubrey W. Fitch), centered around the carrier *Lexington*. In response to Japanese invasion threats against Port Moresby, New Guinea, and the Solomon Islands, Fletcher led his carrier force in the Battle of the Coral Sea (May 4–8), which forced the Japanese to withdraw while the Americans lost the carrier *Lexington*.

Arriving at the end of May at Pearl Habor, Task Force 17 then sortied to help oppose the Japanese attack on Midway Island. At sea, Fletcher assumed tactical command of the three American carriers, *Yorktown, Enterprise,* and *Hornet.* On June 4, American carrier aircraft secured decisive victory by sinking four Japanese carriers, but Fletcher's flagship *Yorktown* was crippled (and sank on June 7) which compelled him to relinquish command to Rear Admiral Raymond Ames Spruance.* For Fletcher's service at Coral Sea and Midway, he was promoted to vice admiral (to date from June 26, 1942) and received the Distinguished Service Medal. During the initial phase of the Guadalcanal operation, Fletcher acted as commander of the Expeditionary Force and the carrier task forces. His carriers on August 24, 1942, fought the Battle of the Eastern Solomons and helped repulse a Japanese attempt to retake Guadalcanal. Wounded on August 31 when his flagship *Saratoga* was torpedoed, Fletcher returned to the United States.

After a well-deserved rest, Fletcher in November 1942 became commandant of the Thirteenth Naval District and also the Northwestern Sea Frontier. His efforts to return to a sea command were unavailing despite the recommendation of his commander in the Pacific, Admiral Chester William Nimitz.* Relinquishing the naval district post in October 1943, Fletcher assumed command of the North Pacific Area which was responsible for combat operations in Alaskan and Aleutian waters. His North Pacific Force, by means of air strikes and warship raids, tied down significant Japanese forces in the Kurile Islands and northern Japan and prepared for the invasion of Paramushiro in the event the Soviet Union entered the war against Japan. In August and September 1945 Fletcher conducted the occupation of northern Honshu and Hokkaido in the Japanese home islands. That December he joined the Navy's General Board which acted in an advisory capacity to the secretary of the navy, and in May 1946 became its chairman. On May 1, 1947, Fletcher was promoted to admiral and retired from the Navy. He died on April 25, 1973, after a long illness.

Frank Jack Fletcher's importance in U.S. naval history centers around his role as commander of fast carrier task forces which fought their Japanese counterparts in several of the classic carrier actions in 1942. Indeed, of the six actual carrier-versus-carrier duels that took place during the Pacific War, Fletcher led American flattops in three: the battles of the Coral Sea (May 1942), Midway (June 1942), and the Eastern Solomons (August 1942). The Battle of the Coral Sea marked a milestone in naval history because it was the first occasion in which opposing task forces relied solely on carrier-borne aircraft for the decisive attacks instead of closing to within gun and torpedo range of each other.

All three of Fletcher's carrier battles resulted in Allied strategic victories, earned at a time when the Japanese menace in the Pacific was paramount and Allied strength had fallen to its lowest point. This, however, has not spared Fletcher from considerable criticism by some naval historians. They consider his command decisions in the Wake Island relief attempt, at the Battle of the Coral Sea, and during his brief participation in the Guadalcanal Campaign to be distinctly controversial. According to these historians, Fletcher at crucial times was unaggressive or timid, with an obsession for refueling his ships when the situation supposedly did not justify diverting them from the mission at hand. These criticisms largely have not survived detailed examination in light of the latest available documentary sources. Especially held against Fletcher was his lack of aviation experience. This was a common trait, however, among most of the early war carrier task force commanders who obtained their posts by virtue of their status as senior flag officers in the Pacific Fleet.

Fletcher never forfeited the respect and confidence of Admiral Nimitz, who entrusted him with the Pacific Fleet's precious carriers during the crucial early months of the war. Despite his recent introduction to carrier aviation, Fletcher secured important victories under extremely difficult conditions in a new form of naval warfare waged against skilled and determined opponents. It was once said of Admiral Sir John Jellicoe in World War I that he was one person who could have lost the war in an afternoon. The same injunction could be equally applied to Fletcher for the spring and summer of 1942. Indeed, his Japanese counterpart at Midway, Vice Admiral Chuichi Nagumo, just may have doomed Japan's chances for victory in the Pacific War through the destruction of his four carriers by Fletcher and Spruance.

BIBLIOGRAPHY

Dyer, George C. *The Amphibians Came to Conquer: The Story of Admiral Richmond Kelly Turner*. 2 vols. Washington, D.C.: U.S. Government Printing Office, 1971.
Lundstrom, John B. *The First South Pacific Campaign: Pacific Fleet Strategy, December 1941–June 1942*. Annapolis, Md.: Naval Institute Press, 1976.

Morison, Samuel Eliot. *History of United States Naval Operations in World War II*. 15 vols. Boston: Atlantic, Little, Brown and Company, 1947–1962.

Potter, E. B. *Nimitz*. Annapolis, Md.: Naval Institute Press, 1976.

Sweetman, Jack. *The Landing at Vera Cruz: 1914*. Annapolis, Md.: Naval Institute Press, 1968.

JOHN B. LUNDSTROM

FLIPPER, Henry Ossian (b. Thomasville, Ga., March 21, 1856; d. Atlanta, Ga., May 3, 1940), Army officer, civil and mining engineer. Flipper was the first black graduate of West Point.

Henry O. Flipper was the eldest of five sons born to slave parents, Festus and Isabella Flipper. His education began in 1864 under the tutelage of John F. Quarles, a slave mechanic. Following the Civil War, he attended the schools of the American Missionary Association. It was while as a freshman at Atlanta University that he applied for, and received, an appointment to the U.S. Military Academy at West Point, New York.

Flipper entered West Point on July 1, 1873. Although five members of his race had preceded him at the Military Academy, none had succeeded in graduating. Ostracized by his white classmates and the frequent butt of cruel insults, Flipper nevertheless worked hard, maintained a dignified bearing, and stoically endured the injustices perpetrated upon him. On June 14, 1877, he graduated fiftieth in a class of seventy-six and accepted a commission as 2d lieutenant in the 10th Cavalry, one of the Army's two Negro mounted regiments. The following year, he published an account of his career at the Military Academy entitled *The Colored Cadet at West Point*.

From 1878 to 1882 Flipper served at Forts Elliott, Concho, Davis, and Quitman, Texas, and at Fort Sill, Indian Territory. While stationed at Fort Sill, he engineered and supervised the drainage of malaria-breeding ponds in the vicinity of the post. The resulting work, known as "Flipper's Ditch," was dedicated as a National Historic Landmark on October 27, 1977. Flipper's other engineering accomplishments included the construction of a wagon road from Fort Sill to Gainesville, Texas, and the installation of a telegraph line from Fort Eliott, Texas to Camp Supply, Indian Territory. He also performed field duty on the Staked Plains and served with distinction in the Victorio Campaign of 1880.

While serving as acting commissary of subsistence at Fort Davis, Texas, Flipper discovered that post funds were missing from his quarters and attempted to conceal the loss until he could find or replace the missing money. Upon learning of the discrepancy in Flipper's accounts, Colonel William Rufus Shafter,* the post commander, arrested the lieutenant and filed court-martial charges. After a lengthy trial that began in November 1881, Flipper was found innocent of embezzlement, but was pronounced guilty of "conduct unbecoming an officer and gentleman." On June 30, 1882, the Army's only black officer was dismissed from the service. Convinced that his arrest and conviction were the result of racial prejudice on the part of Colonel Shafter and other officers at Fort Davis, Flipper spent the remainder of his life protesting the harshness of his sentence and seeking reinstatement in the Army.

Flipper remained on the frontier following his dimissal from the service and, in the course of nearly four decades, became a respected civil and mining engineer in the southwestern United States and in northern Mexico. From 1883 to 1891 he operated in Chihuahua and Sonora as a surveyor of public lands, cartographer for the Banco Minero of Chihuahua, and chief engineer for several American mining companies. Returning to the United States in 1891, he represented the town of Nogales, Arizona, in a land-grant case before the court of private land claims. Impressed by the skill with which Flipper handled the Nogales case, the Justice Department appointed the ex-Army officer special agent. During the course of his work for the Justice Department, Flipper compiled and translated Spanish and Mexican land laws, conducted field surveys, prepared court briefs, and testified as an expert witness on penmanship.

Returning to northern Mexico in 1901, Flipper spent eleven years as resident engineer for the Balvanera Mining Company, Colonel William C. Green's Gold-Silver Company, and finally for Albert Fall's Sierra Mining Company. While in Green's employ, he devoted a considerable amount of time to researching the legend of the Lost Tayopa Mine in the Sierra Madre.

Upon the outbreak of revolution in Mexico, Flipper in 1912 moved to El Paso, Texas, where he continued to perform his duties as representative of the Sierra Mining Company. During this period, he also sent detailed reports of chaotic political affairs in Mexico to Albert Fall, now U.S. senator from New Mexico, whose sub-committee was investigating the impact of disorder in Mexico upon American economic interests south of the border. In 1919 Fall summoned Flipper to Washington to serve as translator and interpreter for the senate subcommittee on Mexican internal affairs. With Fall's appointment as secretary of the interior in 1921, Flipper became an assistant, working with the commission responsible for the location, construction, and operation of Alaskan railroads.

Flipper left the Interior Department in 1923 and accepted a position in Caracas, Venezuela, as engineer for William F. Buckley's Pantepec Oil Company. During his seven-year residence in Latin America, he translated and published an edition of Venezuela's mining laws and statutes. Returning to the United States in 1931, Flipper lived out the remainder of life in the Atlanta home of his brother, Bishop Joseph Flipper of the African Methodist Episcopal Church.

Henry O. Flipper exemplified a rare combination of strength of character and force of intellect in the face of overwhelming adversity. As a young and lonely cadet at West Point, he resolved that "the kind of treatment we are to receive at the hands of others depends entirely upon ourselves," and developed an unswerving conviction that "there is a certain dignity in enduring [prejudice] which evokes praise from those who indulge it, and also often discovers to them their error and its injustice." With the eyes of the entire nation upon him, Henry

Flipper patiently endured social ostracism and racial hostility to become the first black graduate of the U.S. Military Academy. The example he set remained to guide black cadets who followed in his footsteps. Today, the Academy presents an annual award to the graduate who best typifies the high personal standards of its first black graduate.

During his brief career as the only black officer in the U.S. Army, Flipper displayed a degree of competence, diligence, and thorough professionalism that won the respect, if not always affection, of the vast majority of officers with whom he served. Unjustly driven from the Army, and thereafter shunned by the embarrassed leaders of his own race, Henry Flipper adhered all the more tenaciously to the convictions he had formed at West Point. During a forty-eight-year career as a civil and mining engineer, Flipper achieved a measure of respect and prominence previously denied blacks in the engineering profession and in government service. His translations of Mexican and Venezuelan mining and land laws became standard references, his technical expertise as a surveyor and engineer saved the United States large tracts of public lands in the Southwest, and his unique linguistic skills and legal knowledge made him a valuable witness before both congressional committees and the Supreme Court. As an assistant to the secretary of the interior, he established yet another precedent for a member of his race.

As a civilian, Henry Flipper no doubt created for himself a far more productive life than he could have achieved had he remained in the Army. He never ceased to think of himself as an Army officer, however, and he never surrendered the struggle for reinstatement. Finally in December 1976, the Department of the Army granted Flipper an honorable discharge dated June 30, 1882, and a bust of the U.S. Military Academy's first black graduate was unveiled at West Point, New York. On February 10, 1978, the remains of Lieutenant Henry O. Flipper were removed from an unmarked grave in an Atlanta cemetery and on the following day were reentered with full military honors beside his parents in Old Magnolia Cemetery in Thomasville, Georgia.

BIBLIOGRAPHY

Dinges, Bruce J. "The Court-Martial of Lieutenant Henry O. Flipper: An Example of Black-White Relationships in the Army, 1881." *The American West* 9 (January 1972): 12–17, 59–61.

Flipper, Henry O. *The Colored Cadet at West Point*. New York: Homer Lee and Company, 1878; reprinted, New York: Arno Press, 1969.

———. *Negro Frontiersman: The Western Memoirs of Henry O. Flipper*. Edited by Theodore D. Harris. El Paso: Texas Western College Press, 1963.

McClung, Donald R. "Second Lieutenant Henry O. Flipper: A Negro Officer on the West Texas Frontier." *West Texas Historical Association Year Book* 47 (1971): 20–31.

Warner, Ezra J. "A Black Man in the Long Gray Line." *American History Illustrated* 4 (January 1970): 30–38.

Wilson, Steve. "Henry O. Flipper." *Oklahoma Today* 28 (Summer 1978): 33–36.

BRUCE J. DINGES

FOOTE, Andrew Hull (b. New Haven, Conn., September 12, 1806; d. New York City, N.Y., June 26, 1863), naval officer. Foote is best known as commander of the Mississippi Flotilla, 1861–1862, during the Civil War.

Andrew Hull Foote was born into a prominent Connecticut family that traced its Puritan roots in New England back to 1630. His father, Samuel Foote, was U.S. senator (1827–1833) and governor of Connecticut (1834–1835). Andrew applied for an appointment as an acting midshipman in the U.S. Navy in 1821. In the years prior to the founding of the Naval Academy, officers were trained through a slow apprentice system that required many years of sea duty. His appointment did not arrive, and through his father's influence he attended the U.S. Military Academy at West Point. In less than a year, Foote's Navy appointment came through, and he left the Military Academy to become an acting midshipman.

On December 4, 1822, Foote was ordered to the 10-gun schooner *Grampus*, a vessel in the West Indies Squadron under Captain David Porter.* The "mosquito fleet" cruised the Caribbean in search of pirates. Midshipman Foote's first cruise ended in April 1827, and by August, Foote was aboard the 18-gun sloop-of-war *Natchez*, sailing again for the West Indies. While aboard the *Natchez*, Foote discussed religious and moral issues with a fellow officer. He rationalized that if violence was a necessary and unavoidable part of naval duty, then the Navy should be led by good Christian men.

In 1840 he was assigned his first shore duty as commandant of the Naval Asylum at Philadelphia, where he became an advocate of temperance. In 1843 he was transferred to the 44-gun frigate *Cumberland*, and Foote carried his ideas about temperance with him. Over the course of a year, through lay preaching and example, he was able to get the ship's complement of four hundred men to sign temperance pledges. If they relinquished their daily allotment of whiskey (sometimes called "grog"), the crewmen could each receive an additional amount of pay, equivalent to the value of the spirits. Although the daily consumption of whiskey on the *Cumberland* at sea eventually reached nil, the crew was not above drinking on shore. Nevertheless, the *Cumberland* became the first "temperance ship" in the U.S. Navy. Using it as an example, Foote pressed Congress to eliminate the whiskey ration and prohibit flogging. Other officers followed Foote's lead, and strides were made in the 1840s towards social reform in the Navy.

For the next ten years, Foote rotated between shore and sea duty. He sat out the Mexican War as commandant of the Boston Navy Yard. In 1849 he was detailed to the brig *Perry* to suppress the African slave trade. In 1856 Commander

Foote was on the China Station commanding the 20-gun sloop *Portsmouth* and two other ships. The small force was to protect American interests at Whampoa, south of Canton. Relations had been strained between the Chinese and foreigners, and as the American vessels passed the forts guarding Whampoa, Chinese gunners fired upon but did not strike his ships. Irritated that the Chinese offered no apology, Foote landed marines and bombarded the forts over a three-day period. American forces reportedly lost 29 men, and the Chinese 250.

When the Civil War broke out, Foote was in command of the New York Navy Yard. He was promoted to captain in June 1861 and was sent to relieve Commander John Rodgers, Jr.* who was in control of Union naval forces of Western waters. The post was a curious amalgam of tasks requiring tact as well as combat skill. The Western operations were in turmoil. Under unclear authority from the War Department, Rodgers had purchased, armed, and armored with timber a number of river steamers.

Upon arrival at the Army operations center at Cairo, Illinois, Foote set about to man the available gunboats and secure enough sailors for the seven ironclad gunboats under construction by James Buchanan Eads* in nearby Mound City, Illinois, and St. Louis, Missouri. Setting up an office in a storefront in Cairo, Foote found that his title did not carry any weight with either the army or commercial steamboaters. Because Cairo was filled with steamboat captains, Foote petitioned and was granted permission to use the nominal title "flag officer" rather than "captain."

After a number of the Eads boats were commissioned, Foote assisted Brigadier General Ulysses Simpson Grant* in a combined operation against Fort Henry built on the Tennessee River above Paducah, Kentucky. The commander at Fort Henry, General Lloyd Tilghman, had sent most of his troops to the more defensible Fort Donelson nearby on the Cumberland River. Fort Henry had been poorly placed, and Foote attacked the works with his gunboats arranged in line of battle abreast. It was ideal for the ships, since their heaviest arms and armor were arranged to fight bow-on. Grant's forces were detained by rain, and Foote, using the *Cincinnati* as his flagship, attacked at the appointed hour on February 6, 1862. Fort Henry's guns were easily disabled, and Tilghman courteously surrendered to Foote over dinner before Grant's troops could arrive. The Union desperately needed a victory, and Foote's defeat of the fort bolstered the North's plummeting morale. Within weeks, Grant prepared for a more serious assault, this time on Fort Donelson located on high bluffs overlooking the Cumberland River near Dover, Tennessee.

On February 13, 1862, Foote approached Fort Donelson using the same line of battle he had used before at Fort Henry. Within a short time the batteries on the bluffs began to take their toll with plunging fire. His ships were damaged and fell out of battle one by one. Foote, aboard the flagship *Cincinnati*, was wounded twice; he ordered his remaining ships to retire and left the capture of Fort Donelson to Grant and his troops. When Foote returned to Cairo for repairs, he realized that his gunboats were not as impregnable as he once thought. Fearing for his own personal safety, he admitted that he would not do battle again unless it was in a more heavily armored flagship.

The next month the Mississippi Flotilla moved south along the Mississippi in support of Union troops moving towards Vicksburg. Island Number 10, heavily armed and fortified, had to be passed by the gunboats. Foote dashed the flotilla past the island during the stormy night of April 4, 1862. Surrounded by naval forces, the defenders of the island surrendered.

Foote's left foot, wounded at Fort Donelson, never healed, and it became infected. Added to a longtime history of migraine headaches and poor eyesight, the continuing pain manifested itself in Foote's decreased performance. As the Vicksburg Campaign developed, Foote seemed more and more retiring. Gideon Welles,* a childhood friend and now secretary of the Navy, sent Captain C. H. Davis from Washington to help Foote. Seeing a graceful way to leave, Foote asked to relinquish his command to Davis. Welles agreed, promoted Foote to rear admiral, and after a period of partial recuperation, Foote became the chief of the Bureau of Equipment and Recruiting in New York City.

The Navy Department was dissatisfied with the abortive naval attack upon Charleston, South Carolina, led by Admiral Samuel Francis Du Pont* on April 6, 1863. Du Pont was relieved of duty, and Secretary Welles sought a trustworthy naval officer who would obediently employ the ironclad monitors amassed off Charleston. Welles realized that Foote was in precarious health and assigned Captain John Adolphus Bernard Dahlgren* as Foote's aide. On June 11, 1863, Foote left his family home in New Haven on his way to Port Royal to assume command of the South Atlantic Blockading Squadron. He paused overnight at the Astor Hotel in New York and fell critically ill. He died there on June 26, 1863.

Foote was an important link between the Army and the Navy in the West. Replacing the controversial John Rodgers, Foote fell to the enormous task of manning the Mississippi Flotilla, turning the Army and civilian recruits into a semblance of a naval fighting force. Foote developed good relations with the Army and the local population. He was officially subject to the Army's orders, but his good fortune at Fort Henry served to elevate the Army's opinion of the Navy and of the capabilities of the new Eads gunboats. The victory at Fort Henry provided a much needed morale boost for the Union and paved the way to Fort Donelson. The combined operations at the two forts helped to secure Missouri, Kentucky, and southern Illinois for the Union.

Given the narrow channels, changeable currents, and cranky gunboats, Foote's tactics on the Mississippi River could not be very sophisticated. The ideal plan was to draw the gunboats up before the fortifications and slug it out until all the land mounts were abandoned or the ships were too damaged to fight. Fighting at Fort Henry and Fort Donelson, therefore, became a matter of Foote's tenacity, the marksmanship of his gunners, and good coordination with the Army. When Foote lost his tenacity through fear and ill-health, he lost his advantage. After his defeat at Fort Donelson, Foote appeared, for several reasons, too "prudent."

Foote's victories during the Civil War were helpful but not essential to the war effort. In behavior he was an exemplary officer, and he possessed excellent administrative skills. He was popular in his time, and perhaps history has been kind to Andrew Hull Foote in deference to his good intentions and personal sacrifice.

BIBLIOGRAPHY

Anderson, Bern. *By Sea and by River: The Naval History of the Civil War*. New York: Alfred A. Knopf, 1962.
Hopping, James M. *Life of Andrew Hull Foote*. New York: Harper, 1874.
Milligan, John D. *Gunboats Down the Mississippi*. Annapolis, Md.: Naval Institute Press, 1965.
Niven, John. *Gideon Welles*. New York: Oxford University Press, 1973.
Reed, Rowena. *Combined Operations in the Civil War*. Annapolis, Md.: Naval Institute Press, 1978.

DANA M. WEGNER

FORBES, John (b. Fifeshire, Scotland, 1707; d. Philadelphia, Pa., March 11, 1759), British brigadier general in the French and Indian War.

Born into a military family, John Forbes studied medicine in his youth but deserted it for an Army career. According to custom, he bought a cornetcy in 1735 in the 2d Royal North British Dragoons, with which he served in Flanders and in his native country during the War of the Austrian Succession. By diligent effort and continued purchases Forbes progressed in his regiment, becoming a quartermaster in 1745 and a lieutenant colonel five years later.

Early in 1757 Forbes was selected to command the 17th Foot. Its assignment to Halifax took him to America to participate in the French and Indian War, which was then going badly for England. That spring his regiment was assigned to reinforce the abortive attempt against Fort Louisbourg. Later the colonel was made the adjutant general under John Campbell, Lord Loudoun,* commander in chief of the king's forces in North America. He performed capably in this position until March 1758, when he assumed a vital new role.

Loudoun had been replaced at the close of 1757 by Major General James Abercromby, who appointed Forbes to lead one of three key expeditions planned for the coming year by Minister William Pitt, nominal head of the British cabinet. Actually, Pitt had chosen Forbes, who was advanced to the rank of brigadier.

The new general was commissioned to take charge of military offense in the Southern colonies, to weaken the French on the frontier there, and to prevent the enemy in that region from succoring Canada. No other operation could accomplish these objectives so quickly as could a vigorous strike against Fort Duquesne. It had been constructed at the Forks of the Ohio River after the expulsion of a small Virginia force in 1754. Subsequently, the French had held that strategic site and from it had marauded the exposed settlements of neighboring colonies. Thus, Forbes chose the manifest target—Duquesne—with a determination to succeed. By no means could Britain afford to repeat Major General Edward Braddock's* failure to eject the French from that bastion in 1755.

That Pitt provided adequate personnel for Forbes' expedition, as he did for the other major campaigns in 1758 (Canada, by way of Lake George; and Louisbourg), demonstrated his deep interest in the Duquesne project and in the American war in general. Forbes' army, eventually nearly seven thousand men, began with a nucleus of some sixteen hundred regular troops—mainly thirteen companies of Highlanders commanded by Lieutenant Colonel Archibald Montgomery and four companies of Royal Americans led by Colonel Henry Bouquet,* a soldier of fortune descended from Huguenots. (The Swiss-born Bouquet was second in command to Forbes.) In addition to the regulars, there were about twenty-seven hundred provincials from Pennsylvania, two thousand from Virginia, three hundred from North Carolina, and one hundred from Maryland. Indians, whom Forbes regarded as essential in view of Braddock's fatal experience, were an unstable element: their numbers varied unpredictably from time to time.

When General Forbes took charge of the Duquesne Campaign, he was all but an invalid. Shortly before, he had written Loudoun, "My Infirmitys are really no joke,... Both legs and thighs being one absolute sight, and the soals of my feet Blistered, so that it was impossible for me to gett abroad." Later, he contracted a bloody flux which so debilitated him that at times he could not mount his horse. A man of lesser will might have given up, but he was made of stern stuff.

In March 1758 Forbes selected Fort Cumberland, in Maryland, as the site for assembling his troops. Thence he would move westwardly over the road Braddock had built three years earlier. But by May 7 the general had abruptly changed his mind, designating Raystown, Pennsylvania, on Juniata Creek, the base for launching the campaign.

Forbes' choice sparked a controversy between Virginia and Pennsylvania, each colony wanting the commercial advantage that would accrue by having the eastern terminus of the Ohio road in or near its own borders. Colonel George Washington,* the Virginia commander, jumped into the dispute immediately, contending in an unsoldierly manner, Forbes thought, for the Braddock route. With remarkable patience Forbes listened to this debate for almost three months. Late in July he decided irrevocably on the Pennsylvania route—an eventual thoroughfare for the westward movement of the American people.

To avoid Braddock's mistakes, the brigadier planned to erect several fortified bases along this route to support his army on its march and, if worst came to worst, to impede a precipitate retreat. The first post, called Fort Bedford, was begun in June at Raystown. Past that base lay ninety miles of dense forest broken only by Indian trails stretching over several mountain ranges. Forbes described this terrain as "impenetrable almost to any thing human save the Indians." The most formidable of the barriers was Laurel Ridge; nine miles beyond it, construction of a fort later named Ligonier was started on Loyalhanna Creek in September. Such road- and fort-building came about only by rigorous exertion of muscle and mind. The rains of an unseasonably wet autumn made Forbes' new clay road extremely difficult to travel.

Grimly mustering his courage despite feebleness, the general reached Raystown at mid-September in a litter slung between two horses. But his presence under such extremity inspired the soldiers to carry out their arduous mission.

When southern Indians, particularly the Cherokee, proved undependable, the general attempted to wean the Indians of the Ohio Valley from their French allegiance. By supporting Pennsylvania's Indian conferences at Philadelphia in July and at Easton in October, and by encouraging the Moravian missionary Christian Frederick Post in two missions to these Indians that summer and fall, Forbes would have already restored Britain's tribal connections by the time he reached the Forks.

Despite Major James Grant's disastrous strike near Fort Duquesne and a retributive French raid against Loyalhanna, the brigadier continued road construction and inched his westering army forward. When he arrived at Fort Ligonier on November 2, five thousand soldiers were encamped there. Ten days later during a second enemy attack near this post, the British captured prisoners whose testimony revealed a defenseless Duquesne: the Indians had deserted, the Canadians had gone home.

Quickly abandoning a plan to winter at Ligonier, Forbes—borne on his hurdle—led the army toward the river. As the British neared the Forks, they heard a great explosion from that direction late on November 24. The next morning the general began the final push with his troops and that evening viewed the desolate ruins of the burnt fort and village. The enemy was nowhere in sight. Duquesne had been destroyed by French hands, not captured by English.

Forbes named the place Pittsburgh and provided for the quartering of a small detachment there that winter. At death's door, he left the Ohio with his army on December 4, making an excruciating journey to Philadelphia. He died there early in the spring and was interred near the altar in Christ Church.

It is singular that a military man's life should be marked best by what happened when his army's inexorable advance became a threat that an entrenched enemy could no longer endure. But such is true of Forbes' career.

The Scot's wartime assignments in supply, in records administration, and in line command had well fitted him to march through the primeval wilderness of the Quaker colony. The pain he suffered steeled his will and enabled him to surmount the difficulties of supplying and transporting troops.

In one sense, Forbes overcame the French by applying a principle he learned from a recent Gallic essay on warfare by Lancelot, Comte de Crissé. This work advocated securing the route toward an enemy post by erecting a series of protective bases.

Although the fall of Louisbourg and Frontenac had rendered the collapse of

Duquesne a likely occurrence, the general's expedition provided the missing causal link. As events turned out, his valor stands as a principal factor in achieving this success. Forbes literally sacrificed his life to win a campaign whose culmination foreshadowed the Anglicizing of the vast interior of the Continent.

BIBLIOGRAPHY

Forbes, John. *Writings of General John Forbes Relating to His Service in North America*. Edited by Alfred Proctor James. Menosha, Wis.: Collegiate Press, 1938.

Freeman, Douglas Southall. *George Washington: A Biography*. Vol. 2. New York: Charles Scribner's Sons, 1948.

Gipson, Lawrence Henry. *The British Empire Before the American Revolution*. Vol. 7. New York: Alfred A. Knopf, 1949.

Leach, Douglas Edward. *Arms for Empire: A Military History of the British Colonies in North America, 1607–1763*. New York: Macmillan Company, 1973.

Parkman, Francis. *Montcalm and Wolfe*. Vol. 2. Boston: Little, Brown and Company, 1884.

Peckham, Howard H. *The Colonial Wars, 1689–1762*. Chicago: University of Chicago Press, 1964.

CHESTER RAYMOND YOUNG

FORREST, Nathan Bedford (b. Chapel Hill, Tenn., July 13, 1821; d. Memphis, Tenn., October 29, 1877), Confederate cavalry leader. Forrest is considered the greatest American cavalryman, a natural military genius.

Nathan B. Forrest was the eldest son of a blacksmith who moved his family in 1834 to north Mississippi, then a wild frontier. On his father's premature death, young Forrest was left, at sixteen, as the breadwinner for a large and destitute family. Although almost totally without formal education, Forrest survived and then prospered. By 1861, he was a millionaire; having made his fortune first by trading horses, then as a slave dealer, and finally from cotton plantations. Widely respected around Memphis where he settled, Forrest was known for his integrity, his kind treatment of slaves, and his courage; he once thwarted a three thousand-man lynch mob with a small pen knife. In 1861 Forrest was authorized to raise a regiment of cavalry which he equipped at his own expense.

Moving into Kentucky with an army under Albert Sydney Johnston*, Forrest quickly distinguished himself in several skirmishes. Serving at Fort Donelson when Ulysses Simpson Grant* attacked, Forrest refused to surrender and slipped out of the besieged garrison with his regiment. At Shiloh, Forrest, without orders, moved to the Confederate extreme right where his men, fighting as infantry, helped win the initial Southern success. Later, Forrest blocked a Union pursuit by conducting a brilliant rearguard action as the Confederate Army returned to Corinth.

Forrest was ordered into middle Tennessee by General Braxton Bragg,* and in July 1862, in the type of startling, strategic raid behind enemy lines that became his hallmark, captured the Union garrison at Murfreesboro. Promoted to brigadier general, Forrest continued to bedevil Union communications until September 25, when Bragg, who viewed Forrest as a mere guerrilla, stripped him of his forces and ordered him with only a small escort to go behind enemy lines to recruit and equip a new army. Forrest was successful in raising, mounting, and equipping his forces at Union expense in west Tennessee and in fighting his way through superior enemy forces pursuing him. He rejoined the Army of the Tennessee in January 1863. Soon he was raiding behind enemy lines again, destroying supplies and railroads, defeating detached garrisons, and defeating or eluding every force sent to contain him.

In April 1863 a Union cavalry column of two thousand men under Colonel Abel Streight struck across the Tennessee River into northern Alabama aiming to disrupt Confederate industry and communications in northern Georgia. Moving fifty miles in thirty-six hours, Forrest was quickly on Streight's trail. Although badly outnumbered, he unremittingly pressured Streight's rearguard day and night for three days through mountainous terrain, driving him nearly 140 miles. Carefully husbanding the strength of his own forces, Forrest rotated those attacking to allow his troops to rest. Constantly driven without rest, Streight's command collapsed and surrendered without a fight almost within sight of their prime objective, Rome, Georgia.

At Chickamauga, Forrest, commanding infantry as well as his own forces, performed brilliantly and was partially responsible for the Southern victory. Bragg, however, stripped Forrest of his command once more. Forrest angrily quit the Army only to be personally mollified by Jefferson Davis* and given an independent command in northern Mississippi. Allowed more latitude to show his genius, Forrest, now a major general, recruited a new army from behind enemy lines in Tennessee and Kentucky.

Forrest commanded cavalry that never numbered more than four thousand, and he kept the Confederate granary of northern Mississippi free of Union control until the dying days of the war. He repelled four major invasions and three times raided deep into Tennessee and Kentucky, twice reaching the Ohio River. Destroying railroads and supply bases, interrupting river communications, over-running isolated garrisons, and defeating any force with the temerity to fight him, Forrest quickly became a legend. In the process he inflicted nearly fifty thousand casualties and tied down important Union forces. When they overran Fort Pillow, Tennessee, Forrest's men fought so ferociously that they were accused of massacring the Negro garrison. At Brice's Crossroads, in June 1864, with twenty-nine hundred men and four guns he attacked and nearly annihilated General Samuel D. Sturgis' eighty-two hundred man, twenty-two gun force invading Mississippi. Forrest first drew the Union cavalry away from the infantry, attacked and defeated it, then drove it back on to the weary, hurrying infantry which in turn was defeated. Then pursuing until men and horses literally collapsed in the road, Forrest captured all of Sturgis' guns, wagons, and seventeen hundred men; there were five hundred others wounded or dead and the remnant was mostly disarmed fugitives.

All of Forrest's successes could not prevent major invasions of the South such as that led by William Tecumseh Sherman.* Pleading vainly to be turned loose on Sherman's supply lines, the very thing the Northerners feared most, Forrest was denied his chance largely because of Bragg's interference. Belatedly promoted to lieutenant general, Forrest was never given a good opportunity to fully demonstrate his genius. Blinded by prejudice against cavalry raiders and Forrest's slave-trading, uneducated background, the high Confederate leaders never gave him a major command.

In December 1864 Forrest moved into middle Tennessee to support John Bell Hood's* offensive against well-equipped and overwhelming Union forces under George Henry Thomas.* Forrest arrived in time to cover the retreat of the Army of the Tennessee after the disastrous Battle of Nashville. In his finest moment, Forrest commanded the hard-pressed rearguard of infantry and cavalry and succeeded in getting Hood's starving, ragged, barefoot, freezing, and almost disarmed army safely across the flooded Tennessee River. Unable to prevent large-scale invasions in 1865 and hearing of Appomattox, Forrest surrendered his few remaining forces at Gainesville, Alabama, on May 5, 1865.

The transition from war to peace was difficult for Forrest, whose fortune had been destroyed and who was accused of heinous crimes by the North. Urging his soldiers to be "good citizens as they had been good soldiers," Forrest at first set an example of peaceful acceptance of Northern domination. Later in the heated politics of Reconstruction Tennessee, Forrest became the head and moving spirit of the Ku Klux Klan. Originally created as an answer to the legal terrorism of Governor William Brownlow whose partisans acted under the color of martial law, the Klan quickly and violently spread to other states where it proved an ideal vehicle for the restoration of white rule. Forrest officially dissolved the Klan in January 1869. By then it had served its purpose in Tennessee and was out of his control elsewhere. Forrest never admitted his role in the Klan.

War's end found Forrest broken in health and finances. Efforts to recoup his fortune involved Forrest in an unsuccessful railroad venture that led to bankruptcy and to endless litigation. Typically, Forrest assumed the debts as a personal burden. Before his death, he had paid off most debts and had maintained a generous charity for the families of his ex-soldiers. Successful in reestablishing cotton plantations, he was making another fortune when he died in 1877 of a lingering, wasting disease, first contracted in 1865 and diagnosed as "chronic dysentery."

Completely ignorant of military tactics and untrained in any aspect of war, Forrest devised his own system of warfare. His primary targets were Union lines of communication, which he struck in sudden and forceful strategic raids, foreshadowing the *blitzkrieg* of a later day. Tactically, Forrest's system was based upon seizing and holding the initiative under almost all conditions. Even on the defensive, Forrest's men charged to meet an attack. Asked to describe his method of making war, Forrest said that he generally tried to "get there first with the most men'' and that he would trade ''fifteen minutes of bulge [initiative] for three days of tactics.'' Once he had the initiative he held it, never relaxing the pressure as long as it was physically possible to maintain it, even if only a handful of troops were available to him. Forrest's offensive thrusts fell first on the front and then on the flanks and rear of his foes. Once he had beaten his enemies, Forrest pursued them with a brutal relentlessness that was extraordinary in military history. This relentlessness was based upon Forrrest's concept of battle as a means to an end, the destruction of the enemy force, and not an end in itself. ''War means fighting and fighting means killing,'' he said; and he wondered, ''What does he fight battles for?'' of a superior who failed to pursue a beaten foe. His troops, incredibly mobile cavalry, often fought on foot as infantry in battle. Later in the war, some Union cavalry commanders began to adopt Forrest's successful dragoon tactics. Artillery played a major role in Forrest's system, and he worked hard to master its technicalities. Occasionally used at long range, more commonly, Forrest's guns were double shotted with canister and, moving with the front ranks, were used as assault weapons. Original and brilliant in his use of improvisations, Forrest won many victories because of his fertile imagination. Repeatedly, his commands were able to cross flooded rivers, twice on grapevine bridges, dominated by enemy gunboats while pursued by larger armies. Several Union units surrendered to Forrest without fighting; he tricked them into believing they were outnumbered, a deception aided by Northern propaganda which painted Forrest as a bloodthirsty monster. Richly varied ruses, deceptions, ambushes, and a quietly efficient scouting and intelligence system were key parts of Forrest's tactical method. He made himself the best informed Confederate general about Union strength and intentions in his region.

A superb quartermaster, Forrest recruited, equipped, and largely subsisted his forces behind enemy lines and mostly with captured goods. His meticulous care for men and horses paid rich military dividends, for Forrest could move his forces faster and farther than any other officer on either side. A stern disciplinarian, the big (six foot-two inch) Forrest often enforced discipline with his fists and unhesitatingly shot down his own men who broke under the stress of battle. He carefully guarded their lives from unnecessary loss and quarreled with several superiors over wasting his men. But in combat he could be ruthless in sacrificing them when it was necessary. Always in the thick of fighting, Forrest led by personal example. Wounded four times, he had twenty-nine horses killed under him and personally killed enemy soldiers in hand-to-hand combat during the war. Forrest is considered to be one of the greatest horse soldiers of his—or any—age.

BIBLIOGRAPHY

Henry, Robert Selph. *As They Saw Forrest*. Jackson, Tenn.: McCowat-Mercer Press, 1956.
———. *''First With the Most'' Forrest*. New York: Bobbs-Merrill Company, 1944.
Jordan, General Thomas, and J. P. Pryor. *The Campaign of Lieut.-Gen. N.B. Forrest,*

and of Forrest's Cavalry. New York: Blelock and Company, 1868; reprint, Dayton, Ohio: Morningside Bookshop, 1977 (original 1867).

Morton, John W. *The Artillery of Nathan Bedford Forrest's Cavalry.* Nashville, Tenn.: Publishing House of the Methodist Episcopal Church, 1909.

Wyeth, John Allen. *That Devil Forrest.* New York: Harper and Brothers, 1959 (original edition, 1899).

WALTER E. PITTMAN

FORRESTAL, James Vincent (b. Beacon, N.Y., February 15, 1892; d. Bethesda, Md., May 19, 1949), first secretary of defense. Forrestal is considered a major architect of the legislation creating the Department of Defense.

James Forrestal was the son of a building contractor and sometime postmaster. After attending local public schools and Dartmouth for a year, he went to Princeton. There he worked so hard earning a living and getting out the *Daily Princetonian* that he failed to obtain credits needed for graduation and left in his senior year. After working briefly as a salesman for two manufacturing companies and as a reporter for the New York *World*, in 1916 he joined the Wall Street firm of William A. Read and Company (later Dillon, Read and Company). Except for a short tour as a naval airman in World War I, he remained with that firm for twenty-four years, quickly rising from bond salesman to partner (1923), vice-president (1926), and president (1938). In 1936 he married Josephine Ogden, a divorcee who edited *Vogue* magazine. Two children were born to them.

With war looming in 1940, Forrrestal volunteered for government service. Found acceptable by Harry Hopkins, in June President Franklin D. Roosevelt, who wanted a man with "a passion for anonymity," appointed him as an administrative assistant in charge of plans to create a Pan-American Union. Only six weeks later, Roosevelt nominated Forrestal to be the first under secretary of the Navy; he received his appointment on August 22. In April 1941 he flew to London and established close liaison with the British Admiralty. After Secretary of the Navy William Franklin Knox* died, on April 28, 1944, Forrestal succeeded him and served in that capacity from May 1944 to September 17, 1947. He then served as the first secretary of defense until March 1949.

Forrestal's forte was in management. Instead of following an active role by providing aggressive leadership—questioning, suggesting alternatives, proposing objectives, and stimulating progress—he played a judicial role—making decisions on the recommendations made to him by the greatest number of advisors he could reach.

Forrestal's duties as under secretary of the Navy included contracts, tax, and legal matters, and liaison with the Army, Bureau of the Budget, and agencies other than those dealing with labor. He certified to the legal soundness of contractual agreements and coordinated the activities of the material bureaus and the procurement aspects of the Office of the Chief of Naval Operations. By supervising production schedules so as to avoid bottlenecks, he was able to produce thirteen hundred ships in just the fifteen months between August 1940 and December 1941.

As secretary of the Navy (1944 to 1947), Forrestal created the Office of the Comptroller to guarantee fiscal responsibility, and he took advice from a top policy group composed of the highest professional and civilian executives in his department. During the last year of the war, he strove to keep the operational momentum going. To this end he visited war fronts in both the Atlantic and Pacific. He opposed the use of atomic bombs against Japan on humanitarian grounds and because he believed the Japanese sought an opportunity to surrender. Believing that retaining the Japanese emperor would provide postwar stability, he also opposed the doctrine of "unconditional surrender" except with respect to Japan's military power. He opposed President Harry S Truman's wishes to create a United Nations trusteeship for the former Japanese trust territories, preferring instead to let the U.S. Navy use them as advanced bases. Moreover, fearing possible Soviet expansion in Europe, he countered quick and severe American demobilization. Finally, he opposed Army and Army Air Corps plans for a unified defense organization headed by a single chief of staff. He was able to so modify the National Security Act of July 26, 1947, that it provided for a loose federation rather than a unitary establishment. With demobilization complete by September 1, 1946, he reorganized the Shore Establishment; divided "consumer" logistics, which he assigned to the chief of naval operations, from "producer" logistics, which he retained in his own office; created a department-wide Office of Naval Material; brought naval aviators to the fore because of the increased importance of the naval air arm; and established an Office of Research and Invention to coordinate and direct all naval work on submarine technology and atomic energy.

In accepting appointment as the first secretary of defense, on September 17, 1947, Forrestal took the first step in ending his life. He had only three civilian assistants. Military personnel were still steeped in the traditions of their own services; the services squabbled over roles and missions (the Air Force wanted to take over naval aviation and deny the Navy large carriers and heavy aircraft that could carry atomic weapons, while the Army wished to take over the Marine Corps); and the Joint Chiefs of Staff (JCS) were unable to provide a unified defense budget. With Truman keeping his budget too low to provide what Forrestal considered adequate defense (the defense budget was $45 billion for fiscal year 1946; $14.5 billion for 1947; and $11.25 billion for 1948) and with Russia now possessing the atomic bomb, Forrestal became increasingly irritable and, at times, unwilling to make decisions. Although he was granted his request for increased authority over the services in the National Security Act Amendments of August 1949, he still could provide defense based only upon a given number of dollars, not upon national security requirements.

In meetings with the JCS and their advisors and then with them and the service secretaries in 1948, Forrestal forced agreement upon primary and secondary roles and missions for the armed services, a step vital to the determination of a unified budget. Whereas the Air Force would relegate the Navy to an auxiliary force conducting antisubmarine warfare and providing sea transportation, he insisted upon forces balanced militarily, not budgetarily. By favoring the Air Force in 1948, however, Congress appeared to approve strategic bombing as the primary strategy. Although the JCS approved the building of a supercarrier by a vote of three to one, the Air Force opposing, Secretary of the Navy John L. Sullivan and Secretary of the Air Force W. Stuart Symington so disagreed with him on how the Defense Department should be operated that Forrestal was placed in an ambivalent position.

It appeared, therefore, that Forrestal could not manage his service leaders as a *troika*. In addition, more so than any other member of the administration, he opposed various Truman policies, such as support for a new Jewish state in Palestine. He also bitterly resented Truman's niggardly treatment of the services. His leaving his post, however, was a direct consequence of Truman's crumbling before Louis A. Johnson's demand that he be given Forrestal's job as a reward for having raised campaign funds for Truman in 1948. Forrestal resigned on March 1, 1949, and Truman, perhaps hypocritically, pinned a Distinguished Service Medal on his coat. Ground between low budgets, squabbling service secretaries and chiefs, and an alcoholic wife, his mind cracked, and on May 22, 1949, he fell to his death from an unguarded window of the Naval Hospital at Bethesda, Maryland.

Forrestal played a crucial role in preparing America for war, conducting war, and then in the forming of postwar security policy. As the first secretary of defense, he strove mightily to have the services cooperate and thus furnish the nation with the utmost security possible with the few funds Truman allotted them. The roles and missions he forced the services to adopt still largely stand.

BIBLIOGRAPHY

Albion, Robert G., and Robert H. Connery. *Forrestal and the Navy*. New York: Columbia University Press, 1962

Coletta, Paolo E. *The U.S. Navy and Defense Unification, 1947–1953*. Newark: University of Delaware Press, 1980.

Davis, Vincent. *The Admirals Lobby*. Chapel Hill: University of North Carolina Press, 1967.

Haynes, Richard F. *The Awesome Power: Harry S. Truman as Commander in Chief*. Baton Rouge: Louisiana State University Press, 1973.

Millis, Walter, with Eugene S. Duffield, ed. *The Forrestal Diaries*. New York: Viking Press, 1951.

PAOLO E. COLETTA

FOULOIS, Benjamin D. (b. December 9, 1879, Washington, Conn.; d. April 25, 1967, Andrews Air Force Base, Md.), aviation pioneer; chief of the Army Air Corps, 1931–1935. Foulois was a key figure in the development of American military aviation.

Benjamin Foulois, born into the middle-class household of Henry and Sara

Foulois, spent his entire childhood in the small New England town of Washington, Connecticut. After eleven years of schooling, young Benjamin went to work in his father's plumbing business. Two years later, with the news of the sinking of the *Maine* and the likelihood of war with Spain, Foulois ran off to New York City to join the Navy. Rejected because of his small stature and lack of seafaring experience, "Benny" enlisted in the 1st U.S. Volunteer Engineers. Thus began a military career that would span the next thirty-seven years.

Foulois served as an enlisted man during the Spanish-American War and the Philippine Insurrection. His coolness in combat and leadership ability resulted in rapid advancement through the ranks; he was tendered a second lieutenant's commission in 1901. Returning from the Philippines in 1905, Foulois enrolled in the Infantry and Cavalry School at Fort Leavenworth. In 1906–1907 he attended the Army Signal School and saw brief service in Cuba. His interest in the potential of military aviation caused him to be detailed to the Signal Corps' new aeronautical division in 1908.

During the next three decades, Foulois actively participated in the growth and development of American military aviation. In 1909 he flew as Orville Wright's passenger during the Army's final acceptance test of the Wright Flyer. A year later he became the Army's one-man Air Force when the War Department ordered him to take the Wright airplane to Texas and "teach himself to fly." In a short time Foulois became an accomplished aviator.

Assigned to ground duty in 1911, Benny soon worked his way back into aviation and subsequently commanded the 1st Aero Squadron in the 1916 Mexican Punitive Expedition against the elusive bandit and revolutionary Pancho Villa. When the United States entered World War I in 1917, Foulois, then a temporary brigadier general, traveled to France to take over the duties of chief of the Air Service, American Expeditionary Force (AEF). Since the aviation pioneer had no previous experience running a large organization, he was ill-equipped to end the chaos prevailing within the rapidly expanding AEF air arm. As a consequence, General John Joseph Pershing* soon replaced him with a nonflyer, the very able Mason Matthews Patrick.* Foulois stayed on as assistant chief.

In succeeding years Foulois filled a variety of billets. Reverting to the rank of major at war's end, he served for a time as chief of the Air Service Liquidation Division; in 1920 he traveled to Berlin as a military attaché. On his return from Europe in 1924, he became a student at the Command and General Staff School. In 1925 he sought appointment as assistant chief of the Air Corps, a position of high prestige. Instead, he was posted to Mitchell Field, New York, as group commander. Two years later, Lieutenant Colonel Foulois advanced to the coveted assistant chief's job which carried with it temporary promotion to the rank of brigadier general. In 1931 the secretary of war elevated him to the post of chief of the Air Corps upon General James Fechet's retirement. During the next four years, under Foulois' watchful eyes and influence, the Army's air organization made great strides toward becoming an effective combat force.

Major General Foulois' years as chief were by no means a time of smooth sailing for either the Air Corps or himself. Budgets remained tight during the Depression years, and the army was less than enthusiastic about the expanding role Foulois and his fellow flyers claimed for military aviation. Yet Foulois' persistent prodding within the War Department, as well as his fiery testimony before congressional committees, continually nudged the Army to rethink and modify its stand on a host of aviation-related matters. These modifications consistently favored the Air Corps' views, producing a better organized, equipped, and doctrinally sound combat air arm.

Benny Foulois' outspokenness was a double-edged sword. In early 1934, without much reflection on the problems involved, he offered the Air Corps' services when President Franklin D. Roosevelt canceled purportedly fraudulent civilian air mail contracts. Disaster resulted when the Army air arm attempted to carry the mail. The Air Corps was neither trained nor equipped for the task, as numerous crashes attested. Yet as a consequence, the secretary of war convened the Baker Board, ensuring that beneficial changes for military aviation would result—changes long advocated by Foulois, such as the creation of a unified air strike force, the General Headquarters (GHQ) Air Force.

A longtime advocate of autonomy for military aviation, Foulois also made reckless charges against the War Department before the House Military Affairs Committee in 1934 (charges that eventually would get him into trouble). One of his claims was that the Army was incapable of properly supervising the development and effective employment of the nation's military air resources. He had taken a similar position before Congress in 1919, but circumstances had changed over the intervening fifteen years. Foulois' renewed open advocacy of autonomy both frightened and angered the General Staff. The Army rushed to accept the GHQ Air Force, hoping the aviators would view it as a palatable alternative to autonomy. At the same time, senior ground officers turned increasingly hostile to Foulois. When, in mid-1934, members of the House Military Affairs Committee unjustly charged him with intentionally misleading them as to the Army's mismanagement of the Air Corps, General Staff officers unofficially supported the committee's stand and stood by and watched as Foulois "stewed in his own juices." Clearly, the chief of the Air Corps had lost his effectiveness within the War Department and before Congress. He remained under a cloud until his retirement in 1935.

During the remaining thirty-two years of his life, Foulois continued to speak and write about the importance of military aviation. The voice of this dedicated air power advocate was not stilled until 1967, when he quietly passed away at Andrews Air Force Base, Maryland.

Small in stature, rather plain in appearance, and by no means a polished public speaker, Benjamin Foulois was not a dynamic, flamboyant figure of the William "Billy" Mitchell* variety. Yet he believed in the potential of air power and fought for its advancement just as ardently as his better known contemporary.

Foulois was never a very effective bureaucrat. He much preferred flying his trusty biplane or visiting the men of the Air Corps' operational units to the tedium of his Washington office. He was a "doer" rather than a deep thinker, possessing a wealth of practical knowledge about military aviation.

Even with his limitations, Foulois did a credible job of advancing the cause of air power. He wanted the Air Corps to grow into a decisive, autonomous striking force, and he worked tirelessly to that end. Time and again during his four years as chief he cajoled the General Staff leadership to accept changes favorable to military aviation.

The results were impressive. Through his efforts the War Department finally acknowledged in 1935 that strategic bombardment had at least some military value. This rather halting endorsement legitimatized continued Air Corps study of strategic air operations, helping to pave the way for American aerial successes over Germany and Japan a decade later. Foulois also won War Department approval for long-range bomber research and development. This helped supply the tools to make strategic bombing a reality during World War II. When Foulois became chief of the Air Corps, bomber range, speed, and payload were little improved over World War I; when he left office, the Air Corps had already tested and begun purchasing the B–17.

Perhaps his greatest contribution was the formation of the GHQ Air Force. Until that organization came to life in 1935, Air Corps combat units had been parceled out to various Army ground commanders. Dispersed throughout the United States and lacking centralized control, bomber, attack, and pursuit squadrons could not be concentrated quickly, either to defend the homeland or to initiate offensive air operations. Foulois campaigned persistently within the War Department during his first two years as chief to have this deficiency remedied. He believed that effective national defense required the immediate creation of a centrally directed strike force containing all Air Corps combat aircraft. The pressure he brought to bear was instrumental in the changed views that evolved within the Army. American air operations in World War II vindicated Foulois' advocacy of the GHQ Air Force concept. The United States was able to concentrate overwhelming aerial might under the direction of a single air commander with telling results.

In the years prior to World War I, General Benjamin Foulois helped establish American military aviation upon a firm foundation. As chief of the Air Corps some two decades later, his actions began the Air Corps on its road to preparedness for World War II.

BIBLIOGRAPHY

Foulois, Benjamin D., and Carroll V. Glines. *From the Wright Brothers to the Astronauts: The Memoirs of Major General Benjamin D. Foulois*. New York: McGraw-Hill, 1968.
Futrell, Robert Frank. *Ideas, Concepts, Doctrine: A History of Basic Thinking in the United States Air Force*. Maxwell Air Force Base, Ala.: 1971.

McClendon, R. Earl. *The Question of Autonomy for the US Air Arm*. Maxwell Air Force
    Base, Ala.: Air University, 1950.
Rutkowski, Edwin H. *The Politics of Military Aviation Procurement, 1926–1934*. Co-
    lumbus: Ohio State University Press, 1966.
Shiner, John F. "The Army Air Arm in Transition: General Benjamin D. Foulois and
    the Air Corps, 1931–35." Unpublished Ph.D. dissertation, Ohio State University,
    1975.

JOHN F. SHINER

FOX, Gustavus Vasa (b. Saugus, Mass., June 13, 1821; d. New York City,
N.Y., October 29, 1883), assistant secretary of the Navy (1861 to 1866).

Gustavus V. Fox was born to Dr. Jesse and Oliva Fox on June 13, 1821, in
Saugus, a small mill town just north of Boston, Massachusetts. After attending
Philips Academy in nearby Andover, Fox entered the U.S. Navy on January 12,
1838. Between 1838 and 1841 he trained on the 18-gun sloop *Cyane* in the
Mediterranean Sea and spent time on duty in Boston and New York. Fox studied
at the Naval School in Philadelphia during the winter of 1843–1844 and became
a passed midshipman upon completion of his studies. During the following
decade the young naval officer served in the African and Far Eastern Squadrons,
the Coast Survey, and as commander of a mail steamship.

In October 1855 Fox married the daughter of Levi Woodbury, a prominent
New Hampshire politician. The marriage deeply influenced Fox's subsequent
career. His new wife insisted that he resign from the Navy in 1856 and become
manager of a textile mill in Lawrence, Massachusetts. But his wife's family
brought Fox back into government service in early 1861 when Montgomery
Blair, who had married another Woodbury daughter, was appointed postmaster
general by President Abraham Lincoln.* Blair invited Fox to meet the new
president to discuss the growing secession crisis. Earlier, when South Carolina
forces had isolated the Federal garrison at Fort Sumter, Fox had concocted a
plan to reinforce the garrison, but the Buchanan administration had ignored his
advice. Lincoln, however, welcomed the former naval officer. The two formed
an immediate bond, and the president enjoyed Fox's quick wit, humorous stories,
and gossipy conversation. Moreover, Lincoln decided to use the New Englander
to break the stalemate in Charleston Harbor by ordering Fox to equip a relief
expedition for Fort Sumter.

Fox eagerly rushed to New York City to ask William H. Aspinwall and other
old shipping cronies to assist in procuring and provisioning vessels. Meanwhile,
back in Washington, Secretary of State William H. Seward undermined Fox's
efforts. Seeking to avoid conflict over Fort Sumter and anxious to direct policy
himself, Seward diverted promised naval support from the Fox relief expedition.
Too late Fox learned that Lincoln had accepted Seward's advice and reassigned
the big warship *Powhatan* to the Florida coast. Fortunately, before Fox could
launch a suicidal mission, Confederate forces initiated hostilities and bombarded

Fort Sumter into surrender. Fox simply transported the battered Union garrison back to New York City.

Though militarily unsuccessful, Fox's expedition reflected Lincoln's determination to place the rebellious South in the position to strike the first blow. Indeed, the president may have thought that it was necessary to sacrifice brave Fox and his force for the Union cause. In any case, politics now dictated the appointment of his loyal servant to a post in the government. The Navy Department seemed a likely place, and the president urged Secretary of the Navy Gideon Welles* to employ Fox as chief clerk. But Welles owed this position to fellow Connecticut newspaperman William Faxon. Congress resolved this sensitive situation in July, 1861 by creating the post of assistant secretary of the Navy for Fox.

As assistant secretary during the Civil War, Fox coordinated overall naval strategy, operations, and personnel assignments. Although deferring to Secretary Welles' final decisions, Fox influenced most departmental policies. The energetic assistant complemented rather than dominated the methodical Welles, and the secretary used the more visible and outspoken Fox to absorb public and political criticisms of the Navy Department. In addition, Welles employed him to present the Navy position directly to the president, investigate graft, and negotiate contracts for naval supplies. In addition, Fox tried, though not always discreetly, to insulate Welles from unhappy naval officers and civilian bureaucrats.

Intensely devoted to the Union and to the Navy, Fox pressed for naval operations that would bring glory to both. To achieve these ends, he advanced schemes placing the Navy at the center of Lincoln's war strategy. Thus, Fox advocated plans to bottle up Rebel naval forces, reduce Confederate fortifications, and capture Southern ports. This policy partly explained his passionate promotion of attacks on Port Royal, New Orleans, and Charleston. The success of the first two outshone the dismal failure of the latter and kept Lincoln satisfied with the Welles-Fox record.

Furthermore, Fox dabbled in naval technology during the war. He often determined departmental adoption of design, machinery, and weapons. After observing at first hand the four-hour battle between the *Monitor* and the *Merrimac*, Fox became an ardent disciple of the tiny turret vessel designed by John Ericsson.* Indeed, despite questions about the *Monitor*'s sailability, speed, and firepower, Fox convinced Welles to ram through legislation for construction of a whole fleet of Ericsson-designed ironclads. Throughout the war, the assistant secretary defended the monitor at the expense of other designs and insisted that this low-freeboard warship was equally capable of reducing fortifications or sinking enemy ironclads.

Fox resigned on May 22, 1866. His governmental service was not quite complete, however. Shortly after leaving office, Fox received a presidential order to carry a congressional resolution of congratulations to Tsar Alexander II of Russia who had recently escaped an assassination attempt. This assignment provided an opportunity for Fox to silence growing criticism about the monitor-class's seaworthiness. Selecting the two-turret *Miantonomoh*, Fox traveled on the first monitor to cross the Atlantic Ocean. Although a wooden escort towed the *Miantonomoh* much of the way to save coal, the iron man-of-war easily withstood the cross-ocean voyage, reinforcing Fox's wartime faith in monitors. In any event, while the assistant secretary carried messages of friendship to the Russian Tsar, Queen Victoria, Napoleon III, and other European notables, at each stop civilian and military observers scrutinized the strange American vessel.

Returning from this triumphant diplomatic trip, Fox embarked on several unsuccessful business ventures. Finally, he moved back to the familiar surroundings of northeastern Massachusetts and settled in the textile town of Lowell. During the next few years, occasional correspondence from his wartime chief and a visit by Grand Duke Alexis of Russia were the only interruptions in his postwar routine. When, five years after Secretary Welles' death, Fox died in New York City on October 29, 1883, few remembered the first assistant secretary of the Navy.

Evaluation of Gustavus V. Fox's contribution to the war effort caused controversy even while he served in the Navy Department, and historians have perpetuated these differences. As assistant secretary, Fox's passion for directing operations and promoting a dominant role for the Navy over the Army in the war endeared him to some, but also created animosities and opposition. David Dixon Porter,* David Glasgow Farragut,* and other naval officers commended his guidance; yet Samuel Francis Du Pont* and Charles Wilkes* believed that Fox destroyed those who held contrary views of the military situation. At the same time, Fox accumulated warm political allies such as Senator James Grimes of Iowa, while engendering the hatred of Congressman Henry Winter Davis of Maryland, an opponent of his Blair connections. Even Gideon Welles' infamous diary clouded Fox's record by suggesting that somehow Fox was both self-serving and unselfish.

Later generations have been equally ambivalent. Some see Fox as the driving force behind the Union Navy and one of Lincoln's most trusted intimates. According to this view, Fox dominated Welles and directed all operations as assistant secretary. Even those who relegate Fox to a subordinate status within the Navy Department are divided in their estimation of his character and contributions. Either he was seen as a courageous and honest official, or as a sly bureaucrat who lied to the Army about naval support in combined operations and directed the seizure of Southern ports simply to provide cheap cotton for his New England textile mills.

Fox's contribution to American military history stood someplace between these opposing images. In fact, Fox never ran the Navy Department, but served instead as an operational coordinator akin to the present chief of naval operations. Departmental disarray in 1861, combined with the pressures of war, presented too great a task for one man, and Secretary Welles ably portioned out responsibilities to Fox. Welles' assistant proved loyal and competent, but at the same time overly zealous and stubborn. Thus, Fox often advanced ill-conceived war plans and inadequately tested weaponry, and ignored such problems as the menace of Confederate commerce raiders. But survival of the Union demanded immediate action, and Fox pressed the Confederacy on all fronts. In the final analysis, Fox's activities led directly to expanded operations that engaged and isolated the South, allowing the Federals to gather its superior resources and crush the rebellious Confederate states.

BIBLIOGRAPHY

Hayes, John D. " 'Captain Fox—He IS the Navy Department,' " U.S. Naval Institute *Proceedings* 91 (September 1965): 64–71.
———, ed. *Samuel Francis Du Pont. A Selection from His Civil War Letters*. 3 Vols. Ithaca, N.Y.: Cornell University Press, 1969.
Niven, John. *Gideon Welles: Lincoln's Secretary of the Navy*. New York: Oxford University Press, 1973.
Reed, Rowena. *Combined Operations in the Civil War*. Annapolis, Md.: Naval Institute Press, 1978.
Thompson, Robert M., and Richard Wainwright, eds. *Confidential Correspondence of Gustavus Vasa Fox: Assistant Secretary of the Navy, 1861–1865*. 2 vols. New York: Naval History Society, 1918–1919.

JEFFERY M. DORWART

FREDENDALL, Lloyd Ralston (b. Wyoming, December 28, 1883; d. La Jolla, Calif., October 4, 1963), Army officer. Fredendall was commander of II Corps in the North African Campaign until replaced by George Smith Patton, Jr.,* on March 6, 1943.

After traveling to Wyoming from New York as a settler, Fredendall's father, Ira Livingston Fredendall, became active in politics and obtained a commission in the Quartermaster Corps during the Spanish-American War. Army life appealed to the elder Fredendall, and he stayed in service after the war. His enthusiasm apparently extended to his son as the younger Fredendall planned a military career with his mother's active support. Senator Joseph Warren of Wyoming obliged the family by appointing him to the U.S. Military Academy, but ineptitude in mathematics led to his early departure. Fredendall lasted only from June 1901 to January 1902. His mother was angry at the dismissal, and Senator Warren appointed him again with no better results. In January 1903 he was dismissed again. Senator Warren offered to appoint him again, but he declined. Instead, he attended MIT and took an examination for an Army commission in 1906. He placed first among seventy applicants and entered the infantry as a second lieutenant, February 13, 1907.

Fredendall's promotion to first lieutenant came in September 1911, and he became a captain in July 1916. As a temporary major, he served as commandant of an officers' training school in France during World War I. He finished the war with the temporary rank of lieutenant colonel. In July 1920 he became a permanent major but had to wait until September 1930 for promotion to permanent lieutenant colonel. He graduated from the Command and General Staff School with distinction (thirtieth in a class of 151) in 1923. The first real indication that he might have more than an ordinary career came in September 1934 with a prestigious appointment to the Inspector General's Department. After receiving promotion to colonel in August 1935, he left the Inspector General's Department in March 1936.

Fredendall became a brigadier general in December 1939, even before the pre-World War II expansion of the Army. In October 1940 he became a major general and received command of the 4th Division at Fort Benning. This was the Army's first completely motorized division. As its commander, Fredendall established his reputation as an excellent trainer of troops. In July 1941 he took command of the II Corps in Wilmington, Delaware. He was its commander in the North Carolina maneuvers of 1941. The following June he transferred to command of the XI Corps in Chicago.

Fredendall had gained the favor of his superiors as a trainer of troops. General Lesley James McNair* named him as one of the three men suitable to be commander of U.S. troops in England. Thus, it came as no surprise that he resumed command of the II Corps when Mark Wayne Clark* relinquished it to become General Dwight David Eisenhower's* deputy commander for the North African invasion. Fredendall was in charge of the landings at Oran and led the II Corps until after the Battle of Kasserine Pass when he was relieved of command on March 6, 1943. His promotion had been approved before he was relieved, and he became a lieutenant general in June 1943. Directly after being relieved, he returned to the United States where he took command of the Second Army in Memphis, Tennessee. He retired due to physical disability in 1946 and lived in La Jolla, California, until his death.

The most important phase of Fredendall's career was obviously his command of the II Corps in North Africa. When General George Catlett Marshall* suggested him for the position, Eisenhower objected but agreed to accept him. Despite Eisenhower's doubts, Fredendall seemed to do well in the operation at Oran. Eisenhower was "confident that reports will show that he has fulfilled every condition of brilliant leadership in a tough situation." In a cable to Marshall, he stated that "I bless the day you urged Fredendall upon me and cheerfully acknowledge that my earlier doubts of him were completely unfounded."

For the next few months, all continued to be well except for Fredendall's mistrust of the British. He told Patton of his fears that U.S. troops would be turned over to the British, leaving Fredendall and Patton to "hold the bag." Eisenhower gave him a gentle reprimand through Lucian King Truscott, Jr.,* for criticizing the British, but expressed complete faith in him. In fact, Eisenhower went so far as to recommend him for a third star in early February 1943.

Trouble in II Corps began in February with the action in Central Tunisia, which culminated with the Battle of Kasserine Pass. In preparation for the battle, Fredendall established his command post some sixty miles from the front in an inaccessible canyon that he made even more secure by blasting dugouts into its rock walls. In his memoirs Eisenhower said, "It was the only time, during the war, that I ever saw a divisional or higher headquarters so concerned over its own safety that it dug itself underground shelters." When Eisenhower visited the front on February 13, he was disturbed to find that two days had been wasted and no minefields had been laid. He was also unhappy with the location of the troops, which had been scattered in often indefensible positions, despite his orders that some forces be held in reserve. Before any changes could be made, the battle was underway.

Other officers were harsher than Eisenhower in their disapproval of Fredendall's conduct. Lucian K. Truscott described him as

> Small in stature, loud and rough in speech, he was outspoken in his opinions and critical of superiors and subordinates alike. He was inclined to jump at conclusions which were not always well founded. He rarely left his command post for personal visits and reconnaissance, yet he was impatient with the recommendations of subordinates more familiar with the terrain and other conditions than he was. General Fredendall had no confidence in the French, no liking for the British in general and for General Anderson in particular, and little more for his own subordinate commanders.

His subordinate commanders thought no better of him. The II Corps consisted of the 1st Infantry Division under Terry Allen, the 1st Armored Division commanded by Orlando Ward, and the 34th Infantry Division under Charles Ryder. Although Ryder was unhappy with Fredendall's leadership, Ward was his severest critic. Between Ward and Fredendall was "an antipathy most unusual." The two were hardly on speaking terms. Ward felt that Fredendall knew nothing of armor and ignored his recommendations through personal dislike. Fredendall believed Ward incompetent and disloyal. Complicating the situation was Brigadier General Paul Robinette, a subordinate of Ward's who felt he knew more about armor than either Ward or Fredendall and tried to maintain his independence from them. The situation had become so bad by February 19 that Fredendall told Truscott "that Ward simply had to be removed" and asked for help in persuading Eisenhower.

On February 20, Eisenhower ordered Ernest Harmon, commander of the 2d Armored Division, to join Fredendall as deputy corps commander and help him control the situation. Then Harmon was to report whether Fredendall or Ward should be relieved. After some difficulty, Harmon arrived at Fredendall's headquarters at about 3:00 A.M. As soon as he arrived, Fredendall asked him if the headquarters should be moved. Harmon did not even know where he was, but he advised against moving, and Fredendall accepted his opinion as authoritative. Eisenhower had explicitly told Fredendall that Harmon's arrival was not to be used as an excuse to relieve Ward, but Fredendall gave him "battlefield command" of the 1st Armored Division. Harmon gives the distinct impression in his memoirs that Fredendall had completely lost control of the situation and himself. After conducting the Battle of Kasserine Pass, Harmon returned to find "the general in bed, showing some effects of several helpings, of whiskey he had taken in celebration of the occasion." Fredendall later maintained that his grogginess was due to lack of sleep rather than drink. Harmon refused to relieve Ward, and Fredendall sent him back to Eisenhower.

When Harmon reported to Eisenhower that Fredendall was "no damned good," Eisenhower asked if he would like to be the new II Corps commander. Harmon felt it would be unethical to replace the man he had condemned and declined. Eisenhower then sent Omar Nelson Bradley* on a fact-finding mission. Bradley found that Fredendall had lost the confidence of his division commanders and the British, who thought he was delaying too long before moving against the Germans. Eisenhower apparently agreed that Fredendall was dragging his feet. On February 22, Eisenhower told him that the Germans should be attacked and that he would take "full responsibility for any disadvantages that might result from vigorous action." Yet Fredendall hesitated to attack, fearing the enemy had "one more shot in his locker." By morning, the Germans had retreated.

Bradley "was certain that Fredendall should be relieved." Eisenhower agreed and named George Patton to succeed him. Patton wrote his wife that Fredendall was a victim of circumstances, but in his diary he seemed to share Harmon's opinion that Fredendall was a "moral and physical coward." When Patton arrived to relieve Fredendall on March 6, 1943, he found "His staff in general poor. Discipline and dress poor....I think Fredendall is either a little nuts or badly scared. He won't fly to Constantine and proposes to leave at 3:30 a.m. by car. That is the safest time on the road."

Fredendall returned to the United States where he became deputy commander of the Second Army in Memphis, Tennessee. After his promotion to lieutenant general became official in June, he took command of it. Eisenhower said that he would be excellent as a trainer of troops, but "one or two personal faults" precluded him from combat command.

BIBLIOGRAPHY

Chandler, Alfred D., et al. eds. *The Papers of Dwight David Eisenhower: The War Years*. Baltimore: Johns Hopkins University Press, 1970.

Harmon, Ernest N. *Combat Commander, Autobiography of a Soldier*. Englewood Cliffs, N.J.: Prentice-Hall, 1970.

Howe, George F. *Northwest Africa: Seizing the Initiative in the West*. Washington, D.C.: Office of the Chief of Military History, 1957.

Truscott, Lucian K. *Command Missions*. New York: E. P. Dutton, 1954

PHILIP D. JONES

FREMONT, John Charles (b. Savannah, Ga., January 21, 1813; d. New York City, N.Y., July 13, 1890); Army officer, explorer, Civil War general, politician.

The son of a French emigré school teacher and his common-law wife, Frémont lived an itinerant life until the death of his father in 1818 when the mother settled in Charleston, South Carolina. He obtained some schooling in science and mathematics at the College of Charleston (1829–1831) and came to the attention of Joel R. Poinsett, who would be the major influence on his early career. After brief service as a mathematics teacher on the warship *Natchez*, Frémont, through Poinsett's influence, secured work with surveying crews plotting the route of the Charleston and Cincinnati Railroad and doing government work in the Cherokee country of North Georgia. He developed a zest for exploration and thus was launched upon the career that would bring him fame.

Having proved himself in these endeavors, Frémont was called to Washington by his patron Poinsett, now secretary of war, and was commissioned a second lieutenant in the U.S. Corps of Topographical Engineers in 1838. He was attached to the expedition of Joseph Nicollet, famous French scientist, who had been directed to explore the region between the upper Mississippi and Missouri rivers. The two became fast friends, and their association provided the young Frémont with excellent training. Upon their return to Washington after two years in the field, they took bachelor quarters together while producing the report and map that culminated the expedition's work.

Poinsett also introduced Frémont to another prominent Washingtonian, Senator Thomas Hart Benton, who would profoundly influence his future career. Much interested in American expansion to the Pacific, Benton provided the young officer with a broad vision of the need for exploring the vast Western territories. While visiting in the Benton home, Frémont frequently had his attentions diverted by the senator's vivacious sixteen-year-old daughter Jessie. They quickly fell deeply in love, and after a year-long expedition to Iowa Territory, whence Benton had sent the young explorer to try to break up the attachment, they eloped on October 19, 1841. Benton quickly reconciled himself to the match under the influence of his strong-willed daughter, and he became his son-in-law's major patron and benefactor.

It was through Benton's influence that Frémont received the command of his first major expedition: a scientific exploration of the Wind River chain of the Rockies in the summer of 1842. He enlisted the valuable aid of two men who would be with him on subsequent expeditions: Kit Carson as guide and Charles Preuss as topographer. They followed the Oregon Trail to South Pass and then explored extensively the Wind River range beyond. His report, which Jessie skillfully helped him prepare, supplemented by Preuss's map, was quite favorably received and ordered printed by Congress, which also authorized a second expedition.

This trip, which would last fourteen months, took Frémont on a vast circuit of the entire West. He explored extensively in the present-day states of Utah, Oregon, and Nevada before recklessly crossing the Sierras in a difficult midwinter passage. Regrouping at Sutter's Fort on the Sacramento, the expedition traversed California to Los Angeles and picked up the Old Spanish Trail toward Santa Fe. Detouring through southern Nevada and Utah, Frémont emerged at Bent's Fort on the Arkansas on July 1, 1844. His subsequent report solidly established his reputation.

In June 1845 Frémont left St. Louis on his third Western expedition—a journey that would prove to be his most controversial adventure, covering as it did the outbreak of the Mexican War. His instructions indicated that he was to survey the rivers and streams around Bent's Fort and to the east of the Rockies. But press accounts anticipated that he would return to the Great Salt Lake region and California, which he did. The expedition went fully armed in obvious expectation—Frémont later claimed under specific instructions—that war might break out, and they would have a role to play.

In early December Frémont reached California where he became embroiled in controversy with local Mexican officials. As a result, he moved north into Oregon. He returned in May 1846, after receiving dispatches from Washington indicating the imminence of war. Whether these directed him to take any active part remains unclear and the subject of historical controversy. Nevertheless, he played a major role in the events that followed, joining the settlers around Sutter's Fort in the Bear Flag Rebellion and cooperating with Commodore Robert Field Stockton,* who initially commanded both American naval and land operations. Their combined forces took Los Angeles in August 1846 and had seemingly won the California struggle. The native population kept up an incipient revolt, however, which Stockton and Frémont put down with the aid of General Stephen Watts Kearny* who had arrived from New Mexico. Thereafter Frémont became involved in a power struggle between Stockton and Kearny, backing the loser Stockton and being brought back a virtual prisoner under court-martial for disobedience. He was found guilty, and his penalty of dismissal was remitted by President James K. Polk who ordered him back to duty. Frémont resigned his commission in indignation.

Frémont now launched a fourth expedition with private funds in the winter of 1848–1849. It was a disastrous passage through the San Juan Mountains with eleven men lost. Thereafter, Frémont concentrated on developing his Mariposa estate in California which produced gold-bearing veins. He served briefly as U.S. senator (1850–1851) following California's admission and made one final expedition in 1853–1854 in search of a suitable pass for a Southern railroad to the Pacific. Most of his time was divided between California and Europe, however, as he sought capital to develop his property. In 1856 the fledgling Republican party named him as its presidential candidate, seeking to capitalize on his hero status and his strong free soil leanings. Although his supporters were active in the field, he himself conducted a quiet campaign, losing to the Democrat James Buchanan by an electoral count of 174 to 114.

The outbreak of the Civil War found Frémont again in Europe. He hastened home to accept a major general's commission from President Abraham Lincoln* and with it the command of the western department with headquarters at St. Louis. Missouri was already being wracked by guerrilla warfare and was threatened by pro-Confederate forces on two fronts. Frémont found it difficult to sort out his priorities and isolated himself from his military subordinates and political leaders. He was plagued by corruption on the part of friends to whom he granted contracts, and he was condemned for the ostentatious display of his staff, many of them Europeans. Serious military setbacks in western Missouri at Wilson's Creek and Lexington, presumably because of his lack of support for field commanders, hurt further. In the midst of the turmoil, he angered Lincoln and Missouri's political leaders by unilaterally proclaiming martial law with the confiscation of Rebel property and the emancipation of their slaves. The president ordered the last part rescinded when Frémont refused to withdraw it voluntarily. Frémont lasted exactly one hundred days. Removed in November 1861, he held command briefly in the spring of 1862 in the Shenandoah Valley Campaign. This was an even less successful venture. Relieved of command shortly thereafter at his own request because of his unwillingness to serve under John Pope,* he played no further role in the war.

The radical wing of the Republican party nominated Frémont for the presidency in 1864—attracted by his antislavery stance in Missouri—but he withdrew before the election. By the end of that year, he had lost his Mariposa property. After the war he engaged in railroad speculation at which he also proved inept. Bankruptcy and litigation followed both at home and in France. Some income was derived from Mrs. Frémont's writing. For a time he served as governor of Arizona Territory (1878–1881), but speculative activities by his friends again proved his undoing. During his last two decades he continually flirted with poverty. Shortly before his death, he was restored with pay to the Army retired list as a major general for pension purposes.

Frémont's accomplishments as an explorer certainly entitle him to rank high among those who opened up the West. There was little of the area beyond the Rockies that he did not cover in one of his expeditions. His detailed and well-written reports with accompanying maps went through many editions and were widely read. Frémont could report to a friend on one occasion that he had encountered many along the trail who thanked him for stirring their interest and who relied on his maps for guidance. His first two expeditions along the Oregon Trail clearly indicated that the journey was not as difficult as might have been anticipated and reinforced earlier pictures of the Northwest as an area well worth the effort. His extensive exploration of the area between the Wasatch and the Sierras, which he aptly termed the "Great Basin," provided the first substantial knowledge of its arid vastness. All of these efforts solidly established Frémont as what Allan Nevins calls the "Pathmarker of the West."

The explorer's later career was tragically anticlimactic. He was not successful as entrepreneur, presidential candidate, or military leader. Only the faith and efforts of the redoubtable Jessie kept the family fortunes on a somewhat even keel. Throughout their long life together, Frémont had no greater admirer than his wife.

BIBLIOGRAPHY

Frémont, John Charles. *Memoirs of My Life: A Retrospect of Fifty Years*. New York: Belford, Clarke and Company, 1887.

Jackson, Donald, and Mary Lou Spence, eds. *The Expeditions of John Charles Frémont*. 2 vols. Urbana: University of Illinois Press, 1970–1973.

Nevins, Allan. *Frémont: Pathmaker of the West*. New York and London: D. Appleton-Century Company, 1939.

Parrish, William E. *Turbulent Partnership: Missouri and the Union, 1861–1865*. Columbia: University of Missouri Press, 1963.

Preuss, Charles. *Exploring with Frémont: The Private Diaries of Charles Preuss, Cartographer for John C. Frémont on His First, Second and Fourth Expeditions to the Far West*. Translated and edited by Erwin G. and Elisabeth K. Gudde. Norman: University of Oklahoma Press, 1958.

WILLIAM E. PARRISH

FUNSTON, Frederick (b. New Carlisle, Ohio, November 9, 1865; d. San Antonio, Tex., February 19, 1917), adventurer; major general, U.S. Army.

Frederick Funston was the son of Edward Hogue and Ann Eliza (Mitchell) Funston. In 1867 the Funston family moved to Iola, Kansas, where young Frederick was raised on the family farm. A voracious reader, he was graduated from Iola High School and taught school for a while before entering the University of Kansas. Uncomfortable with the academic routine of the university, Funston left after only two and a half years and tried his hand at various jobs, including work as a journalist in Fort Smith, Arkansas, and Kansas City, and as a ticket taker on the Atchison, Topeka and Santa Fe Railroad.

In the summer of 1890, through his father's political connections Frederick obtained a position with a U.S. Department of Agriculture expedition to collect grass samples in the Dakotas. The following year he participated in another Department of Agriculture botanical expedition to Death Valley, California. Soon recognized as a competent botanist and fearless expeditionary, Funston was transferred to Alaska in 1892 to collect samples of Alaskan flora. He crossed Alaska on a thirty-five hundred mile trip from the McKenzie River to the Bering Sea, wintered over alone in 1893–1894 and undertook a solo canoe expedition of fifteen hundred miles down the Yukon River which almost cost him his life.

Leaving Alaska in 1894, Funston lectured publicly on his adventures and purchased land on the Gulf Coast of southern Mexico with the intention of establishing a coffee plantation. While seeking financial backing for his plantation venture, he accepted a sinecure as deputy comptroller of the Atchison, Topeka and Santa Fe Railroad in New York City. In the summer of 1896, he chanced to hear a rousing pro-Cuban speech by Civil War General Daniel E. Sickles and enlisted in the cause of Cuban liberation from Spain. Accepted for the artillery service on the strength of having once seen a salute fired to President Rutherford B. Hayes at a county fair in Kansas, he sailed for Cuba in August 1896. In eighteen months of guerrilla warfare as an artillery commander for Maximo Gomez and Calixto Garcia, he proved a quick learner and brave soldier. Funston participated in twenty-two engagements, was wounded several times, and rose to the rank of lieutenant colonel before being captured by the Spaniards and condemned to death late in 1897. He subsequently escaped and returned to the United States in very poor health in January 1898. Acclaimed as a hero, he supported himself by lecturing on his adventures and in favor of the Cuban cause.

After the declaration of war by the United States against Spain, the governor of Kansas offered Funston command of the 20th Kansas Volunteer Infantry Regiment which he accepted on May 13, 1898. While the regiment was encamped at San Francisco awaiting orders to sail for the Philippines, Funston met and married Eda Blankart of Oakland, California, on October 25, 1898.

The 20th Kansas arrived at Manila on November 30, 1898, too late for operations against the Spaniards. Assigned to Arthur MacArthur's* 2d Division, the regiment did see active service in the Malolos Campaign against the Filipino *insurrectos* in 1899. The advance of the 2d Division northward from Manila along the railroad line toward the Lingayen Gulf frequently involved the crossing of rivers under fire, a type of operation in which Funston and the 20th Kansas became especially adept. His exceptional personal bravery and "aggressiveness leavened with judgment" made Funston well-known within the Army, and the newspapers brought him to the notice of the American public as well.

On April 27, 1899, Funston and forty-five soldiers of the 20th Kansas crossed the Rio Grande de Pampanga at Calumpit on a raft and after a hard fight drove twenty-five hundred *insurrectos* from their entrenchments covering the skeleton of a destroyed railroad bridge. For his part in this action Funston was promoted on May 2, 1899, to brigadier general of volunteers and was awarded the Medal of Honor on February 14, 1900. He continued the campaign as a brigade commander and was wounded at Santo Tomas.

The Malolos Campaign ended in May 1899, and in early September the 20th Kansas sailed for home and muster out. Funston, however, was retained in the U.S. Volunteer organization raised to continue the fight against the *insurrectos*, and he returned to the Philippines in late December 1899 to command the 4th District of the Department of Northern Luzon where he carried out a vigorous and successful series of antiguerrilla operations.

Early in 1901, having been refused a commission in the Regular Army, Funston was again preparing to be mustered out when through some captured correspondence he learned the whereabouts of the secret headquarters of the rebel leader, Emilio Aguinaldo. Funston then concocted an elaborate and dangerous scheme to capture Aguinaldo. A small raiding party consisting of a rebel defector as guide, Funston and four other officers posing as captives, and a party of loyal Macabebe tribesmen posing as an *insurrecto* guard left Manila on March 14, 1901, aboard the USS *Vicksburg* and was landed in northern Luzon. They then proceeded through the jungle to the rebel headquarters at Palanan where on

March 23 they successfully captured Aguinaldo, spirited him to the coast, and were picked up by the waiting *Vicksburg* and returned to Manila on March 28. The daring feat was characterized as "the most important single military event of the year in the Philippines" and led directly to negotiations ending the insurrection.

In recognition of his accomplishment, the thirty-six-year-old Funston was commissioned as a brigadier general in the Regular Army on April 1, 1901, by President William McKinley. He returned home in late 1901 to more routine duties as commander successively of the Departments of the Colorado, the Columbia and the Lakes, and the Southwestern Division. Late in 1905 he was assigned to command the Department of California with headquarters at San Francisco. On April 18, 1906, Funston was also in temporary command of the Pacific Division in the absence of Major General Adolphus Washington Greely* when the city was struck by a great earthquake and subsequently ravaged by fire and disorder. Funston immediately ordered federal troops to assist in the rescue and firefighting efforts, and with the concurrence of the mayor of San Francisco he dispatched military patrols to prevent looting and destroy liquor stocks. His forceful, if unauthorized, actions were credited with reducing the loss of life and property, but he was widely criticized for his decision to dynamite fire breaks in the burning city.

Later in 1906 Funston served briefly and disappointingly with the Taft Mission in the second Cuban intervention. He then served as commandant of the Army Service Schools at Fort Leavenworth from 1908 to 1910, and in 1911 he returned for a third tour in the Philippines as commander of the Department of Luzon. In 1913 he was transferred to command the Hawaiian Department and was responsible for improving the defenses of Pearl Harbor during the short-lived crisis with Japan.

In January 1914 Funston was reassigned to command the 2d Division at Texas City, Texas. He subsequently commanded Army troops in the expedition to Vera Cruz in April 1914 and was both commander and military governor of the city until November 1914 when U.S. forces were withdrawn. He acted with great restraint and diplomacy and erected a model municipal government in the occupied city which earned him the praise of his civilian superiors and promotion to major general on November 17, 1914.

Funston received command of the Southern Department in February 1915, and with increasing border troubles in 1916, he was placed in general command of all U.S. troops along the Mexican border. After Pancho Villa's raid on Columbus, New Mexico, on March 9, 1916, Funston recommended immediate pursuit and oversaw the movements of U.S. forces in Mexico led by Brigadier General John Joseph Pershing* in pursuit of Villa.

On February 19, 1917, only a few days after issuing orders for withdrawal of the Punitive Expedition from Mexico, Frederick Funston died suddenly in the lobby of the St. Anthony Hotel in San Antonio, apparently from a heart attack brought on by stress and acute indigestion. General Funston lay in state in the Alamo and was buried at the Presidio of San Francisco on February 24, 1917. He was survived by his widow, a son, and two daughters.

Frederick Funston's untimely death at the age of fifty-one deprived the U.S. Army of perhaps its most capable and vigorous general officer on the eve of America's entry into World War I and provides one of the most provocative ''might have beens'' in modern American military history. Although lacking in formal military training, Funston had repeatedly proven his personal courage, aggressiveness, and tactical skill on battlefields in Cuba and Luzon. His capacity for higher command and the management of large forces under conditions requiring diplomatic and political skills of a high order had been tested and found superb in San Francisco in 1906, Vera Cruz in 1914, and along the Mexican border in 1916–1917. In 1917 he was possibly the United States' best known and most respected major general, and, had he lived, he probably would have been called upon to command the American Expeditionary Forces (AEF) in France. Had that occurred, the subsequent development of the U.S. Army may have been far different. Although American participation in World War I perhaps would have followed the same general lines, the internal structure of the AEF and, consequently of the postwar Army probably would have reflected the more human and less authoritarian character of Funston rather than the cold, elitist formality of John J. Pershing.

The degree to which Pershing's personality influenced the development of the U.S. Army has yet to be fully studied and understood, but it is clear that the subtle effects of his personal likes and dislikes have their residual effects even today. The possible consequences of Funston's elevation to the command of the AEF are, of course, problematic, but it seems likely that a different set of standards, based not so much on outward appearance but on inward values, would have been adopted. Funston had ever demonstrated a great personal modesty and tolerance for the foibles of others, and he clearly never took himself too seriously. An active, compassionate, and intelligent man himself, he sought those qualities in others. Possessed of a bantam physique little calculated to overawe, Funston judged others by their spirit and actual performance rather than by their outward appearance and assumed potential. A varied, adventuresome, and unsheltered life made him at ease with all types of society and largely without pretension or prudishness. Who can say that an army shaped by Funston's personal and professional foibles would not have been better than that molded by those of Pershing?

Frederick Funston was a transitional figure who in his own public career reflected the changing values of the Army and indeed of American society in general. He has been characterized as ''a man whose adventures symbolized a vanishing era of romantic individualism and at the same time represented the new 'manager' of military forces required for overall command in modern war.'' Throughout his life Frederick Funston displayed an unusual ability to change and grow professionally with the times. As only a few of his contemporaries were able to do, he successfully made the transition from the era of small-scale military operations in which the leaders were expected to display nineteenth-century virtues of personal courage and individual initiative to the early twentieth-century in which the officer was required to be a team player and to manage the efforts of others in complex, large-scale military endeavors.

BIBLIOGRAPHY

Crouch, Thomas W. *A Yankee Guerrillero: Frederick Funston and the Cuban Insurrection: 1896–97*. Memphis, Tenn.: Memphis State University Press, 1975.

Funston, Frederick. *Memories of Two Wars: Cuban and Philippine Experiences*. New York: Charles Scribner's Sons, 1911.

Trussell, Colonel John B.B. Jr. "Frederick Funston: The Man Destiny Just Missed." *Military Review* 53, No. 6 (June 1973): 59–73.

CHARLES R. SHRADER

G

GAINES, Edmund Pendleton (b. Culpeper County, Va., March 20, 1777; d. New Orleans, La., June 6, 1849), Army officer; veteran of the War of 1812 and the Florida Wars.

Son of a Revolutionary War veteran who later served in the North Carolina legislature, Edmund P. Gaines grew to manhood on the east Tennessee frontier. At age eighteen he was elected a lieutenant in a volunteer rifle company raised for defense against hostile Indians, and gained a reputation for rash courage. During the "Quasi-War" with France, Gaines entered the Regular Army on January 10, 1799, as an ensign in the 6th Infantry and was quickly promoted (March 3) to second lieutenant; he was discharged from service on June 15, 1800. He reentered the Army on February 16, 1801, as a second lieutenant in the 4th Infantry. Gaines supervised work on the Nashville-Natchez road, was transferred to the 2d Infantry, advanced to first lieutenant on April 27, 1802, and surveyed the boundaries of the Choctaw Nation.

In 1804 Gaines reported for duty at Fort Stoddert (Alabama) in Mississippi Territory, and two years later he assumed command of this outpost near Spanish Florida. Gaines gained the national limelight in February of 1807, when in response to Governor Robert Williams' call, he arrested the celebrated conspirator Aaron Burr, who was visiting a friend near the fort. Gaines later testified at the Burr trial in Richmond, Virginia. His promotion to captain was dated February 28. Gaines commanded in a sensitive region, clashing repeatedly with filbustering groups intent on invading east Florida. Intensely ambitious, he also read law, secured a license to practice, and with a leave of absence in 1811 he became judge of Pascagoula Parish.

With the outbreak of hostilities with Great Britain, Gaines returned to active duty, advancing to the rank of major on March 24, 1812. In July as lieutenant colonel (July 6) in the new 24th Infantry, he helped raise companies in the Knoxville area, and a year later he reported to General William Henry Harrison* on the Ohio. On September 1, 1813, Gaines was made full colonel and adjutant general on Harrison's staff, and participated in the recapture of Detroit. Transferred to the 25th Infantry, he joined General James Wilkinson's* army on the St. Lawrence River, serving as adjutant in Brigadier General Leonard Covington's brigade. In November Gaines ably commanded his regiment in covering the retreat of the American Army from Chrysler's Farm.

From winter quarters at French Mills, Gaines moved his regiment to Sackets Harbor, where he was attached to Major General Jacob Jennings Brown's* staff until his appointment as brigadier general on March 9, 1814. Gaines commanded forces at Sackets Harbor until August when Brown called him to defend Fort Erie, a key bastion on the Niagara River opposite Buffalo. There, in mid-August with two thousand men, Gaines successfully withstood assaults by a superior British force and sustained a disabling wound. He was awarded the brevet of major general for his gallantry, and that fall was voted a medal and commendation by Congress for heroism. Later, the states of New York, Tennessee, and Virginia presented him with ceremonial swords. After briefly commanding the Fourth Military District (Maryland, Pennsylvania, and New York), General Gaines was ordered to recruit men for the defense of New Orleans. He arrived there in January 1815, only to learn that Andrew Jackson* had repulsed the enemy several days before.

In 1815 Gaines was appointed to the army reduction board and was one of three brigadiers assigned to Jackson's Southern Military Division. Back on the Florida frontier, Gaines dealt summarily with problems. When Creek Indians proved reluctant to leave lands they had ceded, he sent troops into the disputed territory, dispersed the dissidents, and ordered survey crews to run the required demarkation lines. Depredations by renegade Creeks from Spanish Florida prompted Gaines to send regulars across the border, an act that precipitated the extended Seminole Wars. When Jackson enlisted volunteers to invade Florida in 1818, Gaines sought to enroll sixteen hundred Creeks and to appoint a brigadier to head the force—an act that brought stern disapproval from superiors. He served with Jackson during the Florida invasion and presided over the celebrated trials of Arbuthnot and Ambrister, British traders who were arrested and executed for inciting border unrest.

In the army reduction of 1821, Gaines emerged as commanding general of the Western Department, an area lying west of a line drawn from Lake Superior southeast to Florida. In the new arrangement, he exchanged command every two years with Winfield Scott,* commanding the Eastern Department. Gaines promoted settlement on the frontier by constructing forts, dispatching expeditions into Indian Country, and urging the development of transportation. During these years he also became embroiled in heated arguments in both government and military circles. He quarreled with Governor John Troup of Georgia over the local use of federal troops and engaged in vitriolic exchanges with Winfield Scott over seniority.

By 1828, when he was passed over for supreme Army command, Gaines was in disfavor with the president and the War Department. Thereafter when such special assignments as Indian outbreaks or removals arose in his jurisdiction, the government sent Scott or some other ranking officer to take charge. Gaines further alienated his superiors by making unauthorized levies for militia to serve in the Black Hawk War, the Seminole fiasco of 1836, and the Texas Revolution. Between 1837 and 1844, Gaines' command was changed several times. In 1837 the east-west line was moved to the Mississippi; in 1842–1844 nine separate departments briefly replaced the divisions.

At the outbreak of the Mexican War in 1846, Gaines precipitously called on Southern governors for troops, and was rebuked by both the War Department and General in Chief Scott. Gaines was relieved of command and ordered before a court of inquiry. He nominally commanded the Eastern Division until 1848 when he was restored to his old jurisdiction. Gaines died a year later in New Orleans of cholera at the age of seventy-two.

Edmund Gaines spent most of his fifty-year military career on the frontier. On the Florida border, he grappled directly and forcefully with problems caused by rough frontiersmen, would-be filibusters, and restless Indian tribes. In this isolated world, he developed fierce independence, rash self-reliance, and a tendency to spark controversy. During the War of 1812 he performed creditably in regimental, staff, and command assignments, and advanced in rank from lieutenant colonel to brevet major general. With the return of peace he was reassigned to the South as a brigadier under Jackson. Elevated to departmental command in 1821, Gaines became increasingly outspoken about ranking officers of the Army, questioned authority, and issued orders that embarrassed government officials. He spent the last decade of his career enjoying the benefits of a large command but exercising little control over its operations. He was allowed token responsibilities in respect for his past services to the republic.

Although a thorn to Army administration, Gaines took great interest in national defense. In 1838 he submitted to the War Department an elaborate plan that urged the construction of floating batteries to guard valuable harbors, the need for additional forts to protect settlers on the frontier, and the building of a railroad system to shuttle troops and supplies between forts. He particularly stressed the advantages of railroads, not only to national security but also to the development of the nation. To advertise his ideas, Gaines wrote letters, prepared memorials, gave lectures, and even helped organize railroad conventions.

A product of the frontier, Edmund Gaines throughout his career reflected the attitudes and ambitions of the lusty young republic. Bold and brash, he repeatedly placed the army on call to support and protect the manifest destiny of its expanding population. In so doing, he greatly enhanced the image of the military as a potent force in the nation's development.

BIBLIOGRAPHY

Elliott, Charles Winslow. *Winfield Scott: The Soldier and the Man*, New York: Macmillan Company, 1937.

Prucha, Francis P. *The Sword of the Republic: The U.S. Army on the Frontier, 1783–1846*. New York: Macmillan Company, 1969.

Silver, James W. *Edmund Pendleton Gaines: Frontier General*. Baton Rouge: Louisiana State University Press, 1949.

                                                        HARWOOD P. HINTON

GATES, Horatio (b. Maldon [?], England, April [?] 1728; d. New York City, N.Y., April 10, 1806), Army officer. Gates' major achievement was the victory at Saratoga in October 1777.

Horatio Gates was born to working-class parents in England and seemingly was fordoomed to a life of menial labor. Yet, for some reason he came under the protection of Horace Walpole and, possibly, Thomas Osborne, duke of Leeds. Thus, in 1749, at the age of twenty-one, he entered the officer corps of the British Army. Serving in America until the end of the Seven Years' War, he saw extensive service and was promoted to major in 1762. As the Army reverted to a peacetime footing, the young officer found himself cut off from advancing to a lieutenant colonelcy because of his lower class social origins. Hence, he retired from the Army and in 1773 moved his family (his wife Dorothy and son Robert) to Virginia, where he settled into a comfortable life on a quiet farm named "Travellers Rest."

When war broke out between Britain and America, Gates quickly made known his support of the patriot party. Having long ago envinced Whiggish political views, he was welcomed into rebellion and on June 17, 1775, Congress appointed him adjutant general with the rank of brigadier general in the Continental Army. During the siege of Boston in the winter of 1775–1776, his extensive knowledge of Army organization helped George Washington* bring order and regularity to the raw troops in Massachusetts. Gates' service led Congress on May 16, 1776, to promote him to major general and to appoint him one month later commander of a patriot Army that had invaded Canada in the previous year. Arriving in New York to assume his new position, he found that the Army was no longer "in Canada" but had retreated into Philip Schuyler's* Northern Department. Since both generals asserted control over these troops, they agreed that Congress must clarify the command problem—which it did in favor of Schuyler. Gates accepted this situation with little grace but was mollified when Schuyler appointed him commander of upstate New York. Thus, he worked closely with Benedict Arnold* in the summer and fall of 1776 to repel Guy Carleton's thrust from Canada up Lake Champlain towards Fort Ticonderoga. In December he led six hundred Continentals to Washington's assistance, after which he assumed command of Philadelphia. He retained this post for only two months before being ordered by Congress on March 25, 1777, back to Ticonderoga to supersede Schuyler.

The continual bickering between congressional proponents of Gates and Schuyler profited no one except John Burgoyne, who threatened invasion of New York in the spring of 1777. But the quarrel had one more round to go before it ceased.

On May 15 Schuyler managed to get Congress to restore him to office, only to have Gates maneuver against him in that body and on August 4 be ordered for the final time to take charge of the Northern army. With the command situation at last clarified, Gates could concentrate upon defeating the enemy; in the battles of Freeman's Farm (September 19) and Bemis Heights (October 7), the American general, ably assisted by Arnold and Daniel Morgan,* fought Burgoyne to a standstill and forced him on October 17 to sign a convention, which provided that his Anglo-German troops would be returned to Europe and not serve again in the war. Although Gates has often been charged with being too hasty in accepting these terms, as well as being dilatory in reporting his victories to Washington, both charges are largely unsubstantiated. Also not proven are arguments by many historians that Gates, as chairman of the Board of War, participated during the winter of 1777–1778 in the so-called Conway Cabal, a supposed scheme by Thomas Conway* to replace Washington with Gates as commander in chief.

After a useful tenure on the Board of War, Gates was ordered by Congress on April 15, 1778, to command once more in the Hudson River Valley. His only ''accomplishment'' during that summer was a ridiculous duel (the second in six months) with James Wilkinson,* an ex-aide, in which Wilkinson fired at him three times with no effect. On October 22 Congress sent Gates to Boston to command the troops of the Eastern Department, and in the spring of 1779, after surlily turning down Washington's offer to command an Indian expedition (the one John Sullivan* would accept), he was posted in Providence. After the British evacuated Newport in October, he requested from Washington, and was granted, leave to retire to ''Travellers Rest.''

On June 13, 1780, Congress asked Gates to take control of the Southern army—or what was left of it—after Benjamin Lincoln's* surrender of Charleston on May 12. ''An Army, without Strength,'' was the way Gates described his new command on July 3; but he quickly organized a little force at Coxe's Mill, North Carolina, and set out toward the enemy to the south. On the night of August 15, he marched from Rugeley's Mill with his half-starved and bone-tired army toward Camden, only to encounter a British expedition under Charles, Lord Cornwallis, moving toward him. The next day, August 16, the two armies clashed in the Battle of Camden. Gates' poorly disposed militiamen were routed, and his Continentals, commanded by Johann de Kalb, were so decimated that it took the American general three months to reorganize and rebuild at Hillsborough.

When Congress learned of Gates' debacle, the legislators turned upon their erstwhile favorite and voted to allow Washington to appoint Nathanael Greene* in his stead, until a court of inquiry could make a study of Gates' conduct in the South. Not until August 14, 1782, did Congress rescind its earlier resolution and give the general leave to rejoin the army. With his self-respect belatedly restored, he served as Washington's second-in-command at Newburgh in the winter of 1782–1783 and had some role in fomenting officer unrest during the final, unquiet months of the Continental Army's existence. In late March 1783 he left camp for the last time and went home to the bedside of his ailing wife, who died on June 1.

After the war, Gates lived an active life. He served as president of the Virginia State Society of the Cincinnati and supported the movement toward a stronger national constitution. Since his only son had died in 1780, he was without a family and lonely, but in 1786 he married a rich widow named Mary Vallance; four years later, he sold his Virginia farm and settled on Manhattan. In vigorous old age, he emerged as a Jeffersonian in politics and was elected in 1800 to a term in the New York state legislature. But soon his health began to decline; in 1803 he informed his old friend, Benjamin Rush, that he was so "Lean" that he looked like "a Skeleton." Less than three years later, he was dead at the age of seventy-eight.

To assess Gates' importance in American military history, it is necessary to analyze both his relationship with Washington and his qualities as an Army officer. In fact, these two facets of the man's career cannot be separated, for each contributed to, and modified, the other in important ways. A crucial thing to keep in mind about Gates' career is that it was greatly advanced, especially after 1776, by the support of strongly Whiggish congressmen such as Samuel Adams and James Lovell. These men were for political reasons not inclined to be strongly pro-Washington because they viewed him as being too conservative and militaristic; after 1777 the commander in chief reciprocated their distrust, for he became convinced that his position was endangered by their support of Gates. Therefore, in all likelihood he used the events of the so-called Conway Cabal, including his attacks on Gates, more as a political device to secure his own position than to destroy any real attempt by his critics to have him removed from command of the Army. That he succeeded can be seen in the fact that after 1778 the power of the radical Whigs in Congress was so reduced that the legislature became more supportive of a Regular Army and that Gates' reputation was afterward stained with the unmerited charge of being an enemy of Washington.

Even if his controversy with the commander in chief had not colored men's assessments of Gates' military career, he would be regarded as only a modestly talented man whose greatest martial gift lay in his ability to organize and administer large military forces. As adjutant general at Boston, as commander of the much weakened patriots at Ticonderoga and Crown Point in 1776, as reinvigorator of Schuyler's shaken men on the upper Hudson a year later, and as rebuilder of the shattered American force in the South after Camden, he showed uncommon talents as a restorer of morale and a builder of armies. Against Burgoyne, Gates displayed no flashes of brilliance, but he did show common sense in taking a strongly defensive position on his antagonist's route of march and forcing the British Army to fight on his own terms. He realized that time was on the Americans' side; that Morgan's riflemen could be better used in a static, defensive position; that Burgoyne was an impetuous gambler who "might risque all upon one Throw''; and, finally, that the course of the war to that time confirmed that patriot troops performed better in battle when behind defensive fortifications. All the foregoing, plus Gates' own caution, led him to perform against Burgoyne in such a way as to deserve credit for the American victory.

At Camden, Gates was neither as shrewd nor as lucky as he had been three years earlier. He planned to employ the same strategy against Cornwallis as had worked against Burgoyne: to march his army into a strong, defensive position near the British and force them to attack at disadvantage. However, in attempting this maneuver, he made a series of mistakes that assured his defeat—especially since his latest antagonist refused to follow the script. Marching an underequipped and underfed army too hastily toward the enemy, Gates exhausted his men and left behind in North Carolina a much needed cavalry force that had been weakened at Charleston and was rebuilding. Dividing his forces on the eve of battle by sending a reinforcement of four hundred troops to Thomas Sumter, he set out towards the British with the remainder of his army on a *night march* without adequate cavalry for scouting. Relying too heavily on raw militiamen in the battle itself, he disposed them against regulars and then, remarkably, ordered them to charge into British bayonets—practically a guaranteed formula for disaster. Forced to leave the field of battle while his Continenals under de Kalb were engaged with the enemy, he threw himself open to sarcastic denunciations by his calumniators and did irreparable harm to his reputation.

After Camden, however, Gates' critics would have derided his military talents in any case, for they had eagerly awaited such an opportunity. As Rush declared, ''His defeat... gave more pleasure than pain to thousands.'' Thus, they took advantage of the general's discomfiture to ''prove'' that he was not responsible for Burgoyne's defeat (the credit was given largely to Arnold), and his reputation was fixed for a century and a half. Yet, the historical record indicates that for all his faults and missteps, Gates still deserves laurels for his administrative talents and his victory at Saratoga.

BIBLIOGRAPHY

Billias, George A. ''Horatio Gates: Professional Soldier.'' In *George Washington's Generals*. Edited by George A. Billias. New York: William Morrow, 1964.

Knollenberg, Bernhard. *Washington and the Revolution, a Reappraisal: Gates, Conway, and the Continental Congress*. New York: Macmillan Company, 1940.

Nelson, Paul David.*General Horatio Gates: A Biography*. Baton Rouge: Louisiana State University Press, 1976.

Patterson, Samuel White. *Horatio Gates: Defender of American Liberties*. New York: Columbia University Press, 1941.

Shipton, Clifford K., ed. *Sibley's Harvard Graduates*. Vol. 12, Boston: Massachusetts Historical Society, 1962.

PAUL D. NELSON

GAVIN, James Maurice (b. New York City, N.Y., March 22, 1907). Army officer, airborne commander, military strategist and tactician.

James Maurice Gavin entered the Army at the age of seventeen in 1924 as a private and retired at the age of fifty-one in 1958 as a lieutenant general. His rise in the Army was meteoric, and his retirement deliberately premature. Along the way he acquired the reputation of being one of the military's finest, boldest, and most independent analytical minds.

Gavin, orphaned at age two and unable to find a challenging job after being raised in the coal mining town of Mount Carmel, Pennsylvania, did not let modest beginnings deter his rise to the top of his chosen profession. From private in April of 1924 he rose to private first class and then corporal before entering the U.S. Military Academy at West Point in July 1925. Upon graduation in 1929, he was commissioned a second lieutenant of Infantry. It would be five years before he made first lieutenant and five more years before he made captain, but the World War II years saw him rapidly advance. He was promoted to major in October 1941, lieutenant colonel in February 1942, and colonel in September 1942. He received his brigadier general's star in September 1943 and in October 1944 made major general. In March 1955 he was promoted to lieutenant general, the rank with which he retired in 1958.

In his first dozen years of commissioned service, Gavin served in the usual variety of posts for a young infantry officer at home and abroad. After three months duty as a flying student at Brooks Field, Texas, he had tours successively with the 25th Infantry at Camp Harry S. Jones, Arizona; the Infantry School at Fort Benning, Georgia; the 38th and 29th Infantries at Fort Sill, Oklahoma; the 57th Infantry (Philippine Scouts) at Fort William McKinley, Philippine Islands; and the 7th Infantry at Vancouver Barracks, Washington. In August 1940 he became an instructor in the Department of Tactics at the U.S. Military Academy.

After one year at the Academy, Gavin made the decision that would set him on the road to fame—he became a paratrooper. The Army was experimenting with a Parachute School at Fort Benning, and Gavin saw the possibilities of airborne warfare. In August 1941 he obtained a transfer to the Provisional Parachute Group at Benning and, upon graduation from the training school, was assigned to the 503d Parachute Battalion. In December he was named plans and training officer of the group. From February to April 1942 he attended the Command and General Staff School at Fort Leavenworth, and, upon graduation, returned to duty with airborne troops at Fort Bragg, North Carolina. In July 1942 he assumed command of the 505th Parachute Infantry Regiment which in January 1943 was assigned to the 82d Airborne Division. Gavin and the 82d would be together for almost the entire remainder of World War II.

Gavin would go with the 82d from Sicily to Salerno to Normandy to Nijemegen, Holland, to the Ardennes to the Elbe and, finally to Berlin. Gavin led the 505th Parachute Combat Team in a night drop into Sicily on July 9, 1943, that spearheaded that invasion. He commanded the regiment in a parachute landing on Salerno Bay, Italy, on September 14 to reinforce the American beachhead. In October Gavin became assistant division commander of the 82d. From November 1943 until February 1944 he served as airborne advisor to the supreme commander in London before returning to the division to prepare for the Normandy invasion. In that invasion on the night of June 5–6, 1944, he commanded the parachute assault section of the division. Upon the return of the 82d to England, Gavin on August 15 assumed command of the division. He commanded the division in the airborne operations in the vicinity of Nijmegen, Holland, in September 1944, as part of the ill-fated MARKET-GARDEN, a combined airborne and ground offensive that was designed to get across the Rhine and clear the way to victory over Germany by the end of 1944. The 82d then fought alongside regular infantry troops during the Battle of the Bulge, the German offensive in the Ardennes in December. The division next fought through central Germany until the surrender of the German Army in May 1945. In July the 82d took up station in Berlin, and Gavin assumed the additional duty of American representative on the City Kommandantura. In December he and the division returned to Fort Bragg, North Carolina.

In March 1948 Gavin left his airborne command for tours of duty in the United States and abroad in various high-level command and staff positions. He was chief of staff of the Fifth Army at Chicago until April 1949, when he became the Army member of the Weapons Systems Evaluation Group in the Office of the Secretary of Defense in Washington, D.C. In June 1951 he became chief of staff of allied forces in Southern Europe and, in December 1952 commanding general of the U.S. VII Corps in Germany. In March 1953 he returned to Washington, D.C., to serve as G–3, Department of the Army. In March 1955 he became deputy chief of staff for plans and research and in October chief of research and development. While serving in Washington, Gavin found himself directly opposed to the ''new look'' in defense policy whereby the administration of President Dwight David Eisenhower* stressed strategic nuclear retaliatory power at the expense of conventional weapons. Rather than provide lip-service to a policy with which he disagreed, Gavin retired in 1958 in order to tell ''the American people directly what I thought was wrong with the U.S. Defense picture.'' A few months later Gavin published *War and Peace in the Space Age*. In the book, he outlined his ideas on the need of a flexible response to world crises, a response that should include the means to fight a limited war.

Gavin proved to be a prolific writer on military affairs. In 1947 he had published *Airborne Warfare*, which for some time was a standard text for paratroopers. Among his other books are *Crisis Now*, a 1968 study of the Vietnam problem, and *On to Berlin*, a 1978 account of his experiences with airborne troops during World War II.

In addition to writing and speaking on matters of national security, Gavin interrupted his highly successful business career to serve as ambassador to France for eighteen months during the administration of President John F. Kennedy. He left his position as chairman of the board of Arthur D. Little, Inc., in 1977, to become a consultant to that firm. He currently resides in Cambridge, Massachusetts.

As with the 82d itself, Gavin won combat decorations with good cause for his airborne leadership both in theory and practice. He was a pioneer in developing airborne operations, especially in the use of small unit attack groups, and remained the airborne's champion in the larger strategic arena. In combat, he led brilliantly and courageously, receiving the Distinguished Service Cross for his actions under fire in Sicily and a Bronze Oak Leaf Cluster to the Distinguished Service Cross for his actions in Normandy. Even though MARKET-GARDEN failed, Gavin's unit did well, despite the fact that their operations, as all others, did not go as planned. Indeed, after the 82d's efforts at Nijmegen, Lieutenant General Miles C. Dempsey, the commander of the British Second Army ground forces in the operation, told Gavin: "I'm proud to meet the commanding general of the greatest division in the world today." Throughout Gavin's combat leadership of airborne troops, he implemented his belief that successful airborne combat required boldness, courage, and speed of movement—in short, the emulation of cavalry troops. Gavin was known for his calmness under fire. Perhaps one veteran put it best: "He could jump higher, shout louder, spit farther and fight harder than any man I ever saw."

Gavin's leadership and courage were also sorely tested in peace. He believed that the Army had to be able to fight limited wars, especially by using a highly mobile airborne cavalry force. Gavin saw many of his proposals for developing the capacity to fight limited wars accepted and developed by the Army during the administrations of Presidents Kennedy and Lyndon B. Johnson. The fact that the war in Vietnam went badly for the United States does not mean that the strategy of flexible response was proved inadequate. Rather, the American failure in Vietnam stemmed from a misunderstanding of the civil dimensions of that conflict and from various specific decisions along the way.

What emerges, then, is a soldier of courage and imagination who in the end left his beloved army to serve his country in a way he thought he must—by speaking to the national security issues of his time.

BIBLIOGRAPHY

Buchanan, Albert Russell. *The United States and World War II*. 2 vols. New York: Harper and Row, 1964.

Gavin, James M. *On to Berlin: Battles of an Airborne Commander, 1943–1946*. New York: Viking Press, 1978.

———. *War and Peace in the Space Age*. New York: Harper and Row, 1958.

———, and Hadley, Arthur T. *Crisis Now*. New York: Random House, 1968.

Marshall, S.L.A. *Night Drop*. Boston: Little, Brown and Company, 1962.

Ridgway, Matthew B. *Soldier*. New York: Harper, 1956.

Ryan, Cornelius. *A Bridge Too Far*. New York: Simon and Schuster, 1974.

                                                              JOSEPH P. HOBBS

GEIGER, Roy Stanley (b. Middleburg, Fla., January 25, 1885; d. Bethesda, Md., January 23, 1947), Marine Corps officer. Geiger was a pioneer Marine aviator and commanded troops in amphibious operations during World War II.

Born to the large family of a county school superintendent, Roy Geiger developed into a strapping young man. He made enough money for tuition at Florida State Normal School at Deland and in 1904 enrolled as a law student in the John B. Stetson University, earning the bachelor of laws in 1907. Geiger passed the bar examination but practiced law only briefly. He enlisted in the Marine Corps in November 1907.

Geiger served for more than a year as an enlisted man before he was commissioned a second lieutenant in 1909. Following two years of shipboard assignments, he was sent to Nicaragua as a part of the constabulary force. Promoted to first lieutenant (1915), he opted for pilot training the next year. He completed the aviator's course at the Navy Flying School in Pensacola, Florida, and pinned on wings soon after he was promoted to captain.

The United States entered World War I in April 1917. Preparing to go to Europe, Captain Geiger trained an aviation detachment at Coconut Grove Naval Air Station near Miami, Florida. In July 1918 the provisional 1st Marine Aviation Force, under the command of Major Alfred Cunningham, deployed to France, where British pilots and mechanics trained them in the use of Britain's DH–4 two-seater bomber. Cunningham's Marines operated four DH-4 squadrons, one of them commanded by Geiger. During October and November the Marines flew fourteen major missions and dropped twenty-seven thousand pounds of bombs on German targets.

In 1920 Geiger was promoted to major, and during the next two decades he gained valuable experience and education. He flew planes in Haiti (1919–1921) and led the 1st Aviation Group of the 3d Marine Brigade at Quantico, Virginia (1921–1924). Geiger distinguished himself at the U.S. Army Command and General Staff School at Fort Leavenworth, Kansas (1924–1925). After commanding the air station at Quantico, he attended the Army War College in Washington, D.C. (1928–1929). He returned to Quantico as commander of Aircraft Squadrons, East Coast Expeditionary Force. In November 1931 Geiger became director of Marine Corps Aviation in Washington. He was promoted to lieutenant colonel in 1934 and held the directorship until May 1935. For the next four years he was stationed at Quantico and had charge of Marine Air Group One, 1st Marine Brigade of the Fleet Marine Force.

In 1939 Geiger began studying at the Naval War College and by March 1941 had finished the requirements of the senior and advanced courses. He was promoted to colonel (1936) and brigadier general (1941). Late in 1941 he returned to Quantico to lead the 1st Marine Aircraft Wing, Fleet Marine Force.

During World War II Geiger held a number of important commands. In September 1942 he took his pilots to Henderson Field on Guadalcanal in the Solomon Islands. Geiger's airmen helped the Navy to beat back the Japanese, making significant contributions to the first Allied victory in the Pacific. From May to October 1943 Geiger again served as director of Marine Corps Aviation in Washington, D.C., but returned to the Pacific to take part in the campaign on Bougainville. Subsequently, Geiger directed the III Amphibious Corps through several campaigns. The first of these returned Guam to American control (July–August 1944). Second, he participated in the controversial invasion of Peleliu (September–October 1944). Geiger's field service climaxed in the battle for Okinawa (April–June 1945), where he temporarily commanded the Tenth Army. This was the first time a field army had come under the command of a Marine general or an aviation officer.

With the war all but over, Geiger was posted to Pearl Harbor as lieutenant general and commander of the Fleet Marine Force, Pacific. In 1946 he observed the American atomic test on Bikini Island and made recommendations on the organization of the postwar Marine Corps. He had been suffering for some time with problems in his circulatory system and died in 1947.

By 1942 Roy Geiger had built a reputation as a top-flight pilot who believed that Marine infantrymen would benefit directly from the close support of Marine aviation. Geiger set down on Guadalcanal (codenamed ''Cactus'') about a month after the initial American landings. Geiger's amalgam of Marines, Army aviators, and ship-less Navy carrier pilots was dubbed the ''Cactus Air Force.'' Japanese pressure against Guadalcanal mounted steadily. In October, during the showdown in the air over ''Cactus,'' shortages of spare parts, fuel, ammunition, and bombs were normal at Henderson Field. Geiger's pilots flew in any available aircraft—fighters, torpedo-bombers, and dive bombers, once using the general's PBY Catalina Flying Boat on a bombing run. At the height of the fighting, Geiger commanded more than one thousand men, including pilots, mechanics, and support personnel. Geiger sent his men against enemy aircraft as well as troop transports and warships. Furthermore, Cactus pilots hit the Japanese on the ground, assisting the 1st Marine Division (under Major General Alexander Archer Vandegrift*) and various U.S. Army units. Geiger's losses were heavy; on some days less than twenty planes were fit to fly. Geiger lost more than one hundred planes and pilots. Two hundred airmen were wounded. But the Cactus Air Force shot down four hundred Japanese aircraft, sank ten ships, and damaged several others. Geiger and his men were instrumental in capturing Guadalcanal from the Japanese.

Subsequently, the American strategy was to ''island-hop'' toward Japan, taking some islands for the use of airfields and ports, but bypassing and isolating others. This approach used plans developed in part by Major Earl H. Ellis* during the 1920s. On Bougainville, Geiger served for a month as deputy commander of the I Marine Amphibious Corps under General Vandegrift. He took command of ''IMAC'' in November, 1943 (when Vandegrift was made commandant of the Marine Corps) and gained valuable experience in conducting jungle warfare. Geiger changed the direction of his career from aviation to ground combat.

Under the direction of Lieutenant General Holland McTyeire Smith,* Geiger participated in the campaign for the Marianas Islands and was the senior commander ashore on Guam. Prior to that assault, however, the fight for Saipan provided lessons for Geiger. There had not been enough accurate pre-invasion naval gunfire against Saipan. In twenty-nine days of fighting on Saipan, the Americans lost more than three thousand killed and over thirteen thousand wounded. After fourteen days of naval shelling delivered by ships under Admiral Richard L. "Close-in" Conolly and bombing by naval and Marine air units, Geiger's III Amphibious Corps landed on Guam. The pre-invasion preparations against Guam served as a model of such bombardments. In twenty-one days of fierce combat Geiger's forces suffered fourteen hundred killed and more than five thousand wounded, about half the casualties Americans sustained on Saipan. The entire Guam operation serves as one of the best examples of cooperation among the Navy, Marines, and the Army during World War II.

The assault on Peleliu (in the Palau Islands) had been planned as a stepping stone to the recapture of the Philippines, aiming toward a landing on Mindinao. By September 1944, however, the Japanese had sustained severe losses; the Americans boldly decided instead to strike directly to Leyte. The American high command, including General Douglas MacArthur,* Admiral Chester William Nimitz,* and the Joint Chiefs of Staff, approved the change of plans, but after some discussion, the assault on Peleliu proceeded, though the need for it had been reduced by changing the main line of approach on the Philippines. The fighting in the Palaus was overshadowed by the spectacular successes around Leyte.

Geiger's principal subordinate, Marine Major General William Rupertus, predicted that Peleliu would be taken in four days. After a week of fighting with no immediate end in sight, Rupertus declined Geiger's suggestion to bring in a regiment of the Army's 81st Infantry Division to reinforce the 1st Marine Division. Evidently, Rupertus wanted Peleliu to be an all-Marine campaign. The fighting was bitter, especially against the fortified caves and bunkers of Peleliu's Umurbrogol Ridge. The 1st Marine Regiment (under Colonel Lewis Burwell Puller*) suffered 50 percent casualties and was replaced on Geiger's order and over Rupertus' objections. Eventually, the island was secured but at great cost (more than nine thousand American casualties) and after two months of combat.

Taking Peleliu remains a controversial step in the Pacific War. Admiral William Frederick Halsey, Jr.,* believed that the invasion was unnecessary because of the move toward Leyte. Admiral Jesse Barrett Oldendorf,* whose ships inflicted little damage on Japanese emplacements, thought that the assault on Peleliu should not have been made. Furthermore, Geiger and Rupertus did not see eye to eye on use of the 81st Infantry. Geiger should have committed Army regiments to battle earlier, despite Rupertus' ill-conceived opposition. Nevertheless, as the authors of the official Marine Corps history point out, the capture of the Palaus did yield some positive points. American bombers flew from Angaur and inflicted damage on Japanese positions on Luzon. Holding the Palaus reduced the number of air and submarine bases from which the Japanese could interdict America's supply line. Finally, Ulithi Atoll became a major American base for the invasion of Okinawa.

Okinawa lies only four hundred miles from Japan, and the Americans intended to use it as a base for several airfields. To take Okinawa the Allies delivered the heaviest pre-invasion barrage of the island war, under the supervision of Admiral Richmond Kelly Turner.* Command of the invasion force was unusual in that it was to be led by an Army officer, Lieutenant General Simon B. Buckner, rather than a Marine.

The invasion of Okinawa commenced on April 1, 1945. After two weeks the Marines and soldiers had made little gains in yard-by-yard advances against the stout Japanese defenses. Japanese kamikazes pounded the U.S. Navy, inflicting fearful losses in men and ships. Despite sound advice from Geiger and other Marines (including Vandegrift), Buckner rejected a plan to make an amphibious landing to flank the Japanese. Instead, the infantrymen slugged slowly in a grinding campaign that resulted in the highest casualties of an American amphibious battle. The Tenth Army sustained more than sixty-five thousand casualties of all types (killed, wounded, missing, accident, disease); almost ten thousand sailors were killed and wounded; the Japanese sunk thirty-six American ships and shot down 763 U.S. airplanes (April–June 1945).

Okinawa was the culmination of all that the Marine Corps had trained and fought for. Without attempting a flanking amphibious assault, there appeared to be no choice other than a campaign of attrition. Naval officers and Marines criticized Buckner for his handling of the Okinawa fighting. Repercussions of his refusal to order a second amphibious assault reached all the way to Admiral Nimitz, who squelched the criticism temporarily by supporting Buckner's tactical choice. The Marines' criticism of Buckner added to the enmity between the Army and the Marine Corps after the war, and casts doubt on conclusions that the Okinawa Campaign was any model of interservice harmony.

On June 18, 1945, Buckner was killed by Japanese artillery fire. Geiger succeeded to the command of the Tenth Army for five days, until relieved by Lieutenant General Joseph Warren Stilwell.* Although officially Geiger was the only Marine general to command a field army, previously Holland Smith had charge of a force comprising about six divisions in the Marianas Campaign. Unofficially, American procedures limited Marines to corps commands in the field.

Geiger served as a Marine for nearly forty years. During that time he saw the Corps grow from a colonial constabulary to a mighty amphibious strike force. He participated in several significant Pacific campaigns, bringing a pilot's keen eye to amphibious operations.

BIBLIOGRAPHY

Heinl, Robert D. *Soldiers of the Sea: The U.S. Marine Corps, 1775–1962*. Annapolis, Md.: Naval Institute Press, 1962.

Millett, Allan R. *Semper Fidelis: The History of the United States Marine Corps*. New York: Macmillan Company, 1980.

Shaw, Henry I., et al. *History of U.S. Marine Corps Operations in World War II*. 5 vols. Washington, D.C.: U.S. Government Printing Office, 1958–1971.

Sherrod, Robert. *History of Marine Corps Aviation in World War II*. Washington, D.C.: Combat Forces Press, 1952.

Willock, Roger, *Unaccustomed to Fear: A Biography of General Roy S. Geiger, USMC*. Princeton, N.J.: Privately printed, 1968.

JOSEPH G. DAWSON III

GERONIMO (b. near headwaters of the Gila River [near Clifton], Ariz., 1829?; d. Fort Sill, Okla., February 17, 1909), Chiricahua Apache Indian Leader.

Geronimo (Goyakla, or "one who yawns") married several times during his life, but Mexicans killed his first wife, his mother, and his children near Janos, Chihuahua, Mexico, in 1858. Thereafter he vowed to obtain revenge. He fought alongside Cochise in 1861 and probably participated with him in 1862 in the ambush of General James H. Carleton's California troops at Apache Pass, Arizona. Geronimo continued raiding both sides of the U.S.–Mexican border until the 1870s.

In response to the Apache defense in the Southwest, the U.S. Army dispatched General George Crook* to Arizona in 1871. He launched a campaign against the Apaches in 1872, and soon Cochise and Geronimo ceased raiding. The tribes were allowed to live near their native areas in Arizona and New Mexico, and relations improved between the Indians and whites. However, in 1875 the federal government embarked on its concentration program, thereby inaugurating eleven more years of warfare. Partially as a result of this policy, Geronimo became a Patriot renegade. While government officials justified the new policy on the basis of economy, Crook and others familiar with local conditions advised the government not to implement the plan. Crook was then transferred in March 1875 to the Northern Plains.

In June 1876 government officials called for Geronimo and his band to move to San Carlos, Arizona, but he refused and led his band off the reservation. Later that same year Geronimo met with Indian Agent John Clum, who with his Indian Police Force tricked Geronimo and arrested him and his band. This was the only time he was ever captured. Geronimo and his followers arrived at San Carlos in May 1877 and remained there until April 1878 when the wily leader and his followers left the reservation. They fled into the Guadalupe Mountains near the present Arizona–New Mexico border. Geronimo made his headquarters there until December 1879 when he returned to the San Carlos reservation. By then his band was starving, and all members were exhausted from the constant pursuit of the Army. Geronimo remained on the reservation until soldiers appeared there in 1881. Frightened that the soldiers were going to punish him for raids committed by other Apaches, Geronimo again led his followers off the reservation and into the Sierra Madre Mountains of Mexico.

Until 1883 the Apaches raided in Sonora, Chihuahua, and other border regions. However, by that year General Crook had been reassigned to Arizona. Determined to locate Geronimo, he enlisted Apache scouts to assist in this task. In May 1883 Crook crossed into Mexico, where he met Geronimo and demanded that the Apaches surrender. Some of the Indians agreed, and this group of 325 Indians arrived at San Carlos in June. Geronimo would not join those who surrendered until February 1884. Once at San Carlos, Geronimo and his band remained until the spring of 1885, when they were moved near Turkey Creek. Fearful of their future and unwilling to remain in this less than satisfactory place, Geronimo and his band fled the reservation again on May 17, 1885, raiding and killing as they headed for Mexico once more.

Finally, on January 8, 1886, Captain Emmett Crawford and his men picked up the hostiles' trail in Mexico. Two days later Crawford caught up with Geronimo, and the two talked about Geronimo's surrender. While awaiting a final answer from the Apaches, Crawford and his men were attacked by Mexican troops. Crawford died in the fight.

Subsequently, Geronimo agreed to talk to General Crook in Cañon de los Embudos. On March 25, 1886, Crook and Geronimo parleyed. Geronimo finally agreed to surrender, and Crook departed believing that he had settled the affair. Unfortunately, itinerent whiskey peddlers had sold the Indians liquor; they had gotten drunk and had begun to have serious doubts about the surrender. During the night of March 28, Geronimo led forty-one of his band, including men, women, and children back toward Mexico. The rest of the Apaches continued to Fort Bowie, Arizona. Crook was unaware of these developments and probably unaware that Geronimo had not trusted him. Meanwhile, Crook cabled General Philip Henry Sheridan* of the surrender, and the terms he had promised. Angrily, Sheridan replied that the president of the United States had ordered only unconditional surrender, and thus the terms were not acceptable. On March 30, 1886, Crook advised Sheridan of the Geronimo outbreak. Sheridan was dissatisfied with Crook's actions, and Crook asked to be relieved of his command.

Brigadier General Nelson Appleton Miles,* who did not have Crook's understanding of Apaches, assumed command on April 12, 1886. Miles enjoyed no success. To divert attention from his failures in the field, Miles forced one hundred Apaches to move from the reservation near Fort Apache to other quarters some distance away from Geronimo's band. During August 1886 various government officials concluded that all of these peaceable Apaches should be sent to Fort Marion, Florida, where they would be held virtually as prisoners of war. Acting on this conclusion, Miles sent Lieutenant Charles B. Gatewood and a white interpreter, along with Apache scouts, to try to find Geronimo. Gatewood and his scouts crossed into Mexico and followed the trail of some of Geronimo's band who had just left the Mexican village of Fronteras after obtaining supplies. This tactic led them to Geronimo, who agreed to talk to Gatewood. Gatewood related that Miles had told him the Indians would be sent first to Fort Marion and then be reunited with their families. Eventually, they would be allowed to come back to the Southwest. On August 24 the Apaches agreed to meet Miles at Skeleton Canyon, where the official surrender would occur. Miles stalled before heading to the rendezvous, for he knew his promises were only tactics used to capture the hostiles.

After surrendering to the Army, Geronimo and his warriors were sent to Fort Pickens, Florida, not to Fort Marion where their families would be quartered. They were not united with their families until April 1887, when the women and children joined the warriors at Fort Pickens. In May 1888 Geronimo and his band were sent to Mount Vernon Barracks, Alabama, near Mobile, where they would remain for more than seven years. Many Indians died in this low and damp environment. In October 1894 Geronimo and his followers finally were sent to Fort Sill, Indian Territory, where they remained as prisoners of war until 1913.

During his stay at Fort Sill, Geronimo passed the time caring for his garden and livestock, selling autographed pictures of himself, and occasionally posing for artists such as E. A. Burbank or talking to historians such as S. M. Barrett. Geronimo even attended several national or regional celebrations, where he was billed as "the hostile savage Apache Chief Geronimo." Some of the appearances he made included the Trans-Mississippi and International Exposition held at Omaha, Nebraska (1898), the Pan-American Exposition at Buffalo, New York (1901), and the Louisiana Purchase Exposition at St. Louis, Missouri (1904). In 1905 Geronimo rode in the inaugural parade of President Theodore Roosevelt* in Washington, D.C. Geronimo died at Fort Sill on February 17, 1909, still a prisoner of war. He had spent the last twenty-seven years of his life in captivity.

Geronimo was a superior guerrilla soldier. He led his men on various raids on both sides of the international border, striking fear into the hearts of both Mexicans and Americans, and then seemingly vanished into the mountains or deserts. Two nations, with well-organized armies, were unable to snare this elusive Apache and his band.

Geronimo's leadership ability is best illustrated by some of the examples of the campaign to capture him. In 1881 he and his band were temporarily on a reservation, when Army soldiers appeared and frightened him into fleeing to Mexico. He led the Army far south into the Sierra Madre Mountains, where he knew well the old Apache haunts. While there he decided to return to San Carlos and force some Apaches of another band to join him. To do so, he split up his men, recrossed the international border, and arrived at the reservation unseen. After abducting the Apaches he wanted, he and his warriors fled toward Mexico. This time the Army was in hot pursuit and remained doggedly on the trail. Soldiers caught up with the Apaches in the mountains and attacked. Geronimo and his men held off six troops of Army cavalrymen, thereby giving their families time to flee deeper into Mexico. The Apaches lost fourteen warriors in the fight, killed some soldiers, and, as historian Angie Debo has written, "conducted their exodus with almost incredible skill and success." Before reaching safety, the weary Apaches had to fight Mexican soldiers at Aliso Creek, where both sides suffered heavy losses. During June and July 1885 U.S. Army patrols chased the Apaches back and forth across the border with no success. Meanwhile, the Apaches killed thirty-eight civilians and captured or ran off 250 head of livestock.

When General Miles assumed command of the region from General Crook, he recognized the difficulty of locating the Apaches. He requested two thousand more men, which would bring his troop strength to five thousand, before he could promise any success. Despite all of Miles' men and supplies, the Army was totally unable to track down or even to catch a glimpse of the Apache raiders. In the end, only the willingness of Apache scouts to track their brethren allowed Lieutenant Gatewood to locate the old leader and convince him to surrender. Significantly, Geronimo would brag later that he was never actually captured in combat, but tricked by the white men who lied to him. Geronimo's lightning tactics of guerrilla warfare were consistently too much for the armies of both Mexico and the United States.

BIBLIOGRAPHY

Betzinez, Jason. *I Fought with Geronimo*. Edited by Wilber S. Nye. Harrisburg, Pa.: Stackpole, 1959.
Debo, Angie. *Geronimo: The Man, His Times, His Place*. Norman: University of Oklahoma Press, 1976.
Thrapp, Dan L. *The Conquest of Apacheria*. Norman: University of Oklahoma Press, 1967.
———. *General Crook and the Sierra Madre Adventure*. Norman: University of Oklahoma Press, 1972.

JOSEPH A. STOUT, JR.

GIBBON, John (b. Holmesburg, Pa., April 20, 1827; d. Baltimore, Md., February 6, 1896), Army officer. Gibbon was one of the Union Army's best small-unit generals in the Civil War.

John Gibbon accompanied his family to Charlotte, North Carolina, from Philadelphia, Pennsylvania, in 1838. His father was the chief assayer at the U.S. Mint in Charlotte. Gibbon was appointed to the U.S. Military Academy at West Point in 1842 from North Carolina. Although an average student in most respects, his lack of a formal education and failure to adjust to West Point's rigid disciplinary standards placed him in academic difficulties. Because of deficiencies in English grammar, he was given the option of leaving or repeating his second year. Gibbon chose to repeat and was graduated in 1847, ranking twentieth in a class of thirty-eight. As a result of the repeated year, he missed combat experience in the Mexican War.

Although his initial posting was to the 3d Artillery, Gibbon transferred to the 4th Artillery in 1847 and received his commission as second lieutenant in the Regular Army. During the early 1850s Gibbon served in Florida, assisting in the removal of Seminole Indians to Oklahoma. During this time he developed a deep sympathy for the Indian, and during his career always dealt fairly with them.

Gibbon was assigned to West Point as instructor of artillery tactics in 1855, and was promoted to captain in 1859. During these years American artillery was highly regarded for both battlefield skill and technical advancement. After he took up his new duties, Gibbon discovered that there was no textbook suitable for classroom use that discussed all the recent changes in ordnance. In order to fill this gap, he turned his class lecture notes into *The Artillerist's Manual* (1859). The book was used at West Point during the Civil War years and for several decades afterward.

In 1859 Gibbon received the command of Battery B, 4th Artillery, and was ordered to Utah Territory. His unit was stationed at Camp Floyd, and later at Fort Crittenden, and was concerned with keeping order in the predominantly Mormon territory. The approaching Civil War caused a good deal of personal trouble for Gibbon. He was from a southern state, and his parents were Democrats and slaveowners. After the lower South seceded, Gibbon was forced to choose between the U.S. Army and his adopted state. An incident during Sunday parade at Fort Crittenden crystallized his resolve to remain with the Union. While officer of the day, he allowed the playing of "Dixie" by the post band. Three officers brought charges of disloyalty and treason against him. Gibbon replied with a vigorous denial and convinced his superiors of his loyalty. His commanding officer, Philip St. George Cooke,* supported Gibbon during the entire affair. Gibbon ultimately chose to fight for the Union, but three of his brothers joined the Confederate Army.

The Fort Crittenden troops returned to the East during the spring of 1861. When Gibbon arrived in Washington, D.C., after the Battle of First Bull Run, he received the position of chief of artillery in the division of Major General Irwin McDowell.* Gibbon revealed conspicuous talents in the areas of training and discipline, and showed that he could understand and manage volunteer soldiers. His promotion to brigadier general of volunteers was confirmed on May 7, 1862, and he left the artillery to become commander of the 1st Brigade, I Corps, Army of the Potomac. The irrepressible western soldiers who made up the four regiments in the brigade initially resented his firm discipline and rule-bound manner, but Gibbon soon gained their respect by his sense of justice, his professionalism, and his insight into the Civil War soldier's nature. By shrewdly deciding to have the soldiers in the brigade wear distinctive black hats, Gibbon helped them to feel unique, and following his thorough training program, the four regiments soon became an outstanding combat formation. His brigade's performance at Second Manassas and during the Antietam Campaign (when it became known as the "Iron Brigade") vindicated Gibbon's efforts. Although he left the brigade in November 1862 for the command of an infantry division, he always associated himself with the Iron Brigade, and its members with him.

Gibbon's Civil War career was characterized by a great deal of combat experience, and solid, if not spectacular, leadership. After leading a division of the I Corps at Fredericksburg (where he was wounded), Gibbon moved to the II Corps, where he served until 1865. His role at Chancellorsville was minor, but at Gettysburg his division played a major role in repulsing Pickett's charge (led by George Edward Pickett*) on the third day. At the climax of the charge,

Gibbon was badly wounded but returned to his division in time to command it during the 1864 campaign against Richmond led by Ulysses Simpson Grant.*

The years 1864–1865 brought Gibbon professional and personal disappointment. He was unable to obtain a corps command, despite promotion to major general of volunteers, and he found himself becoming disenchanted with the bloody fighting and increasingly radical tone of the war. Moreover, his close relationship with his corps commander, Major General Winfield Scott Hancock,* deteriorated rapidly. During the Petersburg Campaign, Gibbon almost resigned his commission and was considering a civilian career. However, his hope of a permanent corps command was fulfilled in 1865, when he received a posting to the XXIV Corps, Army of the James. In March and April this formation played a major role in forcing the lines of the Petersburg defenses, and pursued General Robert Edward Lee* to Appomattox Court House. At the surrender of the Army of Northern Virginia, Gibbon acted as one of the three Union surrender commissioners.

After the Civil War, except for a short period of service in the East, Gibbon served in the Far West until his retirement. In 1866 he was made colonel in the Regular Army and was given command of the 36th Infantry Regiment. After a brief period of service guarding the construction line of the Union Pacific Railroad, the regiment was disbanded, and Gibbon was transferred to the 7th Infantry in Montana. Brigadier General Alfred Terry* chose him to lead the infantry during the campaign against the Sioux in 1876, and it was Gibbon's column that discovered the survivors of the 7th Cavalry after the defeat of George Armstrong Custer* at the Little Big Horn. The following year Gibbon led a small force of his regiment in an effort to block the retreat of Chief Joseph* and the Nez Perce over the Bitterroot Mountains and into Montana. His understrength command attacked the Nez Perce camp at Big Hole, Montana. The quick reaction of the Nez Perce and the regiment's lack of firepower led to an Indian victory. The Nez Perce were able to hold off Gibbon while making a retreat. During the battle, Gibbon was wounded for the third time in his military career. General Nelson Appleton Miles* eventually forced the Nez Perce to surrender.

Promoted to brigadier general in the Regular Army, Gibbon assumed command of the Department of the Columbia in 1885. He played a major, although deliberately understated, role in quelling the anti-Chinese riots in Seattle in 1886. Although Gibbon put Seattle under martial law, he was uneasy about using soldiers in a police role and superseding civilian authority. He kept his interference to a minimum and managed to ensure a safe departure of the Chinese and the swift restoration of civilian governance. He retired in 1891 after having served as commander of the Department of the Pacific for five years. He lived in Baltimore until his death on February 6, 1896.

Gibbon participated in two of the most important Indian campaigns in the post-Civil War era. He was a good example of an infantry commander fighting against an elusive, mounted foe. Although he did not serve in the South during

Reconstruction as did Philip Henry Sheridan,* Edward Richard Sprigg Canby,* and John McAllister Schofield,* Gibbon had to declare martial law in Seattle, an example of the noncombat duties that the Army was called upon to perform in the nineteenth century.

John Gibbon was regarded by his contemporaries as a capable infantry commander and an excellent trainer and disciplinarian. Despite a tendency to become involved in bureaucratic and personality disputes, he held the loyalty of his subordinates and the esteem of many of his superiors. His reputation rests largely on his Civil War performance, especially his creation of the Iron Brigade and his outstanding defense at Gettysburg. As leader commander of the Iron Brigade, Gibbon became one of the Union Army's best small-unit generals. Throughout the war, he was acknowledged as one of the handful of West Pointers who had excellent insight into the nature of the American volunteer soldier.

BIBLIOGRAPHY

Beal, Merrill D. *"I Will Fight No More Forever": Chief Joseph and the Nez Perce War.* Seattle: University of Washington Press, 1963.

Catton, Bruce. *Mr. Lincoln's Army.* Garden City, N.Y.: Doubleday and Company, 1951.

Gray, John S. *Centennial Campaign: The Sioux War of 1876.* Fort Collins, Colo.: Old Army Press, 1976.

Lavery, Dennis S. "John Gibbon and the Old Army: Portrait of An American Professional Soldier." Unpublished Ph.D. dissertation, Pennsylvania State University, 1974.

Tucker, Glenn. *High Tide at Gettysburg.* Indianapolis: Bobbs–Merrill, 1958.

Utley, Robert M. *Frontier Regulars: The United States Army and the Indian, 1866–1891.* New York: Macmillan Company, 1973.

DENNIS S. LAVERY

GOETHALS, George Washington (b. Brooklyn, N.Y., June 29, 1858; d. New York City, N.Y., January 21, 1928), Army officer, engineer, administrator. Goethals gained worldwide fame as builder of the Panama Canal.

George W. Goethals was of Dutch ancestry; his name translates from the original as "stiff-necked." He attended Brooklyn public schools and the College of the City of New York before winning an appointment to West Point. Christened George "William," Goethals neglected to write out his middle name when registering at West Point. A presumptuous registrar recorded the "W" as "Washington" and refused to change it when Goethals attempted to set the record straight. He was president of his class each year and graduated second, without a single demerit, in a class of fifty-two in 1880.

His career in the Engineer Corps (1882–1905) was impressive and covered all grades from second lieutenant to colonel. Among his most impressive details were: duty in the Northwest (1882–1884); improvements on the Ohio (1884–1885) and Tennessee rivers (1889–1894); assistant to the chief engineer of the U.S. Army (1894–1898); and instructor in civil and military engineering at West

Point (1885–1889; 1898–1900). In 1903 he was chosen to serve on the new General Staff as a specialist in coastal defenses.

On February 18, 1907, Goethals, then a lieutenant colonel, was retired from the General Staff in order to serve at the Panama Canal as the third of its chief engineers, replacing John F. Stevens. President Theodore Roosevelt,* recognizing the need for a permanent policy and an aggressive executive, appointed Goethals chief engineer and chairman of the Isthmian Canal Commission with a veto power. An executive order on January 8, 1908, gave him sole authority and responsibility for the administration of the canal project; the other six commission members were merely figureheads.

Goethals used his considerable administrative talents to solve the monumental complexities facing him in the areas of engineering, labor, housing and sanitation, supply and accounting, and law enforcement. The engineering problems were herculean, but by study and diligence Goethals and his staff solved the complicated problems of lock construction and slide recurrences. The Canal was not an engineering feat alone. Goethals considered the most difficult part of his work to be what he termed the "human element." At its peak in 1913, the work force topped forty-four thousand men from around the world. Goethals worked diligently to keep morale up and to allay the fears of the workers concerning military rule. He recognized that a healthy and contented work force was a productive one. While he insisted on the fundamental rules of military discipline, he dressed only in civilian clothes. He began a weekly official paper, *The Canal Record*, which kept the men fully informed, recorded their progress, and also built esprit de corps. A complete judicial system was instituted. Yet each Sunday from 8:00 A.M. to 1:00 P.M. Goethals customarily held "Sunday Court"; he listened to worker grievances ranging from job-related questions of wages and hours to alimony matters and marital disputes. His decisions gained him a reputation for fairness. He was always accessible to Canal employees, and to many he became a hero.

Goethals was indefatigable in his efforts to master the most detailed information on all aspects of the Canal work. Riding around in his bright yellow motor car, dubbed "the yellow peril," the chief engineer was seemingly everywhere at once supervising everything. Even so, he was not an autocrat. Goethals believed in delegation of authority. He built a finely honed organization, part civilian and part military, to cope with the questions of engineering, sanitation, and supply. Under the direction of Dr. William Crawford Gorgas,* the Sanitation Department worked successfully to eliminate the sources of yellow fever and malaria infections. One of Goethals' former students, Robert E. Wood, was the chief quartermaster of the Canal and director of the Panama Railroad. He established an efficient, self-sustaining supply system and the housing and feeding of the labor force. The 40.3-mile canal was completed in record time—six months earlier than anticipated—and hailed as an engineering marvel as it opened to world commerce in August 1914. Goethals became a national hero and in recognition of his accomplishments received the thanks of Congress on March 4,

1915, and was promoted two grades, from colonel to major general. He served as the first civil governor of the Canal Zone (1914–1916). At his own request, on November 15, 1916, he was transferred to the Army retired list and at about that time served as chairman of the board appointed to report on the Adamson Eight-Hour Law which threatened to precipitate a great railroad strike.

From April to July 1917 Goethals was general manager and chairman of the Executive Committee of the United States Shipping Board Emergency Fleet Corporation. Promised full authority to build wooden ships, Goethals soon clashed with Shipping Board President William Denman when he attempted to take control of the shipbuilding program and expand it to include steel ships. The dual authority issue could not be resolved, and both men resigned in July 1917. Many argued that this lack of centralized authority paralyzed the American shipbuilding program.

Goethals was recalled to active duty on December 18, 1917, as acting quartermaster general, replacing Henry Granville Sharpe* who had come under attack. Nine days later he was given additional duty as ''director'' of a new agency of the War Department, part of a General Staff reorganization effort, the Storage and Traffic Division. A virtually nationwide industrial and transportation paralysis in the bitter winter of 1917–1918 led to criticism of the supply system and demands for a more coordinated effort. As acting quartermaster general, Goethals was determined to relieve the Quartermaster Corps of its traditionally diverse activities and to make it a large purchasing organization rather than a military operation. Another of his goals was to eliminate excessive dependence on civilian assistance by bringing procurement under military control. Three reorganizations of the Corps, in January, April, and August of 1918, accomplished this goal.

As director of Storage and Traffic, Goethals sought to control the intricate flow of troops within the United States and supplies from the factory to France. Established within the division, Embarkation, Inland Traffic, and Storage departments eliminated much of the confusion and congestion. Recognizing the lack of storage facilities, Goethals supervised the building of additional warehouses along the eastern coast, which by the time of the armistice had increased storage fivefold.

In April 1918 further reorganization of the General Staff led to the creation of the Purchase, Storage, and Traffic Division, with Goethals as director. An Army program, which all adhered to, meant correcting the inefficiencies of the bureau system of supply. The five major bureaus had no uniform organization, practice, or nomenclature. Each fought Goethals' plan to coordinate their procurement, finances, storage, and distribution. Assisted by Brigadier General Hugh Johnson, Robert Thorne, and Gerard Swope, Goethals succeeded in establishing a system of interbureau procurement and standardization of bureau recordkeeping, priority, and requirement schedules. He built liaison with other agencies, such as the War Industries Board, by a parallel committee system. He himself served on the Priorities Committee.

Effective control over supply bureau operations did not come until the August

26 reorganization of the Purchase, Storage, and Traffic Division, suggested by Goethals. Between September and the November Armistice, the bureaus were consolidated along functional lines under the director of Purchase, Storage, and Traffic. Goethals' function was executive, not merely supervisory, making him commanding general in the field of supply. In 1918 he was awarded the Distinguished Service Medal for conspicuous service in reorganizing the Quartermaster Corps. On March 4, 1919, he again retired and returned to the practice of his profession as head of an engineering firm. He died of cancer in 1928 and was buried at West Point.

Goethals' claim to fame justifiably centers around his extraordinary seven years spent in building the Panama Canal. His authority was commensurate with his responsibility. The Canal was both an administrative and engineering feat. Goethals was a military manager, committed to the principles of modern industrial management, guided by rationalist principles of centralized control and decentralized operations. He made authoritarian rule acceptable, effective, and popular, He believed that problems could be solved by knowledge, effective organization, and visionary management.

Less heralded but no less creditable were his activities in supplying and transporting American troops at home and abroad during World War I. Although his achievements as acting quartermaster general and director of Purchase, Storage, and Traffic were neither as dazzling nor as lasting as his Canal work, they deserve recognition. Goethals hoped to handle supply organizations along the same management lines as during his years with the Canal. Through the various reorganizations of 1918, he hoped to produce a single, centralized, vertically integrated supply agency—a model of effective and efficient management. By a chain of command and a sophisticated statistical system, he fought off efforts from within and outside the War Department to fragment the work of supply. His reforms were only a limited success. He never had authority to equal his responsibilities. The reforms followed in rapid succession, and Goethals floundered in an organizational maze he never fully controlled. Resistance to change and innovation was deep-seated in the bureau system. The bureau heads felt that Goethals' supply reorganizations produced inefficiency and gave them responsibility for distribution, yet no control over procurement. By the end of 1918 the bureaus had virtually disappeared, absorbed by the consolidated service of supply. In the 1920s the bureaus regained their independence.

BIBLIOGRAPHY

Beaver, Daniel R. "George W. Goethals and the Problem of Military Supply." *Some Pathways in Twentieth Century History*. Detroit, Mich.: Wayne State University Press, 1969.

Bishop, Joseph B., and Farnham. *Goethals, Genius of the Panama Canal*. New York: Harper and Row Publishers, 1930.

Hewes, James E., Jr. *From Root to McNamara: Army Reorganization and Administration 1900–1963*. Washington, D.C.: Department of the Army, 1975.

McCullough, David. *The Path Between The Seas*. New York: Simon and Schuster, 1977.

Risch, Erna. *Quartermaster Support of the Army: A History of the Corps 1775–1939*. Washington, D.C.: U.S. Government Printing Office, 1962.

PHYLLIS ZIMMERMAN

GORDON, John Brown (b. Upson County, Ga., February 6, 1832; d. Miami, Fla., January 9, 1904), Army officer. Gordon was a brigade and corps commander in the Confederate Army during the Civil War.

John Brown Gordon was descended from Scottish forebears who first migrated to America from Aberdeen in 1724. Gordon entered the University of Georgia (then Franklin College) in January 1851 and distinguished himself academically, demonstrating a particular penchant for oratory. He failed to graduate, however, owing to his withdrawal for personal reasons early in his senior year of study. Gordon then studied law privately, secured admission to the Georgia bar, and began practicing in Atlanta. In September 1854 he married Fanny Rebecca Haralson, thus beginning a married life that spanned nearly fifty years. Gordon and his family returned to his father's home in the extreme northwest corner of Georgia, where, in the years prior to the Civil War, Gordon engaged in developing coal mines.

Soon after the Confederates fired on Fort Sumter and President Abraham Lincoln* called for seventy-five thousand volunteers, Gordon was elected captain of a Southern company of volunteers that he helped raise from the mountainous tristate region of Georgia, Alabama, and Tennessee. The state of Alabama accepted these self-styled "Raccoon Roughs" and assigned them as one of the twelve companies of the 6th Alabama regiment. Despite his lack of military training and combat experience, Gordon rose to the colonelcy of the 6th Alabama in April 1862. In his first actual clash of arms during the Peninsula Campaign, he performed admirably and briefly commanded the brigade when his commanding officer, Robert Rodes, was temporarily disabled. Gordon conspicuously led his regiment at the "Bloody Lane" at Antietam, where he suffered five separate wounds. He was appointed brigadier general in November 1862, but owing to the seriousness of his wounds, he was not confirmed until May 7, 1863. When he rejoined the Army of Northern Virginia, Gordon commanded a Georgia brigade at the battles of Chancellorsville and Gettysburg, receiving high praise for the handling of his troops.

As Gordon was entrusted with increasingly greater command responsibility during the final year of the war, he rose to the demands of each new situation. His conduct in the Wilderness and in the battles around Spotsylvania Court House in the spring of 1864 was brilliant. Gordon's actions at the Mule Shoe salient on May 12 prevented a major Federal breakthrough—one that would have threatened the very existence of Robert Edward Lee's* army—and resulted in the Georgian's promotion to major general two days later. He then led a division under Jubal Early* in the Shenandoah Valley, and upon his return to the trenches around Petersburg in late 1864, Gordon assumed command of the II Corps.

During the last winter of the war, Gordon became a close confidant of Lee. Gordon also planned and led the army's last desperate assault against Fort Stedman in March 1865.

On the retreat from Petersburg, Gordon's troops fought primarily as the rearguard and were still heavily engaged when the final truce was ordered. Gordon was one of the three Confederates assigned the task of drawing up the details of the formal surrender with the three Union generals. In one of the truly dramatic scenes in American military history—the surrender of the Army of Northern Virginia at Appomattox Court House on April 12, 1865—Gordon rode at the head of the Confederate surrender column. Douglas Southall Freeman stated that had the final order of march been arranged to recognize the ones who had fought the hardest and the best during the last year of the war, first place would rightly have gone to Gordon. In his final speech to his men, Gordon eloquently appealed to them to return home in peace, to obey the laws, and to aid in rebuilding and reuniting the country.

After the surrender, Gordon returned to Georgia as one of the South's most beloved generals and, quite naturally, drifted into politics owing to his natural ability and his fame as a military leader. In August 1866 he attended the National Union Convention in Philadelphia in hopes of moderating the Radicals' influence upon Reconstruction. Although he was defeated in a bid to become governor of Georgia, Gordon established himself as one of the mainstays of the Democratic party in the state. His exact involvement with the Ku Klux Klan remains shrouded in uncertainty; nonetheless, it is reasonably certain that he was at least titular head of the Klan in Georgia. With his election to the U.S. Senate in 1873, Gordon established himself as a spokesman not only for Georgia but also for the South as a whole, earnestly pleading for an end to the federally supported Republican governments in the South and a restoration of home rule. In the final act of Reconstruction—the Compromise of 1877—Gordon was prominently involved in the discussions at the Wormley Hotel in Washington, D.C. Gordon resigned from the Senate in 1879 but remained influential in Georgia, joining with U.S. Senator Joseph E. Brown and Governor Alfred H. Colquitt to form Georgia's "Bourbon Triumvirate" which controlled state politics for more than a decade. As spokesmen dedicated to the cause of the commerical and industrial "New South," these three prominent Georgians brought new industries and especially railroads to Georgia. Gordon was elected governor of Georgia in 1886. His reelection in 1888 paved the way for his return to the U.S. Senate in 1890. Upon completion of this full senatorial term, Gordon permanently retired from politics in 1897.

In his final years of life, Gordon continued to devote himself to soothing the wounds of the Civil War. In addition to numerous speaking engagements within the South, Gordon traveled throughout the North dedicating monuments and lecturing, usually delivering his famous speech "The Last Days of The Confederacy." He served as commander in chief of the United Confederate Veterans from its formation in 1890 until his death in 1904.

In spite of his want of formal schooling in the science of war, John Brown Gordon displayed the boldness, vigilance, aggressiveness, and sound military sense necessary for high command on every battlefield upon which he fought. He possessed immense physical and moral courage, presented a martial appearance, and excelled at inspiring his men through both words and deeds. Gordon's rise from captain to corps commander was unmatched in the Army of Northern Virginia. Only five Confederate soldiers rose to corps command without the benefit of previous military instruction, and of these, only Gordon failed to receive his warranted promotion to lieutenant general. Despite this oversight, Gordon exercised the authority of that rank and proved equal to its demands and responsibilities.

More important than Gordon's military contributions during the Civil War were his postwar efforts at national reconciliation. Few, if any, Confederate veterans emerged from the war more respected than the "Gallant Gordon." Though often spoken of as the "Very Embodiment of the Lost Cause," Gordon refused to dwell upon the sectional differences that precipitated the war. Instead, he readily acknowledged defeat, strove to effect reunion as quickly as possible, and came to believe it was best that the Southern quest for independence had been thwarted. Both Southerners and Northerners recognized the Georgian as a legitimate spokesman for the South. Within two weeks of taking his Senate seat, Gordon became the first ex-Confederate to be afforded the honor of presiding over the Senate during the vice-president's absence.

Gordon was also instrumental in helping bring a new economic order to Georgia and the South. Gordon's own speculative adventures were as numerous as they were diverse and allowed him to become one of the South's most prominent railroad promoters. These economic changes were wholly consistent with Gordon's efforts at national pacification, for during the postwar years Gordon preached a new sense of national identity—one supplanting sectional antagonism and replacing it with a common commitment to the growth of a strong and united nation.

BIBLIOGRAPHY

Freeman, Douglas Southall. *Lee's Lieutenant's: A Study in Command*. 3 vols. New York: Charles Scribner's Sons, 1942–1944.
Gordon, John B. *Reminiscences of the Civil War*. New York: Charles Scribner's Sons, 1903.
Tankersley, Allen P. *John B. Gordon: A Study in Gallantry*. Atlanta, Ga.: Whitehall Press, 1955.

RALPH L. ECKERT

GORGAS, Josiah (b. Running Pumps, Pa., July 1, 1818; d. Tuscaloosa, Ala., May 15, 1883), Army officer. Gorgas served as chief of ordnance for the Confederacy during the Civil War.

Gorgas came from an undistinguished family and probably would not have been able to have a higher education if he had not been appointed to the U.S. Military Academy. At West Point, he compiled an excellent record and was graduated sixth in a class of fifty-two in 1841. Gorgas chose the Ordnance Corps as his branch of service and received his first assignment at the Watervliet arsenal near Troy, New York. During the years 1845–1846, Gorgas visited Europe and observed the armies of most of the major powers.

He returned to the United States on the eve of the Mexican War and later served with the artillery siege train of the Army under General Winfield Scott* at the Battle of Vera Cruz. Scott assigned Gorgas as chief of ordnance at the Vera Cruz supply depot. There Gorgas performed well, forwarding supplies to Scott's army and gaining thorough training in logistics under wartime conditions.

Following the Mexican War, Gorgas served at a half dozen arsenals in the United States. In 1853 he married Amelia Gayle, daughter of a prominent Alabama politician, while stationed at Mount Vernon Arsenal near Mobile. During this same assignment, Gorgas repaired and improved Fort Pickens near Pensacola, Florida. Ironically, his operations there later enabled the U.S Army to hold the post when the Civil War broke out.

On March 21, 1861, Gorgas resigned his commission as captain in the U.S. Army, effective April 3. Confederate President Jefferson Davis* offered Gorgas a position in the Confederate service, which he accepted. He became chief of ordnance with the rank of major of artillery on April 8, 1861. Gorgas found that the agrarian South had few arms, little ammunition, and practically no industries to manufacture such munitions. This made it necessary for him to look elsewhere to furnish the Confederate armies with necessary equipment. Battlefield captures would provide some weapons and ammunition, but such captures could not be counted upon until the war was well underway. Gorgas recognized that the Confederacy had to import ordnance supplies from Europe. He chose Caleb Huse as the agent to purchase munitions, and his choice proved to be a great benefit to the young nation's struggle.

The Confederate War Department gave Gorgas complete control over scarce raw materials and first priority in transporting these materials and finished products. This made his job considerably easier than it might have been otherwise. To procure raw materials and to supervise manufacturers, Gorgas chose subordinates who performed their tasks reliably and efficiently under adverse circumstances. George W. Rains supervised powder manufacturing, and Isaac M. St. John headed the Nitre Corps (later the Nitre and Mining Bureau). With raw materials in competent hands, Gorgas turned his attention to domestic armaments production. He overhauled and enlarged existing arsenals and started ordnance shops, laboratories, leather works, and depots at various locations. Some of these facilities were government-owned, while others operated under contracts with private individuals, including Joseph Reid Anderson.* He ordered the conversion of Anderson's Tredegar Iron Works in Richmond and the Etowah Foundry in Georgia into cannon manufacturing firms.

Gorgas organized blockade running operations to bring in supplies which his agents purchased in Europe. He was one of the first officers in the Confederate high command to recognize the importance of blockade running and often had to conduct this business with little cooperation (and sometimes outright interference), from other officials. Until the summer of 1863, Gorgas supervised government blockade runners. Once the business had become efficient, he shifted its direction into the hands of a capable subordinate. By 1863 blockade running and domestic production had provided enough arms and ammunition to supply all of the Confederate armies for coming campaigns. Gorgas offset the tremendous losses in arms, artillery, ammunition, and raw materials which resulted from the reverses of that year by importations through the blockade. It is a tribute to the efficiency of Gorgas' operations that Union Major General Ulysses Simpson Grant* replaced the older weapons of some of his regiments with imported rifles captured at Vicksburg.

As a reward for the excellent job he had done, Gorgas received promotion to the rank of brigadier general on November 10, 1864. He made his way to Danville, Virginia, when the Confederates evacuated Richmond in April 1865. The bureau continued to function until the surrender of the Army under General Joseph Eggleston Johnston* in North Carolina, another tribute to Gorgas' efficiency as an administrator. Gorgas surrendered himself and gave his parole at Washington, South Carolina, on May 14, 1865.

In 1866 Gorgas established the Briarfield Iron Works near Ashby, Alabama, but the business failed. Three years later he accepted a position as director of the Junior Department of the University of the South at Sewanee, Tennessee, and became vice chancellor of the school in 1872. By the time he left the university, in 1878, Gorgas had helped transform it into a first-rate institution. He became president of the University of Alabama in 1878 but resigned in mid-1879 due to ill-health. Gorgas died of a brain tumor at Tuscaloosa.

Gorgas' biographer has argued that he contributed more than any man except Robert Edward Lee* to the successes enjoyed by the Confederacy. Any objective analysis of Gorgas' career will support this contention. Certainly the Confederate armies could not have continued to have weapons and ammunition as long as they did without his efforts.

There was actually very little indication in Gorgas' prewar career that he would demonstrate as much ability as he did. His performance at the Vera Cruz depot during the Mexican War undoubtedly taught him how to conduct ordnance operations under trying circumstances, and he put that experience to good use during the Civil War. Difficult, if not nearly impossible, conditions seemed to bring out the best in Gorgas. This ability to rise above adversity is one of the marks of the high-quality soldier, whether on field duty or in supporting services.

One of the keys to Gorgas' success as the head of a supply bureau was his skill in organizing and administering his command. He chose subordinates who performed their appointed tasks as well as anyone could have expected. Some of these men developed gradually while Gorgas directly supervised their sections.

He assumed all of the responsibilities and worries of high-level administration in his bureau, which freed his subordinates to concentrate on their immediate objectives. They operated so efficiently that Gorgas did not need to interfere in their affairs. Unlike other supply departments, Gorgas' bureau functioned like a well-oiled machine throughout the war. There was thus no need for the War Department's high command to interfere in Gorgas' operations.

Gorgas did not allow himself to become bogged down in trivial details, another key to his success. The reliability of his subordinates made it unnecessary for him to worry about many day-to-day matters. But as bureau chief, Gorgas continually encouraged research and invention by his officers. His command tested artillery fuses and various types of powder and projectiles. It even looked into the possibility of using steam-driven motors to move field artillery.

Gorgas could have done much more to make the Confederacy a success if reverses in the field had not deprived him of needed raw materials, ports, and skilled workmen. As it was, Gorgas established a system of manufactures and importations that permitted the agrarian South to compete on a nearly equal basis with the industrial North.

BIBLIOGRAPHY

Goff, Richard D. *Confederate Supply*. Durham, N.C.: Duke University Press, 1969.
————, ed. *The Civil War Diary of General Josiah Gorgas*. University: University of Alabama Press, 1947.
Vandiver, Frank E. *Ploughshares Into Swords: Josiah Gorgas and Confederate Ordnance*. Austin: University of Texas Press, 1952.

ARTHUR W. BERGERON, JR.

GORGAS, William Crawford (b. Toulminville, Ala., October 3, 1854; d. London, England, July 4, 1920), surgeon general. Gorgas is renowned for his work in eradicating yellow fever.

Born on the Gayle plantation near Mobile, home of his maternal grandfather, John Gayle, a former governor of Alabama, William Crawford Gorgas grew up in the South during its most tumultuous years. He spent his childhood in Richmond, where his father, Josiah Gorgas,* was chief of ordnance of the Confederacy during the Civil War. There Gorgas acquired a love of the military inspired by the constant visits of Confederate war heroes. After the war, he moved briefly with his family to Baltimore, then to Brierfield, Alabama, and in 1869 to Sewanee, Tennessee, where his father was made head of the new Episcopal University of the South.

At first a preparatory student and then an undergraduate, Gorgas received his B.A. degree from the University of the South in 1875. Against the advice of his father, who had a low opinion of military opportunities, he entered Bellevue Medical School in 1876 as a means of becoming an Army officer through the Medical Corps. (He was not able to get an appointment to West Point.) Without relinquishing his love for cannon and shell, he picked up an enthusiasm for medicine at Bellevue, graduating in June 1879.

After interning at Bellevue, Gorgas entered the Army Medical Department in June 1880 and spent the next eighteen years in Southern and Western frontier posts, where he had an opportunity to observe yellow fever. In the early 1880s, he fought an epidemic of the disease at Fort Brown, Texas, and became infected; thereafter he was immune. As the years passed, Gorgas' experiences at Fort Brown aroused his interest in yellow fever, which he continued to study, and he became something of a specialist on the disease. As a result, the surgeon general sent Gorgas wherever a yellow fever epidemic broke out. He spent ten years at Fort Barrancas (Pensacola Bay), an area notorious for epidemics.

When the Spanish-American War started in 1898, Gorgas was made head of the yellow fever hospital at Siboney, Cuba. As increasing numbers of American soldiers contracted the disease, he stepped up his sanitary campaign. Gorgas joined the scientific experiments of Walter Reed* who concluded that the scourge was carried by mosquitoes. Thus convinced, Gorgas vowed that he would rid Havana of the pests. Gorgas kept his vow. As chief sanitary officer at the end of the war, he cleaned up Havana, eliminated mosquitoes and their breeding places, and in three months eradicated yellow fever from the city for the first time in 150 years.

Gorgas' success in Havana led him back to Washington in late 1902, where Congress made him a colonel and sent him as representative of the U.S. Army to the First Egyptian Medical Congress with specific instructions to investigate yellow fever at the Suez Canal in preparation for his assignment to Panama. After his trip to Suez, Gorgas went to the Isthmus of Panama, the "whiteman's grave," returned home, and studied the disease for two years.

In 1904 he was appointed chief sanitary officer in Panama. Despite much opposition and discouragement from senators and Canal commission members, who thought expenditures for sanitary improvement extravagant, Gorgas plunged into his work. Employing the same methods used in Havana, he eliminated the disease from the Isthmus in less than a year and enabled construction of the Canal to take place. President Theodore Roosevelt* visited the Canal in November 1906, and assigned Gorgas to serve on the Isthmithian Commission, with authority to carry out long-term sanitary measures.

Gorgas' reputation as an eminent sanitarian rose at home and abroad. In 1908 Gorgas became president of the American Medical Association. Several universities including Brown, Pennsylvania, Harvard, Johns Hopkins, Alabama, and his alma mater, the University of the South, conferred honorary degrees on him. In 1913 the Transvaal Chamber of Mines invited Gorgas to visit South Africa and give advice on how to control pneumonia among the Negro mineworkers. Gorgas had protected the West Indian Negro laborers in the Canal Zone by eliminating overcrowded barracks and building small cabins where healthy individuals could breathe germ-free air.

In January 1914 he was appointed surgeon general of the U.S. Army with the rank of brigadier general. Continuing his work and interest in yellow fever,

Gorgas went to South America in 1916 under the auspices of the International Health Board, a Rockefeller foundation, to outline plans for the eradication of the disease. However, once World War I started this work stopped. As surgeon general during the Great War, Gorgas accented preventive medicine, directing that the Army be provided with wholesale vaccination antitoxin, and serum against infectious diseases.

After retiring from active duty in 1918, he continued his work with the International Health Board, journeying to South Africa in 1920 to investigate yellow fever. Stopping on the way to pick up honors in Europe, Gorgas suffered a stroke of apoplexy in London, dying one month later, after being knighted by King George V.

Gorgas is best known as an Army doctor and surgeon general who was a conqueror of yellow fever. Fighting disease his whole life enabled him to become a world-renowned authority on yellow fever and the first among all sanitarians. When he became sanitary officer in Havana, the city was one of the dirtiest in the world. Yellow fever, typhus, typhoid, dysentery, and other infectious diseases abounded. Flies, mosquitoes, and filth were everywhere. At first, Gorgas segregated the sick and enforced strict quarantine. Then he divided the city into districts, issued sanitary regulations, and conducted an amazingly efficient cleanup campaign, which reached into homes, offices, backyards, roofs, and cellars. Gorgas' campaign eliminated mosquitoes and their breeding places, and established the methods of eradication of yellow fever that are followed to this day. Using the same careful planning and attention to detail, Gorgas eliminated yellow fever from Panama, controlled pneumonia, and then tackled malaria and typhoid. His efforts made the Isthmus a pleasant place to live and the construction of the Panama Canal possible.

As Gorgas' scientific reputation rose, he accepted invitations from abroad to advise several nations on sanitary and health problems. As head of the International Health Board, he outlined health programs, notably for South America and Africa. He received the accolades of the world's top scientists and the honors of foreign governments. Gorgas was more than a superior Army doctor: he was a medical crusader who did as much as any man in history to make tropical lands healthful.

BIBLIOGRAPHY

Ashburn, P.M. *A History of the Medical Department of the United States Army*. Boston: Houghton Mifflin Company; Cambridge, Mass.: Riverside Press, 1929.
Dolan, Edward F., Jr., and H. T. Silver. *William Crawford Gorgas: Warrior in White*. New York: Dodd, Mead and Company, 1968.
Gibson, John M. *Physician to the World: The Life of General William C. Gorgas*. Durham, N.C.: Duke University Press, 1950.

Gorgas, Marie D., and Burton J. Hendrick. *William Crawford Gorgas: His Life and Work*. Garden City, N.Y.: Doubleday, Page and Company, 1924.

Wilson, Charles M. *Ambassadors in White. The Story of American Tropical Medicine*. New York: Henry Holt and Company, 1942.

MARY E. CONDON

GRANT, Ulysses Simpson (b. Point Pleasant, Ohio, April 27, 1822; d. Mount McGregor, N.Y., July 23, 1885), Army officer. Grant is considered a "Great Captain" by military historians.

Grant was the first of six children born to Jesse Root and Hannah Simpson Grant. His father was a tanner, a Whig in politics, a Methodist, and Mason. The Grants christened their first-born Hiram Ulysses, but the name was subsequently reversed. Grant was educated in local schools and helped in the family tannery, farmed, and hauled wood.

In the winter of 1838–1839, Jesse Grant secured an appointment to the U.S. Military Academy for his son. Entertaining no plans for a career in the military, Grant reluctantly entered the class of 1843. Because of an error by the appointing congressman, he was registered as Ulysses Simpson Grant, and he had to retain the name. At West Point, he failed to distinguish himself academically and collected his share of demerits. He was graduated twenty-first in a class of thirty-nine, which included thirteen other future Civil War generals, ten who fought for the North and three the South.

Grant was ordered to Jefferson Barracks, Missouri, near St. Louis, where as a brevet second lieutenant he reported to the 4th Infantry Regiment. In 1845 he joined the army of General Zachary Taylor* at Corpus Christi, Texas. Although he had little sympathy with his nation's goals in the Mexican War, Grant served with distinction in Taylor's campaign through the Battle of Monterrey (1846), and as a regimental quartermaster in the army of General Winfield Scott* on his campaign inland from Vera Cruz to Mexico City. By the end of the war, Grant was a first lieutenant with brevets for gallantry at Molino del Rey and Chapultepec (1847).

In August 1848 he married Julia Dent, sister of a West Point classmate. The couple had four children—three boys and a girl. After tours of duty in New York and Michigan, in 1852 Grant was assigned to the Far West and left his wife and first-born son in St. Louis. He was stationed at Fort Vancouver, Washington Territory, until promoted to captain in 1853 and then ordered to Fort Humboldt, California. Humboldt was a dreary post commanded by a martinet, Captain Robert C. Buchanan. Lonely, bored, and disenchanted with the Army, Grant drank too much. After a reprimand by Buchanan, Grant resigned from the service in 1854.

Grant rejoined his family near St. Louis. A trying six years ensued—years of privation, menial pursuits, limited prospects, and despondence. He successively sought to earn a livelihood as a farmer, firewood salesman, real estate agent, bill collector, candidate for county engineer, and customhouse clerk. He was unsuccessful in these ventures. In 1860 he moved to Galena, Illinois, to work in obscurity as a clerk in a leather-goods store managed by two of his brothers. The next year the Civil War started.

In the weeks following the firing on Fort Sumter and the call by President Abraham Lincoln* for seventy-five thousand volunteers, Grant drilled a company of Galena volunteers and then clerked in the office of the Illinois adjutant-general. His applications for field duty elicited no response. But on June 17, 1861, the governor of Illinois named Grant colonel of the 21st Illinois Volunteer Infantry. After a few weeks in a camp of instruction, Grant's regiment was ordered to Missouri. There he was made a brigadier general of volunteers and placed in command of the District of Southeast Missouri, headquartered at Cairo, Illinois.

Grant secured permission from his reluctant superior, General Henry Wager Halleck,* to make an amphibious thrust up the Tennessee River against Fort Henry. The Confederate fort fell to Union gunboats on February 6, 1862. Grant exploited this success by marching on nearby Fort Donelson, on the Cumberland, which was captured on February 16, along with its more than fourteen thousand defenders. These victories had immediate and far-reaching repercussions—the Confederates were compelled to abandon southern Kentucky, and much of middle and west Tennessee, including the Nashville industrial complex. "Unconditional Surrender" Grant became a household word in the North, while a grateful President Lincoln appointed Grant a major general of volunteers.

On April 6, 1862, the Confederate Army under General Albert Sidney Johnston* surprised Grant at Pittsburg Landing, Tennessee, near Shiloh Church. Although the Federals were driven from their camps and back on the landing, Grant did not panic. When darkness closed in, the Union lines had stabilized. Reinforced by troops under General Don Carlos Buell,* Grant counterattacked the next day, recovered the initiative, and forced the Confederates to retire in Corinth, Mississippi.

Bloody Shiloh had been a costly victory, and Grant's conduct before the battle became a subject of controversy. General Halleck hastened to the front and assumed command as the army closed in on Corinth; Grant became Halleck's second-in-command. But in July Halleck was called to Washington to become general in chief, and Grant resumed command of the Army of the Tennessee.

In November Grant's columns marched south, and his objectives were to capture Vicksburg, Mississippi, and secure control of the 240 miles of the Mississippi River between Vicksburg and Port Hudson, Louisiana. During the winter, on four occasions he sought to bypass Vicksburg but failed, and it appeared he might be replaced. On March 20, 1863, Grant made a fateful decision. He started his army on a march southward through the Louisiana parishes. In mid-April Rear Admiral David Dixon Porter* passed the Vicksburg batteries with his gunboats and transports, rendezvousing with Grant's army thirty river-miles south of the city. On April 30 Grant crossed the Mississippi with twenty-four thousand men and sixty cannon. During the next eighteen days Grant conducted one of history's great campaigns. Striking rapidly inland, he met and defeated the Confederates in five battles. One Southern army under General John C. Pemberton was invested in Vicksburg, while a second under General Joseph Eggleston Johnston* was scattered. Grant's efforts to storm Vicksburg failed. But cut off from supplies and reinforcement, Pemberton surrendered, along with 29,500 Confederates and large quantitites of war material, to General Grant on July 4, 1863, after a harrowing forty-seven day siege. Port Hudson fell to General N. P. Banks on July 9, and the Union again controlled the Mississippi from Cairo to the Gulf. Grant was hailed in the press and on the street, and was promoted to major general in the Regular Army.

That autumn Grant was placed in command of the Division of the Mississippi and ordered to relieve the army of General William Starke Rosecrans,* beleaguered in Chattanooga following its mid-September defeat at Chickamauga. After replacing Rosecrans with General George Henry Thomas,* Grant implemented a plan for supplying and reinforcing the army holed up in Chattanooga. Upon the arrival of four divisions under General William Tecumseh Sherman* from Vicksburg, Grant took the offensive. On November 23 the attack opened, to be climaxed by the surge up Missionary Ridge two days later. The Confederate Army under General Braxton Bragg* was swept from the field.

On March 2, 1864, Grant was promoted to lieutenant general and soon after was placed in command of the armies of the United States. Realizing that the way to victory was to crush the two major Confederate armies, Grant made his plans. In Virginia there would be a coordinated thrust by three Union armies directed at the Army of Northern Virginia, commanded by Robert Edward Lee,* while in northwest Georgia, General Sherman would hammer the Army of the Tennessee, commanded by General Joseph E. Johnston. Grant established his headquarters, not in Washington, but with the Army of the Potomac, then commanded by General George Gordon Meade.*

The Union armies took the offensive in the first week of May 1864. At the Wilderness (May 5–6) Meade's Army of the Potomac suffered frightful casualties, but unlike his predecessors Grant did not recoil. He directed Meade's columns to pass around Lee's right flank. Lee won that race, and after being successively fought to a standstill at Spotsylvania, the North Anna, and Cold Harbor, Grant employed his superior numbers to turn Lee's right and inch his way closer to Richmond. Union losses were staggering and by mid-June equaled Lee's strength at the beginning of the campaign. The North could replace its casualties, however; the South could not.

Stealing a march on Lee, the Army of the Potomac crossed to the south side of the James River and moved against Petersburg. A terrible four-day battle (June 15–18) ensued, but the Confederates held and Grant was unable to slip in Richmond's back door. This led to nine months of siege warfare, during which time the Union armies south of the James slowly extended their rifle-pits and forts westward to cut or threaten the railroads and roads over which Lee supplied his army. North of the James, the Federals inched their way toward Richmond.

Besides initiating and coordinating these movements, Grant maintained contact with his other army commanders to ensure that his strategic goals were implemented and proper priorities were given to the allocation of reinforcements and supplies. Especially significant was his decision to place General Philip Henry Sheridan* in charge of an army with the mission of destroying the Confederacy's economic resources and military power in the Shenandoah Valley.

Sheridan's victory at Five Forks (April 1, 1865) proved decisive, and the next day Grant hurled the armies of the Potomac and the James against Lee's attenuated and undermanned Petersburg lines, scoring massive breakthroughs. On the night of April 2 the Confederates evacuated Petersburg and Richmond and retreated to the west in hopes of rendezvousing with Johnston's army in North Carolina.

At Appomattox Court House, Lee found his route blocked by Sheridan's cavalry, while the Army of the Potomac slashed at his rear. On Palm Sunday, April 9, in the parlor of the Wilmer McLean House, Lee surrendered his army to General Grant. Grant's terms were generous and well received by the Confederates. Before another seven weeks passed, the other Southern armies laid down their arms and America's bloodiest war was history.

Universally esteemed, Grant continued as head of the Army, and in 1866 President Andrew Johnson named him General of the Army, a rank unused since 1799. At first, Grant sought to maintain a neutral stance in the increasingly acrimonious quarrels over Reconstruction policies between President Johnson and Congress, controlled by the Radical Republicans. Grant gradually shifted his position and became linked with the Radicals.

Nominated by the Republicans for the presidency in 1868, he defeated Democrat Horatio Seymour by a whopping electoral vote, though his margin in the popular vote was surprisingly small. Grant was easily reelected to a second term in 1872, thumping Horace Greeley. Grant was well trained for the military but ill-prepared for the White House. He looked to important congressmen and senators for guidance. Personally honest but politically naive, Grant made several unfortunate choices for cabinet officers and other advisors; a number of these men proved to be corrupt or incompetent, and a series of scandals rocked his administration.

Grant retired from public office in 1877, but in 1880 he again sought the Republican presidential nomination. He lost out to James A. Garfield. Two years later, Grant joined a New York brokerage firm, Grant and Ward, in which his name was exploited. In mid-1884 the enterprise failed, throwing Grant into bankruptcy.

Grant was now stricken with cancer of the throat. To provide for his family, in a race against death Grant wrote his *Personal Memoirs*. A classic military account, his memoirs were a financial success, earning for his heirs more than $450,000. In July 1885, a few days after laying aside his pen, the pain-wracked and speechless old soldier died.

Ulysses S. Grant certainly merits inclusion on any roll of the "Great Captains." In February 1862 he first demonstrated his abilities as a strategist and tactician, a rare combination. Although others had earlier pointed to the Tennessee and Cumberland rivers as the vulnerable point in the Confederate front, it was Grant who proceeded against Fort Henry and then exploited the subsequent breakthrough, closing in on Fort Donelson. At a key moment in the Donelson fighting, on February 15, he made decisions that turned apparent defeat into victory.

At Shiloh, Grant demonstrated other facets of his character—a bulldog-like determination and nerves of steel. He arrived on the field at midmorning on April 6 to find his army in disarray. Some units were grimly contesting the Confederate surge, others had not yet engaged, and many soldiers had panicked. Grant kept his nerve. He encouraged his troops and formed new lines; the Confederate onslaught slowed, and the tide turned.

The Vicksburg Campaign was Grant's masterpiece. His strategic concept was bold. Appreciating the value of the Navy, he employed it to give a new dimension to riverine warfare. Securing his bridgehead across the Mississippi at the Battle of Port Gibson (May 1, 1863), Grant marched his columns northeast rather than north. His object in taking the indirect approach was twofold—the capture of Vicksburg *and* the destruction of Pemberton's army. He made no effort to hold the countryside as his army struck inland. Instead, at frequent intervals until mid-May, large, heavily guarded wagon trains left Grand Gulf on the Mississippi to reinforce Grant's columns as they outmaneuvered and beat the Confederates in detail.

At Chattanooga, Grant carefully built up a superior striking force and then dealt Bragg's Confederates a fearful blow. As at Vicksburg, victory in this campaign called for an appreciation by Grant of the logistics involved in supplying and reinforcing tens of thousands of soldiers.

Upon assuming command of the Union armies, Grant demonstrated a keen strategic insight and a strength of will that brought victory to the North. His relations with his principal subordinates, particularly General Meade, with whose army he traveled, are lessons in the art of command. Grant established goals, oversaw logistics, and coordinated movements, while the Army leaders were responsible for tactical control and day-to-day operations of their commands. He did intervene, on occasion, if the situation warranted. Although terrible in attack and relentless in pursuit, Grant at Vicksburg and Appomattox was magnanimous in victory.

BIBLIOGRAPHY

Catton, Bruce. *Grant Moves South*. Boston: Little, Brown and Company, 1960.
———. *Grant Takes Command*. Boston: Little, Brown and Company, 1968.
Fuller, J. F. C. *The Generalship of Ulysses S. Grant*. New York: Dodd, Mead, and Company, 1929; reprint, Bloomington: Indiana University Press, 1958.

Grant, Ulysses S. *Personal Memoirs of U.S. Grant.* 2 vols. New York: J. J. Little and
    Company, 1885.
Lewis, Lloyd. *Captain Sam Grant.* Boston: Little, Brown and Company, 1950.
McFeely, William. *Grant: A Biography.* New York: W. W. Norton and Company, 1981.
Woodward, William E. *Meet General Grant.* New York: Horace Liveright, 1928.

EDWIN C. BEARSS

GRAVES, William Sidney (b. Mount Calm, Tex., March 27, 1865; d. Shrewsbury, N.J., February 27, 1940), Army officer; commander, American Expeditionary Force, Siberia, 1918–1920.

Graves was the son of Evelyn (Bennett) and Andrew C. Graves, a Baptist
minister who became a Confederate colonel, who had driven their covered wagon
from Tennessee to Texas in the footsteps of Sam Houston. After completing
such primary schools as were available, William attended Baylor University
briefly and then entered the U.S. Military Academy, graduating on June 12,
1889. He was commissioned a second lieutenant of infantry and assigned to the
7th Regiment, then stationed at Fort Logan, Colorado, where he remained on
duty until June 30, 1896, with the exception of a little less than a year at Camp
Pilot, Butte, Wyoming, 1890–1891.

Until November 1899 Lieutenant Graves served as aide to Brigadier General
Henry C. Merriam, first at headquarters, Department of the Columbia, and later
at headquarters, Department of the Colorado. This assignment was a fortunate
choice for the young officer, as Colonel Merriam had achieved a brilliant record
during the Civil War and was an example of efficiency and fairness to his
subordinates. In February 1891 Graves married Catherine Boyd from Maine,
who was visiting her uncle, Colonel Merriam.

Lieutenant Graves served with troops until Colonel Merriam's promotion,
when he became aide de camp and, later judge advocate and adjutant general
of the Colorado Department. He was greatly disappointed at not having served
with the regiment in Cuba during the Spanish-American War and, in 1899, a
year after reaching the grade of captain, he secured assignment to the 20th
Infantry in Manila. With two brief exceptions, he was to remain with this
regiment until 1914. Much of his service was as a company commander. He
participated in campaigns against the insurgents in northern Luzon, Batangas,
and Mindanao, and was cited for gallantry in action against *insurrectos* at Co-
loocan, Batangas, on December 21, 1901.

Returning to the United States in April 1902, he took station at Columbus
Barracks, Ohio, where he served with his regiment and in command of a company
of recruits until August of the same year. He then served at Fort Sheridan,
Illinois, until October 26, 1903, when he was ordered to the Philippines a second
time. This tour in the Orient continued until March 1, 1906.

Returning to the United States, Captain Graves was assigned to the Presidio
of Monterey, California, where he remained until December 1907, except for a
month's duty during the earthquake and fire in San Francisco in the spring of

1906. Thereafter, he went to Los Angeles for duty on general recruiting service, where he continued until detailed as a member of the General Staff on April 15, 1909, when he was ordered to Washington, D.C., for duty. He served in the national capital until July 10, 1912.

From January 20, 1911, Graves was secretary of the General Staff. Promoted to the rank of major on March 11, 1911, he no doubt felt that he was well established in his career and that the course ahead lay straight. Yet, the short time he served as secretary of the General Staff set the course of his subsequent official life and resulted in his appointment to the mission that was to determine his place in history.

On July 14, 1912, he joined his regiment, still the 20th Infantry, at Fort Douglas, Utah, where he served until November 27, 1913. At that time he was assigned to El Paso, Texas, in command of the Border Patrol until August 12, 1914. Recalled to Washington again for further duty with the General Staff Corps, he was again detailed as secretary. He continued on that duty until March 22, 1918. It was there that he was first introduced to the secretary of war, Newton Diehl Baker,* when Baker took over the portfolio in 1916.

During this interval General Graves was promoted three times—from lieutenant colonel, July 1, 1916, to brigadier general, National Army, December 17, 1917. From May 30 to July 23, 1917, he was on a special confidential mission in Europe. When he returned, he brought with him for delivery to the War Department, General John Joseph Pershing's * scheme of organization of the then nebulous American Expeditionary Force (AEF). On December 18, 1917, he was detailed as assistant to the chief of staff and served in that capacity until his promotion to major general, National Army, on June 26, 1918. The difficulties of this position were apparent with the formation of the National Army and the incessant requests and political pressure to which the offices of the War Department were subjected. Colonel Graves' unfailing tact, coupled with his quiet determination and fairness, won him the respect and confidence of the secretary of war and the various chiefs under whom he served. By prearrangement with General Peyton Conway March,* the chief of staff, General Graves was then ordered to Camp Fremont, California, to command the 8th Division, which was then training for service in France. In August he was appointed commander of the AEF to Siberia as part of an Allied expeditionary force. He sailed for Vladivostok early in July and remained there with his troops until April 1920, when the forces were recalled. From Siberia General Graves went to the Philippines, where he served at headquarters of the Philippine Department, Manila, until October. Returning to the United States, he assumed command of the 1st Infantry Brigade at Camp (now Fort) Dix, New Jersey. He continued on duty there and at Fort Wadsworth, New York, until September 14, 1922, commanding the 1st Division at Forts Wadsworth and Hamilton, until July 1925, when he was promoted to major general, Regular Army. On July 16, 1925, he assumed command of the VI Corps Area, with headquarters at Chicago; he served at Chicago until November 1, 1926, when he was transferred to the Panama Canal

Department. There he remained until April 1, 1928, when he was ordered back to the United States to await retirement. He was retired, at his own request, after more than forty years' service, on September 4, 1928.

Following retirement he made his home at Shrewsbury, New Jersey, where his residence on Sycamore Avenue became a shrine for former members of the AEF in Siberia. He died there on February 27, 1940, and was buried in Arlington.

General Graves' reputation properly depends upon his performance as commander of the AEF in Siberia. When Graves received his orders personally from the secretary of war in Kansas City, the dramatic interview concluded with some prophetic words from Secretary Baker: ''You will be walking on eggs loaded with dynamite; watch your step.'' Graves' instructions were explained in an aide memoire drafted by President Woodrow Wilson himself. The purpose of the expedition was to help Czecho-Slovak troops, attacked by enemy prisoners of war, to consolidate their forces and ''affect their repatriation by way of Vladivostok'' to fight on the Western Front; and to steady any efforts at self-government or self-defense in which the Russians themselves might be willing to accept assistance. Graves was also warned that the Japanese purpose would be to expand on the Asian mainland and its policy ''to keep the various Russian forces apart and oppose any strong Russian central authority.''

In his book *America's Siberian Adventure*, published in 1931 after his retirement, General Graves tells the essential facts and repeatedly corrects the impression that the forces of the United States were in Siberia to fight the Soviet government or to support any factions in opposition to the Bolsheviks. His instructions were definite in that they forbade any interference in the internal affairs of the Russian people, and he personally was entirely in sympathy with this point of view. This led to continual conflict with the ideas of the State Department and the Red Cross, as well as with the commanders of other Allied forces who went so far as to bring pressure in Washington and before the Supreme War Council to secure his removal. General Graves, however, had been selected by Baker and General March because of their confidence in his capabilities, and both they and President Wilson strongly supported him in his conduct and interpretation of his instructions.

What the author, in his modest narrative, did not bring out was his proper estimate of the situation amid the storm of hostile criticism his action aroused, not only in Siberia but also in much of the press in the United States. He avoided the most tragic difficulties of the North Russian expedition by refusing to submit his command to the senior Allied officer, a Japanese. Although directed to deliver arms purchased in America by the Kerensky government to the armies of Admiral Kolchak, he refused to carry out his orders when he learned that these arms were to be supplied to local Cossacks for possible use against Americans. Although confronted by vastly superior forces, he refused to be intimidated and dared the Japanese-supported factions to provoke a crisis.

Thirteen years later when General Graves' book reached Vienna, his explanation of his respect for the Russian right of self-determination provoked General Constantin Sakharoff, who had commanded the Kolchak White Russian forces in Siberia, to challenge him to a duel by Transatlantic mail. General Graves chose to ignore the challenge.

For his service in Siberia and as assistant to the chief of staff during World War I, General Graves was awarded the Distinguished Service Medal by the U.S. government. He was also awarded the Czechoslovak War Cross, the Japanese Order of the Rising Sun, Second Class, the Chinese Medal, Grand Cordon of the Order of the Wen Hu (Striped Tiger), Second Class, and the Italian Order of the Crown.

BIBLIOGRAPHY

Graves, William Sidney. *America's Siberian Adventure, 1918–1920*. New York: Jonathan Cape and Harrison Smith, 1931.

———. "If Japan Fights." *Current History* 40 (June 1934): 273–79.

Kendall, Sylvian G. *American Soldiers in Siberia*. New York: Richard R. Smith, 1945.

O'Connor, Richard. "Yanks in Siberia." *American Heritage* 25 (August 1974): 10–17.

Unterberger, Betty M. *America's Siberian Expedition, 1918–1920: A Study of National Policy*. Durham, N.C.: Duke University Press, 1956.

———, ed. *American Intervention in the Russian Civil War*. Lexington: D.C. Heath and Company, 1969.

BETTY MILLER UNTERBERGER

GREELY, Adolphus Washington (b. Newburyport, Mass., March 27, 1844; d. Washington, D.C., October 20, 1935), Army officer; Civil War veteran; Arctic explorer; chief signal officer, U.S. Army; major general.

Adolphus W. Greely was descended from forebears of English origin who for nine generations had lived and worked with their hands in coastal New England. The son of John Balch Greely, a shoemaker, and Frances D. (Cobb) Greely, he absorbed in his youth the qualities of determination, resourcefulness, and respect for knowledge which were to mark his long and active adult life. In 1860 he was graduated from Brown High School in Newburyport, and the following year, aged seventeen years, he enlisted as a private soldier in the 19th Massachusetts Volunteer Infantry with which he served through many of the bloodiest battles of the Civil War. He took part in the Battle of Ball's Bluff, the major engagements of the Peninsula Campaign, and the battles of Antietam and Fredericksburg. Thrice wounded (twice within minutes, in face and thigh, at Antietam), he rose from private to sergeant in the 19th Massachusetts and in 1863 accepted a commission in the 81st U.S. Colored Troops with which he served at the siege of Port Hudson. He completed the war as a brevet major of volunteers and commanded Negro troops in the delicate task of occupation duty in New Orleans from 1865 to 1867.

In 1867 Greely was commissioned as a second lieutenant in the Regular Army. Assigned to the 36th Infantry, he saw frontier service at Fort Sanders, Wyoming, and at Fort Douglas, Utah. He occupied his spare moments with the study of telegraphy and electricity. Thus, he was well-prepared when, at the end of 1867, he was unexpectedly detailed for service with the Signal Corps. He served as signal officer on the staff of General Eugene C. Carr during the 1869 campaign in Nebraska against the Cheyennes under Tall Bull which culminated in the Battle of Summit Springs. He also served at Fort Laramie before being assigned to Washington, D.C., in 1870 to assist Brigadier General Albert J. Myer in the organization of the U.S. Weather Bureau. During 1872–1873 Greely gathered data and formulated methods for the River and Flood Service, and he was soon recognized as an expert meteorologist.

Greely's early reputation in the Signal Corps was made by his aggressiveness and efficiency as the Corps' "trouble-shooter" in the construction of military telegraph lines. In 1875 he successfully completed the construction of a line across the state of Texas, ingeniously using juniper poles imported from the Great Dismal Swamp of Virginia to string lines across the treeless prairie. In 1876 he took six months' leave in Europe to recover his health and returned to rebuild hurricane-damaged telegraph lines from Cape Hatteras, North Carolina, to Cape Henry, Virginia. The following year he was again called upon by General Myer to rebuild the line from Santa Fe, New Mexico, to San Diego, California. Greely's arduous and often dangerous construction duties provided the opportunity for him to develop the physical stamina, administrative acumen, and leadership skill that characterized his later service.

In the course of his duties with the Signal Corps' Weather Bureau, Greely became interested in climatology and other aspects of scientific georgraphy. He also became an intimate of Captain Henry Howgate and a supporter of Howgate's Arctic expeditionary schemes. In 1880–1881 the U.S. government organized an expedition to participate with other nations in the establishment and operation of a number of circumpolar stations to study Arctic weather and climate. Lieutenant Greely volunteered and was chosen to command the station planned for the shore of Lady Franklin Bay opposite the western coast of Greenland. Greely and his party of twenty-four men arrived at their station on August 11, 1881, and established Fort Conger. Although hastily organized, the expedition was generously equipped and was supplied with rations sufficient for two years. Under Greely's direction the members of the expedition amassed an important collection of data on Arctic weather and tidal conditions, studied the flora and fauna of the region, and carried out a very successful program of exploration and discovery.

When the relief vessels scheduled for 1882 and 1883 failed to reach Fort Conger, Greely, following his orders, ended the scientific activities of the expedition, abandoned Fort Conger on August 9, 1883, and proceeded southward toward the prearranged rendezvous location. The party encountered extremely difficult conditions but negotiated the fifty-one-day, five hundred-mile passage safely, arriving at Cape Sabine on Bedford Pym Island intact but exhausted and with supplies already running low. At Cape Sabine they established Camp Clay to await the hoped-for arrival of relief. The ship dispatched for that purpose was crushed in the ice without reaching the Greely party, and the subsequent winter became a nightmare of starvation and despair. Supplementing their scanty stores with lichens, a few small shrimp, and, finally, their sealskin clothing and the sinews used to bind together the sledges, the party was steadily reduced by accident, exposure, starvation, and one official execution, ordered by Greely for a soldier guilty of the theft of food. Between January and June of 1884, eighteen of the twenty-five members of the expedition perished. This period was characterized by both heroic self-sacrifice and the darker aspects of human behavior. Despite his own failing health, Greely maintained control of the dwindling survivors with the help of a few dedicated subordinates, notably Sergeant David L. Brainard, and thus managed to avoid a final, catastrophic disintegration of the group. By June 22, 1884, the handful of survivors were, with one exception, confined to their sleeping bags and were within hours of death from malnutrition and disease when the relief expedition under the command of Captain Winfield Scott Schley,* mounted at the insistence of Mrs. Greely and a few friends over the opposition of the Secretary of War Robert Todd Lincoln, finally located the survivors and returned six of them to their homes.

The scientific achievements of the expedition and the hardships endured by the survivors as well as the stirring rescue were soon forgotten amid titillating accusations of murder and cannibalism during the sojourn at Camp Clay. Greely was blamed for the tragic outcome of the affair, but he was eventually absolved when it became apparent that most of the tragedy was made in Washington and that the startling practice of cannibalism was confined to members of the party who had died before the arrival of relief, partly in consequence of their own reprehensible activity.

The scientific data salvaged along with the wracked bodies of the survivors proved of great value to our knowledge of the earth's climate and tidal patterns. In due time the soundness of Greely's judgment and the skill of his leadership became clearly established, and he received credit for his magnificent accomplishments. He was widely acclaimed as a hero in Europe, and in 1886 he received the Founder's Medal of the Royal Geographical Society of London and the Roquette Medal of the Société de Géographie of Paris. In 1923 the American Geographical Society belatedly awarded him its Charles P. Daly Medal. Official recognition was somewhat delayed but came in a spectacular manner. From May 1873 Greely had held the rank of first lieutenant in the 5th U.S. Cavalry. He missed a normal promotion to captain while in the Arctic but was finally advanced to that rank in June 1886. In March 1887 President Grover Cleveland appointed him chief signal officer of the Army with the rank of brigadier general, in which position and grade he served for the next nineteen years. He was the first volunteer private soldier of the Civil War to reach Regular Army general officer rank.

During his long tenure as chief signal officer, Greely proved both an astute politician and an innovative administrator. He fought successfully to keep the Signal Corps in existence and ensured that it was staffed with capable officers of proven scientific expertise. He reformed and supervised the operations of the

Weather Bureau until it was transferred to the Department of Agriculture in 1891 on his recommendation. He also oversaw the construction of tens of thousands of miles of military telegraph and undersea cable, and he was the moving force in adapting the developing technology of the late nineteenth century to military purposes. Under his direction, the Signal Corps introduced the use of wireless telegraphy, the automobile, the airplane, and many other modern devices. As the U.S. delegate to the International Telegraph Congress in London and the International Wireless Telegraph Congress in Berlin in 1903, he also worked successfully to involve the United States in international agreements on communications.

Having refused promotion in the Line of the Army to direct the Signal Corps' activities in the Spanish-American War, Greely was promoted to major general in February 1906 and was assigned to command the Pacific Division. There he was responsible for the coordination of all offical relief activities in San Francisco following the great earthquake and fire of 1906. He subsequently commanded the Northern Division and ended the Ute Rebellion of 1905–1906 without bloodshed. His final assignment was as commander of the Department of the Columbia.

In March 1908 Adolphus W. Greely was retired for age, a retirement that in no way reduced his active contribution to national life. Following an around-the-world trip in 1909, he occupied himself with writing and various public service endeavors. He was one of the founders of the National Geographic Society in 1888 and remained one of its trustees until his death. It was to that Society's collection that he donated the majority of his personal library, including many volumes on Arctic exploration and several hundred scrapbooks of his own compilation. He was active in a wide range of fraternal and service organizations, and he helped to establish the first free public library in the District of Columbia, was the first president of the Explorer's Club of New York, and was one of the six original founders of the Cosmos Club in Washington. His wife, Henrietta H.C. Nesmith Greely, whom he married in 1878 and by whom he fathered six children, was a founder of the Daughters of the American Revolution. In 1911 General Greely was recalled to active duty to represent the United States and President William Howard Taft at the coronation of George V of England.

On his ninety-first birthday, on March 27, 1935, Adolphus W. Greely was presented with a special Congressional Medal of Honor, the second American so honored for peacetime service. (Charles Lindbergh was the first.) He died on October 20, 1935, at Walter Reed Army Hospital in Washington attended by Brigadier General (Retired) David L. Brainard who had shared with him an earlier approach to death in the frozen hut at Cape Sabine. He was buried with full military honors at Arlington National Cemetery.

Adolphus W. Greely's long and active life spanned the central half of the history of the nation which he so faithfully served. As a small child he saw a veteran of the Revolution on parade, and in later life he associated with men who were to become veterans of a second world war. He witnessed the development of the United States from a rural, predominantly agricultural land rent by civil war at home and despised abroad into an urban, industrial, and united world power. He himself played an active role in bringing about that transformation.

Early in his life, Greely proved himself a man of action and a soldier in some of the hardest fighting of the Civil War. He combatted both the elements and the hostile Indians as he opened the West and tied the nation together with military telegraph lines. His greatest personal challenge came as leader of the ill-fated Lady Franklin Bay Expedition and provided a story of unparalleled human courage and endurance.

Greely achieved lasting international fame as a result of his personal fortitude in the Arctic, but he always claimed that his detailed scientific work was far more important. Indeed, when the data collected by the 1881–1884 Arctic Expedition are added to Greely's earlier studies of the floods and climate of the Mississippi Valley, his claim to have significantly improved man's knowledge of the earth's geography, climate, and tidal conditions is fully justified. Much of the data which he collected is still useful today. Greely's accomplishments in the scientific field are all the more striking in that his scientific knowledge was entirely self-taught.

Unhampered by the conservatism and lack of vision that seized so many of his contemporaries, Greely skillfully and enthusiastically led the Signal Corps and the Army into the modern era of advanced technology. Under his guidance as chief signal officer the Army added to its means of defending the nation such instruments of modern science as the radio, the automobile, and the airplane. In his memoirs Greely commented that his most important official act in peacetime was the expenditure of $50,000 in 1898 to convince Samuel P. Langley to produce a flying machine for war purposes. Although Langley's experiments were unsuccessful, they encouraged the Wright brothers and led to the perfection of manned, powered flight five years later. Greely's ability to foresee the usefulness of such inventions and his willingness to patiently and persistently promote their inclusion in the national arsenal, often against great opposition, contributed to the emergence of the U.S. Army as one of the world's most technologically advanced military forces.

Although known as a demanding taskmaster to his subordinates, Greely was unfailingly attentive to the human needs of those who shared his long march through life. As a measure of his basic humility and concern for others in each of his annual reports as chief signal officer he attributed the achievements of his bureau to the responsible officers and men by name, a practice his successors did not continue. He modestly bore his great fame as an explorer, scientist, and military leader, and he skillfully used his friendships and acquaintances with political and scientific leaders of many nations to the advantage of his own.

Adolphus W. Greely is perhaps the foremost example of the small, but important, group of soldier-scientist-adventurers who led the nation into the twentieth century. He was favored by fortune in that his long military career was dedicated to the building up rather than the tearing down of nations. At Greely's death Acting Secretary of War Harry H. Woodring succinctly summarized his career: "The career of General Greely is a striking example of the contributions a soldier may make to civilization. The army salutes a brave comrade, a great leader, a distinguished scientist, a devoted servant of the Republic."

BIBLIOGRAPHY

Greely, Adolphus W. *Reminiscences of Adventure and Service: A Record of Sixty-Five Years.* New York: Charles Scribner's Sons, 1927.
————. *Three Years of Arctic Service.* New York: Charles Scribner's Sons, 1894.
Mitchell, William, *General Greely: The Story of a Great American.* New York: G. P. Putnam's Sons, 1936.
Todd, A. L. *Abandoned: The Story of the Greely Arctic Expedition, 1881–1884.* New York: McGraw-Hill, 1961.

CHARLES R. SHRADER

GREENE, Nathanael (b. Warwick, R.I., July 27, 1742 OS; d. Mulberry Grove, Savannah, Ga., June 19, 1786), general in the War of Independence.

Little in Green's earlier years suggested he would one day have a prominent role in a revolution. Because his Quaker parents, Nathanael and Mary Mott Greene, favored hard work and minimal education, he went to work early in the family-owned forge and mills, learning each job—from anchorsmith to merchant. Largely self-educated, he read widely and later became a fluent letter writer.

Until England closed the port of Boston in 1774, Greene showed slight interest in public affairs. Then, repudiating his Quaker pacifism, he helped found the Kentish Guards. Prevented by a slight limp from being elected an officer, he consented to serve as private, using his spare time to study military treatises. Six months later, in May 1775, for obscure reasons, the Assembly bypassed veteran officers of the French and Indian War to appoint Greene brigadier general of the Rhode Island Army of Observation. Within weeks he had three regiments uniformed, equipped, and encamped near Boston. When his brigade was taken into the Continental Army in June 1775, he became, at thirty-two, the army's youngest general.

The stalemate at Boston and Long Island in 1775–1776 provided Greene an opportunity to learn from veteran soldiers as well as from books and to adapt his practical knowledge to military needs. His career before December 1776, however, was not impressive. After preparing Long Island's defenses, he was made major general in August 1776, but he fell ill before British General William Howe attacked. At Harlem Heights in September he acquitted himself well, but two months later, as commander of Forts Washington and Lee, he watched across the Hudson (with George Washington*) as Howe's army overran Mount Washington, taking twenty-eight hundred prisoners. It was a bitter lesson; never again would he be caught without an avenue of retreat.

The stigma was largely erased in December 1776 by General George Washington's* daring attack on Trenton, which Greene helped to plan and execute. At Brandywine in September 1777, Greene's division marched four miles in forty-five minutes to check the British in a fierce engagement after they turned Washington's flank. During the night offensive at Germantown in October, Greene's column penetrated enemy lines before realizing that Sullivan had had to retreat in fog. Willard Wallace called his disengagement and retreat "remarkable achievements."

At Valley Forge in February 1778, a congressional committee urged the quartermaster post on Greene. Reluctant to leave the "line of splendor" for a chaotic department, he did so finally because of Washington's desperation and his own fear for the patriot cause. Although he offered to accept a general's salary, his assistants insisted on traditional commissions, and Congress set a 1 percent commission for the three.

As head of the sprawling department of three thousand employees, Greene made enormous improvements in the face of shortages and rapidly depreciating currency. Depreciation also brought criticism of Greene and his assistants as commissions in Continental dollars rose astronomically and some people irrationally blamed them for high prices. Even more damaging was the profiteering of some agents, whose misdeeds smeared the entire department. Greene's relations with Congress became increasingly strained, and in August 1780 he resigned.

During Greene's tenure as quartermaster, Washington often sought his advice and occasionally assigned him active duty: in June 1778 near the end of the Battle of Monmouth he repulsed a column under Cornwallis; in August 1778 in Rhode Island he defended John Sullivan's right against strong attacks; and in June 1780 at Springfield, New Jersey, he turned back Baron Knyphausen's five thousand men with half the number.

In October 1780, with Charles Cornwallis controlling Georgia and South Carolina after defeating Horatio Gates* at Camden, Congress approved Washington's choice of Greene to command the Southern army. En route south, he was promised Henry ("Light-horse Harry") Lee's* legion, and in Maryland and Virginia he pleaded for more men and supplies. He left a subordinate, Baron Frederic William Steuben,* in Virginia to raise men. En route he also familiarized himself with the South through maps. His ability to imprint the topography of a region in his mind from maps or observation was part of his genius. His quartermaster experience helped him keep a constant assessment of each region's supply potential.

At Charlotte, North Carolina, on December 3, 1780, he took command from Gates of a hungry, ragged, ill-equipped army of one thousand Continentals and twelve hundred militiamen. Although Greene remained in the South until August 1783, he won his military laurels in the first nine months. Tactical victories eluded him, but with an inferior army he adopted a successful strategy of mobility, of doing with what he had, of using finesse where he lacked strength, of strategic retreats to save his army for another day. He became especially adept at winning the cooperation of partisan leaders. Above all, he never gave in to discouragement. "We fight," he wrote, "get beat, rise, and fight again."

The one tactical victory of his Southern campaign was Daniel Morgan's* destruction of Guy Carleton's legion at Cowpens on January 17, 1781. Greene had prepared the way by the unorthodox move of dividing his small army. With supplies exhausted around Charlotte, he had accompanied eleven hundred men to a more bountiful and defensible area seventy miles southeast at Cheraw, South Carolina. He sent Morgan westward with six hundred men to attract militia and to watch Cornwallis' army of four thousand men, which lay between them. After Cowpens, Greene headed north to rendezvous with Morgan, who was now in retreat before Cornwallis. In Greene's and Morgan's race to cross the Dan River (where Greene had ordered boats built), they not only eluded Cornwallis but also caused him to destroy most of his wagons and supplies in fruitless pursuit. Greene soon recrossed the Dan to encourage North Carolina patriots.

Despite the loss of Morgan (from ill-health) and many militiamen, additional troops brought Greene's numbers to forty-two hundred. That scarcely a fifth of these men had seen action did not deter him from confronting Cornwallis' two thousand veterans. Although Cornwallis had not replaced his wagons and baggage, he accepted Greene's challenge. On a hill near Guilford Court House, North Carolina, Greene deployed his men in three lines as Morgan had done at Cowpens, the militia in front to fire several times before retreating. At noon on March 15, Cornwallis attacked across an open field. Unfortunately, the North Carolina militia fired only once and ran, but Virginia militia and Continental infantry and cavalry fought furiously—until Greene withdrew rather than risk further loss. Cornwallis kept the field, but 30 percent of his men lay dead or wounded as compared with only 6 percent of Greene's. Cornwallis' army was finished as a fighting force. He stumbled toward the coast at Wilmington, whence he later departed for Virginia—and Yorktown.

Greene, reduced to fifteen hundred Continentals by militia withdrawals, headed south, where eight thousand British held nine interior posts plus Charleston and Savannah. Although he was defeated by Lord Rawdon at Hobkirk's Hill on April 19 and was forced to abandon the siege of Fort 96 in June, he succeeded in four months—with the help of partisans under Francis Marion,* Thomas Sumter, and Andrew Pickens*—in clearing the British from the interior. His men covered nine hundred miles in the sweltering heat.

On September 8, with twenty-two hundred men, Greene made a surprise attack on Colonel Alexander Stewart's army at Eutaw Springs. Seasoned veterans declared it the hardest fought battle of the war. Greene was near victory when one of his regiments, in overrunning the British camp, found food and rum. At the same time, Stewart's right, ensconced in a thicket and a brick house, took a heavy toll of Greene's cavalry. When Stewart's retreating column turned and made a stand, Greene withdrew. Both sides were near exhaustion. A fourth of Greene's troops and a third of Stewart's were casualties. The battle was a draw, but the campaign was Greene's when Stewart withdrew to Charleston. For Eutaw Springs, Greene's praises were sung North and South.

Victory at Yorktown did not bring peace to the South. The British still held Charleston and Savannah and gave indications of strengthening them. Moreover, the Whigs and Tories continued regularly to plunder and kill each other. As important as Greene's military achievements were his efforts to reconcile the warring factions and to restore civil government.

In gratitude, South Carolina and Georgia gave him estates, while North Carolina gave him western land. In June 1782 his wife joined him and was with him when he entered Charleston after the British evacuation in December 1782.

The following months were trouble-filled. No sooner had he coped with mutiny than he was accused of profiteering, charges that arose when two former aides were discovered to be partners of John Banks, whose firm had provided Greene's army with food and uniforms. To bolster his credit, Banks had hinted that Greene was to become a partner. Although vindicated by associates (and later by Alexander Hamilton), Greene suffered from the charges. Even worse was Banks' bankruptcy, which left Greene owing thousands of dollars—a debt that shortened his life. Ten years after his death, Congress reimbursed his family.

Greene returned north in August 1783 to a hero's acclaim. Two years later he moved to Georgia and was struggling to make his estates profitable, when he died suddenly on June 19, 1786. He was survived by Catharine and five children under eleven years of age.

Greene's early death denied him a place in the popular pantheon of Revolutionary heroes, although he was fully appreciated by his contemporaries. Many would have applauded Alexander Hamilton when, in his eulogy of Greene, he spoke of his "universal and pervading genius." Not all military historians would agree, but none would deny his genius. British historian J. W. Fortescue called Greene a "very noble character [who] seems to me to stand little if at all lower than Washington as a general in the field." Douglas Southall Freeman thought that next to Washington, Greene had done "the most in the field to achieve Independence." Another historian, Christopher Ward, called him Washington's "right arm" and said that "in the opinion of some well qualified judges he was Washington's superior, both as a strategist and as a tactician."

BIBLIOGRAPHY

Greene, Nathanael. *The Papers of General Nathanael Greene*. Edited by Richard K. Showman, Robert E. McCarthy, and Margaret Cobb. Chapel Hill: University of North Carolina Press, 1976–.

Thayer, Theodore. *Nathanael Greene: Strategist of the American Revolution*. New York: Twayne Publishers, 1960.

Treacy, M. F. *Prelude to Yorktown: The Southern Campaign of Nathanael Greene, 1780–81*. Chapel Hill: University of North Carolina Press, 1963.

Wallace, Willard M. *Appeal to Arms: A Military History of the American Revolution*. New York: Harper and Brothers, 1951.

RICHARD K. SHOWMAN

GRIERSON, Benjamin Henry (b. Pittsburgh, Pa., July 8, 1826; d. Omena, Mich., August 31, 1911), Army officer. Grierson conducted a dramatic raid from La Grange, Tenn., to Baton Rouge, La., during the Civil War and commanded the 10th U.S. Cavalry, 1866–1888.

The youngest of five surviving children born to Scotch-Irish immigrants, Benjamin H. Grierson spent his formative years on a farm on the outskirts of Youngstown, Ohio. A kick from a horse nearly ended Grierson's life at the age of eight and left the future cavalryman with permanent facial scars which, as an adult, he attempted to conceal beneath a full beard. Grierson mastered a wide variety of musical instruments and, at the age of thirteen, assumed the direction of the Youngstown band. In 1851 he moved to Illinois where he taught music in Jacksonville and nearby Springfield. Following his marriage in 1854 to Alice Kirk, he entered the produce business in Meredosia, Illinois. Forced into bankruptcy in the wake of the financial panic of 1857, Grierson on the eve of the Civil War was a thirty-four-year-old failure.

During his residence in Illinois, Grierson campaigned vigorously for the Republican party. In May 1861, he traveled to Springfield at the request of his friend, Republican Governor Richard Yates, and shortly thereafter accepted a position as volunteer aide to Brigadier General Benjamin M. Prentiss. During the first months of the Civil War, Grierson gained valuable experience as a staff officer in southern Illinois and in northern and eastern Missouri.

Governor Yates, in October 1861, commissioned Grierson major in the 6th Illinois Cavalry and, the following April, elevated him to the rank of colonel. Grierson spent much of 1862 chasing guerrilla forces in west Tennessee and in northern Mississippi. When Confederate cavalry under Major General Earl Van Dorn destroyed the Union supply depot at Holly Springs, Mississippi, on December 20, 1862, Grierson distinguished himself in close and aggressive pursuit of the Rebel raiders.

Grierson's activities in the District of West Tennessee brought him to the favorable attention of Generals William Tecumseh Sherman* and Ulysses Simpson Grant.* In the spring of 1863 Grant selected the Illinois colonel to conduct a mounted raid designed to divert Confederate attention while a Union army crossed the Mississippi River below Vicksburg and attacked the river citadel from the rear. On April 17 Grierson left La Grange, Tennessee, at the head of seventeen hundred troopers and six small pieces of artillery. Employing a dazzling combination of speed and deception that left pursuers confused and outdistanced, Grierson's raiders traversed the entire state of Mississippi destroying track, equipment, telegraph lines, and government stores, and creating panic among civilians and soldiers before emerging virtually unscathed at Baton Rouge, Louisiana, on May 2. Grant pronounced the raid "one of the most brilliant cavalry exploits of the war." As a reward for his spectacular accomplishment, on June 3, 1863, Grierson was commissioned brigadier general of volunteers. Major General Nathaniel P. Banks, meanwhile, detained Grierson in the Department of the Gulf as commander of cavalry during the siege of Port Hudson, Louisiana. With the fall of that last Confederate stronghold along the Mississippi River on July 8, 1863, Grierson returned to west Tennessee, where he assumed command of the cavalry division of the XVI Army Corps.

During the spring and summer of 1864, Grierson participated in operations against Nathan Bedford Forrest* in northern Mississippi. In February he accompanied Brigadier General William Sooy Smith's ill-fated expedition to West Point; on June 10 he commanded Union cavalry at the Battle of Brice's Cross Roads—Forrest's greatest victory; and the following month he gained some revenge by sharing in Major General A. J. Smith's defeat of Forrest near Tupelo. Also in July 1864, Grierson assumed command of the Cavalry Corps, District of West Tennessee.

With the reorganization of the Union cavalry in the West under Brevet Major General James H. Wilson,* Grierson on November 6, 1864, was assigned to command the 4th Division, Cavalry Corps, Military Division of the Mississippi. Although five weeks later Wilson abruptly relieved Grierson of his command, Major General Napoleon J. T. Dana detained the experienced cavalry officer in the Department of the Mississippi. From December 21, 1864, to January 5, 1865, Grierson conducted a destructive raid against Confederate lines of communication in Mississippi in an effort to prevent supplies from reaching the battered army under General John Bell Hood* as they retreated from Nashville, Tennessee. Impressed by Grierson's performance, Grant in February of 1865 dispatched the Illinois cavalryman, as brevet major general of volunteers, to New Orleans to organize the cavalry under Major General Edward Richard Sprigg Canby* in the Military Division of West Mississippi. At the close of the war, Grierson was operating at the head of four thousand troopers in the interior of Alabama.

Following Confederate surrender east of the Mississippi, Grierson returned to New Orleans to organize cavalry for service under Generals George Armstrong Custer* and Wesley Merritt* in Texas. Upon completing his duties in Louisiana, Grierson on September 16, 1865, assumed command of the District of Huntsville, Alabama, where he remained until his discharge from the Army on January 15, 1866. Summoned to Washington, D.C., in March to testify before a subcommittee of the Joint Committee on Reconstruction, Grierson successfully lobbied for reinstatement in the service and discharge (on April 30, 1866) at the full rank of major general of volunteers.

On July 28, 1866, Grierson reentered the Army as colonel of the 10th U.S. Cavalry—one of the Army's two black mounted regiments. In almost a quarter-century of service on the Southwestern frontier, Grierson compiled an enviable record for both himself and the legendary "Buffalo Soldiers" whom he organized and commanded. During the unsettled postwar decade on the Central Plains, he served at posts in Kansas and the Indian Territory, supervised the construction of Fort Sill, and commanded the District of the Indian Territory (1868–1869). When, in 1871, a band of Kiowas under Satanta, Satank, and Big Tree attacked a wagon train near Fort Richardson, Texas, narrrowly missing a party that included General Sherman, Grierson saw to the arrest of the Indian leaders. In 1873 Grierson temporarily relinquished command of the 10th Cavalry to serve as superintendent of the General Mounted Recruiting Service at St. Louis, Missouri.

In April 1875, Grierson rejoined his regiment at Fort Concho, Texas. As commander of the District of the Pecos from 1878 to 1881, he secured the trans-Pecos region from the frequent incursion of Apache raiders from New Mexico. In March and April 1880, Grierson and a large detachment of the 10th Cavalry marched to Fort Stanton, New Mexico, where they cooperated with Colonel Edward Hatch in disarming the Mescalero Apaches and returning them to their reservation. Late that same summer, Grierson drove Victorio and his renegade band of Apaches into Mexico, where they were eventually captured or killed, thereby ending the Indian threat to west Texas.

During the spring of 1885, the 3d and 10th Cavalry regiments exchanged stations, and Grierson took post at Whipple Barracks, Arizona Territory, and later occupied Fort Grant. In November of the following year, he was assigned to command the District of New Mexico with headquarters at Santa Fe. On December 1, 1888, Grierson relinquished command of the 10th Cavalry to succeed General Nelson Appleton Miles* at Los Angeles as commander of the Department of Arizona.

On July 8, 1890, Benjamin H. Grierson retired from the Army with the rank of brigadier general. The ex-soldier spent the remaining twenty-one years of his life in quiet retirement at his family home in Jacksonville, Illinois. At the time of his death at his summer cottage in Omena, Michigan, Grierson was one of five surviving major generals of the Civil War.

Grierson's reputation rests largely upon the success of his 1863 cavalry raid through Mississippi. Coming after Union reverses, followed by stalemate, in the East and the West, the flawlessly executed dash through six hundred miles of enemy territory sent a frenzy of excitement through a war-weary North. In terms of objectives, execution, and physical and psychological effects, "Grierson's Raid" ranks among the most brilliant mounted exploits of the Civil War.

Unfortunately, the celebrity of the "Great Raid" has overshadowed Grierson's almost unique reputation among federal cavalrymen for effectiveness and dependability. Sherman, whose distrust of cavalry was profound, nonetheless recommended Grierson in 1862 as "the best Cavalry officer I have yet had," and in 1867 confidently informed General Winfield Scott Hancock* that "you have only to tell him what you want done and he will do it with a will." Grant, likewise, assured General Canby that "with Grierson, I am satisfied you would either find him at the appointed place in time or you would find him holding an enemy." Few other cavalrymen, North or South, enjoyed such confidence.

It is equally unfortunate that historians have generally overlooked Grierson's fruitful, if unglamorous, postwar career. An outsider in an officer corps dominated by a cohesive West Point fraternity and a humanitarian in an era of glory-seeking Indian-fighters, he endured a quarter-century of frustration and loneliness in the unswerving performance of thankless duty at remote frontier outposts. Although Grierson demonstrated strategic and tactical ability during the Victorio Campaign, his singular achievements were those of a builder and a peacemaker. As commander of one of the Regular Army's first black regiments, he instilled pride in the face of racial prejudice and molded the 10th Cavalry into one of the finest mounted units on the Western frontier. Under his direction, the 10th Cavalry opened thousands of miles of roads, strung telegraph lines, established military posts and subposts, and rendered remote regions of the West safe for settlement. Finally, as a firm believer in President Grant's peace policy, Grierson established rare cooperation between the Army and Indian agents in an effort to end depredations while at the same time dealing fairly and humanely with Indian tribes.

BIBLIOGRAPHY

Brown, D. Alexander. *Grierson's Raid*. Urbana: University of Illinois Press, 1954.

Glass, E.L.N., comp. and ed. *The History of the Tenth Cavalry 1866–1921*. Tucson: Acme Printing Company, 1921; reprinted Fort Collins, Colo.: Old Army Press, 1969.

Leckie, William H. *The Buffalo Soldiers: A Narrative of the Negro Cavalry in the West*. Norman: University of Oklahoma Press, 1967.

Nye, W.S. *Carbine and Lance: The Story of Old Fort Sill*. Norman: University of Oklahoma Press, 1969.

BRUCE J. DINGES

GROVES, Leslie Richard (b. Albany, N.Y., August 17, 1896; d. Washington, D.C., July 13, 1970), Army officer, engineer. Groves had a key role in the development of the atomic bomb as the officer-in-charge of the Manhattan Project.

Leslie Groves was named for his father, a Presbyterian minister who, a short time after the birth of his son, became an Army chaplain. Young Groves lived with his family at various Army posts in the Western United States and in Cuba and the Philippines until he entered the University of Washington in 1913. Spending only a year there, he transferred to the Massachusetts Institute of Technology for two years, and then in 1916 received an appointment to the U.S. Military Academy. Enrolled in the prescribed war-shortened emergency course, he graduated fourth in his class, November 1, 1918. Commissioned in the Corps of Engineers, he continued his professional education at the Engineer School, Camp Humphreys (now Fort Belvoir), Virginia, from 1918 to 1921, except for a few months of service in France in 1919.

In the decade and a half following his graduation from the Engineer School, Groves held a series of typical engineer assignments. He served as a company commander with the 3d Engineers in Hawaii (1922–1925) and then as assistant to the district engineer in Galveston, Texas (1925–1927). From 1927 to 1931, he was a company commander with the 1st Engineers in Nicaragua. Following four years (1931–1935) in the Office of the Chief of Engineers in Washington, during which time he advanced to the rank of captain, he prepared for assignment to higher command by attendance at the Command and General Staff School (1935–1936) and, after a two-year stint as assistant to the division engineer in the Missouri River District, at the Army War College (1938–1939).

Groves was serving on the War Department General Staff when World War II began in Europe and, by late 1940, had become fully involved in the massive military construction program undertaken by the United States to provide facilities for a vastly expanded army. Starting as personal assistant to Major General Edmund B. Gregory, the quartermaster general, who had been a close friend of his father, Groves, now a major, held a series of key assignments in the Construction Division, which in December 1941 was transferred from the Office of the Quartermaster General to the Office of the Chief of Engineers (OCE). As chief of the Operations Branch, with the temporary rank of colonel, and then as deputy chief, Construction Division (OCE), he oversaw expenditure of hundreds of millions of dollars on the building of training camps, munitions plants, and a new headquarters for a greatly expanded War Department, the Pentagon.

By late 1942 the peak of military construction in the United States had passed, and Groves sought an assignment overseas. He was very disappointed when he was ordered instead to take command on September 17 of the Manhattan Project, the cover name for the program to develop and produce an atomic bomb. Groves already knew something of this highly secret project, because in June 1942 President Franklin D. Roosevelt had directed the Army to take over administration of its construction aspects. He was aware that basic research, begun in 1939 and carried out in various government and university laboratories under contracts administered by the Office of Scientific Research and Development (OSRD) and predecessor organizations, had established the feasibility of an atomic weapon. In the summer of 1942 he and other Corps of Engineer officers had supported their colleague, Colonel James C. Marshall, who had been assigned to form and head the Manhattan District as the organization to carry out the army's atomic responsibilities. Meanwhile, leaders of the atomic project, including Secretary of War Henry Lewis Stimson,* Vannevar Bush, head of OSRD, and James B. Conant, chairman of the National Defense Research Committee, had concluded that it was going to be an enterprise so complex and vast in scope that an engineer district would not be able to cope with all of its problems. Their solution was to appoint a military leader of general officer rank to be in overall charge of the project and provide him with a committee to make important policy decisions.

With his record of exceptional success in carrying out difficult construction projects, Groves was a logical choice for the position of officer-in-charge of the atomic project. Promoted to the rank of brigadier general on the assumption of his new assignment, Groves, acting in effect as executive secretary of the Military Policy Committee, quickly secured approval of measures that established his dominant control over the rapidly expanding atomic bomb program. Making maximum use of the authority granted to him to use existing facilities of the Corps of Engineers and other Army agencies, Groves succeeded, in spite of severe wartime shortages and competition from other vital programs, in securing for Manhattan the priority ratings, the land, materials, tools, manpower, and other requirements essential to development of the atomic bomb.

From late 1942 to the summer of 1945 Groves provided the leadership and coordination essential to convert results of research and development earlier carried out in laboratories at Columbia University, the University of Chicago, the University of California, and many other institutions, into facilities needed to manufacture fissionable materials and to design and build an atomic bomb. Thus, he directly oversaw site acquisition and plant and community construction and operation of the Clinton Engineer Works in east Tennessee for producing fissionable uranium, the Hanford Engineer Works in south central Washington for manufacturing plutonium, and the Los Alamos Laboratory in north central New Mexico for bond development. By early 1945 Groves, promoted to major general (temporary) in March 1944, was directing activities from his small headquarters in Washington, D.C. The project employed nearly 129,000 workers and would ultimately cost more than $2 billion. It culminated in a successful test of an atomic device at Alamogordo, New Mexico, on July 16, 1945.

Because of the unique character of the wartime atomic project and the circumstances surrounding its development, Groves became involved to an unusual degree in high-level planning and policymaking concerning interchange of atomic information with Great Britain, employment of the bomb against Japan, and domestic and international control of atomic energy after World War II. Because of stringent security requirements and the enormous potential importance of an atomic weapon, he had frequently to deal directly on a regular basis with wartime leaders at the highest level, including Stimson, General George Catlett Marshall,* the chief of staff, and the president himself.

Following the bombing of Hiroshima and Nagasaki and the surrender of Japan in August 1945, Groves and other army leaders expected the Army to be promptly relieved of responsibility for the atomic project. But the long controversy over enactment of peacetime legislation forced Groves to continue as head of the project until establishment of the Atomic Energy Commission at the close of 1946. Groves then became commanding general of the Armed Forces Special Weapons Project, the joint atomic organization for the Army and Navy. Promoted to lieutenant general (temporary) in January 1948, he retired a month later to become vice-president for research in the Remington division of the Sperry Rand Corporation, Stamford, Connecticut. Moving back to Washington, D.C., in 1961, he lived in retirement until his death in 1970. Groves married Grace Hulbert Wilson on February 10, 1922. His son, Richard Hulbert, a 1945 graduate of the U.S. Military Academy, followed him in a career in the Army Corps of Engineers. Groves' own account of his administration of the atomic bomb project, *Now It Can Be Told: The Story of the Manhattan Project*, appeared in 1962.

History seems likely to include General Groves in that notable group of Corps of Engineer officers who are remembered for their exceptional accomplishments as builders of projects of unusual difficulty and great national significance. His construction achievements, particularly those for the atomic bomb project, certainly rank with Brigadier General Montgomery Cunningham Meigs'* building of Washington, D.C.'s water supply system and Major General George Washington Goethals'* construction of the Panama Canal. As an administrator of wartime construction projects Groves was energetic, hard-working, aggressive to a fault, and single-minded, yet adaptable when flexibility was necessary. By the time of his assignment to Manhattan, he had both the education and experience requisite to effective management of a project requiring coordination of scientists, engineers, contractors, and plant operators in carrying out highly technical and complex construction and operations more or less on schedule in spite of often severe shortages of manpower and materials. He displayed great resourcefulness in making maximum use of the authority he had been granted to use the Corps of Engineers, the rest of the Army, and other government agencies, to meet the essential requirements of the atomic project.

In retrospect, some have suggested that the Army's participation, and therefore Groves' involvement, in the atomic bomb project was not necessary at all; that science along with civilian industry's aid could have built the fissionable materials plants and perfected the bomb. Some have even asserted that the Army's entry into the project brought an unfortunate bureaucratization, perhaps most dramatically exemplified in the policy of compartmentalization and other aspects of security, that unnecessarily restricted and slowed development of the bomb. Such a policy, it is claimed, left a legacy of resentment and suspicion among scientists and others, which subsequently found expression after the war in the long and bitter controversy over enactment of legislation for peacetime control of atomic energy. Without either affirming or denying the merit of such criticisms, the fact remains that under the leadership of Groves and the Army, the Manhattan Project successfully produced fissionable materials and fabricated atomic bombs, an accomplishment that most would agree was one of mankind's most significant technical and military achievements.

BIBLIOGRAPHY

Compton, Arthur Holly. *Atomic Quest: A Personal Narrative*. New York: Oxford University Press, 1956.

Fine, Lenore, and Jesse A. Remington. *The Corps of Engineers: Construction in the United States*. (*U.S. Army in World War II* series.) Washington, D.C.: U.S. Government Printing Office, 1972.

Groueff, Stephane. *Manhattan Project: The Untold Story of the Making of the Atomic Bomb*. Boston: Little, Brown and Company, 1967.

Groves, Leslie R. *Now It Can Be Told: The Story of the Manhattan Project*. New York: Harper and Brothers, 1962.

Hewlett, Richard G., and Oscar E. Anderson, Jr. *The New World, 1939/1946*. Vol. I of *A History of the United States Atomic Energy Commission*. University Park: Pennsylvania State University Press, 1962.

Laurence, William L. *Dawn Over Zero: The Story of the Atomic Bomb*. 2d ed. enlarged. Westport, Conn.: Greenwood Press, 1972.

Smyth, Henry DeWolf. *Atomic Energy for Military Purposes: The Official Report on the Development of the Atomic Bomb under the Auspices of the United States Government, 1940–1945*. Princeton, N.J.: Princeton University Press, 1945.

VINCENT C. JONES